Romano **AMERIO**

IOTA UNUM

A Study of Changes in the Catholic Church in the XXth Century

Translated from the Second Italian Edition
by
Rev. Fr. John P. Parsons

SARTO HOUSE
PO-Box 270611
Kansas City, MO-64127-0611

ISBN 0-9639032-1-7

Fifth Printing - September 2004

10   9   8   7   6   5

CONTENTS

CHAPTER I

The Crisis

CHAPTER II

Historical Sketch: The Crises of the Church

CHAPTER III

The Preparation of The Council

CHAPTER IV

The Course of The Council

CHAPTER V

The Post-Conciliar Period

CHAPTER VI

The Post-Conciliar Church. Paul VI

CHAPTER VII

The Crisis of the Priesthood

CHAPTER VIII

The Church and Youth

CHAPTER IX
The Church and Women

CHAPTER X
Somatolatry and Penance

CHAPTER XI
Religious and Social Movements

CHAPTER XII

Schools

CHAPTER XIII

Catechetics

CHAPTER XIV
The Religious Orders

CHAPTER XV
Pyrrhonism

CHAPTER XVI
Dialogue

CHAPTER XVII

Mobilism

CHAPTER XVIII

The Virtue of Faith

CHAPTER XIX

The Virtue of Hope

CHAPTER XX

The Virtue of Charity

CHAPTER XXI

The Natural Law

CHAPTER XXII

Divorce

CHAPTER XXIII

Sodomy

CHAPTER XXIV

Abortion

CHAPTER XXV
Suicide

CHAPTER XXVI
The Death Penalty

CHAPTER XXVII
War

CHAPTER XXVIII
Situation Ethics

CHAPTER XXIX
Globality and Graduality

CHAPTER XXX
The Autonomy of Values

CHAPTER XXXI
Work, Technology and Contemplation

CHAPTER XXXII
Civilization and Secondary Christianity

CHAPTER XXXIII

Democracy in the Church

CHAPTER XXXIV

Theology and Philosophy in the Post-Conciliar Period

CHAPTER XXXV

Ecumenism

CHAPTER XXXVI

The Sacraments. Baptism

CHAPTER XXXVII

The Eucharist

CHAPTER XXXVIII

Liturgical Reform

CHAPTER XXXIX

The Sacrament of Matrimony

CHAPTER XL

Theodicy

CHAPTER XLI

Eschatology

Epilogue

ROMANO AMERIO

Romano Amerio, of Italian nationality, was born in Lugano, Switzerland in 1905. He obtained his doctorate in Philosophy from the Catholic University of Milan in 1927. He was the disciple of Fr. Gemelli, the founder of the University. A rare distinction, he was declared citizen of honor by the city of Lugano, where from 1928 to 1970 he taught Philosophy, Greek, and Latin at the Academy. He is renowned for his philosophical studies of the thought of Antonio Rosmini, and for a critical edition of the monumental work of Manzoni, *Osservazioni sulla morale cattolica*. These philosophico-theological studies are considered as irreplaceable for the bibliography of the greatest philosopher and poet of the 19th century.

He is able to speak with unusual competence about the work of the Central Preparatory Commission of Vatican II, which prepared the drafts of the schemas that were to be discussed at the Council.

The Bishop of Lugano, His Excellency Jelmini, was a member of that Commission, and he chose Professor Amerio to work with him as his *peritus* in studying the schemas and in drafting his comments. Professor Amerio thus gained a close working knowledge of all the documents of Vatican II.

Professor Amerio now lives in retirement in northern Italy and occasionally gives conferences on the crisis in the Church.

Iota Unum was published in Italy in 1985 by one of the most renowned publishing houses in Italy, Ricciardi. It obtained an immediate critical success. One critic, writing in the Roman daily *Il Tempo*, said: "In an era of undeniable crisis, the greatest gift that an elder of the faithful can make to his Church is to speak clearly."

D. april 1997

NOTICE TO THE READER

There are no differing keys (as the current phrase goes) in which this book can be read. The meaning to be attributed to it is the meaning that it has, taken univocally in its immediate literal and grammatical sense. There are thus no intentions, or purposes or beliefs hidden in it, which others can devote themselves to finding, beyond or apart from those which the author put there. The author's meaning is not different from the meaning of the book, except of course in the places where he has written badly, that is, said what he did not mean to say. The author has no desire to return to the past, because to entertain such a desire would be to desire a return of human development to some previous stage of its own becoming, and would thus bring it to an end. That kind of fulfillment within earthly life is irreconcilable with the other worldly outlook that dominates the work. Even the *res antiquae*, the "ancient things," in the motto drawn from Ennius at the beginning of the book, does not refer to things that are chronologically prior to our time, but to things that are ontologically prior to the whole of time, and belong to a changeless vision of the good. If the book has any ulterior reference, it is to the world of changeless values alone. The reader should not seek any other.

LIST OF ABBREVIATIONS

A.A.S.	Acta Apostolicae Sedis
C.I.D.S	Centro informazione documentazione sociale
Denzinger	Enchiridion Symbolorum, 1955
D.V.	*Dei Verbum*
G.S.	*Gaudium et Spes*
H.V.	*Humanae Vitae*
I.C.I.	Informations catholiques internationales
L.G.	*Lumen Gentium*
O.R.	Osservatore Romano
O.T.	*Optatam Totius*
P.L.	Patrologia Latina
R.I.	Relazioni internazionali
S.C.	*Sacrosanctum Concilium*
U.R.	*Unitatis Redintegratio*

Italicized titles refer to decrees of the Second Vatican Council, except for the encyclical *Humanae Vitae* of 1968.

IOTA UNUM

A Study of Changes
in the Catholic Church
in the XXth Century

Iota unum non praeteribit
Not one jot, nor one tittle shall pass away.
(Mt. 5:18)

Miscuit in medio eius spiritum vertiginis
The Lord hath mingled in the midst
thereof the spirit of giddiness.
(Is. 19:14)

Moribus antiquis stat res romana virisque
Old-fashioned ways and men make Rome
stand strong.
(Ennius)

CHAPTER I

THE CRISIS

1. Methodological and linguistic definitions.

A precise use of words makes for a sound argument. Of its nature, an argument is a movement from one idea to another brought about in a regulated way by means of logical connections; it is not a movement by random methods or imaginary steps. Hence an initial definition of terms is the foundation of clarity, coherence and legitimacy in argument.

On the title page of this book I have preferred to use the word *change* rather than *crisis* for two reasons. The first is because crisis, linguistically, refers to an event at a point in time and does not go well with the idea of duration. Doctors contrast a critical or decisive day with the course of the disease, which is a process which takes place over time. The phenomenon with which this book deals is diachronic and extends over several decades. Secondly, a crisis is a moment of decision coming between one essential state and another, that is, between one state of being and another different by nature. The biological transition from life to death, or the theological transition from innocence to sin are instances of such crises. On the other hand, merely accidental change occurring within a given thing does not constitute a crisis.

So, if one were to speak precisely, the word *crisis* would only be used when an extraordinary historical development had taken shape, giving birth to a fundamental change in the nature of human life. A change can indeed be a crisis, but it is not a presupposition of our inquiry that the changes which we study in this book necessarily are such. We will, however, adopt the general usage and apply the word *crisis* to phenomena which approximate to a crisis, even though they do not fulfill the definition we have given.

To avoid possible accusations of over-selectivity regarding the great mass of evidence and documentation available, we

have adopted the following criterion. Having to demonstrate
the changes in the Church, we have not based our argument on
random parts of the almost infinite material relating to it, but
have relied on documents which illustrate the mind of the
Church in a relatively authoritative manner. The evidence we
will produce consists of conciliar texts, acts of the Holy See,
papal allocutions, statements by cardinals and bishops, declarations of episcopal conferences and articles in the *Osservatore
Romano.* Our book consists of official and semi-official declarations of the thinking of the hierarchical Church. It is true we
have also cited books, words and doings from outside these circles, but only as proof of the development and expansion of
positions already expressed in the first category of evidence, or
implicitly but necessarily contained within it. Our enquiry is
partial in its subject matter (what enquiry is not?) but we are
not partial in our point of view.

2. Denial of the crisis.

Some authors deny the existence of the present confusion in
the Church[1] or else deny its specific character by attributing it
to the duality and antagonism which exists between the Church
and the world, between the kingdom of God and the kingdom
of man; an antagonism inherent in the nature of the world and
of the Church. This denial seems to us inadequate, because the
essential opposition here is not between the Gospel and the
world which Christ comes to save, that is, the world understood
as the totality of creation, but rather between the Gospel and
the world for which Christ does not pray;[2] that is, the world
inasmuch as it is *in maligno positus,*[3] infected by sin and oriented towards sin. This essential opposition can diminish or
increase depending on the extent to which the world as a whole
does or does not converge with the world of evil, but we must
never forget the distinction or take as essential an opposition
which is in fact merely accidental, and variable in its scope and
intensity.

---

[1] See the great inquiry in the magazine *Esprit,* August-September
    1964.
[2] John, 17:19.
[3] "In the power of the evil one." I John, 5:19.

3. The error of secondary Christianity.

The fact that the opposition between the Church and the world does vary, disproves the opinion of those who deny that the Church has penetrated the world better at some periods than at others and has, at those periods, been more successful in realizing Christianity in practice. Mediaeval Christendom, in comparison with the modern era, was just such a period. Those who deny that there are such specially favored periods base their case chiefly on the continued occurrence of wars, slavery, the oppression of the poor, hunger and ignorance, which they claim are incompatible with religion and, in fact, demonstrate its ineffectiveness. These faults in the human race past and present show, it would seem, that it is neither redeemed nor redeemable by Christianity. Such a point of view is perhaps the result of what we will call *secondary Christianity*: religion judged by its secondary and subordinate effects on civilization, these being given prime importance and valued more than its transcendent and specifically religious effects. The notion of religion and progress in play here is one we will consider later on (See paragraphs 207-8 and 218-20).

4. The crisis as failure to adapt.

A more common opinion is that the crisis in the Church is due to a failure to adapt to a progressing modern civilization and that the crisis should be overcome by an opening or, in the expression of John XXIII, an *aggiornamento* of the spirit of religion, bringing it into harmony with the spirit of the age.

It should be remembered in this regard that the Church penetrates the world from its very nature as its leaven,[4] and it can be seen historically to have influenced every facet of the world's life: did it not prescribe even such things as calendars and food? So great did this influence become that the Church was accused of encroaching on temporal matters to the point where a purging or removal of its influence was allegedly needed. The fact is, that the Church's adaptation to its circumstances in the world is a law of its being, established by a God who Himself condescended to become man, and it is also a law of history, shown by the Church's continually increasing or decreasing influence on the world's affairs.

---

[4] Luke, 13:21.

This adaptation, however, which pertains to the very nature of the Church, does not consist in the Church's conforming itself to the world: *Nolite conformari huic saeculo*,[5] but rather in adjusting its own contradiction of the world to various historical circumstances; changing that inevitable contrariety without setting it aside. Thus, when confronted with paganism, Christianity displayed an opposing excellence of its own, overcoming polytheism, idolatry, the slavery of the senses and the lust for fame and power by raising the whole of earthly life to a theotropic goal never even imagined by the ancients. Nevertheless, in giving expression to their antagonism to the world, Christians lived in the world as beings having an earthly purpose. In the *Letter to Diognetus* they appear as indistinguishable from pagans in all the ordinary practices of life.[6]

5. Adapting the Church's contradiction of the world.

Analogously, when confronted by the barbarians the Church did not adopt barbarism, but clad herself in civilization; in the thirteenth century when confronted with violence and greed she took on the spirit of meekness and poverty in the great Franciscan movement; she did not adopt renascent Aristotelianism but forcefully rejected the doctrines of the mortality of the soul, the eternity of the world, the creativity of the creature and the denial of Providence, thus opposing all the essential errors of the Gentiles. Given the fact that these are the principal tenets of Aristotelianism, scholasticism could be called a dearistotelianizing Aristotelianism. Tommaso Campanella sees an allegorical allusion to this process in the cutting of the hair and nails of the fair woman taken prisoner.[7] Later still, the Church did not adapt to Lutheran subjectivism by subjectivizing Scripture and religion in general, but by reforming, that is, formulating anew, her own principle of authority. Lastly, in the nineteenth century storms of rationalism and scientism, she did not adjust by watering or narrowing down the deposit of faith but by condemning the principle of the independence of reason. When the subjectivist impulse reappeared in Modernism, the Church did not accept it either but blocked it and reproved it.

---

[5] "Do not be conformed to this world." Romans 12:2.
[6] Rouët de Journel, *Enchiridion Patristicum*, 97.
[7] Deuteronomy 21:12.

One can therefore conclude to a general rule that while Catholicism's antagonism to the world is unchanging, the forms of the antagonism change when the state of the world requires a change in that opposition to be declared and maintained on particular points of belief or in particular historical circumstances. Thus the Church exalts poverty when the world (and the Church herself) worships riches, mortification of the flesh when the world follows the enticements of the three appetites,[8] reason when the world turns to illogicality and sentimentalism, faith when the world is swollen with the pride of knowledge.

The contemporary Church, by contrast, is on the lookout for "points of convergence between the Church's thinking and the mentality characteristic of our time."[9]

6. Further denial of the crisis.

There are those, though they are not very many, who deny the existence of the present confusion in the Church, and there are even some who regard this *articulus temporum*[10] as a time of renewal and reflowering. Denial of the crisis can find support in some speeches of Paul VI, but these are counterbalanced and abundantly outweighed by as many, in fact more, statements to the contrary. Pope Paul's speech of 22 February 1970 bears a remarkable witness to his thought.[11] After having admitted that religion is in decline, the Pope maintains nonetheless that it would be an "error to go no further than the human and sociological side of the question, because a meeting with God can arise from processes which escape purely scientific calculation." It would seem that what God can do with what theologians call His absolute power is here being confused with what He can do by His ordinate power within the really existing order of nature and salvation which He has established by His free decree.[12] The problem of the crisis is evaded by this confusion. By bringing in the idea of an act of God performed outside the order which He has in fact established, the religious crisis deplored from the historical point of view ceases to be deplorable. It is indeed very

---

8 Cf. I John, 2:16. [Translator's note.]
9 O.R., 25 July 1974.
10 "Period of time."
11 Papal speeches will always be cited with the date on which they appeared in the *Osservatore Romano*.
12 *Summa Theologica*, I,q.25,a.5 *ad primum*.

true that "a meeting with God can come about despite a hostile attitude to religion," but it is *nihil ad rem.*[13] If one turns to considering what God can do by His absolute power, one has entered the realms of the miraculous. It then becomes possible to ignore contradictions and to maintain, as the Pope does in another address, that "the more modern man is averse to the supernatural, the more he is disposed towards it." Why not indeed, if one considers the absolute power of God?

7. The Pope recognizes the loss of direction.

On many occasions when his spirit rebelled against the *loquimini nobis placentia,*[14] Paul VI outlined the decay of religion in dramatic terms. In his speech to the Lombard College in Rome on 7 December 1968 he said "The Church is in a disturbed period of self-criticism, or what would better be called self-demolition. It is an acute and complicated upheaval which nobody would have expected after the council. It is almost as if the Church were attacking herself." I need not emphasize the famous speech of 30 June 1972 in which the Pope said that he sensed "that from somewhere or other the smoke of Satan has entered the temple of God." "In the Church too," he went on,[15] "this state of uncertainty reigns. It was believed that after the council a sunny day in the Church's history would dawn, but instead there came a day of clouds, storms and darkness." In a later passage which has similarly become famous, the Pope gave the reasons for the general breakdown as being the action of the Devil, that is, of an evil force who is a damned person; thus placing the whole of his historical analysis within the bounds of orthodox aetiology which sees in the *princeps huius mundi*[16] (the "world" here really does mean opposition to God) not simply a metaphor for merely human sin, or for the Kantian *radikal Böse,*[17] but a person, really conflicting, or cooperating, with the human will. In his speech of 18 July 1975 the Pope went on from diagnosis and aetiology to consider the right cure for the Church's historic sickness, and showed how well he understood internal dissolution was damaging the Church more than any

---

[13] "Irrelevant to the matter."
[14] "Tell us what pleases us." Isaiah, 30:10.
[15] On 7 December 1968. [Translator's note.]
[16] "The prince of this world."
[17] "Fundamental evil."

attack from outside. With vehement and touching emotion he exclaimed "Enough of internal dissent within the Church! Enough of a disintegrating interpretation of pluralism! Enough of Catholics attacking each other at the price of their own necessary unity! Enough of disobedience described as freedom!"

The confusion is still acknowledged by his successors. John Paul II described the state of the Church in these terms at a conference on missions given among Catholic populations: "We must admit realistically and with feelings of deep pain, that Christians today in large measure feel lost, confused, perplexed and even disappointed; ideas opposed to the truth which has been revealed and always taught are being scattered abroad in abundance; heresies, in the full and proper sense of the word, have been spread in the area of dogma and morals, creating doubts, confusions and rebellions; the liturgy has been tampered with; immersed in an intellectual and moral relativism and therefore in permissiveness, Christians are tempted by atheism, agnosticism, vaguely moral enlightenment and by a sociological Christianity devoid of defined dogmas or an objective morality."[18]

8. Pseudo-positivity of the crisis.
False philosophy of religion.

Some people go further than denying the crisis and attempt to present it as something positive. They base their argument on biological analogies and talk about ferments and crises of growth. These are "circiterisms"[19] and metaphors which have no place in a logical argument or an historical analysis. As for ferments, which have become a commonplace of discussion in post-conciliar literature, used by those who want to beautify the ugly, one can indeed draw biological analogies, but one must distinguish ferments of life from those that accompany death. One should not, for example, confuse *saccaromycetes aceti* with *saccaromycetes vini*. Not every fermenting substance produces a

---

[18] O.R., 7 February 1981.

[19] "Circiterism." This seems to me to be a necessary term to express a typical characteristic of the contemporary world both inside and outside the Church. It comes from the Latin adverb *circiter* (= about, more or less). The word was much used by Giordano Bruno in his *Dialogues*. We borrow it from him as perfectly apt for its object.

plus, or an improvement. The decay of a corpse is a powerful pollulation of life but it presupposes the disintegration of a higher kind of being.

To say that we are confronted with a crisis of growth is to forget the pathological nature of growing fevers, which do not in fact occur in the normal growth of organisms, whether of the animal or vegetable kingdom. Furthermore, since any growth which may occur will only become apparent in the future, those who use these biological analogies are arguing in a vicious circle, since they are not at present in a position to show that growth, rather than corruption, will be the real outcome of the crisis.

Introducing another poetic analogy, the *Osservatore Romano* of 23 July 1972 states that the present groanings of the Church are not those of death but of birth, since a new being, in fact a new Church, is about to appear in the world. But can a new Church be born? Here, under the attractions of poetic metaphor and an amalgam of ideas, there lurks the notion of something which, according to the Catholic system of things, cannot possibly occur; namely the notion that the change which the Church experiences over time can amount to a fundamental change, a substantial mutation, a change from one thing into something quite distinct. According to the Catholic system, change in the Church consists of change in accidentals and in historical circumstances, amidst which the substance of religion remains the same, without innovation. The only newness known to orthodox ecclesiology is the eschatological newness of the new heaven and the new earth in which, by means of the judgment of all judgments, there will be a final and eternal reordering of the whole creation, freed not from its finitude but from the imperfections of sin.

In the past, other versions of such a reordering have been proposed, in which it was imagined as an event in earthly history inaugurating the reign of the Holy Spirit; but such versions are heretical deviations. The Church changes but does not mutate. Fundamental innovations do not occur in the Church. The new heaven and the new earth, the new Jerusalem, the new song, the new name of God Himself, do not belong to this world of time, but to the world above. The attempt to force Christianity to go beyond itself, to create *une forme inconnue de religion, une religion que personne ne pouvait imaginer et décrire jusqu'ici,* as Teilhard de Chardin[20] boldly wrote, is a paralogism in logic and an error in religion. It is a paralogism, because if the Christian religion is to become something wholly different from itself, then there is no one subject to which the terms of the argument relate and there is thus no continuity between the present and future Church. It is a religious error because the kingdom which does not originate from this world experiences temporal change only as accidental to its being and not as affecting its substance. Of this substance *iota unum non praeteribit.* Not one jot will change. Teilhard could only forecast that Christianity could go beyond itself by forgetting that going outside oneself, that passing one's limit, means dying (*ultima linea mors*),[21] and that Christianity would thus have to die in his view in order to live. We will address this argument again in paragraphs 53 and 54.

9. Further admissions of a crisis.

The being of every entity is identical with its internal unity, whether it be a physical individual or a social and moral one. If a physical organism is dismembered and divided, the individual existent perishes and is changed into something other. If an association of minds diverges and opinions and wills are divided, the conspiring of the parts *in unum*[22] ceases, and the community perishes. So in the Church too, which is certainly a society, internal dissolution damages unity and consequently the Church's very being. Damage to the Church's unity is fully recognized in Pope Paul's speech of 30 August 1973 which laments "the division, the disintegration which has now unfortunately entered various circles within the Church" and which declares that "the re-establishment of spiritual and practical unity within the Church is today one of the Church's most grave and pressing problems." In his speech of 23 November 1973 the Pope deals with the aetiology of the enormous confusion and con-

---

[20] "An unknown form of religion, a religion which nobody could imagine or describe hitherto." See the edition of his complete works, Vol. VII, p.405. Terms such as *surhumaniser le Christ, métachristianisme, Dieu transchrétien* and the like, demonstrate both an aptitude for neologisms and a weakness of thought in the famous Jesuit.

[21] "Death is the last goal." Horace.

[22] "Into one."

fesses his own mistake, admitting that "the opening to the world
became a veritable invasion of the Church by worldly thinking."
This invasion deprives the Church of its power to oppose the
world and robs it of its own specific character. The equivocal
use of the first person plural in this speech is striking. "We," he
says, "have perhaps been too weak and imprudent." Is it "we" or
"We"?

10. Positive interpretation of the crisis.
False philosophy of religion.

The spurious optimism with which some people regard
declining faith, social apostasy, abandonment of worship and
depravation of morals, is born of a false philosophy of religion.
It is said that the crisis is a good thing because it obliges the
Church to take stock of itself and to look for a solution.[23] The
Pelagian denial of evil is implicit in these assertions. If it is true
that evils are the occasion of goods, they remain nonetheless
evils, and do not cause any goods as such. A cure is undoubtedly related to and conditioned by an illness, but it is not a
good inherent in the illness or caused by it.

Catholic philosophy has never fallen into this confusion
and St. Thomas teaches that *eventus sequens non facit actum
malum, qui erat bonus, nec bonum, qui erat malus.*[24] Only the
mental habit of "circiterism" typical of our age makes it possible
to regard the crisis as positive by fixing one's attention on the
positive results which are allegedly to flow from it. These results, as St. Thomas quite deliberately expresses it, are not the
effects of evil, (only defects pertain to evil) but are simply events
related to the evil and brought about by other causes. The line
of causality producing any good consequences related to the
crisis does not run through the crisis itself. The latter remains
simply a crisis. The true line of causality producing good is
something independent.

Clearly, the whole metaphysic of evil is involved in this
question and we do not wish to enter into that subject here, but
in the face of spurious optimism it is important to drive home
that a happy event relating to evil is not an effect of evil but an
increase in good which evil of itself is incapable of producing,

---

[23] Cf. I.C.I., No.285, 1 April 1967, p.7.
[24] *Summa Theologica*, I,II,q.20,a.5. "A following event does not
make an act which was good bad, nor an act which was bad good."

just as persecution does not of itself produce martyrdom, nor suffering itself produce wisdom (Aeschylus), nor trial itself produce an increase in merit, nor heresy itself produce a clarification of the truth.[25] To attribute a good to the crisis when that good is extrinsic to it and proceeds from other causes, implies a defective understanding of the workings of Providence. In the providential order of things, good and evil retain their intrinsic natures (being and non-being, efficiency and deficiency) while taking their place in a system which is itself good. What is good is the system, not the evils which form part of it; even if one can by catachresis call them good evils as Niccolo Tommaseo does. This view of the providential order of things enables one to see how *al mondo di su, quel di giù torni,*[26] and enables one to see too how a creature's departure from the right path, and even its damnation, can be fitted by Providence into that final order of things which constitutes the ultimate purpose of the universe; the glory of God and of His elect.

11. Further false philosophy of religion.

The good result which is to follow upon the Church's crisis is therefore *a posteriori* and does not change the negative character of the crisis itself; still less does it render the crisis desirable, as some people dare to claim. This spurious optimism offends by assigning evil a fertility which only good really possesses. St. Augustine gave the doctrine a very apt formulation in his *De Continentia:*[27] *Tanta quippe est omnipotentia eius ut etiam de malis possit facere bona sive parcendo, sive sanando, sive ad utilitatem coaptando atque vertendo, sive etiam vindicando: omnia namque ista bona sunt.*[28] It is not the case that in some later phase of its being, evil generates good; it is only a different and

---

[25] To say that evil is good, because it gives an opportunity for good, is an error made by S. Maggiolini in O.R. of 12 January 1983, where he goes as far as to say: "All is grace, even sin." Grace is concerned with sin, but it is not to be identified with sin.

[26] "The lower world turns towards the higher." Dante's *Paradiso* IX,108.

[27] *Patrologia Latina* (P.L.) 40,358.

[28] "His omnipotence is so great that it can even make goods out of evils, whether by showing mercy, or by healing, or by suiting and turning to some useful end, or even by punishing: and all these are goods."

positive entity (ultimately God) which can do so. That evils, even though ordered by Providence, cannot become good, appears very clearly in the last case mentioned by St. Augustine; that of vindictive justice. It is good that sins be punished by damnation, but such sins are not therefore good. Thus it is that, according to Catholic theology, the blessed rejoice in that just order in which Providence has placed sinners, but do not rejoice in their sins, which remain evils. The existence of virtues conditional on the existence of defects, constitutes a chain of causality in which certain goods depend on certain evils. Thus repentance is conditional upon the existence of sin, mercy on the existence of misfortune, and forgiveness on the existence of guilt. This does not mean, however, that sin, misfortune and guilt are good, as is the virtue which is conditional upon them.

CHAPTER II

HISTORICAL SKETCH:
THE CRISES OF THE CHURCH

12. The crises of the Church: Jerusalem (50 A.D.).

It is a habit of the present day to regard contemporary phenomena as altogether new and as bearing no comparison with past events either in kind or in degree. Thus the present crisis and the present renewal are allegedly without parallel in Church history. We shall see later on how much truth there is in this assertion, but for the moment it is worth drawing attention to previous crises in the Church, recognized by historians.

We believe that the Council of Jerusalem, of about the year 50 A.D. should be mentioned first of all. It was the primordial and fundamental crisis, or moment of separation, in religious matters between the Synagogue and Christianity; and since separation is the opposite of syncretism, the famous decree brought by Judas and Silas to the church at Antioch, which consisted of Christians who had come over from paganism, cut off at birth that syncretism of the Gospel and the Torah which would have deprived the new message of its originality and its transcendence.

The Council of Jerusalem was critical from another point of view as well; because it separated once and for all theoretical from practical decisions; principles from their application; and did so not by adjusting principles but by adjusting their application to changing circumstances, which adjustment is made in religious matters under the inspiration of charity. The famous confrontation between Peter and Paul at Antioch, which occurred after the two apostles had agreed at Jerusalem that the Jewish law was outdated, that is, had been surpassed, turned not on a principle but on its application or, as Tertullian puts it, on *conversationis vitium, non praedicationis.*[1] What Paul and later, as the event showed, Peter and the whole Church disapproved of, was Peter's practice of making concessions to the ritual instincts of the brethren who had come over from the Synagogue; which differed from his practice regarding those who had come over from idolatry. These were differences about practical matters or, if you will, errors resulting from not seeing, or not seeing clearly, the connection between a principle and a particular situation. They were disagreements and mistakes of the sort which have continued to occur in the Church, from Paschal II when he repudiated the concordat he had signed with the Emperor Henry V, to Clement XIV when he suppressed the Society of Jesus thus contradicting the *non possumus*[2] of his predecessors, to Pius VII when he retracted the agreements he had made with Napoleon, accused himself publicly of having given scandal to the Church and punished himself by not saying Mass for a time. The distinction between the changeable disciplinary, juridical and political sphere, and the unchangeable sphere of the *porro unum est necessarium*,[3] was first drawn by the Council of Jerusalem and constitutes the Church's first crisis: the historical sphere was clearly distinguished from the sphere of dogma.

13. The Nicene crisis (325 A.D.).

The crisis of Nicea marks the separation of the dogmatic from the philosophical, and thus emphasizes the supernatural and mysterious cast of the Christian religion. Arianism constituted an attempt to deflower the originality of the primitive *kerygma* by placing it within the great current of Gnosticism. Gnosticism undermined the idea of transcendence and removed the notion of creation, by asserting that the whole of reality was included in a graded scale of beings ascending from Matter to Intellect. To maintain that the Word was not consubstantial with the Father but like Him, satisfied the yearnings of the human understanding, but it removed the specific content of the Faith, which proclaims the existence of a single subject for the following two propositions: this individual here is a man, and: this same individual here is God. With the conciliar definitions

---

[1] "A defect in behavior, not in teaching." *De Praescriptione Hereticorum*, 23.

[2] "We cannot."

[3] "There is only one thing necessary." Luke, 10:42.

of Nicea, and subsequently of Ephesus (431) and Chalcedon (451), the Church distanced herself from the ancient conception of a god as the perfection of the human, and of religion as the cultivation of this-worldly values to the exclusion of anything lying beyond. Jesus Christ could not be a god in the manner of Caesar or the divine Augusti, or of the gods of Epicurus who although immortal, perfect and blessed, were of one substance with the substance of man. He could not be something falling within the limits of previous philosophical speculation; instead He had to be that thing different from everything, but not alien, which no philosophy had ever imagined or which, if it had, had regarded as madness. In short, God ceases to be the most inaccessible grade of a perfection common to both man and god, and becomes instead a nature transcending anything human. Christ is not called the God-Man after the fashion of the pagans, that is, by a maximal approximation to the divine perfection, nor by a moral intimacy with God (Nestorius), nor in the manner of the Stoic paradox according to which the wise man is equal, indeed superior, to God inasmuch as God is blessed by nature but a wise man by his own exertions. Christ is ontologically man and ontologically God, and hence His ontological theandric constitution is a mystery.

This mystery does not contradict reason, because of the very concept which the new religion brought with it of the nature of the divine essence; namely that it is a Monotriad, a Three-in-One, in the midst of which the Infinite thinks and loves itself precisely as infinite; and therefore that it stands beyond the limits in which the created intellect operates. If one denies that reason can submit itself to Reason, one denies it access to the supernatural. What is more, by denying this submission, one denies reason a proper knowledge of itself, because one would be denying that it knows itself as limited and that it therefore recognizes something beyond its own limit.

The Nicene crisis was thus a decisive moment in the history of religion, and since every crisis separates an entity from what is alien to it, and simultaneously preserves the essential character of that entity, one can say quite simply that the Christian religion was saved at Nicea.

14. The deviations of the Middle Ages.

The many grave disturbances which the Church experienced in the Middle Ages were not true crises since through

them all the Church was never in danger of changing its nature
or dissolving itself into something else. Low moral standards
among the clergy and lust for riches and power disfigure the
face of the Church, but do not attack its essence by attempting
to alter its foundations.

It is appropriate here to formulate the law of the historical
conservation of the Church, a law which also constitutes her
ultimate apologetic criterion. The Church is founded on the
Word Incarnate, that is, on a divinely revealed truth. She is also
given sufficient energies to conform her own life to that truth: it
is a dogma of faith that virtue is always possible. Nonetheless,
the Church is only in danger of perishing if she loses the truth,
not if she fails to live up to it. The pilgrim Church is, as it were,
simultaneously condemned to imperfection in her activity, and
to repentance: in the modern phrase, the Church is in a continual state of conversion. She is not destroyed when human
weakness conflicts with her own teaching (that contradiction is
inherent in the Church's pilgrim condition); but she *is* destroyed
when corruption reaches the level of corroding dogma, and of
preaching in theory the corruptions which exist in practice.

So it was that the Church combatted the movements that
disturbed her in the Middle Ages, but condemned them only
when, for example, the practice of poverty became a theology of
poverty which would have completely disqualified the Church
from owning any earthly goods. For the same reason, the decay
in clerical morals, which the eleventh century reforms so vigorously combatted, was not a true crisis. Nor was the conflict with
the Empire, despite the fact that the Church was trying to free
herself from the feudal servitude implicit in clerical marriage
and in political domination over the bishops. The Catharist and
Albigensian movement of the thirteenth century, and the further ramification of the Fraticelli, were not true crises either.
These movements, which were begotten of huge overflows of
feeling, and compounded with economic and political movements, were rarely translated into speculative formulae.[4] When
they were so translated, as for example in the regressive doctrine
foretelling a return to apostolic simplicity, or in the myth of the
equality of all the faithful at the level of the priesthood, or in
the theology of the Third Age of the Holy Spirit following on
the age of the Son, which had itself followed on the age of the

---

[4] This is not the case with the Catharists. [Translator's note.]

Father, such doctrinal deviations found the hierarchical Church ready and able to exercise its office of teaching and correcting, in which it was often helped by the temporal power which held the structure of society together. The truths of faith were contested but not corrupted, and the teaching office of the Church did not cease to function.

15. The crisis of the Lutheran secession. The breadth of the Christian ideal.

The great eastern schism left the whole structure of the Catholic faith untouched. The Byzantines did not even directly deny the primacy of the Bishop of Rome, and an act of reunion could be signed at Florence in 1439. The heretical movements, which aimed at purging the Church of its worldly accretions, were powerless to put the Church in danger by causing it to change from one kind of thing to another. The real crisis came with Luther, who changed doctrine from top to bottom by repudiating the principle on which it rested.

The historical reasons for the great movement of religious revolution in Germany can hardly be understood unless one considers them in the context of the Renaissance. The latter is often understood as the restoration of the pagan principle of the absolute naturalness and this-worldliness of man, and thus as something incompatible with Christianity which is seen as a despising of this world. It seems to us that this one-eyed view does not accord with the nature of Christianity. Christianity, based as it is on a God-Man Who is the restorer and completer of all things, broadens rather than narrows the mentality of the believer, and enables him to grasp and to elevate everything that is in conformity with the creative plan, which itself has as its goal the glorification of man joined to God in the theandric Christ.

With powerful mystical sentiment, mediaeval civilization certainly expressed an essential aspect of religion, namely the relativization of all earthly reality and its projection towards a heavenly goal. Some would say, however, that the force with which that aspect was lived out went beyond due limits, and led to the setting aside or mortification of values which do not need mortifying, but coordination among themselves and subordination to heaven. I would say the same. The mediaevals seem unable to conceive of an ideal Christian except in the form of a Franciscan friar.[5] When, by contrast, we remember the breadth of the Christian idea, it becomes clear that the Renaissance was a revival of that breadth, leading the Christian religion to realize the kinship uniting it to past civilizations within which, buried in sleep, there lay the values of natural religion, ideal beauty, the civic life and such treasures as the *Phaedo*, the *Metaphysics*, the Venus of Cnidos, the Parthenon, Homer and Virgil.

Religion has an expressive capacity much greater than can appear in any one period: it comes out in successive developments which are not always complete in themselves but which, taken as a whole, tend towards a progressive perfection. This growth is hinted at in the Gospel parables of the seed, and in St. Paul's references to the Church as an organism that grows up to the full measure of perfection.

Nor should it be thought that this assimilation of classical culture began with the Renaissance and the flight of Greek refugees from Islam, since it was in fact begun long before, in the midst of the Dark Ages, by the monastic preservation of Greek and Latin authors. They were preserved not because the monks found incentives or nourishment for their devotion in Virgil and Horace, but because, quite distinct from the all-pervasive ascetical inspiration of that period, the monks appreciated another ideal which although not ascetic, was nonetheless religious if Christianity does, as I have maintained, acknowledge the value of earthly things while directing them towards heaven. Furthermore, the blending of ancient civilization with the Christian idea had already happened before the Renaissance in the primordial form of intellectual development, namely poetry; especially in Dante's *Divine Comedy*, in which the myths, thought and aspirations of the classical world are powerfully combined with the Christian outlook in a daring synthesis. The limbo of the pagans, for example, in which the light of natural wisdom, while not bringing salvation, nonetheless preserves man from the fullness of damnation, is an outstanding intuition of the mediaeval genius, which was well aware of the spiritual spaciousness of the Christian ideal that both includes, and extends beyond, the ascetic world of the cloister.

---

[5] Luigi Tosti, *Prolegomeni alla storia universale della Chiesa*, Rome 1888, p.322.

16. Further breadth of the Christian ideal. Its limits.

This breadth of the Christian idea, due to its possessing latent aspects destined to be made manifest through historical developments, is a reality running through the whole of Christian thought and is linked theologically to the unity which exists between the cycle of the creation and the cycle of the Incarnation, the same divine Word being present in both. Even without considering the theological causes of this breadth, an examination of historical events is enough to make its existence apparent, inasmuch as contrasting schools and styles have coexisted in the same place. Bellarmine and Suarez lay the foundations of democracy and popular sovereignty while Bossuet justifies royal autocracy; Franciscan asceticism preaches the casting aside of all earthly goods whether material or intellectual while Jesuit realism builds cities, organizes states and mobilizes all the goods of this world *ad majorem Dei gloriam*. The Cluniacs decorate even the pavements of their churches with colors, gold and gems while the Cistercians reduce sacred buildings to their bare architecture. Molina makes much of the freedom and autonomous power of the human will, asserting it capable of checking divine predestination, and lowering the divine knowledge to the level of dependence on human events, while Thomists exalt the absolute efficacy of the divine decree. The Jesuits proclaim a broad way to salvation while the Dominicans proclaim the fewness of the elect. The casuists enlarge the role of the individual conscience when confronted with a law while the rigorists give the law preponderance over human calculation about the circumstances of an act. Franciscanism itself, with its founder's blessing of both Friar Elias and Friar Bernard, contains two spirits which, by their separations and reconciliations under the influence of a higher inspiration, explain the internal struggles in the order.[6]

If one forgets this essential spaciousness of Catholicism, the distance between one form of orthodoxy and another will seem as great as that between orthodoxy and heterodoxy. This is exactly how it did seem to the authors of opposed and mutually accusatory schools of thought, but it was not how it seemed to the magisterium of the Church, which always intervened to forbid mutual accusation and to safeguard religious unity at a higher level. Because this breadth was not grasped by Sainte-

---

[6] A. Gemelli, *Il Francescanesimo*, 3rd ed., Milan 1936, p.40.

Beuve, it seemed to him too amazing *que le même nom de chrétien s'applique également aux uns et aux autres* (he had in mind
the laxists and the rigorists). *Il n'y a pas d'élasticité qui aille
jusque là.*[7] Chesterton very perceptively made this breadth the
main criterion in his apologetic for Catholicism. Jacob's prophetic saying should be remembered: *Vere Dominus est in loco
isto et ego nesciebam.*[8]

It is nonetheless necessary to indicate the limits of this large
view of the Catholic religion, which we too regard as a decisive
historical criterion. The large view must not lead to an all embracing Pyrrhonism, which consumes and syncretizes contradictories, rather than things which merely differ. It is legitimate to
talk in terms of a broad view when several ideas are seen as a
coherent whole, in which there is a genuine plurality of ideas:
that is, when one idea is not destroyed by the contrasts it has
with another. It is, however, impossible for a human, or any
other mind, to make contradictory terms, that is, true and false,
hold together. A coexistence of that sort would be possible only
on an impossible condition; namely if thought were not oriented toward the being of things, or if being and non-being
were equivalent. Catholicism grants logic precedence over every
other form of mental activity, and logic embraces a plurality of
values within its own truth, but it cannot embrace a plurality
consisting of values and anti-values. A spuriously broad view of
religion leads to theoretical and moral indifference, that is, to an
inability to create an order in living.

17. The denial of the Catholic principle
in Lutheran doctrine.

It is therefore a question of seeing how Luther's doctrine
could not be included in the broad ambit of the Catholic system, and how his attack called into question the principle of the
whole system, rather than this or that corollary.

---

[7] "That the same name of Christian should be applied equally to the
one group and the other....No kind of elasticity could stretch that
far." Cited in F. Ruffini, *La vita religiosa di A. Manzoni*, Bari
1931, Vol.I, p.416.

[8] "Truly God is in this place and I knew it not." Genesis, 28:16.

[9] Pyrrhon of Elis (c.365-275 B.C.), founder of the Sceptics, who held
that knowledge of the nature of things is unattainable. [Translator's
note.]

Inasmuch as it is a rejection of Catholic first principles, Lutheranism is theologically irrefutable. When confronted with Lutheranism, Catholic apologetic finds itself in the position neatly outlined by St. Thomas:[10] it can solve the opponent's objections, but not to the opponent's satisfaction, since he rejects the principle on which the argument refuting him is based. For Luther was not merely rejecting this or that article within the body of Catholic doctrine, (though of course he did do that as well) but rather rejecting the principle underlying them all, which is the divine authority of the Church. Bible and tradition are only authorities for the believer because the Church possesses them; and possesses them not simply materially or philologically, but possesses the meaning of them, which she historically unveils little by little.

Luther, on the other hand, places both the Bible and its meaning in the hands of the individual believer, rejects any mediating role for the Church, entrusts everything to the individual's private lights and replaces the authority of an institution by an immediacy of feeling which prevails over all else. The conscience is detached from the teaching office of the Church, and an individual's impressions, especially if they are vivid and irresistible, are made superior to any other rule and are held to establish a right both to believe, and to proclaim what is believed. What the ancient Pyrrhonism does to philosophical knowledge, Protestant Pyrrhonism does to religious knowledge. The Church, which is the historic and moral continuation of Christ the God-Man, is deprived of its native authority, while the liveliness of an individual's impressions is called "faith" and declared to be an immediate gift of grace. The supremacy of this individual conscience removes the foundation of all the articles of faith, because they stand or fall according to whether the individual conscience assents to, or dissents from them. Thus divine authority, which is the sustaining principle of Catholicism, is extirpated and with it go the dogmas of the faith: it is no longer the divine authority of the Church which guarantees them, but subjective individual impressions. Thus, if heresy consists in holding a truth to have been revealed, not on the authority of its having been revealed, but because it accords with a subjective perception, one can say that in Lutheranism the whole concept of faith is converted into the concept of her-

---

[10] *Summa Theologica*, I,q.1,a.8.

esy, because the divine word is accepted only inasmuch as it receives the form of an individual conviction. It is not the thing which demands assent, but assent which gives value to the thing. If then, by an internal logic, this criticism of divine authority as a theological principle becomes a criticism of the authority of reason as a philosophical principle, that is no more than might have been expected *a priori*, and it is also confirmed *a posteriori* by the historical development of German thought, right up to the fully developed forms of immanentist rationalism.

18. Luther's heresy, continued. The bull *Exsurge Domine*.

The germ of the formidable religious revolution occasioned by Luther is all contained in the 41 articles condemned by Leo X in the bull *Exsurge Domine* of 15 June 1520, though the Pope was certainly unaware of just how far the rebellion of human thought was to go. As we have already said, the principle of private judgment is really implicit in every heresy, and each time the Church lifts her voice against a particular theological opinion contrary to the faith, that principle is implicitly rebutted even when it is not explicitly mentioned. In this instance, however, the principle is expressly stated in at least one of the condemned articles.

In this series of condemned propositions, it is difficult to tell which ones the bull intends to reprove as actually heretical, because, in accordance with Roman curial usage, after having listed the 41 propositions, the bull condemns them one and all collectively *tamquam respective haereticos, aut scandalosos, aut falsos, aut piarum aurium offensivos vel simplicium mentium seductivos.*[11] This lack of distinction makes it difficult to discern how the censures are to be distributed, and opens the field to debate among theologians: an heretical assertion that injures Catholic doctrine is an altogether different thing from a saying that might mislead the simple, as the latter constitutes a sin against prudence and charity, but not against faith.

The propositions contain, in a developed form, Luther's doctrine of penance, in which he teaches that the whole efficacy of sacramental penance rests on the feeling the penitent has of

---

[11] "As respectively heretical, or scandalous, or false, or offensive to pious ears, or seductive of simple minds."

being absolved. Some articles invalidate the idea of the freedom of the will, which is said to be moved entirely by grace and to remain *de solo titulo*.[12] Others deal with the supremacy of a Council over the Pope, the uselessness of indulgences, the impossibility of good works, and the death penalty for heretics, which Luther held to be contrary to the will of the Holy Spirit.

There is, however, one article, No.29, in which the heresy of private judgment in the choice of beliefs is openly professed by Luther. This article, stating the true principle of the whole movement, remains as the only really memorable one: *Via nobis facta est enervandi auctoritatem Conciliorum et libere contradicendi eorum gestis et confidenter confitendi quidquid verum videtur*.[13] Here the fundamental root, the ultimate criterion, is made plain: it is private judgment that gives authority to whatever *seems* to be true. Of the two sides of a mental act, the one which apprehends objective being and the other, which is the subjective act of apprehension, it is no longer the objective being apprehended, but the act of apprehension itself which predominates. To express myself in scholastic terms, it is *id quo intelligitur*[14] that predominates over *id quod intelligitur*.[15] If in article 27 Luther proceeds to remove the fixing of articles of faith and moral law from the hands of the Church, he does no more than translate article 29 from the individual to the social aspect of religion.

In conclusion, the soul of the Lutheran secession was not a question of indulgences, the Mass, the sacraments, the Papacy, priestly celibacy, or the predestination and justification of the sinner: it was an intolerance that the human race carries about fixed fast in its heart and which Luther had the daring to manifest openly: the intolerance of authority. Because the Church is the collective historical body of the God-Man, it draws its organic unity from a divine principle. In such a context, what could man be, but a part, living by unity with that principle and by obedience to it? The man who breaks that link loses the forming principle of the Christian religion.

---

[12] "In name only."

[13] "The way is open for us to deprive Councils of their authority and to contradict their acts freely and to profess confidently whatever seems to be true."

[14] "That by which it is understood."

[15] "That which is understood."

19. The principle of independence
and abuses in the Church.

Once the crisis is seen in these terms, the consideration of
the moral faults of the clergy and the institutional corruption
that followed from it becomes a secondary question, even
though it remains important as the historical cause that touched
off the assertion of the principle of private judgment. There
were certainly enormous abuses of the sacred on the part of the
Church's ministers: one could cite the monstrous example of
Alexander VI threatening his concubine with excommunication
unless she returned *ad vomitum*.[16] Nonetheless, quite apart from
the fact that an abuse does not justify rejecting the thing abused,
there is also the fact that the reform of the Church could only
happen, and in the event did happen, in an orthodox way,
thanks to men who were always convinced that Catholics could
not be acting rightly unless they had the seal of approval of
those same churchmen whose vices they continued to castigate,
even while recognizing their authority: and in this they were like
their predecessors St. Francis of Assisi, St. Dominic, St. Catherine of Siena and the founders of religious orders in the fourteenth and fifteenth centuries. The reason why the corruption
of shepherds caused only a dispersal of sheep, rather than a true
crisis, was that malpractice was not erected into a dogmatic theory as it was by Luther. A theory is unlimited, since it contains
in its universality a potential infinity of acts, whereas acts themselves are always limited. Thus if the theoretical dogma is preserved, the health-giving principle remains undamaged, and
through it the whole of practical action is saved.

20. Why casuistry did not create a crisis in the Church.

We cannot pass on without saying a word about the phenomenon of casuistry, although it did not create a true crisis in
the Church. Gioberti and some modern authors maintain that
it was a real crisis and indeed the cause of the decline of Catholicism.[17]

---

[16] "To her old sins." Cf. II Peter, 2:22. The threatening letter is published by G. Picotti in *Rivista di storia della Chiesa in Italia*, 1951,
p.258.
[17] L.R. Bruckberger, *Lettre à Jean Paul II*, Paris 1979, p.101.

First and foremost it was not a crisis because fundamentally casuistry is entirely reasonable and necessary. As the discipline which tells man how to apply to individual actions ethical rules which of their nature are universal, theological casuistry has a function analogous to legal casuistry, or jurisprudence, and is begotten of the necessary and ever present imperatives of moral action. Its further development was encouraged by the Council of Trent which, by declaring that the priest exercises his office in the sacrament of penance *per modum iudicii*,[18] emphasized the need for a body of teaching, dealing with individual cases, which would translate the Church's precepts and the moral law into practical application. Thus far, there is nothing reprehensible about casuistry.

What was reprehensible was its tendency to remove the difficulties of moral obligation and to make the observance of the gospel law easy, by accommodating it to human weakness. Equally reprehensible was the wholly philosophic and rational principle of probability, which placed free will and individual judgment above the imperatives of the law. So, according to Caramuel, whom St. Alphonsus Liguori called "the prince of the laxists," one ought to make room for a variety of opinions about what is good and evil, all of them admissible and helpful provided they have some degree of probability about them, because in his words *divina bonitas diversa ingenia hominibus contulit, quibus diversa inter se homines iudicia rerum ferrent, et se recte gerere arbitrarentur.*[19] Here there is some trace of the Lutheran principle of private judgment, as opposed to the Catholic one of authority.

On the other hand, casuistic theories which gave pride of place to subjective impressions in determining one's moral choices were moderated by the penitent's submission of his conscience to the authority of a confessor, and thus in some sense to the authority of the Church. Casuistry was more a science among the clergy, because of their role as moral advisors, than a moral decline in the popular conscience. The great bulk of books of casuistry published at that period were *Praxis Confessariorum*, and only rarely *Praxis Poenitentium.*[20] It was, however,

---

[18] "By way of judging."

[19] "The divine goodness has given different characters to men, by which men may form different judgments of affairs among themselves, and believe themselves to be acting rightly."

[20] Guides for Confessors, not Guides for Penitents.

easy to drift from benign criteria for evaluating past actions, which is what casuistry was to begin with, to relaxed criteria about actions to be performed in the future.

Casuistry did not amount to a crisis, because the principle that one is free to choose what law one is bound by was never expressly formulated. Thus the many propositions condemned by Alexander VII in 1665 and 1666 contain solutions to cases rather than any error of principle. Therefore it does not follow, as Pascal thought it did, that the Church's censure of casuistry proves the latter was capable of inducing a fully blown crisis in Catholicism.

21. The revolution in France.

The revolution in France, whatever one may say about the violent and evil deeds that disfigure it, is rightly identified with the principles of '89. They would not be principles if they were merely a promulgation of rights. In fact, they are genuinely principles, that is, assumptions about the truth, which it is not permitted to judge and which judge everything else. They are positions antithetical to the Catholic principle of authority. In that respect the French events of '89 are historically unimaginable without the nailing up of the 95 theses on All Saint's Eve 1517, not because the theses taken individually were subversive, but because the *spiritus agitans molem*[21] was. That spirit was bound to bring to birth all that was in fact born of it; bound not by the wickedness of men, nor by the obstinacy of corrupt churchmen, nor by the ineptitude of hierarchies, but by the most terrible of all driving and regulating energies in the human *pandaemonium*: logical necessity.

Many people maintain that a rich and abundant mixture of ideas collided with Catholicism during the revolution and that the causes of the latter were not all philosophical and religious. I would agree, just as I would about the Protestant reform. If I conceive of the revolution's disorderly combat of ideas as being not a *proelium mixtum*[22] but a combat of spirits, a battle of essences, it is because I see in it a vast and fundamental shift

---

[21] "Spirit moving the whole."
[22] "Mixed battle."

which, in Lucretius's stupendous image *funditus hu-manam...vitam turbat ab imo.*[23]

All Catholic authors of the nineteenth century, not least among them those usually classed as liberals, took up the task of criticizing the principles of the revolution. Manzoni does it in his essay *Sulla Rivoluzione Francese*, which modern historiography attempts to discredit and cast into oblivion. Father Francesco Soave does it in his acute little work *Vera idea della Rivoluzione di Francia* (Milan 1793), which is today also condemned to Erebus. Rosmini does it in his *Filosofia del diritto*, paragraphs 2080-92, in terms of a clash between individual and social rights. I am well aware that a benign interpretation has been forced upon the principles of the French Revolution by Catholic thinkers and worldly clerics, Catholic politicians and publicists. They maintain that the principles were the unfolding of Christian ideas that needed to be unfolded, but which were not at once recognized for what they were at the time of their unfolding. There are statements to this effect by senior churchmen and even by contemporary Popes. We will deal with these later on, less fleetingly than in this present swift historical sketch.[24] It is however undeniable, and for more than a century it was seen to be undeniable, that the revolution in France set in motion a new spirit, a genuinely new principle, which can neither be subordinated to the Catholic principle nor combined with it on an equal basis.

22. The principle of independence.
The *Auctorem Fidei*.

Anyone who glances through Denzinger's famous *Enchiridion* might be surprised to find that among the doctrinal documents of the period in which the great convulsion of the French Revolution occurred, there are none which directly concern the theoretical presuppositions underlying the reforming legislation passed by the succession of assemblies which preceded the Consulate and the Empire. Bonaparte, the mediator between two ages, finally abolished the most arrogant and anti-Catholic features of the seven successive constitutions of the 1790s, but left intact the fundamental informing principle of

---

[23] "Disturbs human life most profoundly from its depths." *De Rerum Natura III*, 38.

[24] See paragraph 225.

the modern age, which underlay all the innovations. That principle, as I have remarked several times, is the setting up of human values on a purely human, independent and self-subsistent basis, and the consequent overthrow of authority.

Liberty, equality and fraternity were not values that had gone unrecognized by ancient Greek wisdom, or that had not been given universal import by the Christian religion. Where else could they have come from? The Stoics had made them dependent on a natural *Logos* enlightening every man who came into the world; even if such enlightenment was ineffective, as the history of slavery, for example, proves. Christianity, on the other hand, had made them dependent on the supernatural *Logos* Who became man, enlightening and effectively moving man's heart. Since a natural *Logos* is ideal, not real, it cannot truly be the principle on which all depends, nor consequently can it be revered and obeyed unconditionally. The true principle is a supremely real being that includes the Idea and which, in Christianity, has made itself a created reality by means of the Incarnation.

The God-Man, Who is ontologically an individual, becomes a social individual in the Church. The latter, according to St. Paul's famous teaching, is the mystical body of the former; hence dependence on Christ is reflected in dependence on the Church. This is the principle of authority which rules the whole theological organism. It was impugned by the Lutheran revolution because, as has been said, that revolution substituted private judgment in religious matters for the rule of authority. The correlative of authority is obedience, and one could equally well say that the first principle of Catholicism is either authority or obedience; as appears in the famous Pauline passages about the God-Man being obedient, and obedient even unto death, that is, with the whole of His life. He was obedient not primarily to save man (though it is legitimate to put it that way) but rather in order that the creature should bow before the Creator and give Him that entire and absolute homage which is the very goal of creation. That is why the Church of Christ always draws people to cooperate together, through obedience and abnegation, and to merge themselves in that collective individual which is the mystical Body of Christ, taking the individual and his acts out of their isolation and abolishing any sort of dependence which is not subordinate to dependence on God.

The political independence of man taught by the revolution was contained in the religious independence taught by Luther and later by the Jansenists. In this regard Pius VI's constitution *Auctorem Fidei* (1794) condemning religious independence, has an importance equal to Pius X's encyclical *Pascendi* (1907). When they reproduced the two documents entire in their famous *Enchiridion Symbolorum*, the Jesuit Denzinger and his coeditors displayed a far-sighted grasp of doctrine. In the *Auctorem Fidei* too, there are only a few articles of fundamental importance, and a good many more which apply these fundamentals as a kind of added ornament. The fundamental articles are the ones condemned as heretical; the others receive lesser censures. Setting aside the universal Church, the Pistoians made the particular church the mediator between the individual and the divine Word, thus allotting it the place Luther had given to subjective impressions; and although this pluralized and dispersed the principle of authority somewhat less than did Luther's much vaunted principle of private judgment, it effected a shift in authority from the universal to the particular just the same.

As generally happens in calls for reform, the Pistoians alleged that there had been a general obscuring of important religious truths in the Church in recent centuries (Proposition 1). This allegation was contrary to the nature of the Church, for in her, truth is indefectible and can never be obscured in her official teaching. This proposition, which could fundamentally be considered as an historical judgment, is followed by others also condemned as heretical, which state that authority to teach doctrines of the faith and to govern the ecclesial community resides in the community itself and is communicated by the community to its pastors. This time it is not the private judgment of an individual person, but of an individual church which is set up as the ultimate authority: a universal authority is replaced by an authority which, although still social, is nonetheless individual. There is still an obedience to the divine Word, but only insofar as that Word is conveyed through the medium of what might be called the private judgment of the diocesan church. That the pope is head of the Church as its minister, deriving his authority from it rather than from Christ, is also condemned as heresy; it is a corollary of the principle that authority resides in the community.

23. The crisis of the Church
during the French Revolution.

Prior to the revolution of the masses, royal absolutism had already effected its own revolution and had freed itself from its moral obedience to the Church, renewed the despotism of the *lex regia* whereby *quidquid principi placet vigorem habet legis*,[25] and had reinforced itself by imbibing the spirit of Lutheran freedom of conscience. On the one hand the new Caesarism had asserted the ruler's independence of those laws of the Church which had hitherto strengthened and tempered royal power for the protection of the people. On the other hand, it had absorbed the privileges, franchises, immunities, and immemorial customs which had guaranteed the liberties of the subject. Few writers attempt to establish to what extent the huge revolutionary disturbance was simply a reaction of the social mechanism, and to what extent philosophical aspirations or conspiracies played a part in it. In any case, events proceeded on an enormous scale and eradicated principles and convictions like a *ventus exurens et siccans*;[26] defection and apostasy took a third of the clergy, compensated for by instances of unvanquished resistance even to the point of martyrdom; priests and bishops contracted marriages (subsequently convalidated by the Concordat of 1801, except in the case of bishops); churches and religious houses were profaned and destroyed (of three hundred churches in Paris, only thirty-seven remained as churches); religious symbols were rejected, scattered or banned (so that Cardinal Consalvi and his suite wore lay dress when they came to Paris to negotiate the Concordat); dissoluteness in manners grew and there were licentious and wayward reforms in public worship and instruction, and sacrilegious compoundings of the patriotic with the religious. The Civil Constitution of the Clergy adopted in July 1790 and condemned by Pius VI in the March of the following year, contained a real error in principle, in that it secularized the Church and abolished it as a society prior to, and independent of, the state. If it had remained in force, it would have wiped every Catholic influence and institution off the face of French soil; but it succumbed to the rejection of almost all the bishops and the vast majority of priests, and to the policies of compromise adopted by Bonaparte.

---

[25] "Whatever pleases the prince has the force of law."
[26] "A scorching and drying wind."

Hence the condemnation of the Civil Constitution of the Clergy is a doctrinal document concerning the very substance of the Catholic religion. It is surprising that Denzinger omitted it.

The total separation of Church and state was deemed an error by the framers of the *Syllabus*, but at least it allows the two societies, theocratic and democratic, to continue to exist, each with its own nature and aim. How much more fatal then is the error of absorbing the Church into the state, and of identifying the latter with human society in all its aspects. The French Revolution, reduced to its logical essence, represented a genuine crisis of Catholic principle, because even though it did not succeed in translating the principle of independence into social practice, it did implant that principle, which removes the religious, moral and social orders from their center, and tends towards the complete dislocation of the social organism.

Nonetheless, it is legitimate to doubt that this violent shock to Catholicism really did constitute a crisis, if one remembers there is no true crisis when the mystical body is attacked, so to speak, in its sensitive soul but not in its intellectual or mental one, and when the nucleus, being endowed with the charism of indefectibility, remains undamaged, even though confusion may be spreading through all the physiological operations of the body.

24. The *Syllabus* of Pius IX.

The famous list of modern errors annexed to the encyclical *Quanta Cura* of 8 December 1864 is today repudiated by certain theologians, who are trying to combine Catholicism with those very errors. Alternatively, it is passed over in silence, or beset by authors who, to avoid offending that world which the *Syllabus* did offend, boldly interpret it as the gateway to a further development of error, maintaining that the progress of thought in our century has shown that at heart the errors in question were truths. Or lastly, its doctrinal significance, that is its permanent significance, is flatly denied and it is presented as merely a passing episode in the Church's mistaken policy of opposition to the spirit of the age. Even in the *Osservatore Romano* of 31 May 1980, a French historian associates this outstanding doctrinal document with "a flare-up of ultramontane, monarchical clericalism." Denzinger and his successors displayed both their *sensus fidei* and their *sensus logicae* when they included it entire in their *Enchiridion*.

Disputes and differences arose at once concerning the import of the *Syllabus* in relation to Catholic doctrine. Monseigneur Dupanloup, the Bishop of Orléans, restricted the scope of its condemnations. On the other hand the *Civiltà Cattolica*, which then enjoyed great authority, put forward a strict interpretation, recognizing that the *Syllabus* condemned the principle upon which the whole of the modern world rests. Antireligious writers, who on the essential point were no less clear sighted than the Jesuits, opposed the *Syllabus* because they saw it contained a condemnation of modern civilization. Some of the condemned propositions gave rise to disputes in the area of practical moral conduct. Such were No.75 on the incompatibility of the papacy's temporal and spiritual powers, and No.76 maintaining that the abolition of the Papal States would be good for the welfare of the Church. According to the *Civiltà Cattolica*, anyone who disagreed with the *Syllabus* on those points could not be given sacramental absolution. The clergy of Paris, presided over by their archbishop, decided on the contrary that such a person could be absolved. In an instruction given to the members of his Institute before the *Syllabus* came out, Antonio Rosmini too had maintained the same position.[27]

A feature clearly proclaimed on the very title page of the papal document is, however, more important than the opinions of moral theologians on the extent of the obligations the *Syllabus* imposed on the faithful. It intends to enumerate *praecipuos nostrae aetatis errores.*[28] In the last of the articles however, which constitutes a synthesis of the whole papal condemnation, these errors are identified with the very substance of *modern civilization*, which is thus totally condemned in its principles, but not in the totality of its parts.

Because it contains very few condemnations of particular theological points, and a very sweeping condemnation of the dominant errors of the age, it would seem that the *Syllabus* should be taken more as a denunciation of the state of the world than of the condition of the Church, and that the gist of its teaching lies in its condemnation of the *spirit of the age.*

Of the eighty articles in the document, few stand out for anyone looking for matters of universal importance, but these few are indeed decisive.

---

[27] See on this point the cited edition of the *Morale Cattolica*, Vol.III, pp.340-3.

[28] "The principal errors of our age."

An independent reason, which makes no reference to God, recognizes no law but its own (autonomy), rests on no force but its own immanent strength, and deems itself capable of carrying man and the world to the fulfillment of their destiny, is condemned by the censure of the third proposition. The fifth condemned proposition makes reason an absolute norm, and describes the supernatural as a product and stage of natural thought: it therefore denies the dependence of the created word on the uncreated Word standing infinitely above it; the perfection of divine revelation thus consists in human consciousness of the divine, and in the reduction of dogmas to rational theorems. Proposition No.58 is of equal importance, because it proclaims the individual's ethical decisions to be independent of any absolute norm transcending his own mind, hence the proposition constitutes the reflection in practical reason of these same errors. The juridical application of No.58 is condemned in No.59; namely that human law is duly constituted by human action alone, prescinding from any relation to a moral law; the event is the foundation of justice, and its principle is not the divine Idea, but contingent reality.

Thus, taken as a whole, the *Syllabus* can be seen more as a denunciation of the modern world than as a symptom of a crisis in the Church, because the propositions which it draws together relate to a contradiction between the world and Catholicism rather than to an internal contradiction between the Church and its own principles, and, as we saw at the outset, it is precisely the latter which constitutes the definition of a crisis. It was grasped both by the world and by the Church that this was the meaning of the *Syllabus*.

The condemnation of modern thought proceeds from the *Syllabus* to Vatican I. The preparatory schema *de doctrina catholica* observes it to be characteristic of the age that rather than attacking particular points which leave the first principle of religion untouched, *homines generatim a veritatibus et bonis supernaturalibus aversi fere in humana solum ratione et in naturali ordine rerum conquiescere atque in his totam suam perfectionem et felicitatem consequi se posse existimant.*[29]

---

[29] "Men in general have turned away from supernatural truths and goods and believe they can be content with human reason and the natural order of things alone, and can attain in them their full perfection and happiness."

Hence, the difference between the state of affairs envisaged by the *Syllabus*, and that of the Church in the present confusion, lies precisely in the fact that the demands and claims of the world, which were then external to the Church and opposed by her, have now been internalized within her, and the antagonism between the Church and world abandoned, whether by keeping quiet about it, and thus renewing the mediaeval adage *tace et florebunt omnia,*[30] or by softening it to render it tolerable, or, most commonly, by weakening the force of Catholicism through making it so broad as to embrace not the totality of truth, but a syncretistic totality of truth and falsehood.

The condemnation of the spirit of the age is certainly undeniable, and can be neither avoided nor softened, since that spirit is essentially marked by the errors here condemned. The enormous silence within the bosom of the Church which is intended to extinguish the papal pronouncement of 1864, and thanks to which it was acceptable that Vatican II should not mention it even once, can never annihilate the *Syllabus of Errors*, even though it has succeeded in making its very name a thing to be derided or abhorred.

25. The spirit of the age. Alexander Manzoni.

In the second part of his *Morale Cattolica*,[31] in a chapter called in fact "The Spirit of the Age," which is the most troubled not only in that work, but in the whole of his writings, Alexander Manzoni[32] is confronted with the same problems as ourselves: that is, whether the spirit of the age is compatible with the Catholic religion or not. He finds his solution by a process of analysis and discernment. Rejecting a false systematization which would accept all or condemn all, Manzoni examines article by article the various parts of that heterogeneous compound of ideas; true, useful, sound, false, irreligious and harmful. Having extracted the good elements, he shows that they were contained in religion and are derived from it and that the fault, if there had been one, had lain in not drawing them out, but leaving it to the enemies of religion to do so. Thus, the analysis of the spirit of one age should not be made by the light

---

[30] "Keep quiet and all will be well."

[31] See op.cit. Vol.II, pp.413-59 and Vol.III, pp.323-9.

[32] Alexander Manzoni (1785-1873), Catholic apologist and the most famous of Italian novelists. [Translator's note.]

of the spirit of another, whether past or present, but by the light of religious truth, which illuminates changing intellects as generations take their course, while itself standing, changeless, above all periods by a kind of *ucronia*.[33] By comparing the dominant opinions in a society at a given time, it is possible to effect that philosophic rather than charismatic *discretio spirituum*[34] which does not accept or reject a composite whole *en bloc*, but discerns merits and demerits by a transhistorical criterion.

But here a doubt arises. Is the spirit of an age a compound that can be broken up into its component parts, or is it something (I am not going to define it) which holds a compound together and gives its parts an existence other than they have merely as parts? Is not the spirit that *quid* which informs the parts, and thus brings them out of multiplicity and division into a definite and unmistakable unity, as an individual undivided in itself and divided from everything else?

The point Manzoni makes in those pages remains certain at any rate; that the spirit of an age should not be judged historically, but by a timeless criterion, that is, by religion and not by history. Of course, this criterion will not be accepted by someone holding an axiology which rejects true, noumenal values; but it is the Catholic criterion, and we intend to use it here in order to discern where the crisis lies. That kind of criterion is therefore not only a legitimate one, but *the only one legitimate*.

Judgments which Catholicism and systems opposed to it make about the worth of the same object, for example the value and dignity of the human person, may seem identical; but the identity is only apparent, since Catholicism finds the reason for this dignity where the other systems do not. In both cases man is loved, but in the one he is deemed lovable in himself, while in the other he is not; it is rather a higher principle, Lovable in Itself, which makes him lovable in turn.

By this example one can grasp what it is that constitutes the spirit of an age, a society or a system. It is the *ultimate* ground, irreducible to anything further back, which renders each moment of the system or the age intelligible; the *caput mortuum*,[35]

---

[33] "Timelessness." I expounded the Manzonian solution at length in an address to the Arcadian Academy on 24 April 1979, now published in its *Atti* pp.21-44.

[34] "Discernment of spirits."

[35] "Fixed point."

that is, that final idea in which the whole is resolved and which is not itself resolvable into anything else. Thus the spirit of an age is not a *complex* of ideas, but what unifies such a complex, and cannot itself be broken up. The spirit of the age is the analogue in social life of what the Bible calls the *tree* or *heart* in the life of an individual person;[36] the place whence spring a man's thoughts, good or evil, saving or damning, and whence the good or bad fruit proceeds, according to whether the tree or heart be good or bad itself. From the religious point of view, man is radically good or radically bad, and his destiny turns on the moment of death.[37]

26. The modernist crisis. The second *Syllabus*.

The crisis stated in the *Syllabus* was a crisis of the world more than of the Church. The crisis stated in the second syllabus, constituted by the decree *Lamentabili* of 3 July 1907 and the encyclical *Pascendi* of 8 September of the same year, was, on the contrary, a crisis of the Church itself. The difference between Pius X's document and Pius IX's is obvious from their titles: Pius IX was listing *praecipuos nostrae aetatis errores*,[38] Pius X denounces *errores modernistarum de Ecclesia, revelatione, Christo et sacramentis*.[39] Every philosophy contains a potential theology. The purely theological matters contemplated in the teaching of Pius X, are the mature fruit of that philosophy of independence condemned in the first *Syllabus*. As the titles differ, so does the nature of the 65 condemned propositions. They no longer concern a spiritual state of affairs pertaining to the world but external to the Church; they concern rather the corrosion of the Catholic mind itself; they no longer concern the separate parts of a system, but the spirit immanent in them all.

That is also made plain by the fact, noted in the encyclical, that the modernist *plures agit personas ac velut in se commiscet*,[40] being at once an historian, a critic, an apologist and a reformer. I do not believe that Pius X was making a moral condemnation

---

[36] Matthew, 7:17 and 15:18.
[37] See paragraph 202.
[38] "The leading errors of our age."
[39] "The errors of the modernists concerning the Church, revelation, Christ and the sacraments."
[40] "Mixes in itself, as it were, several characters, and plays their parts."

of trickery or hypocrisy (plurality of masks) when he noted the existence of this variety of characters, even though traces of a certain Achitophellian[41] deception are perhaps to be seen in some of the propagators of the doctrines in question; as they are, are they not, in some of their opponents? I believe rather that the multiplicity of characters or masks shows that the document is not condemning separate limbs, but a single spirit, which is ultimately the spirit of independence.

To proceed in the same manner as we did in the case of the first *Syllabus*, we will examine some of the document's principal articles in order to show its condemnation of this spirit. Proposition No.59 condemns the error that man subjects unchanging revealed truth to his changing judgment, thus subordinating truth to history. This sort of reduction of the truth to an advancing human sentiment, which proposes and reproposes the *datum* of religion as a kind of unknowable *noumenon*, is also rejected in article No.20, as it removes the "religious sense" from its dependence on the authority of the Church.[42] It is expressly admitted that the Church is reduced to the task of merely registering and sanctioning opinions dominant in the *Ecclesia discens*,[43] which is in reality no longer being taught at all. By denying that revealed truth can oblige one to give an internal or personal assent, as distinct from a merely external assent as a member of the Church, proposition No.7 asserts the existence in each individual of an intimate core of independence from truth; so that truth is binding by virtue of being subjectively apprehended, rather than by virtue of its being true.

Proposition No.58 is no less weighty: *Veritas non est immutabilis plus quam ipse homo, quippe quae cum ipso, in ipso et per ipsum evolvitur.*[44] Two sorts of independence are proclaimed here. First, man as an historic being is made independent of

---

[41] See II Samuel, 15-17.

[42] The heart of modernism is really this: that the religious soul draws the object and motive of its own faith from within itself, and not from outside. This is the diagnosis given by Cardinal Mercier in his Lenten Pastoral of 1908.

[43] "The learning Church." A standard phrase distinguishing the main body of believers *Ecclesia discens* from the bishops, or sometimes the clergy at large, who are the teaching Church *Ecclesia docens*. [Translator's note].

[44] "Truth is no more unchangeable than man himself, since it evolves with him, in him and through him."

man as a nature, the latter being entirely absorbed in the historicity of the former. The proposition amounts to a denial of
the existence of the eternal idea containing the exemplars of real
natures, a denial of that indisputable element of platonism
without which the idea of God collapses. The second independence proclaimed is, more generally, that of reason from Reason.
Human reason, which we know is the greatest container in the
world,[45] is nonetheless itself contained in another container,
which is the divine mind. This second container is denied in
proposition No.58. The assumption made in the condemned
article to the effect that truth develops with, in and through
man, is therefore false. It does develop in that way, but not
wholly. It is not true that truth comes to be as man comes to be:
it is created intellects that undergo change, even the intellects of
believers, even those of the social body which is the Church;
they all tend towards the same truth, by their own activity
which varies from individual to individual, from generation to
generation and from civilization to civilization. This alleged
independence of the mind from immutable truth tends to confer a kind of *mobilism* on the entire content of religion, as also
on its container, the mind.[46]

Proposition No.65 seems to me to be of great interest and
to provide much food for thought when compared with the last
proposition of the *Syllabus*. Pius IX declared Catholicism incompatible with modern *civilization*. Pius X condemns whoever
says it is incompatible with modern *science*.

So the Church then is incompatible with modern civilization, but modern civilization is not to be identified with science. Religion is compatible with human thought, not in the
sense that it passively submits to all the forms, some of them
mistaken, through which the history of thought may wander,
but in the sense that it is always compatible with that truth at
which thought's wanderings are directed. The document expresses this difference by proclaiming religion compatible with
true science. In any event, we have two condemned propositions: *Catholicism is compatible with modern civilization* (Pius
IX) and *Catholicism is incompatible with true science* (Pius X).
From a comparison of the two condemnations, it becomes clear
that modern civilization and true science do not correspond.

---

[45] Rosmini, *Teosofia*, III, 1090, nat. ed., Vol. XIV, Milan 1941. See
     indices, for the word *Idea*.
[46] See paragraphs 157-62.

While the Church distinguishes between modern civilization and true science, she does not cease condemning the spirit of the age. There can be knowledge which is true in a civilization which is false, but it is then garbed in a false spirit of which it must be stripped, by a kind of reclaiming action, so that it can be reclothed in the truth which is found in the Catholic system and so be regulated by its true principle.

27. The pre-conciliar crisis and the third *Syllabus*.

In this brief historical overview our intention is to outline cursorily some previous crises in the Church. We are almost entirely ignoring their political aspects, saying nothing about their social repercussions, and are hardly touching on disciplinary changes, since the Church's discipline depends on its doctrine.

Examining crises in the Church, we have found that they only occur when a contradiction of the constitutive and governing principles of the Church arises within the Church itself, rather than in the world outside. This kind of contradiction of principle is the "constant," as mathematicians put it, of all crises. The crisis which had arisen in the world outside the Church and been demonstrated in the first *Syllabus*, and which, at the beginning of this century, had again been identified by Pius X when it began to spread into the Church's internal life, was recognized yet once more by Pius XII in a third syllabus, when it had become widespread within the Church towards the middle of the century. The third syllabus is the encyclical *Humani Generis* of 12 August 1950 and, with the texts of the Second Vatican Council, it constitutes the Church's principal doctrinal pronouncement since Pius X.

In the formation of the Church's collective identity, there are moments of *memory*, when certain parts of the deposit of faith are brought to attention, and moments of *oblivion*, when certain parts of the Catholic system are not adverted to and are left in obscurity.[47] This is an effect of the limited attention of the mind, which cannot concentrate on everything all the time, and the mind's capacity to be directed to one thing or another is the great fact on which the art of education, and at a lower level that of propaganda, is based. Since it is a necessary part of human nature, it can neither be regretted nor eliminated. A rela-

---

[47] We will discuss this forgetfulness in paragraph 330ff.

tive inadvertence of this sort must not, however, be allowed to turn into the abolition of parts of the Catholic system. This or that aspect of the whole is highlighted or obscured by the course of history, but these aspects are not created or destroyed in the consciousness of the Church by such prominence or the lack of it.

When the main current of opinion in the Church drifts towards obscuring certain truths, the teaching Church must forcefully uphold them so as to preserve the Catholic system whole and entire, even if the main current is not much interested in the truths concerned. Thus the undeniable fact that the three syllabuses are at present ignored does not rob them of the outstanding importance they intrinsically have. One cannot help noticing in this connection that it is precisely the coherence and continuity of these papal pronouncements which constitute their chief fault in the eyes of the innovators, since the Church's emphatic reiteration of its teaching is held to block further development. In fact the Church dwells in a timeless truth by which she judges time. The Church's motto is *bis in idem*, or *pluries in idem*, or even *semper in idem*,[48] because she stands in a continual and unbreakable relationship with the first truth, so that when she judges the changing events which are truth's escort through time, it is the truth, not the events, which drives her on.

28. *Humani Generis* (1950).

The categorical character of the encyclical's title immediately attracts attention by not employing the more reserved expressions of other doctrinal pronouncements. Instead of the usual formula *non videntur consonare*[49] or something similar (which is in fact used here regarding polygenism), it is declared at the outset that the opinions to be dealt with are of a kind *quae catholicae doctrinae fundamenta subruere minantur.*[50] It is only a threatened or prospective ruin, but the threat is real: not *subruere videntur,*[51] but *subruere minantur.* The errors are such

---

[48] "Twice, several times, always the same."
[49] "Do not appear to harmonize."
[50] "Which threaten to undermine the foundations of Catholic doctrine."
[51] "Seem to undermine."

as to threaten Catholic doctrine, even if they have not over-thrown it completely.

In the introduction to this catalogue, one characteristic of the crisis is mentioned which signals its importance and marks its novelty. The error which once came *ab extra*, from outside the Church, now comes *ab intra*; it is no longer a case of an external assault, but of an intestine evil; no longer an attempt to demolish the Church, but, in the famous phrase of Paul VI, *a self-demolition of the Church*. But there should be no room for false opinions in the Church, because in it human reason, without prejudice to its natural capacities, is always strengthened and widened in its scope by Revelation. The fundamental error however is precisely the *postulate of independence* from Revelation, and the errors which the encyclical is to describe are merely forms or denominations of it. So the Pyrrhonism essential to the modern mentality will mean our knowledge is not a grasping of the real, but merely the product of ever changing impressions of an ever elusive reality. Knowledge is independent of truth.

Existentialism is also based on this principle of independence. For it, existing things have no relation to the divine ideas, those prior essences which participate in the absoluteness of the divine being. The encyclical reproves the modern mentality, not inasmuch as it is modern, but inasmuch as it claims to detach itself from that firmament of unchangeable values, and to give itself over wholly and solely to present existence. Even with corrections, this mentality cannot be reconciled with Catholic dogma.[52]

The following articles trace the descent of further errors, relating them all back to the error of creaturely independence. *Historicism*, being the consideration of existence detached from any fixed essence, finds reality only in movement, and gives rise to a universal *mobilism*. Indeed, once one does deny the tran-stemporal element in every temporal thing, which consists precisely in its fixed nature, being dissolves into becoming, to the exclusion of any abiding reality, even though in fact the latter is necessary in order to conceive of the very notion of becoming.[53]

The condemnation of *sentimentalism* too,[54] is simply a condemnation of feeling when not viewed in the context of man as

---

[52] Denzinger, 2323.

[53] Denzinger, loc. cit.

[54] Denzinger, 2324.

a whole. At the core of man is an essential relation to his own reason, and at the core of reason is an essence which, though created, participates in the absolute. The theoretical core of Pius XII's document is that Pyrrhonism, existentialism, mobilism and sentimentalism all draw their origin from a principle of independence, opposed to the principle on which Catholicism rests. The censure of particular errors deriving from this fundamental error is purely secondary and accessory, be they the denial of the possibility of metaphysics (whether Thomistic or not), the assertion of a universal evolutionism, scriptural criticism, religious naturalism, and other specific religious errors (among the most important being the denial of transubstantiation); and one should set these apart at a secondary level when one is trying to establish just where the very principle of Catholicism itself is being attacked. That principle is that everything anthropological depends on the divine, and that to deny this dependence is, as the document declares, to dissolve the foundations of every possible axiology.[55]

---

[55] Denzinger, 2323.

CHAPTER III

THE PREPARATION
OF THE COUNCIL

29. The Second Vatican Council. Its preparation.

It seems that Pius XI may at one time have considered reconvening the Vatican Council interrupted by the violent events of 1870; what is certain, from the testimony of Domenico Cardinal Tardini, is that Pius XII pondered the suitability of either reconvening the old council or summoning a new one, and that he had the relevant considerations examined by a commission appointed for the purpose. The commission decided against either course. Perhaps it seemed that the doctrine of the encyclical *Humani Generis* was itself enough to correct whatever errors were appearing in the Church. Perhaps it was thought that no prejudice should be done to the papal government, which the authority of a council might lessen or seem to lessen. Perhaps it was sensed that a council would be pervaded by a democratic spirit incompatible with Catholic principle. Perhaps the Pope was influenced by his habitual feeling that his full responsibility meant he should have an indivisible fullness of power; whence it happened that at his death many important positions in the Curia were vacant. No great weight was given at that time to the alleged benefits of the bishops of the world knowing, and talking to, each other; such thinking betrays democratic leanings, and it was not then believed that merely bringing men together meant either that they really knew each other, or that they understood the matters they were considering. The proposal to call a council was set aside. From the point of view of the See of Peter, there is a long standing suspicion hanging over the idea of a council. Cardinal Pallavicino, the historian of the Council of Trent, found an image to express it: "In the mystical heavens of the Church, one cannot imagine a conjunction more difficult to arrange, or more fraught with dangerous influence, than a general council."[1]

The announcement of the calling of a council came upon the world quite unexpectedly, due, as John XXIII himself said, to a sudden inspiration. In the case of Vatican I, an enquiry among the cardinals had been held as early as 1864, and a majority of them had been in favor of calling a council. A few had been against; in order to avoid airing and aggravating disagreements, or because the relevant errors had already been condemned, or because conditions in the Church could not be changed without the assistance of the states.[2]

In the case of Vatican II, there were no prior consultations as to whether the council was necessary or opportune; the decision came from John XXIII by the exercise of his ordinary charism, or perhaps by the influence of an extraordinary one.[3] On 15 July 1959 the Pope established the central preparatory commission, which contained a large majority of cardinals and a number of patriarchs, archbishops and bishops, chosen according to an indeterminate criterion by which it remained unclear whether doctrine, or prudence in administration, or a relation of special trust with the Pope was the determining factor. This central commission sent out to the bishops of the world a questionnaire concerning the matters that should be dealt with; it collected and classified their opinions, itself established lesser commissions, and drew up the schemas that were to be submitted to the ecumenical gathering.

The bishops' replies reveal at the outset some of the tendencies which were to prevail at the council, and not uncommonly display, through their straying on to irrelevant or useless matters, an inability to stick to the point. At Vatican I there had also been far-fetched proposals. There had been suggestions in favor of Rosmini or St. Thomas; important subjects certainly, but other suggestions had descended to the problem of Catholic servants in non-Catholic households, the blessing of cemeteries and other small disciplinary questions, quite disproportionate to the scope of an ecumenical council.

---

[1]   Mansi, Vol.49, p.28.

[2]   Mansi, Vol.49, p.34. The opinion of Cardinal Roberti.

[3]   The Pope himself said that the idea of calling a council was a divine inspiration, and John Paul II said the same in his speech of 26 November 1981 commemorating the centenary of Roncalli's birth.

All in all, there was a uniform inspiration to the preparation of Vatican II which expressed, so it seemed, the Pope's intentions.[4] The opposition, in this preparatory period, acted less in the internal than in the external arena, delaying its full activity until the plenary period of the council.

30. Paradoxical outcome of the Council.

The outcome of Vatican II was quite different from what had been foreshadowed by its preparation: indeed, as we will see, the preparations were immediately and entirely set aside.[5] The council was born, so to speak, of itself, independently of the preparation which had been made for it. In certain respects, Vatican II could be said to have turned out like the Council of Trent, which, as Sarpi[6] maintains at the beginning of his *History*, "emerged with a form and a result quite contrary to the plans of those who brought it about, and dismaying to those who had done all they could to hinder it"; contrary to the designs of those who supported a Catholic reform which would reduce the powers of the Court of Rome, contrary to the fears of that very Court[7] which, according to the Servite, tried to frustrate its success at every turn. Sarpi draws a conclusion regarding the divine operations, and a religious maxim from all this: the paradoxical outcome of the Council of Trent is a "clear evidence for resign-

---

4   In fact, the Pope gave unmeasured praise to the preparatory work in a radio message to the faithful of the world, on 11 September 1962, speaking of "a superabundant richness of elements of a doctrinal and pastoral kind."

5   The paradoxical outcome of the council, the breaking of the council rules, and the setting aside of the council that had been prepared, are passed over in silence by works recounting the course of the great assembly. See for example the synthesis of the council given by Mgr Poupard, pro-President of the Secretariat for Non-Believers, in *Esprit et Vie*, 1983, pp.241ff. To counterbalance the omission of matters as important as these, we will examine them at some little length.

6   Paolo Sarpi (1552-1623) was a Servite friar who wrote an anti-papal history of the Council of Trent. [Translator's note.]

7   The contrast set up by Sarpi is only apparent. His outcome contrary to the fears of the Roman Court was in fact an outcome that the latter wanted. Trent did not really have a paradoxical outcome at all.

ing our thoughts to God and for not trusting human prudence."[8]

As at Trent, in Sarpi's version, so at Vatican II, events
turned out quite differently from what had been prepared; quite
differently from the projections, as they say. It is not that there
are no modernizing strands of thought apparent in the preparatory phase.[9] They did not, however, leave the deep and definite
impression on the collection of preliminary schemas that they
were subsequently to make upon the final documents promulgated by the council. Thus, for example, in the schema on the
liturgy, a flexibility aimed at accommodating different national
characters was proposed, but it was restricted to mission territories and no mention was made of the altogether subjective
demand for creativity on the part of the celebrant. The practice
of communal absolution, to the detriment of individual confession, aimed at easing moral demands, was indeed proposed in
the schema *de sacramentis*. Even the ordination to the priesthood of married men (though not of women) found a place in
the schema *de ordine sacro*. The schema *de libertate religiosa*
(Cardinal Bea), one of the most troubled and disputed of the
ecumenical assembly, put forward in substance the great novelty
which was in the end adopted, apparently removing Catholic
doctrine from the ordinary path canonized and always maintained by the Church.[10]

The utilitarian principle is characteristic of modern pragmatism and activism, which see value in productivity (whether
of objects, or of work, as the case may be) but which ignore the
immanent, non-transitive operations of the person, placing

---

[8]   *Istoria del Concilio Tridentino*, Bari 1935, Vol.I, p.4. For an ex-
     amination of this point see R. Amerio, *Il Sarpi dei pensieri
     filosofici inediti*, Turin 1950, pp.8-9 and in particular the inconsis-
     tency between the letter and the fundamental thought of the text.
     Sarpi is in fact wholly intent on showing the power of human man-
     agement in the conduct of the council.

[9]   I can speak with a certain amount of knowledge of the labors of the
     central preparatory commission, since Mgr Angelo Jelmini, Bishop
     of Lugano and a member of the commission, closely associated me
     with the study of the schemas and the drawing up of his opinions,
     and I thus got to know all the documents.

[10] See the *Catechism of the Catholic Church*, paragraph 2106.
     [Translator's note.]

them below transitive activities having their effect *ad extra*.[11] Nonetheless, it too found express formulation in the schema *de disciplina cleri*, which advanced the idea that bishops and priests should be ineligible for office on reaching a given age, and should retire. The fruit of this tendency to activism was the *motu proprio, Ingravescentem aetatem*, which institutes a *deminutio capitis*[12] for cardinals over the age of eighty. One particular request concerning the cassock paved the way for the custom of wearing lay dress, thus obscuring the specific difference between the priest and the layman, and leading to the neglect of the rule which made the cassock obligatory during the performance of ministerial functions. Particular opinions of the broader theological schools also crop up in the preparatory work. It was requested, for example, that a debatable proposition regarding the limbo of infants, and even of adults, should be accepted as conciliar teaching. This subject was completely omitted,[13] as being too close to the thorny dogma of predestination, of which the council says nothing, but the broad pelagian spirit which it presupposes pervaded post-conciliar theological thinking, as we will show later on.

The influence of those who wanted to make innovations in the training of the clergy, clearly shown during the preparatory period, was even more obvious during the meetings of the full council (schema *de sacrorum alumnis formandis*). The Church's long standing educational tradition, which has been given shape in the seminary system, implies that priests ought to be formed in a particular way, corresponding to the particular ontological and moral character of their consecrated state. The schema requested instead that the formation of the clergy be assimilated as far as at all possible to that of the laity; hence the *ratio studiorum* of seminaries ought to be modeled on those of the state, and clerical culture in general should lose all the specific differences distinguishing it from that of the laity. The grounds given for this innovation were those which became the oft-repeated theme of the council; that the Church's personnel should con-

---

[11] See paragraph 216-17.
[12] Incapacity to vote.
[13] See Delhaye-Gueret-Tombeur, *Concilium Vaticanum II, Concordance, Index, Listes de fréquence, Tables comparatives*, Louvain 1974. *Praedestinatio* and *Praedestinare* occur only three times: twice for Our Lady and once in a citation of Romans 8:29.

form to the world, in order to perform their specific teaching and sanctifying tasks in the world.

Similarly, on the question of reunion of non-Catholic Christians, there were voices heard which ignored the difference between the Protestants on the one hand; without the priesthood, without a hierarchy, without the apostolic succession and without, or almost without, sacraments; and on the other hand the Orthodox, who have almost everything in common with Catholics, except the primacy and infallibility. At the previous council, Pius IX had drawn a very clear distinction: he sent papal representatives bearing letters of invitation to the eastern patriarchs (who all replied that they could not come) but he did not recognize the different Protestant denominations as churches, regarding them as simple associations, and issued a call *ad omnes protestantes*,[14] inviting them, not to take part in the council, but to return to that unity from which they had been separated. The latitudinarian attitude, which appeared in the preparatory period, rests on an implicit partial equality between Catholics and non-Catholics, and was initially only a minority point of view, but it was subsequently responsible for the invitation of Protestant observers on the same basis as the Orthodox and made itself felt in the decree *de oecumenismo*.[15]

There is one last element common to the preparatory period and to the final result: the general optimism which colored the diagnoses and forecasts of a minority of the central preparatory commission. In the fifth section, *de laicis*, of the schema *de Ecclesia*, there appeared the idea that growth in the scientific understanding of nature, that is, an extension of that kingdom of technology which is modern culture, was also an extension of human dignity and happiness; but this was rejected by the majority, who insisted on the indifferent nature of technical progress: it extends the possible field of moral activity, but the latter is not intrinsically assisted by it. Nonetheless, this theme of the domination of the earth by means of technology, attained sacral status[16] in the final document and came to pervade all postconciliar theological thinking. The promotion of technology to the status of a force which civilizes and morally improves mankind, gave rise to the notion that the world *as such* progresses, and also aroused a gale of optimism. Optimism was in fact to

---

[14] "To all Protestants."
[15] See paragraphs 245-47.
[16] See paragraph 218.

preside over the entire outlook of the plenary meetings of the council and to obscure the real state of Catholicism from sight.

It is worth recording the criticisms which one Father on the central preparatory commission made of the overly rosy description of the state of the world, and of the state of the Church in the world.

"I do not approve of the description of the state of the Church given here with such exuberance, more in hope than in truth. Why, and in comparison with what period, do you speak of an *increased religious fervor*? Should not statistical facts, as they are called, be kept before us, from which it is clear that the worship of God, Catholic belief and public morals are, among many people, collapsing and indeed almost in ruins? Are not men's minds generally alienated from the Catholic religion: the state being separate from the Church, philosophy from the dogmas of faith, the investigation of the world from reverence for the Creator, technical discoveries from conformity with the moral order? Does the Church not labor under a shortage of workers in the sacred ministry? Are not many parts of Holy Church cruelly trampled underfoot by the Giants and Minotaurs who strut about the world, or fallen into schism, as among the Chinese? Has not the enemy devastated our missions among unbelievers, which had been planted and watered with such zeal and such charity? Is not atheism lauded no longer merely by private persons, but (what is altogether unheard of) by whole nations, and upheld by the laws of the state? Are not our numbers diminishing proportionally every day, while Mahommedanism and Paganism increase greatly? We are now a fifth part of the human race, who recently were a quarter. Are not our morals turning pagan, by divorce, abortion, euthanasia, sodomy and the pursuit of Mammon?"[17]

The speaker concluded by saying that his diagnosis proceeded *humano more*,[18] in view of historical facts, leaving out what the Providence of God could do for His Church "beyond the bounds of human thinking," and outside the established pattern of His action.

---

[17] The original Latin is given in the Italian edition. [Translator's note.]

[18] "Humanly speaking."

31. Paradoxical outcome of the Council, continued. The Roman Synod.

Apart from the comparison between the final documents and those first proposed, three principal facts make the paradoxical outcome of the council apparent: *the falseness of the forecasts* made by the Pope and others who prepared it; the *fruitlessness of the Roman synod* called by John XXIII as an anticipation of it; and the almost immediate *nullification* of the decree *Veterum Sapientia*, which was meant to foreshadow the cultural cast of the post-conciliar Church.

Pope John intended the council to be a great act of renewal and functional adaptation for the Church and thought he had adequately prepared it to be such, but nonetheless cherished the prospect that it would all be over within a few months;[19] thinking perhaps of Lateran I under Callistus II in 1123, which three hundred prelates concluded in nineteen days, or of Lateran II under Innocent II in 1139, which a thousand prelates concluded in seventeen days. In fact the council opened on 11 October 1962 and closed on 8 December 1965, thus lasting intermittently for three years. All expectations were overthrown because of the aborting of the council which had been prepared, and the successive elaboration of another quite different council which generated itself.

The Roman synod was planned and summoned by John XXIII as a solemn forerunner of the larger gathering, which it was meant to prefigure and anticipate. The Pope himself said precisely that, to the clergy and faithful of Rome in an allocution of 29 June 1960. Because of that intention, the synod's importance was universally recognized as extending beyond the diocese of Rome to the whole Catholic world. Its importance was compared to that which the provincial synods held by St. Charles Borromeo had had with respect to the Council of

---

[19] That is apparent from the *positio* of the preliminary proceedings for the beatification of Pope John, which became known through an indiscretion on the part of the journalist F. D'Andrea. See *Il Giornale Nuovo* of 3 January 1979. It is also clear from the Pope's own words at the audience of 13 October 1962, which led to the belief that the council could be over by Christmas. [When speaking to the crowds in St. Peter's Square on the evening of 11 October, the day the council opened, Pope John said that it *potesse finire prima di Natale*. "It could finish before Christmas." Translator's note.]

Trent. New life was given to the old saying that the whole Catholic world should wish to model itself on the Church of Rome. The fact that the Pope immediately ordered the texts of the Roman synod to be translated into Italian and all the principal languages, also makes it clear that in his mind it was intended to play an important exemplary role.

The texts of the Roman synod promulgated on 25, 26 and 27 January 1960 constitute a complete reversion of the Church to its proper nature; we mean not merely to its supernatural essence (that can never be lost) but to its historical nature, a returning of the institution to its principles, as Machiavelli put it.

The synod in fact proposed a vigorous restoration at every level of ecclesial life. The discipline of the clergy was modeled on the traditional pattern formulated at the Council of Trent, and based on two principles which had always been accepted and practiced. The first is that of the peculiar character of the person consecrated to God, supernaturally enabled to do Christ's work, and thus clearly separated from the laity (*sacred* means *separate*). The second, which follows from the first, is that of an ascetical education and a sacrificial life, which is the differentiating mark of the clergy as a body, though individuals can take up an ascetical life in the lay state. The synod therefore prescribed for the clergy a whole style of behavior quite distinct from that of laymen. That style demands ecclesiastical dress, sobriety in diet, the avoiding of public entertainments and a flight from profane things. The distinct character of the clergy's cultural formation was also reaffirmed, and the outlines were given of the system which the Pope solemnly sanctioned the year after in *Veterum Sapientia*. The Pope also ordered that the *Catechism* of the Council of Trent should be republished, but the order was ignored. It was not until 1981 that, by private initiative, a translation was published in Italy.[20]

The liturgical legislation of the synod is no less significant: the use of Latin is solemnly confirmed, all attempts at creativity on the part of the celebrant, which would reduce the liturgical action of the Church to the level of a simple exercise of private piety, are condemned. The need to baptize infants as soon as possible is emphasized, a tabernacle in the traditional form and

---

20 O.R., 5-6 July 1982. [*Edizioni Paoline* in Italy published a new edition of the *Catechism* in 1961 which sold very well; however the translation was rather free and inexact. Translator's note.]

position is prescribed, Gregorian Chant is ordered, newly composed popular songs are submitted to the approval of the
bishop, all appearance of worldliness is forbidden in churches
by a general prohibition of such things as the giving of concerts
and performances, the selling of pictures or printed matter, the
giving of free rein to photographers and the lighting of candles
by all and sundry (one ought to get the priest to do it). The
ancient sacred rigor is re-established regarding sacred spaces,
forbidding women entry to the altar area. Lastly, altars facing
the congregation are to be allowed only by way of an exception,
which it is up to the diocesan bishop to make.

Anybody can see that this massive reaffirmation of traditional discipline, which the synod wanted, was contradicted and
negated in almost every detail by the effects of the council. And
so the Roman synod, which was to have been an exemplary
foreshadowing of the council, fell within a few years into the
Erebus of oblivion, and is indeed *tanquam non fuerit.*[21] As an
instance of this nullification I may say that having searched for
the texts of the Roman synod in diocesan curias and archives, I
could not find them there and had to get them from secular
public libraries.[22]

32. Paradoxical outcome of the Council, continued. *Veterum Sapientia.*

The use of the Latin language is, not metaphysically but
historically, connatural to the Catholic Church, and is closely
connected even in the popular mind with things ecclesiastical. It
also constitutes an important instrument and sign of historical
continuity in the Church. Since there is no internal reality
without its appropriate external manifestation, and since the
internal realities arise, fluctuate, and are honored or abased together with their external manifestations, the Church has always

---

[21] "As if it had never been." In O.R. of 4 June 1981, with the usual
loquimini nobis placentia, i.e., "Tell us what we want to hear," it
says that the renewal of the Church was begun under John XXIII
with the holding of the Roman synod and the opening of the
council, and that "the two ended up being amalgamated." Yes, if
"amalgamate" means "annihilate." The synod is not cited by the
council even once.

[22] *Prima Romana Synodus, A.D. MDCCCCLX, Typ. polyglotta Vati-
cana, 1960.*

believed that the external manifestation which is the Latin language should be maintained permanently, in order to preserve the internal reality of the Church. This is all the more true when one is dealing with a linguistic phenomenon in which the fusion of form and substance, of the external and the internal, is quite indissoluble. In fact, the ruin of Latin after Vatican II was accompanied by many of the symptoms of the "self-destruction" of the Church which Paul VI deplored.

We will discuss the value of Latin later.[23] Here we only want to touch upon that difference we are studying between the preparatory inspiration of the council and its actual result.

By *Veterum Sapientia* John XXIII wanted to bring about a return of the Church to its own principles, this return being necessary in his mind for the renewal of the Church in its own proper nature at the present *articulus temporum*.

The Pope attributed a very special importance to the document, and the solemnities with which he surrounded its promulgation in St. Peter's, in the presence of the cardinals and of the whole Roman clergy, are unique in the history of the present century. The outstanding importance of *Veterum Sapientia* is not destroyed by the oblivion to which it was immediately dispatched, nor by its historical lack of success; values are not values only when they are accepted. Its importance comes from its perfect conformity with the historic reality which is the Church.

The encyclical is above all an *affirmation of continuity*. The Church's culture is continuous with that of the Greco-Roman world, first and foremost because Christian literature has been since its beginnings Greek and Latin literature. The Bible comes in Greek swaddling clothes, the oldest creeds are Greek and Latin, the Roman Church is Latin from the middle of the third century, the councils of the early centuries know no other language than Greek. This is a continuity internal to the Church whereby all its ages are bound together. But there is also what might be called an external continuity which crosses beyond the bounds of the Christian era and gathers up the whole of the wisdom of the pagans. We will not indeed start talking about *Saint Socrates*, but we cannot ignore the teaching of the Greek and Latin Fathers, recalled by the Pope in a passage from Tertullian, according to which there is a continuity between the

---

[23] See paragraphs 278-79.

world of thought in which the wisdom of the ancients lived, *veterum sapientia*, and the world of thought elaborated after the revelation of the Incarnate Word.

Christian thought developed a content that had been supernaturally revealed, but it also took to itself a content revealed naturally by the light of created reason. Thus the classical world is not extraneous to Christianity. The latter has as its essence a sphere of truths above our natural lights, and unattainable by them, but it includes nonetheless the sphere of every truth which human thought can reach. Christian culture is thus prepared for and awaited "obedientially," in the mediaeval phrase, by the wisdom of the ancients, because no truth, no justice, no beauty, remain foreign to it. Christianity is therefore in harmony with, rather than opposed to, the ancient culture, and has always been sustained by the latter; and sustained not merely by turning it into a handmaid and making a purely pragmatic use of it, as is commonly asserted, but by carrying it on her bosom, as something that already was, but was to be made even greater by being made holy. I do not wish to disguise the fact that the relationship between Christianity and the ancient world, mutually congenial though they may be, entails some rather delicate questions and requires one to keep a firm hold on the distinction between the rational and the suprarational. It is impossible to sustain Tertullian's overly quoted formula *anima naturaliter christiana*,[24] because it amounts to calling something *naturally supernatural.* One must tread carefully to avoid the dangers which naturalism and historicism pose for a Christian religion which is essentially supernatural and suprahistorical. The idea that Christianity stretches across time and cultural change is nonetheless necessary, true and Catholic, albeit difficult. I shelter under the authority of St. Augustine, when he asserts this continuity in an abrupt and all-embracing fashion, straddling centuries and forms of worship: *Nam res ipsa, quae nunc christiana religio nuncupatur, erat apud antiquos nec defuit ab initio generis humani.*[25]

The practical and disciplinary section of *Veterum Sapientia* is as crystal clear as its doctrine. It is the very precision of its requirements that led to its nullification, when it was not

---

[24] "Naturally Christian soul."

[25] *Retractationes*, I, ch.13. "The thing which is now called the Christian religion existed among the ancients, and has never been lacking since the beginning of the human race."

backed up by papal authority. It decrees that the ecclesiastical *ratio studiorum* should regain its own distinctive character, deriving from the specific nature of a *homo clericus*; that substance should thus be put back into the teaching of the traditional disciplines, principally Latin and Greek; and that in order to achieve this, secular subjects which had come in or been expanded through the tendency to copy the secular syllabus, should be dropped or abridged. It lays down that in seminaries, the fundamental subjects such as dogmatic and moral theology should be taught in Latin from Latin textbooks, and that if there were any teachers who were unable or unwilling to use Latin, they should be replaced within a reasonable period. As the coping stone of this Apostolic Constitution intended to foster a general revival of Latin in the Church, the Pope decreed the establishment of a Higher Latin Institute, designed to train Latinists for the Catholic world at large, and to bring out a dictionary of modern Latin.[26]

The general collapse of the use of Latin, following as it did upon a project for its general restoration, provides a further proof of the paradoxical outcome of the council. *Veterum Sapientia*, being concerned as it was with an historically essential facet of Catholicism, called for an outstanding effort on the part of the authorities issuing it, and an harmonious response on the part of those responsible for its implementation. What was needed was the practical force displayed, for example, in the great reform of Italian schools by Giovanni Gentile,[27] which fixed the form of the syllabus for half a century. Thousands of

---

[26] In reality, the demise of Latin in the post-conciliar Church has been obvious. Even at the International Thomistic Congress of 1974, Latin was not listed as one of the official languages. It was subsequently admitted after I had protested by a letter of 1 October 1973 to the Master General of the Dominicans, Fr. Aniceto Fernandez. He had a reply sent to me on 18 October, accepting both the protest and the request. "We had considered it ourselves," he says, "first and foremost because it is the language of St. Thomas." There is no need to add that very few papers were delivered in Latin. The delatinization of the Thomistic Congresses was complete in 1980, when not one of the twenty-nine contributions was in Latin. There could not be a clearer proof of the transition to a multilingual Church, in which Latin is nonetheless alien.

[27] Giovanni Gentile (1875-1944) was an idealist philosopher, and Minister for Education (1922-1924). [Translator's note.]

teachers who then found themselves in a position analogous to that in which *Veterum Sapientia* placed teachers of sacred literature, were mercilessly obliged either to conform or to resign. The reform of ecclesiastical studies, however, was annihilated in very short order, having met opposition from many quarters for a variety of reasons, principally in Germany in a book by one Winninger, bearing a preface by the Bishop of Strasbourg. The Pope, having stood firm to start with, later gave orders that the implementation of the document should not be insisted on; those who would have had the duty of putting it into effect imitated this papal weakness, and *Veterum Sapientia*, which had been so loudly praised as useful and opportune, was completely wiped from memory and is not cited in any conciliar document. Some biographies of John XXIII do not mention it at all, just as if it did not exist, and never had; while the more arrogant accounts mention it simply as an error. There is not, in the whole history of the Church, another instance of a document's being so solemnly emphasized, and then being so unceremoniously cast out so soon afterwards, like the corpse of an executed criminal.

The question remains, however, whether it was struck out of the book of the living because of the unwisdom shown in promulgating it, or because of the lack of courage shown when it came to demanding its implementation.

33. The aims of the First Vatican Council.

From the beginnings of conciliar gatherings in the Church during the apostolic period, up as far as Vatican I, an ecumenical council had always been summoned with one or more of three objectives, which were called the *causa fidei*, the *causa unionis* and the *causa reformationis*.[28] At the councils of the early centuries, the second and third objectives were implicit in the first, and were not explicitly formulated, but obviously by settling questions of faith, such as that of the union between the human and the divine in Christ, social harmony was re-established in the Church through the overcoming of doctrinal divisions. Thanks to the connection between doctrine and discipline, the laws of the Church's action were thereby re-established no less than the rule of faith. The subject of union was brought forcibly to the Church's attention later on by the

---

[28] The interests of the faith, of unity or of reform.

schisms of Photius and Michael Cerularius, and later still by the great division in Germany. Unity was the predominant issue at the councils of Lyons (1274) and Florence (1439). Lastly, having been in need of attention for centuries, due to the corruption of clerical manners, the overweening worldly power of the Roman Curia and the luxurious pomp of the Papacy, the subject of reform had also been dealt with at the Council of Trent (1545-1563).

These three ends were also pursued at Vatican I: the call to non-Catholics gave rise to a huge literature and wide ranging arguments. The *causa unionis* was made the responsibility of one of the four main preparatory commissions, as was the *causa reformationis*, and this gave rise to a swarm of petitions and suggestions, proving clearly enough how nothing resulted, even in those days, from the activities of small groups and camarillas. The breadth of the hopes aroused is shown by the variety and daring of the suggestions made. There were those even in the middle of the nineteenth century who wanted the council to forbid the death penalty; who proposed that *si quis bellum incipiat, anathema sit,*[29] who called for the abolition of the celibacy of the Latin clergy; and who favored the election of bishops by democratic suffrage. The proposal made by the Capuchin Antonio da Reschio gave clearest expression to the desire for a militant organization of the Catholic masses.[30] He envisaged that the whole mass of the Catholic population, from children to adults, from celibates to married people, should be divided up into "congregations," and that the members of the congregations should not form friendships, or marry, or mix in any other way with non-members. In effect this meant separation not only from those outside the Church, or outside the practicing Church, but even from anyone inside the Church who would not join the mass organization; *tamquam castrorum acies ordinata.*[31] The Capuchin's idea was inspired by pagan, Jesuit or utopian models, and envisaged the perfect society in terms of external organization according to a rational scheme.

Despite these extravagances and veins of modernizing thought, the preparation made for Vatican I succeeded in imposing a definite direction on the council, which guaranteed the Church's unity in the face of the world. As regards the *causa*

---

[29] "Let anyone who begins a war be anathema."
[30] Mansi, Vol.49, p.456.
[31] "Drawn up like a battle line." (Cf. Cant. 6:9).

fidei, the errors identified in the *Syllabus* were condemned again, either explicitly or implicitly. As regards the *causa unionis*, it was asserted once more that unity must necessarily come about through reunion, or the accession of non-Catholic denominations to the Roman Church, as the center of unity. As regards the *causa reformationis*, the principle that all the faithful are subject to the natural law, and to the divine law possessed by the Church, was renewed. The definition of the Pope's infallible teaching authority put the seal on that truth.

34. The aims of Vatican II. Pastorality.

The three traditional aims can all be recognized in the ends pursued by Vatican II, even though they are set forth and emphasized in various ways, so that one or another of them is primarily addressed or stressed at a particular time. They are, however, all swallowed up in a somewhat novel concept expressed by the word *pastoral*.

In the decree *Presbyterorum Ordinis*, paragraph No.12 gives a threefold aim to the council: the *internal renewal* of the Church (this seems to affect both faith and reform), the *spread of the Gospel* in the world (this seems to concern the faith, inasmuch as it is *non servanda, sed propaganda*)[32] and lastly, *dialogue with the modern world* (which seems to be *de fide propaganda* or, as is said these days, *de evangelizando mundo*).[33]

In his speech opening its second period of meetings, Paul VI gave the council four goals. The first is the Church's *taking account of itself*. It seemed to the Pope that "the truth about the Church of Christ ought to be explored, organized and expressed," and that "what the Church thinks of itself should be defined, but not by dogmatic definitions." A shade of subjectivism can be seen here. What really matters is what the Church is, not what the Church thinks about itself.

The second goal is *reform*, that is, the effort of the Church to correct itself and bring itself back into conformity with its divine model (without drawing a distinction between an essential constitutive conformity, which can never be lost, and an accidentally perfectionable conformity, which is always to be sought). The Pope considers a reform of this sort to imply a reawakening of spiritual energies already latent in the bosom of

---

[32] "Not to be kept, but to be spread."
[33] "About propagating the faith, evangelizing the world."

the Church: it is a question of realizing and perfecting the Church as it exists through time.

The third goal takes up the theme of the *causa unionis*. The Pope says this goal "concerns other Christians" and that the Catholic Church alone can offer them perfect ecclesiastical unity. He thus seems to stay within the bounds of traditional doctrine: namely, that union already has its definite center, around which the scattered and separated parts must concentrate. He adds that "recent movements still in full course among the Christian communities separated from us, show that union can only be attained through unity in faith, in participation in the same sacraments, and in the organic harmony of a single ecclesiastical government." He thus reaffirms the need of a threefold agreement in dogmatic, sacramental and hierarchical matters. He does however presuppose that the desire for unity among those separated is a desire for dogma, sacraments and a hierarchy of the sort found in the Catholic Church. The Protestants, on the other hand, understand unity as a mutual drawing together by which all denominations move towards a single center, which, although perhaps found within the Christian body as a whole, cannot be identified with the center of unity which the Roman Church professes to be, to possess and to communicate to others.[34]

The council's ecumenism is thus impaired by a fundamental ambiguity, hanging as it does between the concept of conversion as a *reversion* to the Catholic center, and conversion as a response to a need common to all denominations, Catholic and non-Catholic, for a center beyond and above them all.

The fourth goal of the council is "to throw out a bridge to the modern world." By opening a conversation of this sort the Church "*discovers* and strengthens its missionary vocation," that is, its essential purpose of evangelizing mankind. The term *discover* goes well beyond the meaning for which the Pope employs it, since the Church has always spread the Gospel, and when new journeys and voyages discovered new countries, customs and religions and showed Christendom was only, in Campanella's[35] phrase, a finger of the world, the Church was soon possessed by a missionary spirit, Campanella himself made the first

---

[34] See paragraph 245ff.
[35] Tommaso Campanella (1568-1639) was a Dominican and a philosopher. [Translator's note.]

attempt at a missionary and comparative theology, and Rome created the Congregation for the Propagation of the Faith.

The Pope conceives of dialogue with the world as being identical with the service the Church must give to the world, and he expands the idea of service so far as to say expressly that the Fathers of the council have not been called together to deal with *their own affairs*, those of the Church, but with *those of the world*. The idea that the Church's service of the world is aimed at making the world serve Christ, of whom the Church is the historical prolongation, and that the dominion of the Church does not imply servitude for man, but rather his elevation and his lordship, is here little in evidence. It seems the Pope, without bothering to draw distinctions, wishes to fly from the slightest trace or suspicion of claiming dominion of any kind, and that he sees service and conquest as contradictories; but Christ Himself said "I have overcome the world."

35. Expectations concerning the Council.

Having said something about the council's goals, it is appropriate to mention the expectations held, and the forecasts made, about the effects that would flow from it. Goals are set by the will; forecasts, however, have to do with feelings and often with hopes. The term *triumphalism* was invented to portray a supposed attitude of the Church in the past, without stopping to realize that that portrayal was contradicted both by the Church's sufferings in recent centuries under attacks from the modern state, and by the accusation, which the critics made simultaneously, that the Church was defensively isolating herself as something separate from the world. Triumphalist or not, the general tone of the forecasts made is nonetheless hopeful and optimistic, despite occasional bursts of realism. The hope is not, however, of the theological sort caused by supernatural certainties, and concerned with the state of things in the world to come, but an historical and worldly hope based on guesses and forecasts generated by the desires of the forecaster, or by what seems to be happening to humanity.

In his speech opening the second period of the council, Paul VI displays the state of the modern world, with its religious persecutions, its atheism adopted as a principle of social life, its neglect of the knowledge of God, and its greed for riches and pleasures. "At the sight of such things" the Pope says "we *ought* to be dismayed rather than comforted, saddened rather than cheered." But, as can be seen, the Pope uses a conditional mood and does not turn his hypothetical dismay into a positive statement. He follows instead the footsteps of John XXIII, who, in his opening speech of 11 October 1962 forecasts a "universal irradiation of the truth, right direction of individual, domestic and social life." In Paul VI's speech, optimism not only colors the forecasts, but implants itself firmly in the consideration of the present state of the Church. When one compares his words here with opposing statements made on other occasions, one can see the great breadth of the variation between the extremes in his thinking, and the strength of the Pope's ability to forget one extreme while he was dwelling upon another: "Let us rejoice, brethren: when was the Church ever as conscious of itself, when was it ever so *happy* and so *harmonious* and so ready for the fulfillment of its mission?"

Cardinal Traglia, the Vicar of Rome, abandoned the rhetorical question and frankly asserted: "*Never* has the Catholic Church been so closely united around its head, never has it had a clergy so morally and intellectually exemplary as at present; nor is there any risk of a rupture in its organization. A crisis in the Church is not what the council has to deal with."[36] A judgment like that can only be explained by a very excited state of mind, or a very defective knowledge of history.

An excited state of mind also seems to be the origin of Paul VI's statement in his sermon on 18 November 1965: "No other council in the history of the Church of God has had such ample proportions, such assiduous and tranquil labors, or such varied and interesting themes." It is undoubtedly true that Vatican II was the greatest of the councils in terms of numbers attending, logistical organization, and agitation of public opinion, but these are simply attendant circumstances rather than what makes a council important. There were only two hundred easterners and three Latins at Ephesus in 431, and Trent opened with only sixty bishops. Thanks to the enormous modern apparatus of information, which works merely by stamping images on the mind, the imposing exterior of Vatican II was very successful in stirring the world's attention, and created a conciliar opinion much more important than the actual council. In an age when things are what they are because of the way they are presented, and when things are worth as much as people can be

---

[36] O.R., 9 October 1962.

persuaded they are worth, the council necessarily made a great stir in public opinion, and that very fact was deemed to confer greatness on the council. Neither the council Fathers nor the Pope himself were immune to this inflationary tendency. In a letter of 29 June 1975, admittedly polemical since addressed to Monseigneur Lefebvre, Paul VI declared that Vatican II is a council "which has no less authority (than others), and which in some respects is even more important than the Council of Nicea."

Comparisons between one council and another are dangerous, since one needs to specify in what respect the comparison is being made. If one looks to their practical effectiveness one will find that, for example, Lateran V (1512-1517) achieved nothing regarding the *causa reformationis* with which it was principally concerned, since its reforming decrees were a dead letter; but that its dogmatic decrees were important since they excluded neoaristotelianism, by condemning those who taught that the soul was mortal. Only at Trent were doctrinal clarification and practical measures equally significant, but even Trent failed entirely in the *causa unionis* for which it had primarily been summoned.

Leaving aside all comparisons between one council and another, one can still compare one sort of council with another, and it then becomes apparent that the dogmatic sort, which fix immutable doctrine, are more important than the pastoral sort, which are dominated by historical circumstances and only promulgate transient and changeable decrees about practical matters. Then again, every dogmatic council makes decrees of a pastoral kind, based on doctrine. The proposal to deal with doctrine first and pastoral matters second was rejected at Vatican II.[37] There are no dogmatic pronouncements in Vatican II's teachings which are more than repetitions of the teaching of previous councils. The *Note* on the theological standing of the doctrine taught by the council, released by its Secretary General, Mgr Pericle Felici on 16 November 1965, established that in view of the pastoral nature of the council: *Sancta Synodus tantum de rebus fidei vel morum ab Ecclesia tenenda definit quae ut talia aperte ipsa declaravit.*[38] As a matter of fact, no part of the

---

[37] M. Lefebvre, *Un évêque parle*, Jarzé 1976, p.104.

[38] "The Holy Synod only makes a definition regarding matters of faith and morals to be held by the Church when it openly declares that it is doing so."

council's decrees is declared to constitute a dogmatic definition, but it is well understood that where a doctrine already defined in the past is reaffirmed, there can be no doubt about its theological status. However, to return to the comparison between types of council, it must be firmly maintained that the dogmatic sort are the more important, as a consequence of a philosophical truth prior to all theological propositions, and also as something revealed in Scripture. The metaphysical procession of being gives priority to knowledge rather than to the will, to theory rather than to practice: *In principio erat Verbum.*[39] If it is not based on knowledge, the action of ecclesiastical authority in making arrangements and giving orders has no foundation. That pragmatic tendency which influenced the council on so many occasions influences judgments on this matter as well.

36. Cardinal Montini's forecasts. His minimalism.

Particular mention should be made of the forecasts of Cardinal Giovanni Battista Montini, Archbishop of Milan, in a book on the future council, published by the Catholic University of that city. It is a remarkable document even considered in itself, but even more remarkable for the light it sheds on the continuities and discontinuities in papal thinking, by which I mean the undeniable continuity which is evident in certain directions, and the gap that yawns between the initial optimism and the final pessimism of Paul's pontificate. The text is as follows: "The council should trace the line of Christian relativism, laying down how far the Catholic religion must act as the iron guardian of absolute values, and how far it can and *must* bend in its approach, in its *connaturality* with human life as it exists in time."[40]

Some defects of wording, such as "bend in its connaturality," could make it difficult to expound the sense of this statement, but its fundamental meaning is clear enough. It would seem that the council is not to prepare for an expansion of Catholicism, but to adjust it so that its supernatural element is reduced to a minimum, and so that it chimes in to the greatest possible extent with the world, which is deemed, if the words

---

[39] "In the beginning was the Word." John, 1:1.

[40] O.R., 8-9 October 1962. All the emphases printed in the texts cited are our own, and are made so that the parts of the text commented on stand out clearly.

are to be taken as they stand, to be connatural with it. So the Church is not, as the common image has it, to be the leaven of the world that causes it to rise, nor to work its way into humanity and change its foundations; rather, it should itself be impregnated with the world, because then it will be able to impregnate the world in turn.

A statement like this presupposes that the Church now finds itself obliged to make a compromise with the world, in the way that Clement XIV felt it had to compromise in the eighteenth century, when he brought himself to suppress the Jesuits. It is a judgment based on a cautious rather than a courageous prudence. It also traces a course of action for the council based on a presupposition which the Catholic religion can hardly accept. The supposition is that man must be accepted as he is; but Catholicism takes him as he is, while not accepting him as he is, since he is corrupt: religion always keeps in view what man should be like, precisely so that it can heal him of his corruption and save him.

If one sets aside the familiar predictions of a flourishing revival which Montini made as Pope, and connects his declaration of 1962 with the one he made on 18 February 1976, it can be seen to have a paradoxical importance: "We should not be afraid of the prospect of one day being perhaps a minority, we will not be embarrassed at unpopularity...it will not matter to us if *we are defeated*, as long as we are witnesses to the truth and to the freedom of the sons of God." The prospect of increasing misfortune, almost of extinction, which opened in the Church in 1968, is even more apparent in the cry of the Pope's tragic prayer at the requiem of Aldo Moro: "A sense of pessimism has *annihilated* so many calm hopes and shaken our trust in the goodness of the human race." The man laments, but the Pope laments still more, close to the shadowy line,[41] and confronted with the shattered assumptions of his whole pontificate.[42]

---

[41] Pope Paul was within three months of his own death as he spoke. [Translator's note.]

[42] G. Andreotti, *Diario* 1976-1979, Rome 1981, p.224, says that it appeared the Pope was "almost reproaching the Lord for what had happened." [The English reader must be aware of the nature, duration and symbolic political and religious significance of the relation between Moro and the Pope, in order to grasp the full force of these remarks. Translator's note.]

37. Catastrophal predictions.

The term is not used here in its sinister sense, but with its neutral meaning of a complete about-turn. These were the forecasts of those who foresaw and pursued a radical change in Catholicism. Mgr Schmitt, Bishop of Metz, openly admits as much: *La situation de civilisation que nous vivons entraîne des changements non seulement dans notre comportement extérieur, mais dans la conception même que nous nous faisons tant de la création que du salut apporté par Jésus Christ.*[43] The doctrine underlying this prediction, although confused, was subsequently embraced both at the popular level and in the activity of organized groups which imposed important elements of their thinking on the council. Those who dare to attribute to John XXIII the intention of "blowing up the Stalinist monolith of the Catholic Church from inside"[44] are propagators of the catastrophal scenario. So too are the disciples of the confused and poetical theocosmologism of Teilhard de Chardin: *Je pense que le grand fait religieux actuel est l'éveil d'une Religion nouvelle qui fait, petit à petit, adorer le Monde et qui est indispensable à l'humanité pour qu'elle continue a travailler. Il est donc capital que nous montrions le Christianisme comme capable de diviniser le nisus et l'opus naturels humains.*[45] The Holy Office's *monitum* against Teilhard effectively became obsolete by the time of John XXIII's death.[46] Rightly convinced of the essential irreformabil-

---

[43] Cited in *Itinéraires*, n.160, p.106. "The cultural situation we are living in entails changes not only in our external behavior, but in the very notion we have of *creation* and of the *salvation* brought by Jesus Christ."

[44] *Corriere della Sera*, 21 April 1967.

[45] Journal, p.220. "I think the great religious fact of the present time is the awakening of a new religion which, bit by bit, is leading to the worship of the world, and which is indispensable to humanity in order that it may continue to labor. It is therefore of capital importance that we should show that Christianity is able to divinize the natural human *nisus* and *opus*."

[46] 1981 saw proof of the internal disorganization of the Roman Curia, which often abandons any attempt at coherence. When the Institut Catholique in Paris celebrated the centenary of Teilhard de Chardin's birth, the Secretary of State, Cardinal Casaroli, sent the Institute's president, Mgr Poupard, a message praising the Jesuit's merits and saying how much the Church owed him. Since Teilhard had been the object of a monitum from the Holy Office in 1962, declar-

ity of the Church, the innovators propose to push the Church beyond itself, in search of a metachristianity, to use the Teilhardian term, because a *renewed* religion is a *new* religion. It is supposed that in order to avoid dying, Christianity has to undergo a mutation in the genetic and Teilhardian sense. But if religion has to go beyond itself in order not to die, the formula contains a contradiction, since it amounts to saying that Christianity has to die in order not to die. In French Catholicism before the war there were already ideas about a radical change in the Church, and Cardinal Saliège wrote: "There have been unforeseen biological changes which have the appearance of a new species. Are we now witnessing a kind of change that will profoundly modify the human structure, by which I mean the mental and psychological structure of humanity? This question, which philosophers will regard as impertinent, will be able to be answered in five hundred years."[47]

---

ing that there were "ambiguities and grave errors" in his work, this homage paid to him by the Holy See caused a scandal, and entailed a "rephrasing" of the commendation, which was in fact a retraction.

[47] Cited in J. Guitton, *Scrivere come si ricorda*, Alba 1975, p.319.

CHAPTER IV

THE COURSE OF THE COUNCIL

38. The opening address. Antagonism with the world. Freedom of the Church.

The opening speech of the council, made by John XXIII on 11 October 1962, is a complex document, and there is evidence that this is partly because the Pope's thought is given in a version influenced by someone else. Even the establishment of the precise text gives rise to canonical and philological problems. To give the gist of it, we will present the substance of what it says under a few headings.

In the first place, the speech begins with an energetic reaffirmation of the *aut aut*[1] presented to men by the Catholic Church which, by ordering the things of time to an eternal destiny, rejects neutrality or ambivalence as between the world and the life of heaven. As well as citing the prophetic text of Luke 2:34 which says that Christ will be a sign of contradiction, for the rise and *fall* of many, the Pope also cites the even more decisive text of Luke 11:23: *Qui non est mecum, contra me est.*[2] These texts were never again cited in conciliar documents, because the council proceeded to seek out those aspects of life upon which the world and the Church can meet and unite their efforts, rather than those upon which they are opposed and clash. The perfect conformity of this part of the opening address with Catholic thinking is also apparent when the Pope asserts "that men have the duty to move toward the acquisition of heavenly goods, whether taken individually, or socially united": this is the traditional concept of the absolute lordship of God, which not only affects human affairs at the individual

---

[1] "Either or."
[2] "Whoever is not with Me is against Me."

level, but at the level of societies, and which creates the religious obligations of the state.

The second outstanding point in the speech is the condemnation of the pessimism of those who "see only ruin and calamity in modern times." The Pope admits there is a general alienation from concern for spiritual things discernible in the behavior of the modern world, but believes it to be counterbalanced by the advantage that "the conditions of modern life have removed those innumerable obstacles by which the children of the world once impeded the free action of the Church." The historical reference could have two meanings, and it is unclear whether, on the one hand, the Pope was thinking of the improper interference which the Empire and the absolute monarchies used to exert in the Church when everything ultimately depended on religion, or whether, on the other, he was thinking of the harassment the Church has been subjected to by liberal states since the eighteenth century, in an age in which the exclusion of religion from the civil sphere has brought society to its present condition. It would seem he had the former in mind rather than the latter, but it should be remembered that the Church continually struggled, both theoretically and practically, against subordination to the civil power, particularly in the matter of the appointment of bishops and investiture of ecclesiastical property. One need only remember how much these things were deplored by Rosmini.

Even the so-called right of veto in papal elections was only a pragmatic concession and was treated as null and void on several occasions, as at the conclaves which elected Julius III (1550), Marcellus II (1555), Innocent X (1644), and was abolished after the one which elected St. Pius X (1903); that is, whenever courage prevailed over political considerations.

The Pope's optimistic assessment of the Church's present freedom is certainly in accordance with facts where the Roman Church itself is concerned, freed as it is from the yoke of its temporal rule, but is cruelly contradicted by the reality of the Church's circumstances in many countries, where it is today in chains. Indeed, the striking absence of whole episcopates, prevented by their governments from coming to the council was something the Pope could not but deplore; he confessed he "felt a very real sorrow at the absence we note here today of many bishops, imprisoned for their faithfulness to Christ." One should also remember that the unfortunate servitude which sometimes arose in past centuries was an aspect of the mutual compenetration of religion and society, and resulted from an insufficiently clear mutual ordering of religious and civil values, which were treated as an indivisible whole, structured by religion. The present freedom proceeds, on the contrary, from a delegitimization of the Church's authority in the minds of the men of the age, overcome as they are by their quest for well-being, and by doctrinal indifference.

When one is talking about the liberty of the council, the salient and half secret point that should be noted is the restriction on the council's liberty to which John XXIII had agreed a few months earlier, in making an accord with the Orthodox Church by which the patriarchate of Moscow accepted the papal invitation to send observers to the council, while the Pope for his part guaranteed the council would refrain from condemning communism. The negotiations took place at Metz in August 1962, and all the details of time and place were given at a press conference by Mgr Schmitt, the bishop of that diocese.[3] The negotiations ended in an agreement signed by Metropolitan Nikodim for the Orthodox Church and Cardinal Tisserant, the Dean of the Sacred College of Cardinals, for the Holy See. News of the agreement was given in *France Nouvelle*, the central bulletin of the French communist party, in the edition of 16-22 January 1963 in these terms: *Parce que le système socialiste mondial manifeste d'une façon incontestable sa supériorité et qu'il est fort de l'approbation de centaines et centaines de millions d'hommes, l'Eglise ne peut plus se satisfaire de l'anticommunisme grossier. Elle a même pris l'engagement à l'occasion de son dialogue avec l'Eglise orthodoxe russe, qu'il n'y aurait pas dans le Concile d'attaque directe contre le régime communiste.*[4] On the Catholic side, the daily *La Croix* of 15 February 1963 gave notice of the agreement, concluding: *A la suite de cet entretien Mgr Nicodème accepta que quelqu'un se rende à Moscou pour porter une invita-*

---

[3] See the newspaper *Le Lorrain*, 9 February 1963.

[4] "Because the world socialist system is showing its superiority in an uncontestable fashion, and is strong through the support of hundreds and hundreds of millions of men, the Church can no longer be content with crude anti-communism. As part of its dialogue with the Russian Orthodox Church, it has even promised *there will be no direct attack on the communist system at the council.*"

*tion, à condition que soient données des garanties en ce qui con-
cerne l'attitude apolitique du Concile.*[5]

Moscow's condition, namely that the council should say
nothing about communism, was not therefore a secret, but the
isolated publication of it made no impression on general opinion, as it was not taken up by the press at large and circulated;
either because of the apathetic and anaesthetized attitude to
communism common in clerical circles, or because the Pope
took action to impose silence in the matter. Nonetheless the
agreement had a powerful, albeit silent, effect on the course of
the council when requests for a renewal of the condemnation of
communism were rejected in order to observe this agreement to
say nothing about it.

The truth about the Metz agreements was impressively
confirmed recently in a letter from Mgr Georges Roche, who
was Cardinal Tisserant's secretary for thirty years. This Roman
prelate spoke publicly on the matter in order to vindicate Cardinal Tisserant of the charges made against him by Jean Madi-
ran, and he entirely confirmed the existence of the agreement
between Rome and Moscow, adding that the initiative for the
talks was taken by John XXIII personally, at the suggestion of
Cardinal Montini, and that Tisserant *a reçu des ordres formels,
tant pour signer l'accord que pour en surveiller pendant le Concile
l'exacte exécution.*[6]

So it was that the council refrained from condemning
communism, and in its *Acta* the very word, which had been so
frequent in papal documents up to that moment, does not occur.[7] The great gathering made specific statements about totali-
tarianism, capitalism and colonialism, but hid its opinion on
communism inside its generic judgment on totalitarian ideologies.

---

[5] "Following on this conversation, Mgr Nikodim agreed that someone
should go to Moscow carrying an invitation, *on condition that
guarantees were given concerning the apolitical attitude of the
council.*"

[6] Mgr Roche's letter in *Itinéraires*, No.285, p.153. "Received explicit
orders, both as to the signing of the accord and to ensuring that it
was fully observed during the council."

[7] See the cited *Concordantiae*, where the word *communism* never appears.

The weakening of the logical sense, which is characteristic of the spirit of the age, has taken from the Church too its repugnance to mutually contradictory assertions. The opening speech of the council lauds the freedom of the contemporary Church at a time when, as the speech itself recognizes, many bishops are in prison for their faithfulness to Christ and when, thanks to an agreement sought by the Pope the council finds itself bound by a commitment not to condemn communism. This contradiction, although important, remains nonetheless secondary in comparison to that fundamental contradiction by which the renewal of the Church is based on an opening to the world, while the most important, essential and decisive of the world's problems, namely communism, is left out of account.

39. The opening speech.
Ambiguities of text and meaning.

The third subject in the Pope's speech concerns the very hinge on which the council turns: how Catholic truth can be communicated to the modern world "pure and whole, without attenuations or alterations, but at the same time in such a way that the minds of our contemporaries are aided in their duty of assenting to it."

Anyone studying the matter is confronted at this point with an unexpected obstacle. When it comes to a Pope's words, the official text which has the status of expressing his thoughts is as a rule the Latin alone. No translation has this authority unless it has been recognized as official. That is why the *Osservatore Romano* always states that a *private* translation is being given when it prints its Italian translation after the Latin text. Given the fact, however, that the Latin text is the work of a group of translators working on a text originally drawn up by the Pope in Italian, it would seem legitimate to appeal to the original wording, where that is known, and to take that as a criterion for interpreting the Latin. One would thus reverse the authority of the two texts, giving preference to the Italian version, which is in fact the original, rather than to the official Latin, which is in fact a translation. Philologically this reversal is legitimate, but canonically it is not, because it is the policy of the Apostolic See that its thought is contained in the Latin wording alone.

Now, the discrepancies between the Latin text of the opening speech and its Italian version are such as to change its

meaning. It also happens that in subsequent theological writing
the Italian, rather than the official Latin, has been followed. The
discrepancy is so great that we seem to be presented with a
paraphrase rather than a translation. The original says the following: *Oportet ut haec doctrina certa et immutabilis cui fidele
obsequium est praestandum, ea ratione pervestigetur et exponatur
quam tempora postulant.*[8] The Italian translation carried by the
Osservatore Romano of 12 October 1962, and subsequently reproduced in all the Italian editions of the council texts, reads:
*Anche questa però studiata ed esposta attraverso le forme
dell'indagine e della formulazione letteraria del pensiero moderno.*[9]
The French version likewise says: *La doctrine doit être étudiée et
exposée suivant les méthodes de recherche et de présentation dont use
la pensée moderne.*[10]
   The differences between the original and the translations
are inescapable. It is one thing to say that a new consideration
and exposition of perennial Catholic doctrine should be carried
out in a manner appropriate to the times (a broad and all embracing idea); and quite another that it should be carried out
following contemporary methods of thought, that is contemporary philosophy. For example: it is one thing to present Catholic
doctrine in a manner appropriate to the *citeriorità
(Diesseitigkeit)*[11] peculiar to the contemporary state of mind, and
quite another that it should be considered and expounded *following that same mentality.* For the approach to the modern
mentality to be made correctly, one should not adopt the methods, let us say, of marxist analysis or existentialist phenomenol-
ogy, but rather, formulate the Catholic opposition to the modern mentality in the most effective manner.
   In short, the question here is the one the Pope passes to in
the following section, "how to repress error." We will discuss
this in the following section. But not without first making some

---

[8] "It is appropriate that this certain and unchangeable doctrine, to
which faithful loyalty must be shown, should be examined and expounded in the manner which the times demand."

[9] "But this too should be studied and expounded through the forms of
enquiry and of literary expression belonging to modern thought."

[10] "This doctrine ought to be studied and expounded following the
methods of research and presentation which modern thought uses."

[11] "Hitherness, this-sidedness," i.e., immanence or this-worldliness.
[Translator's note.]

remarks in passing. First, the difference of meaning arising from the discrepancy in the translations witnesses to the loss of that accuracy which used to characterize the Curia in the drawing up of its documents. Second, the difference in meaning resurfaced in the Pope's subsequent addresses, as he quoted his words of 11 October sometimes in Latin and sometimes in translation.[12] Third, the variant contained in the translations, which was soon spread about to the detriment of the Latin version and made the basis of discussion on the subject, contradicts the original, whereas the translations agree among themselves. This agreement gives ground for speculating that there may have been an attempt, whether spontaneous or organized, to give the speech a modernizing meaning which may not have been in the Pope's mind.

40. The opening speech. A new attitude towards error.

The passage in the speech which distinguishes between the unchangeable substance of Catholic teaching and the changeability of its expressions, gives rise to the same uncertainty. The official text reads as follows: *Est enim aliud ipsum depositum fidei, seu veritates, quae veneranda doctrina nostra continentur, aliud modus quo eaedem enuntiantur, eodem tamen sensu eademque sententia. Huic quippe modo plurimum tribuendum est, et patientia si opus fuerit, in eo elaborandum, scilicet eae inducendae erunt rationes res exponendo, quae cum magisterio, cuius indoles praesertim pastoralis est, magis congruant.*[13] The Italian translation reads: *Altra è la sostanza dell'antica dottrina del "depositum fidei" e altra è la formulazione del suo rivestimento, ed è di questo che*

---

12 Mgr Villot, auxiliary bishop of Lyons, confirms in *Echo-Liberté* of 13 January 1963 that the Pope quoted himself in the Italian version in his Christmas address to the cardinals.

13 "The deposit of faith itself, or the truths which are contained in our venerable doctrine, are one thing; the manner in which they are set forth, though with the same sense and the same meaning, is another. Much attention must be given to this matter, and patience if needed be in elaborating it; that is, in the exposition of the subject, those considerations which are most in accordance with the predominantly pastoral character of the magisterium should be given prominence."

devesi con pazienza tener gran conto, tutto misurando nella forma e
proporzione di un magistero a carattere prevalentemente pastorale.[14]

The divergence is so great as to admit of only two hypotheses: either the Italian translator was attempting a paraphrase, or the translation is in fact the original text. If the Italian is the original, it must have appeared convoluted and imprecise (what in fact is "the formulation of its clothing"?) so that the Latin translator tried to gather its general sense and, being dominated by traditional ideas, failed to notice how great a novelty the original version contained. What is very noticeable is the *omission* of the words *eodem tamen sensu eademque sententia* which are an implicit quotation of a classic text of St. Vincent of Lerins, and which are bound up with the Catholic understanding of the relation between the truth to be believed and the formula in which it is expressed.

In the Latin text John XXIII is simply reaffirming that dogmatic truth admits of a variety of forms of expression, but that the variety concerns the act of communication, and never the truth communicated. The Pope's thinking, as he specifically asserts, is a continuation of the teaching that "shines forth in the conciliar decrees of Trent and Vatican I."

The attitude to be adopted in regard to error is on the other hand a definite novelty, and is openly announced as being a new departure for the Church. The Church, so the Pope says, is not to set aside or weaken its opposition to error, but "she prefers today to make use of the medicine of mercy, rather than of the arms of severity."[15] She resists error "by showing the validity of her teaching, rather than by issuing condemnations." This setting up of the principle of mercy as opposed to severity ignores the fact that in the mind of the Church *the condemnation of error is itself a work of mercy*, since by pinning down error those

---

[14] "The substance of the ancient doctrine of the deposit of faith is one thing, the formulation of its clothing is another, and much attention must be patiently given to this fact, everything being measured in accordance with the predominantly pastoral character of the Church's teaching office."

[15] During the preparation of the Roman synod, which maintained the Church's traditional teaching methods, the Pope had already accepted the suggestion that some norms should be relaxed, and had said to Mgr Felici (who recounts the event in O.R. of 25 April 1981): "The imposition of rules is not liked these days." He does not say "is of no use," but "is not liked."

laboring under it are corrected and others are preserved from falling into it. Furthermore, mercy and severity cannot exist, properly speaking, in regard to error, because they are moral virtues which have persons as their object, while the intellect recoils from error by the logical act that opposes a false conclusion. Since mercy is sorrow at another's misfortune accompanied by a desire to help him,[16] the methods of mercy can only be applied to the *person in error*, whom one helps by confuting his error and presenting him with the truth; and can never be applied to his *error* itself, which is a logical entity that cannot experience misfortune. Moreover, the Pope reduces by half the amount of help that can be offered, since he restricts the whole duty of the Church regarding the person in error to the mere presentation of the truth: this is alleged to be enough in itself to undo the error, without directly opposing it. The logical work of *confutation* is to be omitted to make way for a mere *didascalia*[17] on the truth, trusting that it will be sufficient to destroy error and procure assent.

This papal teaching constitutes an important *change* in the Catholic Church, and is based on a peculiar view of the intellectual state of modern man. The Pope makes the paradoxical assertion that men today are so profoundly affected by false and harmful ideas in moral matters that "*at last* it seems men of themselves," that is without refutations and condemnations, "are disposed to condemn them; in particular those ways of behaving which despise God and His law." One can indeed maintain that a purely theoretical error will cure itself, since it arises from purely logical causes; but it is difficult to understand the proposition that a practical error about life's activities will cure itself, since that sort of error arises from judgments in which the non-necessary elements of thought are involved. This optimistic interpretation of events, asserting that *at last* error is about to recognize and correct itself, is difficult enough to accept in theory; but it is also bluntly *refuted by facts*. Events were still maturing at the time the Pope spoke, but in the following decade they came to full fruition. Men did not change their minds regarding their errors, but became entrenched in them instead, and gave them the force of law. The public and universal acceptance of these errors became obvious with the adoption

---

[16] *Summa Theologica*, II,II,q.30,a.1.
[17] "Direct instruction."

of divorce and abortion. The behavior of Christian peoples was entirely altered thereby and their civil legislation, until recently modeled on canon law, was changed into something completely profane no longer having a shade of the sacred about it. On this point, papal foresight indisputably failed.[18]

41. Rejection of the council preparations. The breaking of the council rules.

As we have said, a distinctive feature of Vatican II is its *paradoxical outcome*, by which all the preparatory work that usually directs the debates, marks the outlook and foreshadows the results of a council, was nullified and rejected from the first session onward, as successive spirits and tendencies followed one upon another.[19] This departure from the original plan did not happen as a result of a decision made by the council itself, operating within its duly established rules, but by an act *breaking the council's legal framework*, which although not prominent in accounts given of these events, is now certain in its main outlines.

When the schema on the sources of revelation which the preparatory commission had drawn up came under discussion at the thirty-third session, the doctrine it propounded aroused a lively difference of opinion, although it had already been sifted by numerous meetings of bishops and experts. Those Fathers who were more attached to the Tridentine formula stating that revelation is contained *in libris scriptis et sine scripto traditioni-bus*,[20] taken as two sources, found themselves at odds with those who were keen to reaffirm Catholic doctrine in terms less unpalatable to those separated brethren who reject tradition. The very lively disagreement between the two groups led to a pro-

---

[18] This change entirely escaped the attention of the O.R. of 21 November 1981, in its article *Punti fermi per camminare con la storia* which, analyzing Italian legislation during the previous thirty years, notices only "the wonderful evolutionary and adaptive capacity" of the legislation itself.

[19] This salient fact about Vatican II is always passed over in silence. M. Giusti, prefect of the Vatican Secret Archive, makes no mention of it, writing on the twentieth anniversary of the work of the preparatory commission.

[20] "In written books and in unwritten traditions." Session IV of the Council of Trent.

posal on 21 November that discussion should be discontinued and the schema entirely redrafted.[21] When the votes had been collected, it was discovered that the move to suspend discussion did not have the two-thirds majority that the council's rules required on all procedural questions. The secretary general therefore reported that: "The results of the voting mean that the examination of individual chapters of the schema under discussion will be continued in the coming days." However, at the opening of the thirty-fourth session on the following day, it was announced in four languages as well as Latin that, in view of the prolonged and laborious debate which might be expected, the Holy Father had decided to have the schema recast by a new commission, in order to shorten it and to make the general principles defined by Trent and Vatican I stand out better.

This intervention, which at one blow reversed the council's decision and departed from the regulations governing the gathering, certainly constituted a *breaking of the legal framework* and a move from a collegial to a monarchical method of proceeding. I do not go so far as to say this breaking of procedure marked the beginning of a new doctrine, but it did signify the beginning of a new doctrinal orientation. The behind the scenes activity which led to this sudden change in papal policy is today public knowledge,[22] but it is considerably less important than the exercise of power superimposing itself on the due legal structure of the council. The result of the vote could have been challenged by the Pope if there had been a fault in procedure, or if a change in the rules had been introduced, as in fact happened under Paul VI, who decreed a simply majority would do. In the circumstances in which it happened, however, this intervention constituted a classic case of a Pope imposing his authority on a council, and is all the more remarkable in that

---

[21] One must admit that the official account given in the O.R. has a comical flavor to it: "all the Fathers recognize the schema has been studied with the greatest care, being the fruit of the work of theologians and bishops from a great variety of nations." How then could it be decided that it was unfit to be advanced?

[22] It is clear from the very objective account of this episode given by Phillipe Delhaye in the *Ami du Clergé*, 1964, pp.534-5, that that night, towards ten o'clock, Pope John received Cardinal Léger and the Canadian bishops, and that there were discussions between Cardinal Ottaviani and Cardinal Bea, spokesmen for the two conflicting schools of thought.

the Pope was at that time portrayed as a protector of the council's freedom. The exercise of authority was not, however, something the Pope did on his own initiative, but the result of complaints and demands by those who treated the two-thirds majority required by the council rules as a "legal fiction" and ignored it in order to get the Pope to accept the rule of a bare majority.

42. The breaking of the Council's legal framework, continued.

The predominantly modernizing tendency of the council, which was responsible for the rejection of three years' preparatory work carried out under Pope John's aegis, was apparent even in the very first meeting on 13 October. That day, the council was due to elect its members (sixteen out of twenty-four) on the ten commissions which were to examine the draft documents drawn up by the preparatory commission. The council secretariat had distributed copies of the ten requisite forms, each having blank spaces in which to write the names chosen. It had also published the list of the members of the preconciliar commissions from whom the drafts had come. This procedure was obviously designed to favor an organic continuity between the drafting stage and the formulation of the final documents. This is in accordance with traditional practice. It also answers a very urgent need, since nobody can better present a document than those who have studied, refined and finally drafted it. Nor did it prejudice the electors' freedom, since they remained completely at liberty to set aside the members of the preconciliar commissions when choosing those who were to form the conciliar ones. The only objection which could be made was that since the council had opened only three days earlier, an election might appear to be unduly hasty and insufficiently considered, given that the members of the vast and heterogeneous gathering knew each other so little.

To a good number of Fathers, this procedural step seemed to amount to an attempt to force the issue, and was resented in consequence. Cardinal Achille Liénart, one of the nine presidents of the council, voiced their point of view at the opening of the session. When he had asked the president of the session, Cardinal Tisserant, for permission to speak, and had been refused in accordance with the rules on the grounds that the session had been called in order to proceed to a vote, not in order to debate as to whether a vote should be held, Cardinal Liénart seized the microphone, thus violating due legal process, and read a declaration amidst the applause of many of those present: it was impossible to proceed to a vote without first having information about those to be selected and without there first being consultations among the electors and the national conferences of bishops. The vote did not take place, the session was adjourned, and the commissions subsequently formed contained large numbers of men who had had nothing to do with the preconciliar work.

Cardinal Liénart's action was regarded by the press as a *coup* by which the Bishop of Lille *infléchissait la marche du Concile et entrait dans l'histoire*.[23] All observers recognize his action as a genuinely decisive point in the course of the ecumenical council; one of those points at which history is concentrated for a moment, and whence great consequences flow. Liénart himself interprets the event in his memoirs as a charismatic inspiration, conscious (at least *a posteriori*) of the effects of his intervention, and keen to exclude the idea that it might have been premeditated or prearranged: *Je n'ai parlé que parce que je me suis trouvé contraint de le faire par une force supérieure en laquelle je doit reconnaître celle de l'Esprit Saint.*[24] Thus, according to John XXIII, the council was called by command of the Holy Spirit, and the council which John prepared was then promptly turned on its head by the same Holy Spirit, working through a French cardinal. We now have an open confession of this repudiation of the council as originally conceived, from Fr. Chenu, one of the spokesmen of the modernizing school.[25] The eminent Dominican, and his brother in the order Fr. Congar, were upset by their reading of the preparatory commissions' texts, which appeared

---

23   "Deflected the course of the council and made history." *Figaro*, 9 December 1976. The account of events we have given is based on Liénart's own memoirs, published posthumously in 1976 under the title *Vatican II*, by the faculty of theology at Lille. It agrees with the account given by Fr. Wiltgen S.V.D., in *The Rhine flows into the Tiber*, Paris 1975 (translation of the American edition of 1966), p.17, which however says nothing about the illegality of the Frenchman's action.

24   "I only spoke because I felt constrained to do so by a higher force, in which I feel obliged to recognize that of the Holy Spirit."

25   I.C.I., No.577, 15 August 1982, p.41.

to them to be abstract, antiquated and foreign to the inspirations of contemporary humanity, and they took action to get the council to go beyond this restricted compass, and to open itself to the world's requirements, by persuading it to proclaim a new orientation in a message addressed to humanity at large. Fr. Chenu says the message *impliquait une critique sévère du contenu et de l'esprit du travail de la Commission officielle préparatoire.*[26] The text to be put forward in council was approved by John XXIII, and by Cardinals Liénart, Garrone, Frings, Döpfner, Alfrink, Montini and Léger. It emphasized the following points: that the modern world desires the Gospel, that all civilizations contain a hidden urge towards Christ, that the human race constitutes a single fraternal whole beyond the bounds of frontiers, governments and religions, and that the Church struggles for peace, development and human dignity. The text, which was entrusted to Cardinal Liénart, was subsequently altered in some parts, without relieving it of its original anthropocentric and worldly character, but the alterations were not liked by those who had promoted the document in the first place. It was passed by two thousand five hundred Fathers on 20 October. Fr. Chenu's statement about the effect of the document is significant: *Le message saisit efficacement l'opinion publique par son existence même. Les pistes ouvertes furent presque toujours suivies par les délibérations et les orientations du Concile.*[27]

43. Consequences of breaking the legal framework. Whether there was a conspiracy.

The consequences which flowed from the events of 13 October and 22 November were very important: a reshaping of the ten conciliar commissions, and the elimination of the whole of the preparatory work, so that of the twenty original schemas, only the one on the liturgy remained. The general spirit of the texts was changed, as was their style, in that they abandoned the classical structure in which disciplinary decrees followed upon a

---

[26] "Implied a severe criticism *of the content and the spirit* of the work of the official preparatory commission."

[27] "The message managed to seize public attention by its very existence. The paths opened up were *almost always followed* in the deliberations and orientations of the council."

doctrinal section. To a certain extent, the council was self-created, atypical and unforeseen.

At this point, anyone studying the council must ask himself whether the unexpected change in its course was due to a concerted plan made before the council, and outside it, or whether it was an effect of the natural dynamism of the council itself. The former opinion is held by adherents of the traditional, curial school of thought. They go so far as to recall the instance of the *latrocinium*[28] at Ephesus: the holding of a council after its preparations had been destroyed seems to them to be explicable only by concerted action, well organized by a group of very determined men. A conspiracy also seems to be proved by what the French Academician, Jean Guitton, relates of something told him by Cardinal Tisserant.[29] When showing Guitton a painting made from a photograph, which depicted Tisserant himself and six other cardinals, the Dean of the Sacred College said: *Ce tableau est historique ou plutôt il est symbolique. Il représente la réunion que nous avions eu avant l'ouverture du Concile où nous avons décidé de bloquer la première séance en refusant des règles tyranniques établies par Jean XXIII.*[30] The chief instrument used by the modernizing conspirators, mainly French, German and Canadian, was the working alliance of the bishops from those areas; while the opposing group was the *Coetus Internationalis Patrum*, dominated by bishops from the Latin world.

One must nevertheless ask whether a conspiracy, in the political sense, is here being confused with the common action natural to members of an assembly who find themselves drawn together by their common opinions and interpretations of history, and thus by a common set of intentions. It is undeniable that any body of individuals which comes together for a particular reason to fulfill some social function, is subject to some influences of some sort or another. Without them, it cannot constitute itself as a true working body, and move from being a multitude of atoms to being an organic group. Influences of this

---

[28] "Robbers' council," of A.D.449.

[29] J. Guitton, *Paul VI secret*, Paris 1979, p.123.

[30] "This picture is historic, or rather, symbolic. It shows the meeting we had before the opening of the council, when we decided to block the first session by refusing to accept the tyrannical rules laid down by John XXIII."

sort have been felt at every council, as part of its structure not as
something extraneous, and they do not constitute a defect.
Whether all relevant influences arose within the councils themselves in this way, or whether some of them came from outside
political interference need not be determined here.

It is well known how great the sway of the Emperor and
other sovereigns was at the Council of Trent, and how important papal intervention was too, leading Sarpi to remark with
bitter mockery that "the Holy Spirit arrived from Rome in a
saddle bag." At Vatican I Pius IX played a major role, as was
appropriate, given that as head of the Church he was also head
of the council.

It is the very concept of an assembly, of whatever kind,
which implies not only the legitimacy but the necessity of influences of this sort. The existence of an assembly, as such, is the
result of a collection of individuals establishing themselves as a
unity. What brings about this fusion if not the working of such
influences? Violent influences have indeed played their part in
history, and according to one school of thought, which we do
not accept, it is precisely the violent events, the ruptures rather
than the influences properly so-called, which alter the course of
what happens. Whatever the answer to that question may be, it
is certain that a group of men met together in an assembly can
only get beyond the atomistic stage and be shaped by a common thought as a result of a conspiring together of minds. A
council, which is a group of men of some standing, in virtue of
their merits, learning and disinterestedness, does indeed have a
different sort of dynamism from that of the crowd, which Manzoni called a vile body, entered successively by contrary spirits
which drive it either towards atrocious injustice and bloodshed,
or towards justice and right behavior. It seems to be true, both
psychologically and historically, that any gathering becomes an
organic whole only if there is a conspiration of minds, giving
character and organization to the mass. The truth is so obvious
that the Second Vatican Council's rules recommended, in paragraph No.3 of article No.57, that Fathers of like minds in their
theological and pastoral views should form groups to uphold
their opinions in council, or have them upheld by their
spokesmen.

That there can be unique and privileged moments which
determine an entire series of events, and which shape the course
of the future, such as were Cardinal Liénart's action on 13 Oc-

tober and the breaking of the rules on 22 November 1962, is historically and providentially true, as can be seen in our article relating this truth to a famous historical event.[31]

44. Papal action at Vatican II. The *Nota praevia*.

John XXIII used his authority to renounce the council that had been prepared, to unleash the radical effects that flowed from that action, and to comply with the direction which the council wanted to take once continuity with its preparatory stages had been broken. Some individual decisions which John XXIII took, without involving the council in them, were of an unusual sort. One such was the inclusion of the name of St. Joseph in the canon of the Mass, to which no changes had been made since the time of Pope St. Gregory the Great. Its addition was promptly and sharply criticized, either on the grounds of its probable anti-ecumenical effect, or because it seemed merely to be satisfying a personal wish of the Pope's, despite the fact that it had been desired for some time by a good many people in the Church. In practice,[32] St. Joseph's name was not mentioned for long, and disappeared into the Erebus of oblivion, together with those other of Pope John's doings that did not find favor with the conciliar consensus.

Although Paul VI generally supported the modernizing tendency in the council, which had made its first appearance in the opening speech, he felt obliged to part company with it and to use his own papal authority at some points in the debate.

The first of these points concerned the principle of collegiality, until then implicit in Catholic ecclesiology, but which the Pope thought should be drawn out explicitly, and which subsequently became one of the chief criteria for reforming the Church. The council's proposed text on the subject was defective, whether because of the novelty of the subject, or because of the unforeseen nature of the discussion on a matter of which the preparatory commission had said nothing, or because of the delicacy of the relationship between the primacy of Peter and the collegiality of the whole episcopal body. Paul VI decided

---

[31] *Bollettino Storico della Svizzera italiana*, I, 1978, Il luganese Carlo Francesco Caselli negoziatore del Concordato napoleonico. Especially the note to p.68.

[32] That is, because the Roman Canon is now so rarely used. [Translator's note.]

that the council's theological commission should issue a *Nota praevia* which would clarify and formulate what the constitution *Lumen Gentium* had said about collegiality. The terms of this clarification were such as to put beyond question the Catholic doctrine about the Pope's primacy over the whole Church and over each of its members individually, in both government and teaching. As the First Vatican Council had said, papal definitions in matters of faith and morals are irreformable *ex sese et non ex consensu Ecclesiae*[33] and therefore not by consent of the bishops as a college.

The *Nota praevia* rejects the familiar notion of collegiality, according to which the Pope alone is the subject of supreme authority in the Church, sharing his authority as he wills with the whole body of bishops summoned by him to a council. In this view, supreme authority is collegial only through being communicated at the discretion of the Pope. But the *Nota praevia* also rejects the novel theory that supreme authority in the Church is lodged in the college together with the Pope, and never without the Pope, who is its head, but in such a way that when the Pope exercises supreme power, even alone, he exercises it precisely as head of the college, and therefore as a representative of the college, which he is obliged to consult in order to express its opinion. This view is influenced by the theory that authority derives from the multitude, and is hard to reconcile with the divine constitution of the Church. Rejecting both of these theories, the *Nota praevia* holds firmly to the view that supreme authority does indeed reside in the college of bishops united to their head, but that the head can exercise it independently of the college, while the college cannot exercise it independently of the head.

It is difficult to say whether Vatican II's tendency to release itself from any strict continuity with tradition, and to create for itself atypical forms, customs and procedures, should be attributed to the modernizing spirit which enveloped and directed it, or to the mind and character of Paul VI. Probably each should be attributed its proportionate part in the process. The result was a renewal, or rather an innovation in the Church's being, which affected structures, rites, language, discipline, attitudes and aspirations, in short the whole face which the Church was to present to the new world. In this regard one should note the

---

[33] "Of themselves, and not by the consent of the Church."

peculiar character of the *Nota praevia*, even as regards its form. In the first place, in the whole history of the Church's councils, there is no other example of a gloss of this sort being added and organically joined to a dogmatic constitution such as *Lumen Gentium*. Secondly, it seems inexplicable, after so many consultations, corrections and revisions and the acceptance and rejection of so many amendments, that the council should issue a doctrinal document so imperfect as to require an explanatory note at the very moment of its promulgation. A final curiosity of the *Nota praevia* is that although it is meant to be read *previous* to the constitution to which it is attached, it is printed *after* it.

45. Further papal action at Vatican II. Interventions on mariological doctrine. On missions. On the moral law of marriage.

The second papal intervention concerned devotion to Our Lady. The dominant view was that, as something peculiar to the Catholic religion, devotion to Our Lady should be only briefly treated at a council which had given pride of place to the *causa unionis*. It was thought a single chapter on Our Lady ought to be enough, and the separate schema envisaged by the preparatory commission was not necessary. From its beginning, the council was in fact under the influence of German theological schools, themselves influenced by a Protestant mariology which it was thought undesirable to contradict. Protestantism, like Islam, accords merely a certain reverence to Our Lady, but rejects that full and unique veneration which the Church accords in a very special way to the Mother of Jesus. Among the many titles with which Catholic devotion has surrounded the Virgin some, even most, are the fruit of the poetic imagination and vivid affectionate feelings of Christian peoples, while others presuppose or generate a theological proposition. The Coronation of the Virgin has, for example, been the subject of magnificent works of art, but has not figured in theology; while the Assumption has figured in both art and theology and was finally given dogmatic status by Pius XII in 1950. The grounds for the dogma of the Assumption lie in the profound ontological connections between the unique character of the God-Man and the person of His Mother.

Paul VI wanted one of these many titles, *Mother of the Church*, to be officially approved in the schema on the Blessed Virgin, or rather in the chapter of the schema on the Church to which the former schema had been reduced. The council wished otherwise. The title is based on both theological and anthropological considerations: since Mary is truly the Mother of Christ, and since Christ is head of the Church and in a sense the "contracted" Church (just as the Church, to use Nicholas of Cusa's phrase, is the "expanded Christ") the step from Mother of Christ to Mother of the Church is beyond criticism. But the majority of the council objected to the proposed proclamation, on the grounds that the title was of the same kind as those that range from the poetic to the speculative, are of uncertain meaning, lack a theological basis, and obstruct the way to Christian unity. Acting on his own authority, the Holy Father proceeded to make the solemn proclamation in his speech closing the third session of the council on 21 November 1964, and was received in silence by an assembly usually quick to applaud.

The Pope's act gave rise to strong complaints since the title had been struck out of the schema by the theological commission (despite an impressive number of votes in its favor) and the Bishop of Cuernavaca had actually criticized it on the council floor. The incident illustrates the internal dissensions in the council and the anti-papal spirit of the modernizing party. In the face of these facts, one cannot accept an assertion made by Cardinal Bea. He was right when he said that since there had been no specific vote by the council on whether to accord the title to the Virgin or not, it was not fair to oppose the unstated desire of the council to the authoritatively expressed will of the Pope. The Cardinal went beyond the bounds of logic however when he tried to prove the Pope and council were in agreement, by arguing that the title *Mater Ecclesiae* was implicitly contained in the whole mariological teaching expounded in the constitution. An implicit teaching is, however, a teaching *in potentia*, and somebody who refuses to make it explicit, that is to teach it *in actu*, is certainly at odds with somebody who does want it made thus explicit. The statement made by Cardinal Bea, who was one of the opponents, is merely a sign of respect or reparation directed at the Pope. It rests on a sophistical line of argument which would equate the implicit with the explicit, and is designed to rob the incident of its significance. Someone who refuses to make an implicit proposition explicit is not of the same mind as someone who wants it made explicit, because by not wanting it made explicit, the latter does not really want it at all.

The Pope's intervention on 6 November 1964, requesting the speedy acceptance of the document on missions, which was principally opposed by bishops from Africa and heads of missionary orders, also revealed the difference of view between the body of the council and its head. The schema was rejected, rewritten and re-presented during the fourth session of the council.

Paul VI's intervention concerning the doctrine of marriage was both more definite and more serious. Since new theories had been bruited about on the floor of the council, even by cardinals such as Léger and Suenens, which reduced the importance of the procreative purpose of marriage and opened the way to its frustration by elevating its unitive end and the gift of self to an equal or higher level, Paul VI sent the commission four amendments, with orders to insert them in the schema. The illicitness of artificial contraceptives was to be explicitly taught. It was also to be declared that procreation is not an incidental or parallel end of marriage when compared to the expressing of conjugal love, but rather something necessary and primary. All of the amendments were supported by texts from Pius XI's *Casti Connubii*, which were also to be inserted. The amendments were accepted but the texts of Pius XI were not.

The question of contraceptives was meanwhile referred to a papal commission and subsequently decided by the encyclical *Humanae Vitae* of 1968, which we will treat later.[34] Thus the conciliar commission excluded the texts of Pius XI, but Paul VI in the end insisted on their being added to the schema that the council approved during its fourth session.

46. Synthesis of the council in the closing speech of the fourth session. Comparison with St. Pius X. Church and world.

The closing speech of the whole council is in effect the one made by Paul VI on 7 December at the end of the fourth ses-

---

[34] See paragraphs 62 and 63.

sion, since the one he made on 8 December[35] is merely salutary and ceremonial. The dominant spirit appears more clearly than it does in the individual interventions which the Pope had made during the course of events. The speech gives a better idea of what was in Pope Paul's mind than the conciliar texts themselves. The speech has an *optimistic air* which links it to Pope John's opening address: the agreement between the Fathers is "marvelous," the closing session is "stupendous." The individual parts of the Pope's summing up are all merged in what might be called the optimistic coloring of the whole; the council is "deliberately very optimistic." The somber elements, which the Pope cannot but notice, and which he does not fail to mention, are bathed in the glow of an optimistic outlook. Thus the diagnosis of the present state of the world turns out to be ultimately and openly positive. The Pope admits that the Catholic conception of life has been generally dislodged and sees "in the great religions of the peoples of the world too, disturbance and decline of a sort not experienced before." An exception should perhaps have been made here at least so far as concerns Islam, which has experienced new growth and an increase in morale during the course of this century. The Pope clearly recognizes in the speech that there is a general tendency among modern men towards immanence (*Diesseitigkeit*) and a growing boredom with any kind of ulteriority or transcendence (*Jenseitigkeit*). But having made this precise diagnosis of the wavering of the modern spirit, the Pope leaves it all within the realm of mere description, and fails to see in the crisis a fundamental opposition in principle to Catholic axiology, which is fundamentally *transcendent.*

St. Pius X in his encyclical *Supremi Pontificatus* had made the same diagnosis as Paul VI, and had also recognized that the spirit of modern man is a spirit of independence which directs the whole of creation towards man himself and aims at man's own deification. But St. Pius X had also recognized that this-worldliness had the character of a fundamental principle, and had therefore bluntly drawn attention to the antagonism which objectively means that, quite apart from personal illusions or wishes, worldliness will necessarily clash with Catholic principle: the latter sees reality as from God and for God, while the former sees it from man and for man. The two Popes therefore

---

[35] The last day of the council. [Translator's note.]

this PPG seems like the hour of ~~the~~ legitimate criticism / VII speed / everyone / S. Paul in S. Paul in Scripture! / IMMANENCE vs TRANSCENDENCE.

The Course of the Council   95

agree in their diagnosis of the state of the world, but differ in the value judgment they make on it. Just as St. Pius X, citing St. Paul[36] saw modern man making himself a god and claiming adoration, so Paul VI explicitly says that "the religion of the God Who made Himself man, has met the religion (for such it is) of man who makes himself God." Pope Paul however, ignoring the fact that the confrontation involves rival principles, thinks that thanks to the council the confrontation has not produced a clash, or a struggle, or an anathema, but an immense sympathy and a new attention to the needs of man on the part of the Church. Going on to meet the objection that by bending in the direction of the world, indeed almost running after it, the Church is being deflected from its own theocentric course and moving in an anthropocentric direction, the Pope replies that in so doing the Church is not *deviating* towards the world but *turning* towards it.

At this point one asks oneself: turning towards the world in order to join it, or in order to attract it to the Church? The Church's duty of proclaiming the truth does indeed derive from her duty of exercising charity towards the human race. The harshness with which doctrinal correction has at times been exercised becomes monstrous if it becomes separated from charity, and if one forgets that there is a *caritas severitatis* as well as a *caritas suavitatis*.[37] The challenge is to avoid misrepresenting the truth for the sake of charity and to approach modern man in his anthropocentric orbit; but in order to invert his movement, not to reinforce it. There are not two centers of reality, there is a single center and there are epicycles. And I am not sure that Paul VI made it clear enough in his speech that Christian humanism can only serve an instrumental purpose, given that charity cannot accept, even momentarily, as the ultimate goal, what the anthropocentric view holds indeed to be ultimate: the triumph and divinization of man.

The imprecision of the speech is also apparent in its adoption of two contradictory formulas, that is, that "in order to know man, one must know God." According to Catholic doctrine there is a knowledge of God by natural means which is possible for all men, and a knowledge of God which is revealed only supernaturally. There are likewise two corresponding sorts

---

[36] II Thessalonians, 2:4.
[37] "Severe charity, as well as gentle charity."

of knowledge about man. But to assert, without drawing these distinctions, that to know man one must know God and that to know God one must know man, does not establish the well grounded interrelation between the two sorts of knowledge which can be recognized in the Catholic formulation of the matter; it establishes instead a vicious circle in which the mind would find no valid point of departure either for knowing man or for knowing God. This whole line of argument regarding man and God can be extended to the field of loving as well as knowing. In fact the Pope says that in order to love God one must love man, but he is silent about the fact that it is God who makes man lovable and that the reason one is duty bound to love man is that one is similarly bound to love God.

To sum up, the heart of the final speech lies in the *new relation of the Church to the world*. In this regard, the closing speech of the council is an extremely important document for anyone wishing to investigate the conciliar changes and the nature of those tendencies underlying the council which post-conciliar developments would accentuate and reveal. These developments are mixed with others deriving from the coexisting but contrasting tendencies which were at work during the council. We will now trace their course in the complex, disturbed and ambiguous tangle of the post-conciliar Church.

CHAPTER V

THE POST-CONCILIAR PERIOD

47. Leaving the Council behind.
The spirit of the Council.

As we have seen, the council broke with all the preparations that had been made for it, and took the form of an *outstripping of the council that had been prepared*. After its closure, the post-conciliar period which ought to have seen the implementation of the council became in turn a period in which the council itself was left behind. Papal addresses have often lamented the occurrence of this process; Paul VI for example spoke explicitly about it on 31 January 1972, drawing attention to "minorities which are small, but bold and of very disintegrating effect." The numerous voices of those who regard the conciliar innovations as insufficient, and call for a Vatican III, bear witness to the occurrence of the same process: their proposed council would force the Church to take the step forward which she refused, or hesitated, to take at the council just concluded.

This process of going beyond the council is particularly obvious in liturgical matters, with the Mass being transformed into something altogether different from what it had been; in institutional matters, which have been enveloped by a spirit of democratic consultation and perpetual referendum on every subject; and is still more obvious in the general mentality now prevailing, open as it is to compromises with doctrines alien to Catholicism.

This outstripping of the council happened in the name of the complex, ambiguous, diverse and confusing thing called *the spirit of the council*. Thus the council outstripped, and indeed abandoned, its own preparation, while the spirit of the council outstripped the council itself.

The idea of a *spirit of the council* is not something clear or distinct; it is a metaphor which strictly speaking means the council's breath. Reduced to its logical essence, spirit represents the ruling principle which guides a man in performing all his activities. The Bible speaks of the spirit of Moses, and says that God took the spirit of Moses and bestowed it on the seventy elders.[1] The spirit of Elijah entered into his disciple Elisha.[2] References to the spirit of the Lord are innumerable. In all these passages, the spirit is what precedes and directs all of man's acts as a *primum movens*.[3] The seventy elders who begin to prophesy when God sends the spirit of Moses upon them, have the same governing idea, the same prime mover as Moses. The spirit of Elijah dwelling in Elisha is Elijah's governing spirit, become now the governing spirit in Elisha. The spirit of the Lord is the Lord Himself, inasmuch as He makes Himself the knowledge and the motivating principle of those who have His spirit. In the same way, the spirit of the council is the ideal principle motivating and vivifying the council's activities, to use a Stoic phrase, it is the "ruling principle" of the council.

That having been said, it is obvious that the spirit of the council, namely that which underlies its decrees and constitutes its *a priori* principle, is neither wholly identical with the letter of the council nor wholly independent of it. How does a deliberative body express itself if not in its regulations and deliberations? Thus the appeal to the spirit of the council is a doubtful proceeding, especially when made by those who want to go beyond its decrees; it is a convenient pretext for attributing to the council a particular individual's desire for change.

It should be noted that since the spirit of the council is nothing other than its ruling principle, to posit the existence at the council of several spirits would be to posit the existence of several councils, and some authors have indeed maintained that this constitutes the council's *richness*. The supposition that the council has several spirits arises from the uncertainty and confusion which disfigure some conciliar documents, and which give grounds for the theory that the council was surpassed by its own spirit.

---

[1] Numbers, 11:25.
[2] IV Kings, 2:15.
[3] "First mover."

48. Leaving the Council behind.
Ambiguous character of the conciliar texts.

In fact, this going beyond the council by an appeal to its spirit is sometimes effected by a frank surpassing of the letter of its decrees, and sometimes by a widening or distortion of their terms.

These are *frankly surpassed* whenever post-conciliar thought has adopted, as being conciliar, ideas which the council's texts neither support nor even mention. The word *pluralism*, for example, is used only three times, and then always in reference to civil society.[4] Similarly, the idea of *authenticity*, as the criterion of the moral and religious worth of any human attitude, does not appear in any document; and if the word *authenticus* does occur eight times, it is always used in its philological and canonical sense, referring to the authentic Scriptures, the authentic magisterium, or authentic tradition, and never in the sense of that air of psychological immediacy which is today lauded as a sure sign of genuine religion. Finally, the word *democracy* and its derivatives is not found anywhere in the council's texts, though it does occur in the index of some approved editions of conciliar documents. Nonetheless, the modernization of the post-conciliar Church has been in large measure a process of democratization.

The provisions of the council are also frankly abandoned whenever its letter is ignored, and the reforms unfold in directions contrary to those which the council actually decreed. The most conspicuous example of this is the universal elimination of the *Latin language* from the Latin rites, despite the fact that according to article 36 of the Constitution on the Liturgy its use was to be maintained in the Roman rite; in fact it has been effectively banned, and both the didactic and the sacrificial parts of the Mass have everywhere been celebrated in the vernacular languages.[5]

The more general procedure, however, has not been to abandon the council thus baldly but rather to appeal to its spirit and so to introduce new words designed to insinuate particular ideas, exploiting to this end the imprecision of the conciliar

---

[4] See the cited *Concordantiae* of Vatican II regarding these words.
[5] See paragraphs 277-83.

documents themselves.[6] It is highly significant in this regard
that, although the council, as is customary, left behind it a
commission for the authentic interpretation of its decrees, that
commission never issued any interpretations and is never referred to by anyone. The post-conciliar period was thus devoted
to the *interpretation* of the council rather than to its *implementation*. Since an authentic interpretation was lacking, those
points on which the mind of the council appeared uncertain
and open to question were thrown open to dispute among
theologians, with the resulting grave damage to the Church's
unity which Paul VI deplored in his speech of 7 December
1968.[7] The ambiguous nature of the conciliar texts thus provides support both for a novel and a traditional interpretation,
and generates a whole hermeneutical enterprise of such importance that we cannot but make brief reference to it here.[8]

49. Novel hermeneutic of the Council. Semantic change. The word "dialogue."

The depth of the change which has taken place in the
Church in the post-conciliar period can be similarly deduced
from the great changes which have occurred in its language. I
need hardly mention the disappearance of such words as *hell,
heaven* and *predestination*, all of them to do with doctrines
which are not mentioned even once in the conciliar texts. Since
words follow ideas, their disappearance suggests the disappearance or at least the eclipse of concepts which were once very
prominent in the Catholic system.

---

[6] This imprecision is admitted by an important witness, Pericle Cardinal Felici, sometime general secretary of the council, who says
the constitution *Gaudium et Spes, maiore litura* (i.e., with greater
polishing) could have been improved in some of its formulations.
O.R., 23 July 1975. *Gaudium et Spes* was in part originally drafted
in French.

[7] See paragraph 7.

[8] The council's lack of precision is admitted even by those theologians most faithful to the Roman See, who attempt to acquit the
council of blame in the matter. But it is obvious that the need to
defend the univocal meaning of the council is itself an indication of
its equivocal character. See, for example, the defense made by
Philippe Delhaye, *Le métaconcile*, in *Esprit et Vie*, 1980, pp.513ff.

Semantic transposition is also a great vehicle for innovation. So, for example, to call the parish priest a *pastoral worker*, the Mass a *Supper*, authority and every kind of office a *service*, and spontaneity even of a reprehensible sort *authenticity*, suggests a change in these concepts when they are referred to by the latter terms.

The *neologism*, generally a philological monstrosity, is sometimes designed to signify new ideas (for example *conscientise*), but is more often the product of a desire for novelty, as can be seen in the use of *presbyter* rather than *priest*, or *diaconia* rather than *service*, or *eucharist* instead of *Mass*. Even in the introduction of new terms for old, there is generally a hidden change in the concept involved or at least a change of nuance.

Some words that had never been used in papal documents and which occurred only in specific fields have acquired an enormous popularity in the short space of a few years. The most notable of these is the word *dialogue*, which was previously unused in the Church. Vatican II used it twenty-eight times and coined the famous formula which expresses the axis or main intention of the council: *dialogue with the world* and *mutual dialogue* between the Church and the world.[10] The word became a category embracing the whole of reality, going far beyond the ambit of logic and rhetoric within which it had previously been confined. Everything had a dialogical structure. Some even went so far as to imagine a dialogical structure in the divine essence (considered as one, not as three), a dialogical structure in the Church, in religion, in the family, in peace, in truth and so on. Everything becomes dialogue, and truth *in facto esse*[11] dissolves into its own *fieri*[12] as dialogue.[13]

---

[9] *Gaudium et Spes*, 43.

[10] *Mutual* seems somewhat redundant, since if only the Church talks there is no dialogue, but a monologue.

[11] "As an acquired fact."

[12] "Process of becoming."

[13] See further paragraphs 151-6. The use of the word "manichaean" to describe any definite opposition between two things, including the opposition between good and evil, is also very significant, implying as it does a denial of axiological absolutes. Anyone who calls some kind of moral behavior bad, is immediately accused of manichaeanism.

50. Novel hermeneutic of the Council, continued. "Circiterisms." Use of the conjunction "but." Deepening understanding.

The "circiterism" is something which occurs frequently in the arguments of the innovators. It consists in referring to an indistinct and confused term as if it were something well established and defined, and then extracting or excluding from it the element one needs to extract or exclude. The term *spirit of the council*, or indeed *the council*, is just such an expression. I remember instances in pastoral practice, of priestly innovators violating quite definite rules which had been in no way altered since the council, and replying to the faithful, who were amazed at their arbitrary proceedings, by referring them to "the council."

I do not deny that a knowing subject can only direct his attention successively to the various parts of a complex whole, given, on the one hand, that the *intentio*[14] of the intellect is incapable of contemplating all sides of it at once, and on the other, that the exercise of thought is free. I do, however, maintain that this mode of operation, natural to the intellect, must not be confused with that deliberate diversion of attention which the will can impose on the workings of the mind so that, as the Gospel puts it, it fails to see what it sees and to grasp what it knows.[15] The first kind of mental operation occurs in genuine research, which of its nature proceeds step by step, but the second does not deserve to be called research, since it imposes on facts a manner of viewing them which originates in one's subjective inclinations.

It is also common to talk about a *message*, and a *code* by which one reads and deciphers the message. The notion of a *reading* has replaced that of the *knowledge* of something, thus replacing the binding force of univocal knowledge with a plurality of possible readings. It is alleged that a single message can be read in different keys: if it is orthodox, it can be deciphered in a heterodox key; if heterodox, in an orthodox key. This method, however, forgets that the text has a primitive, inherent, obvious and literal sense of its own, which must be understood before any reading, and that it sometimes does not admit of

---

[14] "Concentration or attention."
[15] Matthew, 13:13.

being read with the key with which the second reading proposes to read it. The conciliar texts, like any others, have, independent of the reading that may be made of them, an obvious and univocal readability, that is, a literal sense which is the basis of any other sense which may be found in them. Hermeneutical perfection consists in reducing the second reading to the first, which gives the true sense of the text. The Church, moreover, has never proceeded in any other way.

The technique adopted by innovators in the post-conciliar period thus consists in illuminating or obscuring, glossing or reinforcing, individual parts of a text or of a truth. This is merely the abuse of that faculty of abstraction which the mind necessarily exercises when it examines any complex whole. It is a necessary condition of all discursive knowledge arrived at in time, as distinct from angelic intuition.

To this they add another technique, characteristic of those who disseminate error: that of hiding one truth behind another so as to be able to behave as if the hidden truth were not only hidden but simply non-existent. When the Church, for example, is defined as the *People of God on a journey*, the other side of the truth is hidden, namely that the Church also includes the blessed who have already reached the end of the journey, and that they are the more important part of the Church, since they are the part in which the purpose of the Church and of the universe has been fulfilled. In the next stage, the truth which was still part of the message but which has been put in the background will end up being dropped from the message altogether, through the rejection of the cult of the saints.

The procedure we have described is often effected by using the conjunction *but*. One has merely to know the full meaning of words in order to recognize the hidden intention of this school of interpreters. For example, to attack the principle of the religious life they write: *Le fondement de la vie religieuse n'est pas remis en question, mais son style de réalisation.*[16] Again, to get round the dogma of the virginity of Our Lady *in partu*[17] they say that doubts are possible *non d'ailleurs sur la croyance elle-même dont nul ne conteste les titres dogmatiques, mais sur son objet exacte, dont il ne serait pas assuré qu'il comprenne le miracle de*

---

[16] "The foundations of the religious life are not in question, *but* the style of its realization." Report of the *Union des Supérieurs de France*, 3 vols. cited in *Itinéraires*, No.155, 1971, p.43.

[17] "While giving birth."

l'enfantement sans lésion corporelle.[18] And to attack the enclosure of nuns they write: *La cloître doit être maintenue, mais elle doit être adaptée selon les conditions des temps et des lieux.*[19]

The particle *mais*[20] is equivalent to *magis*,[21] from which it derives, and thus while appearing to maintain one's position on the virginity of Our Lady, on the religious life and on the enclosure of nuns, one is asserting that what is *more* important than a principle, are the ways of adapting it to times and places. But what sort of principle is inferior rather than superior to its realizations? Is it not obvious that there are styles which destroy, rather than express, the fundamentals they are meant to embody? At this rate one might just as well say that the fundamentals of gothic style are not in dispute, only the way they are realized; and then proceed to abolish the pointed arch.

This use of *but* often occurs in the speeches of the council fathers, when they lay down in their principal assertion something which will be destroyed by the *but* in a secondary assertion, so that the latter becomes what is principally asserted. So too at the Synod of Bishops in 1980, French language group B wrote: "The group adheres without reserve to *Humanae Vitae, but* the dichotomy between the rigidity of law and pastoral flexibility must be overcome." Thus adherence to the encyclical becomes purely verbal, because bending the law to conform with human weakness is *more* important than the encyclical's teaching.[22] The formula of those who wanted the admission of divorced and remarried people to the Eucharist was more forthright: *Il ne s'agit pas de renoncer à l'exigence évangelique, mais de reconnaître la possibilité pour tous d'être réintégrés dans la communion ecclésiale.*[23]

---

[18] "Not concerning the belief itself, the dogmatic credentials of which are not contested by anyone, *but* as to its exact object, which does not necessarily include the miracle of giving birth without rupture of the body." See J.H. Nicolas, *La virginité de Marie*, Fribourg, Switzerland 1957, p.18, who argues against the unorthodox thesis of A. Mitterer, *Dogma und Biologie*, Vienna 1952.

[19] "Enclosure must be maintained, *but* it must be adapted according to circumstances of time and place." *Supérieurs de France*, op. cit.

[20] French *mais*; English "but"; Italian *ma*.

[21] Latin for "more."

[22] O.R., 15 October 1980.

[23] "It is not a question of abandoning the demands of the Gospel, *but* of recognizing the possibility that all people can be reintegrated

At the same Synod on the Family in 1980, the use of the word *deepening*[24] cropped up among the innovators. While seeking the abandonment of the doctrine taught in *Humanae Vitae*, they confessed complete adherence to it, but asked that the doctrine be *deepened*; meaning not that it be strengthened by new arguments, but changed into something else. The process of deepening would apparently consist in searching and searching until one arrived at an opposite conclusion.

Even more important is the fact that "circiterisms" were sometimes used in the drawing up of the conciliar documents themselves. These inexact formulations were deliberately introduced so that post-conciliar hermeneutics could gloss or reinforce whichever ideas it liked. *Nous l'exprimons d'une façon diplomatique, mais après le Concile nous tirerons les conclusions implicites.*[25] It is a diplomatic style, that is, as the word itself implies, *double*, in which the text is formulated to accord with its interpretation, thus reversing the natural order of thinking and writing.

51. Features of the post-conciliar period. The universality of the change.

The primary characteristic of the post-conciliar period is an *all-embracing change* affecting every aspect of the Church, whether internal or external. From this point of view, Vatican II has given vent to such enormous mental energies as to deserve a unique place in the series of general councils. The very universality of the change effected leads to the question of whether we are not confronted with a *substantial mutation*, as mentioned in paragraphs 33-35, analogous to what, in biological terms, is called an idiovariation. The question arises as to whether a change from one kind of religion to another is not underway, as many in both lay and clerical circles do not hesitate to assert. Were that the case, the birth of the new would entail the death

into the ecclesial community." I.C.I., No.555, 13 October 1980, p.12.

[24] *Approfondimento* in Italian, with a connotation of exploration and research.

[25] "We will express it in a *diplomatic* way, but after the council we will draw out the implicit conclusions." Statement by Fr. Schillebeeckx in the Dutch magazine *De Bazuin*, No.16, 1965, quoted in French translation in *Itinéraires*, No.155, 1971, p.40.

of the old, as in biology or metaphysics. The age of Vatican II would then be a *magnus articulus temporum*,[26] the climax of one of those cycles which the human spirit undergoes in its perpetual revolving upon itself. Or, putting the question in other terms: might not the age of Vatican II be the one that provided proof of the *pure historicity* of the Catholic religion, which is tantamount to proof of its non-divinity?

The change can be described as more or less all-embracing in its extent.[27] Of the three sets of attitudes which sum up in themselves the essence of religion, namely things to be believed, things to be hoped for and things to be loved, there is not one that has not been touched and has not tended to change. In the intellectual sphere, the notion of *faith* has been changed from an act of the intellect into an act of the person, and from adhesion to revealed truth into an attitude to life, thus encroaching on the sphere of hope.[28] *Hope* lowers its object, becoming an aspiration and a belief about a purely earthly liberation and transformation.[29] *Charity*, which like faith and hope has a formally supernatural object,[30] similarly lowers its object and turns towards man; and we have already seen in the closing speech of the council how man was introduced as a pre-condition to the love of God.

These three sets of human attitudes, which concern the *mind*, are not the only things touched by the innovations; the *sensory* side, as it were, of the religious believer has also been affected. For the sense of sight, there have been changes in forms of dress, in sacred furnishings, in altars, architecture, lights and gestures. For the sense of touch, the great innovation has been being able to touch that thing which reverence for the Sacred used to render untouchable. For the sense of taste, there is drinking from the chalice. For the sense of smell, there has been the loss, more or less, of the sweet smelling incense which

---

[26] "Great point in time," i.e., a turning point of the ages.

[27] P. Hegy in an essay published in the collection *Théologie historique*, edited by Fr. Daniélou, maintains that "this council has touched every area of religious life, except the organization of ecclesiastical power," and that Vatican II "is not only a revolution...but an incomplete revolution." *L'autorité dans le catholicisme contemporain*, Paris 1975, pp.15-17.

[28] See paragraph 164.

[29] See paragraph 168.

[30] See paragraph 169.

was used in sacred rites to sanctify the living and the dead. The sense of hearing has experienced the deepest and most widespread change, as regards language, which has ever happened on the face of the earth, the reform having changed a language affecting half a billion men. It has also changed musical styles from melodious to percussive, and banished from the Church that Gregorian chant, with which for centuries "the daughters of music"[31] had soothed and conquered the hearts of men.

I am, moreover, leaving aside here what will have to be said later concerning innovations in the structures of the Church, in legal institutions, in nomenclature, in philosophy and theology, in coexistence with civil society, in the understanding of marriage—in short, in the relation of religion to civilization in general.

This raises the difficult question of the *relation between the essence of a thing and its accidental parts*, between the essence of the Church and its accidents. Is it not possible that all the things we have listed pertaining to the Church, whether individually or generically, could be reformed and yet leave the Church unchanged?

Yes, but three points must be noted. First: there are those things that the scholastics called *absolute accidents*, that is, accidents which are not indeed identical with the substance of something, but without which it does not exist. These are such things as quantity in corporeal substances, and in the case of the Church, faith.

Second: although there are accidental parts to the life of the Church, she cannot assume and abandon any and every accidental quality indifferently, because, just as every entity has certain accidents and not others (a ship one hundred stades long, as Aristotle remarked, is no longer a ship) and as, for example, the body has extension but lacks consciousness, so the Church too has certain accidents and not others, and there are such things as accidents which are incompatible with the Church's essence, and which destroy it. The Church's great historical struggle has been to reject those accidental forms which would have destroyed her nature, whether by insinuating themselves from within, or by being imposed upon her from without. Was not monophysitism, for example, an accident pertaining to the way one understood Christ's divinity? And was not

---

[31] Ecclesiastes, 12:4.

Luther's spirit of private judgment an accident pertaining to the way one understood the action of the Holy Spirit?

Third: the things we have listed as being affected by the post-conciliar change are indeed accidents in the life of the Church, but accidents should not be regarded as matters of indifference, which can be or not be, be in one way or be in another, without thereby changing the nature of the Church. This is not the place to conduct a full metaphysical debate or to appeal to St. Thomas's *De ente et essentia.* It is, however, essential to remember that the substance of the Church exists only in her accidents, and that an unexpressed substance, that is, one without any accidents, is a nullity, a non-existent. The entire existence of an individual across time is, furthermore, contained in his acts of intellect and will: and what are intellection and volition but accidental realities which *occur,* come and go, emerge and disappear? Yet one's moral destiny, salvation or damnation, depends on just those accidents. So too the whole life of the Church in time is her life as it exists in accidentalities and contingencies. How then can one fail to recognize her accidentals as important, and indeed *substantially* important? Are not changes in accidental forms accidental and historical changes, occurring within the unchangeable nature of the Church? And if all the accidents were to change, how would we be able to tell that the substance of the Church had not changed? What remains of a human person when his whole accidental and historical expression is changed? What remains of Socrates without the ecstasy of Potidaea, without the conversations in the market place, without the Five Hundred and the hemlock? What remains of Campanella without the five tortures, the Calabrian conspiracy, the betrayals and the sufferings? What remains of Napoleon without the Consulate, Austerlitz and Waterloo? Yet all these things are accidental to the man himself. The Platonists, who separated essences from historical events, said the essences could be found beyond the sphere of the planets. And where, pray, are we to find them?

52. The post-conciliar period, continued. The New Man. *Gaudium et Spes* 30. Depth of the change.

As one examines the various movements, whether progressive or regressive, which have disturbed the Church across the centuries, one often discovers *catastrophal* ones, that is, ones which have sought to change the Church from top to bottom, and through her, to change the whole of humanity. These are an effect of that spirit of independence which yearns to dissolve the bonds of the past in order to throw itself forward regardless, meaning quite literally without a backward glance. Not, therefore, a reform within the limits provided by the very nature of the Church, and in accordance with certain established arrangements which are accepted as given, but a movement of regeneration which invents a new nature for the Church and for man, sets them on another basis and redefines their limits. Not something new within the institution, but new institutions. Not the relative independence of a development germinating organically in dependence on a past which is in turn dependent on a foundation given *semel pro semper*,[32] but independence pure and simple, of the sort which is today called *creative*.

There are many instances of this sort of attempt. Without searching too far afield for examples, and adducing heretical earthly eschatologies from the Third Age of the Holy Spirit, it is enough to remember the direction the Catholic renewal took in the last century in the ardent imagination of de Lamennais, as seen in his letters published by Perin.[33] The Breton abbé was convinced the Church was about to undergo wholesale reform and a profound transformation, which was quite certain to happen even though the exact shape of the reform was as yet unforeseeable: but in any case, a new condition of the Church was imminent, as was a *new era* of which God Himself would lay the foundations by a new revelation. I will not delay in order to show that this creation of a *new man* is characteristic of the modern Revolution, and coincides exactly with the one aimed at, in more esoteric form, by Hitlerian Nazism. According to Hitler, man's solar cycle was coming to an end, and the new man, who would put down the old humanity, was already appearing with his new nature.[34]

Gaudium et Spes, paragraph No.30, contains a very extraordinary passage on this subject. It says that the moral obligation which ought to take pride of place in contemporary humanity is social solidarity, nurtured by the exercise and spread

---

[32] "Once and for all."

[33] In *Mélanges de politique et économie*, Louvain 1882.

[34] See Hitler's *Tischreden* (Tabletalk), related by H. Rauschning, *Hitler m'a dit*, Paris 1939, particularly chapter XLII.

of virtue, *ut vere novi homines et artifices novae humanitatis exsistant cum necessario auxilio divinae gratiae.*[35]

The word *novus* occurs two hundred and twelve times in Vatican II; much more frequently than in any other council. This large figure includes frequent use of the word in its obvious sense of a relative newness affecting the qualities or accidental properties of things. Thus there is mention of the New Testament (obviously), of new means of communication, new obstacles to the practice of the Faith, new situations, new problems and so on. But in the passage cited (and perhaps too in *Gaudium et Spes* 1 *nova exsurgit humanitatis condicio*[36]), the word is taken in its more narrow and rigorous sense. It is not merely a case of a new quality or new perfection arising in man, but rather of a novelty in virtue of which the basis of humanity is changed, and there is a *new creature* in the fullest sense of the term.

Paul VI repeatedly proclaimed the newness of conciliar thought: "The important words of the council are newness and updating...the word *newness* has been given to us as an order, as a program."[37]

It is appropriate to emphasize at this point that Catholic theology, indeed the Catholic Faith, knows of only *three radical kinds of newness*, capable of bringing about a new state of humanity and, as it were, of transnaturalizing it. The first is defective, and is the one by which man fell, by reason of a primordial fault, from a state of integrity and supernatural existence. The second is restorative and perfective, and is the one by which the grace of Christ restores the original state of human nature and, indeed, elevates that nature above its original condition. The third is completive of the whole order of things, and is the one by which, at the end of time, man endowed with grace is also beatified and glorified in a supreme assimilation of the creature to the Creator, an assimilation which, *in via Thomae*[38] just as much as *in via Scoti*,[39] is the very purpose of the universe. It is therefore not possible to imagine a new humanity which, while remaining in the present order of the world, goes beyond that

---

[35] "So that genuinely new men, makers of a new humanity, may arise with the necessary help of divine grace."
[36] "A new state of humanity is appearing."
[37] O.R., 3 July 1974.
[38] "In Thomist theology."
[39] "In Scotist theology."

condition of newness to which man has been brought by the grace of Christ. That kind of transcendence does occur, but lies in the realms of hope and is destined to be realized at the last instant of each creature's existence, when there will be a new earth and a new heaven.

Scripture uses the verb *to create* in its strict sense when speaking about grace, because man does not receive merely a new power or quality from grace, but a *new existence*, something affecting his very nature. Just as creation is the passage from non-existence to existence in the natural order, so grace is the passage from non-existence to existence in the supernatural, and is discontinuous with the former and altogether original, in such a way as to constitute a *new creature*,[40] a *new man*.[41] This newness, which begins in the essence of the soul during our earthly life, envelops the whole of our mental activity and in the final metamorphosis of the world will envelop our bodies as well. Apart from this newness, which bestows upon man (by acting upon that something of the divine reality which exists in the human self) a new existence which is ontological and not merely moral, the Catholic religion knows of no *innovation* or *regeneration* or *addition* to man's being. Whence we must conclude that the council's *novi homines* should be understood not in the strong sense of a change of nature, but in the weak sense of a great revival within the body of the Church and of human society. In fact, the formula has often been understood in its strict and unacceptable sense, and has invested the post-conciliar period in an aura of ambiguity and utopianism.

53. Impossibility of radical change in the Church.

And yet, from among the episcopate, voices are heard speaking quite unmistakably about a change in fundamental matters. It would seem that the crisis in the Church is not a kind of suffering which must be undergone in order to survive, but a suffering which generates another kind of being. According to Cardinal Marty, the Archbishop of Paris, the newness consists in a *fundamental option* by which *l'Eglise est sortie d'elle*

---

[40] II Corinthians, 5:17.
[41] Ephesians, 4:24. For this doctrine see *Summa Theologica*, I,II, q.114, ad.1,2 and 4 as well as Rosmini's *Antropologia soprannaturale*, lib. I, cap.IV, a.2 (National Edition, Vol. XXVII, p.44) and St. Thomas's *Comm. in Epist. II ad Cor.* V,17, lect. IV.

même pour dire le message[42] and thus to become missionary. Mgr Matagrin, the Bishop of Grenoble, is no less explicit and talks of a *révolution copernicienne, par laquelle (l'Eglise) s'est décentrée d'elle-même, de ses institutions, pour se centrer sur Dieu et sur les hommes.*[43] But to be centered on two centers, God and man, is not a coherent idea, even though it may be a nice verbal formula. This supposed fundamental option, that is, this assertion of a new foundation, is from the Catholic point of view absurd. Firstly, because the Church's coming out from the Church means nothing other than apostasy. Secondly, because as I Corinthians 3:1 says: "No man can lay any other foundation different from that which has been laid, which is Christ Jesus."[44] Thirdly, because it is not legitimate to reject the Church in its continuous historical reality: Apostolic, Constantinian, Gregorian, Tridentine; and to leap the centuries systematically, as Fr. Congar admits he wishes to do: *le dessein est d'enjamber quinze siècles.*[45] Fourthly, because it is not legitimate to equate the Church's going forth into the world in missionary activity with the Church's going forth from itself. The latter is a movement from its own existence, while the former is the propagation and the expansion into the world of the Church's own being. It is, moreover, historically incongruous to call the contemporary Church, which no longer converts anyone, "missionary," while at the same time denying that character to the Church which in times not far from our own converted Gemelli, Papini, Psichari, Claudel, Péguy, etc., and while keeping quiet, of course, about the missions of the *Propaganda Fide* which were so flourishing and glorious until very recently.

Fr. Congar repeatedly states that the Church of Pius IX and Pius XII is finished. As if it were Catholic to talk about the Church of this or that pope, or the Church of Vatican II, instead of the universal and eternal Church *at* Vatican II! Mgr Pogge, the Archbishop of Avignon, says[46] quite literally that the Church of Vatican II is *new* and that the Holy Spirit is inces-

---

[42] "The Church has come out of itself to spread the message."
[43] "Copernican revolution, by which (the Church) has ceased being centered on itself and its institutions, in order to Centre itself on God and men." I.C.I., No.586, 15 April 1983, p.30.
[44] It is said elsewhere that the foundation is the Apostles, but see St. Thomas in his commentary on this place.
[45] "The aim is to skip fifteen centuries."
[46] O.R., 3 September 1976.

santly drawing it out of its staticity. The novelty consists, according to the bishop, in a new definition of itself, that is, in the discovery of its new nature, and the new nature consists in "having begun once more to love the world, to open itself to the world, and to become dialogue."

This conviction that a great innovation has occurred in the Church, attested by the universal change in everything from ideas to material objects to terminology, is also apparent in the continual reference made to *the faith of the Second Vatican Council*, while abandoning reference to the one Catholic Faith, which is the faith of all the councils.[47] It is no less obvious in Paul VI's appeal for obedience as due to himself and to the council, rather than as due to his predecessors and to the Church as a whole. I do not deny the fact that the faith of a later council sums up the faith of all earlier ones. But one must not detach and isolate things which are connected, or forget that if the Church is one *in space*, it is even more one *in time*; it is the social existence of Christ in history.

In conclusion one could say, with the merely relative precision inevitable in all historical analogies, that the Church in our age finds itself in the opposite situation to that pertaining at the time of the Council of Constance: then there were several popes and one Church, now we have one pope and several Churches; the conciliar one, and the Churches of the past which we are to regard as belonging to other ages and as having no authority.

---

[47] The reduction of the Church to Vatican II, that is, the simultaneous negation of both the historical and the suprahistorical aspect of the Church, has been the inspiring idea behind whole movements in the post-conciliar period. In the study meeting held by *Comunione e Liberazione* at Rome in October 1982, the eschatological character of the Church was rightly emphasized, but without being sufficiently aware of the opposition which the innovating tendency raises against that aspect of the Church, by putting all the emphasis on man's earthly duties; it was alleged that while man seeks Heaven, Heaven throws him back down to his earthly tasks. The meeting was entirely based on the idea that the Catholic's duty today consists in putting the council into effect. See O.R., 4-5 October 1982.

54. The impossibility of radical newness, continued.

The idea of a radical change, advanced in all sorts of metaphors and "circiterisms" that fail to convey precisely what they intend because of the badness of their style, is naturally linked to the idea of the *creation* of a new Church. Indeed, once one has refused to recognize that there is a continuity in the Church's development, based on a foundation which does not change, the Church's life will necessarily appear as an incessant act of creation, or process *ex nihilo*. At the Italian Church Assembly of 1976 Mgr Giuseppe Franceschi, the Archbishop of Ferrara, said in one of the principal addresses: "The real problem is to invent the present and to find in it paths of development to a future which will be truly human." But "to invent the present" is a compounding of words conveying no intelligible meaning, and if one invents the present, what need is there to find in it paths of development for the future? Why not invent the future as well forthwith? Creation has neither presuppositions nor lines of development: *ex nihilo fit quidlibet.*[49] But to deal with vague statements of this sort rigorously in grammar and in logic does nothing to resolve the question; it merely makes one recognize the general "circiterism" of the episcopate.[50]

We have already drawn attention to the impossibility of there being anything new in the fundamentals of the Church, the impossibility of a rebirth which would replace one set of foundations with another. Man is reborn in baptism, and his rebirth excludes a third birth, which could be no more than an epiphenomenon of the second, a kind of monstrosity. Antonio Rosmini calls this notion a heresy in set terms. The Christian is one who has been reborn and it is through such rebirth that the Church herself is reborn; hence, as there is no higher level of life for a Christian other than the eschatological, there is no higher level of life for the Church herself.[51]

History shows that changes in the Church are built upon a perduring foundation, without change to that foundation itself.

---

[49] "From nothing you can make whatever you like."

[50] "Circiterism" = from the Latin *circiter* which signifies "around": this word indicates an imprecise and inexact expression which revolves around a notion without defining it exactly. [Translator's note.]

[51] A. Rosmini, *Risposta ad Agostino Theiner*, Part I, ch.2 (National Edition, Vol. XLII, p.12).

All genuine reforms within the Church have been based on old foundations; none have attempted to lay new ones. To attempt to lay them is the essential characteristic of heresy, from the Gnosticism of the first centuries, to Catharism and the other mediaeval heresies regarding poverty, to the great German heresy of the sixteenth century. I will give two examples.

Savonarola brought about a great upsurge in the religious spirit of the Florentine people, breaking with worldliness, but not with the people's life as citizens, or with the beauties of the arts, or with intellectual culture. Although the movement he began was broad and deep, and although he resisted the Pope, he was quite clear that he was not promoting anything radically new in religious matters, no *saltus in aliud genus*.[48] The root remains what it has always been; the foundations have been laid once for all. His words in his sermon on Ruth and Micah are unambiguous: "I say indeed there must be a renewal. But the faith will not change, nor our belief, the Gospel law will not change, nor ecclesiastical authority."[49]

An analogous set of circumstances arose in the early seventeenth century, when Christians overtly influenced by contemporary learning came to believe in an incongruous link between faith and philosophy, as the result of new discoveries in the natural sciences. Some of them thought that the profound change in the manner of viewing the physical universe carried with it a similar change in the idea of man, a rejection of religious certainties and an incipient secularization of the world. This drastic interpretation of cultural change was rejected by the very authors of that change, such as Galileo, Castelli, Campanella and those others who could maintain the distinction between philosophy and theology: and thus the true upshot of the conflict was to restore to theology its properly theological character. Campanella indeed drew up proposals for a universal reform of the sciences and of life, based on new astronomical discoveries and anomalies (as he thought them), and on the discovery of new lands and new races, but he kept the renewal within the ambit not only of Catholicism but of the papal, Roman Church. To those who thought, like the contemporary playwright Berthold Brecht, that the revolution in astronomy would extend to the whole of life, Galileo addressed this warn-

---

[48] "Leap into another kind of being."
[49] National Edition, Vol. I, Rome 1955, p.188.

ing: "To those who are disturbed at the prospect of having to change the whole of philosophy, it must be shown that such is not the case, and that the theory of the soul, of generation, of meteors and of animals remains the same."[50] Genuine reforms, whether in human knowledge or in religion, do not deny the fixity of human nature; they admit the existence of an unchanging element upon which man constructs the legitimate novelty of his own historical period.

The theologians of the *Centre des pastorales des sacrements*, an institution controlled by the bishops of France, have said that: *L'Eglise ne peut être universellement signe de salut qu'à la condition de mourir en elle-même...d'accepter de voir des institutions, qui ont fait leurs preuves, devenir caduques...de voir une formulation doctrinale remaniée* and have decreed that *lorsqu'il y a conflit entre les personnes et la foi c'est la foi qui doit plier.*[51] Here the description of radical change has become a theory, and given the official status which the Centre enjoys, the Church's teaching authority is also involved, thus showing that the problem is not confined within the realm of the doctrinal perversions and aberrations of private individuals.

It is thus unnecessary to introduce the analysis of the crisis in the Church made by persons outside it, who concur in maintaining that the Church has "made a decision about those aspects of its tradition to be put forward and those which are to be radically modified" thus coming to terms with the modern world.[52] This coming to terms requires a movement in the direction of the immanent, which Vatican II is alleged to have begun involuntarily, and which tends to abolish law in favor of love, logic in favor of the spiritual, the individual in favor of the

---

[50] National Edition, Vol. VII, Florence 1933, p.541.

[51] "The Church can only be a sign of salvation universally if it dies to itself...and is content to see familiar institutions decay...to see doctrinal formulas reworked" and have decreed that "when there is a conflict between persons and faith, it is faith that must bend." In the booklet *De quel Dieu les sacrements sont signe*, published by the *Centre Jean Bart*, s.l., 1975, pp.14-15, Mgr Cadotsch, secretary of the Swiss episcopal conference, maintains that the Church is changing and theology today is critico-interrogative (*kritisch-fragende*). In *Das neue Volk*, 1980, No.31.

[52] N. Abbagnano, *Il Giornale Nuovo*, 7 July 1977.

collective, authority in favor of independence, and the council itself in favor of the spirit of the council.[53]

55. The denigration of the historical Church.

The present denigration of the Church's past by clergy and laity is in lively contrast with the courage and pride with which Catholicism confronted its adversaries in centuries past. It used to be recognized that the Church had adversaries and indeed enemies, and Catholics simultaneously waged war on error while exercising charity towards their opponents. Where truth forbade the defense of human failings, reverence would cover the shame as Shem and Japeth covered their father Noah.[54] In the wake of the radical innovation which has occurred in the Church, and the consequent rupture of historical continuity, respect and reverence have been replaced by the censure and repudiation of the past.

Respect and reverence derive from a feeling of dependence on something, some principle on which we depend either for existence, as in the case of our parents or our country, or for some benefit, as in the case of our teachers. Those feelings involve an awareness of continuity between those who offer and receive respect, so that what we revere is something in ourselves, to which we in some respect owe our existence. But if the Church should die to itself and break with its past so as to rise as a new creature, the past is not something that should be appropriated and lived out, but something from which one should detach oneself and then repudiate; and reverence and respect for it will thus vanish. The very words *respect* and *reverence* include the idea of a *looking backward*, for which there is no room in a Church projected towards the future, a Church which sees the destruction of its past as a condition of its own rebirth. During the council itself there were already signs of a certain pusillanimity in defending the Church's past, a vice which is opposed to the pagan *constantia* and to Christian fortitude; and the syn-

---

[53] This is what is maintained, for example, by Fr. P.de Locht in I.C.I., No.518, 15 September 1977, p.5 and by Fr. Cosmao O.P. on Swiss Romande television on 8 September 1977: "In fact it is the Church which has changed very profoundly, particularly because it has ended up accepting what has happened in Europe since the end of the eighteenth century."

[54] Genesis, 9:23.

drome subsequently developed rapidly. I will not go into what
the innovators have said about Luther, the Inquisition, the Cru-
sades and St. Francis. The great saints of Catholicism are treated
either as forerunners of modernity or as being of no importance. I pass rather to the denigration of the Church and the
exaltation of those outside it.

This denigration of the Church is a commonplace with the
clergy of the post-conciliar period. By a piece of mental confusion combined with an accommodation to the opinions of the
world, they forget that one's duties towards the truth are not
only binding when one's enemies are involved, but also apply in
one's own case; one need not be unjust to oneself in order to be
just to others.

The French bishop, Mgr Ancel, blames the Church for the
problems of the modern world because *aux problèmes réels nous
ne fournissons que des réponses insuffisantes.*[55] Who, first of all, is
meant by *we*: we Catholics? the Church? we pastors? Secondly,
it is false in the Catholic view of things to say that errors are
born from the lack of satisfactory solutions, since in fact errors
always coexist both with the problems and with those true solutions which the Church permanently possesses and teaches, so
far as the essentials of man's moral destiny are concerned. It is
moreover ironical that those who say that error is necessary in
the search for truth, should then say that the search for truth is
impeded by error. Error has its own responsibilities, which
should not be loaded upon those who are not in error.

Pierre Pierrard repudiates the whole polemic waged against
anticlericalism by the Catholics of the nineteenth century, and
even writes that the slogan *Le cléricalisme, voilà l'ennemi*, previously regarded as wicked, is now appropriated by priests themselves, since the Church's past has been a negation of the Gospel.[56]

The Franciscan, Nazzareno Fabretti, writing with a great
many loose theological expressions in the *Gazzetta del popolo* of
23 January 1970 on the subject of ecclesiastical celibacy, accuses
the Church of committing crime throughout its history when
he writes that virginity, celibacy and the denial of the flesh
having been imposed by sheer authority, without a corresponding conviction or objective possibility of choice, on millions of

---

[55] "We only provide inadequate responses to genuine problems." Rev.
Boegner, *L'exigence oecumenique*, Paris 1968, p.291.
[56] *Le prêtre aujourd'hui*, Paris 1968.

seminarians and priests, represent one of the greatest abuses which history records." Mgr G. Martinoli, the Bishop of Lugano, maintains that religion is responsible for Marxism and that if Catholics had behaved differently, atheistic socialism would not have arisen.[57] The same Mgr Martinoli says: "The Christian religion is now presenting itself with a new face: it is no longer made up of little practices, exteriority, great feast days and much noise: the Christian religion consists essentially in a relationship with Jesus Christ."[58] Mgr G. Leclercq would have it that the people responsible for the defection of the masses are the priests who baptized them.[59]

Cardinal Garrone states that: "If the modern world is dechristianized, it is not because it rejects Christ, but because we have not given Him to it."[60] At the Italian church assembly of 1976, the conclusions of the principal *relator*, Professor Bolgiani, on the recent history of the Church in Italy were entirely negative: the bishops had been nonentities, there had been compromises with political power, and a lack of openness to any renewal.[61] Cardinal Léger, the Archbishop of Montreal, went so far as to say that "if religious practice is decreasing, it is not a sign that people are losing the faith because, in my humble opinion, they never had it, I mean a personal faith."[62] According to the Cardinal, the Christian people in the past cannot have had true faith. The false notion of faith underlying these statements will be explained further on. Finally, S. Barreau, author of the book *La reconnaissance, ou qu'est-ce que la foi* writes: *Pour ma part je crois que depuis le XIII siècle il y a peu d'évangelisation dans l'Eglise.*[63]

56. Critique of the denigration of the Church.

This line of accusation, which has taken the place of Catholic apologetics and even of an exposition of Catholic

[57] *Il Giornale del popolo*, Lugano, 6 July 1969.
[58] *Giornale del popolo*, 6 September 1971.
[59] *Où va l'Eglise d'aujourd'hui*, Tournai 1969.
[60] O.R., 12 July 1979.
[61] O.R., 3-4 November 1976.
[62] Interview in I.C.I., No.287, 1 May 1967.
[63] "For my part I believe there has been very little evangelization in the Church since the thirteenth century." I.C.I., No.309, 1 April 1968.

tradition, is first and foremost *superficial*, because it assumes that the efficient and determining cause of one man's error is to be found in the errors of others. The thesis contains a veiled denial of personal freedom and responsibility. It is also *erroneous*, because it implies that those who are to blame for others' errors are themselves the only real agents, the others being simply secondary characters or even mere matter acted upon by the first group or by history. The thesis is also *irreligious* and generates an idea which is at odds with theological and teleological truths. Consistently applying this accusatory line of thought would lead to belaboring Christ Himself with responsibility for the opposition He met with from men, blaming Him for not having revealed Himself appropriately or sufficiently, for not having entirely dissipated doubts about His divinity, in short, for not having done His duty as savior of the world. The accusation rebounds from the Church to Christ; from the social individual of the Church to the personal individual of its founder. The truth is that the attainment of the Church's end is not a fact of history, but of religion and of faith, and consequently one cannot consider the Church's activity as if it were a purely human enterprise, since that activity is essentially spiritual and other-worldly, even though it occurs in time. The accusatory line of thought savors of that theological superficiality characteristic of the innovators who, having entirely set aside the doctrine of predestination, are no longer able to grasp either the depths of human freedom, which they contradictorily claim depends on the freedom of other people, or the depths of the mystery of redemption. In his Christmas message for 1981, John Paul II expounded the theological depth of the Christian mystery very well.[64] The birth of the God-Man, come into this world, is certainly the heart of it, but it is equally mysterious that from the moment of His birth onward the world has not received Him and continues to refuse to receive Him. This mysterious non-reception of the Word pertains to the very depths of our religion, and the attempt to find its causes in the failings of the Church is a sign of spiritual aridity.

As prefigured in Isaiah 5:4, and re-echoed in the marvelous liturgy of Good Friday, Christ asks the human race: *Quid est, quod debui ultra facere, et non feci?*[65] To which the moderns seem

---

[64] O.R., 26-27 December 1981.
[65] "What more should I have done, that I have not done?"

to reply: *Ultra, ultra debuisti facere et non fecisti.*[66] Their reply to Christ's lament is: *Appensus es in statera et inventus es minus habens.*[67] Christ's preaching and miracle working left the majority in their unbelief, many in their sins, and all with a tendency to sin. Was the redemption therefore a failure? Those who accuse the Church are ignorant not only of the psychology of freedom, with its attendant mystery, and of the theology of predestination, with its hidden depths, but of the first law of God's dealings with creation, by which the pattern of God's manifestation *ad extra* is directed back towards the glory of God *ad intra.* The grammatical distinction between suasion and persuasion is itself sufficient to explain the history of the Church: *Ecclesia veritatem suadet, non autem persuadet,*[68] since history is the theater of both divine predestination and human freedom.

57. False view of the early Church.

One paradoxical result of the denigration of the historical Church by the new fashion in historiography[69] has been the unmeasured lauding of the early Church and the claim that its spirit and customs are being restored. The early Church is presented as a community of the perfect, inspired by charity and following the commands of the Gospel to the letter.

The truth is rather that the Church has always been a mixed multitude, a field of wheat and tares, a mixture of good men and bad. The evidence begins with St. Paul. One need only remember the abuses at the *agape,* the factions among the faithful, the moral lapses, the apostasy in persecution. In St. Cyprian's experience, in the third century, the mass of Christians aposta-

---

[66] "More, more shouldst thou have done, and hast not done."

[67] "Thou hast been weighed in the balance and found wanting." Daniel 5:27.

[68] "The Church counsels the truth, but does not impose it."

[69] There have been refutations of this denigration of the historical Church. One notable one was made by Mgr Vincent, the Bishop of Bayonne, read on Vatican Radio on 7 March 1981, and published subsequently in his diocesan bulletin. He refutes the articles of accusation one by one: that the Church was merely ritual, that the Bible was unknown, that there was no appreciation of the liturgy, that there was an obsession with matters of sex. The bishop remarks that: "This opposing of the past to the present has about it something infantile, caricaturistic and unhealthy."

tized at the first news of persecution, before the real danger had even begun. *Ad prima statim verba minantis inimici maximus fratrum numerus fidem suam prodidit....Non expectaverunt saltem ut ascenderent apprehensi, ut interrogati negarent...ultro ad forum currere* etc.[70] And was it not in the early Christian centuries that there was a great sprouting of heresies and schisms, of which St. Augustine numbers fully eighty-seven kinds in his *De haeresibus ad Quodvultdeum*, ranging from the most deep and widespread, such as Arianism, Pelagianism and Manichaeism, to local and extraordinary kinds like Gaianism and Ophitism?[71]

This retrospective lauding of preconstantinian Christianity, on which the schemes for renewal of the Church are based, is thus historically groundless, as Christianity is at all periods the mixed thing portrayed in the parable of the tares. Wolbero, the Abbot of St. Pantaleon, even writes that the Church contains the city of God and the city of the devil,[72] I think mistakenly, because, as St. Augustine teaches, it is the world, not the Church, which contains the two cities.

We do not therefore imply that it is impossible to distinguish between one era and another: as well as the injunction not to judge: *Nolite iudicare*,[73] we also read: *Nolite iudicare secundum faciem, sed iustum iudicium iudicate.*[74] The actions of both individuals and generations are matter for this difficult operation. The criterion of judgment is the unchanging reality of religion, to which human changes are in different degrees conformed. Historical judgments about religious matters are in this regard no different from, for example, judgments about aesthetics. Just as any beautiful work is measured against the type towards which it tends (a fact attested to by the labor of an artist, who knows when the ideal is being approximated to and when it is not), and is comparable with other works so measured, so too the various historical periods of Christianity can be measured

---

[70] *De lapsis*, 4 and 5. "At the first threatening words of the enemy the greater part of the faithful (i.e., the great majority) betrayed their faith. They did not even wait to be at least arrested, and to make their denial after interrogation...running off to the forum unnecessarily."

[71] P.L., 42, 17-50.

[72] P.L., 195, 1062.

[73] Luke, 6:37.

[74] John, 7:24. "Do not judge according to appearances, but judge justly."

against the inspiring principle of the Christian religion itself, and then compared one with another. Hence it is that a period of crisis can be defined as one when the Church distances itself so much from its inspiring principle as to put itself in danger. Let it be noted, however, that we will not arbitrarily privilege one historical period as the yardstick by which to measure another, judging the present state of the Church by comparing it with, for example, the mediaeval period; all are to be measured against a suprahistorical and unchanging standard, which depends on the divine unchangeability, and is thus the genuine measure of them all.

CHAPTER VI

THE POST-CONCILIAR CHURCH. PAUL VI

58. Sanctity of the Church. An apologetical principle.

That the Church is holy is a dogma of the Faith, included in the creed, but the theological definition of that holiness is a difficult business. We are not here concerned with canonized holiness, which has indeed varied in style with the centuries: the holiness of the Emperor St. Henry II is markedly different to that of St. John Bosco, as is that of St. Joan of Arc from that of St. Therese of Lisieux. There is furthermore a gap between the heroic virtue of the canonized saint, and the holiness inherent in anybody who is merely in a state of grace.

In the *Summa Theologica*, III,q.8,a.3 *ad secundum,* and in the Catechism of the Council of Trent, in the section on the creed, it is explained how the sins of the baptized do not prejudice the holiness of the Church, but this remains nonetheless a complex notion which only a rigorous distinction can render clear. A definite distinction must be drawn between the natural element, and the supernatural element which produces the new creature; between the subjective and the objective element; between the historical element and the suprahistorical element which operates within it.

Firstly, the Church is objectively holy because it is the body which has the God-Man as its head. In union with that head it becomes itself theandric: no profane body can be conceived as living in union with a holy head. Secondly, it is objectively holy because it possesses the Eucharist which is in its very essence the Sacred and the Sanctifier: all the sacraments derive from the Eucharist. Thirdly, it is holy because it possesses revealed truth in an indefectible and infallible way. The fundamental principle of Catholic apologetics must be located here: the Church cannot display, throughout its history, an uninterrupted sequence of activity in perfect conformity with the requirements of the Gospel, but it can point to an uninterrupted teaching of the truth: the holiness of the Church is to be located in the latter, not the former. It follows from this that those who belong to the Church will find themselves preaching a doctrine which is better than their own deeds. No man can preach himself, beset by weakness and failure; he can only re-preach the doctrine taught by the God-Man, or better, preach the person of the God-Man Himself. Thus truth too is a constituent element in the holiness of the Church, and is forever attached to the Word and for ever at odds with corruption, including one's own.

The holiness of the Church is revealed in what could be called a subjective way in the holiness of its members, that is, in all those who live in grace as vital members of the mystical body. It appears in an outstanding and obvious way in its canonized members, whom grace and their own activity have pushed onward to the highest levels of virtue. This holiness did not fail, be it noted once again, even in the periods of the greatest corruption in Christian society and among the clergy; an age when the papacy was depraved by pagan influences saw the flourishing of Catherine of Bologna (†1464), Bernardino of Feltre (†1494), Catherine dei Fieschi (†1510), Francis of Paola (†1507), Jeanne de Valois (†1503) as well as many reformers such as Girolamo Savonarola (†1498).

Considerations and facts of this sort, however, do not clear the field of all objections. Paul VI conceded to the Church's critics the fact that "the history of the Church has many long pages that are not at all edifying"[1] but he did not distinguish clearly enough between the objective holiness of the Church and the subjective holiness of its members. In another address he put it in these terms: "The Church *ought* to be holy and good, it ought to be as Christ intended and designed it to be, and sometimes we see that it is not worthy of the title."[2] It would seem that the Pope is turning an objective note of the Church into a subjective one. It is indeed true that Christians *ought* to be holy, and they are inasmuch as they live in a state of grace, but the Church *is* holy. It is not Christians who make the Church holy, but the Church that makes them holy. It is also true that the biblical affirmation of the irreproachable holiness

---

[1] O.R., 6 June 1972.
[2] O.R., 28 February 1972.

of the Church *non habentem maculam aut rugam*[3] is applicable to the Church in time only in an initial and partial way, despite the fact that it is indeed holy. All the Fathers take that absolute flawlessness as connected with the final eschatological purification rather than with the Church's pilgrim state in time.

59. The catholicity of the Church. Objection. The Church as a principle of division. Paul VI.

Another aspect of the denigration of the Church should not, it seems to me, be passed over in silence, given that it was referred to by Paul VI on 24 December 1965. "The Church, with its demanding and precise attitude to dogma, impedes free conversation and harmony among men; it is a *principle of division* in the world rather than of union. How are division, disagreement and dispute compatible with its catholicity and its sanctity?"

The Pope replies to this difficulty by saying that Catholicism is a principle of *distinction* among men, but not of *division*. The distinction is, he says, "of the same sort as that involved in the case of language, culture, art or profession." Then, correcting himself: "It is true that Christianity can be a cause of separation and contrast, deriving from the good it bestows upon humanity: the light shines in the darkness and thus diversifies the zones of human space. But it is not of its nature to struggle against men, if it struggles at all, it is for them." This seems a feeble and risky kind of apologetic.

To equate differences between religions to differences of language, culture and even occupation, is to lower religion, the highest good, to the level of goods which, even if superior in their kind, still belong to a lower order. There is no true or absolute language, art or occupation; there *is* a true and absolute religion. In any case, even interpreting the division as a mere distinction, the Pope does not succeed in removing the difficulty he had proposed, and with which he was logically confronted. The drawing of any distinction can reduce but not eliminate the contradictory element found in distinct things, which will always prevent a perfect commonality between them, since it always includes something which separates one of them from the other. Hence the Pope moves away from the order of faith, with its demanding and precise attitude to dogma, to the

---

[3] Ephesians, 5:27. "Having neither spot nor wrinkle."

order of charity, or rather of liberty, and talks of "respect for whatever there is of truth and of worth in every religion and in every human opinion, with the intention *specially* of promoting civil harmony, and collaboration in every sort of good activity." I will not enter into the question of religious liberty. It is enough to note that in this section of the Pope's message the principle of unity among men is no longer religion but liberty, and that therefore the objection which the Pope intended to tackle remains unresolved, namely that Catholicism is a principle of division. What is needed to produce union is a principle that is truly unifying, and which goes beyond religious divisions, and this principle according to Paul VI is liberty.

Perhaps the solution to the contrast between the universality of Catholicism and its determinate character, by which it causes oppositions and divisions, is to be sought at a supernatural and theological level rather than at the level of some principle of natural philosophy, such as liberty and philanthropy. It should not be forgotten that in holy writ itself Christ is proclaimed as a *sign of contradiction*[4] and that the life of individual Christians and of the Church is described as a *warfare*. We must therefore have recourse to that higher principle governing God's relations with creation, namely predestination, which is from beginning to end a mystery bound up with division, separation and election.[5] This kind of contrapositioning, which never exceeds the bounds of justice, is not at odds either with the goal of the universe or with the glory of God, provided that one does not assume that the divine design has failed of its end simply because some men have failed to realize their own potential destiny. To believe the former sort of failure has occurred merely because the latter has, is possible only if one confuses the goal of the universe with the goal of each man in particular; only if one says, with *Gaudium et Spes* 24, that man is a creature which God willed for *its own sake* rather than for *His own sake*, in short, only if one indulges the anthropocentric tendencies of the modern mentality and, to put it in theological terms, if one abandons the distinction between antecedent predestination, which concerns humanity *in solidum*[6] and consequent predestination which concerns men *divisim*.[7]

---

[4] Luke, 2:34.
[5] Matthew, 25:31-46.
[6] "As a whole."
[7] "As individuals."

60. The unity of the post-conciliar Church.

We are treating of the notes of the Church in the post-conciliar period by grouping together the phenomena of growth under the idea of dependence, which seems to us a characteristic principle of Catholicism, and the phenomena of decline under the opposing idea of independence. For it is the spirit of independence which has generated the radicalness of the changes, and the radicalness coincides in turn with that demand to create a new world which has led to a discontinuity with the past and a denigration of the historical Church. We must now examine what effect the spirit of independence has had on the unity of the Church.

In the dramatic speech of 30 August 1973, already cited, Paul VI bewails "the division, the dispersal which is now unfortunately encountered in certain circles in the Church" and says indeed that "the *recomposition* of spiritual and practical unity within the Church is today one of the Church's most grave and urgent problems." The schismatic situation is all the more grave in that those who have in substance separated themselves claim not to be separate, and those whose responsibility it is to declare that the separated are in fact separate, wait instead for the schismatics to admit that that is what they are. "They would like" says the Pope "to have their own official membership of the Church legalized, allegedly in the name of tolerance, thus removing any possibility of being in a state of schism or of self-excommunication."

In his speech of 20 November 1976, the Pope returned to the situation "of those sons of the Church who, without declaring an official canonical break with the Church on their part, are nonetheless in an abnormal relation with her." These assertions seem to give a subjective character to a matter of fact which the Church is competent to ascertain, since the feeling of being united to the Church is not enough to create and sustain real unity. The Church is endowed with an organ which knows when unity has been broken and which has the objective function of declaring the fact, when necessary, and which cannot properly limit itself to confirming the admissions of those who are in substance already cut off from the Church. When expressing his "great sorrow at the phenomenon which is spreading like an epidemic *in the cultural sphere* of our ecclesial community," the Pope was using a turn of phrase designed to mask and reduce a phenomenon which in fact affected the hierarchical

sphere, since the formation of isolated and autonomous groups
was agreed to by episcopal conferences. The Pope went on to
say that disunity in the Church was the result of pluralism: this
ought to be limited to the manner in which the faith is formulated, but has come to trespass on the substance of the faith itself; it ought to be confined within theological circles, but has
come to cause dissent among the bishops. In the same speech
the Pope pointed out very clearly that a disunited Church cannot possibly bring about union among all Christians, or indeed
among all men.

In his speech of 29 November 1973, talking of people who
claim to make Church (as they put it) simply by claiming to be
the Church, Paul VI made the following lenient judgment on
the schismatic situation: "Some defend this ambiguous position
with *reasons which are plausible in themselves, that is with the
intention* of correcting certain regrettable and debatable human
aspects of the Church, or to advance its culture and spirituality,
or to put the Church in step with the changing times, and they
thus disrupt the communion to which they wish to remain
joined." The peculiar part of this address is the description of
the *intention* of improving the Church as a *plausible reason*, as if
intentions could right a false line of thought, like that of those
who claim to be in the Church independently of the Church, as
if any departure from ecclesial unity had to be deliberate and
formalized by the deserters in order for there to be a true schism
in the Church. Is it not quite a common attitude historically, in
clashes of this sort, that those who separate themselves claim
not to be separate, and even say they are more united to the
Church than the Church is itself? Do not all schismatics claim
to belong to the true Church, from which the Catholic Church
has in some way separated itself?

61. The Church disunited in the hierarchy.

The rock-like unity of the Church, whether loved or
loathed, has been replaced in the post-conciliar Church by a
disunity which is in turn equally loved or loathed. We will discuss disunity in matters of faith later on. At this point we simply state the *facts* concerning disunity in the hierarchy.

Mgr Gijsen, the Bishop of Roermond, has said in reference
to the pluralism of the Dutch church that a meeting of minds is
impossible within the Church if it means a meeting between
those who want to belong to one Church and those who want

to belong to another. It would then, he says, be a meeting between churches rather than within the Church. Replying to someone who had asked him whether the differences among the Dutch bishops were so great as to justify talking of different churches, he said "certainly" and explained that his colleagues in the Dutch episcopate claim the Roman Church stands on the same level as the Dutch, thus denying the Catholic dogma of the primacy of Peter and his successors.[8] The bishop's diagnosis exactly corresponds with that of Protestant communities: "The reality is that we are no longer confronted with one Catholicism, but with different types of Catholicism."[9]

The importance of these different testimonies to the internal discord within Catholicism becomes all the more obvious when one remembers that the peaceful harmony of the Roman Church has always been contrasted, whether for praise or blame, with the varieties of Protestantism. Up until the council, the fragmentation which the principle of private judgment had generated in Protestantism was a commonplace of Catholic apologetics.

Episcopal pluralism certainly becomes apparent when there are contradictory statements on the same points. In 1974, for example, the demands of the synod of Würzburg regarding the admission of bigamous divorcees to the sacraments, and the participation of heterodox people in the Eucharist were rejected by the German bishops, but identical proposals were made and accepted by the synod and bishops of Switzerland. Even within the bosom of the same episcopal conference individual members take dissenting and independent stands. This is an effect of the collegial system, which works by majorities and deprives each of the bishops of the minority of his own authority while not specifying what degree of acquiescence is due to the conference's decisions, or whence any supposed duty of acquiescence is derived. Thus the individual bishop is stripped of his own authority on the one hand, while on the other he is licensed to judge not only his own conference, but all other bishops and conferences as well.[10]

---

8   *Giornale del popolo*, 28 October 1972.
9   *La voce evangelica*, September 1971. The official organ of the Italian speaking Protestant community of Switzerland.
10 The Bishop of Chur, Mgr Vonderach, in a letter of 10 April 1981 did not hesitate to admit: *Als einzelner Bischof bin ich machtlos.*

In 1974 Mgr Riobé, the Bishop of Orléans, openly defended the catechist chaplains of France whom the episcopal conference and Cardinal Marty had expressly censured.[11] When Cardinal Döpfner, the Archbishop of Munich, had allowed the basilica of St. Boniface in Munich to be used for the performance of *Ave Eva, oder der Fall Mariä*[12] which insults Our Lady, he received public criticism and protest from Mgr Graber, the Bishop of Regensburg. The Bishop of Cuernavaca, Mgr Arceo, was disowned by the Mexican episcopal conference when he maintained that Marxism was a necessary component of Christianity.[13] The Bishop of Rotterdam, Mgr Simonis, walked out of the Third Dutch Pastoral Colloquium which his brothers in the episcopate continued to attend, conniving at proposals to ordain women and married men,[14] while Mgr Gijsen, the Bishop of Roermond, effectively separated himself from the rest of the Dutch bishops by establishing his own seminary and rejecting the new forms of clerical training. When Mgr Simonis had declared it an error to assert that the Catholic Church was only a part of the Church, he was contradicted by Mgr Ernst, the Bishop of Breda, and Mgr Groot declared that Mgr Simonis's doctrine was "squarely opposed to the teaching of Vatican II."[15]

The bishops of a single country are often in disagreement on political questions. In the Mexican presidential elections of 1982, the majority recommended one candidate while a large minority supported one from an opposing party.[16]

There is a sharp contrast between the French and Italian bishops regarding communism. The Italians said being a Christian was incompatible with adherence to atheistic Marxism: freedom of political choice was limited by this objective incompatibility. The French bishops, on the other hand, decided at their meeting in 1975 to withdraw their official authorization from all youth, Catholic Action and workers' movements and *donner liberté aux mouvements de faire les options politiques qu'ils*

"As an individual bishop I am powerless." The letter is among my papers.
[11] I.C.I., No.537, 1979, p.49.
[12] "Hail Eve, or the Fall of Mary."
[13] *Der Fels*, August 1978, p.252.
[14] *Das Neue Volk*, 1978, No.47.
[15] I.C.I., No.449, 1974, p.27.
[16] I.C.I., No.577, 15 August 1982, p.53.

désirent.[17] All specifically Catholic social movements were suppressed because *aucun mouvement ne peut jamais exprimer en lui seul la plénitude du témoignage chrétien évangelique.*[18] Apart from the discrepancy in teaching between the two episcopates, what is important here is the motive inspiring the French. They presuppose that every possible kind of witness is simply a species belonging to the same genus, and that there are no species opposed to the genus. They also implicitly accuse the Catholic Church of being defective and of needing the aid of Marxism in order to give an integral witness, and foresee a kind of social syncretism in which contrasting ideas are completely obliterated and effaced.[19]

62. The Church disunited over *Humanae Vitae.*

The famous encyclical *Humanae Vitae* of 25 July 1968 gave rise to the most widespread, important and, in some respects, arrogant display of dissent within the Church. Almost all the episcopal conferences published a document about it, some supporting and some dissenting. Documents from bishops on the occasion of papal teachings or decisions are not a new thing in the Church; one need only remember how many letters from bishops to the people of their dioceses appeared under Pius IX. What is new is that such letters should express judgment rather than give assent, as if the principle *Prima sedes a nemine iudicatur*[20] had vanished. Everybody knows how lively the opposition to the definition of the doctrine of papal infallibility was in 1870, either as regards the content of the doctrine or the opportuneness of defining it, and how much controversy there was both in historico-theological debate and on the council floor. The German bishops were not agreed as to what attitude to take

---

[17] "Give the movements freedom to make the political choices they prefer."

[18] "No single movement can ever express the fullness of evangelical Christian witness." I.C.I., No.492, 1975, p.7.

[19] See paragraphs 111-13. The Italian episcopate was also divided with, for example, Mgr Borromeo, the Bishop of Pesaro, and the magazine *Renovatio* under the influence of Cardinal Siri, disagreeing with Cardinal Pellegrino about relations between Church and state. I.C.I., No.279, 1967, p.33.

[20] "The first See is judged by none." [Gratian's Decree, A.D.1140; cf. Canon 1404. Translator's note.]

towards the writings of Döllinger, which were condemned by
Mgr Ketteler, the Bishop of Mainz, but tolerated by others.
Once the doctrine had been proclaimed, however, all those who
had opposed a definition adhered within a few months to the
one that had been made, with the exception of Strossmayer,
who waited until 1881. Papal definitions used not only to fix
the outlines of a disputed truth, but to settle the dispute, it being absurd that the Church's teaching should be subject to a
perpetual referendum.

Because Vatican II had established the specific principle of
collegiality, and the general idea of the corresponsibility of everyone for everything, Paul VI's encyclical became a text open to
different readings, in accordance with the hermeneutic we discussed in paragraph 50. Not just the bishops, but theologians,
pastoral councils, national synods and the mass of ordinary
people whether believers or not, joined in the process of debat-
ing and censuring the papal teaching.

I will not attempt to cite the numberless publications on
the encyclical, but limit myself to dissent by the bishops. Certainly, in pronouncing as he did, against the majority of experts
on his own commission, against a large number of theologians,
against the mentality of the age, and against the expectations
which had been aroused by authoritative declarations and by his
own attitude, and also (as some would have it) against his own
opinion as a *doctor privatus*,[21] Paul VI performed the most important act of his own pontificate. This is so not only because
he set forth once more the essence of the old established teaching based on natural and supernatural truths, but also because
the Pope's action, coming as it did in a context of dissent within
the Church and exposing it to the full light of day, was very
obviously an instance of one of those acts of the papal teaching
authority which bind *ex sese et non ex consensu Ecclesiae*,[22] as
Vatican I put it.

Dissent from the teaching was serious, widespread and
public, and was apparent not only in episcopal documents but

---

[21] "Private theologian." By rights one should discuss at this point that
most disturbing of all mysteries concerning the Petrine ministry: is
it possible, and how is it possible, for a pope to give judgment
against his own convictions? What is this duality of persons? What
is the role of the pope's confessor, who is the judge of his conscience?

[22] "Of themselves and not by the consent of the Church."

in a myriad of publications on how to read and apply the encyclical, all of them pushing it in the desired direction.

The encyclical was attacked and misrepresented in the religious columns of magazines with a wide circulation. The misrepresentation of it in addresses and articles by the well-known Jesuit, Father Giacomo Perico, deserves special mention. In *Amica*, a weekly with a circulation of seventy thousand, he wrote: "It is inaccurate to talk about new orientations in an absolute sense. What can be said is that *certain churchmen* in the past have given unduly restrictive interpretations of conjugal morality. *That was a mistake*."[23] The facts have been inverted here: it was not some churchmen, but the Church, all the Popes including Paul VI, and the whole of tradition which held the restrictive opinion. *Some churchmen* who held the opposing point of view were condemned. Fr. Perico kept up his misrepresentation of *Humanae Vitae* in courses of aggiornamento for the clergy, and in the *Giornale del popolo* of 22 March 1972. I discussed his opinion in two articles in the same paper on 8 and 29 April. He alleged that "the norm contained in the encyclical regarding the use of contraceptives is clear: married couples ought not to have recourse to contraceptive techniques." No, the encyclical says they *must not*. To change the Pope's imperative into a conditional is to misrepresent the encyclical.[24]

Objections to the encyclical related either to its *authority* or its *teaching*. Cardinal Döpfner, the Archbishop of Munich, a supporter of contraceptives, stated: "I will now get in touch with the other bishops to see what help can be offered to the faithful."[25] It appears that in his view the faithful were to be helped against an encyclical which amounted to a hostile act directed against the human race. In America, where the bishops, it seems, had slyly anticipated the Pope's decision and set up a contraceptive assistance program, the reaction was sharp. Attacking its own bishop, Cardinal O'Boyle, the Catholic University of Washington not only refused to accept the doctrine, in a declaration supported by two hundred theologians, but also attacked the Pope for rejecting the opinion of the majority on

---

23 *Amica*, 12 August 1969.
24 The force of the Italian *non dovrebbero*, as opposed to *non devono* cannot be rendered in natural English. [Translator's note.]
25 *Corriere della sera*, 30 July 1968.

the papal commission, and for not consulting the episcopal college.[26]

Although they had generally been in favor of contraceptives, the German bishops accepted the teaching of Paul VI, but conceded the faithful the right to dissent in both theory and practice, on the grounds of the non-infallible authority of the document, thus referring them ultimately to the private judgment of their conscience, "provided that the dissenter asks himself in conscience whether he can allow himself to dissent in a responsible way before God."[27] In their view, rejection "does not mean a fundamental rejection of papal authority." Perhaps, indeed, it does not mean a rejection of the foundations of that authority, but it certainly does mean a rejection of its concrete acts. There was a sensational demonstration of dissent in the German church at the *Katholikentag* at Essen in September 1968: amidst calls for the Pope's resignation, the meeting discussed a resolution demanding a revision of the encyclical, and proceeded to pass it by an overwhelming majority, of five thousand to ninety, in the presence of the papal legate Gustavo Cardinal Testa and the whole German episcopate. The *Osservatore Romano* replied on 9 September, publishing a message from the Pope recalling German Catholics to faith and obedience.[28] The rejection of the encyclical continued nonetheless with the Swiss synod of 1972, the German synod of Würzburg and the Königstein declaration. The principal Swiss Catholic daily, *Das Vaterland*, refuses to this day to desist or relent in its opposition. The division of German Catholics, among themselves and from the See of Rome, continues and becomes ever more obvious. The *Katholikentag* of 1982 was opposed by a so-called "base *Katholikentag*" made up of dissenting Catholics, held simultaneously and in parallel. The dissenters demand indiscriminate access to the Eucharist, the priesthood for women, and the abolition of priestly celibacy, while also celebrating a different Mass.[29]

---

[26] I.C.I., No.317-18, 1968, suppl., p. xix.

[27] Text in *Humanae Vitae*, ed. I.C.A.S., Collana di studi e documenti, No.15 Rome 1968, p.98.

[28] R.I., 1968, p.878.

[29] I.C.I., No.579, October 1982, pp.15ff. The magazine also states that there are two types of Catholic in Germany, though they believe themselves to form a single body.

63. The Church disunited concerning the encyclical, continued.

A deep division became apparent even in the English Church, where Mgr Roberts, the former Archbishop of Bombay, strongly attacked the encyclical and opposed Mgr Beck, the Archbishop of Liverpool, on the radio. *The Tablet*, the principal English Catholic publication, and generally orthodox, caused widespread surprise by a protest against the encyclical, demanding "the right and duty to protest when conscience demands":[30] conscience operating by the light of private judgment is here made the supreme rule of morality.

Opposition to *Humanae Vitae* was general in the Dutch church, which was beset by disputes, assertions of independence and preschismatic experimentation. Even if he was not totally silent on the believer's obligation to form his conscience by the teaching of the magisterium, Cardinal Alfrink maintained that since the encyclical was not pronounced with infallible authority, "individual conscience remains the most important norm." The Vicar-General of the diocese of Breda stated on television that the faithful should continue to be guided by their own conscience. The commission of the pastoral council on the family described the encyclical as "incomprehensible and disappointing" and said it would continue on its own course. They all agreed that the matter defined by the Pope remained open and debatable.

The same ultimate authority of individual conscience was the principal theme of the Canadian bishops. They also introduced the concept of a conflict of duties, which could only be weighed and decided by the spouses, because only they could know the unique circumstances in which those duties had to be fulfilled.[31]

The French bishops' divergence from papal teaching was more obvious. They maintained that in a conflict of duties the conscience may *rechercher devant Dieu quel devoir en l'occurrence est majeur,*[32] thus contradicting the doctrine of *Humanae Vitae,* paragraph 10, which states that it is never licit to will an act which is intrinsically disordered and consequently unworthy of the human person, even if one intends to safeguard the good of

---

[30] I.C.I., No.317-18, 1968, suppl., p. xiv.

[31] I.C.A.S., ed. cit, pp.92, 94 and 118.

[32] "Seek before God which duty is in practice greater."

an individual or family. It is clear that they are misrepresenting the traditional, and papally accepted, theory which allows for that sort of weighing up of choices only when an intrinsically disordered act, such as frustrating conception, is not involved: what is intrinsically illicit never becomes licit in any circumstances. A supposed conflict of duties is purely subjective and psychological, never objective and moral. What is more, to teach that moral duties are to be waived whenever they encounter difficulties which are "humanly" insupportable, is an error which religion has always fought, since from the religious perspective no difficulty can take precedence over one's duty.

The French bishops' position was indirectly criticized by a notice published in the *Osservatore Romano* of 13 September 1968 denying that their position had been approved by the Holy See. Even though it said in its usual euphemistic way on 13 January 1969 that "no episcopate has questioned the doctrinal principles recalled by the Pope,"[33] the paper was forced to admit that "some of the bishops' expressions could cause concern as to the true meaning of their utterances."[34]

Resistance to *Humanae Vitae* in Italy was more muted but no less widespread. I cite opposition to the encyclical from *Famiglia cristiana*, the weekly published by the Paulists, with a circulation of one and a half million copies, on sale in all parishes. In its issue of 23 May and 20 June 1976 Father Bernard Häring, C.Ss.R., defended contraception and adopted the French bishops' line. The *Osservatore Romano* attacked and re-

---

[33] This sort of euphemism is standard among high ecclesiastics whenever they talk about *Humanae Vitae*, and is kept up, for example, by Mgr Martini, the Archbishop of Milan, in his press conference during the 1980 synod of bishops. See *Il Giornale nuovo*, 17 October 1980.

[34] At the colloquium organized by the French school at Rome on the subject of Paul VI and the modernity of the Church, Jean-Luc Pouthier said in his address on *Humanae Vitae* that "after having been presented and commented upon in inadequate terms, *Humanae Vitae* was completely *put in the shade*, and the moment seems now to have come to take a new look at the document which appears extraordinary today in many respects." O.R., 5 June 1983.

futed him on 14 July 1976 but he continued to teach against the encyclical.[35]

64. The Dutch schism.

Dissent in the Dutch church was of the sharpest kind[36] and, supported by the majority of the country's bishops, it amounted to doubting whether the Pope had any authority unless he exercised it collegially. As a general rule, the Roman Church weakened the bonds of its unity in the post-conciliar period, not only where they had been too tight, but also in cases where the local churches had been bound to each other by means of their common links with Rome. It forgot the great maxim of the art of politics: that the greater the mass and the more diverse the compound in which unity is to be maintained, the stronger the weight of authority needs to be. This cardinal principle of politics was recognized and acted upon by the ancients. Tacitus[37] has Galba saying, as he chooses Piso as his successor, that the great mass of the empire cannot be kept in equilibrium without a single guide. The need for an arrangement of this sort was generally given as the historical justification for the transition of Rome from a republic to a monarchy. At the opening of the third session of the council on 14 September 1964, Paul VI also remarked that "the vaster the catholic extension of the Church becomes, the more she stands in need of a central guide in the interests of unity." The application of the difficult principle of collegiality led to a clash with the central principle that unifies diversities while at the same time preserving and sustaining them in their proper places, within the organic unity of the body of the Church.

---

[35] Fr. Häring went so far in his campaign as to describe as immoral the practice of periodic continence which the Pope had recommended. See the refutation of this in O.R., 6 August 1977.

[36] I will not expand upon the frequent cases of the clergy of whole dioceses refusing to receive a bishop appointed by Rome. It happened at Botucatu in Brazil, but Mgr Zioni stood up to an attempt to make him resign, describing the rebels as "priests of low intellectual level." I.C.I., No.315, 1 July 1968, p.8. The nomination of Mgr Mamie as auxiliary to Mgr Carrière, Bishop of Fribourg in Switzerland, also aroused opposition among the clergy. *Corriere della sera*, 21 August 1968.

[37] *Hist.*, I,16.

The abscess opened, as the doctors say, with the Dutch pastoral council, a large assembly representative of all groups in the Church, meeting with the bishops present. By a nine to one majority the meeting voted for the abolition of priestly celibacy, the employment of secularized priests in pastoral positions, the ordination of women, the right of bishops to exercise a deliberative vote on papal decrees, and of the laity to do the same regarding rulings by their bishops.

In order to meet "the wish of many people wanting to know what the Holy See's attitude to the Dutch council is" the *Osservatore Romano* of 13 January 1970 published an autograph letter by Paul VI to the Dutch bishops. The letter is typical of the character of Paul's pontificate: the eye sees the damage and the error, but neither by medicine nor by cautery nor by knife, is the hand put to the evil to combat and cure it. The Pope "cannot disguise the fact that certain projects and reports accepted by the bishops as a basis for discussion and certain doctrinal statements in them leave him perplexed and seem to him to merit serious reservations." He then expresses "well founded reservations about the criteria for the representation of Dutch Catholics at the plenary assembly." He is "profoundly struck" by the fact that Vatican II is "very rarely cited" and the thinking and proposals of the Dutch gathering "do not seem to harmonize at all with conciliar and papal acts. In particular the mission of the Church is represented as purely earthly, the priestly ministry as being an office conferred by the community, priesthood is dissociated from celibacy and attributed to women, and not a word is said of the pope except to minimize his responsibilities and the powers bestowed upon him by Christ."

After this catalogue of errors, sometimes affecting the essence of the Church, such as the denial of the sacramental priesthood and the Petrine primacy, the Pope concludes, in the original French, with these words: *Notre responsabilité de Pasteur de l'Eglise universelle Nous oblige à vous demander en toute franchise: que pensez-vous que Nous puissions faire pour vous aider, pour renforcer votre autorité, pour vous permettre de surmonter les difficultés présentes de l'Eglise en Hollande?*[38] In view of the Pope's previous account of the Dutch attack on essential articles of the

---

[38] "Our responsibility as Shepherd of the universal Church obliges Us to ask you in all frankness: what do you think that We can do to help you, to *strengthen your authority*, to enable you to overcome the present difficulties of the Church in Holland?"

Catholic system, with the bishops either consenting or conniving, what was required was that the bishops be invited to reaffirm the faith of the Church on those points, but instead of demanding such a reaffirmation, Paul offers the Dutch bishops his service to help them strengthen their authority, when in fact it is not theirs but his own which is not being recognized: to help them, he says, to overcome the difficulties of the Church in Holland, when the difficulties of the universal Church are the real issue. The words the Pope addresses to Cardinal Alfrink would be more suitable if he had been opposed to the schism. The words the Pope uses to console himself also have a peculiar sound: "strengthened by the support of *so many* brothers in the episcopate." It is a hard thing for the Pope not to be able to say *all*, and to have to rest merely upon the strength of a large number, which is not a principle in any order of moral values.

The weakness of Paul VI's attitude is apparent *a posteriori* as well, in that in an interview with the *Corriere della sera* on 30 January, that is after the papal letter had been sent to him, Cardinal Alfrink continued to assert that the main points criticized by the Pope should not be resolved by central authority, "but according to the principle of collegiality, that is, by the episcopal college of the whole world, of which the Pope is the head." The bishop was forgetting that the college is only consultative and that its authority, even thus limited, comes from the Pope. When he went on to state that "a schism can only occur on a matter of faith," he was lapsing into a formal error and confusing schism with heresy, since schism is a separation from the discipline of the Church and a rejection of authority. St. Thomas treats it as a sin against charity, while heresy is one against faith.[39]

65. The renunciation of authority.
A confidence of Paul VI.

The external fact is the disunity of the Church, visible in the disunity of the bishops among themselves, and with the Pope. The internal fact producing it is the *renunciation* that is, the non-functioning, of papal authority itself, from which the renunciation of all other authority derives.

In whatever social setting it is exercised, authority has a necessary and some would say a constitutive function in society,

---

[39] *Summa Theologica*, II,II,qq.11 and 39.

because a society is always a collection of free wills that needs to be unified. The role of authority is to effect this unification, which is not a reduction of all wills *ad unum*, but a coordination of their freedom by a united intent. It must direct men's freedom towards a social goal, by laying down the means, that is the order, in which it will be reached. Authority thus has a double function: it is merely *rational* in as far as it discovers and promulgates the order by which a society will operate; but it is *practical* in as far as it *commands* that order, by arranging the parts of the social organization in accordance with it. This second act of authority is *governing*.

Now, the peculiar feature of the pontificate of Paul VI was the tendency to shift the papacy from governing to admonishing or, in scholastic terminology, to restrict the field of *preceptive* law, which imposes an obligation, and to enlarge the field of *directive* law, which formulates a rule without imposing any obligation to observe it. The government of the Church thus loses half its scope, or to put it biblically, the hand of the Lord is foreshortened.[40] This *breviatio manus* can have several causes: an imperfect understanding of the evils to be dealt with, a lack of moral strength, or even a prudential calculation that to set one's hand to correct the admitted evils would not cure them but only make them worse.

Papa Montini was temperamentally inclined to favor this enervation of his authority by a side of his character which can be seen in his private diaries and which he admitted to the Sacred College in his speech of 22 June 1972, on the ninth anniversary of his election: "Perhaps the Lord did not call me to this service because I have any special aptitude for it, or in order that I should *govern* the Church and save it in its present difficulties, but in order that I should *suffer* something for the Church and make it clear that He and no other is guiding and saving it." This is a remarkable confession.[41] It is quite beyond the limits of expectation, whether looked at from an historical or theological point of view, for Peter to be backward in the service of guiding the barque of the Church (*to govern* is in fact derived from the nautical expression *to pilot*) which has been given to him by Christ, and to take refuge in a desire to suffer for the Church.

---

[40] Isaiah, 59:1.

[41] Pope John had a diametrically opposite view, saying to his doctor on his deathbed: "A pope dies at night, because he *governs* the Church by day." [A joke, surely? Translator's note.]

The papal office entails a service of working and governing. The exercise of government was, however, alien to Montini's character and vocation: the man could not find it within him to bring together his soul and his circumstances: *peregrinum est opus eius ab eo.*[42] Furthermore, in letting his own inclinations take precedence over the demands of his office, the Pope seems to imply that there is more humility in suffering than in working to fulfill his functions. I am not sure the idea is justified: is it necessarily more humble to set oneself the goal of suffering for the Church than to admit that one must work for it?

That the Pope saw his task as giving directions rather than prescriptive commands, led him to think that the giving of such directions summed up the whole nature of the Petrine ministry. This is very clear in a letter to Archbishop Lefebvre.[43] Having recognized that the Church is in a very serious condition, beset by a collapse in faith, dogmatic deviations, and a rejection of subordination to hierarchical authority, the Pope also recognizes that it is pre-eminently his task to "identify and correct" the deviations and goes on to declare that he has never stopped raising his voice to refute wild or excessive systems, whether theoretical or practical. Lastly he protests that: *Re quidem vera nihil unquam nec ullo modo omisimus quin sollicitudinem Nostram servandae in Ecclesia fidelitatis erga veri nominis Traditionem testificaremur.*[44] Now, acts of government have always been reckoned as pertaining to the highest office in the Church, that is acts of a commanding and binding power, without which even the teaching of the truths of the faith remains a merely theoretical and academic business. Two things are needed to maintain truth. First: *remove the error* from the doctrinal sphere, which is done by refuting erroneous arguments and showing that they are not convincing. Second: *remove the person in error*, that is depose him from office, which is done by an act of the Church's authority. If this pontifical service is not performed, it would seem unjustified to say that *all* means have been used to maintain the doctrine of the Church: we are in the presence of a *breviatio manus Domini.*[45] As a consequence, a narrowed idea of

---

[42] Isaiah, 28:21. "His work is foreign to him."

[43] O.R., 2 December 1975.

[44] "In actual fact we have never at any time or in any way failed to give evidence of Our concern to preserve in the Church a faithfulness to Tradition, properly so called."

[45] "A foreshortening of the arm of the Lord."

authority and obedience is spread abroad, without meeting any effective resistance, and ideas about freedom and open debate are correspondingly broadened.

The origin of this whole *breviatio manus* lies quite clearly in the opening speech of the Second Vatican Council, which announced an end to the condemnation of error, a policy which was maintained by Paul VI throughout the whole of his pontificate. As a teacher, he held to the traditional formulas expressing the orthodox faith, but as a pastor, he did not prevent the free circulation of unorthodox ideas, assuming that they would of themselves eventually take an orthodox form and become compatible with truth. Errors were identified and the Catholic faith reiterated, but specific persons were not condemned for their erroneous teaching, and the schismatic situation in the Church was disguised and tolerated.[46]

It was John Paul II who began to restore the full ambit of papal government, whether by individually condemning and removing some teachers of error, or by re-establishing Catholic principles in the Church in Holland by means of an extraordinary synod of the bishops of that province, held in Rome.

Paul VI preferred to give speeches and warnings which recalled people to their duty without condemning them, made them aware of something without putting them under an obligation, and gave directions without insisting that they be followed. In his solemn apostolic exhortation *Paterna* of 8 December 1974, addressed to the whole Catholic world, the Pope denounces those who "attempt to destroy the Church from within" (while euphemistically comforting himself that such people were relatively rare); he enlarges on the subject of refusal of obedience to an authority which is accused of "upholding a system and apparatus of ecclesiastical power"; he deplores a theological pluralism in rebellion against the magisterium; he protests loudly *adversus talem agendi modum perfidum*;[47] he goes so far as to apply to himself the defense of his own episcopal authority which St. John Chrysostom made: *Quamdiu in hac sede sedemus, quamdiu praesidemus, habemus et auctoritatem et virtutem, etiamsi simus indigni.*[48] The Pope laments and denounces and defends and accuses, but in the very act of defend-

---

[46] See paragraph 64.

[47] "Against such a dishonest way of proceeding."

[48] "As long as we sit in this See, as long as we preside, we have power and authority, even though we are unworthy."

ing authority he reduces it to a warning: as if merely a party in the case rather than the judge, he makes the accusation but will not pass sentence.

The general effect of a renunciation of authority is to bring authority into disrepute and to lead it to be ignored by those who are subject to it, since a subject cannot hold a higher view of authority than authority holds of itself. One French archbishop has said: *Aujourd'hui l'Eglise n'a plus à enseigner, à commander, à condamner, mais à aider les hommes à vivre et à s'épanouir.*[49] And to descend from the Palatine to the Suburra, at a round table of priests, organized by the newspaper *L'Espresso* in 1969, it was maintained that the Pope was like a layman, or to be precise, that he was like a policeman set on a stand higher than other people so that he can direct the traffic. It is alleged that the ever present disputes which make the Church today so different from the historical and preconciliar Church, are the distinctive feature of authentic religion and a symptom of the Church's vitality, rather than an abnormal or pathological phenomenon. There is never a papal document on which the episcopates of the world fail to take up their own position, and in their train, but independently of them, theologians and the laity do the same, contradicting each other in their turn. A host of documents is thus churned out, displaying a disorderly variety in which authority is multiplied and so nullified.

66. An historic parallel. Paul VI and Pius IX.

The disjunction between the holding of the supreme office and the exercise of its powers, which we have noted in Paul VI, has a precedent in the pontificate of Pius IX, not because he limited his spiritual functions by refusing to make condemnations, but because he limited his secular authority by refusing to exercise certain powers inherent in it. Antonio Rosmini's criticism of Pius IX's political policies, made in a letter of May 1848 to Cardinal Castracane,[50] can be applied to the religious policies

---

[49] "Today the Church no longer has to teach, command and condemn, but to help men to live and develop." *Courrier de Rome*, No.137, 5 December 1974, p.7.

[50] This can be read in his *Epistolario Completo*, Casale 1892, Vol. X, pp.312-9. The comments that Manzoni made on the letter on 23 May 1848, when it had been shown to him by Rosmini, are significant. See *Epistolario*, cit. Vol. II, p.447.

of Paul VI. "A prince who neither prevents anarchy nor makes any effort to prevent it, who allows people to do everything that he declares he does not want done, and who indirectly supports things that are done against his expressed wish, does not seem to be fulfilling the duties which pertain to his principate." Rosmini was thinking of Pius IX's foreign policy, that is his refusal, because of his high regard for his office as universal pastor, to make the military alliances which Rosmini believed were imposed upon him by his duties as an Italian ruler. There is an analogy in the psychological situation of the two popes. One case shows the difficulties which the union of spiritual primacy and a temporal dominion create for the latter. The other shows the incompatibility of the possession of a spiritual primacy and a refusal to use the authority inherent in it. If the character of the Catholic priesthood seemed to Pius IX incompatible with his exercising all the functions of a temporal ruler, his only course was to give up those functions altogether, or to overcome his reluctance to exercise them. Similarly, since the exercise of authority seemed to Paul VI to be incompatible with a pastoral ministry, he had no other choice than to give up the supreme government (and there were signs that he might do so)[51] or else to carry out a complete restoration of the way authority was being exercised. The difference between the two cases lies in the fact that with Pius IX the element to be renounced was something extrinsic, which had been useful to the spiritual power, but which could be set aside without doing that power any harm; while with Paul VI, what had been given up was intrinsic to the spiritual government, and to give it up was to derange the Church's internal workings, which are based on the idea of subordination, not independence. Although he failed to use his full political force, Pius IX still ran the risk of using his spiritual authority improperly in political matters; he did refuse to wage war, but he excommunicated the combatants all the same. In Paul VI's case, the temporal power had been wholly or almost wholly lost, and he rightly trusted to his spiritual authority, but at the same time reduced it by half through fear of using it in an

---

[51] The sure sign of the possibility of his abdication is that the reformed rules governing a conclave, promulgated in 1975, allow for the possibility that the papacy may be vacant because of the resignation of the pope, which had never previously been envisaged. See *Gazzetta Ticinese*, "*Paolo VI come Celestino V?*" 2 and 9 July 1977.

unspiritual way; dealing with error by commands and penalties was for him an abuse, something repugnant to the true nature of the Church and appropriate for temporal rather than spiritual matters.[52]

67. Government and authority.

It is important nonetheless to state that for Paul VI this renunciation of authority did not mean a renunciation of dogmatic principles, which he in fact forcibly reaffirmed in his major doctrinal encyclicals such as *Humanae Vitae*, on marriage, and *Mysterium Fidei*, on the Eucharist. He also asserted the principle of the plenitude of papal power to *iudicare omnia*,[53] referring expressly to the famous bull *Unam sanctam* of Boniface VIII, in a speech made on 22 October 1970: everything is subject to the keys of Peter. The renunciation simply means that doctrinal assertions were separated from that exercise of authority, in the form of commands and sanctions, which, in the Church's tradition, is designed to support them. Man is still under an obligation to obey, but the Church has no corresponding right to require that obedience. It is as if men were not united socially, but simply left in isolation with their own private judgment: the authority of the Church is therefore never the ultimate determinant of what a Christian does.

In his speech of 18 June 1970 Pope Paul spoke at length about papal authority in a fully Catholic sense; while describing the Petrine primacy as a service, he nonetheless declared: "The

---

[52] There are some extraordinary examples of this reduction of authority to a merely didactic function. When the Tübingen theologian Herbert Haag denied the Catholic doctrine about the devil in the book *Abschied vom Teufel* "Goodbye to the devil," proceedings were begun against him in Rome but soon dropped, and the only response to his denial was a document from the Congregation for the Doctrine of the Faith reaffirming the traditional teaching. Haag continued to make statements incompatible with Catholic doctrine. On the feast of the Immaculate Conception 1981 he preached a sermon in the main church in Lucerne expressly denying two very important doctrines: the Immaculate Conception and original sin. See the text of the sermon published by Haag himself in *Luzerner Neueste Nachrichten*, No.43, 1982. It seems that episcopal authority believes it can put down error without checking a man who goes around spreading it.

[53] "Judge all things."

fact that Jesus Christ has willed His Church to be governed in a spirit of service does not mean that the Church should not have the power of hierarchical government: the conferral of the keys on Peter does mean something." The Pope recalls the fact that the authority of the apostles is none other than the authority of Christ Himself transmitted to them, and does not disguise the fact that it is a power *in virga*,[54] a power to punish and to consign to Satan. It is thus undeniable that Paul's renunciation of authority was accompanied by an assertion of the existence of that authority without any *breviatio manus*, and equally undeniable that this paradox was characteristic of Paul's style, but uncharacteristic of the Church in general. The presentation of authority as a kind of service is quite usual in Catholicism, which sees the whole of life in that light: the catechism says that man is born "to know, love and *serve* God." It should not therefore seem odd that authority itself is seen as a kind of service. When the Pope uses the title of *servus servorum Dei*, originally assumed by Pope St. Gregory the Great as a description of the power of the Supreme Keys, one must remember that the formula *servus servorum* is not a genitive of object, as if the pope were the one who serves the servants of God, but an hebraic genitive signifying a superlative sense as in *saecula saeculorum, virgo virginum, caeli caelorum*,[55] and so on. The formula therefore means that the pope is the servant of God more than all others, the servant of God *par excellence*, not that he is the servant of those who are the servants of God. Were it otherwise, the formula would tend to imply that the pope was the servant of men rather than of God, and would also imply that only the pope was not a servant of God, while everyone else was.

Finally, it is important to emphasize that if authority is a service to those over whom it is exercised, the fact that it is a service does not take away from it the element of inequality which is essential to its existence and in virtue of which the one giving orders is *as such* more important than the one receiving them. Authority and obedience cannot therefore be brought together on a basis of perfect equality. In fact the very word *authority* (coming from *augere*, to augment) shows that someone who is invested with it is endowed with some increase over and

---

[54] "Of the rod."

[55] Literally: age of ages, virgin of virgins, heaven of heavens, but in fact: all ages, greatest of virgins, highest heaven.

above his own person, and suggests a transcendent relation of the sort which has always been recognized in Catholic philosophy.

68. The renunciation of authority, continued. The affair of the French catechism.

The renunciation of authority, even as applied to doctrinal affairs, which had been begun by John XXIII and pursued by Paul VI, was continued by John Paul II. The new catechism put out by the French bishops is at odds with Catholic doctrine on some important points,[56] and also abandons the usual form of catechisms. In an address delivered in Lyons and Paris in January 1983, Cardinal Ratzinger criticized its mistaken inspiration at some length. This seemed to be a warning and a correction. But the same renunciation of authority which had been manifested in the case of the Dutch catechism, and in the feeble condemnation of Hans Küng, whose false teaching had been allowed to continue unchecked, meant that Cardinal Ratzinger withdrew his criticisms almost at once, and his withdrawal could then be publicized by the French bishops in *La Croix* on 19 March 1983. There we read that the Cardinal *entendait traiter de la situation globale de la catéchèse, et non désavouer le travail catéchétique en France. Nous avons pu de vive voix vérifier récemment notre accord avec lui sur tous les points.*[57]

Cardinal Ratzinger's retraction shows the point to which Roman authority has retreated in the face of the emancipated bishops. Although canon 775 of the new Code of Canon Law lays down that episcopal conferences cannot publish catechisms for their territories without the prior approval of the Holy See, the French bishops promulgated theirs without approval and even forbade the use of any other text, thus prohibiting even the catechisms of the Council of Trent and of St. Pius X. After having spoken in his address of the *misère de la catéchèse nouvelle,*[58] and of *désagrégation,*[59] he now seems at one with the

---

[56] As we will show in paragraph 136.

[57] "Intended to discuss the overall catechetical situation, not to disavow catechetical work done in France. We have recently been able to establish face to face our full agreement with him on all points."

[58] "Misery of the new catechetics."

[59] "Breakup."

French bishops in valuing and praising that same misery and breakup.

Not even the natural resentment of a member of the Curia for this despising of Roman authority, or a concern for personal coherence succeeded in evoking a display of fortitude. St. Thomas teaches that fortitude, inasmuch as it means resoluteness of spirit, is not only a special virtue concerned principally with offering resistance, but also the general "form" of all the virtues. We have already mentioned[60] the *breviatio manus* which consists in reducing the role of authority to the mere giving of warnings. These warnings ought at least to be coherent, and free of pliable opportunism. It seems, however, that they are merely verbal declarations, and that the voice of the Church has been reduced to being simply an echo of the fashions of the world. Cardinal Ratzinger's retraction is typical of the post-conciliar Church and demonstrates all the main problems that beset it: the decay of papal authority, the emancipation of the episcopal conferences, the dissension in the Church, and a decline in the force of logic and in attachment to dogmatic truths.

Another display of the decline of authority in the Church and of incoherence in its acts, which now drift with the times, can be had from examining the proposals Papa Luciani made during his short pontificate. He said it was his intention to "conserve *intact the great discipline* of the Church" and addressed his collaborators who were, he said, "called to a *strict following* of the Pope's wishes and to the honor of an activity which commits them to holiness of life, a spirit of obedience, the works of the apostolate and to a strong and exemplary love of the Church."[61] Everyone knows from subsequent events the response there has been to this statement of aims.

The renunciation of authority is not merely a prudent bending of a principle in the light of contemporary circumstances: it has instead itself become a principle. The Prefect for the Congregation of the Clergy, Silvio Cardinal Oddi, admitted as much at a conference of eight hundred members of "Catholics United for the Faith" held at Arlington in the United States in July 1983. The Cardinal admitted that there was confusion about the faith and said that many catechists today choose certain articles of the *depositum fidei*[62] which they are

---

[60] See paragraph 65.
[61] O.R., 29 September 1983.
[62] "Deposit of faith."

going to believe, and abandon all the rest. Doctrines such as the divinity of Christ, the virginity of the Mother of God, original sin, the real presence in the Eucharist, the absoluteness of moral obligation, hell and the primacy of Peter are publicly denied by theologians and bishops in pulpits and in academic chairs. The Prefect for the Congregation of the Clergy was insistently asked why the Holy See did not remove those who taught error, such as Fr. Curran, who had for years been openly attacking *Humanae Vitae*, and who teaches the licitness of sodomy. Why was it that the Holy See did not correct and disavow those bishops, such as Mgr Gerety, who depart from sound doctrine and protect those who corrupt the faith? The Cardinal replied that "The Church no longer imposes punishments. She hopes instead to persuade those who err." She has chosen this course "perhaps because she does not have precise information about the different cases in which error arises, perhaps because she thinks it imprudent to take energetic measures, perhaps too because she wants to avoid causing an even greater scandal through disobedience. The Church believes it is better to tolerate certain errors in the hope that when certain difficulties have been overcome, the person in error will reject his error and return to the Church."[63]

This is an admission of the *breviatio manus* we discussed in paragraphs 65-67 and an assertion of the innovation announced in the opening speech of the council:[64] error contains within itself the means of its own correction, and there is no need to assist the process: it is enough to let it unfold, and it will correct itself. Charity is held to be synonymous with tolerance, indulgence takes precedence over severity, the common good of the ecclesial community is overlooked in the interests of a misused individual liberty, the *sensus logicus*[65] and the virtue of fortitude proper to the Church are lost. The reality is that the Church ought to preserve and defend the truth with all the means available to a perfect society.[66]

---

63   The whole text of Cardinal Oddi's speech appeared in a German version in *Der Fels*, September 1983, pp.261-64.

64   See paragraphs 38-39.

65   "Logical sense."

66   A *societas perfecta* or perfect society is one containing within itself all the means necessary to its own existence and government. [Translator's note.]

69. Character of Paul VI. Self-portrait. Cardinal Gut.

There is room for debate *ad infinitum* on the character of Paul VI. It seems to some that he was paralyzed by an excessive breadth of vision. If St. Thomas's profound theory about how we make a decision is correct, then to decide is to put an end to the intellect's contemplation of different possible courses of action; and thus the greater the number of possibilities considered, that is the wider the view the intellect has, the longer it takes to break off and make a decision. That is Jean Guitton's analysis of Paul VI's character[67] and it is one shared by John XXIII. Other people, however, think it is not a question of character but of a far reaching plan which was always perfectly clear in Pope Paul's mind. What he was aiming at was an adaptation of the Church to the spirit of the age, with the goal of taking over direction of the whole human race, at a purely humanitarian level, and so Pope Paul proceeded cautiously, leaning now to one side and now to the other, acting quite voluntarily and not under constraint, and moving always in the direction of the pre-established goal. Others believe that the Pope did have such a goal in mind, but that in leaning to one side or the other he was driven by circumstances. This view would seem to be confirmed by the self-portrait that Paul VI sketched on 15 December 1969, borrowing a nautical simile from St. Gregory the Great. The Pope presents himself as a pilot who sometimes takes the waves with the prow head on and sometimes dodges their force by turning the ship to the side, but is forever tossed about and under stress. In either of the two latter interpretations it is clear that what the Pope does is adjusted to circumstances and is partly passive, as indeed is all human activity; but in the latter of the two views, passive reaction is the dominant element, and the one which stamps the character of Paul's pontificate.

A remark made by Cardinal Gut, the Prefect of the Congregation for Divine Worship, apropos of liturgical abuses is relevant here. *Beaucoup de prêtres ont fait ce qui leur plaisait. Ils se sont imposés. Les initiatives prises sans autorisation on ne pouvait plus bien souvent les arrêter. Dans sa grande bonté et sa sagesse le Saint Père a alors cédé, souvent contre son gré.*[68] It is obvious that

---

[67] Op. cit., p.14.
[68] *Documentation Catholique*, No.1551, p.18. "Many priests did whatever they liked. They imposed their own personalities. Very

giving in to those who break the law is neither goodness nor wisdom, unless one gives in after a struggle and maintains the law at least by protesting. Furthermore, since wisdom is a practical discernment of the means appropriate to the attainment of an end, it can hardly be reconciled with the idea of giving up that end. Giving up the law could also be seen as joining what had proved to be the larger party in the Church. It could be equivalent to a decision to change the law in a way the majority desired, thus making it more acceptable and easier to follow. In disciplinary matters this is a plausible point of view, but hardly very plausible when the law is abandoned to support a riotous minority instead of the obedient majority.

The latter occurred regarding the option of taking communion in the hand, which two-thirds of the bishops of the world had said they did not support. The option was granted first of all to the French who had improperly introduced it, and requests were then made that it be extended to the whole world. That an abuse should be the grounds for abrogating a law has never been admitted, or regarded as admissible. It was, however, precisely what happened in the case of the scheme for the radical reform of the Mass, which, having been proposed to the bishops and rejected by them, was nonetheless taken up and promulgated for use everywhere, under pressure from powerful people.

70. Yes and no in the post-conciliar Church.

Renunciation of authority brings with it uncertainty and flux regarding the law. By receding from its own positions, authority denies and contradicts itself, giving rise to a *sic et non*[69] in which doctrinal certainty and practical stability are lost. The old adage *lex dubia non obligat*[70] applied to the situation we have described leads to a failing authority seconding the successive impositions of those who rebel against it, and the rebels thus become the source of law.

Uncertainty about the law, created by the hesitations of authority, is very obvious in the whole liturgical reform, which

---

often unauthorized initiatives could not be stopped. In his great goodness and wisdom, the Holy Father then made concessions, often against his own inclinations."

[69] "Yes and no."

[70] "A doubtful law does not bind."

was carried through in disorderly fashion by the withdrawal of prohibitions, the repeated broadening of options and the introduction of experimental practices: from this uncertainty, and from the introduction of the principle that the celebrant should be creative, there arose a vast variety of celebrations: while the official rite contained only four canons, thousands of canons were produced, with book upon book suggesting new ones, drawn up by diocesan liturgical commissions or by private individuals, some of this with the approval of the Holy See. This multiplicity of ritual forms is deplored by those who approved the liturgical reform originally, and is complained of by those who dislike it.

The most obvious evidence of the breakup of the Catholic rites through the renunciation of authority is to be found in the almost total disappearance of *prescriptive rubrics*, the frequency of rubrics which merely advise or recommend, and in the multiplication of possible alternatives: the celebrant will make this gesture, or he will not, or he will make another one according to circumstances of time and place which, except in one or two instances, are left to his own judgment. It should also be remembered that since many faculties which were previously reserved to the Holy See have been devolved upon the bishops, the bishops are now the judges of how they should be used, and thus new discrepancies are created between nation and nation, diocese and diocese, and even between one parish and another. This discrepancy can be seen, for instance, in the practice of communion in the hand, which is permitted in universal law, practiced in some countries, more or less obligatory in others, and forbidden in yet others.[71]

The *sic* of the law and the *non* of an authority which refuses to enforce it sometimes come together in strikingly illogical ways as, for example, in *Notitiae*, the bulletin of the Congregation of Divine Worship, 1969 ed., p.351, which publishes si-

---

[71] There was much comment on the action of John Paul II when, during a visit to France, he placed the host in Madame Giscard D'Estaing's mouth while she held out her hands to receive the host for herself. A photograph appears in *Der Fels*, July 1980, p.229. Even if the event shows what the Pope's personal preference is, it is still a further proof of the peculiar state of the law in the Church today, because according to the norms applying in France, there is an absolutely free choice between the two ways of receiving the Eucharist.

multaneously an *Instructio* forbidding something and a decree permitting the same thing.

The vacillation of authority in the matter of the order in which children should receive the two sacraments of Penance and the Eucharist is just as apparent. Some episcopal conferences kept the old practice of making a sacramental confession before receiving Holy Communion for the first time, while others made a change by reversing the order for not very convincing psychological reasons. Not convincing, because if the child is allegedly too immature to understand its own sinfulness, how is it mature enough to understand the real presence in the sacrament? The German episcopal conference first of all decreed, in agreement with Cardinal Döpfner, that children should be admitted to the Eucharist without first making a confession, then, a few years later, in agreement with Cardinal Ratzinger, Döpfner's successor, it decreed that first communion should be preceded by confession.

It is obvious that uncertainty about the law, which has become something very changeable and which is in practice applied diversely in accordance with the differing opinions of differing people, has had the effect of increasing the importance placed on private judgment, and of producing a multiplicity of individual choices in which the organic unity of the Church is eclipsed and disappears.

71. The renunciation of authority, continued. The reform of the Holy Office.

At this point a word must be said about the reform of the Holy Office, promulgated by the *motu proprio, Integrae servandae* of 7 December 1965 and by the subsequent notification *Post litteras apostolicas* of 14 June 1966. The notification expresses the renunciation of authority in the clearest possible way and makes it clear that there are to be no more obligations imposed by law, only obligations imposed by conscience, through its relationship with the moral law. It states that the Index of Forbidden Books remains *morally* binding, but *no longer has the force of ecclesiastical law* with its attendant censures. The reason for making it no longer binding is that the Christian people are presumed to have such religious and intellectual maturity as to be lights unto themselves. Indeed we read in the document that "the Church trusts that such maturity exists in the Christian people." Historians will have to decide whether this supposed

maturity actually existed, and whether it was grounds for abolishing the prohibition. The Church moreover places "the firm-
est hope in the vigilant care of ordinaries[72] whose duty it is to
examine and prevent the publication of harmful books, and
where necessary, to reprove and admonish the authors." It is all
too obvious that this supposed doctrinal vigilance on the part of
ordinaries is a *modus irrealis*[73] since their doctrine is neither
firm, nor concordant nor, at times, sound; nor can ordinaries
prevent the publication of harmful books if they are not given
the right to demand that books be submitted to their judgment
in advance. But in fact, as is stated in the decree of 19 March
1975, the Church confines itself to *enixe commendare*[74] that
priests should not publish without the permission of their bishops; and that bishops should guard the faith and require that
books on matters of faith and morals should be submitted to
them by authors, who have however no corresponding obligation to submit them. The Church asks lastly that all the faithful
cooperate with their pastors in this matter.

The entire disciplinary reform is based upon the hidden assumption that individuals are *immediately* subject to the law,
without the mediation of any authority, and that they may be
presumed to have a maturity which, in the older view, the
Church was trying to give them through the whole of its legislative activity. It is also clear that there has been a transition
from the realm of commands and prohibitions to that of mere
directions and exhortations, in which error is identified, but the
person in error is not disciplined, since it is supposed, in accordance with what was said in the opening speech at the council,
that error will of itself generate its own refutation and produce
assent to the truths opposed to it.

So far as reading books is concerned, the freedom the
Church now allows the faithful is the ordinary freedom that
anyone has, subject to the moral law. But is it right to allow the
same freedom where the writing of books is concerned, given
that publishing is not a private and passing activity, but something public, permanent and independent of the author, and
which produces effects beyond his control? The state ought to

---

[72] i.e., Bishops.

[73] "Unreal mode," i.e., in grammar, a proposition containing a condition which is not realized: thus what is contingent on it is not realized either.

[74] "Strongly recommending."

grant such freedom, but the state is based on different principles
from the Church; principles which are not specifically religious.
In the Church, a different set of first principles leads to a different set of conclusions. The abolition of the *Index librorum pro-
hibitorum* is a renunciation of authority: it purports to maintain
the prohibitions entailed by the moral law, but refuses to say,
specifically, what they are; that is, it refers the consciences of the
faithful to universal principles so that they can make the particular application of them themselves.

The post-conciliar Church did not officially allow an absolute liberty in the publishing of books, and reserved the right to
judge their orthodoxy with a view to the common good. The
Church has a duty to *preserve* its members from error, as well as
to *teach* Catholic doctrine whole and entire. Both duties were
acknowledged in the opening speech of the council[75] but the
first was merged with the second: it was alleged that teaching
alone was enough to enable the Christian to preserve himself
from error, since he was deemed able to protect himself by his
own sound judgments.

When Paul III originally established the Congregation of
the Holy Office in 1542, its aim was "to combat heresies and
consequently to repress offenses against the faith." Paul VI
thinks "it seems better that the defense of the faith should be
made by means of a commitment to foster doctrine, so that
while errors are corrected and those in error are sweetly recalled
to better counsels, those who proclaim the Gospel receive new
strength." As in Pope John's opening speech, these loving methods are based on two presuppositions: first, that provided error
is allowed to develop, it will find its way to truth; and second,
that either because of his natural constitution or because of the
point that civilization has now reached, man has achieved such
a state of maturity that, "the faithful will follow the Church's
path more fully and lovingly...if the content of the faith and the
nature of morals are (merely) demonstrated."

72. Critique of the reform of the Holy Office.

In paragraphs 40 and 41, I have already touched on the
connection this position has with an anthropocentric mentality,
and I will do so again later. I want here simply to point out the
juridical and psychological confusion of persons with things

[75] See paragraph 40.

which underlies the reforms. There used to be an Index of Forbidden Books, not an Index of Forbidden Authors. This distinction continues to be ignored in disputes about the reform, just as it was in the implementation of the reform itself. Is there anything wrong, as people allege, in passing judgment on a book without hearing the author's explanations? There would be, if the meaning of a precise piece of writing had to be gathered from the author's intentions or from the explanation he gave of it, rather than from the writing itself. A book is a thing in itself which has, indeed is, its own meaning. It is made up of words, and words are more than the person who utters them, since they have an objective meaning set within them. A writer needs to know how to make his subjective meaning come together with the objective meaning of his language. One can intend to say something that is not in fact said, and hence the mark of good writing, that is of true writing, is to say what one really wanted to. The mark of bad writing is, conversely, to say what was not intended. Thus a book can profess atheism, while its author believes himself a theist.

The additions an author makes to a book, once it has been published, do not alter the nature of the book. Even if, *per impossibile*, they were to change its nature and make it quite irreproachable, no notice should be taken of that insofar as the already circulating book is concerned. The reason for this is obvious. The justificatory additions an author may subsequently make cannot accompany his books wherever they go; they run their course alone: *Parve sine me, liber, ibis in urbem.*[76]

It is a matter of distinguishing between one thing and another, between a person and a book. A matter of recognizing, as

---

[76] "You will go, little book, to Rome without me." Ovid. One publication can only be corrected or disowned by another. In itself, it has an unchanging meaning which can only be "retracted" (both in the sense of "rehandled" and of "withdrawn") by the appearance of another publication. Under the new rules, the Holy Office listens to the author's defense and requests that the clarifications which he has given to bring the book within the bounds of orthodoxy be published by him. If the author refuses to publish them, the whole business becomes even more unpleasant. That is what happened in Fr. Schillebeeckx's case. See *Le Monde*, 10 December 1980. He refused to publish the statements he had made to the Holy Office, which in turn limited itself to publishing the letter in which it listed the corrections he was to incorporate.

Plato did,[77] that a book is not like a person in conversation, who can turn this way and that to make himself understood by somebody questioning him, and who can clarify, refine and explain: a book always says the same thing, namely what its words express when taken in their natural sense, and that is all.

Nor let it be said that words do not have a meaning of their own within a given idiom: they may lack meaning sitting in a dictionary, but they certainly have meaning in a particular act of speech. If they did not, what would all the critics in the world be doing? Do they refrain from making judgment until they have been able to speak to the author? Do they ask an author for the meaning of his works, or do they extract it from the work itself? And of course great masterpieces, including the very greatest in each language, which are the source of the poetry, and indeed of the whole culture of a particular people, have no owner; they attain to a kind of superhuman impersonality. But nobody has ever thought their value cannot be judged because their authors are unknown. So far from the comprehension of a work depending on a knowledge of its sometimes rather obscure author, such as Shakespeare or Homer (if the latter was a single individual, which Wolf[78] denies), one could maintain, as Flaubert did, that the personal character of the author should not enter into the work and that a perfect writer is one who makes posterity think he never existed.

But to return to the reform of the Holy Office, a writer's intention cannot prevent written words from expressing error if error is what they express. The fixed meaning of words is the basis of all communication between men. It is not a question of judging the state of someone's conscience, but of knowing the meaning of words. Nor is it true that in examining books the Holy Office did not pay attention to every aspect of the work in question. Every aspect of *the book* was precisely what it did examine; not the intentions of its author. Nor should anyone adduce the example of the Inquisition's repeated long interviews with Giordano Bruno between 1582 and 1600, because the conversations were in that case not concerned with the true meaning of the philosopher's books, but with getting him to repent and retract. Benedict XIV[79] decreed in his day that a consultor should be specifically delegated to defend a book under

---

[77] Protagoras, 329A.

[78] Friedrich Wolf (1759-1824), Homeric scholar. [Translator's note.]

[79] Pope from 1740 to 1758. [Translator's note.]

examination, not by expounding the author's intentions but by interpreting the words of the text in their proper sense; and this practice was, I believe, maintained. Thus the accusations made against the established procedures stem from a failure to understand the objective and independent nature of every piece of writing; in short, from a failure in the art of literary criticism.[80]

73. Change in the Roman Curia. Lack of precision.

The passion for innovation enveloped the whole Curia, not only reordering its traditional form, as St. Pius X had done in 1908 following the example of many of his predecessors, but also changing the functions of long established congregations. All the names were changed. The Congregation for the Propagation of the Faith became the Congregation for the Evangelization of Peoples, and the Congregation of the Consistory became the Congregation for Bishops. New congregations were created with the title of commissions, councils or secretariats: one for Christian unity, one for non-Christian religions, one for non-believers, one for social communications, one for the apostolate of the laity, and so on. The change in names is not without its significance. The *propagation* of the faith carried with it the notion of the expansion of Catholicism among unbelieving peoples, while the concept of evangelization is generic and is already applied to pastoral activity among people who are already Christian, and even to the very act of living as a Christian, thus merging a specific activity in a more general one.

It has been common since the council to say that the Roman Curia has exercised an influence opposed to the reforming intentions of the council and the pope. The fact is that the Curia, as the organ of papal government, has always been an organ effecting changes in the Church, and that all the transformations which have taken place and are taking place in Catholicism in the twentieth century have been brought about through using the Curia. The reform of the Holy Office, which signified

---

[80] I find the apologia for the Holy Office made by Mgr Hamer in the O.R., 13 July 1974, somewhat peculiar in that it does not address the fundamental issue, namely that a book has a reality of its own, quite apart from its author. I think the same defect is evident in Mgr Landucci's study in *Renovatio*, 1981, p.363, in that he thinks the provisions for safeguarding the rights of the author in the new *Ratio agendi* are very commendable.

and brought about the completely new post-conciliar mentality, bears the signature of Cardinal Ottaviani, its prefect, whom the innovators tend to regard as the incarnation of the preconciliar spirit. Indeed, as we saw in paragraph 69, disobedience to Roman norms achieved its end through successive ratification by the Curia, which abandoned its own positions and turned abuses into laws.

Our subject here, however, is the change in the formal and technical workings of the Curia. First of all one should note the decline in the standard of curial Latin. If one goes back to the chiseled, adamantine style of Gregory XVI's[81] documents or the elegance of Leo XIII's,[82] one can see in comparison the loss of nobility, lucidity and precision in the curial style. The Latin of Vatican II was often deplored as miserable by the council fathers who nonetheless approved the content of the documents. Furthermore, some of the main texts, such as *Gaudium et Spes*, were originally drafted in French, thus breaking the canons of curial procedure, whereby the Latin text is meant to be original and authentic, and giving rise to the hermeneutical uncertainty we mentioned in paragraph 39.

A notable instance of this uncertainty passing from the grammatical to the juridical field is the apostolic constitution of 3 April 1969. In its final paragraph we read: *Ex his quae hactenus de novo Missali Romano exposuimus, quiddam nunc cogere et efficere placet.*[83] But the translations that were immediately put into circulation give the phrase this meaning: *Nous voulons donner force de loi à tout ce que Nous avons exposé*[84] and the Italian version: *Vogliamo dare forza di legge a quanto abbiamo esposto,*[85] or: *Quanto abbiamo qui stabilito e ordinato, vogliamo che rimanga valido ed efficace ora e in futuro.*[86]

---

81 Pope from 1831 to 1846. [Translator's note.]

82 Pope from 1878 to 1903. [Translator's note.]

83 "From the things which we have set forth regarding the new Roman Missal we now wish to sum up certain elements and draw a conclusion."

84 *Documentation Catholique*, No.1541, p.517. "We wish to give the force of law to all that we have set forth."

85 O.R., 12 April 1969. "We wish to give the force of law to what we have set forth."

86 *Messale Romano* published by the Italian Episcopal Conference, Rome 1969. "What we have here established and ordained, we wish to remain valid and effective now and in the future."

It is not our intention to enter a philological debate on this curial, or rather papal, text, but we should note how the clarity and rigor of the curial style have been lost in a passage as important as this. Declaring ourselves incompetent to decide the philological question, we will confine ourselves to noting what seems undeniable, that is that the bad or, in Cicero's sense, "unused" Latin prevents one immediately seizing what the legislation means, and so opens the way to opposing readings: one which sees in the formula nothing more than a stylistic flourish (but in that case it is hard to see what "conclusion" the author is referring to, as the signature and date of the document follow immediately); and another which sees an intention to give the force of law to everything which has been set out (but in that case the problem is that *quiddam* is not at all the same as *quidquid*, yet that is what the translations have assumed). A necessary consequence of the imprecision and uncertainty attending the whole business is the unpleasant fact that there are now three different official versions of the constitution, varying among themselves through additions and omissions.

74. Change in the Roman Curia, continued. Cultural inadequacies.

Apart from bad Latin and a lack of precision, the Curia can be criticized for the cultural inadequacy implicit in recent papal documents, which were for centuries distinguished by an irreproachable perfection. We will give separate treatment to article 7 of the constitution *Missale Romanum*, which contained a definition of the Mass at odds with the Catholic understanding of it, stating that the Mass was a *meeting*, instead of a *sacrificial act*, with the result that the constitution had to be altered after a few months to get rid of its open departure from the teaching of the Church.[87] We give now a few examples of defective knowledge, culpable negligence and lack of attention to detail, on the part of those who serve the pope, remembering that a pope's official documents should never be allowed to damage his standing, particularly in matters of teaching or of special solemnity.

In his speech on 2 August 1969 at Kampala in Black Africa, Paul VI praised the African Church of Tertullian, St. Cyprian and St. Augustine as if it had been a black church, when in fact

---

[87] See paragraphs 273-4.

it was entirely Latin. He also listed among the great men of the African church one "Octavius of Miletus," who never existed but who, if he had, would not have been African. There was an Optatus of Milevis, but he was a writer of secondary importance and uncertain orthodoxy.

Elsewhere, talking about unpredictable things which sometimes interrupt men's plans, the Pope cited chapter seven of Machiavelli's *Prince*, giving Valentine's words saying that he "had thought of everything except the possibility that he would die suddenly." But the unforeseen thing was not that he died (if it had been, how would he have been able to talk about it later?) but that he found himself at death's door, when Alexander VI was dying, that is, when he would otherwise have been executing his plan to take over the state for himself.[88]

In another speech the Pope said that "the council decided to revive the *word* and the idea of *collegiality.*" But the word is not used in any of the conciliar texts[89] and although the Pope might well have inserted it in them at the time of their drafting, he could not thereafter make it be there when it was not. In his speech of 9 March 1972, he talks about the gift of freedom *che l'uomo a Dio fa simigliante,*[90] but that is a slip because Dante is not there referring to freedom but to the order of the world which makes the creature like the Creator, inasmuch as that order is an impression upon the creation of an idea in the divine intellect.

It is still stranger that this imprecision should extend even to quotations from Scripture. On 26 July 1970 the Pope quoted Galatians 5:6 as if it said that "faith makes charity operative" while St. Paul says the opposite, that is that charity makes faith operative, which was how the same passage was correctly translated in another speech of 3 August 1978.

Without going into the general opposition between the Pope's optimism and the actual state of the world and the Church, one can find particular statements that contradict the facts. In a speech of 27 November 1969 justifying the abandonment of Latin in the liturgy, the Pope said that Latin

---

[88] Valentine, otherwise known as Cesare Borgia, was the illegitimate son of Alexander VI Borgia. The events referred to occurred at the time of that pope's death in 1503. Cesare was killed in a brawl in Navarre in 1507. [Translator's note.]

[89] See the cited *Concordantiae.*

[90] Dante's *Paradiso*, I, 105. "Which makes men like to God."

"remains in official documents and in ecclesiastical teaching."
But in almost all ecclesiastical universities and seminaries
teaching is now given in the national language and at meetings
of the Synod of Bishops the assembly breaks up, after the plenary opening session, into *circuli minores*[91] corresponding to
language groups. The Curia itself is now multilingual and I
have among my papers a letter from Cardinal Wright, Prefect of
the Congregation of the Clergy, headed (in English)
"Congregation of the Clergy." Apparently in the drawing up of
this particular papal speech, some non-papal hand has trans-
gressed the limits on the use of the word "remain."

No one should allow the respect that is owed to so venerable an organ of the papacy as the Roman Curia to be reduced
in his own mind by the incubus of these lapses into imprecision. The truth of the matter is, nonetheless, that inadequacies
among the Pope's assistants are particularly embarrassing precisely because the seat of highest authority in the Church ought
to be the one most immune from all reproach, and because the
Pope in a sense personally incarnates the whole culture of the
Catholic Church. Even if Pope Paul was not aware of the very
real deficiencies of his assistants in drawing up documents, preparing speeches and looking up authors and quotations, he had
nonetheless a very clear idea of the high standards required in
those who work for a pope. In fact he said to Jean Guitton: *La
moindre inexactitude, le moindre lapsus dans la bouche d'un Pape
ne peut se tolérer.*[92]

The failings we have noticed do not perhaps show any
profound cultural deficiencies, but they are indicative of a lack
of diligence and precision which affect even the Pope himself. A
master craftsman cannot vouch for the excellence of all the work
done by his subordinates, but the general quality of the assistants whom he employs necessarily reflects on his own powers
of discernment. All the doings of an authority's agents are doings of that authority, and either keep up or lower its prestige.
There are still those who remember the commotion when a
head of government quoted a saying of Protagoras in a very important speech, and attributed it to Anaxagoras.

---

[91] "Small circles."
[92] Op. cit., p.13. "The least inexactitude, the smallest lapse, in the
mouth of a Pope is intolerable."

75. The Church's renunciation in its relations with states.

The renunciation of authority which we have explored within the Church, in the case of the reform of the Holy Office, is also apparent in relations with states, in the form of an agreement by the Church to join in the general process of international détente. The tendency is clearly there, but we will not go into any great detail in a subject which is not directly relevant to a book such as this and would involve our giving opinions on various famous events. We will, however, note the removal of Joseph Cardinal Mindszenty from the primatial see of Hungary, and the voluntary humiliation of the papal delegation at the installation of the new Patriarch of Constantinople in 1971, at which Cardinal Willebrands and the rest of the papal representatives listened to the accusations directed at the Roman Church without any word or mark of protest. We note lastly the sympathy that Paul VI showed to the schismatical Catholic Church in China, which Pius XII had condemned in two encyclicals in 1956. We will deal at greater length with the more typical of the actions that show the renunciatory attitude the Church has adopted towards the modern state.

The revision of the Italian concordat of 1929 is the most outstanding example of the change the Catholic Church has made in its philosophy and theology as far as relations between Church and State are concerned. The attack on first principles had already begun during the long process of negotiation, in an article in the *Osservatore Romano* of 3 December 1976 in which it was stated that the Church would condescend to sacrifice principles in order to demonstrate its own flexibility. The new agreement covered in fourteen articles matters to which the agreement of 1929 had devoted more than forty. This alone suggested that many mixed matters[93] had been abandoned to the civil power, with the Church ceasing to have any say in them. There were three decisive changes. The first is laid down in article No.1 of the additional protocol and reads as follows: "The principle, originally recognized in the Lateran Pacts, that the Catholic religion is the sole religion of the Italian state, is held to be no longer in force."[94] This provision of the new agreement

---

[93] i.e., Matters in which both Church and state might have a voice. [Translator's note.]

[94] R.I., 1984, p.257.

implies the abandonment of the Catholic principle according to which man's religious obligations go beyond the individual sphere and embrace the civil community: this should, as a community, have a positive concern for the ultimate destination of human society, which is a life transcending our present state. Acknowledging God is a social duty, not merely an individual one. Even if it were felt undesirable to attempt to uphold this principle from a theological point of view, given the nature of contemporary society, it might still have been upheld for historical reasons. That is, prescinding from the suprahistorical value that religion claims to have, it would still have been possible to recognize its value as an integral and important part of the historic life of the Italian nation, on the same basis as its language, art and culture. This is the thesis upheld by Paul VI[95] when he said religion was a distinctive but not a divisive characteristic of civil society. It should also be said that with a greater degree of finesse in Vatican diplomacy, a way would have been found of giving less open expression to such a drastic concession, by which the Church accepted a divorce between social values and religious truth. It should have been possible to lay down not that the principle "is held to be no longer in force," but that "the Holy See takes note that the Italian state declares it considers the principle to be no longer in force." The substantial change here is obvious: the Church is today calling *laicità*[96] what it yesterday described as *laicismo*[97] and condemned as an illegitimately equal treatment of unequal views of life.

Lastly, if the agreements signed on 12 February 1984 reshape the concordat of 1929, as everyone recognizes they do, they also attack the treaty regularizing the sovereignty and temporal independence of the papacy. The possibility of abandoning the concordat while leaving the treaty intact, which Mussolini had raised in a speech in parliament, was promptly excluded by Pius XI who said: *simul stabunt aut simul cadent.*[98] I do not know how legitimate it is to abrogate a clause in one agreement without noting that in so doing one is abrogating a clause in another, but it is a fact (little noticed in speeches and in the press) that article 1 of the additional protocol signed on 18 February 1984 tacitly abrogates articles 1 and 2 of the treaty of

---

[95] See paragraph 59.
[96] "Laicity," i.e., secularity. [Translator's note.]
[97] "Laicism," i.e., secularism. [Translator's note.]
[98] "They will stand or fall together."

1929 which specify that: "Italy recognizes and reaffirms the principle by which the Catholic, Apostolic and Roman religion is the sole religion of the state." As a result, article 13 of the new concordat which says: "The foregoing arrangements constitute changes to the Lateran concordat" is false because of what it fails to say: they constitute a change to the treaty as well.[99]

76. The revision of the concordat, continued.

The second change concerns the regulation of marriage. By the 1929 concordat, Italy recognized the civil effects of canonical marriages and decreed they should be recorded in the civil registry office. With the introduction of divorce,[100] these arrangements had been unilaterally modified: the state withdrew from divorced persons the status of a spouse, which in the Church's eyes they retained forever. Article 8 of the 1984 agreement continued to recognize the civil effects of a canonical marriage, but gave the state the right not to accord such recognition if the requirements of canon law did not conform in a particular case to the norms of civil law.

The third change concerns education. Instead of the obligation to attend Catholic religious instruction at school, recognized by the 1929 concordat, article 9 of the new one states: "The Italian republic, recognizing the value of religious culture, and taking account of the fact that Catholic principles are part of the historic patrimony of the Italian people, will continue to ensure the teaching of the Catholic religion in schools. Each person is acknowledged to have the right of availing or not availing himself of such teaching." This right of choice will be exercised by "students or their parents." An obligatory system, tempered by the right to be dispensed from attending on the grounds of freedom of conscience, was thus replaced by an optional system by which instruction in the Catholic religion is

---

[99] In 1929, the Holy See, under Pope Pius XI, and the Italian state, of which Mussolini was prime minister, signed the Lateran Treaty by which the sovereignty of the Holy See was recognized and the borders of the present Vatican City State were established. At the same time a concordat, of the sort which the Holy See has with various sovereign states, was also signed with Italy, regulating the status of the Catholic Church in that country. These are the agreements the author refers to. [Translator's note.]

[100] In 1970, and upheld at a referendum in 1974. [Translator's note.]

left entirely up to the free choice of the individual. The Catholic religion is no longer part of the system of values recognized by Italian society, and that society is no longer bound by it; when recognized, values do impose an obligation. It is no longer the Catholic religion, as Catholic, that the state recognizes, but the Catholic religion inasmuch as it is an historically important form of religious expression. Here we have the notion that *natural religion* is the nucleus of all religions, giving them what value they have. This is, as we have often said, the fundamental principle of the modern age.

Those negotiating on the part of the Holy See stuck to their accommodating and renunciatory line when it came to a vital point of educational policy. Requests for financial aid from the state for private schools, or for families who make use of them were not supported, and played no major role in the negotiation although Italian Catholics had staged many demonstrations in support of their right to such assistance, as a consequence of a pluralist approach to the matter, and had asked that Italy should make the same arrangements as many other democracies in Europe and in the world at large.

The revision of the concordat gave rise to a good deal of dissimulation, intended to disguise the extent of the change by covering it with a fictitious historical continuity that could only be secured by changing the meaning of words and weakening the logical coherence of the Church's thinking. Dispassionate observers recognized the extent of the change nonetheless. One such observer said: "The concordat is too different from the old one for its novelty to be called in question: it embarks on a new course of which the outcome cannot be foreseen."[101] The writer recalls the doctrine of Pius XI on the objective superiority of the goals pursued by the Church and concludes "it is clear how profoundly the Catholic Church has changed in recent years."

The thinking in the official Vatican journal of 19 February was altogether different; it maintained that "the new concordat is the solid and well-founded fruit of the agreements of 1929." This statement would be true if words meant the opposite of what they do, and if changing one's principles were the same as developing them, getting them to bear fruit and "maintaining the concordat in its integrity." The subsequent statement that "the principles of the Catholic religion remain intact" provokes

---

[101] R.I., 1984, p.246.

the obvious distinction that they do indeed remain intact amidst error or persecution, but that they certainly do not remain intact in the law, morals or social life of a state that professes and practices their opposite. The Pope himself took part in this attempt to change reality by changing the meaning of words; this attempt to derive from forms of words a satisfaction which actual events did not afford. In his speech of 20 February he said: "The revision of the concordat is a sign of renewed harmony between state and Church in Italy." But is not divorce out of harmony with indissolubility? Does not the Church believe that abortion violates the ban on killing which stems from natural moral law? Is not indifferentism in public schools regarding religious instruction at odds with the Catholic's duty to inform himself about his own religion? The fact of the matter is that in the axiology of the Italian republic there is room for literacy, physical education, health, work, social security, the arts and letters, but the value which, according to Catholic doctrine, is the foundation and consummation of them all is left out and relegated to the private sphere guaranteed by individual liberty.[102]

Geno Pampaloni discusses the growing convergence between Church and state in Italy in an article called "The Narrowing of the Tiber"[103] but he mistakenly considers it to be the result of "a weakening of secularity," when it is in fact due to a draining of Catholicism of what makes it specifically Catholic: it is not the state that is bending to suit religion, but religion that is bending to suit the state, and thus, as it were, de-religionizing itself. Borrowing a term from the vocabulary of Italian politics, Pampaloni calls this a *compromesso storico*.[104] At its broadest and deepest, however, it is nothing less than that

---

[102] The Pope's judgment receives a sharp rebuff from a remark by Cardinal Ballestrero, the President of the Italian Episcopal Conference, in O.R. of 25 November 1983: "Our country is terribly detached from the Church because the principles which inspire it in almost all its choices and ways of behaving are no longer those of the Gospel."

[103] *Il Tevere più stretto*, in *Il Giornale*, 6 January 1984.

[104] "Historic compromise." A term used, mainly in the 1970's, to refer to a possible coalition between the Italian Christian Democrats and Communists. [Translator's note.]

fundamental shift which is preparing the ground for a humanitarian cosmopolis and a universal confusion of religions.[105]

77. The Church of Paul VI.
His speeches of September 1974.

Pope Paul could not permanently maintain his natural disposition to disguise the difficulties the Church was experiencing, since it entailed a kind of forcing of his own mind, given the open admission of those difficulties which he often made, and which we mentioned in paragraph 7. These admissions reached their climax in two speeches of 11 and 18 September 1974, which astonished world opinion, were printed entire by the main journals of historical and political studies[106] and were the object of much comment from the editor of the *Osservatore Romano*.

The fact becoming apparent in both West and East is "the massive advance of a dechristianizing secularism." Having recognized the theoretical and practical hostility of the modern world towards religion in general and Catholicism in particular, the Pope, overcome by a spiritual sadness, admits not only that it seems impossible for religion to flourish in such a world, but that, "to a superficial observer, the Church seems an impossible thing in our day, and even seems doomed to die out and be replaced by a simpler and more experimental, rational and scientific conception of the world, without dogmas, without hierarchies, without limits to the possibilities of enjoying existence, without the Cross of Christ." The Church remains a great institution "but let us open our eyes: it is today, in certain respects, *experiencing great suffering, radical tension and corrosive contradictions.*" The Pope wonders whether the world still needs the Church to teach the values of charity, respect for rights, or solidarity, given that, "*the world does all this, and it would seem, does it better*" and that its success in doing so seems to justify the abandonment of religious practice by whole peoples, the irreligiousness of secularism, emancipation from the moral law, the defection of priests and also of "the faithful who are no longer worried about being unfaithful." In short the Pope puts forward the idea that Christianity is superfluous, and that the modern

---

[105] The author uses the term *teocrasia*, derived from the Greek, and meaning a "mixture of gods." [Translator's note.]

[106] R.I., 1974, p.932.

world could be emptied of all religion: one might call it the advent of "man the mini-god."

The Pope rightly sees an important element of the present crisis in the fact that the Church is trembling before the assault of forces internal to itself, not those outside. That is exactly the criterion we have adopted for discerning whether or not there has been a crisis in the Church's history.[107] "A great range of these evils do not assail the Church from without, but afflict it, weaken it and enervate it *from within*. The heart is filled with bitterness." The novelty does not lie in evils arising from among the clergy; evils have often come from that source in the past. The Pope is well aware that the new element is what he called *self-demolition* in his famous speech at the Lombard College. That expression is inadmissible dogmatically, and in fact was never used again by the Pope, because the Church is essentially constructive rather than destructive; but when understood historically, it is appropriate.

When approaching the question of the solution to this crisis, if the Pope were to remain in the realm of facts and of reasonable conjectures based upon them, he would find himself in a cleft stick. So, in his conclusion he moves from the historical level, on which the Church is experiencing suffering and decline, to the level of faith, on which the believer's spirit is sustained by a divine promise that *non praevalebunt*.[108] This movement to the so-called argument based on faith has become common in Catholic apologetics since the council. It is doubtful whether it is a logical transition to make. The diagnosis he has already given, identifying the world's sickness as stemming from alienation from God, desacralization and a complete *Diesseitigkeit*, is itself an argument based on faith. Only faith sees a ruin in what looks to the unbeliever like the perfecting and progress of the human race.

78. Paul VI's unrealistic moments.

There are two ways in which Paul VI overcomes the sadness caused by contemplating the present state of the Church. The legitimate and only true and traditional way is to admit that facts are as they are, and then to examine them in the light of a genuinely Catholic philosophical and theological analysis. The

---

[107] See paragraphs 2, 12 and 19.
[108] "They will not prevail." Matthew, 16:18.

illegitimate way is a product of the old psychological habit of believing things are the way you want them to be, which leads to the mind's refusing to recognize what it does really know, because it would be unpleasant to do so. The mind then senses the way things are through its contact with reality, but does not admit the state of affairs to itself or to others. Examples of this phenomenon abound in the writings of moral philosophers and biblical prophets, to whom the people cried *loquimini nobis placentia,*[109] which is, at times, what each individual says to himself as well. Perhaps some words in a letter Montini wrote as a young man show the first signs of this predominance of imagination over the perception of facts: "I am convinced that one of my thoughts, a thought from my own soul, is worth more to me than anything in the world."

Only those who are unaware of what Augustine called the *latebrae*[110] and Manzoni the *guazzabuglio*[111] of the human heart, including the heart of a pope, will be surprised to find side by side in the same speech by Paul VI a sadness justified by reality, and a triumphalism which shrouds or transforms or even reverses the reality of a situation. In his speech of 16 November 1970, for example, the Pope had vividly depicted the unhappy state of the post-conciliar Church. Externally there was "an oppressive legal system in so many countries" which bound the Church: it "suffers and struggles as far as it can and survives because God helps it." Internally "it is for everyone a cause of surprise, pain and scandal to see that within the Church itself there arise disturbances and unfaithfulness, often on the part of those who ought to be most loyal and exemplary because of the commitments they have made and the graces they have received." He also mentions "doctrinal aberrations," "a casting aside of the authority of the Church," a general moral license, a "lack of concern for discipline" among the clergy.

But then, despite this grave state of affairs which he has just described so articulately, the Pope goes on to see something positive in the situation, even to see "marvelous signs of vitality, spirituality and sanctity." He can only see them vaguely, and only vaguely say what they are, since he is carried away by his imagination. Even in the heart of the doctrinal errors he had so energetically condemned in the encyclical *Mysterium Fidei*, the

---

[109] "Tell us what we want to hear."
[110] "Hiding places."
[111] "Medley or mixture."

Pope detects some reason for satisfaction, because in the very heresies denying the real presence he can see "a praiseworthy desire to examine this great mystery and explore its inexhaustible riches." His tendency not to quench the smoldering wick here lapses into approving attempts to diminish and dissolve a mystery.

In other addresses too his tendency to lapse into unreality led Pope Paul to mistake the products of his own imagining for the reality of the world around. By a sort of general synecdoche, some minute and irrelevant part of the whole is endowed with an imaginary exponential power and projected onto a grand scale so as to be proof of a general trend. As Arnobius says, it is like denying a mountain is made of earth because there is a nugget of gold buried in it, or denying that a decayed and suffering man is sick, because he has a healthy fingernail.

Perhaps the greatest example of this *gratissimus error*[112] is Pope Paul's speech on the twelfth anniversary of his coronation, reported on 23 June 1975. Having said that "Vatican II has indeed begun a new era in the life of the Church in our time" he praises "the *vast harmony* of the whole Church with its supreme pastor and its bishops"; this being said at a time when almost all the episcopates of the world were sitting in judgment on papal encyclicals and putting forward teachings of their own. This is said after the *Katholikentag* at Essen had done the things we mentioned in paragraph 62. Three weeks later the Pope was struck by a fit of forgetfulness regarding this "vast harmony" when he said: "Enough of internal dissent within the Church! Enough of a disintegrating interpretation of pluralism! Enough of Catholics attacking each other at the price of their own necessary unity!"[113] Similarly, to say that "the council has made us understand the vertical dimension of life" presupposes that the pre-conciliar Church was turned toward the world rather than towards heaven, and thus contradicts the principal and professed aim of the council right from its beginning, which was to adjust the direction of Catholicism by reconciling it to recent historical developments, insofar as any adjustment was to be made at all. The Pope says further that "the fruits of the liturgical reform today appear *in their splendor*"; but a few weeks previously Rheims cathedral had, with the approval of its bishop,

---

[112] "Welcome untruth."
[113] O.R., 18 July 1975.

been so profaned that people had asked for it to be reconsecrated; arbitrarily altered liturgies were multiplying without limit in France, illegal eucharistic prayers by the hundred were circulating in defiance of Roman decrees, and the *Missa cum pueris*[114] was provoking strong complaints throughout the Catholic world. In conclusion, the Pope declared in a sweeping statement, that would hardly have been justified even in periods of genuine spiritual unity, that "the teachings of the council have entered into daily life and have become the staple food of Christian life and thought." If by *Christian life* the Pope means those small circles into which it had already retreated, anticipating the forecast he was to make the following year[115] and abandoning the main bulk of society, then his assertion is valid, as one would expect it to be.[116] If, on the other hand, the Pope's analysis is meant to apply to the whole world and the whole contemporary Church, then his words are altogether at odds with the decline in morals, the urban violence that is turning cities into jungles,[117] the adoption of atheist constitutions (which are a very recent phenomenon in human history), the cynical disregard of international law, and with the spread of divorce, abortion and euthanasia.

There is in this anniversary speech a lack of critical thinking that veils historical realities and sometimes reverses them by dismissing the dark background of the picture as merely a few shadows. This one-eyed view of the situation is taken up by the official journal of the Holy See which, being unable to ignore realities entirely, makes a distinction between "fundamental

---

[114] "Children's Mass."

[115] See paragraph 36.

[116] It is certainly not valid, however, for the See of Peter which is the city of Rome, where, according to statistics given in O.R. on 19 November 1970, 80% of people said they were Catholic, but half of those did not believe in heaven and hell. Nor is it valid in the light of subsequent events, since in May 1981 only 22% of Romans voted against abortion. [In the national referendum held on the matter in that month. The national figures were 20 million in favor of abortion and 10 million against. Translator's note.]

[117] To such a point that, after Pope Paul's time, some countries celebrated "a day of hate" in 1984; like the days for mothers, the sick, for flowers, and all the other secular festivals which are now replacing the religious feasts of the liturgy.

health" and visible appearances.[118] If such a distinction were legitimate, any judgment about the state of the Church would become an esoteric operation that common sense, whether in the Church or in the world, would be incapable of performing. This, however, is not the case, because even though it is true that the most important element in the Church is an invisible principle that works in the depths of consciences to produce acts which in themselves are invisible, it is also true that that invisible element exists in history and appears in the deeds it produces. Insofar as it exists in the visible world, the Church is an earthly reality like the Kingdom of France, as Bellarmine[119] said. I will not go so far as to apply to the contemporary Church Tacitus's words about the decaying Roman world, namely that *corrumpere et corrumpi saeculum vocatur*[120] but nor will I be like the biblical antelopes that maintained their confidence, and deliberately ignored the fact that they were captured, until the very moment they fell into the nets.[121]

[118] O.R., 24 December 1976.
[119] St. Robert Bellarmine S.J., 1542-1621, Cardinal and Doctor of the Church. [Translator's note.]
[120] "To corrupt and to be corrupted is what is called the world." *Germania*, 19.
[121] Isaiah, 51:20.

CHAPTER VII

THE CRISIS OF THE PRIESTHOOD

79. The defection of priests.

There was not much Pope Paul's disinclination to be sad about the sad events besetting the Church could do in the face of a statistically charted defection of priests apparent in the Church at large.[1] The Pope discusses this thorny and painful matter in two speeches. On Holy Saturday 1971, while recalling the paschal drama of the God-Man who was deserted by His disciples and betrayed by His friend, the Pope drew an analogy between Judas and the apostasy of priests. He says at the outset that "one must distinguish one case from another, one must understand, sympathize, forgive, be patient, and one must always love." But then he described those who defect or apostatize as "unfortunates or deserters," spoke of "base earthly reasons" that move them and deplored the "moral mediocrity that thinks it natural and logical to break a promise one has given after long consideration."[2] The Pope's heart is vexed by the evidence and, not being able to remove all guilt from the act of apostasy, he reduces it somewhat by using the expression "unfortunates or deserters." But desertion is not an alternative to misfortune; those who have fallen away are unfortunate precisely because they have done so.

---

[1]   In the *Annuarium statisticum* for 1980 a slowing down in the decline in the number of priests appeared, and there were some signs of a revival. The rate of priestly ordinations rose from 1.40% to 1.41% of priests. Defections decreased by half. The total number of Catholic priests nonetheless fell by 0.6% over the year. Male and female religious continued to decrease, but females rather more, with a fall of 1.4% as opposed to 1.1% over the previous year. In general the decline is in Europe and the increase in Africa. O.R., 28 May 1982.

[2]   O.R., 10 April, 1971.

Speaking to the Roman clergy in February 1978 about priestly defections, the Pope said: "We are oppressed by the statistics, disconcerted by the casuistry, the reasons do indeed demand a reverent compassion, but they cause us great pain. The feeble kind of strength that the weak have found in order to abandon their commitment amazes us." The Pope talks of a "mania for laicization" which has "undone the traditional image of the priesthood" and, by a somewhat improbable process "has removed from some men's hearts the sacred reverence due to their own persons."[3]

The Pope's dismay stemmed partly from the scale of the phenomenon and partly from the depth of the decay it suggests. The point here is not that the priests have behaved badly by breaking their commitment to celibacy, because that had already happened in earlier times without the priests in question apostatizing; rather it is the appearance of a new sort of corruption, which consists in a *refusal to acknowledge the nature of things*, and in the preposterous attempt to turn a priest into a nonpriest; his new state is of course parasitic on the old.

In considering the statistics one should remember that the sacramental character of the priesthood can never be lost; hence what they reveal is how many have ceased to act as priests in either of two available ways: a dispensation from the Holy See or an arbitrary and unilateral break. The latter is not a new thing in the Church's history. During the revolution in France, twenty-four thousand of the twenty-nine thousand priests who had taken the oath to uphold the Civil Constitution of the Clergy apostatized, as did twenty-one of the eighty-three constitutional bishops, of whom ten later married.[4] Under St. Pius X quite a number abandoned the cloth because of difficulties with the faith or a desire for independence. Until the council, however, it was a rare thing, each case would arouse interest or scandal, and the defrocked priest was a theme for novels.

What is new about the defection of priests in the postconciliar Church is not so much the extraordinarily large numbers involved, but the legalization of these defections by the Holy See, through a widespread use of dispensations *pro gratia*.[5] This removes a priest's right to exercise his ministry, and reduces

---

[3] O.R., 11 February, 1978.
[4] P. Christophe, *Les choix du clergé dans les Révolutions de 1789, 1830 et 1848*, Lille 1975, t. 1, p.150.
[5] "As a favor."

him to the state of an ordinary layman, thus making the indelible character he received in ordination inactive and meaningless. It was indeed rare in the past for priests to be reduced to the lay state as a punishment, but it was even rarer for them to be reduced *pro gratia* by reason of a lack of due consent, similar to a defective consent in marriage. Apart from the period of the French Revolution, apostate bishops have been a very rare thing in the Church's history. The famous cases are those of Vergerio, the Bishop of Capo d'Istria at the time of the Council of Trent; de Dominis, the Archbishop of Spalato under Paul V; Seldnizky, the Bishop of Breslau under Gregory XVI and, more than a century later, Mgr Mario Radavero, auxiliary bishop of Lima and formerly a father of the Second Vatican Council.[6]

80. The canonical legitimation of priestly defections.

As we have said, the change in the way the Church has dealt with and evaluated priestly defections is the new thing in question here, rather than the disproportionately large numbers involved in comparison to the pre-conciliar period.[7] Recent human history contains nothing that has not happened in the past, so far as mere physical events are concerned. That is why the ancient author could say *Nihil est iam factum quod non factum sit prius.*[8] The important and novel element is the moral judgment that the mind makes, and it alone is the indication of the real direction of events.

The Pope may have been dismayed by the number of defections, but the practice of dispensation nonetheless became habitual, after having long been unknown, and that changed the moral and juridical character of the abandonment of the priesthood, removing from it the air of defection it had once had. A very senior person in the Roman Curia, whose task it was to look after the procedures, told me that the reductions to the lay state, which happened by the thousand in the years from 1964 to 1978, were once so unusual that many people, even members of the clergy, were not even aware that such a canonical proce-

---

[6] O.R., 23 March 1969.
[7] Another novelty is that members of the hierarchy have joined the movement against celibacy. Cardinal Léger says for example: "One might wonder whether the institution could not be reconsidered." I.C.I., No.279, 1 January 1967, p.40.
[8] "Nothing is now done which was not done before."

dure existed. It can be seen from the *Tabularum statisticarum collectio* of 1969 and the *Annuarium statisticum Ecclesiae* of 1976, published by the Secretariat of State, that in the whole Catholic world during those seven years the total number of priests fell from 413,000 to 343,000, and members of religious orders from 208,000 to 165,000. The 1978 edition of the same *Annuarium statisticum* reveals that defections numbered 3,690 in 1973 and 2,037 in 1978. Dispensations ceased almost entirely from October 1978 by order of John Paul II.[9] Although these defections have thinned the ranks, their real importance lies in the fact that they were legitimized by the granting of dispensations on an enormous scale. Canon law laid down[10] that by being reduced to the lay state a cleric lost clerical offices, benefices and privileges, but remained bound to celibacy. The only clerics to be released from it were those whose ordinations could be proved invalid through lack of consent.[11] It would seem that in the recent jurisprudence of the Holy See, lack of consent is no longer to be judged by a man's dispositions at the time of ordination, but by subsequent experiences of unsuitability or moral discontent during his life as an ordained priest. It is this same criterion that the diocesan tribunals of the United States tried to introduce in marriage annulment cases, and that Paul VI criticized and rejected in 1977. By this criterion, the very fact that a priest asks at any given moment to return to the lay state becomes a proof that he was immature and incapable of giving a valid consent at the time of his original commitment. The possibility that there may have been a subsequent act of consent and thus a convalidation, which would prevent a dispensation from celibacy under canon 214, is also ignored. As with the American tribunals, we are here confronted by a veiled denial of the importance of every individual moral act and a

---

[9] Papa Wojtyla's decision was strongly criticized by the innovators. See for example the interview with H. Herrmann, the Professor of Canon Law at the University of Tübingen, in the weekly *Der Spiegel*, 6 October 1981: *Warum sollen wir uns noch zu einem Kreis von Menschen zählen wollen, der das Evangelium von der Liebe ständig verrät?* "Why should we still want ourselves to be counted as belonging to a group of people that permanently betrays the Gospel of love?"

[10] In canons 211-14.

[11] Canon 214.

tacit adoption of the principle of globality.[12] Each individual
moral act is stripped of importance, so that the sum total of
such acts can be invested with it. Perhaps the fundamental reason for decline in priestly vocations, that accompanied the increasing number of defections, was this trivialization of the
commitment involved, which robs the priesthood of the air of
totality and *permanence* that appeals to the noblest part of human nature, by persevering through trial and hardship. It is
certainly true that, as John Paul II has said, these defections are
"an anti-sign, an anti-witness, which has contributed to the dis-
appointment of the council's hopes."[13]

The crisis among the clergy has been explained by the usual
references to sociological and psychological factors, which are
not true causes, while the moral factor has been ignored. The
origins of the phenomenon are principally spiritual and operate
at two levels. Firstly, at a purely religious level, there is an im-
poverished understanding of freedom, whereby man is held to
be incapable of joining his free will absolutely to something
which is itself absolute, but his free will is, conversely, held to be
entitled to untie any existing bond. There is an obvious analogy
with divorce. It too is based on the idea that it is impossible for
the human will to bind itself unconditionally; based, that is, on
the denial of anything unconditional.

Secondly, beyond this failure to understand that liberty is a
capacity to bestow an absolute character on a possibility of our
own choosing, and thus to instill an indefectible coherence into
one's life, there is also, at the supernatural level, a failure in
faith, that is, doubt about the existence of the absolute to which
a priest dedicates himself, and to which there can be no authentic dedication unless it is *de jure* absolute. This failure, which
could right itself or be righted, is instead abetted by the dispensation that the supreme authority grants. There is thus a vicious
circle, whereby liberty is thought to be denied by an insistence
on absolutes, when in fact the latter is precisely what is needed
if a mature liberty is to be attained. The granting of dispensations and the abandonment of obligations was in itself a scandal
and a sign of moral weakness and of a diminished sense of personal worth, as well as a cause of scandal when comparisons
were made with lay people bound by the indissoluble bonds of

[12] See paragraphs 201-3.
[13] O.R., 20 May 1979.

marriage. The granting of dispensations was soon stopped by John Paul II. On 14 October 1980 the Congregation for the Doctrine of the Faith promulgated a document establishing a stricter regime whereby grounds for dispensation are reduced to two, and two only: a defective consent to the act of ordination, and error by the superior in agreeing to ordain.[14]

81. Attempts to reform the Catholic priesthood.

The numerous proposals for a reformed priesthood that are now bruited about by the gigantic megaphone of public opinion, have not the slightest novelty about them since they have cropped up repeatedly during the Church's history; being put forward usually in an unorthodox spirit as by the Cathari, the Hussites and Luther, but being sometimes simply an innocent aberration, as in the case of the celebrated Cardinal Angelo Mai, a better philologist than theologian,[15] who wanted the clergy to be given the right to request a release from sacred orders at any time. The reasons underlying these proposals for a reformed priesthood can all be reduced to a denial of essences, that is of fixed natures in things, and in a desire to cross the frontiers that delimit those essences and that, by delimiting them, cause them to be what they are.

The complaint is heard that priests are kept in a subordinate state without full responsibility for their own acts and it is urged that they be "given back the right to control their own lives" by being given the right to marry, work in factories, publish books and air their own opinions.[16] This last demand is out of touch with facts, since the Catholic clergy have never been allowed to speak out more fully, more easily or louder than they do at present. Priests can publish books without prior approval from their bishops, issue statements, hold protest meetings, speak on radio and television, go onto the streets to demonstrate against papal decrees, mix with non-Catholics and take

---

[14] *Documentation Catholique*, No.566, October 1980 and *Esprit et Vie*, 1981, p.77.

[15] Angelo Cardinal Mai (1782-1854), noted antiquary and Prefect of the Vatican Library. [Translator's note.] See *Nuova Antologia*, January 1934, p.80, *Memorie di Leonetto Cipriani*.

[16] These were the requests made at a meeting of laity and priests held at Bologna and reported in *La Stampa* of 28 September 1969.

full part in their meetings. The relaxation of canonical discipline at once became an ever-present and influential reality.

Indeed, under cover of the authority derived from their ordination, many priests preach their own ephemeral and transient opinions as if they were the message of the Gospel and the doctrine of the Church; that is, they preach themselves or something of their own. In so doing, they are committing a typical and historically familiar clericalist abuse, which once stemmed from a confusion of religion and politics but now stems from a detachment from Catholic doctrine, and aims to remodel dogma and dislocate the Church's organization. Priests thus enjoy not simply the authority they derive from their ordination, but an authority which is in practice much wider, because they use their position illegitimately to invest their own private opinions with the authority of the Church.

That a priest should demand greater power "to control his own life" (what man does?) suggests a weakening of faith, and a weakened understanding of the dignity of the priesthood, which faith alone can make one grasp. How can one who has the authority to produce the Body of the Lord sacramentally and to forgive sins, thus changing human hearts, feel he is inferior and lacking in responsibility except as a result of a clouding of the mind and an eclipse of faith? This feeling of inferiority comes from a priest's having forgotten the true purpose of the priesthood, which is to provide men with the sacred, and from thinking of the priestly state as being a state like any other, that is, something in which one seeks to achieve one's own potential and make one's own contribution to the world.

82. Critique of the critique of the Catholic priesthood. Don Mazzolari.

Priests are said to suffer because they find themselves in the midst of an indifferent or hostile world which is not open to what they want to do and which passes them by without coming into contact with them. The psalmist's verse with which the First Vatican Council opened is not appropriate to today's priest: *Euntes ibant et flebant mittentes semina sua, venientes autem venient cum exsultatione portantes manipulos suos.*[17] Today's priests weep both sowing the seed and returning, because they

---

[17] Psalm 125:6. "Going forth, they went weeping carrying their seed, but returning they will come exulting carrying their sheaves."

lack the sheaves that gladden the heart. Certainly a priest is in a difficult position, but the difficulty is an original and essential element in what he is; it was no easier for the apostles, nor were they promised it would be. It is particularly incongruous to complain at length about the alienation of the priesthood from society and then to turn around and accuse the ages of faith of being triumphalist because during them there was no such alienation, because the tension between the two had been absorbed into the structures of an integrated Christendom.

Don Mazzolari observes that "the priest suffers from having to preach words that demand a higher standard than is realized in his own life, and by which his life is condemned." But every man is in that position vis-à-vis the moral law and the standards of the Gospel; the tension is not restricted to priests. To realize that no one can preach moral truths in his own name, one need only recall the distinction between the ideal and real orders of being, which is necessary to the existence of moral obligation, since it is derived from the attempt to unite the two; nobody's virtue is equal to the ideal preached. To base preaching on anything other than the truth of what is preached, would involve measuring its validity by the moral worth of the preacher, as the Hussite heresy implied. Preaching would thus become impossible. If what gave a priest a right to preach were a moral level equal to the demands he made, even the most holy priest would abstain from preaching. In fact, however, "it is necessary that many men, that all men, preach a morality more perfect than their own behavior. The ministry...involves weak men, who sometimes give in to their passions, preaching an austere and perfect morality. No one can accuse them of hypocrisy, because they speak as ones commissioned to do so, and speak with conviction, and they confess implicitly and sometimes explicitly that they are far from the perfection they teach...Unfortunately it sometimes happens that preaching descends to the level of behavior, but this is an abuse: without the ministry however, it would be the rule."[18] The inadequacies of a priest's life are simply an instance of the inadequacies in all men's lives when compared to the ideal. The conclusion to be drawn is that we should have *humility*, not an *anguish* stemming from pride.

---

[18] A. Manzoni, *Osservazioni sulla morale cattolica*, ed. cit. Vol. III, p.135.

Then again, the human capacities a priest has do not vanish simply because he is a priest, since the exercise of the ministry affords opportunities for the unlimited employment of all the talents, zeal and ability an individual may have; opportunities to do everything that makes for personal excellence. Is not Church history full of beautiful ideas, charitable undertakings and teaching organizations, that give ample opportunity for people to develop their potential, even though they are not allowed to preach themselves? Where, outside the Church, does one so often find the name of a particular individual used as the name of whole bodies of men, united together in their opinions and aims and works?

83. Universal priesthood and ordained priesthood.

The fundamental error of the criticisms of the Church's historic priesthood, which is the true form of priesthood as such, lies in not recognizing the essence, or fixed nature, of the thing and in reducing it to a merely human and functional level. Catholic doctrine sees within the priesthood an essential, not merely a functional, difference between the priest and the layman: an ontological difference due to the character impressed upon the soul by the sacrament of orders. The new theology revives old heretical doctrines, which came together to produce the Lutheran abolition of the priesthood, and disguises the difference that exists between the universal priesthood of baptized believers and the sacramental priesthood which is proper to priests alone. Through baptism, man is joined to the mystical body of Christ and consecrated to the worship of God by a sharing in the priesthood of Christ, the only man who has ever offered God due worship in the most perfect way. Over and above this baptismal character, the priest receives in ordination a further character which is a sort of reinforcement of the first. Thanks to ordination he is capable of performing acts *in persona Christi*[19] of which laymen are incapable. The first among these are the act which produces the eucharistic presence and the act of forgiving sins. The tendency of the theological innovators is to dissolve the second priesthood in the first, and to reduce the priest to the same level as all Christians. They maintain that the priest has a special function in the diverse makeup of the Church, just as every Christian has. This special function is be-

---

[19] "In the person of Christ."

stowed upon him by the community and does not imply any *ontological difference* with respect to the layman, "nor should the ministry be considered as something higher."[20] So then "the priest's importance consists in having been baptized like any other Christian."[21] The difference between essences, or natures, is thus denied through a rejection of the sacramental priesthood, and that reduces the differentiated and organic structure of the Church to something formless and homogeneous.[22]

This thesis is expounded explicitly in a book by R.S. Bunnik, which is a good example of the thinking dominant in the Dutch church and its center for theological training.[23] "The universal priesthood must be seen as a basic category of the People of God, while the particular ministry is only a functional category" and is "a sociological necessity emanating from below." From the universal priesthood being the basis of the particular one (which indeed it is since an ordinand must have been baptized) this Dutch theologian goes on to deny that ordination sets a man on a new basis from which new acts proceed which were impossible simply on the basis of baptism; although baptism gives an active capacity to do some things, it gives only a passive capacity to do others, among which are the receiving of the Eucharist and of holy orders.

This paralogism concerning the priesthood runs in tandem with another concerning the position of the Church in the world. The author maintains that "the conciliar Church is progressively discovering that in the final analysis the Church and the world constitute *one and the same divine reality*." Thus the natures of things are first dissolved and then compounded; the ordained priesthood is confused with the priesthood deriving from baptism, and the supernatural theandric nature of the

[20] C.I.D.S., 1969, p.488.
[21] Ibid., p.227.
[22] Mgr Riobé, the Bishop of Orléans, displayed his own position quite unequivocally in a statement to the French bishops' conference, published in *Le Monde* on 11 November 1972, in which he proposed that with the consent of the bishop, lay people should be temporarily instituted by the community to fulfill the functions of an ordained priest.
[23] *Prêtres des temps nouveaux*, translated from the Dutch by Denise Moeyskens, Tournai, 1969. The passages quoted are on pp.64 and 43. Fr. Schillebeeckx supports the same idea.

Church is confused with the whole undifferentiated mass of the human race.

84. Critique of the saying "a priest is a man like other men."

This theological compounding of separate things has come to be commonly accepted and has in part caused, and in part been caused by, the wide dissemination of certain authors' opinions. The idea is that "a priest is a man like other men." This statement is false and superficial both theologically and historically. Theologically, because it clashes with the doctrine of the sacrament of orders, which some Christians receive and others do not, and by which they are differentiated ontologically, and thus functionally. Historically, men are not equal in civil society, except in their essential nature considered in the abstract apart from those concrete circumstances by which that nature is differentiated. To say a priest is a man like others, who are not priests, is even falser than saying a doctor is a man like others, who are not doctors. No, he is not a man like all others, he is a man who is a priest. All men are not priest-men, just as all men are not doctor-men. Watching how people behave is enough to show that everyone can draw a distinction between doctors and non-doctors, priests and non-priests. In some emergencies they send for a doctor, in others for a priest. The innovators fix their attention on the abstract identity of human nature and reject the special supernatural character that the priesthood introduces into the human race, and by which a priest is separate: *Segregate mihi Saulum et Barnabam.*[24]

Obvious practical consequences flow from this error. Today's priest should do manual work, because he can only fulfill his own destiny by working, and only by working can he discover the ordinary human life which reveals God's purposes for the world. Thus work is taken as either man's end, or as a *sine qua non* for reaching his end, and contemplation and suffering are ranked below utilitarian productivity. Being a man like all others, the priest will demand the right to marry, dress as he wishes and take an active part in social and political struggles; so too he will join revolutionary struggles that look upon a brother as an enemy to struggle against, unjust though this be.

---

[24] Acts 13:2. "Set apart for me Saul and Barnabas."

The complaint that priests are cut off from the world is unjustified. Firstly, because they are set apart, as Christ set apart His apostles, precisely in order to be sent into the world. That ordinary people understood what sacramental ordination added to these men apart, was so obvious until recent times that even common sayings whether in received speech or in dialect bore witness to it. These adages distinguish between the man and his priesthood, and avoid offending the priesthood even when designed to offend the man. They keep the man separate from the cloth, taken as a sign of the priesthood, and from "what he ministers," namely the sacred.

Secondly, historically, there is no support for the idea that the clergy have been separate from the world in the sense complained of by the innovators. Both what are called the secular clergy, and the regular clergy, are within the world, though separated from it. The most triumphant demonstration that the clergy's separateness does not cut them off from the world lies in the fact that it was the regular clergy, those more separated from the world, the men in the cloisters, who exercised not only the most powerful religious but the most powerful civil effects in the world around. They shaped civilization for centuries, even gave birth to it, since they were the ones who produced the structures of culture, and of social life, from agriculture to poetry, from architecture to philosophy, from music to theology. To take a misused image and to give it its legitimate meaning, the clergy are the yeast that made the dough rise, but they do not become the dough. Chemists are well aware that enzymes contain something antagonistic to the substances they cause to ferment.

CHAPTER VIII

THE CHURCH AND YOUTH

85. Change in the post-conciliar Church regarding youth. The delicate task of education.

There are other aspects of human life that the Church views differently since the council. The *deminutio capitis*[1] based on age, which was imposed by Paul VI in his decree *Ingravescentem aetatem*, was an indirect sign of the new attitude it has adopted towards youth. The new view is directly expressed in other documents.

From ancient times down to our own, youth has been regarded by philosophy, ethics, art and common sense as a time of natural and moral imperfection, that is, incompleteness. St. Augustine goes so far as to call the desire to return to childhood stupidity and folly, and writes in this sermon *Ad iuvenes*[2] *flos aetatis, periculum tentationis,*[3] insisting on youth's moral immaturity. Because his reason is not yet settled and is liable to go awry, a young man is *cereus in vitium flecti,*[4] and in his youth needs a ruler, adviser and teacher. He needs a light to see that life has a moral goal, and practical help to mold and transform his natural inclinations in accordance with the rational order of things. All the great Catholic educators from Benedict of Nursia to Ignatius of Loyola, Joseph Calasanz, John Baptist de la Salle and John Bosco made this idea the basis of Catholic education. The young person is a subject possessing freedom and must be trained to use his freedom in such a way that he himself chooses that one thing for the choosing of which our freedom has been given us; namely, to choose to do our duty, since religion sees

---

[1] "Loss of rights" (to vote).
[2] "To young people."
[3] "The flower of youth involves the danger of temptation."
[4] "As flexible as wax to vice." Horace, *Ars poetica*, 163.

no other end to life than this. The delicacy of the educator's task comes from the fact that its *object* is a being who is a *subject*, and that its goal is the perfecting of that subject. It is acting upon human freedom not in order to limit it but to make it really free. In this respect the act of educating is an imitation of divine causality which, according to Thomistic theory, produces a man's free actions even in their very freedom.[5]

The Church's attitude to youth cannot ignore the difference between the imperfect and the relatively more perfect, the ignorant and the relatively more informed. It cannot set aside the differences between things and treat young people as mature, learners as experts, lessers as greaters and (here the fundamental error returns) in the final analysis, the dependent as independent.

86. Character of youth. Critique of life as joy.

The profound Thomistic theory of potency and act assists a student of human nature in considering the nature of youth, by supporting him in seeking out the essential characteristics of that stage of life, and by stopping him being led astray by prevailing opinion.

Given that youth is the beginning of life, it is important that a view of the whole of life ahead be presented to it and that it keep that view in mind; a view of the goal in which the beginner's potential will be realized, the form in which his powers will unfold. Life is difficult, or, if you prefer, serious. Firstly, this is because man's nature is weak and in its finitude it collides with the finitude of other men and of the things around, all these finitudes tending to trespass on each other. Secondly, it is part of the Catholic faith that man is fallen and inclined to evil. Man's disorderly propensities mean that he is beset by opposing attractions and that his condition is one of struggle, of war, even of siege. That there is a potency within life which must be

---

[5]   One could also say that education is an imitation of divine causality according to Molinism, inasmuch as education sets up circumstances favorable to the right choice. [The references are to the internal Catholic debate c.1600 and since, concerning the operation of man's will in response to grace. Luis de Molina S.J.(1535-1600) emphasized the freedom of the will while Dominic Banez O.P. (1528-1604), a follower of St. Thomas, emphasized the power of grace. Translator's note.]

brought out means that life is not only difficult but interesting, since interest consists in having something lying within (*inter est*).[6] This does not mean, however, that man should *realize himself*, in the current phrase, but rather that he should be transformed by *realizing the values* for which he is created and which call him to that transformation. It is curious that when post-conciliar theology so often uses the word *metanoia*, which means a transformation of the mind, it should go on to put so much emphasis on the realization of the self. It is pleasant to go with one's inclination, and rough to resist one's own ego in order to mold it. The difficulty of it is recognized in philosophy, poetic adages, politics and myths. Every good is acquired or achieved at the price of effort. The Greek sage says the gods have put sweat between us and excellence, and Horace says: *multa tulit fecitque puer, sudavit et alsit.*[7] It was a commonplace of education in ancient times that human life is a combat and an effort, and the letter upsilon became a symbol of the fact, but not the upsilon with equally sloping arms, Y, but the Pythagorean one with one arm upright and the other bent, Ⴒ . Antiquity also applied to life the much told tale of Hercules at the fork in the road.

Life is today unrealistically presented to young people as joy, taking joy to mean the partial sort that comforts the soul *in via*[8] rather than the full joy which satisfies it only *in termino*.[9] The hardness of human life, which used so often to be referred to in prayers as a vale of tears, is denied or disguised. Since the result of this change in emphasis is to depict happiness as a man's natural state and thus as something due to him, the new ideal is to prepare a path for the young man which is *secura d'ogn'intoppo e d'ogni sbarro*.[10] Thus every obstacle they have to overcome is seen by young people as an injustice, and barriers are looked upon not as tests, but as a scandal. Adults have abandoned the exercise of their authority through a desire to please, since they cannot believe they will be loved unless they flatter and please their children. The prophet's warning applies

---

6 "It is inside."
7 *Ars Poetica*, 413. "Much he bore and did as a boy, he sweated and grew cold."
8 "On the way," sc. through life.
9 "At the destination," sc. in heaven.
10 Dante's *Purgatorio*, XXXIII, 42. "Safe from every obstacle and every barrier."

to them: *Vae quae consuunt pulvillos sub omni cubito manus et faciunt cervicalia sub capite universae aetatis.*[11]

87. Paul VI's speeches to youth.

All the themes of the *juvenilism* of the contemporary world, in which the Church shares, come together in Pope Paul's speech to a group of hippies who had come to Rome for a peace demonstration in April 1971. The Pope sketches and enumerates with praise those "secret values" young people are searching for. The first is *spontaneity*, which doesn't strike the Pope as being at odds with searching, even though a sought spontaneity ceases to be spontaneous. Nor does spontaneity seem to him at odds with morality, even though the latter involves considered intentions, superimposes itself upon spontaneity, and can clash with it.

The second value is "liberation from certain formal and conventional ties." The Pope does not specify what they are. As for forms, they are the substance itself as it appears, that is as it enters the world. And as for conventions, they are what is agreed upon, that is they are consents, and are good things if they are consents to good things.

The third value is "the need to be themselves." But it is not made clear what self it is that the young person should realize and in which he should recognize his identity: there are in fact many selves in a free nature, which can be transformed into many guises. The true self does not demand that the young person realize himself any old how but that he be transformed and even become other than he is. The words of the Gospel, furthermore, will bear no gloss: *abneget semetipsum.*[12] The day before, the Pope had been exhorting to *metanoia*. So then, is it realize yourself, or transform yourself?

The fourth value is an enthusiasm "to live and interpret your own times." The Pope, however, offers the young people no interpretative key to their own times, since he does not point out that from the religious point of view, man must seek out the non-ephemeral among the ephemeral things of his own time, that is, seek out the last end that perdures through it all. Having thus developed his argument without any explicitly religious

---

[11] Ezechiel, 13:18. "Woe to those who embroider cushions for every elbow and make pillows for heads of every age."

[12] Luke, 9:23. "Let him deny himself."

reference, Paul VI somewhat unexpectedly concludes by saying: "We think that in this interior search of yours you notice the need for God." The Pope is here certainly speaking speculatively rather than with his authority as teacher.

The interpretation of youth the Pope gave in his speech of 3 January 1972 is even more openly at odds with the traditional one. In it he describes a "natural detachment from the past," a "quick critical spirit" and "intuitive foresight" as positive qualities of youth. These qualities do not really fit with a true psychology of youth, and they are not positive. To detach oneself from the past is a moral, historical and religious impossibility: one need only remember that for a Christian the direction of the whole of one's life follows from one's baptism, which is antecedently there, and baptism depends on the family, which is antecendently there, and the family depends on the Church, which is a massive antecedent reality. That young people have a critical spirit, that is, a discerning judgment, is difficult to maintain if one recognizes the element of growth there is in man's makeup, that is, if one distinguishes between his mature and immature state and admits that at the beginning of life a person finds himself under an obligation to become what as yet he is not. Lastly, foresight is a very new discovery in the youthful psyche, which has always been seen as a *tardus provisor*,[13] someone who is slow to foresee not only events in the outer world, but his own good. In fact, *temeritas est florentis aetatis, prudentia senescentis*.[14]

But this enthusiasm for Hebe[15] drives the Pope to declare that "young people are the prophetic vanguard of the joint cause of justice and peace," because "first and foremost they have a greater sense of justice than others," and "adults are on their side," obviously as reserves while the young are the front line troops.

It is not difficult to detect in Pope Paul's speech a peculiar reversal of roles, by which those who ought to follow are followed and the immature are made examples for the mature. Attributing an innate sense of justice to youth finds no support in any Catholic interpretation of life. It would seem that the Pope was carried away by an enthusiasm contracted from the

---

[13] Horace, *Ars Poetica*, 164. "One slow to foresee."

[14] Cicero, *De senectute*, VI, 20. "Temerity belongs to the flower of a man's age, prudence to one who is growing old."

[15] Greek goddess of youth. [Translator's note.]

youthful energy around about and lapsed into a sort of doxol-
ogy of youth. This same lapse into youthful enthusiasm made
him on another occasion change the letter of Scripture to read
"young people" instead of "children"[16] in support of his assertion that "it was young people who recognized the divinity of
Christ."[17]

88. Juvenilism in the Church, continued.
The Swiss bishops.

To prove that this cult of Hebe is not confined to the papacy, but spread through every level of the Church, I will not
cite the almost infinite writings of priests and laymen, but a
document produced by the Swiss episcopal conference for the
national day in 1969. It says that "youthful protest advances the
values of authenticity, availability, respect for man, impatience
with mediocrity and the denunciation of oppression, values
which on closer inspection harmonize with the Gospel."

It is easy to see the Swiss bishops are rather vague in their
logic. Authenticity, in the Catholic sense, does not consist in
putting oneself forward as one naturally is, but in becoming
what one ought to be, that is it consists ultimately in humility.
Availability is in itself neutral and becomes good only through
the good for which a man makes himself available. Respect for
man would exclude despising the human past and repudiating
the historical Church. Impatience with mediocrity, besides being vague, (mediocrity in what?) is opposed to the wisdom of
the ancients, at odds with the virtue of being content with what
is available, and incompatible with poverty of spirit.

That we are "in the presence of new human and religious
goals" is a statement that privileges the new simply because it is
new and forgets that there is no new creation apart from the
one re-founded in the God-Man, and there are no goals other
than the ones He prescribed.[18] When the bishops go on to point
to young people "as a sign of the times and as *the voice of God
himself*" to the whole of contemporary Christendom, their
choice of words is absurd because of its undue adulation; even
more absurd than saying *vox populi vox Dei*,[19] because it makes

---

[16] Matthew, 21:15.
[17] O.R., 12 April 1976.
[18] See paragraphs 53 and 54.
[19] "The voice of the people is the voice of God."

the largely unreflective voice of youth an organ of the divine will and almost a text of divine revelation. To praise the fact "that young people want to be protagonists" clashes with the Catholic principle of humility and with obedience, since the Church does not belong solely to the young and everyone cannot have first place: this protagonism fails to recognize the role of other people. To recognize their rights is part of both religion and justice.

In concluding this analysis of the new attitude the world and the Church have towards youth, we note that here too there has been a semantic shift, and that the words paternal and paternalistic have become terms of disapproval, as if a father's education, precisely as a father, were not a commendable use of his wisdom and love, and as if the whole method of instruction were not paternal. But then, anyone can see that in a system in which worth is judged in terms of self-expression and a refusal to imitate anything, the first thing to be rejected will be paternal dependence. Setting aside the claims made by some people, whether clergy or laity, the truth is that youth is a time of potential and incompleteness that cannot be held up as an ideal state or taken as a model. In fact youth is much directed towards the future and its hopes, which can only be realized as youth vanishes and is lost. The myth of Hebe turns into the myth of Psyche. If youth moreover is divinized, the young are driven to pessimism by being made to want a perpetual youth they cannot have. Youth is directed towards non-youth, and maturity must be modeled not upon it, but upon an achieved wisdom. No stage of life has another stage of its own, or anybody else's life, as the model for its own development. The model for any stage is provided by the deontological, or duty orientated nature of man, which must be grasped and lived out at every stage of life, irrespective of age. Here too a dizzy spirit has turned the dependent towards independence and the insufficient towards self-sufficiency.

CHAPTER IX

THE CHURCH AND WOMEN

89. The Church and Feminism.

The accommodation of the Church to the world apparent in the idolizing of youth, also shows itself in support for feminism, which from its beginnings has been a program for the emancipation of women, and for their complete equality with men. For strictly doctrinal reasons this equality could not go as far as equality in the priesthood, since tradition, which is a source of doctrine, has constantly excluded that possibility, and the exclusion is a matter of divine positive law. The council's closing message to women on 8 December 1965 was very reserved about their worldly advancement. It said "the hour has come when the vocation of women will be fulfilled in its completeness," but that vocation was depicted in traditional terms, as "the care of the hearth, love of life, a feeling for the cradle." The message exhorted women "to transmit to your children the traditions of your fathers." The positive role of the Church in the matter was made very clear since it "is proud to have elevated and liberated women, to have made their fundamental equality with men shine out down the course of the centuries, though endowed with their own characteristics." Post-conciliar developments generally went beyond these ideas and supported the urge for emancipation and equality rather than the preservation of traditional values.

As with every other doctrine of faith and morals, the impossibility of conferring the priesthood on women was forcefully reaffirmed by Paul VI, in a letter to the Anglican primate,[1] but by the *breviatio manus* that we have said characterized his pontificate,[2] feminist demands were not effectively opposed or

---

[1] O.R., 21 August 1971.
[2] See paragraph 65.

contained. Among other doctrinally erroneous demands, which
were glossed over by the Holy See's official journal as "a statement of the facts regarding the feelings of the laity," the third
world congress on the apostolate of the laity, held in Rome in
October 1967, expressed the wish "that a serious doctrinal study
should establish the position of women in the sacramental order."[3] In France there is a Joan of Arc Association that presses
for the priesthood for women, while in the United States, without any objection from the bishops, there is an active national
convention of American religious sisters that makes the same
demand. The movement's arrogance was displayed, and the
world was amazed, on the occasion of John Paul II's visit to
America, when Sister Theresa Kane, the convention's president,
confronted the Supreme Pontiff unannounced claiming women
had a right to be admitted to the priesthood, and urged Christians to stop giving any help to the Church until that right was
recognized.[4] At the international conference on women held at
Copenhagen, Bishop Cordes, the Holy See's delegate, said that
"the Catholic Church *now* rejoices at the thirst for a *fully free
and human life* which lies at the origin of the great movement
for the liberation of women," letting it be understood that "after
two thousand years of Christianity this fully human life had too
often been denied them. In fact it still cannot be said that
women have been accepted in the way the Creator and Christ
want, that is for themselves, *as fully responsible human persons.*"[5]
The feminist streak has shown up again in the Church in sensational displays, as when the feminist president of the Catholic
youth association of Bavaria repeated the American sister's gesture, during John Paul II's visit.[6]

Two elements of the innovators' thinking can be clearly seen
in the movement: firstly, the adoption of feminist terminology;
secondly, the denigration of the historical Church.

Speaking to a large female audience, John Paul II adopted a
feminist view of history: "It is sad to see how women in the
course of the centuries have been so humiliated and maltreated."[7] Since these words seem to inculpate Christian centu-

---

³ O.R., 21 October 1967.
⁴ I.C.I., No.544, 1979, p.41.
⁵ O.R., French edition, 12 August 1980.
⁶ R.I., 1980, p.1057.
⁷ O.R., 1 May 1979.

ries too, the *Osservatore Romano* tried[8] to make a defensive distinction, by blaming the alleged injustice and vexation on the failings of Christians, rather than on the Church. There is no evading the issue that way though, because the Church's responsibility for the general run of behavior in centuries in which the whole of civilization was shaped by its spirit and its regulations cannot legitimately be denied, as it can be today when society as a whole has defected from the Church and attacks it. It is also peculiar to try to acquit the Church of any faults in the past, and yet to blame it for a crisis that has arisen precisely because the modern world has abandoned the Church.[9]

Historical truth forbids supporting this denigration of the Church, and indeed obliges one to counterattack. The first large women's movement to be organized this century was Women's Catholic Action, created by Benedict XV, who well outlined its motives and goals in an audience given in 1917: "The changed conditions of the times have broadened the field of women's activities: an apostolate in the midst of the world has replaced the more intimate and restricted activities that women used to perform within the domestic walls."

In the face of all the ancient civilizations that held women in subjection by their male despotism, their sacred prostitution and their divorce more or less at will, it was Christianity alone that freed women from a deplorable servitude by sanctifying marriage and making it unbreakable, by teaching the supernatural equality of man and woman, by raising the status of both virginity and marriage and lastly by raising the human race to a height it would never have imagined for itself, through the recognition of a woman as the Mother of God.

The permanent and inviolable rights of women in an indissoluble marriage were defended against male despotism by the Roman pontiffs on several controversial occasions. I do not deny that in the famous cases of the Emperor Lothair, Philip Augustus (whose wife Ingeburg uttered the memorable cry "Evil France, evil France. Rome, Rome!"), Henry IV of France, Henry VIII of England and Napoleon, political considerations operated at a secondary level for or against the primary religious issue at stake, namely indissolubility. But it *was* at a secondary

[8] O.R., 4 May 1979.
[9] See paragraph 55.

level that they operated, while the powerful principle of the equality of the sexes in marriage was always acknowledged to take precedence over them. Outside the Roman Church, history affords no examples of a priesthood rising up with all its moral force in defense of a woman's rights.

90. Critique of Feminism. Feminism as masculinism.

In modern society there have been changes in customs and social arrangements which, in part, cannot but be reflected in the life of the Church through a necessary conformation of Catholicism to changeable historical circumstances; such changes have always affected the customs, mentality, rights and external appearances of the Church, but these are merely *circumstantial* changes, that is, changes in behavior and methods that *stand around* the essence of Christian life and that change precisely in order to keep it the same, without touching it themselves.

How much of the change occurring at any given historical moment would compromise Christian life and how much can be incorporated into applying and advancing the latter, it is difficult to decide;[10] the Church's task is to preserve and develop Catholic principles, moderating the existential spirit of novelty by reference to the essential spirit of conservation, which Paul VI said made the Church "intransigently conservative."[11] The Church cannot pull up or dry out her own roots in order to graft herself onto others.

When it comes to feminism, we are once again dealing with attempts to weaken the principle of dependence, so as to unshackle and unbind things which, both by nature and revelation, come to us as dependent and confined. Catholicism rejects dependence of man upon man. The dependence that it upholds is that of man upon his own nature; a dependence that shuts out the principle of a creaturely creativity. Since natures in themselves are uncreated divine forms, and since as actually existing, they are participations in those forms, which have been brought forth by the act of creating, man's dependence on his own nature is ultimately a dependence on primal Being. The man who becomes aware of this dependence and takes it to

---

[10] See paragraph 25.
[11] See O.R., 23 January 1972.

himself, is making an act of *moral obedience* to the being of God. Thus the fundamental mistake of modern feminism is that, by misunderstanding the natural particularities of the female side of the human creature, it has taken upon itself to claim for women not those things that belong to all human nature as such, but things that only seem to belong to human nature when it is considered with the natural particularities of the male. Feminism thus resolves itself into an imitation of the masculine, entailing a consequent loss of those characteristics that human nature possesses in virtue of the duality of the sexes. In this regard, feminism is a conspicuous example of that abuse of abstraction from which egalitarianism is born: it claims to strip a particular person of the lineaments stamped upon him by nature. In the last analysis, feminism redounds not to the exaltation of women, but to the obliteration of the feminine and its total reduction to the masculine. In its last unfoldings it is, as can already be seen, the negation of marriage and the family, which canonize the distinction of male and female. The moral equality of the sexes does not therefore remove the natural particularities of women, or abolish the maintenance of the inner life of the family as their primary task, or take away their role as doers of things that cannot be transferred to the other sex. John Paul II's apostolic exhortation *Familiaris consortio* of 15 December 1981, which sums up the findings of the synod of bishops held to discuss the family, says that the mentality by which *censetur honor mulieris magis ex opere foris facto oriri quam ex domestico*[12] should be rejected. It declares that society should be organized in such a way *ut uxores matresque re non cogantur opus foris facere, necnon ut earum familiae possint digne vivere ac prosperari etiam cum illae omnes curas in propriam familiam intendunt.*[13] The Pope is here reverting to a thought he had touched on when calling for prayers for the same synod of bishops: *Est profecto ita! Necesse est familiae nostrae aetatis ad pristi-*

---

[12] *Familiaris consortio*, 23. "A woman's standing is thought to come more from external works than domestic ones."

[13] Ibid., 25. "That wives and mothers should not in fact be forced to work outside, and so that their families may be able to live fittingly and to prosper even if they devote all their time to their own families."

num statum revocentur.[14] Mother Teresa of Calcutta takes up the same theme: "The woman is the heart of the family. If we have great problems today it is because the woman is no longer the heart of the family, and when the child comes home it no longer finds a mother there to welcome it."[15]

Feminism is thus in fact a form of *masculinism* without realizing it, and takes masculinity, rather than the true feminine prototype, as its model. When it talks about emancipating women from men, it does not mean to make men respect women by binding men to faithfulness and conjugal chastity, but rather it means to turn women into as great libertines as men. In its maddest form, the demand for emancipation produces an unnatural egalitarianism that rejects not only the alleged inferiority of women, but even some advantages that civilization accords to the female sex. So special provisions in the law in favor of women who are pregnant or who have just given birth, bans on imposing heavy work on women, social payments to widows when widowers get none, and any special protection of mothers of families, are all rejected as signs of inequality. All this because "this traditional division of functions and duties between men and women weakens women's position in the labor market."[16] To assert an equality between unequals is to be at odds with the variety of created being, that is, the assertion breaks to pieces on the principle of non-contradiction; its real bias, however, is a pride that refuses one's own good when it comes from occupying a less than equal position that is regarded as humiliating, when in fact the position is part of life's rich variety.

91. Feminist theology.

The loss of the right vocabulary to express ideas, doctrinal confusion, historical inexactitude and the general desire to agree with the spirit of the age have also produced a feminist theology. This theology, which is a contradiction in terms since theology means a consideration of God, puts the subject who is theologizing in the place of the object whom theology considers, and

---

[14] "It is indeed the case! The families of our time must be summoned back to their old condition."

[15] Interview in the *Giornale nuovo*, 29 December 1980.

[16] "Report of the Federal Commission for Women's Issues," Berne 1980.

makes women the light by which women's concerns are to be examined. In real theology women are considered in the light of revelation and in relation to God, who is the formal object of theology.

The Holy See's newspaper has not been immune to this feminist theology. I will not go into the attempt to remove the idea of fatherhood from the Lord's prayer. It is motivated by a distaste for the masculine gender in grammar, which is often used for superlatives. It was this same distaste that made the American episcopal conference replace the word "man" in the liturgy with the word "people." But I want to concentrate on the *Osservatore Romano* of 1 December 1978, which denigrates the historical Church, to which feminine values, so it maintains, have been revealed by contemporary feminism after two millennia, and which presents Christian women as wanting "to be considered as persons and consequently to be able to act as such, as beings who realize and express themselves."[17] Obviously thinking does not always precede speaking, and what is said is therefore not always even intelligible. But to say for two thousand years the Church has honored, catechized, given sacraments to, given legal rights to and even canonized, beings to whom it denied the status of persons, is a mere compounding of words; and if anything can be deciphered from it, it is simply the ignorance of the authoress as to what constitutes a person, freedom, the goal of Christian life and the nature of the Church.[18]

The attempt by a religious sister[19] to introduce the feminine gender into the Holy Trinity by making the Holy Spirit a *Spirita Santa* is even more rash. Historical ignorance encourages insolence on the sister's part, to the point of calling the Catholic theology of the Trinity a "very strange anomaly" and a

---

[17] This has become a commonplace, and even a hackneyed one. There is never a discussion, by priests or laity, in which the formula "woman has finally become a person and a subject" does not crop up. For example, I.C.I. No.556, 1980, p.42, *Le nouveau rôle de la femme dans la famille occidentale.*

[18] I protested against the absurdity and impiety of the article in a letter of 3 December 1978 to the editor of the paper who, being *tanquam modo genitus infans* (like a newborn child), seemed to be unaware of the paper's traditional honesty and courtesy and did not deign to reply.

[19] In *Seminari e teologia*, April 1979.

"tremendous equivocation" because it failed to see that the third person of the Trinity is a *Spirita Santa*. The Hebrew word translated into Greek as neuter and into Latin as masculine is in fact feminine and the *Spiritus Sanctus* of our Vulgate is therefore alleged to be a mother-god, a *Spirita Santa*.[20]

It is only historical ignorance that leads anyone to regard the aberrant idea of a *Spirita Santa* as new. It was noted as long ago as Agobard,[21] and the heretics called the *Obsceni* thought the third person was feminine and adored her incarnation in Willhemina of Bohemia. From a theoretical point of view the logical and biological monstrosities that follow from this aberration are repellent. The Blessed Virgin would have been overshadowed in Matthew 1:18 by a feminine being, and thus Jesus would have been born of two women. If the third person of the Trinity is a Mother, then, since "she" proceeds from the Son, we would have the absurdity of a mother originating from her son. These theological implications of the sister's point of view show that, for her, refraining from writing is much more difficult than writing.

This introduction of the feminine into the Trinity is mistakenly alleged to have been initiated and supported in a speech given by Pope John Paul I, in which he said, on the basis of a passage in Isaiah, that God is a mother. The passage is, however, concerned with the divine mercy and says that God is like a mother, because "even if a mother forgets the child in her womb, the Lord will never forget Israel."[22] This is a beautiful poetic image for the measurelessness of the divine mercy, on which John Paul II subsequently wrote his encyclical *Dives in Misericordia*, rather than an image designed to convey the femininity of God.

Giovanni Testori, a literary convert not altogether free of a tendency to exaggerate and extrapolate for effect, has gone so far as to say that "Our Lady had become part of the Trinity." The conclusion is to be drawn that feminist theology is attempting

---

[20] This feminist theology within Catholicism is one of the points used to advance the cause of union with non-Catholics. The final document of the World Council of Churches in Vancouver in 1983 contained demands not only that the priesthood be bestowed on women but that the Holy Spirit be declared to be "God the Mother." See O.R., 10 August 1983.

[21] P.L., 104, 163.

[22] Isaiah, 49:15.

to apply *ad intra* attributes of God that only apply *ad extra*, and is fixing on the Trinity a sexuality only found among creatures and which is wholly equivocal when predicated of the three divine persons.

92. The Church's egalitarian tradition. Subordination and superordination of women.

This injection of male and female equality into the inner life of the Trinity is less acceptable than the Jacobin assertion of female superiority, based on the *Genesis* account, in which woman is created after man as a more perfect creature, and one requiring a higher grade of creative activity.[23]

But any kind of feminism clashes with the natural order that differentiates the two sexes by making them reciprocally subordinate. This harmonized difference is not a mere social effect, as some biologists have attempted to maintain, which would disappear or be reversed with the disappearance or reversal of the social forces producing it. It is in fact a difference inherent in human nature. Without it human nature would be incomplete because it is archetypically conceived as existing in this duality. The significance of Adam's loneliness lies in the fact that it is the loneliness of a being crying out for its own fulfillment.

I will not go into the metaphysical aspect of the duality of the sexes, involving the direction of the two entities into a unity, nor will I invoke the myth of the androgenes, which is an adumbration of conjugal union. I simply note that because each sex is coordinate with the other, the element of *subordination* which is undeniably and naturally present in the conjugal act[24] does not alter the fact that the common end, be it procreation or the gift of self, puts the two partners on an absolutely equal level. Nor does that subordination mean that the naturally dif-

---

[23] *Giacobini Italiani*, Bari, 1964, Vol. II, p.459. *La causa delle donne*. Anonymous.

[24] That the man is the active principle and the woman the passive one in the act of union seems to me something recognized by the ancients and undeniable by the moderns: the "fiasco" of erotic experience is something only experienced by the man, because only the male takes the active part in the union. See Stendhal, *De l'amour*, Paris, no date, in the chapter devoted to *Fiasco*. Ovid's *Amores*, III, VII, is the classic description of the phenomenon.

ferentiated functions of the two regarding the consequences of the act of union are not of the same moral or social worth. The notion of woman as a *masculus occasionatus*, that is, a defective man, and therefore inferior, is not part of Catholic teaching; but the coordination of the two unequals in an equalizing unity is. Beside the *physiological subordination* of the woman, there is in this union of unequals an undeniable *psychological superordination* on her part in the order of attraction, since she, rather than the man, puts out the pollen of seduction, and the man is only active in conjugal *congressus* after he has fallen subject to her solicitations at the stage of the *aggressus*. Because of this reciprocal subordination the old controversy, much discussed in literature, as to which sex was stronger in love loses its meaning, and the facts relating to Messalina, or the mythological Hercules, or the famous *placet* of the Queen of Aragon become mere anecdotes.[25] If the reported facts had been true, they would only have been oddities that do not disprove the reciprocal influences we have mentioned.

The woman's predominance is particularly expressed within the domestic setting; John Paul II has deliberately distanced himself from the innovators' views in an important document promulgated as a *Charter of the Rights of the Family* in 1983. The Pope teaches that the natural place in which women express their personalities is the family and that their particular task is the bringing up of children. Work away from home is a disorder to be corrected. Article 10 on wages says that they "ought to be such as not to force mothers to work away from home, to the detriment of family life and the upbringing of children in particular." We have seen how the Pope seemed to call for a restoration of traditional family life when asking for prayers for the synod of bishops on the family.[26] This papal teaching was soon openly contradicted, however, by a congress of Catholic women which took up the new view: "No woman considers it a good thing not to have the experience of working away from home, or plans to do housework all her life."[27]

---

[25] For Messalina see Juvenal, VI, 129-30; for Hercules, Statius, *Silv*, III, 1, 42; for the Queen of Aragon, Montaigne, *Essais*, Paris 1950, p.956.

[26] See paragraph 90.

[27] O.R., 1 April 1984.

93. The subordination of women in Catholic tradition.

From the religious point of view, both the equality and the subordination of the two sexes have a supernatural aspect to them. According to the account given in *Genesis*[28] and referred to by St. Paul[29] woman is derived from man to take away his feeling of loneliness, so that emerging from the sleep sent upon him by God, he found himself "man and woman." Woman thus is second to man in creation. She is subject to man, but not because he is the end for which she exists. The end is the same for both and superior to both. St. Paul says forcefully that with respect to that end "there is neither man nor woman,"[30] just as there is neither Jew nor Gentile, slave nor free. Not that all these do not exist, with all their different qualities, but that all the baptized have put on the same Christ and *to that extent* all their differences have been taken away. There is no distinction between persons in the order of grace. All have been made members of Christ and filled with the same life. St. Paul nonetheless says[31] women should be subordinate, thus taking on what had been laid down in *Genesis: Mulieres, subditae estote viris sicut oportet in Domino,*[32] where the original word would be perhaps better translated by a reflexive verb than by a participle used as a noun, since the meaning of the Greek is rather "of yourselves subject yourselves."[33] It is important that the text also provides the manner and limit of this subjection, which is to be *in Domino,*[34] that is it is to have as its rule the service due to the Lord, which is a liberating service. The connection of *in Domino* to *subditae estote* thus provides the ultimate reason for subjecting oneself to a husband, and that reason is certainly not the husband himself, but the First Principle of all obedience. Christian freedom is not enfranchisement from all order and subordination, but a choosing to be subject to a particular order. As

---

[28] Genesis, 2:21-2.
[29] I Corinthians, 11:8.
[30] Galatians, 3:28.
[31] Colossians, 3:18.
[32] "Wives, be obedient to your husbands, as is fitting in the Lord."
[33] Nor should it be forgotten that Ephesians 5:21 calls spouses "subject one to another," as John Paul II noted in his speech of 3 August 1982.
[34] "In the Lord."

St. Paul[35] explains, the act of being subject to a husband is a being subject to the Lord.[36]

It is not possible to explain away the subordination of woman to man by reference to historical circumstances, as is now usually done, in imitation of Marxist historiography, with every Catholic principle or institution that is out of fashion in the modern world. It comes from the divine law at the beginnings of the human race. It comes from the different nature of the two sexes, one stamped with an instinct to govern and to procreate, the other with an instinct to be led and to be attached to a spouse. It comes with the reiterated authority of revelation[37] which preaches a non-servile subjection to a succession of theologically subordinate beings, the Apostle saying that "of every man the head is Christ, the head then of the wife is the husband and the head of Christ is God." Subordination is thus sculpted in man's nature, considered not in the abstract of humanity, but as really existing, stamped with the two sexes. To deny the legitimacy of such subordination is yet again an effect of a fallacious and flawed kind of abstraction, by which one arrives at a generic essence through stripping actual beings of their specific, individuating characteristics, and then taking that essence as reality. It is a reality, but not in its abstract form, only in its individual and concrete expression. Feminists take the abstraction as a reality to which rights can be attributed, when in fact they can only be given to real entities: the right of a workman to his salary does not come from his being a man but from his being an actual workman.

One could object that historically the subordinate position that women have occupied in the Church has been that of servants rather than that of companions. One could adduce in evidence certain derogatory judgments made by, mainly Greek, Fathers of the Church, and some discriminations in the liturgy. Among the patristic passages would be the one from Clement of Alexandria: "Every woman ought to die with shame at the thought of being a woman."[38] Being banned from the priest-

---

[35] Ephesians, 5:22.

[36] Ephesians, 5:24 is decisive on this point, where the subjection of a woman to her husband is modeled on that of the Church to Christ: "As the Church is subject to Christ, so are women to their husbands in all things."

[37] I Corinthians, 11:3.

[38] Clement of Alexandria, *Paedagogus*, 2.

hood cannot be counted as an undue liturgical discrimination, because it is a matter of divine positive law. Among the more visible and well-known discriminations, until the recent liturgical changes, was the banning of women from the sanctuary areas of churches; but this was not a discrimination between sexes but between clerics and laity, illustrated by the fact that St. Charles Borromeo, for example, maintained the bar even against ruling sovereigns. The heavier penances which women had to perform, in now distant centuries, for the same sin were, on the other hand, genuine discriminations on the grounds of sex, as was the custom of banning women from the Eucharist at certain times. Some of these discriminations are connected with the notion, sanctioned by the Old Testament, that the impurity involved in certain physiological events is inseparable from moral impurity. In some of these instances, men and women were treated alike.

94. Defense of the Church's doctrine and practice concerning women.

In making any judgment on the alleged inferiority of women in the Church, two considerations must be kept in mind.

First, the natural inequality we have discussed[39] can give grounds for allocation of different rights to the two sexes, without prejudicing that equality on a higher level which is so clearly maintained by the same Clement of Alexandria: "There is but one and the same faith for man and woman, there is for both a single Church, a single temperance, a single modesty. The same too are food, marriage is the same, and breathing, seeing, learning, knowledge, hope, obedience, love, grace, salvation and virtue."[40] The particular rights of each person are not derived, as are their common rights, from their abstract nature, but from their concrete nature in the circumstances in which it actually exists.

The historical character of the Church, and the development through time of its beliefs and practices must also be considered. Orthodoxy and orthopraxis are in principle unchangeable, but they are sharpened and unfolded and applied with the passage of time. As to orthodoxy, it is obvious that the clear and

---

[39] See paragraph 93.
[40] *Paedagogus*, 1:10.

full understanding of Our Lady's immaculate dignity came after the indistinct and partial understanding the early Church and the Apostles themselves had of it.[41] I leave aside the doctrines of grace, papal infallibility, the Assumption and many other points of faith that the Church of the twentieth century possesses in a much more developed and distinct way than did the ancient Church.

As for orthodoxy, so for orthopraxis. The Catholic Church has always believed the two sexes have the same worth and the same end, so that the natural difference, and fitting subordination that go with it, end in a final equality; the unnatural differences that come from corruption and concupiscence are a different matter. This is the unchanging strand in the teaching. Its legitimate consequences, however, are manifested through an historical development of the Christian mind; and the deductions which are to be drawn from it are made step by step amidst delays and deviations, particularly if they are remote conclusions which are harder to reach because of the subtlety of the principle on which they rest. Slavery, for example, even when recognized in civil law, is transcended by Christians' spiritual brotherhood and common moral goal. These implicitly demand its abolition. Religion in fact gradually removed slavery from civil law.

The belief that the Christian religion has suppressed and maltreated women has become a commonplace of the innovators' propaganda and is largely accepted by those who grant, without historical or philosophical proof, that women have in centuries past had the status of objects, that they have not been persons, and furthermore, that this has been their own fault because they accepted servitude without recognizing it for what it was.[42] The truth is that, as in much of contemporary thought-

---

[41] I do not accept the improbable view that the Apostles had, but did not publish, a perfect knowledge of all the truths of faith that have been recognized gradually since their day.

[42] See the articles *Sulla condizione femminile* in *Vita e pensiero*, May-August 1975. This assumption is granted therein from the outset and the articles are moreover imbued with Freudianism, Marxism and historicism. Heterodox authors are quoted, the whole Catholic tradition is neglected and St. Augustine and St. Thomas are ignored. Even the language is spoiled by inaccurate expressions of every sort. See too O.R., 4 May 1979, which accepts that women have been universally mistreated in the past. The commonly ac-

a kind of historiographical synecdoche is here at work, that isolates a part and takes it for the whole. There have been times in Church history when the conclusions that ought to have been drawn from principles have been unclear, because the principles have been allowed to become unclear. Practice and then, to a lesser extent, theory, have lapsed into illegitimate conclusions that are incompatible with the principles in question. What should be asked about a principle, however, is what its legitimate consequences are, rather than what consequences human passions can abstract from it arbitrarily. The centuries during which Christianity flourished are the centuries in which the dignity of women was recognized and in which their influence upon the world was most largely displayed.

95. Catholicism's elevation of women.

I set aside the holy women to whom St. Paul pays so much honor, by name, in his letters. I set aside St. Mary Magdalene's first place as a witness to the Resurrection. I will not enter a discussion which could continue almost indefinitely regarding the orders of virgins and widows, whose religious and moral excellence was praised in the writings of all the Fathers from Tertullian to Augustine. Any such discussion would be not only long but difficult, since the modern mind lacks the wings to rise to the height at which what is precious is prized and the perfection of virtue admired.

I turn instead to the large part that good women on the imperial thrones of both East and West had in the evolution of the Christian world; women such as Helena and Theodora II. Later when barbarism was being civilized and tamed, women such as Theodolinda, Clothilde and Radegonde exercised an influence greater than that of any woman in the modern period.[43]

---

cepted truth that Christianity raised the status of women has been replaced by a commonly accepted error that it lowered it.

[43] It should be noted that women had importance and influence in the life of Athens and that Epicurus admitted them to his school. That caused surprise, and even three centuries later Cicero could write in reference to Leontium, a female disciple of Epicurus: *Leontium contra Theophrastum scribere ausa est, scito illa quidem sermone et attico, sed tamen...* "Leontium dared to write against Theophrastus, admittedly in a somewhat refined way, but nevertheless ...."

In the monasteries of France and Germany women reached
very high levels both culturally and in the government of their
orders. During the Carolingian renaissance it was a woman,
Doda, who wrote the first treatise on the education of children.
Later in the great monasteries which were the seed beds of every
aspect of that civilization, a very high cultural level was reached,
partly by the efforts of women. Heloise, abbess of the convent
of the Holy Spirit in the twelfth century, taught her nuns Greek
and Hebrew, thus renewing the instruction St. Jerome gave his
female disciples at Rome and Bethlehem. Hildegarde, Abbess of
Bingen, also in the twelfth century, wrote on natural history and
medicine; Rosvita, the Abbess of Gandersheim, composed Latin
comedies and had them acted. These are all signs of a cultural
level just as high as that of male contemporaries, and one which
was not confined to isolated cases.

The part women played in meetings to promote the Truce
of God and to moderate the savagery of warfare in the mediaeval period deserves special attention. How far equality went is
particularly apparent from the fact that in twin monasteries of
men and women, the government of both communities was
entrusted to women in more than one instance.[44] Until the
nineteenth century it was not rare for women to take part in
communal assemblies[45] which were the only popular assemblies
in the past, as great national affairs were generally handled by
sovereigns; and if women had to meet a property qualification
to participate, so did men. What ended this participation by
women was the lowering of their status caused by the advent of
a utilitarian, industrial society and the consequent secularization
of the masses. It is worth remembering, however, that women
traditionally had voted in their local communities in Austria,
Switzerland and indeed the Papal States.

It was the poetry of courtly love that put forth the most elevated view of women in the Christian Middle Ages; its theoretical formulation being provided by Andreas Cappellanus.

This does not, however, disprove the generally down-trodden state
of women in pagan society, denounced by all the Fathers.

[44] Abbesses enjoyed the same quasi-episcopal jurisdiction as abbots
over the subjects and territories of their monasteries, including the
whole extent of spiritual and temporal government. See the important work of Adriana Valerio, *La questione femminile nei secoli X-
XII*, Naples, 1983.

[45] The author seems to have Switzerland in mind. [Translator's note.]

Courtly poetry embraces a whole range of sentiments and behavior, based on delicacy of feeling, respect and loyalty. Courtly
love sometimes strayed in the direction of disincarnate love or
an opposing erotic passion, but as a whole remains a proof of
the exalted feelings that the contemplation of the feminine
aroused in mediaeval civilization. In poetry of the Sicilian
school and the *dolce stil nuovo*, the theme of the angelic woman
rose to even greater heights. Dante's *Divina Commedia* also exalts the feminine through the characters of Mary, Beatrice and
the *donne benedette* in the prelude, making them the supreme
means of man's spiritual elevation and the power that brings
him salvation. Once one is aware of the importance of poetry at
that period, one cannot fail to realize the dignity and majesty
religion had brought to women. The distinction between love
and marriage which was a consequence of the exaltation of the
feminine as such, did indeed lean in the direction of a neopla-
tonism incompatible with Christian realism, but the mediaeval
phenomena show irrefutably that Catholicism remained faithful
to the double truth contradicted by modern feminism: namely
that women and men have the same worth and the same end,
but that the two are not the same and must live out their axiological equality in their different ways.

A further proof that Catholicism recognized an equality
between the sexes can be drawn from the influence that women
of great attainments and pronounced mystical inspiration exercised on the government of the Church, on religious movements and on attempts at renewal and reform. One need only
mention the names of Catherine of Siena, Joan of Arc, Catherine of Genoa and Teresa of Avila in order to demonstrate overwhelmingly the fact of this feminine influence in the Church.
Then again there are the numerous women of very active character who founded religious orders and societies, or who persuaded popes to undertake works of universal importance, like
the Mademoiselle Tamisier who promoted the idea of eucharistic congresses in the reign of Pius IX. Above all there are the
hosts of women the Church has honored with canonization,
and those to whom it has given the title of Doctor of the
Church: Catherine of Siena and the Spanish St. Teresa.

96. Decline in morals.

Related to the doctrinal deviation concerning the nature of
women, there is an analogous one concerning the nature of sex-

ual acts. To evaluate this deviation correctly, one should remember that although the greater or lesser frequency with
which certain kinds of behavior recur is important in any sort
of human activity and in morals especially, it is of still greater
significance how that behavior is understood, that is, how the
public conscience judges it. Nobody denies that immodesty is
more widespread than it was in the past, when moral excesses
were confined to small circles and when, even more importantly, they were hidden, not daring to show themselves. Today
our cities wear immodest faces. Modesty was a general characteristic of the Christian centuries; immodesty is the general
characteristic of our own, and to be sure of the fact, one need
only look at the old treatises on love, the books on the government of women, the provisions of civil and canon law and the
confessors' manuals which are primary sources in this field. Intimacy has today lost its shining veil of modesty, and is di-
vulged, displayed and bruited about in the illustrated magazines
devoured by the vulgar horde. Public entertainment, especially
in films, takes sex as its favorite subject and critics provide theoretical support for doing so by decreeing that the breaking of
moral rules is essential to art. Thence there follows a mechanical
progression in obscenity *in infinitum*: from simple fornication
to adultery, to sodomy, to incest, to sodomitic incest, to bestiality, to coprophagia and so on. The established fact of public
coitus is perhaps the ultimate demonstration of contemporary
sexual indulgence; precedents for it can only be found by going
as far back as the Cynic philosophers, and St. Augustine
thought it impossible, even physiologically. It is outdone perhaps by international displays of erotic objects and of porno-
graphic art; the former at Copenhagen in 1969 and the latter at
Hamburg in the same year, opened by the Minister of Culture.

   The Church quickly took up an indulgent attitude to ob-
scene films. Indications that a film should be avoided were
dropped from the Catholic press, the assertion that "present day
morality differs from the crude moralism into which people
often fell in the past" was offered to justify a new attitude, notoriously indecent films were awarded prizes and the new indulgent outlook was presented as a recognition of the maturity of
modern man.

   But as we have said, events are less important than the
meanings they have in people's minds and less important than
the deep rooted, tacitly held opinions on which people base

their judgment. We should therefore examine the phenomenon of modesty a little, to show that the present decline in morals also springs from a denial of natures or essences.

97. Philosophy of modesty. Natural shame.

Far from being, as the moderns pretend, a transient and temporary social phenomenon to be abolished by psychology and sociology, modesty is something connected with man's metaphysical core, and should be studied in anthropology and theology.

Modesty is a species of the genus *shame*: it is shame connected with sexual matters. Shame is in general the feeling accompanying the perception of a defect, and is natural, or moral, depending on whether the defect is in nature or in personal behavior. Nature is ashamed of its own defects, because every nature has to live up to its own archetype; and if by some fault, whether innate or acquired, it falls away from its ideal, it notices the defect and is ashamed of it. Since natures only have real existence in individual entities, so do defects; thus natural shame at some defect becomes the shame of the defective individual.

The objection will be made that such an individual is not at fault and cannot be ashamed at nature's defects. This is a superficial objection. It does not matter that the individual is not to blame for nature's faults: nature is ashamed of its own fault in the individual. The facts of ordinary life show it. No sane person boasts of, or is indifferent to, the fact that he is hunchbacked or crippled or blind. No one considers such defects normal in man in general, or in himself in particular. Merely observing that the individual is not to blame for the defect does not alter the fact that it is there, or take away the shame that nature feels at it.

In this regard the grief and shame that man feels at his own mortality, which is the radical defect in human nature[46] is very

---

[46] A very important and often neglected distinction should be made here between man's original state and his natural state. The former has only ever existed in the first human couple before their fall, and included supernatural and preternatural qualities, freedom from death being one of the latter. Man's truly natural state is the state of that same couple as they would have been without any supernatural or preternatural endowments. Man is therefore now fallen and corrupt with respect to his original state; but that is not to say that

significant. This same feeling extends, with greater or lesser intensity, from mortality to disease and old age, and all other bodily operations that suggest mortality. The activities of nutrition, generation and egestion are performed by man within his own walls and in hiding. Great philosophers and poets have touched on this mystery. Even though he tried to extinguish man's fear of death, Lucretius speaks of man's indignation at being born mortal.[47] Horace knows man feels fear and anger when faced with death because he feels it contradicts his own nature: *mortis formidine et ira.*[48] Gabriele d'Annunzio abhors the shame of decrepitude and death as did Mimnermus in antiquity. But what shame is there, if he is not at fault? The shame is metaphysical: it is indignation at the destruction of a being whose original structure rejects death, it is a shame at a defect which does not belong to the individual as such, but to his nature. Man does not feel shame or indignation at not being winged, since not having wings is not for him a defect; but he does feel such sentiments at not being immortal, since mortality is indeed a defect.

---

death is a defect in his nature. See Pope St. Pius V's condemnation of the teachings of Michael Baius on 1 October 1567, *passim*, but particularly condemned proposition 78. *Immortalitas primi hominis non erat gratiae beneficium, sed naturalis conditio.* "The immortality of the first man was not a gift of grace but a natural condition." *Denzinger*, No.1078 (1956 edition). See also Pope Pius VI's condemnation of the teaching of the Jansenist Synod of Pistoia, on 28 August 1794, especially Propositions 16 and 17, in the latter of which the Pope condemns the notion that *mortem, quae in praesenti statu inflicta est velut iusta poena peccati per iustam subtractionem immortalitatis, non fuisse naturalem conditionem hominis, quasi immortalitas non fuisset gratuitum beneficium, sed naturalis conditio.* "Death, which is inflicted in the present state as a just penalty for sin through the just subtraction of immortality, was not man's natural condition; as if immortality had not been a gratuitous gift, but a natural condition." *Denzinger*, No.1517 (1956 edition). It is in fact the teaching of Doctors of the Church such as St. Thomas Aquinas and St. Robert Bellarmine that human nature, strictly so called, was not damaged at all by the fall and survives intact in *puris naturalibus*, i.e., in its purely natural qualities. [Translator's note.]

[47] *De Rerum Natura*, III, 884.
[48] Epistolae, II, II, 207.

The depth of the phenomenon of shame is also apparent from its involuntary character. Man blushes at his own or another's fault;[49] his face lights up without his willing it. It is not the person who is ashamed, but the person's nature. A brow of bronze and an impassible face are sad signs among people of any race.

98. Personal shame. Reich.

Personal shame is deeper than natural shame because it is caused by a personal moral failing. Its moral character is no longer a mere feeling, but an act whereby one freely acknowledges and detests a voluntary defect, that is, a fault of which one is guilty.

This phenomenon of shame has an even deeper meaning when viewed theologically. The *libido* is the most far reaching form of disobedience at work in human nature, which has been put out of harmony by the disobedience of original sin. Thinking sins of the flesh the worst sort was an exaggeration, indeed a grave error, but was not a mistake that well-instructed people made.[50] Nonetheless, even though it is not synonymous with sin, concupiscence is the most obvious symptom of man's present state, and his inherent tendency to sin. The subjection of the seeing, rational part of man to his blind, instinctive part is in fact at its greatest in carnal union, since the latter is at its height a moment of delirium and confusion of consciousness, in which the very awareness of the unitive meaning of the act is lost. Shame connected with sexual matters can be seen, from the religious point of view, to be profoundly connected with what it means to be human, and all the drama of love and the meaning of moral struggle is lost if modesty is trivialized by confining it to the merely psychological and sociological sphere. It is a sign of the disorder in human nature caused by sin. Through this disorder, the will to exercise moral mastery is itself mastered unless it maintains itself by continual struggle. The will is not bound to concupiscence as Luther thought, but it is bound to a struggle against it, and when it wins a victory it is always a victory for the time being because the struggle is always in progress.

---

[49] Dante, *Paradiso*, XXVII, 32.

[50] In Dante's Hell and Purgatory those guilty of such sins occupy the circles of least punishment, being guilty of a lighter fault.

Thus the modern ideas which dismiss modesty, take away
the element of struggle in order to celebrate self-indulgence as
total victory.

Reich's famous book *The Sexual Revolution* proclaims the
idea that venereal pleasure is the essence of human happiness
and that therefore every barrier blocking the *libido* ought to be
removed as an impediment to happiness. Since conscience is the
greatest barrier because it reasserts itself imperiously whenever it
is violated, emancipation from any conscientious obligation to
modesty becomes synonymous with happiness. Theoretically,
what this entails is the denial of any fixed purpose or law governing sexual activity; practically, it entails the abolition of
marriage, public coitus, unnatural union, indiscriminate sexual
relations and the abolition of clothes. Underlying this eroticism
is a spurious notion of liberty, by which a dependent being denies that it does in fact depend on its own nature.

99. Episcopal documents on sexuality.
Cardinal Colombo. The German bishops.

Many episcopal documents on sexual questions lack theological depth: they condemn immodesty not because it is morally wrong, but simply because it upsets the mechanics of life
and is an impediment to a person's development. Theological
considerations are left out, no connection is made with original
sin, man's divorce from the moral law is not considered, even
the terms chastity and modesty are not used. In his homily at
Pentecost 1971, which dealt with love as the only principle governing sexual union, Giovanni Cardinal Colombo, the Archbishop of Milan, makes no mention of the procreative end of
marriage or of divine law; the only grounds for continence he
mentions are the achievement of personal maturity, without
which "sexuality becomes a cause of psychological blocks, of an
emotional aridity which is sometimes irreparable and which
therefore damages and deforms the process of achieving personal maturity."[51]

The German bishops' pastoral letter[52] also has a non-
Catholic anthropology as its point of departure, since it states
that "sexuality informs the whole of our life, and because body
and soul form a unity, our sexuality determines the soul's sensi-

---

[51] O.R., 5 June 1971.
[52] O.R., 18 July 1973.

tivities and imagination, as well as our thought and our decisions." I do not want to exaggerate the bishops' faults while
making a judgment about these statements, so I will take account of the general theological vagueness of the modern episcopate and refrain from taking the terms they use rigorously.
The underlying anthropology is nonetheless far from the tenets
of any Catholic school, all of which hold that *sexus non est in
anima*.[53] Rationality, not sexuality, is in fact the form of the
whole of life. The classical definition taken up by the Fourth
Lateran Council is: *anima rationalis est forma substantialis corporis*,[54] that is, it is the first principle which gives being to the
whole human individual. To say that sexuality *determines*
thought and the will's decisions, is at odds with man's spirituality. Spirituality consists in the fact that there is an element in the
soul which is not wholly concerned with informing the body,
but is a subsistent form in its own right. This element transcending matter is the source of man's universalizing faculty and
so of that freedom of choice by which man ranges over the
whole universe of good and is not confined within the bounds
of the particular. If sexuality *determines* decisions, decisions are
not free.[55]

The document condemned premarital sexual relations, but
in the passage dealing with them it overturns the traditional
norms of ethics and asceticism regarding modesty, by abandoning the warning about the proximate occasions of sin, so much
emphasized in the past, and it defends familiarities between the
sexes as if putting oneself in the way of temptation were a sign
of moral maturity. "Even if there is a danger that these meetings
might lead to sexual relations and to the forming of relation-
ships at too early a stage, it is not right to reject or seek to avoid
this necessary step towards maturity in man's capacity to love."
Two principles of the Church's moral teaching are avoided here.
The first is theological: namely that since nature has lost its integrity through original sin, and the ruling, rational part of man
has consequently lost its mastery, a tendency to be overwhelmed

---

[53] *Summa Theologica*, Supplement q.39,a.1. "Sex is not in the soul."
[54] "The rational soul is the substantial form of the body."
[55] If one talked like that, one could say that man's sensitive, nutritive
and respiratory faculties "informed" the whole of his life. They do
not; his life is composed of these various things each having its
own value, but what informs the whole and makes man man is his
rationality.

by sexual temptation is part of man's lot. The second point is
more directly moral: merely to get close to sin is indeed not the
same as sinning, and is therefore not wrong in itself; but it is
sinful because of the pride and presumption involved in assuming one has the moral strength to counteract any impulse contrary to the law. The old adage *salus mea in fuga*[56] once the
motto of Catholic asceticism, seems to have been forgotten in
the interests of personal maturity and training in love.

---

[56] "My salvation lies in flight."

CHAPTER X

SOMATOLATRY AND PENANCE

100. Modern Somatolatry and the Church.

If sexuality has often been taken as the very forming principle of the human person, the cult of the body which has become such a notable feature of contemporary culture has been even more widely supported. I am well aware that the cultivation of personal strength and beauty in ancient times was one of the links that bound the Greek cities together in their amphictionies, and that such qualities were celebrated at civic festivals. But these festivals involved the whole of Greek culture, and poets, historians and playwrights were honored at them no less than winners of races and athletic contests; there are no Pindars among modern champions. What we call sporting prowess was only one rather conspicuous element at the ancient festivals. But even in ancient Greece, sporting ability was not much valued when separated from that cultural whole of which it was a part, and the mere pursuit of sports as such was despised by philosophers and ridiculed in comedies. Seneca speaks disdainfully of athletes, *quorum corpora in sagina, animi in macie et veterno sunt*;[1] Epictetus says *abiecti animi esse studio corporis immorari*;[2] Persius mocks "muscular youth";[3] and Plutarch in his *Quaestiones Romanae* even attributes the decline of Greece to the sports ground.

In the tradition of Catholic teaching, the care of the body was considered under the heading of exercise and fitness, and it merged with medical considerations about hygiene. That idea is still apparent in the much used *Manuale dell' educazione umana* published at Milan in 1834 and written by Rev. Antonio Fon-

---

[1]   *Epist. Ad Lucilium*, 88, 19. "Whose bodies are trim, but whose
      souls are thin and lethargic."
[2]   "To spend much time on the body is the sign of an abject soul."
[3]   *Satires*, III, 86.

tana, the Director General of Public Instruction in the province
of Lombardy and Venetia: one of its four books is on "Physical
Education," but includes such things as food, sleep and cleanli-
ness, with only one of the chapters, entitled "On the Exercises
of the Person," having to do with physical education in the
modern sense.

The separation of these elements, the erection of bodily exercise into a special form of human activity and finally its
apotheosis, are all things that have happened in the last century.
Sport fills the lives of professional athletes, absorbs much of the
energy and almost all the attention of the young and has invaded the mentality of enormous masses of people for whom it
is not exercise, but entertainment, as well as the object of
fiercely competitive and combative instincts. Newspapers regularly devote a third of their space to sport and have evolved a set
of flattering metaphors designed to increase the importance of
sports matches; they refer to athletes and their performance as if
referring to the heroes of a great saga, and they confuse the
winning of some competition with the achievement of personal
perfection. In 1971 there was a world championship boxing
match, which turned out to be a display of bestiality and insults, but sports writers, including some of great talent, used the
words "style" and even "philosophy" to describe what were
merely different forms of quasi-homicidal rage, just as they use
"syllogism" and "deduction" to describe the action at a football
match, thus debasing the language. Civic authorities proclaim
the spiritual importance of sport at important matches and assert that "besides being a disciplined activity with a very important goal, sport is a noble expression of civic spirit" and that
"only sport can reconcile the hatreds that divide nations, and so
make men brothers."[4]

This removal of sport from its proper place and the attri-
bution to it of a spiritual importance was not effectively resisted
by the Church which, as if admitting the unjust accusation that
it undermined physical strength through the gnawings of conscience, was afraid to be, or even to seem to be, against the
praise of physical excellence; the Church, instead, gave its support to the prevailing somatolatry of the age, as if its support

---

[4]   The mayor of a Swiss city when opening a sports field. When receiving the Varese football team, John Paul II spoke of sport as "a
noble human activity." O.R., 5 December 1982.

were needed or as if the passion for sport were not already sufficiently inflamed. The only sign of any continuing reserve in the Church's attitude to sport is the absence of a sports column in the *Osservatore Romano*. The hierarchy have followed the trend nonetheless.

It is true that in recent times there have been sporting and gymnastic associations under Catholic aegis, but the religious reference in their names was of the general sort that can be made in connection with any worthy activity. There were Catholic banks, agricultural leagues etc., but they were associations of Catholics rather than Catholic associations.

101. Sport as the perfecting of the human person.

The main grounds for the Church's baptizing of the cult of the body are: firstly, that the physical excellence pursued in sport is a precondition of personal balance; and secondly, that sporting events bring together great numbers of people with different languages, ways of living and political systems, thus helping different peoples to get to know each other, and fostering a fraternal spirit in the world at large: *Manifestationes sportivae ad animi aequilibrium nec non ad fraternas relationes inter homines omnium condicionum, nationum vel diversae stirpis statuendas adiumentum praebent* is how the Second Vatican Council put it.[5]

These two ideas were examined and rejected or corrected by Pius XII in an important address to the national scientific congress on sport, on 8 November 1952.[6] Man's activities derive their character from their proximate end: sport is thus not in the religious sphere because its proximate end is bodily exercise and the conservation or development of physical strength; but that end is ultimately directed at the same goal as all our other proximate ends, namely, the perfection of the person in God. The Pope emphasizes that the ever fuller dominion of the will over its conjoined instrument, the body, is one of the proximate ends of sport. But the body that sport is concerned with is a body that is doomed to be swept away biologically in the stream of death, and although the body man is supernaturally destined

---

[5]   *Gaudium et Spes*, 61. "Sporting events are of assistance in establishing a balanced temperament and fraternal relations between men of all conditions, nations and races."

[6]   *Discorsi ai Medici*, Rome 1959, pp.215ff.

to have is indeed the same body, that body will be one that has
put on an immortality to which bodily strength acquired on
earth contributes nothing.

I note in passing that it is not true that bodily exercise of itself produces moral health. That had already been seen to be
false in ancient times. Juvenal's dictum *mens sana in corpore
sano*[7] has in fact passed into common usage in a mutilated form
that contradicts its real meaning. It does not in fact say that you
will find a healthy mind in a healthy body, but rather that we
ought to pray the gods to give us both: *Orandum est ut sit mens
sana in corpore sano.*[8]

Ascetic principles demand that the whole person be controlled by the requirements of reason, and since sport is subject
to those principles, its goal cannot be merely the intensive use
of one's physical strength: if such use is divorced from the austerity that the spirit should impose upon the body, sport un-
leashes a man's instincts either by its violence or by its sensual
seductions. An awareness of one's own physical strength, and
success in competitions, may be of some use, but they are not
the main part of man's activity, or morally essential, and still less
a goal for one's life. Popular opinion was so mistaken on these
matters that Pius XII thought it necessary to emphasize that a
man is no less truly a man for being no good at sport. It is not
correct to talk about a physical personality and a spiritual personality, because the one person is defined by his higher faculties. Those who do not play sport fulfill God's design just as
well as those who do.[9]

Under the pressure of popular enthusiasm, the distinction
between physical strength and personal perfection is often
dropped. The violent boxing match mentioned earlier was reported by the *Osservatore Romano*[10] under the headline "Blazing
boxing victory," and it went on to say that the universal interest
in the event "could in a certain sense be considered positive"
because "despite everything, mankind is still able to react and

---

[7] "A healthy mind (is in) a healthy body."
[8] *Satires*, X,356. "We ought pray that there be..." etc.
[9] Just how far the somatolatric mentality has advanced since the
making of that speech can be judged by the fact that invalids are
now thought to be unjustly deprived of their fulfillment as persons
unless they engage in sports.
[10] O.R., 20 March 1971.

concentrate on a value, or an event which is assumed to have value." The writer of the article seems to think that the quality of mankind's moral action is determined simply by a capacity to react, and that to pursue a presumed value is as commendable as pursuing a real one. This is the modern dynamist heresy which holds that action is good in itself, independent of its object or end. It is this dynamist thinking that leads the writer to compare the world-wide interest in a boxing match with the interest in the moon landing of 1969 and conclude that "a boxing match represents a moment in life," the only reservation being that "it should not be absolutized." It is all too obvious that the reservation simply means sport is not heaven; it does not criticize the apotheosis of sport in this world, and the author does not intend to distance himself from the prevailing mentality by a condemnation.

102. Sport as an incentive to brotherhood.

The second justification of modern somatolatry is just as mistaken as the first, since sport is no more productive of the virtues of cooperation and respect among men, and peace among nations than it is of the soul's dominion over the body. I do not deny that competitive sport involves obeying the rules of a game, or that the rules are generally observed. If they were not observed, there could be no game, just as there could be no collective human activity without agreed rules.

But the facts of fraud, violence and intolerance belie the common assumptions about sport. As to fraud; in Italy in 1955 whole football teams were banned for having paid the players in opposing teams to let themselves be beaten, and in 1980 widespread fraud was delated to the so-called sports judges. As to violence; the 1953 match between Austria and Yugoslavia led to apologies being exchanged at diplomatic level; in December 1957 in Belfast the Italian footballers were attacked by the crowd and had to be rescued by the police and in 1964 in Lima dozens of people were trampled to death by an infuriated crowd after a match against Argentina. In May 1984 the sports ministers of twenty-two European countries met in Malta to look for remedies to violence on sports grounds and fraud in matches. As for respect for persons, I would prefer not to mention the events of June 1955 on the racing car circuit at Le Mans, but it must be recorded that when a car jumped the barrier not even the deaths of eighty spectators were enough to halt the whole murderous performance. Last of all there is one fact so incredible, that it proves the power of sport to draw out the animosities of whole nations, as well as those of individuals: a football match occasioned a war lasting several months between El Salvador and Honduras, in which three thousand people were killed and twelve thousand driven into exile.[11] Despite events of this sort, Cardinal Dall'Acqua, the Cardinal Vicar of Rome, praised sport and, somewhat myopically, saw in it signs of health, peace, order, religion and perseverance.[12]

The most outstanding example of the Church's support for the somatolatric tendencies of the age is Paul VI's speech for the Twentieth Olympiad at Munich, a speech tragically in contrast with the dreadful events that saddened those games. The speech begins with a glorification of "healthy, strong, agile and beautiful youth," "a revival of the ancient form of classical humanism, unsurpassable in elegance and energy; a youth drunk with its own play and with delight in an activity which is an end in itself, youth freed from the miserly, severe and utilitarian laws of its usual work, cooperating and joyful in the most varied forms of competition designed to produce friendship, not to offend it." The Pope moves on to the usual celebration of youth as an "image and hope of a new, ideal world in which feelings of brotherhood and order reveal peace to us at last." He says young people are fortunate because "they are on an ascending path." The Pope, however, does not ignore Catholic doctrine, and concludes that "sport must be an incentive towards the realization of man's full capacity; it must tend to go beyond itself and reach the transcendent levels of that same humanity on which it has conferred no static perfection, but a tension towards the perfection of the whole." The speech ended with a quotation from the cyclist, Merckx.

A statement by Avery Brundage, the President of the International Olympic Committee, chimes in exactly with Pope Paul's glorification of sport, and draws out all the theological and paratheological meanings of the Pope's address. If one removes the limited reservations the Pope had put on sport as an ultimate ideal, it can be given a religious or semi-religious value. "The olympic spirit" Lord Brundage says, "is the most wide-

[11] R.I., 1969, p.659.
[12] O.R., 20 February 1965.

spread religion of our time, a religion that bears within itself the nucleus of all others."[13]

If one analyses Pope Paul's speech, one can see that none of the four qualities for which the Pope praises youth is a moral good, that is, a virtue; beauty least of all. That youth is "drunk with its own play" cannot be grounds for satisfaction, since religion forbids disproportionateness and drunkenness of any sort, except the sober drunkenness of the Holy Spirit. The demeaning of work on the grounds that it is, apparently, bound to utilitarian laws, seems to overlook the fact that work is in essence a moral activity which can be an occasion for the exercise of many virtues. To say sport is an end unto itself is incomprehensible from the Catholic point of view, since in fact no human activity can be an end in itself, because man himself is not an end unto himself. The true happiness of youth cannot be identified with being on an ascending path; nor can progress in sport be identified with human progress; if anything, it represents the progress of a human being, in accordance with the distinction between these two concepts drawn by St. Thomas. Nor can sport go beyond itself and reach transcendent levels, since it cannot get beyond its own nature and is not part of man's spiritual development. The Pope's final proposition is absolutely correct; sport is not the whole of life, or a religion. But in making this qualification, it ceases to be possible to recognize any kind of specifically moral character to sport: all activities in human life can be a step on the road to perfection, and so can sport, but they all are such in so far as the will can make them play a part in the attainment of a moral goal: they are none of them steps to perfection in themselves, but only by the moral decisions of the will. One must take care not to confuse the natures of things and thus take sport as a form of spirituality. The *Osservatore Romano* forgot this when it said: "Sport benefits from the paschal mystery and becomes an instrument of elevation."[14] Since revelation contains not the tiniest possible reference to any sporting activity on the part of Christ, the paper attempts, in a confusing and imprecise way, to push sport into the mystery of Easter.

---

[13] O.R., 27 July 1972.
[14] O.R., 1 January 1972.

103. Somatolatry in practice.

Events at the 1972 Munich Olympics sharply contrasted with the worship of sport typical of the modern world and at least partly supported by the Church; they contrasted particularly with the spirit of philanthropy and universal friendship which the Olympics are supposed to foster.[15] Obsessive competition and national hatreds were in fact the dominant themes at the games, not philanthropy or humanity. In Baron Coubertin's original scheme, the Olympics were meant to be a competition between individuals, not states, but now contests and victories are seen as those of Russia, America, Italy and so on. The shouting, whistling, or cheering crowds at the contests are divided and divisive. As for honest collaboration, eighteen judges were dismissed for having favored athletes of one side or another and many of the competitors were banned from the games for having used forbidden drugs and stimulants.

The contrast that really dismayed the world was the atrocious and treacherous slaughter of the whole Israeli team by Palestinian terrorists, and the appalling subsequent decision not to suspend the Olympics. The reason given was that "a criminal act must not prevail over the spirit of sport." This is the usual illegitimate comparison of persons with things. It was not a question of letting crime prevail over the spirit of sport, which is in any case a confused idea that everyone can accept precisely because of its confusion, but of respecting and honoring the victims, and not going on as if the dead had not been killed and the assassins were not assassins. This lack of humanity and respect shows the irreligious spirit of the modern Olympics when compared with the ancient.

To judge this modern somatolatry fairly we should remember that factional hatreds often flared up in the Roman circus and the Byzantine hippodrome. Vitellius is notorious for putting the enemies of his team, the Blues, to death; and the people of Constantinople went on the rampage on several occasions, killing and even burning down half the city. Sporting rivalries were quite lively between Christian people in the Middle Ages. Even the religious confraternities, that existed for purposes of devotion and for works of mercy, indulged in jealousies and

---

[15] The Moscow Olympics of 1980 were not attended by the United States, and the Los Angeles ones of 1984 were not attended by Russia.

rivalries until quite recent times. But the point I am making here is not that ugly human passions are a twentieth century novelty. Such passions can concentrate around noble or ignoble objects, and even take over religion and turn it into a heartless and angry hatred. The novelty today is the tendency to detach these passions from their real and merely physical origins, and to put them on a higher level and thus dignify them by putting them into contact with religion, and even with the Christian mystery.

Sport does not of itself have anything to do with the perfecting of the human being or with his destiny, and is of no assistance in attaining either, since excellence in physical attainments is quite compatible with a weakening of the subordination of these lower powers to reason. It is only the exercise of the will that confers any worth on the exercise of physical strength, inasmuch as an exercise of the will can increase the power of a man's reason and the extent of his moral freedom. One should not imagine there is any continuum between the physical and moral orders. There is a leap involved, that only the moral will can make.

104. The penitential spirit and the modern world. Reduction of abstinence and fasts.

The penitential element and the ascetic demands of the Catholic religion have retreated as a necessary consequence of the advance of somatolatry. The retreat seems to have begun with the special indult of 1941 that suspended Friday abstinence from meat, and all fasting except on Ash Wednesday and Good Friday, for the duration of the war. It was not really a retreat, but a normal adaptation of a principle to changed circumstances. The general shortage of food during the war made it difficult to obtain foods that conformed to the Church's requirements, and also decreased the absolute amount of food people were eating. The Church's fasts did actually cut into what people normally ate, as will be realized if one recalls that fasting meant having only one full meal a day, besides a piece of bread in the morning and a light snack at night. Types of food were also laid down, with various sorts being excluded from daily consumption. The eucharistic fast, which is a sign of reverence for the Blessed Sacrament rather than an act of penance, was also mitigated from the time of the introduction of evening

Masses in 1953. Eventually people who had once had to fast from midnight were only obliged to abstain from food for one hour before receiving Holy Communion. The original grounds for relaxing the penitential fasts were the weakness of the modern generation when confronted with increasing war time food shortages and with the general sufferings war imposed. But later, well after the war, penitential discipline was definitively relaxed in 1966 by the abolition of Friday abstinence from meat, except on the Fridays of Lent, and in 1973 the eucharistic fast was reduced, at least in the case of sick people, to a quarter of an hour.[16] Today any kind of Friday abstinence has in fact disappeared. Thus, in the space of a few years, the discipline of fasting has lost all its rigor and then almost vanished. Yet once, as can be seen from Church history, old customs and turns of phrase, fasting was not only a universal practice, but something laid down in civil law, and was the subject of negotiations between governments and the Holy See.

This relaxation produced two effects. One was verbal. The meaning of the word "fast" has changed from going without food for a significant period, so that one had an empty stomach, to meaning merely not eating even if only for a few minutes. Thus in the new sense one can eat one's fill and then be fasting, and as such go to Holy Communion.

The second effect has been to falsify the liturgy, that is to deprive the liturgical formulas of their truth so that they now describe the reverse of what the Church actually practices. The dominant theme of Lent used to be the bodily fast, the Lenten preface saying for instance: *Deus qui corporali ieiunio vitia comprimis, mentem elevas, virtutem largiris et praemia.*[17] But the preface of the *Novus Ordo* only recognizes a very general sort of Lenten fast.[18] On the Tuesday of the first week of Lent one used to pray *ut mens nostra tuo desiderio fulgeat, quae se carnis maceratione castigat*[19] but in current Lenten practice there are no

---

[16] O.R., 1 April 1973.

[17] "O God who by bodily fasting dost repress our faults, raise our minds and grant virtue and its rewards."

[18] The *Novus Ordo* provides four Lenten prefaces, of which the fourth is the traditional one, as just quoted by the author. [Translator's note.]

[19] "That our mind, which controls itself by the weakening of the flesh, may shine forth in its desire for thee."

macerations, and the new liturgical formulas have abandoned the idea, even though it comes straight from St. Paul.[20] The collect for the Saturday of the second week used similarly to say: *ut castigatio carnis assumpta ad nostrarum vegetationem transeat animarum.*[21] The problem of these falsified liturgical texts, at odds as they were with the Church's new practice, was solved by the changing of the texts themselves, so that while remnants of the old system can still be found in them, the general inspiration comes from the modernized views on penance and conforms to the modern world's distaste for mortification.[22]

Fasting has a definite doctrinal basis in Catholicism: it is a particular application of the general duty of mortification, which in turn comes from the doctrine of original sin. Natural inclinations could only be safely trusted, rather than checked, if nature had not been spoilt and left in its concupiscence. Pelagius and Vigilantius derive their doctrine from this same denial of original sin, and in his bitter polemic against Vigilantius, St. Jerome justifiably mocked his opponent by calling him Dormitantius, essentially meaning that he had not woken up to the real condition of human nature. All the reasons for fasting given by theologians stem essentially from the fact that fallen man must be mortified, in order that he may come to life as a new creature. Purely philosophical mortification, as practiced by oriental sects, has no such foundation: they chastise the body for what might be called gymnastic reasons, so that it does not encumber the mind as it otherwise would. All this can be done without any religious motives.

Beyond any such considerations, penitential exercises in Catholicism are principally an expression of sorrow for faults. This sorrow, which is an act of will, constitutes the interior virtue of penance, but given the dual nature of man whereby the spirit does not move without moving the body, exterior penance

---

[20] I Corinthians, 9:27.

[21] "That the chastening of the flesh we have taken on may turn to the nourishing of our souls."

[22] Another sign of the decline in the penitential spirit is the abolition of the period preparatory to Lent, marked by Septuagesima, Sexagesima and Quinquagesima Sundays.

is the necessary accompaniment of interior, and indeed is the
same as interior penance, inasmuch as it is done by the whole
man.

Seen in this light, fasting is an important part of penance;
and it should be remembered that when Christ talks about
"doing justice" he sums up the works of justice under the three
heads of almsgiving, prayer and fasting, which are, as St.
Augustine explains, representative of benevolence, the desire for
God and the control of concupiscence, each being understood
in the widest sense.[23]

In his sermon at Santa Sabina on Ash Wednesday 1967,
Paul VI recalled the Church's teaching that penance is necessary
both for repentance, human nature being fallen, and as a reparation for sins. Fasting is not only a perfecting of the natural
virtue of sobriety, known to the pagans, but something proper
to the Christian religion, which, having made man aware of his
profound evils, has also provided the remedies for them. The
pleasures of taste (which are the part of concupiscence under
consideration here) can indeed be reconciled with sobriety, but
Christianity sees in them a sensual tendency that diverts man
from his true goal, and, in accordance with the knowledge it has
of what lies within a man, Christianity blocks that tendency
before the evil takes hold.

105. The new penitential discipline.

The reform of the rules about fasting actually seems to
change the nature of the restriction by removing the element of
an afflicting of the flesh that was previously so openly admitted,
even in the liturgy, and leaving only the element of regular
moral conduct. But penance involves not merely abstaining
from sumptuous eating, but a cutting down on ordinary sobriety, with a double aim in view: to strengthen the mind's failing
moral energies in its struggle with "the law of the members"[24]
and to expiate the faults that even good people fall into because
of inherited weaknesses.[25] Given that the Church is one body
with many members all of which are united among themselves
and with Christ their head, it is also true that a Christian's

---

[23] *De perfectione vitae hominis*, Ch. VIII, 18 in P.L., 44, 300.

[24] Romans, 7:23.

[25] See Manzoni's pages on fasting in *Osservazioni sulla morale cattolica*, ed. cit. Vol.II, p.284ff.

works of penance are an imitation of, and a sharing in, the penance done by an innocent Christ for a sinful humanity; nor is this reality lessened by the fact that such works derive the whole of their value from the works of Christ himself.

The reform of penitential discipline was accompanied by the denigration of the historical Church that goes hand in hand with the whole process of modernization. In modern times, superficial and irreligious writers have derided the Catholic discipline regarding abstinence, that had been expounded by all the Fathers of the Church in works especially devoted to the subject, often of the highest quality, and that had been unanimously followed for century upon century by thoughtful and obedient generations. These writers failed to distinguish between the depth, beauty and truth contained in the Church's laws, and abuses which are bound to occur in this as in any other religious activity; they failed to recognize the important principle that a doctrine should be judged by its logical consequences rather than by the actions of those who fail to live up to it. The ridicule to which the Church's laws about food have been subjected stems from the world's general distaste for the mortification of the senses and takes as its pretext the fact that such laws can be followed merely materially without attending to, or intending, the high moral purposes to which they are directed. Some Christians, in short, concentrate on this part of the general penitential attitude recommended by the Church and isolate it from the rest. This element then appears incongruous in lives which are otherwise devoted to worldly concerns and pleasures. Worldly and irreligious minds, confronted with the incongruity of these elements of penance, then take the opportunity to mock them and dispense with penance altogether.

The important fact about the present state of the Church is, however, that this superficial spirit, that undervalues and ridicules mortification of the senses, has spread to the clergy, who have thus lost any understanding of, or attachment to, the traditional discipline. To cite just one of the many examples I have collected, the October 1966 bulletin of St. Lawrence's Cathedral in Lugano made cheap fun of the alleged unimportance of the difference between a sole and a steak, or between fried food and salami. This is to ignore the differentiation between foods made both by the law of Moses and by the Church. It seems that the failure to distinguish between the different natures of things has spread even to food.

The grounds for distinguishing between different sorts of food were in part based on old physiological theories now out of date, and since the distinctions are merely a matter of ecclesiastical law they can be altered; with the expansion of Catholicism outside Europe, injunctions to abstain from certain types of food that are not even available in some countries were incongruous and gave grounds for reform. All that being as it may, the Church has no reason to be ashamed of its legislation or to think its doctrine ridiculous; it was in fact perfectly reasonable, based on nature, commanded by Christ and sanctioned by the obedience of generations that were not rougher or less fragile than the present, merely more thoughtful and less sensual.

106. Origins of the reform of penance.

The reform of penitential discipline was driven by two motives, one anthropological and pseudo-spiritual, the other libertarian.

The anthropological consideration was based on a false conception of the reciprocal relations between body and soul. It was thought that bodily gestures could not be expressions of acts of the soul, thus revealing a failure to grasp the nature of the union between the two metaphysical elements that make up man. It was forgotten that acts of the soul do not attain their full authenticity if they remain unexpressed and without effect on sensory experience. It is indeed possible to observe a law designed to mortify the sensually inclined will without actually mortifying that will, that is, it is possible to be materially obedient to a law without accepting what it is aimed to achieve. But this is not peculiar to laws about abstinence; it extends to every moral injunction: one can do just things without being just, observe the requirements of chastity without being chaste, do loving things without being loving, in fact one can play one's part in the theater of virtue while merely wearing virtue's mask and lacking the spirit on which all depends.

Even the material observance of the law produces some unintentional effect, due to the interconnection of all the elements that go to make up man; sensual impulses are less strong in a lean frame and their rebellion against the laws of the spirit is less violent.

The innovators' tendency to dismiss bodily penance is therefore mistaken. Fasting must certainly be accompanied by compunction of heart, and is indeed intended essentially to produce it, but even without such compunction, fasting has a salutary effect and is a reminder not to despise that particular virtue. The tendency the new laws have to refer one to interior mortification rather than to bodily fasts is therefore misguided insofar as it implies any undervaluing of bodily abstinence, which is of use to the whole man; and is even more unacceptable if it is designed to support the commonly held view that the keeping of laws is a hindrance to true penance and that it is hypocritical or materialistic for a Christian to mortify himself by keeping the Church's laws on fasting.

Besides cutting man in half, an insistence on non-bodily penance is not actually possible, because proud thoughts can hardly be got rid of without any external humbling, or irregular sensual desires without restraining the actions of the exterior senses, or the desire to overeat without cutting down on both extravagant and ordinary eating. Even when Christ so strongly condemned making a show of fasting, it was not because it necessarily involved an external form of mortification, but because it was done as a kind of proud display and out of human respect. So far is He from condemning even the observance of minute rules about food and external behavior, that He actually says they are necessary, in association with an interior attitude: *haec oportuit facere et illa non omittere*[26] thus bringing the two together. The evil lay in lacking the spirit, not in following the letter.

Since abstinence from food is only a means towards abstinence from sin, the two are clearly not of equal importance. It is the principle of obedience that gives bodily abstinence its importance: and that principle has been deprived of its force by the reform in the laws of penance through the reduction in the long periods during which abstinence had to be practiced to a mere two days, and through the leaving of all other penance to the supposedly enlightened and mature judgment of the faithful. When John XXIII put out an encyclical on penance, it proclaimed no fast nor even any obligatory day of abstinence, whether from food or secular pleasures. When Paul VI did pro-

---

[26] Matthew, 23:23. "These things should have been done without neglecting the others."

claim a Sunday of prayer and fasting in October 1971, many bishops made no mention of fasting in celebrating it, and left penance as something exclusively interior.

The movement from an explicit positive law to the general obligations of the moral law as the guide on these matters is analogous to what has happened concerning the reading of books.[27] Individuals are left to their private judgment, with liberty being valued above law. In replying to an objection, St. Thomas says that fasts were "not contrary to the liberty of the faithful, but serve instead to impede the slavery of sin."[28] Erasmus took up a position redolent of the spiritualistic heresies of the Middle Ages, making every Christian fast only when he felt the need of it, for the sake of the mortification it effects.

The adulation of liberty has become commonplace in post-conciliar theology and has even penetrated into question and answer columns in magazines. Mgr Ernesto Pisoni, for example, says in reply to a question: "It is simply a matter of a law that derives its justification and its moral value from the free will of the person who chooses to observe it in spirit, since the letter of it is easily got round." A priest here suggests a false understanding of the moral law to a readership of half a million. A man's actions receive their value from their conformity to the law, whereas the value of the law is here being derived from the free act of the man who chooses to obey it. There is a double sophistry involved: first, that the will ought to reject any external law, that is that the dependent ought to be independent; second, that the individual Christian ought to dissociate himself from the bulk of the Church, which is the collective mystical body of Christ, and set himself up as a law unto himself.

107. Penitence and obedience.

Relaxation of penitential practices has been based on the presupposition that the faithful now have a more mature ascetic sense, and on the desire to spiritualize and refine the sorts of mortification involved. The presupposition is at odds with the facts. Christian populations today are generally immersed in an abundance of sensory pleasures and worldly satisfactions; while even those who are not are on the road to the same state of

---

[27] See paragraphs 71 and 72.
[28] *Summa Theologica*, II,II,q.147,a.3 *ad 3*.

abundance. The fact is that the Church's lessening of corporal privations, ostensibly in order to increase interior denial, has led to an almost total disappearance of fasting from the ordinary life of Christian people. The English Cardinal Godfrey's idea that in the midst of this universal loss of the sense of penance, animals should be made to share in Lent, is simply an aberration.

As we have seen, the demise of laws in this matter has meant the overthrow of the value of obedience and the substitution of its opposite. The bulletin of St. Lawrence's Cathedral in Lugano for January 1967 says that as to "whether or not there should be ecclesiastical rules saying what one should or should not do: it is actually better that there should not be any." Elsewhere it is asserted, in comments on the Lombard bishops' pastoral letter abolishing abstinence and rules in these matters, that: "Penance is made free and therefore more meritorious."[29]

Three values are lost in this new teaching. First, the value of doing what the duty of penance requires from a motive of obedience to the Church, and through using the means the Church lays down. Second, the value that comes from performing a penitential act ecclesially in the way described in the traditional liturgy, leaving it to the Church to decide on the way the substance of the duty will be performed, rather than simply doing something individually. Third, the value of giving up one's own will as to the form of penance; that self-abnegation being itself a penance. These values, all of which depend on the fact that the will is bound to observe certain customs and times as laid down, are no longer appreciated as they were in the days when the permitted food was weighed out by ounces and people waited for church bells to ring to signal the end of a fast. The relevant Roman Congregation was asked if there was an obligation to observe particular penitential days, or merely to observe the number of days involved and replied favoring the latter view.[30] Times of corporal penance are thus left to the free choice of individual believers, and the fixed and sacred character of Ash Wednesday and Good Friday ceases to be the immovable thing it had seemed to be.

The idea that abstinence can be replaced by works of mercy undermines the notion of Lenten penance, but has been insti-

[29] Diocesi di Milano, 1967, p.130.
[30] O.R., 9 March 1967.

tutionalized in such things as the "Lenten Sacrifice," a money offering held to be equivalent to corporal mortification. But a monetary sacrifice is no more appropriate to the times than the fasting abandoned on the grounds of its inappropriateness to the times. Christian societies are in large measure rich and well to do, so the monetary offerings are relatively trifling, and of course it is always harder to deny the body than it is to give up some part of one's wealth. The Roman decree of 1966 explicitly confuses the penitential and the non-penitential when it says: "Penitential works can include abstaining from food that one particularly likes; an act of spiritual or corporal charity; the reading of a passage of Sacred Scripture; the giving up of an entertainment or amusement and other acts of mortification." Reading is not an act of mortification, nor is a work of charity. Once the concept of penance is lost, everything becomes a penance. Even in John Paul II's Lenten message for 1984, Lent is made to consist of works of mercy, and fasting does not appear at all.

CHAPTER XI

RELIGIOUS AND SOCIAL MOVEMENTS

108. Renunciation of political and social action.

Since contemporary society is dominated by the idea of possessing the world through the technological application of science to nature, with a view to controlling that nature, the whole of political life has assumed a new character. The *subject* now acting in society is the mass of individuals united in search of the useful; and the *end* society pursues is maximal production and distribution of what it deems useful. The change might be summed up in the *renunciation* by religion of any political and social action.

In the nineteenth century political parties had little organization and were largely based on religious attitudes. The whole liberal age was marked by a split: one party favored the separation of civil life from religious matters, thinking the latter should be left to individual conscience as having nothing to contribute to the public welfare; the other side resisted that trend and thought of religion as being not only part of the historical tradition of the nation, but also, at a suprapolitical and suprahistorical level, as something morally necessary for life in community. The fact of the struggle between the Church and the modern state, the latter setting itself up as an autonomous source of values and thus cutting itself off from the religious roots on which it had grown, explains why the political struggles of the age involved religious values, and took the form either of an attempt to maintain those values within the body of society, or an attempt to confine them within the sphere of individual choice.

The popes of the last century encouraged a great expansion of political and public activity by Catholic groups, either through the creation of distinct political parties that called

themselves Catholic and were inspired by the Church's teachings, or through the establishment of special organizations for
special activities, whether cultural, sporting, charitable or economic.

The struggle of Catholics in the then United Kingdom, a
non-Catholic state, does not fit this pattern, as the Catholics
concerned were mainly Irish and their action was a kind of
prolongation of the wars of religion, as well as being compounded with aspirations to national independence. Catholic
parties operating in states that still gave constitutional recognition to Catholicism are the ones we have in mind. In France
under Louis Philippe, when the monarchy had turned against
the Church, Montalembert and Dupanloup contended for the
rights of religion, but on the new grounds of a right to full freedom pure and simple. The *raison d'être* of the Conservative-
Catholic party in Switzerland was the defense of the rights and
privileges of the Church. It pursued its aim so fervently that the
Catholic cantons decided to band together in a separate league
and leave the Swiss confederation, which actually led to a civil
war. A widespread and active organization named after Pius IX,
the *Piusverein* kept up political action in the form of large
popular meetings. In Belgium and Holland, Catholic forces
were organized in strong organizations that often played a
dominant role in directing national life. The Catholic minority
in the German Empire was impressive in its numbers, powerful
in its organization, secure in its united purpose and strengthened by the high caliber of its leaders, and was able to resist
Bismarck's anti-Catholic policies, forcing him to give in to its
opposition and repeal the laws of the *Kulturkampf.* The Italian
Catholics' status as an ineligible political minority,[1] which was
the result of the dispute between Church and state regarding the
papacy's temporal sovereignty, prevented them from displaying
their real strength. When their ineligibility was removed, however, the Catholic "Popular Party" founded by the priest Luigi

---

[1] Due to two factors: that the papacy from 1870 to 1905 urged
     Catholics in Italy not to cooperate with the usurping new Italian
     state and thus to boycott elections; and that until 1906 the only
     people eligible to vote were the wealthiest ten percent of the male
     population, probably the least Catholic group in Italy. [Translator's
     note.]

Sturzo briefly exercised an important influence in the life of the country, or at least showed what it would have been capable of.[2]

The direction taken after Vatican II meant that Catholic political and social organizations became colorless and, as it were, lost their salt. "If the salt shall lose its savor ...." I am well aware that this is part of a general process whereby all political parties, having lost much of their particular character, are left with certain basic political goals that they share with one another. In the case of the Catholic parties, this process means that having ceased to defend the Church's freedom on any basis unacceptable to other parties, they now defend it on the basis of freedom for all points of view whatsoever.

109. Disappearance or transformation of Catholic parties.

All Catholic parties have thus reduced or watered down the aims for which they were founded, or else have disappeared altogether from the theater of national life. The *Mouvement Républicain Populaire*, that arose in France after the war through the efforts of Maurice Schumann, is an example of one that has vanished.[3] In Switzerland the Catholic Conservative Party abandoned its old name, too redolent of its original character, and calling itself instead the "Christian Democratic Party," adopted a vaguely Christian ideal that includes all the principles of liberal political philosophy. In the canton of Ticino, for example, it has become the "Democratic Popular Party," a name which is devoid of any specific Catholic reference, although making an incongruous double reference to the idea of the people. Following the directions of the local bishop, the party adopted and promoted the policy of changing the constitutional status of the canton from Catholic to a canton of mixed religion. An analogous process took place in Germany, where the *Christliche Demokratische Partei*, the successor of the famous *Centrum*[4] came to have a Catholic and Protestant membership and to adopt the

---

2 Like all other parties, it went into oblivion after Mussolini became Prime Minister in 1922. [Translator's note.]

3 See R.Richet, *La démocratie chrétienne en France. Le Mouvement républicain populaire*, Besançon 1980. To graph the extent of the change, it ought to be remembered that in the first years after the war, the Movement was the strongest party in France.

4 Catholic Centre Party. [Translator's note.]

political principles of liberalism. Spain, which had a political system excluding parties, has witnessed the rise of movements since the death of General Franco that compound a Catholic inspiration with the principles of the modern state. In Belgium and Holland, the collapse of the grounds for the long standing antagonism to the liberalism of the modern state has meant that the formerly very well organized and powerful Catholic movements have similarly lost their savor. Even opposition to communism has been replaced by solidarity with the whole working class, and Catholic social and political movements have adopted positions inclining towards liberalism and communism, while the condemnations of Pius XI and Pius XII are set aside.

The most outstanding example of this renunciation of Catholic character is that of "Christian Democracy" in Italy, which, although it had been in power for thirty years, gradually weakened its opposition to the socialism and communism the nation had given it an imposing mandate to oppose in the elections of 18 April 1948.[5] A measure of just how bitter the opposition to communism was, and of how grave a danger the country was believed to be facing in 1948, is the fact that even the gates of the most strictly enclosed nuns were unlocked so that the sisters could vote against *Hannibal ad portas*.[6] In no democratic country in Europe has the change in political climate and social mentality been as radical as in Italy; which is reflected in the fact that the attitude of the party has changed

---

[5]   The D.C.'s weak opposition to the introduction of divorce was highly significant. When the introduction of the Fortuna-Baslini divorce bill was being discussed in parliament, G. Gonella deplored "the absence of any governmental statement of policy in the chamber. The Government has stated its policy on every bill proposed since 1948, but today, with 15 ministers in office, Christian Democracy has not a word to say." At the national congress of the party, the same Gonella demanded that if the bill were not dropped the Christian Democrats should resign and bring down the government. It seemed to him impossible that with all its strength Christian Democracy should not be able to prevent what a secularist and anti-clerical Italy had rejected for a century. Fr. Gemelli and Mgr Olgiati had also denounced the failings of the Popular Party's program in 1919. It was suggested in *Renovatio*, 1979, pp.402-6 that the Christian Democrat Party should change its name as there was nothing particularly Christian in its activities.

[6]   "Hannibal at the gates."

from one of energetic and combative opposition to secularization, to an attitude of acquiescence and accommodation. In 1948 the great goal of the party was the defeat of socialism and communism, but today it is the reaching of an "historic compromise" with the old enemy.

Ever since the famous statement of Pope Gelasius at the end of the fifth century, which was later reaffirmed by Boniface VIII,[7] the Church has explicitly recognized that it is not the competent authority in political matters, and that in them, laity and clergy are subject to the temporal sovereign; but the Church does claim authority in the whole spiritual field, and in matters that have a spiritual side to them, with clergy and laity being subject to it in these. Since political activity is a means towards the achievement of man's moral good, the Church also claims that even though it is not directly involved in such activity, it can nevertheless pass judgment on the laws of a political community, should those laws hinder the achievement of that goal, or violate natural justice, or infringe the Church's own rights. In a situation where sovereignty is lodged in the whole body of citizens, as it is in most modern regimes, the Church can resist these unjust laws by charting a course of action that Catholic citizens should follow in using their political rights, while avoiding any spirit of hatred or sedition. This view was reaffirmed by John XXIII in his encyclical *Pacem in Terris*, which shows how religious and civil duties can coincide since the good of justice, which is the object of moral activity, is itself a constituent element of the common good, which is the object of political activity. Because of this overlap, Roman Pontiffs have declared the state's law null and void in some historical emergencies. The most recent instance is Pius XI's annulling of the anti-religious laws in Mexico in 1926. Quite apart from that procedure, Catholics have a right to oppose legislation contrary to natural law, and to make use of what share in legislative power they may have while doing so; and the Church has the duty to oppose unjust laws by calling the laity to action.

In our own time, Catholic laity have on occasion carried the day, under the leadership of the hierarchy; but now the Church has almost completely given up using the rights it has in these matters, and has instilled into the laity within each

---

[7] Pope from 1294 to 1303. [Translator's note.]

country that same spirit of surrender it has adopted in its own
direct relations with national governments.

110. The Church's surrender in the Italian campaigns for divorce and abortion.

I will give two examples of this surrender, that so contrasts
with the militant self-assurance of the older Catholic movements, illustrating the examples, as promised, from official
sources rather than from private expressions of opinion.

The first is the fact that the Italian lay movement that opposed divorce, and tried to have it repealed by referendum, was
left isolated and unsupported by the Italian hierarchy.[8] There
was a sharp contrast between the ready assertiveness of innovating priests[9] who openly defended divorce at public meetings,
and the unhelpful and discontented reserve of the bishops, who
seemed to accept the considerations of worldly prudence put
forth by those who opposed the referendum. Giulio Andreotti[10]
says that Paul VI was doubtful about the outcome of the referendum, but essentially opposed to the idea of having one at all.
In fact the Pope said that "*he could not prevent* a group of Italian
Catholics making free use of the means provided by the Italian
constitution to try to cancel a law they *held* to be bad." It would
have been more appropriate for the Pope to encourage, rather
than merely *not prevent*, a democratically legitimate and religiously obligatory movement of Catholics inspired by a spirit of
justice to oppose a law that the conscience of the nation had
rejected up to that point. Forecasts of failure should not have
deterred him from fighting; what makes us safe is the doing of
our duty, not the having of the odds in our favor. But as I have
said, the laity were abandoned by a hierarchy that was less con-

---

[8]   A divorce bill was introduced in the Italian parliament in 1965,
      passed into law in 1970 and upheld in a national referendum in
      1974. [Translator's note.]

[9]   Nominally Catholic magazines like *Il Regno* (Bologna) and *Il
      Gallo* (Genoa) campaigned in favor of divorce. About a hundred
      staff and students at the Catholic University of Milan protested at
      an article by Mgr G.B. Guzzetti that "claims to say once and for all
      what the Church's teaching is." They claimed that "the Catholic
      cannot impose on others what he does through faith."

[10] *A ogni morte di Papa*, Milan 1980, p.121.

cerned to uphold a principle of the natural law than to divine the state of public opinion, in order to follow it.

The Archbishop of Milan, Giovanni Cardinal Colombo, formulated the principle of surrender[11] in these three propositions: first, "A priest who spoke against holding a referendum would not be in step with the Italian episcopate"; second, "A priest who personally collected signatures in favor of holding a referendum would be out of step"; third, "Those priests who try to encourage lay Catholics to act in accordance with their Christianly enlightened conscience are in step with the bishops." Note that it is presented as a matter of keeping in step with bishops when one's first duty in the matter was to inform one's conscience in the light of moral law; that is what it was the clergy's duty to preach, holding to that frankness that led their nineteenth century predecessors to prison for defending points that were not, after all, part of the natural law. Note, secondly, the ban on priests using their own legal right to collect signatures, even though in performance of their religious duties. Note, lastly, the sending of people to their private consciences to make a decision on a matter of natural and positive divine law, that the Church should itself decide. The Cardinal's speech seems to be a refusal by the Church to perform the task of teaching incumbent on it, as the light of the nations. If the *Osservatore Romano* is right to say[12] that religious and civil matters are to be kept separate, it is wrong when it defends the Church's abstention in the divorce controversy; divorce is a mixed religious and civil matter, and anyone who defends its abstention is practically asserting the Church should abstain even in those mixed matters in which it has always claimed competence.

This fundamental refusal to fight for important points of Christian teaching, and for their inclusion in the law, when those points are embarrassing or controversial, is patently obvious in the same Cardinal Colombo's attitude at the time the country was agitated over the proposal to legalize abortion. Preaching in his cathedral, the Archbishop of Milan declared that "the bishops are not trying to get the law to enforce the observance of a moral norm if it were no longer something rec-

---

[11] When it was being debated whether to hold a referendum in order to overturn the law that had introduced divorce. [Translator's note.]

[12] O.R., 5 May 1971.

ognized as such by the majority of consciences."[13] The intrinsically contrasting terms *majority* and *consciences* are put together
in this text. The Archbishop opposes the law introducing abortion, which Vatican II had called a "horrendous crime," because
he thinks there is a majority against it, and thus appears to imply that if a majority of countable consciences were in favor of
this particular crime, the bishops would keep quiet and that
Catholics, as citizens, ought then to reconcile themselves to the
iniquity. Judging by the Archbishop's sermon, it would seem
that the inadmissibility of a civil law depends solely on the consent of the majority; that is, that morality is a human creation
and that in the face of a majority, resistance ought to cease, or at
least tuck itself away in the lonely refuge of a private conscience.

111. The Church and communism in Italy.
The condemnations of 1949 and 1959.

The Church's renunciation of its involvement in civil life
takes the form of referring the Christian to his own opinions
and judgment about the conduct of public life. The Italian
bishops, followed by the Italian Church Assembly of 1976, have
stated that the faithful have complete freedom of choice in political matters, with the sole proviso that their choice be coherent with their religious faith. That is what the Church has always said, ever since democratic constitutions lodged sovereignty in the bulk or in the whole of the citizen body. The difference is, that the decision as to what is actually coherent with
Catholic faith is removed from the hands of the Church's
magisterium, which had decided in the past, and left instead
entirely in the hands of the community. At the assembly of
1976 Fr. Sorge approved the formula: "Join whatever you like,
but stay Christian," adding that the judgment as to whether one
was a Christian or not could not be made individually or arbitrarily "but in harmony with that of the entire Christian community."[14] The replacement of the Church's directions by public
opinion is obvious.[15] Does this expression mean the Church as
an organic union of hierarchy and laity, or the whole Christian

---

[13] O.R., 26 February 1976.

[14] *Corriere della Sera*, 5 November 1976.

[15] Readers in English speaking countries should remember that in the
Italian context almost the entire population is, in one sense, "the
Christian community." [Translator's note.]

body, which is supposed to be manifesting its faith through a majority? Or through some other means? The limit the Church imposes on political freedom of action is analogous to the one she imposes on freedom of theological speculation and on any other sort of liberty, and is designed to guarantee an autonomy that stays within the bounds of Christian law. Since political freedom of choice can range over a very wide area before crossing these bounds, the Church's specifications as to what they are, are few and far between.

The most important specification of this sort is the Holy Office's decree of 28 June 1949 and the extension added to it on 25 March 1959 under John XXIII. The first lays down an excommunication of anyone who professes atheist and materialist communism, and condemns supporting the communist party. The second condemns anyone who votes for the communist party or for any party supporting it. It is clear the second widened the nature of the offense. The first allowed for a distinction between persons professing communism (which had been condemned by Pius XI) and persons who merely supported communists without necessarily believing in communism; and most supporters were of that sort. The second decree is not concerned with beliefs, but with the external act of voting communist. It also condemns a coalition with the communists by any other party, thus affecting the whole political process in those democratic countries having several parties and therefore habitually governed by coalitions.

This political intervention by the Church aroused open conflicts between Italian bishops and the civil authorities. The most famous was the case of Mgr Fiordelli, the Bishop of Prato, who publicly condemned the civil marriage of a communist as concubinage and was taken to court, convicted and then acquitted. When the conviction was announced, Cardinal Lercaro ordered the tolling of a funeral dirge by the church bells of his diocese and Pius XII canceled the ceremonies for the anniversary of his coronation. When an electoral alliance was made with the communists at Aosta, the bishops suspended the Corpus Christi procession; in Sicily Cardinal Ruffini took part in the election campaign, to oppose a particular Christian Democrat candidate, and at Bari the archbishop, Mgr Niccodemo, refused to allow the communist mayor to attend Church services, saying his presence was incompatible with the sacred character of the ceremony. In this last case, it seems to me a distinc-

tion should have been made between the mayor's public and
private capacities and between the city of Bari as a moral entity
and the majority controlling it at a particular moment. It is a
principle of constitutional law that members of parliament not
only represent the people who voted for them, but all the electors. Popes receive the Rome city council each year, even when
there is a communist majority.

112. The Church and communism in France.

We have seen how the Italian bishops have moved from active resistance to abdication in regard to communism. The
transition brought the Italian Church to the point the French
Church had already reached previously when its bishops proclaimed that Christians could take any political course compatible with their own consciences. Since this book is not a
history of the Catholic social movement, I will assume my readers are aware of the general history of that movement in France
before the council, and I will confine my remarks to commenting on the French bishops' document *sur son dialogue avec les
militants chrétiens qui ont fait l'option socialiste.*[16]

The very form of the document constitutes an abdication of
the bishops' authority to teach, direct and give orders. It is designed merely "to echo," and leave intact, the opinions of a
working class that is assumed to be a homogeneous whole. The
Catholic social movement is entirely ignored.

It is impossible to disguise the difference between this style
and that of the papal documents we have referred to in the preceding section. The bishops' document contains various
propositions taken from "Christian workers," who are all assumed to be communists, but no rebuttal or counter statement
except an occasional oblique and ambiguous remark. The
document is designed to help pro-communist Christians "from
within" their spiritual situation, as if the heart of Christianity
somehow lay concealed within their own opinions and merely
needed bringing out; and as if pastoral help could never involve
any opposition in principle to their views, or any possible renunciation of errors on their part, in short, a conversion.
Linked with this outlook, the document contains a confusion

---

[16] In *Documentation Catholique*, 29 May 1972, coll. 471ff. "On its
dialogue with Christians who have taken the socialist option."

between "the action of the Holy Spirit" and workers' agitation;[17] the communist movement, which is perfectly explicable by the ordinary historical forces that drive events, is taken as one of those movements that result from the supernatural impulses of the Holy Spirit:[18] in short the document turns the social struggles of the age into a religious phenomenon. This imprecise, novel and immanentist thinking fails to distinguish between the Holy Spirit and the workings of Providence that draw human events to their predestined goal, and fails to see that the Holy Spirit is the soul *of the Church*, but *not of the human race* as such. The French bishops took these guidelines of 1972 as the basis of their behavior in 1981, when they refused to make any intervention in the electoral campaign that brought a socialist and communist coalition government to power in France, having a platform that heralded the establishment of a frankly atheistic society of Marxist origin. In their document of 10 February 1981 the bishops declared their neutrality regarding all parties and said that they did "not want to influence the personal decisions of the faithful": as if political events were a complete irrelevance, and the Church's magisterium had no duty to form and direct people's consciences. In a further document of 1 June 1981 the bishops profess an absolute neutrality, that is, an inability to judge the various French parties by reference to any absolute Christian standards, adducing as their reason the fact that Christians are to be found in all parts of the political spectrum. They do "not want to support any group or *oppose anyone*, but to draw attention to the essential values involved." Since they see these values in all parties they cannot proscribe or prescribe anything.

The unique character of communism that *Divini Redemptoris* and the other papal decrees had deemed important enough to justify giving orders as to how Christians should behave towards it, is here subjected to a so-called process of re-examination and "depthing," leading to the conclusion that at

---

[17] The communist movement's being thus an effect of the Holy Spirit makes it easier to understand the introduction of Karl Marx into a *Missel des dimanches* (Sunday Mass booklet) promulgated by the French bishops, shortly after the council and again in 1983 in connection with the centenary of Marx's death, where on p.139 we find a commemoration of the founder of communism on 14 March, the day of his death.

[18] Sections 16-17 of the document.

bottom the opposing Christian and communist conceptions of
life have so much in common that there is room for them to
recognize each other's merits. The formula for this is *des valeurs
communes sont donc perçues différemment selon le milieu auquel
on appartient.*[19]

This is an implicit denial of Catholic principle. The document robs man of his capacity to appreciate values in themselves
and asserts he can only perceive them in his own manner; which
in this case does not mean in accordance with the characteristics
of his own psyche, but with those of his social class. Since in
their view the values in question are identical, and all differences
stem from the way they are perceived, the bishops are free to
assert that two contradictory views of reality are merely different
perceptions of the same thing. This form of subjectivism is derived from the Marxist view that perceptions spring from one's
social situation. The French bishops' statement thus fails to recognize the differences between the natures of things. Religion is
in their view not a principle, rather an interpretation and a
manner of speaking. Christian truth is no longer fundamental
and primary, but one interpretation of reality, destined to be
reconciled with other interpretations within a confused whole
which seems sometimes to be justice, and sometimes love.

The refusal to recognize the fundamental quality of the opposition between Christianity and Marxism separates this
document from the teaching of Pius XI, who calls communism
intrinsically evil. The refusal also shows that the framers of the
document favor socialism, because their refusal to admit the
essential perversity of communism is combined with an assertion of the intrinsic perversity of the capitalist system:[20] by refusing to condemn both socialism and capitalism they part company with papal teaching which, from *Rerum Novarum* to
Populorum Progressio, has condemned both equally.

Having mistakenly found the Holy Spirit and Jesus Christ[21]
in the dynamism of the working world, and having placed the
socialist option on an equal footing with Christian commitment, the document proceeds to another, final, confusion stating that when the struggle of Christian communists for greater
justice, fraternity and equality reaches the underlying common

---

[19] Section 29. "Common values are thus perceived differently according to the social setting to which one belongs."

[20] Section 21.

[21] Section 47.

ground that Christians and communists share, it meets, coming from the communist side *une forme réelle de contemplation et de vie missionaire.*[22] Marxist praxis and the class struggle thus take over even that highest place which has traditionally been allotted to contemplation.

113. Committed Christians.

The fundamental error of imagining that contradictions are fundamentally the same thing–different aspects of some fundamental good underlying them both–makes it possible to deprive the theses of the two rival schools of their specific character and thus to deny their opposition. Socialism contradicts two important articles of Catholic social teaching: the principles of private property and of harmony between social classes. John XXIII confirmed "the natural character of the right to property, even as regards the means of production," and hoped property would be more widely diffused,[23] while the French document, adopting a Marxist view, restricts the extent of Pope John's teaching by alleging that forms of property that affect the whole community and dominate the modern economy, and are owned by small numbers of people, are not to be classed as private property and not therefore to be protected under the guarantees of the natural law.

But the most obvious departure from Catholic social doctrine is the identification of the struggle for justice with a struggle between the classes, based on the assumption that justice can only be done by going beyond justice into a form of counter-justice. This in turn assumes that the social order is independent of the moral order, and that the latter must be transcended if we are to restore the former. The truth of the matter is that the provocation of class struggle is a kind of war conducted within each nation, which is intended, according to the teachings of Lenin and Stalin that communists have never rejected, to become a struggle of the international working class when circumstances are right, directed against all other classes throughout the world.

If the class struggle is the means of promoting justice and is also a kind of war, it follows that despite the Church's condem-

---

[22] Section 54. "A real form of contemplation and of missionary life."

[23] *Mater et Magistra*, No.113.

nation, the class struggle counts as a just war and is therefore permissible.

114. Weakening of antitheses.

The weakening of the antithesis between communism and Christianity, which leads logically to liberation theology as we will see in the following section, is due to two things: doctrinal dissent within communism, and the teachings of John XXIII in *Pacem in Terris*.

The first, the so-called breakup of communism, is reflected in the form of the statutes of various communist parties, omitting the requirement that members accept historical materialism, and admitting to the party people who take up the workers' cause under the influence of other philosophical or religious ideals.

This shift had already taken place within the Socialist International; when it was re-established at Frankfurt am Main in 1951, the ninth clause of its preamble laid down: "Democratic socialism is an international movement that does not require rigorous doctrinal uniformity. Whether socialists base their own convictions on Marxism or on other systems of social analysis, or whether they are inspired by religious or humanitarian principles, they all struggle for the same end: a system of social justice, greater prosperity, freedom and world peace."[24] By setting aside specifically Marxist principles such as historical materialism, the rejection of religion, the expropriation of the means of production and the class struggle, it becomes possible to put various heterogeneous movements together under a vague ideology of justice, prosperity and peace.

What the Frankfurt document does to socialism the French bishops' document does to Catholicism: it leaves specifics behind in order to put things on a more generic and confused basis. Justice in papal teaching is quite different from what it is in Marxism, since the popes envisage it as a wider sharing in the use of riches while Marxists envisage it as state ownership of all goods.

The meeting of Catholicism and Marxism has been much assisted by disagreements among Marxist theoreticians. To stay in France, one need only recall Garaudy's version, envisioning a polycentric democracy accompanying democratic centralism, a

---

[24] R.I., 1951, p.576.

version of communism that denies that centralization of power is the only way to install communism; and then there is Althusser who denies the exclusive primacy of economics usually taught by Marxists, and acknowledges a plurality of structures, with economic ones merely having a kind of dominance over the others.[25]

These variations do not effect the essence of communism. They are simply instances of the variety generated by any intellectual theory elaborating a fundamental idea. They could be likened to the different schools of theology, that make interpretations and deductions based on the primary content of faith. A wide field is open to dispute between Thomist, Scotist, Suarezian or Rosminian schools, since the Christian intellect is bound to the formulas of faith but free to speculate otherwise, and is not therefore bound to share the particular opinions of any school.

The various forms of Marxism cannot so enlarge its fundamental principles as to embrace its opposite, nor do they break up or alter its essence. The party, which is the historically influential force in Marxism, has always rejected any variant that would attack fundamental principles. When interviewed by the newspaper *La Croix*, the secretary general of the French communist party, Georges Marchais, stated unambiguously: *Nous ne voulons pas créer d'illusions sur ce point: entre le Marxisme et le christianisme il n'y a pas de conciliation possible, pas de convergence idéologique possible.*[26] This statement entirely accords with the views of President Mitterand, the head of the French socialist-communist coalition, expressed in his book *Ici et maintenant*[27] which is openly anti-religious. It asserts the complete *Diesseitigkeit*[28] of communism, that replaces man's other worldly destiny with a vision of a happiness to be had *here*, in this world, and *now*, not in a future life.

At the origins of the communist movement one finds Lenin saying: "Communists who form alliances with social democrats and Christians *do not cease* to be revolutionaries, because they

---

[25] For the variants of communism see M. Corvez, *Les structuralistes*, Paris, pp.156ff.

[26] "We don't want to create any illusions on this point: no coming to terms, no ideological convergence between Marxism and Christianity is possible."

[27] "Here and Now," Paris 1980.

[28] Immanence, this worldliness.

direct such cooperation towards the end of destroying bourgeois society."[29] This appeal to communist principle is parallel to the appeal to Catholic principle made by Paul VI in his apostolic letter of 14 May 1971 to Cardinal Roy: "A Christian cannot adhere to systems or ideologies that are radically opposed to his faith and his conception of man on substantial points." The *Osservatore Romano*'s denial of the difference between Christianity and Marxism in an article entitled *Cultura, pluralismo e valori*, is very odd. Supported by a very novel line of argument, the idea is there advanced that the opposition identified by Pius XI does not exist. "One must ask if the analytical grid that used to distinguish between a Catholic and a Marxist culture still exists." The author seems *quasi modo genitus infans*[30] and to be unaware of the existence of *Divini Redemptoris* and all the other relevant papal documents.

115. Principles and movements in *Pacem in Terris*.

It is nonetheless apparent that both Catholicism and communism have in fact departed from the logical integralism whereby their two views of life remain forever distinct, without any possibility of a *coincidentia oppositorum*.[31] The incentive for departure on the Catholic side came from a famous passage in John XXIII's encyclical *Pacem in Terris*: "It should be remembered that false philosophical doctrines on the nature, origin and destiny of the universe, and of man, cannot be identified with historical movements that have economic, social, cultural and political goals, even if these movements arose from those doctrines and have drawn, *and still draw*, inspiration from them. For the doctrines remain always the same, once they have been elaborated and defined, while the movements in question, acting in continually evolving historical situations, cannot but be influenced by those situations, and therefore cannot but be subject to profound changes."[32]

John's thesis is derived from the Church's constant teaching that one ought to distinguish between error and the man; between the purely logical aspect of assent, and an assent as the act of a person. A contingent defect in one's convictions does not

---

[29] Quoted in O.R., 5-6 July, 1976.
[30] "Like a newborn child."
[31] "Meeting of opposites."
[32] R.I., 1963, p.506.

alter a person's destination to truth, or the axiological dignity
that derives from it. That dignity comes from man's origin and
his other worldly goal, that no event within this world can remove, and which in fact can never be lost: it is a dignity that
remains even in the damned. But the encyclical moves from this
distinction between a man and his errors, to a distinction between doctrines, and movements inspired by those doctrines,
and it depicts the doctrines as unchangeable and closed within
themselves, while the movements are caught in the flow of history and continually *in fieri*,[33] always open to new events which
will transform them even to the point of making them the reverse of what they were. But the legitimate distinction between
the movement, that is, the mass of men agreeing together, and
the idea inspiring the movement, cannot be so absolute as to
make the doctrines fixed, while leaving the movements subject
to change. Just as the initial movement that sprang from the
doctrine cannot be conceived except as a mass of men agreeing
on that doctrine, so it is impossible to imagine the doctrine remaining without any adherents, and the mass of men nevertheless staying together without any reference to that doctrine,
simply drifting with historical events. The mass moves because
it goes on thinking over its doctrines, and the doctrines share in
historical change precisely because they are the ideas of men in
motion. What, moreover is the history of philosophy, if not the
history of intellectual systems in their development and their
becoming? How can one say that the systems are fixed and that
only the men who think them move?

It would therefore seem that the encyclical obscures the
continuing dialectical nexus between what the masses of a
movement think (granting that they think it less clearly than the
theoreticians) and what they do; and that the encyclical also
implies that what they do has no present connection with an
ideology, that, apparently, did nothing more than start the
movement in the first place. The fact that thought precedes action is overlooked, so that ideologies seem to be begotten by
movements, instead of begetting them. Ideologies do indeed feel
the influence of changeable men, changing in the course of
time, but the essential question remains the same, namely,
whether the changing movements do or do not continue to
draw their inspiration from the principles that gave them birth.

---

[33] "In a process of becoming."

Having neatly divided a movement from its ideology, in order to allow Catholics to join the movement while maintaining
their reservation about the ideology, the encyclical proceeds to
announce another criterion by which Catholics are permitted to
cooperate with alien political forces. "Furthermore," it says,
"who can deny that there are in those movements elements that
are positive and worthy of approval, to the extent that such
movements conform to the dictates of right reason and are the
spokesmen of the just aspirations of the human person?" John's
thesis is redolent of the Church's old and standard practice,
formulated by St. Paul: *Omnia autem probate, quod bonum est
tenete.*[34] But in the Apostle's view of it, it is not a matter of *experiencing*, that is taking a practical part in the movement, but
of *examining* to discern and appropriate in practice whatever
positive elements may be found in some movement.

It nonetheless remains true that the consent and cooperation that are legitimate when men turn their minds to lesser and
contingent ends become illegitimate when they turn them to
supreme and final ends that are mutually incompatible. In the
Catholic view, the whole of political life is subordinate to an
ultimate other-worldly end, while for communism it is directed
exclusively at this world and should repudiate any transcendent
end. Be it noted, communism not only *prescinds* from that end,
as does liberalism, it positively *repudiates* it. So then, if communism is condemned, it is not the subordinate ends it pursues
that are condemned, but its ultimate quest for an absolutely
this-worldly organization of the world, to which its subordinate
activities are directed; a quest incompatible with the ends pursued by religion. The reality is, that when two agents having
contradictory ultimate goals participate in the same works, there
is no cooperation, except in a material sense, because actions
derive their character from the end that is being pursued, and
here the ends are contradictory. The outcome of the material
cooperation will conform to the wishes of whichever party has
been clever enough to get what it wants.[35]

---

[34] I Thessalonians, 5:21. "Test all things, hold to what is good."

[35] When Roncalli was Patriarch of Venice, he expounded the idea of
cooperation between ultimately contradictory forces in a message
to the congress of the Italian Socialist party in 1957, talking about
"common striving towards the ideals of truth, goodness, justice and
peace." See G. Penco, *Storia della Chiesa in Italia*, Milan 1978,
Vol.II, p.568.

The positive elements in the movement are considered in the encyclical as if they were distinctive of communist ideology, when in fact they are primarily religious values, since religion includes natural justice, and they only receive their full significance and force when they are put back into the setting of religious ideals. It is thus not enough just to recognize the values, one must recognize them as part of a larger truth and reclaim them for religion so as to restore them to their full integrity. *Pacem in Terris* does not attempt this process of reclamation, whereby what appears good and reasonable in a movement is plucked out of it, and restored to its religious setting. Instead, the encyclical expatiates on the recognition of values that are allegedly to be found on an equal footing in the movement and in Christianity; values that must therefore be derived from some prior source common to both, and which is thus what actually gives value to both. Just what this true, authentic source of values is, does not appear in the encyclical; nor could it, without the primary value of religion being sacrificed to that original underlying good.

The factitious coherence that men attempt to force upon mutually repellent ideas is not nearly as strong as the abstract coherence of ideas logically interconnected and unstoppably unfolding one from the other. This explains why liberation theology inevitably sprang from Christians opting for a Marxism that contains within it the notion of a class struggle culminating in revolution. As noted in the preceding section, the idea that prevails draws in its wake those of incompatible conviction who cooperate with it; and this is precisely what has happened in the transition from a Marxist political option to the generation of a liberation theology.

116. On Christian socialism. Toniolo. Curci.

The idea of Christian socialism is legitimate. In his *Indirizzi e Concetto Sociale* Guiseppe Toniolo did not attempt to set out a new Christianity, but did envisage a new stage in Christian civilization, in which there would be a renewal of the unity and supernatural quality of religion as against heresy and nationalism, and in conjunction with that, a renewal of society through an organic recomposition of classes whereby the proletariat would be reintegrated into society. The authentic Catholic ideas of mastership and brotherhood would then completely supplant Marxist socialism.

Di un Socialismo Cristiano (1885) by the celebrated Fr.
Curci is even more precise in its thinking, and is entirely inspired by certain social implications of Christianity that had
lain implicit up to that point. Curci appeals to the Christian
notions of wealth and of social living, which respectively entail
the sharing of goods and the proportional, though not absolute,
equality of all members of the body politic. The heart of the
matter is given in Horace's line: *Cur indiget indignus quisquam,
te divite?*[36] The idea of justice is maintained; it is the rich who
insult the guiltless poor as Amos says: *Vaccae pingues quae ca-
lumniam facitis egenis.*[37] Curci is acutely aware of the specially
delicate nature of social reform, judged from a Catholic point of
view. Reform should get rid of injustice towards one part of
society without generating hatred of the other parts. If hatred
takes over, and justice ceases to be the fruit of love, it becomes
instead merely a counter-injustice, and social relations are poi-
soned.

So, Curci's Christian socialism, no less than Toniolo's, rejects the Marxist notion of class war and aims at a social reform
not brought about by violence, or even primarily by law, but as
the fruit of a further moral development of Christendom. Two
essential points of Catholic thinking must be firmly grasped.
The first is that mankind has a transcendent destiny: on earth
we serve, then comes the enjoyment of absolute good. The second is that human activity should never compromise justice,
since no circumstance or utilitarian consideration should ever
be allowed to prevail over it.

117. Father Montuclard's doctrine
and the emptying of the Church.

Both these points are ignored, in theory and in practice, by
Christian movements that embrace Marxism. Through their
entirely this-worldly spirit, such movements are bound to put
transcendent religious goals below economic enfranchisement
and temporal well-being. The process has three stages. First the
goal of temporal justice is made equal in importance to man's
transcendental goal, the two being thus on a par. Then the
earthly goal is emphasized, and otherworldly concerns are re-

---

[36] *Satires*, II,II,103. "Why is any guiltless person poor, when you are
rich?"

[37] *Amos*, 4:1. "Fattened cows that vilify the lean."

stricted, so that the two are no longer equal. Finally the temporal aims are given absolute predominance and what is specifically Christian is either rejected as false or relegated to the sphere of irrelevant private opinion.

The Dominican Fr. Montuclard's book *Les événements et la foi 1940-1952*[38] which expressed the ideals of the *Jeunesse de l'Eglise*[39] movement and which was prohibited by a decree of the Holy Office on 16 March 1953, is important as the forerunner of this tendency.[40] The French bishops had already warned Catholics against the book, even though they had not enforced the Roman decree of 1949 excommunicating communists, and had allowed it to remain a dead letter in France.[41] Later on, a condemnation of Catholic Marxist movements appeared in the *Osservatore Romano*.[42]

The doctrine outlined in the book impugns Catholic teaching on several points and indulges in a denigration of the historical Church, driven by a bitter and acrimonious zeal.

The first departure from Catholic truth is in its understanding of faith. Faith is taken as a feeling of communion with God, or an experience of the divine, devoid of any rational justification or any theoretical formulas expressing its truth.

The second is an echo of the spiritualist heresies of the Middle Ages. Fr. Montuclard in fact maintains that the spiritual

---

[38] "The Faith and current events 1940-1952."

[39] "Youth of the Church."

[40] The present section on Montuclard's doctrine excuses us from a detailed analysis of the document put out by the Congregation for the Doctrine of the Faith in 1984 on certain points of the so-called theology of liberation. That theology's principles are in fact identical to those of Fr. Montuclard that the Holy Office had condemned years before. The old Holy Office's acumen came from Prometheus ("Forethought") not from his brother Epimetheus ("Afterthought"): someone who understands principles also understands the future development of a doctrine.

[41] The *Ami du Clergé*, a review much read by French clergy, replying to a question asking why the decree had not been applied in France, quoted the bishops' provisions in the matter "which signify a definite desire to apply the Roman decree, and see it applied everywhere," but it could not deny the general failure to apply it, and attempted to say this was due to "some oversight." *Ami du Clergé*, 1953, p.267.

[42] O.R., 19 February 1954.

and temporal are quite separate and that the spiritual has no
influence on temporal realities. His doctrine concerning these
two independent orders is applied in such a way as to destroy
the essence of the Church. Of the two sorts of liberation,
namely, that relative temporal liberation represented by such
things as the suppression of slavery and the partial suppression
of war, and spiritual liberation on the other hand, the former is
to be entirely effected by communism and the latter can only
happen as its consequence: *Désormais les hommes demanderont à
la science, à l'action des masses, à la technique, à l'organisation
sociale de réaliser à une bien plus grande échelle cette délivrance
humaine dont l'Eglise avait eu dans le passé à s'occuper par sur-
croît.*[43] Having rendered the Church's social action irrelevant, Fr.
Montuclard goes on to deprive it of any function at all in present conditions by saying that *Les hommes ne s'intéresseront plus à
l'Eglise qu'à partir du moment où ils auront conquis l'humain.*[44]
Christianity therefore has nothing left to do in history, since
what it is really capable of doing in the traditional understanding is here declared unsustainable by the Church's own resources, and everything must wait until the preliminary work of
liberating the human race has been done by communism. Instead of being absolute and primary, Christianity thus becomes
conditional and secondary. Not only is it not allowed to work in
its own way for human liberation, but its own very existence is
made conditional on a prior liberation effected by communism.
Spiritual liberation, that is the kingdom of God, must wait to
be called into being by a secular, or at least an entirely human,
change.

One of communism's primary errors is involved here: it
proposes to liberate some men, namely those who happen to be
alive when earthly liberation is brought about, but it sacrifices
present generations to future ones as if they alone, and not all
men as such, had a truly human destiny. Furthermore, by saying
that our heavenly destiny cannot be reached until the temporal
order has been perfected, the Church is left with nothing to

---

[43] *Les événements et la foi 1940-1952*, p.56. "From now on men will
look to science, mass action, technology and social organization to
bring about, and on a much larger scale, the improving of man's lot
with which the Church has had to busy itself incidentally in the
past."

[44] "Men will henceforth take no interest in the Church until such time
as they have mastered human affairs."

offer and no motive to act in the present circumstances of the world. And in fact if the Church were to draw upon its timeless, supernatural nature and perform here and now its duty of preaching the truth, reminding men of transcendent realities and building up the spiritual man, the achievement of earthly perfection would thereby be hindered. Since in this view man's temporal perfection is a necessary precondition of his spiritual liberation, it is disastrous for humanity to subordinate temporal to spiritual concerns, or even to preserve the two conjointly. Fr. Montuclard says so quite unambiguously: *Non, les ouvriers n'ignorent pas le christianisme. Les paroles chrétiennes que de fois ne les ont-ils pas entendues. Mais ces paroles leur ont paru des attrap-enigauds. Et maintenant que l'on parle de l'enfer, du renoncement, de l'Eglise ou de Dieu ils savent qu'en fait tout cela tend à leur ar-racher des mains les outils du leur propre libération.*[45] This is the old Jacobin idea that, to an unbiased mind, religion is an im-posture designed to disarm justice. There is also the quite un-Catholic insinuation that the kingdom talked about in the Gos-pel is not concerned with making men new creatures, but with installing them in a natural perfection.

The practical conclusion of this axiology is that Christianity is absolutely useless in the present state of the world, and that it should withdraw, contract and keep quiet while awaiting the secular liberation from which alone spiritual liberation can be born; but to what end, one might ask, if man will then have attained human perfection? *Jeunesse de l'Eglise* contains some disturbing words: *Que voulez-vous donc que nous fassions? Il n'y a pour nous qu'une attitude possible et vraie: nous taire, nous taire longtemps, nous taire des années et des années durant, et participer à toute la vie, à tous les combats, à toute la culture latente de cette population ouvrière que sans le vouloir nous avons si souvent trom-pée.*[46]

---

[45] "No, the workers are not unaware of Christianity. How often they have heard Christian words. But these words seemed to be booby traps. Now if anyone talks about hell, or renunciation, the Church or God, they know that in fact all that has the effect of taking the tools of their own liberation out of their hands."

[46] "What should we do then? There is only one right and possible atti-tude for us: to keep quiet, to keep quiet for a long time, to keep quiet for years and years, and to join in the whole life, all the struggles, all the hidden culture of that working population that we have so often unintentionally deceived." (pp.59-60). [This ex-

118. Transition from the Marxist option to liberation theology. The nuncio Zacchi. The document of the seventeen bishops.

Montuclard's emptying or voiding of Christianity links him very obviously to Marxist ideologues. Since they are free from the need to speak carefully, as politicians often do, and also because they are more logical, Marxist theoreticians admit the irreconcilability of Marxism and Christianity as axiomatic. In the large *History of Philosophy*[47] of which the sixth volume appeared in German in 1967, man is defined as a *Naturwesen*, that is a mere part of nature, the history of thought is viewed as a development towards atheism and radical humanism, and the present dialogue with Catholicism is explained as an effect of the cracking of faith in the face of science and the modern mentality. Dialogue is simply a tactical stage and cannot include an agreement on doctrine.

By contrast with the communist's firm logic, the so-called *Gauche du Christ*[48] abounds with people who believe in the positive character of class war and its compatibility with Christianity, and who even see communism as having an intrinsically Christian nature. The papal diplomat Mgr Zacchi said on a visit to Cuba that Fidel Castro's communist regime "is not Christian ideologically, but it is ethically," as if a system that considers the idea of God to be a harmful illusion could be regarded as Christian in any respect and as if a Christian ethic could spring from a non-Christian idea.

The document signed by seventeen bishops from around the world and published by *Témoignage Chrétien* is of more importance.[49] It makes the transition from a positive attitude towards communism, to liberation theology. Mgr Helder Camara, the first signatory and drafter of the document, says the Church does not condemn revolutions that advance the cause of justice, but accepts them, if indeed it does not promote them. This idea is certainly in accordance with Catholic principles, and was

---

traordinary note of self-hatred, and the implicit desire to be legitimated by "the workers" is not uncommon among French Catholics of advanced views. Translator's note.]
[47] *Geschichte der Philosophie, herausgegeben von der Akademie der Wissenschaften der URSS*, Berlin 1967.
[48] "Christian Left."
[49] *Témoignage Chrétien*, 31 August 1967.

fully elaborated by the Spanish theologians of the sixteenth century in protest against royal despotism, but Camara's version of it is mistaken inasmuch as he allows the rebellious group to judge whether their own cause is just, whereas the correct doctrine demands an at least implicit assent from the whole body of society. Non-violent means should moreover be tried according to Catholic social theory, including negotiation, compromise and cooperation. This document makes revolution a naturally legitimate and appropriate means of social reform. Then, by smuggling two disparate ideas into a single phrase, it claims that the Gospel harmonizes with a Marxist revolution because *L'Evangile a toujours été, visiblement ou invisiblement, par l'Eglise ou hors de l'Eglise, le plus puissant ferment des mutations profondes de l'humanité depuis vingt siècles.*[50] The illegitimate transition from the moral transformation brought by Christianity, to revolutionary upheaval is staringly obvious. So is the false nature of the claim that Christianity has been the cause of all the great changes in human society. Were that the case, it would have to be the cause not only of the French Revolution, upon which Mgr Camara actually can see a Christian stamp thanks to his superficial or at least highly debatable analysis of it, but the cause of Islam and of the obviously atheistic Russian revolution as well.[51] The lack of any solid standard of judgment means anything can be detected in anything else, and one set of events can be confused with another.

The document then attacks the Church's collusion with money and crooked wealth, condemns the taking of interest on loans,[52] demands that social justice not be given to the poor but that the poor should themselves extract it from the rich, and openly replaces the harmonious transformation of society with social war. Since it sees Christian values fulfilled in communism rather than Christianity it concludes that: "*L'Eglise ne peut que se*

---

[50] "For twenty centuries, whether visibly or invisibly, through the Church or outside it, the Gospel has always been the most powerful fomenter of profound changes among men."

[51] Remember Lenin's letter to Maxim Gorkij, in which he calls religion "an unspeakable infamy and the most disgusting of diseases."

[52] It is important to distinguish the Church's condemnation of the charging of a price for a loan simply in virtue of the loan, and its approval of the charging of a price for a loan in virtue of the losses incurred or profits foregone, etc., because of the making of the loan. [Translator's note.]

réjouir de voir apparaître dans l'humanité un système social moins éloigné de la morale évangélique. Bien loin de bouder la socialisation, sachons y adhérer avec joie comme à une forme de vie sociale mieux adaptée à notre temps et plus conforme à l'Evangile."[53]

The document of these Seventeen is in sharp contrast to the position Pius XII took in his Christmas message for 1957, when he said that both cooperation, and even dialogue with communism were impossible, the reason being that there cannot be a discussion without a common language, and in this instance the disagreement concerns fundamentals. The Pope then condemned the attitude that the seventeen bishops have subsequently adopted: "With deep regret we must lament the support given by some Catholics, both churchmen and lay people, to these obfuscatory tactics...How can anyone still fail to see that this is the aim of all the insincere agitation that goes under the name of 'Colloquia' and 'Assemblies'? What is the use from our point of view in discussing without a common language, and how is it possible to meet if our paths diverge, that is, if one of the parties rejects and fails to recognize absolute common values?"[54]

119. Judgment on the document of the Seventeen.

The conclusion of the bishops' document is quite unambiguous, but its premises are false. Whether as a system of thought or as the practice of that thought, by the admission of its own theoreticians and by the judgment of all the popes, communism is not merely a social system that bishops can welcome as one of the many possible forms of political organization; it is a complete axiological system intrinsically repugnant to the Catholic system. To equate modern communism with a social system of the sort that prevailed, for example, in the famous Jesuit "Reductions" in Paraguay, is indeed to draw it of its sting, but only by dint of misrepresenting its nature. The movement from the Marxist option to liberation theology is only possible because the seventeen bishops fail to grasp both

---

[53] "The Church cannot but rejoice to see a social system less removed from the morality of the Gospel appear in the world. Far from sulking at socialization, let us be wise enough to adhere to it joyfully as a form of social life better adapted to our times and more in conformity with the Gospel."

[54] R.I., 1957, p.17.

the nature of communism and the nature of Christianity itself. Externally their applause for the class struggle ill accords with the condemnations of the Church's teaching office and also raises questions about the coherence of the hierarchy; internally, the document departs from Catholic thought on at least two points. Because of its defective understanding of God's dealings with the world, it says nothing about the eschatological nature of Christianity, whereby earth is seen as being made for heaven, and a full grasp of man's destiny can only be had from beyond the walls of time. Yet again, because of its faulty view of history the document fails to state that Christianity traces the origin of social injustice to moral disorder, and as a result injustice is to be found throughout the whole body of society and cannot be attributed exclusively to those who enjoy material prosperity. In short, the document lacks calmness of judgment, because the bishops side exclusively with one party, and entirely overlook the Catholic workers' movements that were rejected by the rich; it also lacks that more exalted calm that comes from a religious spirit and which can detect a goal beyond history as it surveys the record of the past. This is no real theory of history, but an immanentist philosophy only interested in liberation from worldly misfortune, and looking only to human self-improvement to achieve it.

120. Options of certain Christians, continued. Mgr Fragoso.

The ignoring of Catholic social doctrine and activity, that cuts the seventeen bishops' document off from the teaching of the Church, also appears in other episcopal pronouncements to the effect that the spiritual liberation brought by Christianity should be placed after the struggle for justice in this world, both in time and in importance. Since religion claims prime importance in life, it cannot abandon that claim without perishing, and so the practical effect of such proposals is not merely to degrade Christianity but to destroy it.

Mgr Fragoso, the Bishop of Crateus in Brazil, openly teaches that the Church's supernatural end should take second place to the struggle for temporal justice. He denies[55] there is any leap or gap between temporal and eternal life, between nature and the supernatural. God's purpose is, he maintains, that

---

[55] In an interview with I.C.I., No.311, 1968, pp.4ff.

this world be just, brotherly and happy; the Kingdom of God is achieved in the present life to such an extent that at the *parousia* the world will continue without drastic change in the eternal kingdom since the new heaven and new earth will have already been realized by that point.[56]

Both the old and the not so old versions of millenarianism, of which the last great statement was made by Campanella, were founded on a legitimate theological premise, namely that Christianity is a theory of the whole of reality and that Christ, the eternal Reason incarnate, should therefore achieve man's temporal perfection, not only his perfection in the spiritual and supernatural sphere; otherwise he would not have completed His own design, as far as earthly matters go. Nonetheless, millenarianism made a firm distinction between heaven and earth, history and eternity, and did not maintain that temporal perfection, that is civilization, was the beginning of the Kingdom.[57] In Mgr Fragoso's case the new heavens and the new earth do not *transcend* but rather *continue* the present creation and so the goal of the world becomes the continuation of the same world; the subjection of all things to God disappears, and the Church is confused with the organizing of the human race. When transcendent realities have been eclipsed, earthly purposes can be preserved with an absoluteness appropriate to ultimate ends, and submission to the laws of obedience and patient fortitude is overthrown by the right to happiness in this present life. Violence becomes the highest Christian duty, immediately connected with moral responsibility: *A la conscience adulte il est reconnu une responsabilité et un droit d'opter pour la violence.*[58]

Problems that properly belong to politics become religious problems and the Church has to take on the problems of hunger, drought, hygiene, population control and everything else that is now included under the term "development." It is the Church's failure in promoting human development that in Mgr

---

[56] One need hardly add that this notion of the Second Coming as something happening in an already complete and perfect world contradicts *ad litteram* the description given of it in Scripture, and by Christ himself, involving errors, escapes, hatreds and disasters.

[57] See R.E. Amerio, *Il sistema teologico di Tommaso Campanella,* Milan and Naples 1972, Ch. VII, pp.272ff.

[58] "An adult conscience is acknowledged to have a responsibility and a right to opt for violence."

Camara's view[59] justifies the accusations Marx made against it: *qui présente à des parias un christianisme passif, aliéné et aliénant, vraiment un opium pour les masses.*[60] Religion's task thus becomes the building up of the *civitas hominis*[61] and the relation between civilization and religion is misrepresented by the compounding of the two.

In this regard Mgr Fragoso's application of his ecclesiological principles to a particular case is interesting inasmuch as it shows his conception of the duties of a Catholic bishop.[62] Having laid down that the Gospel must be lived before being learnt, he discusses his own pastoral action among the peasants of his diocese and says: *Si les paysans travaillent ensemble, s'unissent, s'entraident, s'ils acquièrent le sens de la solidarité, ils vont s'apercevoir que ce qu'ils croient être une fatalité n'est qu'injustice ou défaut d'organisation, ils vont perdre leur religiosité passive en vivant l'Evangile. Après seulement je leur parlerai de Dieu.*[63] It would seem the Bishop of Crateus does not understand the problem of evil, and attributes droughts, floods, earthquakes and frosts to the injustice of the rich and lack of organization. But lack of organization, that is a lack of technology, is not an injustice, but a deficiency inherent in finite reality. Nor does the Bishop give much evidence of being a thinker when he supposes one can live the Gospel without first knowing God. When his interviewer asked whether his people did not run the risk of losing their faith through this mental transformation he replied: *C'est un risque et j'en suis conscient. Mais mon travail peut débouter en trois sortes de résultats. Ne rien changer à la situation actuelle: je considérerais alors que j'ai failli à ma mission. Le seconde: conscientiser les paysans en transformant leur foi: c'est la*

---

[59] Conference in Paris, 25 April 1968, I.C.I., No.312.

[60] "It presents social outcasts with a passive, alienated and alienating Christianity, which is really an opium for the masses."

[61] "The City of Man."

[62] Interview published by F. de Combret in the book *Les trois Brésils, Le Mercure de France*, s.l., 1971, p.154.

[63] "If the peasants work together, unite, help each other and acquire a sense of solidarity, then they will realize that what they have regarded as fate is only injustice or a lack of organization, they will lose their passive religiosity, in living the Gospel. *Only after that* will I talk to them about God."

réussite. Le troisième: conscientiser les paysans mais leur faire perdre la foi: ça n'aurait été qu'un demi succès.[64]

121. Examination of Mgr Fragoso's doctrine.

The movement from a Marxist option to the negation of religion is clear in this case. Firstly, Mgr Fragoso confuses and compounds the spiritual and temporal orders by assigning to the Church the promotion of a certain social order, not as an indirect and consequent responsibility but as a direct and primary concern. Success in that task is therefore his criterion of success in his ministry as a bishop, that is, as a priest. Secondly, he regards letting his people lose their faith as a success, though only partial, provided the loss is compensated for by their conscientization, that is by their conversion to the idea of the *civitas hominis*. This latter is therefore good even apart from and *against* religion. Thirdly, how can there be a genuine raising of consciousness without at least some general knowledge of God? Mgr Fragoso's reservation of the preaching of God to his people until after the *civitas hominis* has been constructed is a vain proceeding.

Lastly, the function Mgr Fragoso assigns to a bishop includes none of those assigned by the Church, namely teaching the truths of faith, sanctifying by the sacraments, and governing and shepherding his people.[65] In his version of things the temporal order is the proper and primary object of pastoral concern, and if the people lose their faith *ch'è principio a la via di salvazione*[66] it seems to him a bishop has only partially, but not entirely, failed in his task, provided he succeeds in advancing civilization.

We may conclude by adding that if the Seventeen are only a fraction of the episcopate, the facts that their doctrine is so odd, that they were not specifically reproved by the Holy See and

---

[64] "It is a risk and I am aware of it. But my work could have one of three results. Change nothing in the present situation: I would take that as a failure of my mission. Second: conscientize the peasants while transforming their faith: that is success. Third: conscientize the peasants but make them lose their faith: that would be only a partial success." (p.154).

[65] *Lumen Gentium*, 24-25.

[66] Dante's *Inferno*, II,30. "Which is the beginning of the way of salvation."

that they received such wide support, mean that their statement is an important indication of the doctrinal weakness of the Catholic episcopate and of the renunciation of the use of ecclesiastical authority.[67]

122. Support for the teaching of the Seventeen.

We have confined ourselves in the preceding paragraph to documents signed by members of the hierarchy, in accordance with the general methodological principle we have adopted, but it must be remembered that a good many bishops who did not sign that document nonetheless supported it, and that they too share this Marxist, or at least entirely secular conception of the purpose of earthly existence.[68] Important movements of clergy and laity do the same. These include *Tercer Mundo* in Brazil, the Columbian movement involving the priest Camillo Torres who was reduced to the lay state and killed in a guerrilla band when about to finish off a wounded soldier; another Columbian movement involving Fr. Lain; and one in Chile involving Fr. Joseph Comblin who believes religion is essentially and entirely a political and indeed a martial art: *Il faudrait susciter des vocations politiques vraies pour susciter des groups résolus à tenter la prise du pouvoir. Il est nécessaire d'étudier la science du pouvoir et l'art de la conquête.*[69]

The university association *Pax Romana* also maintains the notion that Christianity necessarily passes into Marxism, and it says that: *Malgré la déclaration pontificale d'une trentaine*

---

[67] See paragraphs 65 and 66.
[68] Arguing with the Archbishop of Mexico City, the Bishop of Cuernavaca teaches that "in the dialectical variety of Marxist thought, one can very well be faithful to Jesus Christ and be a Marxist" and that "the Marxist critique of religion has helped to liberate Christianity from bourgeois ideology." I.C.I., No.577, 15 August 1982, p.54. [Marx had in fact no original ideas on religion, his views being borrowed entirely from Feuerbach. Translator's note.]
[69] "We ought to raise up people with true political vocations who can in turn raise up groups intent on seizing power. We must study the science of power and the art of conquest." *Note pour le document de base préparatoire à la deuxième Conférence de CELAM*, Recife 1965.

d'années, christianisme et socialisme sont pleinement compatibles.[70]
The arrogant attack upon authority contained in these words is
no less significant than their doctrinal error.[71]

---

[70] "Despite the papal declaration of some thirty years ago, Christianity
and socialism are fully compatible." *Pax Romana* Bulletin, May
1967, p.26.

[71] Despite condemnations by Paul VI and John Paul II, liberation
theology continues to be preached in pulpits and in the mass media. In the Sunday magazine *La fede oggi*, published under the aegis of the Italian episcopal conference and which has Claudio Sorgi
as its theological adviser, a South American priest said on 29
August 1982 that the Gospel does not condemn violence and that
the revolutionary interpretation of the Gospel is the only legitimate
one.

CHAPTER XII

SCHOOLS

123. Schools in the post-conciliar Church.

Turning from communism and revolution to catechetics, the common theme uniting the two subjects is the one that guides all the analyses of this book, namely, the idea of the adjustment of the Church to the spirit of modernity.

The Church's educational activities are carried on in three ways; one direct and two indirect. Firstly, there is catechesis, carried on directly, within the ambit of the Church, in virtue of a divine right independent of the state. Secondly, there are schools maintained by civil society in which religion is taught by agreement between civil and ecclesiastical authorities since that kind of education concerns them both. Thirdly, there are Catholic schools in which the whole of what is taught is shaped by religious belief. The Church's activities in all these areas have been very extensive, even though not always successful. Education is a delicate working upon human freedom and its outcome is not certain since the forces involved are not calculable. If Catholic schools have had their splendid successes, they have also had their paradoxical failures. It should not be forgotten that all the Jacobins had been to Catholic schools.

Up until the Second World War some countries, such as Germany, had public schools of different religious denominations; others, such as the canton of the Ticino in Switzerland, had public schools that were agnostic: religion was an essential and obligatory part of their *ratio studiorum* but students could be dispensed from it in conformity with a constitutional provision for freedom of conscience; others again, like Spain, integrated religious instruction into the teaching as an important aspect of national identity and part of the cultural tradition of the country. This last system made religious instruction obligatory irrespective of the student's personal beliefs. This was a

continuation of the social arrangements that prevailed before
the revolutionary period, when religious as well as civil duties
were included in what students had to learn. These systems often removed the element of freedom that confers moral value
upon one's behavior.

Vatican II's declaration *Gravissimum Educationis* distinguishes two sorts of schools and approves of both. The first are
public schools established and controlled by the state: their general aim is intellectual development, the transmission of cultural
inheritance and professional training. These schools are based
on the principle of prescinding from religion, which, the
council says, is required in view of the pluralism prevailing in
very many countries.[1] The paragraph stating these facts fails to
acknowledge that the ruling principle inspiring education needs
to be something more than a mere respect for pluralism, and it
therefore is at odds with the definition later given of the second,
and specifically Catholic, sort of school. The goal of Catholic
schools includes the goals assigned to public ones, but outstrips
and transmutes them because "it helps the pupil to develop his
own person as a new creature born in baptism and directs the
whole of human culture towards the saving message, in such a
way that all knowledge concerning the world, life and man is
illuminated by faith."[2] The positive worth of an education prescinding from man's religious values is therefore admitted, but
the Church's right to carry on its educational work in its own
schools is also defended. Nonetheless, in the council's view, the
Church's rights in civil society are based upon one of that society's own principles, namely, a freedom in which all sorts of beliefs are held to be equal.

124. Relative necessity of Catholic schools.

The necessity of Catholic schools was re-emphasized by
Paul VI in a speech on 30 December 1969, but as a conditioned
necessity, rather than as one arising from the Church's own system of values. The Pope says: "A Catholic school is a necessity
for anyone who wants a complete and coherent education; it is a
necessity as a complementary experience in the context of modern society; it is necessary where other schools are lacking; it is
also necessary for the Church's own internal use, so that the

---

[1] Paragraphs 5 and 6.
[2] Paragraph 8.

Church does not lose its own ability and power to fulfill its fundamental ministry of teaching." As can be seen from the terms used, a Catholic school is as it were a supererogatory form of education that serves the needs of those wanting a more complete formation, but not the needs of the general run of Christians, who can be formed without a Catholic school. The Pope assigns a Catholic school, as such, a supplementary and a complementary role with respect to state schools, which are assumed to be suitable for giving a complete mental and moral formation.[3] If the context of modern society, which the Pope was considering, is to be taken as implying a pluralistic structure, then as we have said, pluralism would be the ground on which the Catholic school would have its right to exist, and it would continue to exist as long as pluralism prevailed.

125. The Congregation for Catholic Education's document of 16 October 1982.

This document is designed to set out the role of lay Catholics teaching in state schools, and bears the mark of the new pedagogy: it accepts the idea of education as self-education, praises the progress of scholastic institutions in the modern world, sees schools as having an essentially dialectic structure and says nothing about the authority of the teacher.[4] The whole conception of the document labors under an even greater difficulty. It states[5] that in public schools "every teacher gives his teaching, advances certain standards and presents certain values as positive, in the light of his conception of man or of his own ideology." This statement does not correspond with the real state of public schools. In many countries a teacher is obliged to profess and teach a given ideology to the exclusion of any other, and often it is an ideology expressly hostile to Christian doctrine. In many other countries, teachers in public schools are required to prescind from their own religious and philosophical

---

[3]   On 10 April 1968, Benno Cardinal Gut was asked on Italian Swiss television whether today's Church should still run Catholic schools. The answer was that that depended on circumstances and that a Catholic school was not necessary where a good public one existed. The Cardinal added that the Pope in any case wanted there to be Catholic schools anyway.

[4]   Paragraphs 21, 3, 4, 49 and 50.

[5]   Paragraph 47.

beliefs in their teaching, and must not challenge the beliefs of their pupils. Respect for the beliefs of the latter are made the limit of the educational activity of the former. The moral authority which a school inevitably has, is then derived exclusively from the shared beliefs of society at large. These include such natural ethical principles as: seeking good, respecting the rights of one's neighbor, suppressing egoism, doing good to all, being truthful, working together for the common good, revering and honoring one's country. This system was at least possible until states gave up the foundation of natural justice which men had shared as common ground[6] and until they adopted the principle of personal independence, begotten of scepticism and an autonomy autonomous from what is right.[7] Until recently, public schools used to require their teachers to leave their personal opinions behind when they crossed the threshold of the school and to adjust their teaching to the *sensus communis* of natural morality.[8]

This idea of a school is limited, but Catholic: the school lifted minds above passions that wounded and divided and brought them into that light in which teachers and pupils are both aware of the *logos* above their *dialogue*, and more important than it; and in that light they recognized their true fraternity, the deep unity of their own nature.

This pedagogy, based on a distinction between the natural and supernatural orders, is abandoned in Cardinal Baum's document.[9] It moves from *freedom of teaching*, that is from a plurality of schools each homogeneous within itself, to a *freedom for teachers* within the ambit of each school. The document

---

[6]   See paragraphs 174-8.

[7]   See paragraphs 148-9.

[8]   In the *lycée* of the canton of Ticino, at Lugano, between 1898 and 1930 the teachers were political exiles, Italians thoroughly involved in political disputes who had been imbued with passionate ideals vehemently held and had also suffered unjustly: they were on the run from their own anger and that of others. Nonetheless, when they entered the school, such men were able to set aside their high principled and furious passions, leaving them on the shore of the stormy sea whence they had emerged. None of their pupils ever felt that his own religious or political opinions were even touched by a shade of scorn, let alone insulted.

[9]   Cardinal Baum was head of the Congregation for Catholic Education when the 1982 document was issued. [Translator's note.]

says expressly: a school is a relation between persons, that is between teacher and learner. The Church used to say that it is a relation of both to the world of values. It is not the teacher that the pupil has to know; both have to know the world of values and direct their common attention towards it. But just as one man's face is turned towards another's in the reformed liturgy, so is it in the reformed pedagogy. It goes without saying that this pluralism in schools, understood as a pluralism in teaching within the one public school, is an attack on freedom. For it to be otherwise, families that choose a public school would have to have the right to choose the teachers. This sort of pluralism makes a school a place of uncertainty, disagreement and intellectual confusion: the very essence of education, namely unity of knowledge, is lost.

In short, if a school is an institution on which each teacher has a right to impress his personal ideology, the school ceases to be a communion of minds brought about by their communing in an overruling truth. Catholic teachers in public schools will, moreover, find themselves at odds with the nature of such schools, because they are intended to prescind from the specifics of religion precisely in order to be public, that is, open to all.

126. Catholic rejection of Catholic schools.
Mgr Leclercq.

If the reasons for Catholic schools in modern society seem unclear to some people, to others they are non-existent. Both *events* and *theory* are here involved.

In 1967 the Christian Democrats in Württemberg gave up the defense of Catholic schools and joined forces with the socialists to introduce so-called simultaneous schools having a Christian but not a denominational basis. It is particularly significant that in the very act of protesting to the government against the violation of the concordat of 1933, the nuncio Mgr Bafile said: "The Church too is really interested in the creation of *a progressive school system.*"[10]

By a 75% majority, a popular referendum in Bavaria changed the state's constitution in order to introduce non-denominational Christian schools to replace Catholic ones. In Italy in 1967, when two hundred thousand million lire had to be allocated to university construction and the Liberals pro-

---

[10] R.I., 1967, p.395.

posed to allocate something to independent universities including the Catholic University of Milan, the proposal failed because the Christian Democrats abstained in accordance with
agreements they had made with other parties. In some cases, the
abandonment of Catholic schools was influenced by the ecumenical drive, in others, by the Marxist option. In the African
state of Mali, which is a socialist republic, Catholic schools adhere to the state educational syllabus and therefore give lessons
in Marxism. In Ceylon the Catholics decided to hand most of
their schools over to the state, although controlled by Marxists,
so that the young could be more easily integrated into national
life and the Church would become a place of dialogue rather
than a source of tension.[11] In communist countries the episcopate's attitude towards state schools is in harmony with its attitude to communism itself.

Theoretical *opinions* asserting the uselessness and unimportance of Catholic schools today, are no less important than these
events. Mgr Leclercq, the emeritus professor of moral theology
at the Catholic University of Louvain, sees a general incompatibility between Catholic universities and a contemporary
civilization marked by pluralism and averse to any kind of
ghetto. This incompatibility deprives Catholic universities of
their reason for existing. But Mgr Leclercq's argument is not
conclusive and is in fact self-contradictory. Precisely because we
are in a pluralistic world, Catholic universities become normal:
one cannot be in favor of pluralism in the abstract, while rejecting an actual plurality in teaching by asserting that a particular
teaching cannot be part of the plurality.

The second argument used to deprive Catholic universities
of their reason for existing in the contemporary world, is that
they are allegedly obliged to isolate themselves because they aim
to produce minds that are safe and secure and thus they prevent
the mind from coming to grips with modern civilization's opposition to Catholicism: being kept safe like this, in what is
derisorily called a hot house, cannot produce open minds and
strong convictions.

This line of reasoning is alien to Catholic thinking. The
factual answer is that Catholic schools have produced Catholic
men, indeed generations, with open minds and strong convictions. Qualitatively, the argument fails to understand the value

---

[11] I.C.I., No.279, 1 January 1967, pp.25-6.

of security, and thinks of it as something almost degrading and "bourgeois." Security is in actual fact the moral effect of certainty, and, at a higher level, of salvation, when the certainty is that of faith. Certainty and security are the intellectual and psychological faces of a single human condition. Supernatural faith gives the spirit a repose founded not on a renunciation of intellect but on a consistency that leaves no room for doubt.[12]

Nor is the security upon which Catholic teaching is based a flight from wrestling with contemporary opinion, because the believer must be able to give an account to anyone of his supernatural view of things,[13] proportionate with his knowledge of the faith, and if he is a teacher, he is bound by profession to do so. The comparing of different current opinions is a necessary step that thought must take in seeking and maintaining the truth, because nobody can either enquire into or refute an opinion without a process of examination. Indeed, confrontational methods were the characteristic note of scholasticism; in the mediaeval University of Paris the masters offered to respond publicly and without notice to the objections and questions of their pupils in the faculties and even to those of the common people, as can be seen in the vivid depiction of the mentality and spirit of that age provided by St. Thomas's *Quaestiones quodlibetales*. Furthermore, the literary genre of the apologia could not have arisen if religion had imposed isolation: religion is indeed isolated from error, but to effect its isolation it has to confront dialectically all the kinds of opposition that are made to religion. This true sort of isolation from error is alien to the novel theology because the latter is riddled with scepticism. The line of argument we are considering also ignores a fundamental principle of apologetics, namely that one does not have to refute all the objections made to the faith in order for the faith to stand firm.[14]

Another of Mgr Leclercq's arguments concerns epistemology and the relation between different areas of knowledge. He maintains that a Catholic university *confessionalizes* knowledge and interferes with free and impartial enquiry: science repudiates any kind of finality or heteronomy.

At this point the voice of the eminent theologian seems to be an echo of irreligious rationalism. In falling subject to a het-

---

[12] See paragraph 167.
[13] Cf. I Peter, 3:15.
[14] See paragraphs 152-3.

eronomous principle, science is not confessionalized, that is it does not become part of the faith; it remains autonomous in its own order. Even if one wanted it to be of use to faith, how could it be so if it were not constituted as the individual, autonomous, specialized form of knowledge that it is? An extrinsic subordination does not affect the intrinsic autonomy of each area of knowledge. Indeed, this extrinsic subordination sustains the unified field of knowledge, is a necessary condition of any discipline, does not injure the autonomy of any, and is necessary to the architecture of knowing. To give an example: pharmacology is certainly a science, certainly subordinate to medicine and does not function except at the service of medicine but it does not therefore take its laws from medicine. Thus every body of knowledge has its own independence even if it is extrinsically directed at some end.

A final argument advanced by the celebrated professor emeritus from Louvain denies the autonomy, that is the scientific character, of science in the Catholic system, but it seems to me an argument that distorts the nature of epistemology. He asserts that to recognize any other source of truth than human knowing is to make science a slave. Now being part of a whole is not the same as being a slave. No part of the field of knowledge is a slave, even though it be coordinate with and dependent upon other parts. The primal source of both science and faith is objective Reason, that is the Word,[15] and it is only possible to conclude that science and religion cannot be jointly embraced by the same person if one holds one or other of the two following opinions: that revelation contains science, thus returning to the erroneous view of certain theologians at the time of Galileo; or that subjective reason is infinite and does not allow of any knowable object beyond its limit, thus adopting the panlogism of heterodox German idealism.

The fact of the matter is that far from being a mere difference of opinion in a political question, the rejection of Catholic schools is the conscious or unconscious corollary of views at odds with Catholic thought. The specific basis of Catholic schools is removed and they are recast in an alien mold and conformed to the prevailing cultural pluralism and nihilism. The program for the reform of seminaries drawn up at Fribourg

---

[15] See John Paul II's speech to members of the University of Padua, in which he teaches that Christ is the principle of wisdom. O.R., 12 April 1981.

in Switzerland rejects the traditional *ratio studiorum* and lays down that "from the outset a global outlook must be taken, which confronts the problems posed by the existence of other beliefs and unbelief, so that the student does not run *the risk of Christian self-sufficiency*."[16]

To appreciate how far this idea is from Catholic pedagogy, one need only note that the Christian conception of the world is alleged not to have a global character, so it lacks a universal principle; that there is meant to be from the outset a coming to grips with other philosophies, without the students having any criterion whereby they can judge them; lastly, and it is hard to say whether this is more notable for its oddity or its error, the young people are warned about the risk of taking Christianity as something self-sufficient. Thus even though Christianity is a divine teaching, it is alleged to be not enough in itself to satisfy the mind and to grant it rest in the truth; it must be believed as an opinion that needs to be integrated with others in order to have real worth.[17] Hence the progressive loss of originality in Catholic schools, which now model themselves deliberately on state schools as regards their structures, syllabuses, calendar and everything else. As for their culture, they have largely given up a specifically Catholic view of history and have adopted instead points of view that in the nineteenth century were typical of the Church's enemies.[18]

Setting aside the closures, laicization and doctrinal scandals of Catholic schools, we must sum up this treatment of their decline in the post-conciliar period by measuring its extent. The measure was provided by Michael Cardinal Faulhaber, the

---

[16] I.C.I., No.279, 1 January 1967, p.20. Mgr Martinoli, the Bishop of Lugano, is no less explicit in talking to the students of the *Collegio Papio* at Ascona: "I must ask you to deepen your knowledge of Jesus, of the Church and of religion more and more. Broaden your knowledge of other religions and currents of philosophy that are not in harmony with Christianity." See *Palaestra Virtutis*, the annual of the *Collegio Papio*, Ascona, 1971, p.26.

[17] At the Roman colloquium on Europe's Christian roots, Pierre Emmanuel maintained, without opposition, that there is now no specific and independent Catholic culture, since it is the same as the general culture round about. O.R., 26 November 1981.

[18] See for example the text book *Images et récits d'histoire*, Paris 1979, in which the leaders of religious persecution like Gambetta and Jules Ferry are held up as "great" Frenchmen.

Archbishop of Munich, when in 1936, in the thick of the tussle with Hitlerian tyranny, he said: "To close a hundred schools at a stroke is more than destroying a few churches."

127. Modern pedagogy. Catechetics.

In the present state of the Church, it is not the methods of teaching that are the real issue, but the truth of what is being taught; the post-conciliar renewal in catechetics could not but move from pedagogy to doctrine, since pedagogy is in itself an expression of doctrine. The crisis in catechetics is primarily a crisis of content and derives from the Pyrrhonism that has overtaken the Church's thinking. Meeting after meeting on catechetics asks the same question: *Peut-on trouver après Vatican II une doctrine catholique incontestable qui refasse l'unité perdue?*[19]

Modern pedagogy has its remote roots in Rousseau's negative pedagogy which attempted to draw man's education out of man himself, who was supposed to be good by nature; it has its closer origin in the German transcendental philosophy of the late eighteenth century, that regarded the individual as a "moment" of universal spirit. Its most rigorous systematic statement is made in Giovanni Gentile's *Sommario di pedagogia come scienza filosofica* published in 1912, which provided the basis of its author's reform of Italian schools. The pervading theme of that pedagogy is that universal Spirit is the true teacher; our spirits' movement is always contained within itself; Absolute Spirit is nothing other than the act of the individual, and the latter's action is a self-formation having no object or model outside himself.[20]

In the Catholic system too, the true teacher is the universal spirit, that is, the divine Word, "that enlightens every man coming into the world,"[21] and manifests natural truth; but this Spirit is other than the human spirit and transcends the latter, whereas the modern pedagogy holds that there is no transcendence of Spirit over spirit, or of truth over the intellect or of teacher over pupil.

---

[19] "Is it possible after Vatican II to establish an incontestable body of Catholic teaching that will re-establish the unity we have lost?" *Dossier sur le problème de la catéchèse*, Paris 1977, p.36.

[20] Op. cit., IV ed., Bari 1926, p.174.

[21] John, 1:9.

The Christian religion recognizes that apart from the natural light there is also a supernatural light that illuminates the human spirit from above, and makes it capable not indeed of *seeing* truths surpassing the natural sphere, but of assenting to them without seeing them, and of appropriating them to itself. For modern pedagogy on the other hand, reality is self-creation, truth self-knowledge, and teaching self-teaching, because it believes that the true and the good and every other spiritual value are inherent in the spirit itself, in short that the divine is immanent in man.

128. Novel pedagogy.

Let us now proceed to an exact statement of the mistakes in this novel pedagogy. The first error consists in denying and saying nothing about the fact that the mind to be educated depends on the principle that will educate it, and in supposing that truth is a result of personal creativity when it is actually a light the intellect does not create, but finds and indeed finds better the less it mixes its own experiences with the intuition of the truth. Experience is the means of access to the truth, but truth is not something lived, as they say today, but a pure seeing. The *De magistro*, whether of St. Augustine or of St. Thomas, affirms that truth transcends both pupil and teacher and that man does not produce it, but discovers it. Man can indeed read truth in the reality of things without having a teacher. The teacher does not pour knowledge into a pupil, but rather rouses him to personal acts of knowledge. A teacher, already possessing actual knowledge, activates the learner's potential and thus brings him to know things for himself. It is thus radically impossible for teaching to be really self-teaching and education self-education, just as it is metaphysically impossible for a potential being to bring itself into existence. St. Thomas explicitly lays down the thesis that: *Non potest aliquis dici sui ipsius magister vel seipsum docere.*[22]

Here we must recall three important points of Catholic pedagogy. The first is metaphysical: the distinction between potency and act, or the non-creativity of human faculties. The second is axiological: someone who knows is, as such, superior to someone who doesn't. The third is gnoseological: the primacy

---

[22] *De Veritate*, q.XI,a.2. "Nobody can be said to be his own teacher or to teach himself."

of knowledge over moral experience, that is, that all other things being equal, a man's moral life consists in his thought, that is, in the judgment he makes about the goals and activities of his own being.

The second error of the new pedagogy is that the direct aim of teaching is to produce an experience, that the way to that goal is also experience and that abstract knowledge of life is, as they say, merely notional. In fact the proper and formal goal of teaching, including catechetics, is not to produce experience but knowledge. The teacher draws the pupil to proceed from one state of knowing to another by means of a dialectical process of the presentation of ideas. Thus the immediate end of catechesis is not an existential and experiential meeting with the person of Christ (to think it is, is to confuse catechesis with mysticism) but is rather the knowledge of revealed truths and of the preambles to them.

The modernist origin of this pedagogy is obvious to anyone who knows that the fundamental philosophical principle of modernism was that sentiment, or feeling, contains all values within itself and is superior to all theoretical knowledge, the latter being merely an abstraction from the concrete reality which is experience.

129. The knowledge of evil in Catholic teaching.

The moral implications of this pedagogical deviation are quite serious. If knowledge is an experience, that is something lived out, knowledge of good will be experience of good, and knowledge of evil experience of evil, that is, sin: the whole system of Christian ethics and asceticism crumbles. The distinction between the ideal order given in the intellect and the real order given in lived experience disappears. St. Augustine teaches that: *scientiae malorum duae sunt, una qua potentia mentis non latent, altera qua experientia sensibus cohaerent, aliter quippe sciuntur omnia vitia per sapientis doctrinam, aliter per insipientis pessimam vitam.*[23] There is a knowledge of evil which consists in evil being present to the mind and there is another which con-

---

[23] *De Civitate Dei*, XXII, 30. "There are two sorts of knowledge of evils, one by which they do not remain hidden to the power of the mind, another by which they enter the experience of the senses; for the way a wise man's teaching knows all evils is quite different to the way a foolish man's bad life knows them."

sists in taking evil into one's experience. The second sort of knowledge goes beyond knowledge and becomes a moral act by which the spirit chooses what it has come to know, and this unites the ideal and real orders in a lived action. Experiencing should not be confused with knowing; still less made the only source of knowledge. All Catholic asceticism and pedagogy rest on this distinction and it cannot be abolished without the whole structure falling into ruin. The opinion now current even among Catholics, that one must know evil to combat it, is false, or at least it is false to say that one needs to know it experientially, beyond the knowledge of it that comes from knowing and willing the good. The value of chastity, for example, is known all the more the less one has experiential knowledge of its opposite. The Servant of God, Canon Francesco Chiesa spoke very wisely when he said: "Do not say 'we would need to be in that position.' Some things are better known precisely because we are not in that position."[24] The new pedagogy tends to identify learning with experiencing, though it does not do so explicitly, since it can hardly become *ex professo* a pedagogy of sin. This is the origin of its tendency to remove any limits on experience, to free the pupil from the teacher, the lesser from the greater, ethics from law (which is not something experienced, but something obeyed or violated) and strength from reason. The *numquam satis*[25] that Catholic philosophy associates with knowing, the modern pedagogy associates with living. From it, it deduces a right to experience everything in order to know it, a liberty which the innovators extend to the questions of ecclesiastical celibacy, premarital continence, the indissolubility of marriage, and to faithfulness in any of life's undertakings. It is alleged that any commitment the will makes without experientially knowing all the matters involved, is unjust.

The crisis of Catholic schools is at bottom a downgrading of rationality as opposed to experience, and an instance of that

---

[24] See A. Vicolungo *Nova et vetera. Can. Francesco Chiesa*, Edizioni Paoline, Alba 1961. This priest, who was as outstanding in his teaching as in his pastoral charity, was the inspirer and colleague of Don Alberione, the founder of the Society of St. Paul, for promoting Catholic publishing. The Society was subsequently publicly criticized twice by Paul VI for its doctrinal deviations. One can understand why it has removed all the theological works of the Servant of God from its catalogue.

[25] "Never enough."

vitalism typical of contemporary society, that sets no store by a
truth that could contradict life, and values instead whatever is
live, and makes this latter the standard of truth: *vivo, ergo sum.*[26]

130. Teaching and authority. Catechetics.

If one denies that truth transcends teacher and pupil, and
reduces education to self-education, the idea of authority is removed from pedagogy. Authority is a quality attaching to the
sort of act that cannot be reduced to the subjectivity of the person performing it or of the person receiving it; it stands independent of assent or dissent.

It is not therefore surprising that innovators should attack
authoritarian schools and claim that the principle of authority
has no place in pedagogy. Just as in an autonomous morality the
will that makes the laws is a law unto itself, so in an autonomous pedagogy, the person educating himself has no authority
to which he is subject. But if on the other hand truth transcends
the intellect and imposes assent, that is especially the case with
truths of faith that are the objects of catechesis, since they transcend man not merely in the way that all truth does, but in a
unique manner inasmuch as they are revealed truths and must
be assented to not on the strength of evidence but out of respect
for God.

There is therefore a singular incompatibility between
catechesis and self-education. In throwing out the authoritative
character of truth, catechesis ceases to be an appropriation of
the truth and reduces itself to a search for truth, on an absolute
equality with any other teaching.

The enormous movement of catechetical renewal which
followed the council has so far succeeded in destroying every
vestige of traditional catechesis,[27] but has not produced any
common doctrinal outlook or any positive achievement:[28] more

---

[26] "I live, therefore I am."

[27] The *Nuovo catechismo antico* by Franco della Fiore, which is an
attempt at authentic renewal, and was published by the Salesians'
SEI with a commendatory letter from the Secretariat of State, was
subsequently discontinued by decision of the publisher, despite its
good sales. It was republished by ARES in 1981 and 1985.

[28] See paragraph 68 regarding the doctrinal "misery" of the new
catechetics, emphasized by Cardinal Ratzinger in his speeches at
Lyons and Paris in January 1983.

than a few catechisms published by diocesan catechetical centers teem with rash statements, dogmatic errors and aberrations.

This new fangled catechesis can claim some support from a speech made by Paul VI on 10 December 1971, which seems to adopt two principles of the modernized pedagogy: first, that "excessively authoritarian methods should be abandoned in presenting doctrinal content and a more humble and fraternal attitude should be assumed; that of a search for the truth"; second, that "to teach means to be open to dialogue with students, with a due respect for their personality."

The first part of this speech displays a confusion between what is didactic and what is heuristic; between communication of knowledge that is already possessed and enquiring after the truth; between the professorial chair and open debate. Here too we have a case of an inadvertent transition from one essence to another, and an implicit nullification of one of the two. It is indeed true that all the wild weeds in human nature including pride can creep into the act of teaching, but one should not be surprised at that, even though one must be on guard against it continually: that untamed nature lurks in the folds of all human activity. Is it impossible for pride to creep into a dialogue in search of truth? Truth can be taught without the spirit of truth, with the intention of imposing and teaching oneself; but any consideration of human doings should concern itself with their essence, and not treat contingent flaws as if they were in fact that essence.

The elimination of authority is essential to the notion that teaching is self-teaching, by which the spirit draws truth from itself. If truth transcends the mind, it is independent of the intellect that thinks it: it is not the fact of being thought by man, but the fact of being thought by God that makes truth intelligible to man. But in the post-conciliar Church there is a widespread idea that man is self-created and thus there is much talk of self-education, self-teaching, self-government, self-evangelization and even self-redemption: authenticity is held to consist in this autonomy.

This conception of the relation between teacher and pupil, which amounts to a change in the natural state of affairs, is proclaimed openly in a letter from the Secretariat of State to a meeting in Strasbourg of the *Union nationale des parents des écoles de l'enseignement libre.* It says: *Les enseignants sans démissionner de leurs graves responsabilités, deviendront des conseillers, des orientateurs et pourquoi pas? des amis. Les élèves, sans rejeter systématiquement l'ordre et l'organisation, deviendront des corresponsables, des coopérateurs et en un certain sens des coéducateurs.*[29] This conversion of pupils into teachers and vice versa implicitly means the abolition of any true pedagogy and also entails a denigration of all the teaching efforts of the historical Church.

We will discuss the philosophy of dialogue in paragraph 156. To return to Paul VI's speech, which would seem to imply that the Church's previous teaching methods had not been respectful of student's personalities, and that teachers had been neither humble nor ready to serve, one need only point out an essential difference: to dialogue is not the same as to teach. Furthermore, anyone doing a service can only be called upon to provide the service for which he has been called, prepared and authorized; to imagine one can provide any and every service is a form of blindness and pride.

---

[29] "Without giving up their serious responsibilities, teachers will become counselors, directors and, why not?, friends. Without systematically rejecting order and organization, students will become corresponsible, co-workers and in a certain sense, co-educators." O.R., 21 May 1975.

CHAPTER XIII

CATECHETICS

131. The dissolution of catechetics.
The 1977 synod of bishops.

With the removal of the teacher's authority and the reduction of truth to a mere search for truth, the reform of catechetics could not but embrace unorthodox deviations that changed content by changing methods. A congress in Assisi in 1969 on the teaching of religion ended with a document calling for the abandonment of any dogmatic content, that is anything specifically Catholic, and the replacement of the teaching of the Catholic religion by the teaching of the history of religions, since the former was held to be an unjust privilege in a democratic country.

Nor did the 1977 synod of bishops, which discussed the new catechetics, succeed in bringing about any effective change of direction; instead it displayed disagreement among the bishops on first principles, a general lack of logic and above all an inability to stick to the point under discussion. Sticking to the point nonetheless remains the rule of rules in any debate, and to succeed in doing so itself guarantees the argument will get somewhere. At the synod, however, catechetics spilled over into sociology, politics and liberation theology. A few examples will suffice. For the Bishop of Saragossa catechetics "must promote creativity among the pupils, dialogue and active participation, without forgetting that it is an action of the Church." Creativity is in fact a metaphysical and moral absurdity, but even if it were not, it could hardly be the aim of catechesis since in the Christian view man cannot become an end unto himself; the end is given, he simply has to will it. For Fr. Hardy (of the African missions) "catechesis must bring an experience of Christ," which is a proposition that confuses the ideal and the real and strays into the field of mysticism. Catechesis is *per se* and for-

mally to do with knowledge, not experience, even though it is
ordered towards experience, that is towards life's activities. According to Cardinal Pironio "catechesis is unleashed by Christian humanity's profound experience of God and is a more
profound assimilation of love and faith."[1] There is an inkling of
modernism in assertions of that sort. Catechesis is doctrine and
it is not unleashed by the existential experience of believers, because it has a supernatural content that their experience does
not encompass.

Catechesis comes down from a divine teaching and is not
produced by religious experience; it rather produces it. Lastly a
bishop from Kenya declares that "catechesis must commit itself
to denouncing social injustices...and defending initiatives towards the social liberation of the poor,"[2] and thereby lowers the
word of eternal life to an economic and social enterprise.

132. The dissolution of catechetics.
Father Arrupe. Cardinal Benelli.

Pluralism was the synod's dominant theme, more important
even than creativity or social concern; several bishops called for
plurality of catechisms to reflect the color of different national
cultures. Fr. Arrupe, the General of the Jesuits, put the demand
for pluralism in its most extreme form. "The Spirit," he said,
"satisfies man's deep desire to reconcile the apparently contradictory demands of a fundamental unity and an equally fundamental diversity."[3] It would seem from this that the foundation
of human thinking is not identity but contradiction, and that
the Holy Spirit brings about a synthesis between incompatibles,
which the human heart is alleged to desire. The fundamental
illogicality of this is ill-disguised by the adventitious use of the
adverb "apparently." If demands are fundamentally diverse they
cannot be reconciled, that is, made non-diverse at the level of
their roots. They give rise instead to a plurality and diversity in
things. Unity and diversity cannot exist at the same level. Fr.
Arrupe goes on to say that he does not want "complete definitions, because they might lead to an aristocratic and involuted
form" of catechesis. As if truth were to be found in confused
approximations; as if orthodoxy had a negative value and as if

[1]   O.R., 16 October 1977.
[2]   O.R., 7 October 1977.
[3]   O.R., 7 October 1977.

authentic catechesis were begotten by mob rule. The truth of the matter is that here, just as in the case of Christianity and Marxism, things and ideas which are not the same are being taken simply as different ways of looking at the same object. A plurality of catechisms is wanted because of the belief that all the distinctions that give doctrines their specific content are resolvable in some fundamental sameness that surpasses them all.

Speaking to a meeting of teachers of religion, Cardinal Benelli said that religious teaching "should favor an objective meeting with other visions of life that should be known, evaluated, and, it may be, integrated." The Cardinal sees no error in the religious and intellectual world that needs to be rejected, but merely something to integrate. He also says that "the only way to teach the Catholic religion is to propose a way of living." No room for proposing truths having the authority of divine revelation. Lastly the Cardinal gives the student himself the right to "guarantee its validity, because he has already had experience of it."[4]

Two chief characteristics of the new catechesis, that is that it is a search rather than a doctrine and that it attempts to produce existential reactions rather than intellectual conviction, are reflected in attitudes towards a variety of catechisms and towards memorization.[5] Where there is no dogmatic content to be assented to, there cannot be a single universal catechism, since there are no formulas of faith valid for the whole Church, precisely in virtue of that single content. The old methods dating back to the beginning of the Church[6] and continued by the catechisms drawn up at the request of the Council of Trent, and those of St. Robert Bellarmine, St. Peter Canisius, Rosmini and St. Pius X are thus dropped.

The question and answer form was adopted by the German episcopal conference in its catechism but was rejected by the majority of bishops at the 1977 synod. It is well adapted to the didactic, rather than heuristic, form of Catholic catechesis,

---

[4] O.R., 28-29 September 1981.

[5] A real religious syncretism is the result of a plurality of catechisms: in many schools run by religious, other religions are already taught side by side with Catholicism, as a service to non-Catholics and non-Christians.

[6] One thinks of the baptismal creeds used for catechesis in the primitive Church. [Translator's note.]

which answers directly with the truth, and does not ask questions with the methodological presupposition that their answers are in doubt. Even under the socratic method, favored by the opponents of tradition, it is Socrates who knows the truth, and the pupil who has it drawn out of him.

Memorization is discounted and despised by the modern educational theorists as mere parroting, when it is in fact the foundation of all culture, as the ancients showed through the myth of Mnemosyne, Mother of the Muses.[7] It is well suited to catechesis, provided the latter is seen as a communication of knowledge rather than a social activity. For one bishop from Ecuador "catechesis consists not so much in what is heard as what is seen in the person catechizing." This is to make truth which is perceived by the intellect less important than one's personal experience, and to bind the Gospel to the excellence of its preachers rather than to its own intrinsic merits. This anthropocentric shift, by which the effect of catechesis is thought to depend more on the skills of the teacher than on the power of truth, is an error concealing yet again a confusion about the natures of things. It is to make a catechist like an actor or poet, who has power of his own to move men's minds. Catechesis is not the art of moving rhetoric, practiced in the ancient world. If it were, divine truth would not be received whenever rhetorical skill was lacking. This error crops up in the *Dossier sur le problème de catéchèse*[8] even though it is critical of the new catechesis.

133. The dissolution of catechesis.
Le Du. Charlot. Mgr Orchampt.

The intoxicating weed whose influence we have seen in synodal and episcopal documents, sprouted into a wide literature including official catechisms, not to mention private ones which we will set aside in accordance with our methodology.[9]

---

[7] Mnemosyne, "Memory," was the mother of the Muses, the nine goddesses of literature and the arts. [Translator's note.]

[8] Paris, 1977, p.22.

[9] This multiplication is noted by E. Castelli in his introduction to Rosmini's *Catechismo*, National Edition, Vol. XLV: "Within the Catholic Church today, catechisms incorporating more or less desirable changes succeed one another."

The Dutch Catechism, which is an expression of the Dutch church's alienation from orthodoxy, had a striking, widespread and unhappy effect on the Church universal. Two things amazed the world: on the one hand the audacity of its novelties, which extended from the denial of the existence of angels and the devil and the sacramental priesthood, to the rejection of the eucharistic presence and the questioning of the incarnation of the Word; and on the other, the feeble condemnation of it made by the Holy See. After having submitted the catechism to an extraordinary congregation of cardinals, which found errors and omissions of very important articles in it, the Holy See nevertheless let it circulate throughout the world, Catholic and other religious publishing houses vying for the right to print it. Only one condition was attached by the Holy See to its publication, namely that the *correctorium*, represented by the decree that had condemned the catechism, should be attached as an appendix to the *corruptorium* represented by the work itself.

The Dutch Catechism was welcomed everywhere as "the best presentation of the Catholic faith that could be made to modern man." Despite the Holy See's judgment, bishops introduced it into public schools and defended it to parents who, to fulfill their duty to guard their children's faith, withdrew their children from corrupting teaching being given by priests with the same bishops' approval.[10] The Dutch Catechism was only dropped in 1980 after the extraordinary synod of Dutch bishops held in Rome under the presidency of John Paul II.

Many publications that overthrow Scripture, question dogma and corrupt morals have emerged from the catechetical office of the diocese of Paris. John Le Du's book on the ten commandments, for example, entitled *Qui fait la loi?*[11] attacks the historicity of the Sinai covenant, which it calls *une opération frauduleuse effectuée par Moïse pour consolider son autorité.*[12] Le Du fully adopts the idea of a religious imposture propagated by Voltaire out of hatred for the Jews, a perennial source of hatred for Christianity, as is seen very clearly in the case of Nazism. Answering the question which is the book's title, "Who Makes the Law?," Le Du denies the law its divine origin, whether

---

[10] See the letter of 28 October 1964 from Mgr Martinoli, the Bishop of Lugano, to Mr. Walter Moccetti, who had informed the bishop that he had withdrawn his son from religious instruction.

[11] "Who Makes the Law?"

[12] "A fraudulent operation by Moses to consolidate his authority."

through nature or through revelation, and makes it a product of man's evolving consciousness, that is gradually freeing itself from myth; man is secularizing himself and *choisit en définitive quel homme il veut être.*[13]

An even sharper controversy was aroused by the book *Dieu est-il dans l'hostie?*[14] by Fr. Léopold Charlot, the priest in charge of the *Centre régional d'enseignement religieux d'Angers*, and seen in parish display cases. The subject of the book is *la manière dont il faut penser aujourd'hui l'Eucharistie comme présence réelle.*[15] The nub of the argument is that from age to age there are differing ways of understanding the real presence, and that the way proper to our own time is to understand it as a non-real presence, an imaginary and metaphoric presence identical to Beethoven's presence in one of his sonatas and his presence in the feelings of somebody hearing it. Charlot teaches catechumens that the Eucharist was not instituted by Christ at the Last Supper, but by the primitive Christian community. Bread and wine remain substantially bread and wine and are only a conventional sign of the presence of Christ in believers. It is thus absurd that they should be consecrated and reserved with a view to adoration. Indeed, Léopold Charlot advises mothers not to genuflect with their children in front of the tabernacle, to teach them that the Sacrament is not to be adored.

That a priest who has been invested by his bishop with responsibility for catechesis should deny the doctrine of the Eucharist in an official catechism and do so quite calmly, is certainly a scandal, in the strict sense of an act leading others to sin, in this case to sin against faith. But since it is both psychologically and morally true that responsibility runs up, not down, it is an even greater disorder that a blasphemy of this sort should be propagated in a catechism approved by a bishop, since bishops are teachers of the faith and guardians of the flock against the wolves of heresy. If the priest is devout, as it is said Charlot is, and if he is preaching his errors in good faith, the scandal on his part will be merely "material," as classical theology puts it, but the scandal given by the Church is even greater, because the Church as Church thereby appears as teaching error

---

[13] "Definitively choosing what sort of man he wants to be."

[14] "Is God in the host?"

[15] "The way in which we must think of the Eucharist as a real presence today."

and blasphemy in the person of one of its ministers, approved and commissioned by the bishop.

What Mgr Orchampt, the Bishop of Angers, said when he was besieged by a mass of protests from laity and clergy, is embarrassingly symptomatic of the decline in the intellectual lucidity and fortitude of the episcopate. When he was challenged to do something, in accordance with the requirements of canon 336, about the public offense he had given to the faith, he merely replied that: *L'évêque responsable de la foi de son peuple se doit de signaler les dangers de mutilation pour une foi qui se tiendrait à la prospective de ce fascicule...Il se doit d'inviter ceux qui l'utiliseraient à la critique et à l'approfondissement pour le nécessaire effort de renouveau pastoral.*[16] The bishop thus neither condemns nor withdraws the work published by his catechetical Centre; he treats the annihilation of a dogma as its mutilation; he allows the Catholic religion to go on being taught on the basis of a book that attacks it; he does not remove the author from office; he judges Charlot's thesis to be tenable as long as it is not held exclusively, as if holding one of two contradictory views did not exclude the other; and in accordance with the innovators' usual practice, he does not ask for a refutation of the book but for a "deepening," a word which, as we have seen in paragraph 50, is used in the new hermeneutic to mean beating endlessly upon some point of doctrine until it dissolves entirely into the opposite. Lastly the Bishop of Angers persists in maintaining that efforts like Charlot's contribute towards the renewal of the Church.

The Holy See made a sign of disapproval, but it was couched in general terms and put in a mild way. One section of Pope Paul's speech on 17 April 1977 certainly has the Bishop of Angers in view: *Les fidèles s'étonneraient à bon droit que des abus manifestes soient tolérés par ceux qui ont reçu la charge de l'épiscopat, qui signifie depuis les premiers temps de l'Eglise vigilance et unité.*[17] It is also significant that a group of bishops

---

[16] "A bishop responsible for the faith of his people owes it to himself to point out the dangers of mutilation facing a faith confined to the outlook of the booklet...He owes it to himself to invite those who would use the booklet to a critique and a 'deepening,' in order to carry out the pastoral renewal that is needed." *Semaine religieuse du diocèse d'Angers*, 11 November 1976 and 16 January 1977.

[17] "The faithful would be rightly amazed were abuses to be tolerated by those who have received an episcopal charge, which, since the

should resign and delegate their inescapable responsibilities to one bishop, and that he should in turn depend on the unsound opinions of one of his priests. Charlot's book was in the event taken up by all the dioceses of western France.

134. Renewal and vacuity of catechetics in Italy.

Delegation of teaching authority by episcopal conferences to priests of the innovating sort was seen yet again in the case of the Italian commission established to draw up a new catechism, which commission included intellectuals of a Marxist sort who subsequently defected from the Church and stood as electoral candidates on the Communist Party ticket. An arbitrarily interpreted kind of ecumenical concern led the authors of the new *Catechismo dei giovani*,[18] published in Rome in 1979, to assert that there was "a coinciding of Catholic and Protestant exegetical research"; a coinciding that cannot occur, because Protestants do not recognize, over and above their private lights, an exegetical wisdom proceeding from the magisterium of St. Peter. The authors weaken one of the principal articles of Catholic doctrine and move in a modernist direction when they say that the working of miracles did not precede faith, but that faith caused believers to think that miracles had occurred. The idea that the faith is unchangeable is given little prominence in the book, emphasis being placed instead on the new "mobilism" which teaches that the Church is forever listening and searching.

The *Catechismo dei fanciulli*[19] published in 1976 by the Italian Episcopal Conference displays the new tendencies even more clearly, especially in its interpretation of ecumenism. It sees ecumenism as a process of the recognition of values that are contained identically in every religious belief, with a greater or lesser prominence. There is thus never any movement from one religion to another, but only a process of "deepening" the truth one possesses by reference to the truth possessed by others, so that dialogue always brings enrichment to both parties. The children being instructed are detached from what is specific to the Catholic religion, invited to look at the phenomenon of

---

earliest period of the Church's history, has meant vigilance and unity."

[18] "Young People's Catechism."

[19] "Children's Catechism."

religion as a whole and led not to a reaffirming of their belief, but to a continuing search. It is stated that catechesis "ought to help children to work together with all men so that there may be liberty, justice and peace, without however ceasing to recognize faith and the sacraments as the source of spiritual strength." That "however" is significant. It would seem the ultimate criterion a catechism has to meet is that it does not deny the faith and that it recognizes that the sacraments are a source of spiritual strength, as are the beliefs of all the peoples under heaven. What is specific to Catholicism is set aside. Nothing is said about sin, error, God's threats, the redemption, the judgment or our transcendent goal: Christianity, which is either all or nothing, is reduced here to a subsidiary and auxiliary appendage.

135. The Roman catechists' meeting with the Pope.

The emptying of catechesis of its proper content is unequivocally apparent in the Roman catechists' meeting with John Paul II.[20] The Pope draws a distinction between catechesis as a direct work of the Church, and religious teaching in public schools, which is the duty of the state as an organic part of the formation of pupils. He asserts the state's duty to "perform this service for Catholic pupils, who constitute almost the entire body of students," and for their families "who are logically presumed to want an education inspired by their own religious principles." Despite this declaration, the meeting proceeded to draw up proposals and ideas that amount to a rejection of such Catholic teaching. Several speakers reduced Catholicism to a syncretistic Christian religiosity, others reduced it to natural religion, others to an expression of freedom, all of them touched on what is called the priest's crisis of identity. The only motive that could be found to justify the teaching of religion was a cultural need to know the Judaeo-Christian world in order to understand the values that go to make up modern civilization. The only goal that could be found for catechesis was to make students aware of the range of existing ideologies "to enable them subsequently to make free choices," as if a knowledge of things that could be chosen provided a criterion of choice. No specifically Catholic ground could be found for such instruction. Since Catholicism is not the sole bearer of religious values "it ought not to be the only one to go into schools and give les-

---

[20] O.R., 7 March 1981.

sons in religion." Time devoted to religious lessons ought to be pluralized by the admission of every kind of belief. The provisions of the concordat giving a special place to the Catholic religion ought therefore to be abolished.

These Roman priests seem to be continuing the naturalist tradition: they remind one of the syncretistic pantheon portrayed in the circles of Campanella's City of the Sun in which Christ stands beside Osiris, Charon and Mahomet, or of the chapels of certain Renaissance humanists, or of the syncretistic project at Notre Dame de la Garde at Marseilles planned by Mgr Etchégaray. Nothing specifically relating to Catholic truth could be found to justify the teaching; it was asserted instead that "catechists are not paid to do catechesis and teach a faith, they are at the service of the human person." They say that "it is a task of pre-catechesis, pre-evangelization, that the state ought to recognize as a support to personal growth." The clergy's profound loss of direction is obvious, as they stumble about in vague expressions like "personal growth," and allege an opposition between teaching Catholic truth and serving the human person, the former being reduced to a mere support, or the beginning of a process of discovery in which freedom, not truth, is master.

The vacuity of catechesis is openly expressed in the proposals made in the final document, which are: that a Mass be celebrated for students who are about to do exams, that a Schools' Day be held in Rome as elsewhere, that the Pope receive the Roman catechists in audience in the near future, and that he "carry out a visit to a fifth form class in a public school." Anyone can see that the results of this Roman meeting, involving the Pope, are somewhat thin: good results certainly, but completely unrelated to the real nature of the problems debated. There is reason to think that this paucity of content was simply a last resort to prevent the final document reflecting the oddness of the opinions that had been aired, which were hardly in accord with sound philosophy or the Church's traditional practice.

136. Contradiction between the new catechetics and the directives of John Paul II. Cardinal Journet.

The mentality of the clergy evident in the document is all the more noteworthy for being clearly opposed to an apostolic exhortation by John Paul II.[21] While the new catechetics is of an existential sort and is designed to produce an experience of faith, the Pope asserts the intellectual character of catechesis and wants catechumens to be imbued with simple but firm certitudes *quibus ad Dominum magis magisque conoscendum adjuventur.*[22] The new catechetics wants the faith to be adapted to different historical cultures, while the Pope wants the faith to transform each culture: *non esset catechesis si Evangelium ipsum mutaretur cum culturas attingit.*[23] The new catechetics repudiates the principle of authority, the classic question and answer method, and thus the use of memory, while the Pope emphasizes the need to grasp the sayings of Christ, some principal biblical texts, the formulas of faith, the ten commandments, some common prayers and liturgical texts, in a lasting way, that is by memory.[24] The new catechesis is conducted by a dialogue between equals, aimed at discovery and based on the absence of specific truths, while the Pope rejects as dangerous a dialogue which *saepe ad indifferentismum omnia exaequantem delabitur.*[25] The new catechetics sets out to lead the catechumen to an experience of Christ and of the divine, while the Pope calls

---

[21] O.R., 26 October 1979. [The apostolic exhortation is *Catechesi Tradendae*, 1979, whence came the quotations following. Translator's note.]

[22] "By which they can be helped to know the Lord more and more."

[23] "It would not be catechesis if the Gospel itself were to change when it comes into contact with cultures."

[24] The most widespread and obvious effect of the elimination of memorization from catechesis is that children do not know the *Pater* and the *Ave Maria* because they have been taught them neither by their mothers nor by their parish priests. That was the view of Mgr Martinoli, the Bishop of Lugano, given in a sermon in Lugano Cathedral on 20 May 1973. Mgr Orchampt, the President of the Episcopal Commission for Catechesis in France likewise asks that children should again be taught these two prayers. See M. Gillet, *Notre catéchèse*, Paris 1976.

[25] "Often lapses into an indifferentism that regards all things as equal."

catechesis *institutio doctrinae christianae*, that is, an instruction aimed to bring someone to an ever better knowledge and an ever firmer assent to divine truth, not to an ever greater development and affirmation of the catechumen as a person.

The whole present loss of direction in the Church is reflected in the crisis in catechetics. It displays the despising of theoretical knowledge, the uncertainty not only in theology but in dogma, the excessively subjective spirit, the disagreement among bishops,[26] the discord between bishops and the Holy See, the rejection of the fundamental principles of Catholic pedagogy, the worldly and millenarian outlook and the anthropocentric drift of teaching in general.

Gérard Soulages[27] publishes some striking letters by Cardinal Journet on the present state of catechetics. The Cardinal sees it precisely as an effect of the loss of direction by the hierarchy and the internal decay of the Church: *Il serait catastrophique que les évêques, successeurs des Apôtres, soient à la dérive de commissions et de poussées limitées à l'ajustement du monde et au service d'une déchristianisation du peuple chrétien.*[28]

137. Catechesis without catechesis.

The newfangled catechesis is thus characterized by two intrinsically connected stages: a methodological stage, in which it drops the Catholic pedagogy based on the transcendence of the truth over the intellect that discerns it; and a dogmatic stage, in which it drops the certainties of faith and replaces them with subjective examination and choice. The new catechetics launched by the French episcopate with their *Fonds obligatoires*[29] was brought to fulfillment by the promulgation of *Pierres vivantes*[30] in 1982. The appearance of this text without the approval

---

[26] In the course of the Charlot case we have mentioned, Bishop Elchinger (Bishop of Strasbourg 1967-1984) walked out of the episcopal commission because of disagreement on points of doctrine.

[27] In *Dossier sur le problème de catéchèse*, September 1977, p.53.

[28] "It would be catastrophic for the bishops, who are successors of the Apostles, to move in the wake of commissions and pressure groups aimed only at improving the world, and for them to assist a dechristianization of the Christian people."

[29] "Obligatory Sources."

[30] "Living Stones."

of the Holy See, and accompanied by a ban on all other catechisms, thus including the catechisms of the Council of Trent
and of St. Pius X which had recently been reprinted, threatened
to cause an unpleasant conflict between the French bishops and
the Holy See, but in the event it did not. In January 1983 Cardinal Ratzinger, the Prefect of the Congregation for the Doctrine of the Faith, came to Lyons and Paris to address meetings
on the present state of catechetics, or what he called *la misère de
la catéchèse nouvelle,*[31] and aroused strong complaints from the
French bishops, confusion among the clergy and no little disturbance in public opinion.

The Cardinal's complaint against the new catechetics was
that instead of putting forward truths to which the assent of
faith is due, it presents biblical texts explained simply according
to historico-critical methods, leaving it up to the catechumen to
give or withhold his assent. The truths of faith that the Church
proclaims are thus detached from the Church which is their
living context, and put directly before the believer, who is called
upon to act as interpreter and judge; the Bible thus treated in
isolation becomes merely a document subject to historical criticism, and the Church is valued less than personal opinion.

The mistake consists essentially in wanting *dire la foi direc-
tement à partir de la Bible sans faire le détour par le Dogme.*[32] This
amounts to the Lutheran mistake of denying tradition and the
Church's teaching authority, and it also changes the status of the
Bible itself which, when *détachée de l'organisme vivante de
l'Eglise*[33], becomes *un simple musée de choses passées et une collection de livres hétérogènes.*[34] The Church is left at the mercy of
private judgment, and the doctrines of faith at the mercy of
historians and critics: believing in religious truth becomes
something done by an individual, outside the community willed
by Christ. Because the exegesis with which the biblical text is
presented is dominated by rationalistic assumptions that reject

---

[31] "The misery of the new catechetics."

[32] "To put forth the faith directly from the Bible without going via
dogma." Following this pedagogical technique, one arrives at the
absurdity of getting children to deal with the apocryphal writings
and *logia* of Christ while they remain ignorant of the creed, the
sacraments and the principal mysteries of the faith.

[33] "It is detached from the living tradition of the Church."

[34] "A mere museum of the past and a heterogeneous collection of
books."

anything above present human understanding, *on tend aujourd'hui à éviter la difficulté partout où le message de la foi nous met en présence de la matière et à s'en tenir à une perspective symbolique. Cela commence avec la création, continue avec la naissance virginale de Jésus et sa Résurrection, finit avec la Présence réelle du Christ dans le pain at le vin consacrés, avec notre propre résurrection et avec la Parousie du Seigneur.*[35] The doctrinal errors that beset the new catechesis are clearly outlined here. The doctrine of creation is not clearly taught nor does it come at the beginning of instruction: it is mentioned only in chapter nine of *Pierres vivantes* and identified with God's creating of his people by freeing them from slavery. The virgin birth of Christ is given no doctrinal significance since Mary is described merely as *une jeune fille de Palestine que Dieu a choisie pour être la mère de Jésus:*[36] nothing is said about the Immaculate Conception, about Mary's perpetual virginity or about her being the Mother of God. The resurrection at Easter is said to be a spiritual event that was a reality in the faith of the primitive community, and thus in virtue of the logical connection so strongly asserted by St. Paul,[37] the resurrection of the dead in general is merely an opinion. The Ascension is simply a metaphor conveying the moral apotheosis of Christ, since *Pierre vivantes* says in set terms: *Monter au Ciel est une image pour dire qu'il est dans la joie de son Père.*[38] But even a mere man can ascend to the joy of the Father in that sense. Where Scripture says that he ascended to heaven *videntibus illis*[39] the French catechism teaches that *le 40ème jour après Pâques les chrétiens croient que Jésus est au-dessus de tout.*[40] Lastly the Eucharist is reduced to the Christian com-

---

[35] "People tend today to avoid difficulties whenever the message of faith involves matter, by limiting themselves to symbolic interpretations. It begins with the creation, continues with the virgin birth of Jesus and his Resurrection, and ends with the real presence of Christ in the consecrated bread and wine, our own resurrection and the Lord's parousia."

[36] "A young girl in Palestine whom God chose to be the mother of Jesus."

[37] I Corinthians, 15:12ff.

[38] "Going up to heaven is an image to convey the fact that He is in the joy of His Father."

[39] Acts, 1:9. "In their sight."

[40] "On the fortieth day after Easter, the Christians believed that Jesus was above all."

munity's celebration of the memory of the Lord's Supper and the chapter devoted to it in *Pierres vivantes* is called *Des chrétiens se souviennent*.[41] This represents the innovators' theory of transignification and transfinalization, which we will treat in paragraphs 267-75. *Pierres vivantes* cannot disguise the fact that it presents something abnormal and unorthodox to French children as if it were the Catholic faith, even though it does not do so in every article, and proceeds by way of omissions, metaphors and half truths, which become strikingly obvious only if they are compared with the formulas contained in the old catechism.[42]

138. Restoration of Catholic catechetics.

Cardinal Ratzinger says catechesis is a teaching operation, that is, a communication of truths, and its content is the teaching of the Church, that is to say not merely the words of the Bible considered as historical and philological abstractions, but the words of the Bible as they are conserved and communicated to men by the Church. One cannot leave the teaching of doctrine till adolescence, as the French catechism claims, while confronting children directly in the meantime with a Bible whose meaning is to be garnered by being read in different keys: the meaning of the Old Testament, then that of the New, then lastly, what the Bible means for today's Catholic.[43] This application of historicist principles to revelation harmonizes nicely with the modernist belief that the divine is an unknowable *noumenon* that the human spirit clothes and reclothes in a thousand styles that make up the total religious experience of mankind. John Paul II's warning in his speech at Salamanca is applicable to the French catechism: "Be on guard against the dangerous illusion of separating Christ from His Church, and the Church from its magisterium."

---

[41] "Christians remember."

[42] Speaking to the International Council for Catechetics shortly after Cardinal Ratzinger's speech, the Pope reaffirmed the essential link between catechesis and dogma. He said that the task of catechesis was "to transmit the realities expressed in the Creed, to explain them and to ensure that they are integrally lived out." O.R., 16 April 1983.

[43] Be it noted that these three readings of a single text are differentiated typographically by using three colors to distinguish them.

Cardinal Ratzinger emphasizes the permanence of dogma in the face of the historicism of *Pierres vivantes*, a permanence that catechists must expound in a variety of ways, by means of various psychological, literary and didactic methods, while preserving its substantial identity amidst the flux of history. Dogma does not exist in different modes, but there is a variety, indeed an infinity of different ways of expressing it. Catechesis is essentially intellectual and aims to transmit knowledge, not to procure an existential experience or what is called insertion into the mystery of Christ. Truths of faith are indeed taught with a view to their becoming practice, a way of life, but the proper object of catechesis is knowledge, not behavior as such.

The Cardinal wants subject matter arranged following the scheme of the Catechism of the Council of Trent, which was followed throughout the Catholic world until Vatican II. As soon as they are capable of understanding, children should therefore be taught what the Christian should believe, which amounts to an exposition of the Creed; then what he should want and ask God for in prayer, which amounts to explaining the *Pater Noster*; lastly what he ought to do, which amounts to an exposition of the commandments. This threefold division has a great metaphysical and theological depth (though the new catechisms have failed to realize the fact) because it corresponds to the trinitarian constitution of all being, to the internal distinctions within the Holy Trinity itself and to the threefold character of the theological virtues of faith, hope and charity. The treatment of the sacraments follows upon these three parts, and it too as a fourth part is well integrated into Catholic teaching, because it is only with the help of the grace communicated through the sacraments that man becomes able to fulfill the moral law, as confirmed and heightened by the law of the Gospel. Cardinal Ratzinger also mentions the need to involve the memory, and the effectiveness of the question and answer method, which are both well suited to dogmatic matters that are not open to heuristic examination or an existential approach.

Cardinal Ratzinger's serious criticisms of the French catechism lose none of their theoretical and doctrinal force from the fact that, after having expounded them in a speech which when printed ran to twenty pages, he later retracted them in a statement of twenty lines, drawn up in agreement with the French bishops.[44]

---

[44] See paragraphs 60-68 on renunciation of authority.

CHAPTER XIV

THE RELIGIOUS ORDERS

139. The religious orders in the post-conciliar Church.

Since religious orders and institutes take on the supererogatory part of religion, that is, the observance of the evangelical counsels, it is obvious that the loss of direction that has come upon religion as a whole will have dealt a particular blow to that particular part of the Church. In accordance with the *loquimini nobis placentia* by which men tend to adorn their own defects and heighten their own virtues, the serious decay that has occurred in religious orders has been generally disguised through the adoption of John XXIII's optimistic outlook, and by taking change and instability as signs of life.

The decay is nonetheless obvious from the defections of those who had taken up a consecrated life.[1] All religious communities, great and small, male and female, contemplative, active or mixed, if not strictly decimated, have been reduced to a fraction of their former selves in the course of twenty years. According to the official statistics contained in the *Tabularum statisticarum collectio* of 1978 the total number of religious in the world dropped from 208,000 to 165,000 between 1966 and 1977;[2] a fall of almost one-quarter. Nor can one assert, though the attempt is made, that a reduction in numbers has been accompanied by an improvement in quality: quality shows itself in quantity. If numbers of people commit themselves to an ideal, the practice of that ideal can be brought to perfection. The larger the number of people involved in an activity, the larger the minority who excel at it, just as one needs a lot of practice at working in order to work well.

---

[1] See paragraph 79.
[2] The greatest ruin had occurred amongst the Dominicans, falling from 10,000 to 6,000; the Capuchins, 16,000 to 12,000; the Jesuits 36,000 to 26,000 and the Salesians 22,000 to 17,000.

The decay is also proved by the *innovations:*[3] all religious institutes have held special chapters to reshape their constitutions and rules, sometimes in reckless ways, and always with results that have been more destructive than edifying. When asked about the existence of a crisis in religious life, Cardinal Daniélou gave a blunt and distressing answer: *Je pense qu'il y a actuellement une crise très grave de la vie religieuse et qu'il ne faut pas parler de renouvellement, mais plutôt de décadence.*[4] The Cardinal sums up the cause of the decay as being a distorting of the evangelical counsels by taking them as a psychological and sociological outlook rather than as a special state of life structured in accordance with the counsel Christ gives in the Gospels.[5]

This renewal should have been an adaptation of external activities with a view to a more effective pursuit of holiness, which is the goal of the Church in general and of religious life in particular. Relations with the world at large were always in the minds of founders and reformers. When Mahommedans and Christians practiced slavery, the Mercedarians arose to ransom slaves; when epidemics raged there came the Hospitaller Brothers of St. Anthony, the Fatebenefratelli and the Camillans; when the masses had to be taught there were the Scolopi. Not

---

[3] The spirit of novelty also produces a lack of attachment to the founder of the order and can lead to an abandonment of places associated with him. In 1870 Pius IX suggested to Don Bosco that he transfer his works from Turin to Rome and asked: "Would your congregation lose by it?" and the saint was heard to reply: "Holy Father, it would be its ruin." (*Memorie biografiche di Don Bosco,* Vol. IX, p.319.) In 1972 when the Major Chapter of the Salesians moved to Rome, the Rector said: "What then would have been the ruin of the Salesians, has become a necessity a hundred years later, because of radically changed circumstances" (O.R., 9 June 1972). Nor is it any good to claim that Turin continues to be the spiritual center of the order, and that it will be even more so than it was before. This is an abuse of words: a center cannot remain a center when the central organization departs.

[4] M. de Lange, *Dans le sillage des Apôtres,* Paris, 1976, p.223. "I think there is at present a very grave crisis in religious life and that people should not be talking about a renewal, but rather a decay."

[5] Cardinal Ciappi has also called attention to the perversion of reform under the pretext of adapting to the world. O.R., 3 July 1981.

to mention the modern congregations adapted in a thousand ways to meet the needs of society.[6]

Adaptations there have always been, but the general rule of the post-conciliar reforms has been: that reform has without exception been *from the difficult to the easy or less difficult* and *never from the easy to the difficult or more difficult.* It is important to note that this general law of post-conciliar reforms is the reverse of what can be seen in the history of religious communities. All past reforms were begotten by a disgust with weakening of discipline and by a desire for a life that was more spiritual, more prayerful and more austere. The Cistercians, for instance, sprang from the Cluniacs, and the Trappists from the Cistercians. Successive waves of a desire for austerity meant that from the Franciscan Friars Minor there arose the Observant Franciscans, the Reformed Franciscans and the Capuchins, not to mention the heretical Fraticelli; all caused by an ascending and unworldly spirit, never a descending and worldly one of the sort that, for the first time ever, is the inspiration of the reforms in the Church at present.

Reforms today are in large measure drawn up in a new vocabulary, embodying a good deal of monotonous verbiage. In chapters assembled to effect a renewal, a religious order "questions itself," "lets itself be asked," "confronts experiences," "searches for a new identity" (which inadvertently implies that it is becoming something other than itself), "puts in place new working principles," "becomes aware of new questions in the Church" (which means that the ends in view have altered), "addresses the problem of creativity," moves towards "building true communities" (as if for centuries past religious orders had consisted entirely of false communities), thinks of ways of "inserting itself into its context" and so on.[7]

---

6   The Mercedarians, properly the Order of the Blessed Virgin Mary of Mercy, have existed since 1218. The Hospitaller Brothers of St. Anthony flourished c.1095-1777. The Fatebenefratelli ("Do Good Brothers"), properly the Hospital Order of St. John of God, have existed since 1537. The Camillans, properly the Order of Clerks Regular Ministering to the Sick, have existed since 1582. The Scolopi, properly the Order of Clerks Regular of the Mother of God of the Pious Schools, have existed since 1617. [Translator's note.]

7   These expressions are taken from plans for renewal by the Salesians in Latin America, published in the *Bollettino Salesiano*,

140. Change in principles.

As in the case of all parts of the ecclesial body, the crisis among religious is the result of an excessive conforming to the world, and a taking up of the world's positions because one has despaired of winning the world over to one's own. The crisis is an alienation stemming from an incipient loss of one's own essential nature, and from crossing over into what is other. A by no means small or unimportant sign of this alienation is a change in the dress of members of religious orders, inspired by a wish that it should no longer differ from that of secular persons. While it is symptomatic of the loss of the essence of religious life, or at least a loss of the accidental qualities belonging to that essence, it is also a sign of servility. It should not be forgotten that the sometimes extravagant singularity of religious dress was intended to show the singularity of the religious state, and was also an important sign of the Church's liberty and its independence of styles and fashions. From despising the usual ecclesiastical dress, one lapses into despising liturgical dress, and at concelebrations today one sees priests officiating in frankly lay attire.[8]

Religious life is a style of living modeled on the evangelical *counsels* and is therefore objectively more excellent than common Christian life based on the Gospel's *precepts*, since it is the option referred to by Christ when he says *Si vis perfectus esse.*[9] The drift in reform in religious life today is parallel to the one governing the reform of the priesthood. On the one hand there is the obliteration of the difference between the sacramental priesthood and the priesthood of all believers; on the other, of the difference between a state of perfection and the common

September 1978, pp.9-12. But they are common to all reforming chapters. See O.R., passim.

[8] *Esprit et Vie*, 1983, p.190, deplores the negligence of bishops in this matter. Slackness in dress on the part of clergy and religious is condemned by John Paul II in his letter to the Cardinal Vicar for Rome, on 8 September 1982, in which he says the reasons and pretexts advanced in favor of dressing as one wishes are "much more of a merely human character than they are ecclesiological." O.R., 18-19 October 1982. The Cardinal Vicar then published norms valid for all clergy living in Rome, but they have yet to be obeyed.

[9] Matthew, 19:21. "If you would be perfect."

state. What is specific to religious life is washed out or watered down in thought and behavior.

Since man's life is a flux, and the human will perpetually wanders into opposition to the fixed and abiding requirements of the law, a *state* of life implies a fixed order within which that flux can be shaped. A fixed character can then be given to life by the commitment whereby the will binds itself forever to that fixed order, through the triple vow of poverty, chastity and obedience. A falling away from that fixed state is produced by weakening the observance of those vows, and weakening them not by contingent and arbitrary decisions on the part of individuals, but precisely through a canonical relaxation laid down in general chapters called to effect reform.

First of all, the principle of *stability* is gone. The stability that the monk promised according to the Benedictine rule had a double meaning corresponding to the two senses of the word. Reference to the original, inner meaning of a word is often enough to clarify an issue. The Latin *regere* means both *to uphold* and *to direct*. The monastic rule is thus a norm that imposes a direction on life and upholds it simultaneously. The Latin *stare* from which we get *stabilitas* means both to stay put and to stay upright. Religious stability meant both that the monk stayed in his monastery and did not change his abode, and that through doing so he found a means of remaining upright in his moral and religious behavior.

Local stability has today disappeared.[10] Of course for centuries superiors in all religious orders have changed their subjects' places of residence. Indeed canon law expressly allows for a moving around at the behest of superiors. The problem is that a lack of stability has become part of the life of individual communities. Because of the greater mobility of men today, brethren leave their religious houses not only to go traveling, or on holidays, or to pursue amusements often disguised by some cultural or apostolic motive; members of the same community separate from each other by going to live in different places and giving up communal life. Exclaustration,[11] which was once unusual, has now become a normal form of religious life. In place of a cenobitic existence there is a kind of diaspora in which the

---

[10] That depends on what kind of order you have in mind. [Translator's note.]

[11] Permission to live outside the community.

benefits of stability that we have mentioned are lost and community life disappears.

141. The fundamental change.

The whole renewal is moving towards a fundamental shift which, if it were fully carried through, would cause a complete about-turn, amounting to annihilation.[12] This fundamental change is an expression of the anthropocentric revolution that characterizes the present stage of the Church's history.[13] It is apparent in the definition of the ends of religious life, and affects the general principles of morality and religion. The new end assigned to the religious life is the *service of man* rather than the service of God, or rather the service of man identified with the service of God, and it rests upon the false assumption that man's end is not and cannot be his own salvation, because to aim at that would be a kind of theological utilitarianism. Loving man is held to leave no room for loving one's self, and the fact that there is a heavenly reward for pursuing what is right is held to prove that the pursuit of right is a selfish activity.

The goal men used to set before themselves in taking religious vows was explicitly the salvation of their souls. Without going as far back as the original Eastern monasticism, that goal appears in the prologue to the Rule of St. Benedict: *Et si fugientes gehennae poenas ad vitam perpetuam volumus pervenire, dum adhuc vacat et in hoc corpore sumus, currendum et agendum est modo quod in perpetuum nobis expedit.*[14] But this motive is no

---

[12] See paragraphs 39 and 53.

[13] At the meeting of the Union of Superiors General held at Grottaferrata in May 1981 in the presence of Cardinal Pironio, it was said that renewal "has its roots not so much in certain changes that are superficial rather than substantial, as in the genuine Copernican revolution in the relationship with the present world, by the light of which members of religious institutes today seek to discover the meaning of their life as members of those institutes." This is a reference to the complete or "catastrophal" turnaround we mentioned in paragraphs 53-54. The peculiar statement was also made that "The charism of an institute is conveyed to us by its history." It would seem that an institute's history, which is in fact the unfolding of the founder's charism, is instead the thing which gives birth to the charism. O.R., 11 June 1981.

[14] P.L., 66,218. "And if flying from the penalties of hell we wish to arrive at eternal life, while there is still time and we are still in this

less obvious among the great founders of orders in modern times. In 1862 when the secular priest Fr. Lemoyne was thinking of joining St. John Bosco's congregation "to help you to what small extent I can," the saint replied: "No, God's work needs no help from men: come simply for the good of your soul." John Paul II upheld the traditional doctrine when he said in a speech to priests: "Your first apostolic duty is your own sanctification."[15] In the Catholic view of things, the doing of good to one's soul amounts to the perfecting of justice, that is, to the fulfilling of the divine will, and it is by doing that that one serves God and gives him glory. This difficult but true view of things is completely free of any shade of theological utilitarianism.

In the Constitutions of his Institute of Charity, and in his explanations of this point, Antonio Rosmini expresses the goal of all religious life even more clearly: "The Institute of Charity brings together Christians who, aflame with a desire to follow Christ, attend to their own perfection by mutual help and exhortation." In explaining "the proper and specific end" of the religious life, Rosmini writes that it "is to think more than others do about themselves, about their own soul[16] with the purpose of purifying it more and more by divine assistance, and to this end in this Institute a man proposes to make an entire sacrifice of himself to God...and the exercises of St. Ignatius themselves and the missions that the Institute undertakes, are not considered as an end, but as a means to their own sanctification."[17] Lastly the *Opus Dei* founded by the Servant of God Escrivá de Balaguer in 1928, erected as a personal prelature in 1982, and which has 70,000 members, makes personal sanctification by means of the fulfillment of the duties of one's state its principle aim. The formulas "for my salvation," "to go to heaven," "to save my soul" are not peculiar to monastic asceti-

---

body, let us so run our course and now act as will benefit us forever."

[15] O.R., 1 October 1979.

[16] This truth is denied today by both laity and priests. At a symposium in Lugano on "Gospel and Society," Mgr Riboldi, the Bishop of Acerra, condemned anyone who thought that belonging to the Church could be reduced to a commitment to religious perfection and the search for one's own salvation.

[17] *Epistolario Completo*, Vol. VI, p.92, Casale Monferrato 1890, letter to Fr. Reynaudi.

cism, but come from the foundation common to all Christianity and form part of liturgical prayer, ordinary formulas of
prayer, a hundred popular sayings and even of the legal style of
wills and contracts: "for the salvation of my soul," "as a remedy
for my soul." Religious life which used to have the three vows as
its essential elements, has today departed from its original
"vertical" direction and has turned to developing the personality
of its members in this world and in the service of man.[18]

142. The religious virtues in the post-conciliar reform. Chastity. Temperance.

This departure from a transcendent orientation can be seen
in detail in the exercise of the virtues entailed in the vows of
religion. We know that all the virtues are interconnected, and
are indeed a single virtue.[19] If virtue is a habit of the will that
always seeks the eternal law, particular virtuous acts are specific
instances of that habit; thus one can say that all of them are
contained in each one even though they do not appear: *Ita
quaelibet non tantum cohaeret, sed etiam inest alteri, ut qui unam*

----

[18] In an important program broadcast on Swiss television on 7 April
    1982, the Capuchins of the Swiss province gave a clear and wide
    ranging view of the reform of religious orders, as the innovators
    understand it. There was one general principle governing the pres-
    entation of the reforms that had been instituted. It was that depar-
    tures from the Rule were new ways of following the Rule and thus
    by those departures one was truly following the intentions of the
    founder, St. Francis of Assisi. The doings of Capuchins who came
    back from the missions, left their communities, dropped any activi-
    ties properly belonging to religious, said they wanted to set off in
    search of a new experience of God, went about living the life of
    vagabonds or hermits, avoided the obligations they had undertaken,
    followed faith in man as their guiding principle, undertook philan-
    thropic activities and in so doing said they did not mean Catholic
    activities but activities of men drawn together on the basis of com-
    mon faith in man, were all held up as praiseworthy. Poverty did not
    consist, so they said, in not possessing riches, but in sharing riches
    with others. They thus made the usual confusion of the natures of
    things and thought that poverty in imitation of Christ was the same
    as charity towards one's fellow man.
[19] *Summa Theologica*, I,II,q.65.

habet, vere omnes habere dicatur.[20] Conversely, one can say when analyzing the individual virtues of the religious life that a decline in any one of them will be a sign of a decline of religious virtues in general.[21]

As regards chastity, a decline in delicacy and care are obvious in the widespread slackness in clerical dress, in the more frequent mixing of the sexes, even on journeys, and in the abandonment of the precautions adopted even by great and holy men, which are now despised in theory and neglected in practice. It must be admitted that a distaste for chastity is a cause of many of the defections, however that fact may be disguised.

Pope Paul's *motu proprio, Ecclesiae Sanctae* lays down that: "Religious should pay more attention than other Christians to works of penance and mortification."[22] It is a fact that the virtue of temperance that was commanded by the rules of the older orders, and observed both individually and collectively, lasted even in modern orders up to the post-conciliar renewal. Not to mention the bread and water diets of eastern hermits, the oilless diets of certain cenobites, and the meatless ones of the Carthusians, Trappists and Minims, one can say that all religious institutes founded from the Council of Trent right up to modern times prescribed a very abstemious diet in food and drink: in the morning a cup of coffee and a piece of bread, at midday soup, a main course with a vegetable, a piece of fruit, a limited measure of wine;[23] in the evening a soup, a main course

---

[20] St. Bonaventure, *De profectu religionis*, Liber II, cap.24. "Thus each one of them not only joins the others, but is actually in the others, so that someone who has one of them can truly be said to have them all."

[21] To grasp the difference between the old and the new discipline it is useful to read R. Thomas's *La journée monastique*, Paris 1983, which describes the Cistercian use.

[22] Paragraph 22.

[23] The wine was often of poor quality. Don Bosco, for example, used to buy what was left over at the markets and even then watered it down, which led him to joke that: "I have renounced the devil, but not his pomps." See *Memorie Biografiche*, Vol. IV, p.192 (out of print). But the most relevant writing on the subject is the *Apologia ad Guillelmum abbatem* by St. Bernard, which vividly depicts relaxation in some monasteries in the 12th century. It can be found in the first volume of his *Opera Omnia* published by *Scriptorium*

with greens. There is no need to add that fasting and abstinence from meat were practiced on the days laid down by general law. Today in some rich countries the regime is: at breakfast a choice of coffee, chocolate, tea, milk, marmalade, bacon, cheese, yoghurt, bread and biscuits; at lunch an antipasto, soup, a main course with two vegetables, fruit or dessert, bread and coffee, some beer or wine. Halfway through the afternoon there is coffee, tea, milk, biscuits and fruit. Supper is the same as lunch except for the antipasto and the coffee.

I do not want to make the mistake of those who, through ignorance of history, look at all times and ways of behaving in the same light. In making judgments of a mixed historico-moral sort on monastic virtues, the standard of virtue must be firmly grasped, but the relativities of history should not be forgotten. The ferocious mortification of the appetite for food, for which eastern asceticism is famous, was a way of detaching oneself from an ordinary diet that was much less rich and varied to start with than it is today. Mortification is a relative thing, but a mortified diet must be different from the ordinary one. In periods when most people, in Lombardy for example, lived on rye bread often weeks or months old, or on chestnuts, monastic temperance had to cut down even on that scanty diet, and thus reached levels of austerity that are unimaginable today. A monastic regime today has to cut down on an incomparably more sumptuous diet. But it must still cut down. Amidst the relativities of one age and another, the fundamental requirement remains that the diet of consecrated persons should be more modest than what is usual, and it should be recognizable as such. Even in diet, a religious is not a man like other men.

143. Poverty and obedience.

I include temperance under poverty, because it is really part of the humble and modest life that poverty involves. Temperance is poverty in the matter of food, but the non-possession implied by a religious vow of poverty covers more than basics like food; it involves all the paraphernalia that make for an easy life, which must also be renounced or reduced, in accordance, naturally, with the historically relative standards mentioned above. Poverty will not therefore involve lighting the night with

---

Claravallense, Milan 1984, pp.123ff. See also the introduction's treatment of the matter, pp.139-143.

oil lamps or candles in the age of electricity, or adopting the methods of Deuteronomy, 23:12-13 in an age when washrooms are as luxurious as royal apartments and guides to them are even published. Nor will it mean warming oneself by going to a single fireplace in an age when heaters are electric and hot air is directed to whole buildings, blocks or cities. Nor will it mean only communicating by means of letters, delivered by a slow and infrequent postal service, in an age of telephones and telegraphs.

Some things that were unnecessary, ineluctably become necessary through the general developments of technology. The movement whereby what was once superfluous is made necessary to more and more people is now called "progress." The disappearance of individual self-sufficiency is a distinguishing characteristic of contemporary civilization, in which man is assisted and directed to do all that he does. But even if that is the direction that civilization is taking, it is appropriate that men vowed to a state of perfection should withdraw from its excesses. For example, the use of radios and television, which until a few years ago was forbidden in religious communities, was first allowed in common, and has now reached individual cells. The television that daily prints the same images in millions of brains and returns the next day to overprint others in the same brains, like a sheet of paper printed on a thousand times, is the most powerful organ of intellectual corruption in the contemporary world. Nonetheless I will not deny that from those enormous antennae that send out across the world influences more powerful than those of the stars in the celestial spheres, there may come some slight influence that may accidentally be of use to religion. But I do deny that these scraps can legitimate the habitual and uncontrolled use of such technology or become the norm by which to shape the rhythms of religious life. One cannot but be amazed! Certain communities have abandoned the centuries old custom of reciting the night office in church so as to be able to watch television programs that clashed with the keeping of their rule.

144. New concept of religious obedience.

But disobedience is the point on which the drift towards relaxation in religious orders shows itself most clearly. There has been a great change by comparison with former practice, but an even greater one if one considers the departure from former theory. It is by lowering the conception one has of this virtue that one succeeds in lowering its practice. The corruption in theory, and its approval in reforming chapters general, has been achieved by the innovators' usual methods. They do not put forward another definition of something, which would make it obvious that the nature of the thing in question is being changed; they pretend rather that they are taking up merely another *style* or *form* of the same thing.[24] Thus a meeting of major superiors lowers the concept of obedience by dint of lowering the principle of authority and mixing it up with a kind of fraternal relationship: "The accent on authority as service implies a new style of obedience. Obedience must be active and responsible."[25] And it adopts this "circiterism": "Authority and obedience are exercised as two complementary aspects of the same sharing in the offering of Christ." The superiors do not deny that the person being obedient should do the will of God, but they no longer identify that will with the will of the superior, as the continuous teaching of Catholic asceticism does. On the contrary, both the superior and subject "proceed *pari passu* in doing the will of God, which is sought out fraternally by means of a fruitful dialogue."

New ideas are here being put into circulation under cover of familiar terminology. Obedience is not in reality a dialectical attempt to discover what will to obey; it is submission to the will of the superior. It is not a re-examination of the superior's command by the one obeying. Catholic obedience cannot therefore be based on an examination of the quality of the superior or of his orders. The Apostolic Delegate in England was wrong when he said "authority is worth no more than the worth of its arguments."[26] That is true in debate, in which the force of logic is what matters, but not in respect of the authority to govern. It must nonetheless be remembered that the theory of absolute obedience is characteristic of despotisms and is not part of Catholic doctrine. Religion obliges us to disobey someone who commands what is manifestly illicit. This duty of disobedience is the ground of martyrdom.

Nor does obedience seek a coinciding of the wills of subjects and superiors. In the traditional view of obedience, that coinciding is brought about by the subject's making the supe-

---

[24] See paragraphs 49 and 50.

[25] O.R., 18 October 1972.

[26] O.R., 24-25 October 1966.

rior's will his own; but here it is achieved by a coming together from both directions. Obedience as such is completely subjectivized and agreement no longer involves a sacrifice of one's own will by conforming it to somebody else's. In this consensual view, the person who submits is ultimately submitting only to himself. The principle of independence which, as we have seen, produces self-government, self-teaching, self-education and even self-redemption could not but effect religious life and take from obedience what is part of its essence: the tendency to make the subject disappear in order to allow the object to be realized. When confronted with the spirit of independence and egalitarian emancipation, the new sort of obedience vanishes altogether. Thus it was that such *hubris* was displayed in the United States on the occasion of the Pope's visit, when he was publicly confronted by Sister Teresa Kane, the President of the Federation of Religious Sisters in that country. When the Holy See later expelled Sister Mary Mansour from her religious order for continuing to act as director of a state abortion clinic, a thousand religious sisters met in Detroit and rebelled against the Holy See, accusing it of being a male chauvinist authority and of violating human rights, stifling freedom of conscience and even of violating canon law.

145. Rosmini's teaching on religious obedience.

As a measure of how far the reformed concept of religious obedience is from the one the Church has always accepted, I will adduce the thought, not of the lawgivers of the ancient orders, but of a modern founder as distinguished for the depth of his theological speculation as for that of his religious spirit. In his ascetical writings, Antonio Rosmini, the founder of the Institute of Charity approved by the Holy See in 1839, removes any trace of subjectivism from the virtue of obedience and reduces it to its bare essence. Obedience consists in abandoning one's own will, freely, once and for all, into the hands of one's superiors, and in thus renouncing the right to examine the commands one is given. Nevertheless obedience is a supremely rational act, because it is based on a reasoned persuasion, but not the persuasion that the particular thing commanded is appropriate (that was de Lamennais' doctrine) but rather the persuasion that the superior has a legitimate authority to ask what is asked. Philology comes to the aid of asceticism. The Greek verb "I obey" fundamentally means "I am persuaded," but it cannot mean persuaded of the appropriateness of the act, which I would perform of my own free choice, but rather of the commander's right to command. If one reduces obedience to a subjective persuasion of the rightness of the thing commanded the virtue of obedience disappears. Obedience becomes auto-obedience. Rosmini says this in various places. "If one makes the reasonableness of the command the ground for obeying, obedience is destroyed." And more expressly: "One ought to obey in simplicity, without thinking whether the order is right or not, expedient or inexpedient." And again: "the blindness of obedience is the blindness of faith itself." And in a more energetic turn of phrase: "We ought to be victims with Christ and what sacrifices us ought to be the iron of obedience." To one of his order in England he addressed the logical paradox that "A single act of obedience is worth more than the conversion of England."[27]

Rosmini's teaching, which is also the Catholic teaching, is indeed profound because it identifies obedience with the essence of any moral act, which is precisely recognizing a law and submitting to it. It is the direct opposite of the new view, namely that what one does in obedience to a command is simply what one would freely choose to do anyway without a command. Being obedient is, on the contrary, doing what one would not do without the command, and doing it because it is commanded. The change on this point reaches the foundations of morality and theology. Christianity assigns no other goal to the God-Man, or to any human will, than to be obedient to the will of God, whether known naturally or supernaturally. Obedience was lost in the post-conciliar reforms, as Paul VI noted in his speech to the general congregation of the Society of Jesus, in which he said he could not hide "his own amazement and his own pain" at "the strange and sinister suggestions" that were trying to remove the Society from its foundations, as a result of adopting a completely historicist outlook and placing it on a

---

[27] For these five quotations see the *Epistolario ascetico*, Rome 1913, Vols. I, p.308; III, p.255; III, p.91; I, p.567; III, p.211. What religious obedience should be and how a superior should make it his duty to require it can be seen from a letter in which St. Philip Neri excluded two otherwise distinguished Oratorians from becoming his successor because of their lack of this virtue. The letter is quoted in an article by N. Vian in O.R., 16-17 November 1981.

new basis "as if Catholicism did not contain a charism of permanent truth and invincible stability."[28]

In the reform expected or attempted in that famous Society too, there is a spirit of radical innovation sweeping away the essential suprahistorical elements of religion, as well as its expendable historically relative aspects; and all in order to strike in with the world.

146. Obedience and community life.

Since obedience is given to a rule, and it is the rule which gives unity, a weakening in obedience weakens the spirit of unity. An article in the *Osservatore Romano*[29] on the secularization of religious life mentions a reforming chapter in one congregation "which has removed from the founder's constitutions every religious practice (daily Mass, spiritual reading, meditation, examination of conscience, monthly retreat, rosary, etc.) and every form of mortification, and has questioned the value of the vow of obedience by allowing a member the right of conscientious objection in instances in which he wishes to exempt himself from the superiors' orders." The article rightly says that "we are here confronted with an annihilation of religious life." But then, making the usual concessions, it grants that there is something positive in this subversion and annihilation of the religious life, something having "a cathartic function." I really do not see how a tendency that is admittedly destroying religious life can simultaneously be described as "purifying" it.

When the ties of obedience that bind all the members of a community to pursue the institute's ends *in common*, and to attend to the care of one's soul jointly with the other members are dissolved, individuals are left to do the things proper to the religious state as if the community did not exist. Mass is celebrated at any time, prayer is left to the spirituality of each person. Even dress, which was once uniform for all the members of an institute, is left to individual choice and thus styles vary from cassocks, to black suit, to lay dress to overalls and so on. The practice of concelebration is no sufficient corrective to the weakening of community life. Since it is not obligatory and is only adopted by part of the community, it appears more like a sign of division than a sign of unity. Since no religious practice

---

[28] O.R., 17 November 1966.
[29] O.R., 22 December 1972.

is now pursued in common in some communities, communal life among members of the same family is tending to become a mere sharing of board and lodging,[30] or at most a sharing of common work. One cannot justify individual choice as regards religious practice by saying such things need to conform to the individual character of each religious. If that were the aim, there would be no religious institutes: they are intended precisely to pursue in common what the post-conciliar reform is returning to the individual. It is obviously a contradiction in terms to join a community in order to do individually, and on one's own account, things one has joined the community to do in common.

Our final conclusion in this analysis is that the crisis in religious life springs from the adoption of the principle of independence, and from the dissolving of objective values in subjectivity. Community reverts to an inorganic multiplicity: *Chacun dans sa chacunière*.[31] Freedom to judge the superior degenerates into freedom to choose anything one likes, even one's place of residence. It is not for nothing that the office of porter has been abolished in some monasteries. I am not saying that these reforms are not cloaked in a certain plausibility; I am saying the cloak is short.

---

[30] But see paragraph 140.
[31] "Everyone in his own home."

CHAPTER XV

PYRRHONISM

147. Theological setting of the argument.

An analysis of the dizziness or the giddiness and dislocation, that has entered the Church in the twentieth century, could be conducted in purely philosophical terms. In Catholic epistemology however, philosophy is a subordinate discipline that makes reference to a faith that stands above it, and hence a philosophical consideration of things is included as part of a higher view, which philosophy serves without losing its own autonomy.

As we have indicated in the opening paragraphs of this book, and as is generally recognized, the crisis in the Church is a crisis of faith, but the link between man's natural constitution and the supernatural life that is made connatural to him, rather than simply superimposed upon him, means that a Catholic enquirer must look for the origins of the crisis in an order deeper than the purely philosophical.

Underlying the present confusion there is an attack on man's powers of cognition, an attack that has implications for the metaphysical constitution of being in general and of primal Being as well, that is of the Holy Trinity. We will call the attack by its historically expressive name of Pyrrhonism;[1] it is something that attacks the very principle of all certainty, not merely this or that truth of faith or reason, since what it impugns is man's capacity to know any truth at all. There are two points to be made about this wobbling of the axis around which all certainties revolve. First; it is no longer an isolated and esoteric phenomenon, a peculiarity of a particular philosophical school, but something that permeates the mentality of the age and with which Catholic thought has compromised. Second; it affects

---

[1] See note at paragraph 16. [Translator's note.]

theology as well as metaphysics because it penetrates to the constitution of created being and therefore to that of uncreated being as well, the former being an analogical imitation of the latter. As love proceeds from the Word within the Trinity, so life proceeds from thought in the human soul. If one denies the priority of thought over life, of truth over the will, one is attempting a dislocation of the Trinity. If one denies the capacity to grasp being, the expansion of the spirit into its primal loving is left unconnected with truth, loses any regulating norm and degenerates into a mere existence. By turning away from the divine Idea, on the grounds that it is held to be unreachable, human life is reduced to a pure mobilism or becoming, devoid of any ideal values. Were it not for the impossibility on God's side that He should leave his creation to lapse into pure movement, devoid of axiological form, man's world would be a becoming without substance, direction or goal.

A Pyrrhonism that posits a pseudo-absolute alogism (pseudo because thought cannot deny itself) distorts the ontological composition of the Trinity, and reverses its processions, as we have said. If truth is unreachable, the dynamic of life no longer proceeds from the intelligible but precedes it and indeed produces it. The denial of the Idea, as Leopardi[2] acutely saw, is strictly, ultimately and irrefutably a denial of God, because it takes away from human life any trace of eternal and indestructible values. If the will does not proceed from knowledge, but produces and justifies itself, the world is deprived of any rational basis and becomes a kind of meaninglessness. If one denies the capacity of our intellect to form concepts corresponding to the real, the more the mind is unable to apprehend and conceive (that is take with itself) the real, the more it will develop its own operation within itself by producing (that is bringing forth) mere excogitations. These latter will be occasioned by something that touches our faculties but is not present in the concept which we form of it. Hence come all the ancient and modern sophisms that trust in thought while at the same time lacking any confidence that we can grasp the truth.

If thought does not have an essential relation with being, it is not subject to the laws governing being and ceases to be measured because it becomes itself the measurer. Protagoras of

---

[2] Giacomo Leopardi (1798-1837). Italian romantic poet and egotist. [Translator's note.]

Abdera's saying well expresses the independence of thought from being: man is the measure of all things.[3] Gorgias of Leontini's three propositions bear witness to a refusal to grasp the object and to the arrogance of the mind that closes itself upon itself: "Nothing exists. If something existed it would be unknowable. If it were knowable, it would be inexpressible."[4]

The arrogance of controversy has manifested itself in every branch of knowledge, particularly at times when a subjective spirit was in the ascendant. Setting aside the extravagances of the Greek sophists and of those who deny the very existence of Christ, I come to the Pyrrhonism of the contemporary Church.

148. Pyrrhonism in the Church.
Cardinals Léger, Heenan, Alfrink and Suenens.

The root of the confusion in the world and the Church is Pyrrhonism, that is the denial of reason. The charge commonly made, to the effect that modern civilization overestimates the power of reason, is superficial. It would be true if one meant by reason the mind's capacity to calculate and construct, to which we owe technology and our control over the things around us. But that is one of the mind's lesser faculties and is said to be found in spiders and apes. If on the other hand one means the capacity to grasp the being of things and their meaning, and to adhere to them with the will, then the present world is much more inclined to alogism than rationalism. In the third syllabus, Pius XII defended *verum sincerumque cognitionis humanae valorem ac certam et immutabilem veritatis assecutionem*[5] against the spirit of the age. Paul VI nobly declared: "We are the only ones who defend the power of reason."[6] In the doctrinal constitution *Lumen Gentium*, Vatican II repeated the anti-pyrrhonist text of Vatican I: *Deum omnium rerum principium et finem naturali*

---

[3]   Diels, 74 B 1.

[4]   Ibid., 76 B 3. These three propositions are illogical if they are taken without explanation, but become true if they are understood as applying absolutely. It is in fact true that no finite being perfectly is, that is to the full extent that it is possible to be. No thing is perfectly knowable or perfectly expressible by us in an exhaustive sense.

[5]   Denzinger 2320. "The true genuine worth of human knowledge and the certain and immutable attainment of truth."

[6]   O.R., 2 June 1972.

humanae rationis lumine certo cognosci posse.[7] *Gaudium et Spes*
also condemns those who "no longer admit any absolute
truth."[8]

These assertions, however, do not reflect the mentality of a
large part of the council and are in contradiction with post-
conciliar developments. In the 74th sitting Cardinal Léger
maintained: "Many people think that the Church demands a
too monolithic unity. In recent centuries an exaggerated unity
has been introduced into the study of doctrines."[9] It would
seem that the Canadian cardinal can detect a lesser degree of
doctrinal unity in the non-recent centuries, when a death penalty existed in some times and places for people who broke that
unity, and that he is moreover ignorant of the variety of theological schools that are a feature of the Church's life throughout
history. To this historical judgment, Léger attaches a value
judgment of a frankly pyrrhonistic kind: "Certainly the assertion that the Church has the truth can be justified, if the necessary distinctions are made. The knowledge of God, whose
mystery is explored in doctrine, prevents intellectual immobil-
ity."[10] It seems the Cardinal is denying that, whether inside or
outside the Church, there are changeless truths, and that in his
case Pyrrhonism is based upon the divine transcendence, as if
the fact that the infinite cannot be infinitely known by the finite
removed all knowledge, when in fact it is knowledge's foundation. Next the Cardinal misunderstands the passage in St.
Augustine that says we must seek in order to find, and find in
order to seek again, which is actually opposed to Pyrrhonism:
what is found is one thing, what is sought the next time is another, not the same thing over again as if it had not been found
and could not become, in certain conditions, fixed for ever.[11]

Cardinal Heenan noted the relativist scepticism that generally characterizes the Church's teachers: "The magisterium has
survived only in the Pope. It is no longer exercised by the bish-

---

[7] *Lumen Gentium*, 6. "God, the beginning and end of all things can
be certainly known by the natural light of human reason."
[8] *Gaudium et Spes*, 19.
[9] O.R., 25-26 November 1963.
[10] O.R., 25 November 1963.
[11] What John Paul II said in his speech to the European Council for
Nuclear Research during a visit to Geneva is very apt here: "One
must unite the search for truth with the certainty of already knowing the source of truth." O.R., 16 June 1982.

ops and it is rather difficult to get the hierarchy to condemn a false doctrine. Outside Rome the magisterium today is so unsure of itself that it no longer even attempts to lead."[12] This statement certainly condemns the renunciation of authority but it also shows the pyrrhonistic uncertainty that has entered the Church's teaching body. During the fourth session of the council, in a press conference on 23 September 1965 reported by the news agencies, Cardinal Alfrink also notes the phenomenon, but unlike the Englishman, he gives it a positive interpretation, expressing his Pyrrhonism in set terms: "The council has got people thinking and there is hardly a subject in the Church that has not been brought into question." Lastly Cardinal Suenens said to the French Catholic intellectuals' week at Paris in 1966: *La morale est d'abord vive, dynamisme de vie et soumise, à ce titre, à une croissance intérieure, qui écarte toute fixité.*[13] It is obvious that the Cardinal is mixing up morality, an absolute and unchangeable demand that imposes itself on man, and one's moral life that changes in each individual continually from one judgment to the next. Morality is not a subjective dynamism but an absolute rule which is a participation in the divine Reason.

149. The discounting of reason. Sullivan. Innovators' rejection of certainty.

Reason is openly discounted in Jean Sullivan's book *Matinales.*[14] The author denies the distinction between faith and love, on the grounds that it has no scriptural basis and he hence denies there is a crisis of faith in the Church while not even stopping to realize he is implicitly distorting the Trinity. Indeed one cannot talk about a crisis, that is a discernment, when one has

---

[12] O.R., 28 April 1968.

[13] "Morality is first and foremost alive, a dynamism of life, and therefore subject to an interior growth that rejects any kind of fixity." *Documentation Catholique*, No.1468, coll.605-6. This firmness of the mind in truth is seen as an evil; the French bishops in their *Missel pour les dimanches* of 1983 got people to pray *pour les croyants qui sont tentés de s'installer dans leurs certitudes.* "For believers who are tempted to become fixed in their certitudes."

[14] It was reviewed at length in I.C.I., No.506, September 1976, p.40, the most widely read publication of the newfangled sort in France.

no fixed measure, no means of discerning the difference between faith and non-faith, or when one mixes up opposing
ideas in a confused mass and regards them as one. The difference between believing and loving is not, in any case, based
merely on Scripture; it rests on man's nature, in which intellect
and will are really distinct. Their distinction is derived from the
analogous distinction within the Trinity.

It is clear from what Sullivan says about the incompatibility
of faith and certainty that the ignoring of this distinction means
the radical overthrow of rationality: *Les croyants s'imaginent que
la foi va avec la certitude. On leur a mis ça dans la tête! Il faut se
méfier de la certitude. Les certitudes sont généralement fondées sur
quoi? Le non approfondissement des connaissances.*[15]

The book contains a great many absurdities both logical
and religious. If the author is saying that something cannot be
seen and believed simultaneously by the same person, he is
merely stating the obvious and repeating a philosophical truism.
But if he is saying one cannot have certainty about something
that is believed, he is departing from Catholic doctrine. It is a
Catholic dogma that faith involves certainty, and so is the
proposition that such certainty is not the privilege of mystical
or simple souls, but a light common to all the faithful. Secondly, Sullivan overthrows any sound gnoseology when he reverses the relation between certainty and the deepening of one's
knowledge. Certainty is the subjective state of the knower precisely inasmuch as he really is a knower; ignorance is a lack of
knowledge and doubt is less than full knowledge. Sullivan's
views remind one of the impious calumnies of Giordano Bruno,
set forth in his "Dialogues" on holy stupidity. They are accompanied by another more fundamental error to the effect that
certainty and faith block the possibility of acting, so that, in the
author's ill-found phrase, *vivre c'est perdre la foi.*[16] He maintains
that any kind of stability in thought makes it impossible to enter into communion with other minds, and that our own minds
should be kept permanently open to any and every point of
view.

Catholic teaching holds instead that communion involves
something that remains the same amidst the movement of life.

---

[15] "Believers imagine that faith goes with certainty. People have put
that idea into their heads! One should distrust certainty. Certainties
are generally founded on what? A shallowness of knowledge."
[16] "To live is to lose faith."

It also says that life proceeds from thought, not thought from life, just as theologically the Holy Spirit proceeds from the Word, and not vice versa. Human activity is in fact driven by the belief that one possesses truth, and the history of philosophy proves the fact. The Ephectics of antiquity and all other systems that advocate flight from action, seek to reduce our certainties so as to deprive us of motives for action, their optimal goal being a complete lack of certain knowledge that will bring us to the safe haven of complete spiritual ataraxy or detachment.

Certainty is a mental state that follows from a deepening of knowledge, not from shallowness as Sullivan alleges. He denies the existence of any depth that cannot be surpassed, any fundamental principle, any absolute. Pyrrhonism goes hand in hand with its twin, mobilism, and like it, leads to blasphemy: *Vivre c'est aussi perdre la foi et s'apercevoir qu'on est possédé par...C'est pourquoi rencontrer Dieu c'est le renier à l'instant même.*[17] This is just trivial love of paradox, but behind the literary device of paradox there is a denial of the Word and, as Leopardi accurately saw, a denial of God.

150. The discounting of reason, continued. The Padua theologians. The Ariccia theologians. Manchesson.

Let it not be thought that we have picked out and exaggerated one or two cases in order to prove that Pyrrhonism has penetrated the Church. We have pointed them out as symptoms, not as oddities. The widespread mentality they indicate can be gauged from the actions of whole bodies of thinkers, not just from notable individuals.

The Congress of Italian Moral Theologians in Padua in 1970 adopted this proposition: "Since the exercise of reason is systematically included in a particular historical set of circumstances, it cannot be exercised in universal terms." This really does mean the destruction of reason and thus of everything else, including congresses of moral theologians.

The Pyrrhonism of the Ariccia Congress of Theologians, presided over by Cardinal Garrone, the Prefect of the Congregation for Catholic Education is analogous. The Osservatore Romano reported it without criticism.[18] The dominant view

---

[17] "To live is also to lose the faith and to realize that one is possessed by...That is why to meet God is to deny him at the same instant."

[18] O.R., 16 January 1971.

was "no proposition can be held to be absolutely true." There are, it was alleged, no rational prolegomena to theology "because the word of God justifies itself and interprets itself." The contradiction of the Church's theology here is less fundamental than the contradiction of its philosophy. Firstly, since man is a rational creature, his faith cannot be something devoid of reasonableness. Secondly, the word of God would only justify itself, as it is here alleged to do, if it carried with it convincing evidence, since only evidence, immediate or mediate, can justify an assertion. But in fact such evidence is lacking where the message of faith is concerned and it is accepted precisely through faith, and not on the basis of convincing evidence. Thirdly, to say that the word of God interprets itself is a mere concatenation of words, not a meaningful statement. To interpret means literally to place oneself in the middle between a word and its hearer, between the intelligible and the person exercising intellection. The interpreter is a third who mediates between two other things, and so the word of God cannot be said to stand between itself and something else.

The Ariccia theologians go on from the relation between philosophy and theology, straying into the field of the relation between subject and object and state frankly that "to speak in the categories of the man of our time, the theologian must take account of the anthropological shift, which consists in an inversion of the relationship between subject and object and in the impossibility of apprehending the object in itself." That is an explicit formulation of Pyrrhonism and the destruction of Catholic doctrine. Faith presupposes reason. It involves submission by the reason but a submission willed by reason itself. The theological congress's theories are regressive and take philosophy back to pre-Socratic positions. That they were accepted by a congress of Catholic theologians presided over by a cardinal means either that an abuse of language has occurred or that Catholic theology no longer exists.

Pyrrhonism drops its last veil in the conclusion that: "For there to be a valid and effective meeting with contemporary man, one must know the transcendental condition, that is the general structure, of the man of today." If words mean anything, this is to say that "transcendental" means the same thing as "empirical."

This Pyrrhonist vein has not been exhausted in the more recent post-conciliar period, and continues to crop up in official and semi-official statements. The colloquium held at Trieste in January 1982 at the Centre for Theology and Culture, the proceedings of which were published with an introduction by the local bishop, ended by adopting this thesis: "An absolute reason of an idealist or Marxist sort [or any other sort] that unfolds itself in the concrete events of human history does not exist; there is rather an historically given reason, the forms of which change with the changing of cultural contexts. There can be no question of readopting a totalizing metaphysical, philosophical and theological view."[19] This is to invalidate reason, repudiate Providence, deny metaphysics and set aside God.

Yves Manchesson of the Institut Catholique in Paris puts the Church's role in the world in these terms, in a description of the state of the Church in France after the liberation: *L'Eglise essaie de déchiffrer les signes des temps, pense ne pas avoir réponse à tout, cherche moins à préciser une vérité en soi qu'une vérité pour tous les hommes.*[20] These expressions of the respected author seem to us a mere compounding of words. First of all, the Church has never claimed to be the depository of all truths, since there is a whole world of knowledge that God has left to man's investigation and debate: *et mundum tradidit disputationi eorum, ut non inveniat homo opus quod operatus est Deus ab initio usque ad finem.*[21] This sphere comprises what might be called extra-moral matters that do not involve human axiology and teleology, that is matters that do not concern man's ultimate destiny. But the Church is, on the other hand, the depository of all truth without which man cannot fulfill his destiny and the destiny of the world.

Secondly, there is a prodigious carelessness about the meaning of words in talking about a truth that is not true in itself, but is nonetheless a truth for all men, since the latter is surely an instance of the former, that is, a truth that stands and lasts independent of its being apprehended by finite minds. It is not the consent of man that gives truth its value, as some dare

---

[19] O.R., 8 July 1983.
[20] "The Church tries to read the signs of the times, does not think it has the answer to everything, is less concerned to define truth as such than a truth for all men." *Amitiés Catholiques Françaises,* April 1979.
[21] Ecclesiastes, 3:11. "And he gave the world over to their disputing, and man could not fathom the work that God had done from beginning to end."

to assert today; it is the truth that bestows value on human opinions. A truth can exist in relation to man only if it is in itself independent of man: *per prius* it exists in itself *and per posterius* it is true for man.

CHAPTER XVI

DIALOGUE

151. Dialogue and discussionism in the post-conciliar Church. Dialogue in *Ecclesiam Suam*.

The word *dialogue* represents the biggest change in the mentality of the Church after the council, only comparable in its importance with the change wrought by the word *liberty* in the last century. The word was completely unknown and unused in the Church's teaching before the council. It does not occur once in any previous council, or in papal encyclicals, or in sermons or in pastoral practice. In the Vatican II documents it occurs 28 times, twelve of them in the decree on ecumenism *Unitatis Redintegratio*. Nonetheless, through its lightning spread and an enormous broadening in meaning, this word, which is very new in the Catholic Church, became the master-word determining post-conciliar thinking, and a catch-all category in the newfangled mentality.[1] People not only talk about ecumenical dialogue, dialogue between the Church and the world, ecclesial dialogue, but by an enormous catachresis, a dialogical structure is attributed to theology, pedagogy, catechesis, the Trinity, the history of salvation, schools, families, the priesthood, the sacraments, redemption, and to everything else that had existed in the Church for centuries without the concept being in anybody's mind or the word occurring in the language.

---

[1] In the *Osservatore Romano* of 15 March 1971, Cardinal Roy said dialogue was a new experience for the Church and for the world. On 15-16 November 1966, on the other hand, the *Osservatore* said that the Church had always practiced dialogue (mixing it up with controversy and refutation of other arguments) and that if there had been times when it did not practice it, "they were more or less depressed periods."

The movement from a thetic manner of talking, which was appropriate to religion, to a hypothetic and problematic style, is apparent even in the titles of books, which used to teach, but now enquire. Books that were called *Institutiones* or "manuals" or "treatises" on philosophy, theology or any other science have been replaced by "Problems in philosophy," "Problems in theology," and manuals are abhorred and despised precisely because of their positive and apodictic nature. It has happened in all areas: no more nurses' manuals, but problems in nursing; not drivers' manuals but drivers' problems and so on, with everything moving from the certain to the uncertain, the positive to the problematic. It is a decline from an intentional appropriation of real objects by means of knowledge (signified by the syllable *no* in *nosco*, I know) to a simple throwing of the object before the mind (*proballo* in Greek, from which we get *problem*).

In August 1964, devoting a third of his first encyclical *Ecclesiam Suam* to dialogue, Paul VI equated the Church's duty to evangelize the world with a duty to dialogue with the world. But one cannot help noticing that the equation is supported neither by Scripture nor the dictionary. The word *dialogue* never occurs in Scripture and its Latin equivalent *colloquium* is only used in the sense of a meeting between chief persons and of a conversation, never in the modern sense of a group meeting. *Colloquium* on three occasions in the New Testament means a dispute. Evangelization is a proclamation not a dispute or a conversation. The evangelization the Apostles are commanded to undertake in the Gospel is immediately identified with teaching. The very word *angelos* carries the idea of something that is given to be announced, not something thrown into dispute. It is true that Peter and Paul dispute in the synagogues, but it is not a question of dialoguing in the modern sense of a dialogue in search of something, setting out from a position of ostensible ignorance, but rather a dialogue in refutation of errors. The possibility of dialogue disappears, in their case, the moment the disputant is no longer open to persuasion, whether through his obstinacy or his incapacity. This can be seen, for example, in St. Paul's refusal of dialogue on one occasion.[2] Just as Christ spoke with authority: *Erat docens eos sicut potestatem habens*,[3] so the Apostles preached the Gospel in an authoritative

---

[2] Acts, 19:8-9.

[3] Matthew 7:29. "He taught them as one having authority."

manner, not looking to validate it by dialogue. In the same place Christ's positive way of teaching is contrasted with the dialogues of the scribes and pharisees. The heart of the matter is that the Church's message is not a human product, always open to argument, but a revealed message designed to be accepted rather than argued about.

After having equated evangelization with dialogue, *Ecclesiam Suam* denies that evangelization, or preaching the truth, means condemning error, and it identifies condemnations with coercion. The theme of the council's opening speech thus returns.[4]

"Our mission," the encyclical says, "is to announce truths that are undeniable and necessary to salvation; it will not come armed with external coercion, but with the legitimate means of human education." This is a legitimate and traditional manner of approach, as was proved by the fact that immediately after the encyclical's publication, Wisser't Hooft, the Secretary of the World Council of Churches, hastened to state that the Pope's ideal of dialogue as a communication of truth without a reciprocal reply, was not in accordance with ecumenical ideas.[5]

152. Philosophy of dialogue.

The new fangled dialogue is based on "the perpetual problematicity of the Christian subject," as the *Osservatore Romano* puts it,[6] that is, on the impossibility of ever getting to anything that is not itself problematic. In short it denies the old principle, recognized in logic, metaphysics and morality, that *anagke stenai.*[7]

Dialogue first runs into trouble when it is made to coincide with the Church's universal task of evangelization and heralded as a means of spreading truth. *It is impossible for everyone to dialogue.* The possibility of holding a dialogue depends on the knowledge one has of a subject, and not, as is alleged, on the fact of one's liberty or the dignity of one's soul. The right to argue depends on knowledge, not on man's general ordering towards the truth. Socrates said that on matters of gymnastics, one should consult an expert in gymnastics, on horses an expert

---

[4] See paragraph 38.
[5] O.R., 13 September 1964.
[6] O.R., 15 January 1971.
[7] "It is necessary to stop somewhere."

on things equine, on wounds and diseases an expert in medicine and on the running of society an expert in politics. Expertise is a result of effort and study, of reflecting on things methodically and steadily rather than hastily and extempore. Contemporary dialogue presupposes, however, that any man is capable of dialoguing with anyone else on any subject, simply in virtue of being a rational creature. The demand is therefore made that the life of the temporal community and the Church should be arranged so that everyone can participate; not as the Catholic system envisages, by each person contributing his knowledge and playing his own proper part, but by everybody giving his opinion and deciding on everything. The paradox is that this right to argue is being extended to everyone at the very moment when the knowledge that gives an authentic title to join the argument is getting scarcer and feebler even among the Church's teachers.

The next blunder relates to the onus of proof. It is assumed that dialogue can and should satisfy all the objections of an opponent. Now for one man to offer himself to another with the aim of giving him complete intellectual satisfaction on any point of religion is a sign of a moral failing. It is rash for somebody who has asserted a truth to proceed to expose himself to a general, extempore and unlimited discussion. Every subject has many facets; he is familiar with only some, or even one of them. Yet he exposes himself as if he were ready for every objection, impossible to catch off guard, and as if he had anticipated every possible thought that could arise on the matter.

Dialogue labors under yet another difficulty from the side of the inquirer, because it rests on a gratuitous presupposition that St. Augustine perceptively detected in his day. An intellect can be capable of formulating an objection without being capable of understanding the argument that meets the objection. This fact, that an individual's intellectual strength may be greater in raising objections than in understanding replies, is a common cause of error. *Ecce unde plerumque convalescit error, cum homines idonei sunt his rebus interrogandis quibus intelligendis non sunt idonei.*[8]

This disproportion between an intellect's asking a question and understanding a reply is a result of the general difference

---

[8] *De peccatorum meritis et remissione*, lib. III, cap. 8. "Here is a thing that often fosters error; when men are capable of enquiring into things they are not capable of understanding."

between potency and act. Refusal to recognize this difference leads to an illogical conclusion in politics: everyone has by nature a capacity to be able to rule, therefore everyone can rule. It also leads to the illogicality implicit in dialogue: everyone has by nature a capacity to know the truth, therefore everyone actually knows the truth.

In the first book of his *Theodicy*, Antonio Rosmini also teaches that an individual should not trust his own intellectual powers to solve the questions that arise regarding the workings of divine Providence: no individual can be certain that his own intellectual strength is up to meeting all the objections that might face it. This uncertainty as to a person's intellectual capacities is what Descartes ignored in his method, when he imagined that the power of reason was equally strong and equally exercisable in each individual.

153. Appropriateness of dialogue.

In Scripture, evangelization proceeds by teaching not by dialogue. Christ's last command to his disciples was *matheteuein* and *didaskein*, which literally means make disciples of all men, rather as if the Apostles' task consisted in leading the nations to the condition of listeners and disciples, with *matheteuein* as a preliminary grade of *didaskein*, to teach.[9]

Besides lacking a biblical foundation, dialogue is also void of a gnoseological one, because the nature of dialogue is incompatible with a line of argument based on faith. It assumes that the credibility of religion depends on a prior resolution of every particular objection made to it. Now that cannot be had, and cannot be made a precondition for an assent of faith. The correct order is the other way around. Having established even by one convincing consideration that religion is true, the latter is to be held on to even if particular difficulties remain unresolved. As Rosmini teaches,[10] the proposition "the Catholic religion is true" means that there are a great many possible objections that could be raised against it. But it is not necessary to have previously resolved the 15,000 objections in the *Summa Theologica* before one can reasonably assent to Catholicism. Its

[9] In his commentary on Matthew, Paris 1927, p.144, Lagrange translates the first word by *enseigner* and the second by *apprendre*.
[10] *Epistolario*, Vol.VIII, Casale 1891, p.464, letter of 8 June 1843 to Countess Theodora Bielinski.

truth is, in short, not to be garnered synthetically, as a compound of particular truths, and does not imply that entire intellectual satisfaction necessarily accompanies its acceptance; in fact it is assent to that overall truth that leads one on to the particular assents that follow.

Lastly it should be noted that the present idea of dialogue obscures the way of useful ignorance that is appropriate for minds that are incapable of adopting the way of examination, and that adhere firmly to their fundamental assent and do not devote much attention to opposing views, to find out where their error lies. Being afraid of ideas opposed to what they know is certainly true, they keep themselves in ignorance to preserve the truths they already possess, and shut out false ideas and also any true ones that happen to be mixed in with them, without separating the one from the other.

This way of useful ignorance is legitimate in Catholicism, is based on the theoretical principle explained earlier, and is moreover the condition in which the great majority of all religious believers find themselves.[11] It is therefore untrue to say as the *Osservatore Romano* does that "anyone who refuses dialogue is a fanatic, an intolerant person who always ends up being unfaithful to himself and then to the society of which he is part. Anyone who does dialogue gives up isolation and condemnations."[12] To dialogue unconditionally in all circumstances is a sign of rashness, and of the fanaticism that replaces the objective force of truth by one's own subjective capacities.

154. The end of dialogue. Paul VI.
The Secretariat for Non-Believers.

The difference between the old and new sorts of dialogue can be seen very clearly in the ends assigned to them. The new sort, some say, is not directed towards the refuting of error or the converting of one's interlocutor.[13] The new fashioned mentality abhors anything polemical, holding it to be incompatible with charity even though it be in reality an act of charity. The idea of polemics is inseparable from the opposition between

---

[11] The theory of useful ignorance is developed by Manzoni in his *Morale Cattolica*, ed. cit., Vol. II, pp.422-3 and Vol. III, p.131.
[12] O.R., 15-16 November 1965.
[13] See the *Istruzione per il dialogo* published on 28 August 1968 by the Secretariat for Non-Believers.

truth and falsehood. A polemic is aimed precisely at overthrowing any pretended equality between the two. Thus polemic is connatural to thought, since it removes errors in one's own thinking even when it fails to persuade an opponent.

From the Catholic's point of view, the end of dialogue cannot be heuristic, since he is in possession of religious truth, not in search of it. Nor can it be eristic, that is, aimed at winning the argument for its own sake, since its motive and goal is charity. True dialogue is aimed at demonstrating a truth, at producing a conviction in another person, and ultimately at conversion. This was clearly taught by Paul VI in his speech of 27 June 1968: "It is not enough to draw close to others, to talk to them, to assure them of our trust and to seek their good. One must also take steps to convert them. One must preach to get them to come back. One must try to incorporate them into the divine plan, that is one and unique." This is a very important papal utterance, because the Pope was expressly talking about ecumenical dialogue; its importance was confirmed by the fact that the *Osservatore Romano* even printed it in a different type, a unique event.

That notwithstanding, in 1975 the head of the Secretariat for Non-Believers made the following diametrically opposite assertion: "The Secretariat was certainly not created with the intention of proselytizing among non-believers, even if that word is understood in a positive sense; nor with an apologetic intent but rather with the aim of promoting dialogue between believers and unbelievers."[14] When I objected to the author that his text contradicted Pope Paul's assertion, he replied[15] that the Secretariat does nothing without the agreement of higher authority and that the particular article had been seen by the Secretariat of State prior to publication. The letter simply makes the difference between the Pope and the Secretariat for Non-Believers all the more obvious. As to my specific objection, the letter answered that although the Church had the task of converting the world "that does not imply that every step and every organization in the Church is specifically aimed at converting one's interlocutor."

This answer lacks clarity. The Church has a single all-embracing goal which is human salvation, and everything it

---

[14] O.R., 21 August 1975.
[15] In an official letter of 9 September 1975.

does is one particular expression of that goal: when it teaches, it
teaches not baptizes; when it baptizes, it baptizes not teaches;
when it consecrates the Eucharist it consecrates not absolves,
and so on. But all these specific ends are precisely specifications
and actuations of the all-embracing goal, and all of them are
aimed at turning man towards God, that is at conversion. It is
this ultimate end that gives direction to all the Church's subordinate goals, and without it none of the lesser goals would be
pursued.[16] The statement by Paul VI we have quoted asserts
unequivocally that dialogue is aimed at conversion.

155. Whether dialogue is always an enrichment.

De facto, conversion and apologetics have been excluded
from post-conciliar dialogue which is said to be "always a positive exchange"; but that assertion is difficult to accept.

Firstly, as well as a dialogue that converts there is a dialogue
that perverts, by which one party is detached from the truth and
led into error. Or will it be pretended that truth is always effi-
cacious and that error never is?

Secondly, there is the situation where instead of helping the
participants, dialogue presents them with an impossible task. St.
Thomas envisages the case in which it is impossible to prove the
truth to the person one is addressing because there is no jointly
held principle on which to base the argument. All that can then
be done is to prove that the opponent's arguments are not conclusive and that his objections can be met. In such circumstances, it is not true that dialogue has a positive outcome for
both parties and constitutes a mutual enrichment. The dialogue
is unproductive. If its usefulness is then alleged to lie in getting
to know the psychology and ideology of one's partner, the answer is that such things are the province of psychology, and are
not the goal of a religious dialogue; they belong to history, biog-
raphy or sociology. Such knowledge can indeed be useful in
adjusting the dialogue in a manner more appropriate to the
participants, but that is not the same thing as being a mutual
enrichment.

---

[16] *Summa Theologica*, I,II,q.1,a.4.

156. Catholic dialogue.

The aim of Catholic dialogue is persuasion and, at a higher level, conversion of the other party.

Bishop Marafini says "the method of dialogue is understood as a movement converging towards the fullness of truth and a search for deep unity," but it is not quite clear what he means.[17]

There is a tendency to confuse dialogue on natural matters with dialogue concerning supernatural faith. The former is carried on by the light of the reason that all men have in common. Everyone is equal under that light, and above their dialogue, as we have said,[18] they can sense a more important *Logos* that makes them realize they are brothers, profoundly united by their common nature. But in dialogue about the faith, the two parties cannot converge towards the truth or put themselves on a par. The non-believer rejects or doubts in a way the believer cannot.

It might be objected that the believer adopts a process of methodic doubt, analogous to Descartes': the believer adopts an unbelieving position only for the purposes of dialogue. But the difficulty returns: if the doubt or rejection of faith is real, it implies a loss of faith and a sin on the part of the believer. If it is hypothetical or feigned, the dialogue is flawed by a pretense and rests on an immoral basis. There is also the question of whether someone who pretends not to believe what in fact he does, is not sinning against faith, and whether a dialogue based on pretense is not bound to be unproductive as well as wrong. It has been claimed[19] that dialogue is fruitful for the believer's faith, quite apart from being an act of charity. But there is a clear contradiction involved. The article presents a dilemma that "if the Lord Jesus one knows is not the supreme and totalizing truth for man...one will have something other and greater to learn than what one has received by grace." And if on the other hand Christ is that supreme and totalizing truth "one cannot see

---

[17] O.R., 18 December 1971. Cardinal König said when presenting the *Instruction* on dialogue to the press that: "Dialogue puts the partners on an equal footing. The Catholic is not considered as possessing all the truth, but as someone who has faith and is looking for that truth with others, both believers and non-believers." I.C.I., No.322, 15 October 1968, p.20.

[18] In paragraph 125.

[19] In an article on "Faith and dialogue" in O.R., 26-27 December 1981.

how an idea or an experience can be added to him." But then the author casts his dilemma aside and says the believer does in fact gain something to add to his faith by the dialogue "on condition that these new acquisitions are not seen as additions to Christ. They are simply facets, dimensions, aspects of the mystery of Christ which the believer already possesses but discovers thanks to the stimulus of those who, though not Christians consciously, are Christians in concrete fact." This is to say that an addition to knowledge is not an addition to knowledge; that an atheist is an implicit Christian;[20] and that the atheist possesses facets of the Christian mystery which the explicit Christian does not know but which the atheist will suggest to him.

We may conclude by saying that the new sort of dialogue is not Catholic. Firstly, because it has a purely heuristic function, as if the Church in dialogue did not possess the truth and were looking for it, or as if it could prescind from possessing the truth as long as the dialogue lasted. Secondly, because it does not recognize the superior authority of revealed truth, as if there were no longer any distinction in importance between nature and revelation. Thirdly, because it imagines the parties to dialogue are on an equal footing, albeit a merely methodological equality, as if it were not a sin against faith to waive the advantage that comes from divine truth, even as a dialectical ploy. Fourthly, because it postulates that every human philosophical position is unendingly debatable, as if there were not fundamental points of contradiction sufficient to stop a dialogue and leave room only for refutation. Fifthly, because it supposes that dialogue is always fruitful and that "nobody has to sacrifice anything,"[21] as if dialogue could never be corrupting and lead to the uprooting of truth and the implanting of error, and as if nobody had to reject any errors they had previously professed.

Dialogue converging towards a higher and more universal truth does not suit the Catholic Church, because an heuristic process putting the Church on the road to truth does not suit it; what is appropriate for the Church is the act of charity, whereby a truth possessed by grace is communicated to others and they are thereby drawn to that truth, not to the Church as an end in itself. The superiority here is not that of the believer over the

---

[20] See paragraph 253.
[21] O.R., 19 November 1971.

non-believer, but of truth over all parties in dialogue. It should not be thought that the act of one man persuading another of the truth is tantamount to an act of oppression or an attack on the other's freedom. Logical contradiction and an "either or" are part of the structure of reality, not a kind of violence.

The sociological effect of Pyrrhonism, and the discussionism that follows from it, can be seen in the flood of conventions, meetings, commissions and congresses that began with Vatican II. It has also caused the current tendency to regard everything as problematic and to refer all such problems to committees, so that the responsibility that used to be personal and individual has been dispersed within collegial bodies. Discussionism has developed a whole technique of its own; in Rome in 1972 there was a convention of moderators of dialogues, which was designed to train the moderators, as if one could direct a dialogue in general, without any specific knowledge of what the dialogue were about.

CHAPTER XVII

MOBILISM

157. Mobilism in modern philosophy.

Mobilism is to metaphysics what Pyrrhonism, with its attendant discussionism, is to logic. It precedes Pyrrhonism, because doubt about the primacy of being is what causes doubt about the primacy of knowledge. Mobilism is a characteristic of the post-conciliar Church, in which as Cardinal Alfrink says, everything has been put in motion and no part of the Catholic system is free from change: *nihil quietum in causa.*[1]

International organizations take mobilism as being axiomatic. The UNESCO report for 1972 is called *Apprendre à être,*[2] but "to be" is taken as synonymous with "to become" or "to develop." It is said that "the mind should not stop still in definite conclusions" but should "become extremely ready to change." It is consequently asserted that there is "a need to educate thought in such a way that it is ready to hypothesize a multiplicity of solutions" of divergent rather than convergent sorts, and a need to prevent the mind adhering to any definitive opinions.[3] Truth, that is, stability, is not the law of thought; but rather opinion, that is, what fluctuates continually. UNESCO fails to see that of course someone will be directing the movement of opinion that governs opinion, and that the way is thus open to Hobbes' Leviathan.

Gaudium et Spes describes mobilism as a characteristic of modern civilization: *Ita genus humanum a notione magis statica ordinis rerum ad notionem magis dynamicam atque evolutivam transit.*[4] The document later refers to modern man's assertion of

---

[1] "Nothing in the matter is at peace."
[2] "Learning to be." Paris 1972.
[3] O.R., 10 January 1973.
[4] *Gaudium et Spes*, 5. "Thus the human race is moving over from a static to a dynamic and evolutionary idea of the order of things."

human rights and says that this dynamism is positive and in harmony with the Gospel: *Ecclesia ergo iura hominum proclamat et hodierni temporis dynamismum haec iura undique promoventem, agnoscit et magni aestimat.*[5] This second statement is specifically concerned with social movements, but the first embraces the whole of human life and seems to make the moral order subject to the law of mobility, when religion holds it to be immobile and a participant in the divine changelessness. However, if the word dynamism is taken as equivalent to perfecting, the council's thought remains within the bounds of the traditional understanding, which says that all things are perfectionable, and to be perfected, within an order demanding perfection, but which does not perfect itself.

158. Critique of mobilism. Ugo Foscolo. Kolbenheyer.

As seen in the history of philosophy, mobilism is the mentality that values becoming more than being, motion more than rest, action more than the goal. It is typical of modern thought. Heraclitus of Ephesus, in the sixth century before Christ, taught that reality was flux, but that the flux was ruled by an inviolable law which is the Logos. The whole of Christian philosophy has considered becoming as an accidental quality of all finite substances, and that God alone is unchanging. Italian Romanticism, inasmuch as it imitated the German sort, also believed that change is synonymous with life and that therefore the importance of the mind lies in searching for truth, rather than in possessing it. Foscolo, for example, maintains in his *Dell'origine e dell'ufficio della letteratura* that life consists in the agitation of one's feelings, and in the continual change of the thoughts of a spirit aspiring towards a vision of the whole truth. He maintains however that to be forever aspiring is better than attaining: "Unhappy man, were he ever to see it! Perhaps he would have no further reason to live." Goethe's *Faust* is the poem of a man who dreams of satisfying himself by an infinity of successive experiences; he desires, and as soon as he attains his desire, desires again and never reposes in any attained good.

---

[5] *Gaudium et Spes*, 42. "The Church therefore proclaims the rights of men, and recognizes and values the dynamism of the present day that promotes these rights everywhere."

This restlessness was splendidly expressed this century in Guy Kolbenheyer's great trilogy *Paracelsus*:[6] the profound meaning of reality lies in becoming, in the endless change of nascent and dying forms projected by a deceiving hope that never rests in the good it attains. The primacy of becoming brings with it the primacy of action and the unimportance of the end pursued: it is the conquering not the conquest, the coming not the arriving, that matters.

The most complete theoretical systematization of mobilism is Hegel's philosophy: existing being is an infinitely changing process of becoming across time; becoming infects God and takes away his attributes of absolute changelessness and timelessness.

159. Mobilism in the Church.

Within the Church too, the idea has caught on that changeability is a positive quality and should be accepted; it has replaced the ideas of stability and immutability. The religious injunction remains clear nonetheless: *Stabiles estote et immobiles.*[7] The Bishop of Metz says: *La mutation de civilisation que nous vivons entraîne des changements non seulement dans notre comportement extérieur, mais dans la conception que nous nous faisons tant de la création que du salut apporté par Jésus-Christ.*[8] At the microphone of France-Inter the same bishop declared: *La théologie antéconciliare, celle de Trente, est désormais terminée.*[9] Speaking at odds with his strenuous assertions that the Church is unchangeable, even Paul VI himself said that "the Church has entered the movement of a history that evolves and changes."[10] It has become a commonplace in the mentality of this age, learned, half-learned and unlearned, that what matters about an act is not its result, but the act itself, irrespective of the end it has in view, worthy or unworthy: what matters is action itself,

---

[6] Berlin, 1935.
[7] I Corinthians, 15:58. "Be firm and stand fast."
[8] "The change of civilization we are living through brings with it changes not only to our external behavior, but to the ideas we have both of creation and of the salvation brought by Jesus Christ." Metz Diocesan Bulletin, 10 October 1967.
[9] Broadcast on 18 August 1976. "Pre-conciliar theology, the theology of Trent, is henceforth at an end."
[10] O.R., 29 September 1971.

not the value it pursues or attains. It need hardly be said that
this action for action's sake is the very soul of the great modern
political perversions such as Nazism, as Max Picard has shown
in a famous book, that can never be famous enough.[11]

Mgr Illich said when interviewed in his seminary at Cuernavaca: "I believe the Church's function is to participate consciously in all forms of change, in any kind of change. That is
the task Christ has given us. We want a Church whose principal
function is the celebration of change."[12] The style is extravagant,
but the spirit it expresses is exactly the one that *agitat molem*.[13]
The President of the Italian Theological Association taught at a
national convention that "the task of evangelization is to put
any stabilization and absolutization into crisis."[14]

160. Mobilism and the fleeting world. St. Augustine.

As a philosophy of pure becoming, mobilism has a profound significance, acutely perceived by Rosmini in his essay on
the philosophy of Ugo Foscolo, and which Rosmini appropriately calls the philosophy of false hope. Mobilism involves the
denial of the Infinite as the fullness of being and posits the notion of life as the antithesis of God. In her novel *We the Living*,
Ayn Rand makes life itself the supreme good, and God is conceived of as the antithesis of life. To know whether the people
she is speaking to believe in life, as she does, the heroine asks
them whether they believe in God: "If they answer that they
believe in God, I know they don't believe in life."

Mobilism is partly true and partly false. The true part is its
description of finite existence as becoming, fleetingness, transition, unfulfilledness, quest. *This fleeting world* is well known in
religion and in Christian asceticism. The false part is its assertion that the changing reality of finite being is not directed towards an Infinite that does not change and that does satisfy; the
assertion that for man there is only an infinite becoming from
which he can never reach a perfect and unchanging infinitude.
The fleeting world, as religion presents it to man, is wonderfully

---

[11] M. Picard, *Hitler in uns selbst (Hitler in Ourselves)*, Erlenbach-
Zürich 1946.
[12] Quoted in the *Dauphiné Libéré*, 26 February 1968.
[13] "Stirs the whole mass."
[14] O.R., 11 September 1981.

portrayed by St. Augustine[15] who explains it as essentially an ontological deficiency, a lack of being. The things of the world escape the spirit, "which wants to stand and dwell with the things it loves, and is overwhelmed and torn by the motion of fleeting things, to which it attaches itself with the bond of love." It is torn because things flee from it and it would like to hold them fast but can find no place to do so: *in illis enim non est ubi, quia non sunt.*[16] In fact one cannot say of changing things, at any moment of their existence, that they really are, because they are always on the edge of being, in transit towards being, never adequately confirmed in being, always *in fieri* and never *in facto esse.*[17] Thus on the one hand the soul has a fundamental intuition of being and strives for the total reality, while on the other it seems obliged to desire fleetingness, that is, the total devolution of reality into becoming, and an endless succession of changing moments. In fact, however, the soul does not want this *successive infinity* of fleeting things but a simultaneous infinity of a single moment, that is, a moment containing past and future moments in a single whole. And this aggregation and unification is the definition of eternity: *interminabilis vitae tota simul et perfecta possessio.*[18]

The words of Goethe's Doctor Faust to the fleeting moment are relevant here: *Verweil doch! du bist so schön!*[19] The words express the contradictory desire that the moment (a word derived from *movere*, to move) should stand still, that the fleeting not fly, the finite be infinite, the partial be the whole. If life is pure becoming and the religious presupposition that, as St. Augustine says, *anima esse vult et requiescere amat in eis quae amat*[20] is false, then the only reality will be in change and only the complete occurrence of all changes (if that were available) would give the whole of reality. But if, on the other hand, the whole reality is not a becoming but a whole and changeless being, then becoming is only the mode in which creatures participate in that fullness of being and gain access to it.

---

[15] *Confessions*, IV, 10 and 11.
[16] "In them there is no place to hold, because they are not."
[17] "In a state of becoming" rather than "in a state of being."
[18] Boethius's *Consolation of Philosophy*, Book V, Prose 6. "The full, simultaneous and perfect possession of boundless life."
[19] "Stay then, thou art so fair!"
[20] Op. cit. "The soul wishes to be, and it loves to rest in the things it loves."

161. Mobilism in the new theology.

Mobilism has affected the practical attitudes of clergy and laity, who are now apt to value action for its own sake and to undervalue the end to which the action is directed. But it has also affected theology. Mobilism is now diffused in the mentality of the age. The doctrinal sources from which it came are no longer identifiable. They are rather like a now disused dye, the color of which can only be judged from cloth previously tinted with it. This theoretical mobilism that has pervaded Catholic thinking is solemnly professed in a large front page article in the *Osservatore Romano*,[21] which is very important for two reasons. It attacks the doctrine of the unchangeability of the moral law that Paul VI had upheld in *Humanae Vitae*, and which flows from the metaphysical principle of the unchangeability of natures. The article also alleges there is change and becoming within God's own nature.

The article questions the metaphysical foundation of Catholic theology which, in union with Greek philosophy of both the Platonic and Aristotelian schools and in harmony with Jewish tradition, has always regarded God as perfect Being, whose essence is to be and who is therefore not subject to change or becoming, since to become is to be lacking in being, and to come-into-being. God is thus distinct from creatures, whose being is imperfect, changing and temporal. The philosophical understanding of God is also in perfect accord with popular ideas, which reject any shadow of imperfection, non-being or lack of being in God, and see Him as absolute immensity, eternity and totality.

The front page of the Vatican paper bears all those ideas about the changeability of the essential natures of things that it is impossible to reconcile with the Catholic faith, and which that faith has always rejected.

"The fact of being created in the image of God does not fix man in an *immobilism of essence*, but rather devotes him to a *'making himself' in the image of God.* That is why it is legitimate to manipulate his own nature towards a good end." This is to declare legitimate that manipulation of natural generative processes that *Humanae Vitae* has solemnly condemned as illegitimate. It is also to confuse man's *moral* self-making with his *ontological* self-making, which is an absurdity. It is obvious that the

---

[21] O.R., 3 March 1976.

writer's idea of human freedom is not Catholic but existentialist and heterodox. In Catholic teaching, there is an unchangeable nature underlying man's freedom, in conformity with which that freedom has to be exercised, and which specifies how it should be exercised: freedom does not mean creation; still less self-creation.[22]

The rejection of Catholic metaphysics is even more obvious in the following words that plunge God's being into becoming: "The definition of God as *ens a se*, that is, as an active and dynamic essence *that posits itself in being*, offers the key" etc. "Man, analogously to God, creates himself, and can also be *seen to be* an *ens a se*." The Catholic idea of God is here cast aside; namely that he is an *ens a se* not because he self-posits himself, but because he *is*; not because he unfolds his own reality through a perpetual need being perpetually fulfilled, but because he indefectibily and unimprovably possesses his own being. The God expounded in the *Osservatore Romano* is the god of the German idealists, not the God of the Catholic creed; it is the god who says *ego sum qui fio*, not the biblical God who says *ego sum qui sum*.[23]

The mobilistic man outlined here is equally heterodox. One can rightly say that man creates his own moral life, for because of his liberty he is *in manu consilii sui*[24] but it is a metaphysical enormity to say that he creates himself and is an *ens a se*. Even using that expression analogically will not do because it takes away the difference between Creator and creature and lapses into pantheism.

---

[22] In a volume of essays by various authors, *Il problema di Dio in filosofia e in teologia oggi*, Milan 1982, p.34, L. Sartori maintains it is plausible that if God is conceived of as love and freedom "it is not clear that the dimensions of historicity (=becoming) that he might assume, not through necessity or through a need to 'acquire' or to 'grow,' but solely through his freedom, can be held to compromise his infinite perfection." But it is clear that God's freedom does not extend to His own nature, because the Perfect cannot become imperfect, or the Unchangeable changing. [The motive for change is improvement, so a change would prove God had been in need of improvement, and is subject to time as well. Translator's note.]

[23] "I am who becomes" as opposed to "I am who am."

[24] Ecclesiasticus, 15:14. "In the hand of his own counsel."

The writer of the article concludes: "This nature is created by God not as a static reality and as a realization of a divine Idea perfect from the outset but as a dynamic reality designed to *autorealize* itself in the dynamic of history." There are things here that will not bear examination. First, as we have said, man's moral and metaphysical becoming are confused. Second, becoming is taken to be self-creation or, to use Gentile's terminology *autoctisis*, and thus the whole Catholic philosophy of being, which has always refused to attribute creativity to creatures, is rejected.[25] Third, the Word is denied, whether in philosophy or theology, that is, there is a denial that the forms of created and creatable things exist eternally in God. This is to remove the firmament of divine thought that generates the world, time and becoming, and from which the immutability and absoluteness of human values derive. As Leopardi says, the man who denies the Word and the divine ideas, denies God.

We conclude as regards the essentials of mobilism, that becoming should not be thought better than being, nor the dynamic better than the stable, because becoming is an effect of non-being and a sign of imperfection. A creature can become *inasmuch as it does not exist*, and lacks the principle that sustains it in being. It thus has to take on incessantly those determinations of being that it lacks. God, who is being at its most determinate, possesses the whole of being and all its possible determinations, in an absolute simple unity. If the divine action did not sustain it, the creature would fall of itself into non-being: its principle of stability comes to it from outside.

Mobilism is foreign to religion. The task of the Church is not to support and accelerate its movement, but to fix the spirit of man in the *firmamentum veritatis*[26] and to arrest its flight: *siste fugam*[27] as Seneca said.

162. Mobilism in eschatology.

The mobilism that attacks the divine being cannot but attack the participation in that being which constitutes supernatural beatitude. If deity is in becoming, deified man will be too, and man's final state will be not so much a *state* as a *motion* in search of something. This thesis is explicitly professed by

[25] See *Summa Contra Gentiles*, Lib. II cap. 21.
[26] "Firmament of truth."
[27] "Stay your flight."

Father Agostino Trapè, who says that man will indeed find his own integration in the vision of God but it will be a "vision that will be consummated not in staticness, even of a marvelous sort, but in an infinitely *dynamic search* for the Supreme Good. Thus nothing is so opposed to this inexhaustible journeying towards the earthly or heavenly possession of God as any sort of immobilism." I do not believe that the static conception of beatitude, which all schools of Catholic theology have upheld, constitutes the greatest possible opposition to genuine eschatology; I also seem to detect a contradiction in terms in the expression *inexhaustible journeying towards the earthly or heavenly possession*, since it refers to an infinite process of acquisition which excludes the possession of the thing acquired.[28]

Trapè's theory, which had already been anticipated by Gioberti in his *Filosofia della Rivelazione* at quite a different level of philosophical power, is false, because the Church teaches that man's condition as a *comprehensor* is quite different from his condition as a *viator*.[29] To deny this difference is equivalent to removing the special kind of non-temporal duration in which the creature lives when it has been "freed from vanity,"[30] to which it is now subject, that is, freed from becoming and non-being. It is also equivalent to shutting the creature up in time, making eternal life a continuation of time, and canceling both the divine transcendence and our analogical transcendence along with it. God is not looking for himself, he possesses himself; so too the beatified creature will not look for him either any more, but will possess him. In this regard, the idea of eternal life as an infinite continuation of life in time is a regression to the Elysian fields the pagans believed in. They could only imagine an other-worldly happiness as an undisturbed continuation of the delights of this world. Ovid depicts the happiness of the Elysian fields as *antiquae imitamina vitae.*[31]

In the descent into the underworld in the *Aeneid*, happiness consists in athletic games, songs, music and even picnics in verdant meadows.[32] When applied to eschatology, mobilism thus

---

[28] This mobilism regarding our heavenly end is disposed of by simply knowing the distinction between essential and accidental beatitude, and by a reading of Dante's *Paradiso*.

[29] A "comprehender" and a "wayfarer," i.e., in heaven and on earth.

[30] Cf. Romans, 8:20-21.

[31] *Metamorphoses*, IV,445. "Imitations of their old life."

[32] *Aeneid*, VI, 656ff.

leads to a definite immanentism that makes becoming something internal to God and moreover removes the truly transcendent quality of man's goal, by projecting present life into eternity and ignoring the leap to the "new heavens and a new earth."

CHAPTER XVIII

THE VIRTUE OF FAITH

163. Rejection of natural theology.
Cardinal Garrone. Mgr Pisoni.

The denial of the primacy of knowledge over life has pene-trated the Church.[1] Many people today doubt, set aside or deny the Church's teaching concerning the rational preambles of the faith, namely that "The one true God, Creator and Lord, can be known with certainty by the natural light of human reason."[2] The supernatural virtues of hope and charity are thus deprived of their foundation and become mere manifestations of vitality. Keeping to our methodological criterion, we will demonstrate the eclipse of the Church's rational sense by giving two pieces of evidence; one from the Cardinal Prefect of the Congregation for Catholic Education (alias Seminaries and Universities), and one from a priest who with his bishop's authorization, for many years wrote what was called a theological column in one of the most widely read weekly magazines in Italy.

At the Congress of Italian Theologians held in Florence in 1968 Gabriel Marie Cardinal Garrone attributed the crisis in faith to our inability (unnoticed by Teilhard de Chardin) to offer contemporary man a notion of God that is meaningful for him, that is, in accord with his distaste for rationality, reason-ableness and truth. His Eminence detected an excess of theo-retical knowledge in Catholic theology, an intemperance of rea-son, a sort of philosophism. His precise words were these: *Au siècle dernier les théologiens avaient été amenés à affirmer la ca-pacité de la raison humaine à prouver l'existence de Dieu...Les théologiens ont abandonné Dieu entre les mains des philosophes. Nous devons reconnaître que nous nous sommes trompés, car nous*

---

[1] See paragraph 149.
[2] Vatican I, Denzinger 1806.

avons demandé à la philosophie ce qu'elle ne pouvait pas don-ner...Nous devons retrouver les attributs de Dieu, non pas les idées abstraites de la philosophie, mais les noms, les vrais noms de Dieu. Nous avons mission de prêcher non pas des idées mais la foi.[3]

The authority of a particular person does not deprive members of the faithful of their right to compare the teaching of one of the Church's ministers with the teaching of the Church universal. It was not merely the theologians who taught that reason was able to prove the existence of God; it was the Church itself that solemnly taught it, exercising its supreme teaching authority at the First Vatican Council. It will therefore not do to say *nous nous sommes trompés*: it would have to be *l'Eglise s'est trompée.*[4] It is not only the Florence congress that displays this lack of confidence in reason and this "circiterism." It is the whole People of God who today talk half Azotic and half Hebrew.[5] Nonetheless, it would be a bad day for the Church if it were to say to men: "Believe in me, when I don't believe in myself."

When I asked the editors of the journal which referred to the Cardinal's speech[6] whether it had not perhaps misreported the event, and the editors had forwarded my enquiry to the Cardinal, the latter replied to me saying: *Ce texte des I.C.I. ne m'avait pas échappé et j'ai pris avec les responsables le contact qui convient en leur remettant le texte authentique de cette conférence. Je n'ai pas besoin de vous dire que le ton était tout autre.*[7] Since it seemed worth pursuing the matter, I asked I.C.I. to publish the authentic text, and two editors of the review discussed the

---

3 "In the last century theologians had been led to affirm the capacity of human reason to prove the existence of God....Theologians have abandoned God into the hands of the philosophers. We must recognize that we have made a mistake, because we have asked of philosophy what it could not give....We must discover the attributes of God, not the abstract ideas of philosophy, but the names, the true names of God. Our mission is to preach the faith, not ideas."

4 Not "We made a mistake" but "The Church made a mistake."

5 Nehemiah, 13:24.

6 It was mentioned in I.C.I., No.305, 1 February 1968, pp.12-13.

7 "The text in I.C.I. had not escaped my notice and I have made appropriate contact with those in charge by sending them the authentic text of the address. I need hardly tell you that the tone was quite other."

question with Cardinal Garrone in Rome. The Cardinal then declared *préférer ne pas poursuivre l'affaire.*[8]

There is no need to go into the question further. It is obvious, however, from merely reading the texts, that Cardinal Garrone's words contradict Vatican I, just as *not to be able* contradicts *to be able.* It is also a fact that the tone, whether it be A sharp or B flat, does not change the tune of the music, and that the feelings one has when making a judgment can change neither the meaning of the terms nor the value of the judgment.[9] The Cardinal's opinion has a modernist origin, since it is characteristic of modernism to base beliefs on a feeling and an experience of the divine, rather than on a preliminary rational certitude, and to hold that reason *nec ad Deum se erigere potis est nec illius exsistentiam, utut per ea quae videntur, agnoscere.*[10]

In his column called *La posta dell'anima*[11] Mgr Ernesto Pisoni writes: "Human reason alone can certainly show the possibility of the existence of God and therefore prove that the existence of God is credible." This is the precise opposite of the Church's teaching. Reason can prove not only the possibility but the reality of God's existence. One could perhaps also say that God's existence is possible in the sense that it does not involve contradiction; from which St. Anselm would immediately deduce his existence. Non-contradiction is indeed a condition for the possibility of the existence of something. But what the Church teaches is not that God's existence is possible, that is, not absurd, but rather that it is real. "The existence of God is not contrary to reason" says Mgr Pisoni, but he fails to realize that he is thus applying to natural truths a test that is really relevant to supernatural ones. Reason apprehends and sees natural truths, which are its proper intelligible object. It does not apprehend supernatural truths, but has the task of showing that they do not conflict with reason.

---

8   "To prefer not to pursue the matter." The whole correspondence that began with my letter to I.C.I. on 18 February 1968 and ended with this statement of the Cardinal's preference is to be found in the materials for *Iota Unum.*

9   See paragraph 72.

10 Encyclical *Pascendi Dominici Gregis*, Denzinger, 2072. "Can neither reach God nor come to know of his existence by means of visible things."

11 In the magazine *Amica*, 7 July 1973.

164. The theological virtue of faith.

The failure to distinguish between the sphere of the naturally intelligible and the sphere of the superintelligible brings with it a misrepresentation of Catholic doctrine concerning the theological virtues, which we must now examine.

Reason cannot arrive at a demonstration of supernatural truths such as those regarding the Holy Trinity, the God-Man, the resurrection of the body, the real presence in the Eucharist. These are truths proposed by revelation and apprehensible only by faith. But that impossibility does not deprive the act of faith of its rational character: it remains supremely reasonable. By recognizing itself as finite, reason sees that knowable truths can exist beyond its own limit, without being apprehensible by rational evidence. Reason adheres to these truths with an assent; but this assent is produced not by a logical necessity stemming from the evidence, but by a supernatural determinant, namely grace.

Faith is a supernatural virtue, pertaining to our own power of knowing, by which man goes beyond his own limits and assents to things he cannot see precisely because of their being beyond his own limits. According to Catholic teaching faith is a virtue that resides in man's intellect, just as charity resides in the will; it is possible because, as we have said, man's intellect is limited.

The reason for faith is, on one side, this limitation of the intellect,[12] and on the other the authority of the revealed divine word. The fact that there has been a revelation pertains to history, and has to be shown from history. The authority of the divine word is likewise something knowable by reason. It would be a vicious circle to say that man recognizes God's authority on God's authority; the proposed revelation is accepted as authoritative because of arguments showing that it really does come from a God whose authority can be known by an analytical examination of the concept of God itself. All the sources of authority in the Catholic system are thus grounded on reason, and if reason submits to authority it is because reason itself has seen the need of submitting. Thereafter, divine authority be-

---

[12] All sciences are based on faith in that they receive from other sciences knowledge that they do not themselves prove, but believe on the authority of the sciences from which they receive them. This sort of thing also happens in ordinary social life.

comes the criterion that prevails over all others. The things Christians believe are thus certain since the grounds for believing them lie not in some property belonging to the creature, but in the truth of God's own thought.

165. Critique of faith as a search. Lessing.

For the new theology, it is not stability that characterizes real faith, but rather the mobility of an endless searching. People even go so far as to say that an authentic faith must go into crisis, come through temptations and stay as far as possible from a state of rest. Objections to faith should abound because they stimulate us "continually to review and reconquer our own certainties about the Christian message."[13]

This dynamic view of faith is immediately derived from modernism, which holds that faith is produced by a feeling for the divine, and that conceptual truths that the intellect produces are merely changeable expressions of that feeling. More distantly, this view comes from the German transcendental philosophies that value becoming more than being and therefore value perennial doubt more than certainty and seeking more than finding. This is the mentality that Lessing expressed so well in the parable in *Eine Duplik*. "If the infinite and omnipotent God were to give me the option between the gift in his right hand, which is the possessing of the truth, and the gift in his left, which is searching for the truth, I would humbly pray: O Lord, grant that I may search for the truth, for possessing it belongs only to you."[14]

The mistake in this position lies in regarding as humble an attitude that is really an intense form of pride. What is someone really preferring when he prefers searching for truth to truth itself? He is preferring his own subjective movement and the activity of the Ego more than the good that his powers of acting are given him to attain. In short the Object is being valued less than the subject and an anthropocentric view is being adopted that is irreconcilable with religion, which seeks the creature's subjection to the Creator and teaches that in being thus sub-

---

[13] O.R., 15-16 January 1979.

[14] Frankfurt edition 1778, p.10. The passage on the previous page makes the meaning of the parable explicit: "It is not the truth that a man has or thinks he has that gives him his value, but the earnest effort that he has employed in order to attain it."

jected the creature finds its own satisfaction and perfection. The false view that values searching more than the truth is really a form of indifferentism. John Paul II has condemned it in these terms: "Another form of indifferentism towards the truth is to hold that it is more important that men should seek it than find it, on the grounds that definitive truth escapes them altogether."[15] From this there follows the error of "confusing the respect due to each person, whatever his ideas, with denying that an objective truth exists."

166. Critique of faith as tension. The French bishops.

Faith is alleged to consist in a human tension towards God. This view is favored by the document the French bishops published after their plenary meeting in 1968. They expressly repudiate the definition of faith as an adherence of the intellect to revealed truths, and see it instead as an existential adherence and an expression of vital energy: *Longtemps on a présenté la foi comme une adhésion de l'intelligence éclairée par la grâce et appuyée par la parole de Dieu. Aujourd'hui on en est revenu à une conception plus conforme à l'ensemble de l'Ecriture. La foi se présente alors comme une adhésion de tout l'être à la personne de Jésus-Christ. Elle est un acte vital et non plus seulement intellectuel, un acte qui s'adresse à une personne et non plus seulement à une vérité théorique...et de ce fait elle ne saurait être mise en péril par des difficultés théoriques en détail.*[16] So since faith is a vital tension of this sort, it continues to exist irrespective of what one believes, provided the tension lasts.

This attitude is a departure from the Church's tradition. Religion is indeed an attitude of the whole person and not only of the intellect, but the act of faith is an act that a person makes specifically by means of the intellect. One should not confuse

---

[15] O.R., 25 August 1983.

[16] "For a long time faith has been presented as an adherence of the intellect, enlightened by grace and supported by the word of God. Today we have returned to an idea of it that is more in keeping with Scripture as a whole. Faith then is presented as an adherence of one's whole being to the person of Jesus Christ. It is an act of life and no longer simply intellectual, an act addressed to a person and no longer simply to a theoretical truth...and for that reason it would not be endangered by theoretical difficulties on particular points."

priorities and so confuse the theological virtues as a result. Faith is a human virtue pertaining to knowing, not tending. Religion does indeed consist in all three of the theological virtues, but the foundation of the whole is faith, not a tending or tension, which is hope. I do not deny that religion as a whole can be regarded as a tending towards God. But it is false that its essential quality is that tension. First of all because a tension towards God is involved in all the human race's religious experience, including that of people who worship dung and scarab beetles and offer human sacrifice. Secondly, a tension towards God is involved in titanism, in which human energies are turned towards God not in order to revere him but to defy and defeat him. Indeed this tension is supremely present in Satan's religious experience, when he initially tended towards God with all his might, but to supplant him not to adore him. The real essence of true religion consists in subjection, and the principle on which it rests is the intellectual recognition of dependence on God. The principle on which tending or tension rests is one of an initial self-positing or independence.

167. Reasons for the certainty of faith.
Alexander Manzoni.

The innovators depart from the Church's teaching in the matter of the motive for religious belief as well. They say that the motive for believing is that faith brings out the perfect integration of the human person and that entire satisfaction that man seeks. This is one legitimate motive and is recognized as such in Catholic theology, but not as primary and determinant, because the goal of religion is not the satisfying of man, but the fulfilling of the end of creation, which has God himself as its goal. The anthropocentric drive of the new thinking crops up once more. The end that God assigns to man is justice,[17] that is, adherence to the will of God, but hidden within that end is the end God proposes that man should thereby attain, namely beatitude. The first object in man's view must be justice. Beatitude consists in being perfectly just as Christ says: "Blessed are they who hunger and thirst after justice, for they shall be satisfied

---

[17] *Quaerite ergo primum regnum Dei et iustitiam eius*, Matthew, 6:33.

(with justice)."[18] The subjective quest for beatitude must take second place to the triumph of God, its Object.

The ground for the certainty of faith also lies outside the subject. For the believer this certainty is the most unshakable of all certainties, and rises above the unintelligibility of the things revealed and above all historical conditioning. Since revealed truth is such that the human mind can neither discover it nor verify it, the only possible way to ground certainty about it is to receive the truth, simply receive it without any admixture from our side; in other words to shift the grounds of certainty entirely from the side of the subject to that of the Object. The certainty that the believer has about the dogmas of the faith is not based on arguments that have been discovered in the course of history to support their truth, or, as I have said, on the solution of all the objections that are made against them. It is based on a principle that surpasses all conditions, presuppositions and even all historical eventualities. To believe with Catholic faith (that is on the authority of God the primal truth) is to know most firmly that no argument yet devised, or which ever can be devised, will ever avail against the truths that one believes; it is to know that all the objections made against them are inconsequential, false or resolvable and all future objections will be likewise, throughout the whole of time to come *in saecula saeculorum* no matter how far human knowledge may advance.

As Manzoni writes "Have you been able to examine all these objections (against revelation)? Objections of fact, chronology, history, natural history, morality, etc. Have you discussed all the arguments of opponents, and have you discovered they are false, inconsequential?...even if you have, that will not be enough to have faith in the Scriptures. It is possible, it is unfortunately possible that in generations to come...there will be men who will devise new arguments against the truth of the Scriptures; they will fossick through history,...they will claim to have discovered facts which mean the things asserted in the Scriptures appear false. Now you must swear that these books which have not yet been written will be full of errors: do you swear it? If you refuse to, then you must admit that you do not have faith."[19]

---

[18]   Matthew, 5:6.
[19]   *Morale Cattolica*, ed. cit. Vol. II, pp.544-5, and for an analysis of Manzoni's theory, Vol. III, pp.358-9.

Faith is thus an unshakable persuasion admitting of no qualification *rebus sic stantibus,*[20] no historicist scruples, and which leads man into a sphere above history and above time, the sphere of the divine as such, in which *non est transmutatio nec vicissitudinis obumbratio.*[21]

---

[20] "Things being as they are."
[21] James, 1:17. "There is no alteration or shadow of change."

CHAPTER XIX

THE VIRTUE OF HOPE

168. Hybridization of faith and hope. Hebrews 11. Reasonableness of the supernatural virtues.

The abandonment of the intellectual nature of faith and its transformation into a tension or tending, has the effect of altering the nature of revelation so that it is no longer an unveiling of truths inaccessible to man by his natural intellectual powers, and becomes instead a tension or impulsion that directs his energies towards the infinite. The confusion arises because some people believe that an intellectual adherence to supernatural dogmas is an easy thing, or at least easier than adhering to them in practice. In fact, it implies a complete overcoming of the highest faculty in man, which far transcends an easy adherence to imaginary objects provided by mythology. This is because it involves a leap to the supernatural level, which is an act that the whole person performs by means of his intellect. Faith thus has a metaphysical profundity that puts it on a level with the two other theological virtues, hope and charity.

However, inasmuch as modern thought takes faith to be a tension, it tends to turn it into a form of hope, thus spoiling the order of the faculties and moving faith from the cognitional to the appetitive level. This equating of hope and faith comes from existentialism and is allegedly supported by the Pauline definition of faith[1] translated by Dante as: *fede è sustanza di cose sperate ed argomento de le non parventi.*[2] All the Fathers and scholastics rightly understood that faith is the substance, *hypostasis*, or substratum and foundation of hope: supernatural things that are hoped for have as their principle and underlying substance

---

[1] Hebrews, 11:1.

[2] *Paradiso*, XXIV, 64-5. "Faith is substance of things hoped for and argument of things that do not appear."

things that are believed. Faith is thus the thing that substantiates hope, not something substantiated by hope. One hopes for heaven because one believes it is there; one does not believe it is there because one hopes for it.

The moderns have deliberately inverted this order and made faith the daughter of hope, when it is actually the other way round. They say that first, man launches himself in hope towards his world of values and then the values hoped for are made the object of belief and of certainty. This turning of faith into hope has crept into the documents of national synods in aberrant definitions tinged with meaninglessness, as for example the one advanced at the synod in the canton of Ticino which asserted "faith is a speaking of our own hope to ourselves and to God," which, if it were not merely a sign of doctrinal collapse and detachment from theological tradition, could be taken as a semi-official alteration of the relation between faith and hope, given that the synod was presided over by the bishop.

The modernists said, in a false sense, that faith was an experience of God, forgetting that experience of God is not granted in this life, except as a special favor of the sort studied in mystical theology. Nonetheless, it can be called an experience of God if one takes experience in a broad sense as meaning conscious and verifiable acts, which would include all acts of knowing. When speaking to some theologians John Paul II taught that "man transcends the limits of his purely natural consciousness and has an experience of God that he would otherwise be denied." But he explains at once, referring to St. Thomas, that the experience of faith is essentially intellectual: "man can reach a certain understanding of supernatural mysteries thanks to the use of reason, but only insofar as it is based on the unshakable foundations of faith, which is a participation in the very knowledge of God and of the blessed in heaven."[3] Or will somebody allege that man on earth has an *experience* of God like that of the blessed in heaven?

In conclusion, the priority of faith over hope belongs to the basis of the Catholic religion, which is rationality. All the theological virtues have a motive, and what is a motive if not a reason? Their character as motivated acts was clear in the now disused formulas of acts of faith, hope and charity, and in the act of sorrow, all of which were taught in catechisms and used daily

---

[3] O.R., 17 October 1979.

in Christian life. You believe in revelation *because* God exists and is truthful. You hope for eternal salvation and the forgiveness of sins *because* Jesus Christ has merited them and strengthens our wills. You love God *because* he is infinite Good and infinitely lovable, and you love your neighbor, who is not infinitely lovable, *because* you love God who has made him. Lastly, you are sorry for and repent of your sins *because* you have offended God and because you have lost him as your happiness.

Reasonableness or rationality thus dominates all the doings of the Catholic religion, which never takes the dependent creature man as its foundation, but the all sufficient God.[4]

---

[4]   This confusion in theological concepts is often combined with the "circiterism" characteristic of the post-conciliar mentality, that includes disparate ideas under a single expression. In the O.R. of 30 March 1983 a bishop asserts that it is not enough to believe in God; we must also believe in man, because God has believed in man, in Adam, in Eve, in the Apostles, in Judas, etc., "so much so that he tried by every means to save them." Besides contradicting Scripture (Jeremiah, 17:5) and overlooking the classical distinction between *credere Deum, credere Deo* and *credere in Deum* (to believe God is, to believe on God's authority, to believe so as to attain to God) "believing" is obviously being used instead of "loving," thus using words so equivocally that anything could be said about anything.

CHAPTER XX

THE VIRTUE OF CHARITY

169. The Catholic idea of charity.

The mention of the polished and precise theological formulas of the acts of faith, hope and charity that were once in use brings us to the concept of charity, which is today tending to absorb both faith and hope in a single tension.

The primacy of charity, emphasized by St. Paul in a famous place,[1] is indeed recognized by all theologians, whether of intellectualist or voluntarist ilk, not because the other two theological virtues are formally reducible to charity and thus lose their specific nature, but because, as St. Thomas explains[2] the will has the advantage of moving towards the desired object and thus in some sense transfers the known object into the knowing subject: *operatio intellectus completur secundum quod intellectum est in intelligente.*[3] So faith, which is an intellectual virtue, attains God by giving assent to things it does not see; hope attains him by expecting a God it does not possess; but charity attains God *ut in ipso sistat.*[4] Even in this life God is loved, and it is by love that he is attained in heaven too. It is because faith and hope are means to an end that they pass away, but *caritas nunquam excidit.*[5] Faith ceases when God is seen, hope ceases because he is reached, but charity continues in our eschatological state, merely putting aside the imperfection that it had in our life in time.

Quite apart from its being not simply a means to an end, but an act directed towards, and eternal within God, there is a

---

[1]   I Corinthians,13:13.
[2]   *Summa Theologica*, II,II,q.23,a.8.
[3]   "The working of the intellect is carried out inasmuch as the thing understood comes to be in the understander."
[4]   "As he is in himself."
[5]   I Corinthians, 13:8. "Charity never passes away."

more profound theological reason why charity is the chief of
virtues. To the extent that they exist in God's thought, finite
beings cannot cease to be, because the *Logos* of which they are
part is eternally begotten within God's nature. This rose, for
example, could cease to be, but it is impossible that the idea of
this rose should not be; Martin need not have been, but the idea
of Martin had to be. Real things, with their own act of existence, need not have existed and are made to do so only by
God's love.

This profound truth is stupendously expressed by Dante:

Non per aver a sé di bene acquisto
(Ch'esser non può), ma perché suo splendore
Potesse, risplendendo, dir "subsisto,"
In sua etternità, di tempo fore
Fuor d'ogni altro comprender, come i piacque,
S'aperse in nuovi amor l'etterno amore.[6]

The creature proceeds from the divine charity, without
which it would exist in God but not in itself. Nonetheless it is
clear that even the excellence of this creative charity does not
abolish the logical precedence of the Idea, which has an excellence of another sort because it is a greater thing to exist necessarily in the divine Ideas than contingently like the world,
which only exists *per accidens.*[7]

Charity is not only the greatest of the virtues but the one
most specific to Christianity, as the pagans had almost no idea
of God's love for the world or man's love for God. In the *Ni-
comachaean Ethics* Aristotle denies there can be friendship between God and man because of the one's transcendence over the
other, and in the *Symposium* Plato denies it as well on the
grounds that love is the offspring of *Penia*, Need, and implies
poverty.

---

[6]   *Paradiso*, XXIX, 13ff.
      "Not for himself to have a good acquired,
      Which cannot be; but simply that His splendor
      Might in its shining say that 'it existed,'
      In His eternity, what time would render
      That none yet comprehended, at His pleasure
      The eternal love gave forth; new loves' begetter."
[7]   "As an accidental quality," i.e., as an aspect of a substance that lies
      elsewhere.

This excellence of charity is misrepresented by the innovating school. Just as they abolish logic in favor of lived experiences, so they abolish law in favor of love, but in so doing they reduce the Church itself to a formless mass of conflicting loves, because it is law that gives the structure of morals and religion.

170. Life as love. Ugo Spirito.

Ugo Spirito's book *La vita come amore*[8] gives relentlessly coherent theoretical expression to this subsuming of all values, particularly logical ones, under the category of love, and calls the process the sunset of a Christian civilization that has been overly dominated by the *Logos*. Spirito's thesis implies the denial of the Word, that is, as we have said many times but not too often, the denial of the Holy Trinity, the denial of God. The author maintains that the Word is incompatible with *agape* and that love can only be attained by eliminating the duality and opposition between good and evil and thus eliminating the value judgment that gives expression to that opposition. In order to love, one needs an absolute lack of standards that removes any *discretio spirituum*[9] and which, in short, downgrades the principle of contradiction by which evil is not good and should be hated, while good is loved. Ugo Spirito maintains that the world's crisis is strictly and formally the result of judgments that divide man between values and antivalues, things to be loved and to be hated.

Love is indeed the transcendent reality in which all things are one, and indeed of fundamental metaphysical importance. Spirito maintains that it can only really exist when values have been abolished. But there is an intrinsic contradiction in saying that something is lovable because it cannot be judged to be lovable. It is the same vicious circle Pyrrhonism always generates: even if love overcomes the distinction between what is lovable and hateful, we would still need the distinction to be able to choose the lack of distinction as preferable: *utcunque philosophandum est.*[10] It need hardly be said that this theory of life as love abhors absolute judgments and therefore rejects that absolute judgment that is called Hell in ethics. It rejects it not because it asserts that everyone is saved, the just by their justice

---

[8]   *Life as love.*
[9]   "Discernment of spirits."
[10]   "One way or another, we have to go on philosophizing."

and the evil by the mercy of God, but because to a love that is above any contradictories, virtue and crime are one.[11]

171. Love and law.

As the infinite Holy Spirit proceeds from the infinite Word, so in finite spiritual creatures does the will proceed from the intellect, and the denial of these processions means there is an amalgamation of law with love, that is, of intellect with will. The man having charity is then seen as being freed from any law, and law is seen as a merely restrictive and coercive thing. An opposition is thus created between law and the spirit of love, with the former being regarded as typical of pre-Christian man and as contrary to the Gospel. The Catholic teaching is that love contains obedience to law and that the will should conform to the order the law provides. There is no escaping Christ's words: *Si diligitis me, mandata mea servate.*[12] How could love be shown if there were no law? Love does not dissolve the law but fulfills it, just as, metaphysically, the will presupposes the intellect and, if one may so speak, the Holy Spirit presupposes the Word.

The Christian law of grace and the natural moral law both create an obligation; the Gospel is a new law, a new commandment, but a law and a commandment nonetheless. This law has a coercive character because it is endowed with a double sanction: the internal rebukes of one's conscience and, above all, a reward at the end of time. The rejection of law as incompatible with truly moral behavior is quite groundless, because true law is a replica of truly moral behavior. According to unanimous Catholic tradition, the fact that St. Paul says that *lex iusto non est posita*[13] and that men living without revelation, with a merely natural morality *ipsi sibi sunt lex,*[14] does not mean that a law is not given to them, but that it does not have to be imposed upon them. The just man appropriates the law to himself

---

[11] This is also the view of D. Flusser in his *Jésus*, French translation, Paris 1970, pp.92ff. But knowing a little history is enough to be able to recognize how little there is that is new in these modern ideas. The view of life as love is a variant of the heresy of the *Ethicoproscopti* attacked by St. John Damascene in the eighth century.

[12] John, 14:15. "If you love me, keep my commandments."

[13] I Timothy, 1:9. "Law is not imposed on a just man."

[14] Romans, 2:14. "Are a law unto themselves."

through love, and its requirements are no longer extrinsic to him but something that has been internalized. The abiding obligation to observe the law thus becomes a form of free behavior. This view of the matter is of Stoic origin, but is typical of the law of grace in the Christian scheme. St. Thomas teaches[15] that the highest grade of human dignity consists in moving towards the good of one's own volition; the second grade lies in moving towards the good at the instigation of someone else but without compulsion; and the lowest, but still a grade of dignity nonetheless, is to need to be forced to move towards it. In all of these cases, however, it is the requirements of the moral law that ultimately cause the act of the will, that is the act of love. And be it noted. It is not the law that is internal to man and deduced from him; it is man who is internal to the law and deduced from it, because it penetrates and molds his will. The primary thing is the law, not man. As St. Augustine teaches,[16] liberty does not eliminate the law but confirms it, the ruling principle of human life is outside of man: *vitium oritur cum sibi quisque praefidit seque sibi ad vivendum caput facit.*[17]

This discussion of the pre-eminence of law over love, and then of love over law, leads to a consideration of the post-conciliar attack on the existence and absolute quality of the natural law, which is the basis of moral life. The attack has taken various forms: attacks on the very existence of unchanging principles and their replacement by situation ethics or the principles of globality, or of graduality. Then again, there has been a decreasing emphasis on one's individual destiny and a greater emphasis on communitarian salvation.

172. The denial of the natural law. Sartre.

This denial stems from the aberrations we have discussed and especially from the Pyrrhonism and mobilism that have invaded the Church.[18] This attack from all sides on the natural law becomes obvious in the general change in European law that has adopted divorce and abortion and has abolished the laws against sodomy. This change is the most undeniable and

---

[15] Commentary on Romans, 2 lect.III.

[16] *De Spiritu et Littera*, Lib.I, cap.XXX,52. P.L.,44,233.

[17] Op. cit., cap.XII,II, P.L.44,206. "Fault arises when someone trusts in himself and makes himself the ruling principle of his own life."

[18] See paragraphs 148ff and 157ff.

most fearsome sign of the corruption of civilization taking place
at the present moment. We will confine ourselves here to explaining briefly those modern theories which are destructive of
the natural law, and to showing that they imply a radical rejection of essential natures in things.

First of all there is the Sartrian perversion which is not
content to deny the existence of the natural law, but actually
inverts it, thus taking the form of a *justificatio diaboli* or *dia-
bolodicy*[19] as opposed to the traditional *theodicy.*[20] Sartre's theories amount to a celebration of an unrestrainedly evil will; not a
will that happens to go astray because of some underlying evil,
but rather a will that takes the breaking of moral laws as its
guiding principle. It is therefore not simply an avoiding of the
law, which would be limited to ignoring the contrast between
good and evil and the obligation to do good, but an actual inversion, since it is what is wrong, as wrong, that the will seeks to
do. This complete independence of the law changes freedom
into a delirium, in the strict sense of jumping the groove, and
changes autonomy into anomy:[21] "O evil, be thou my good!" as
Satan says in Milton's *Paradise Lost.*

Some Catholic theologians maintain[22] that the ban on
abortion is not an unchangeable requirement of the Gospel law,
and that the latter cannot rightly be imposed on temporal society, since society is based on freedom of choice in moral matters.

Paul VI spoke out against theories that called the reality of
the natural law into question: "The moral norm in its constant
principles, both those of the natural law and those of the Gospel, cannot undergo change. We admit, however, that it can be
subject to uncertainties as regards the deepening of these principles through speculation or as regards their logical development and their practical application."[23] The Pope here reiterates
the classical teaching of the grand tradition of Greco-Roman
philosophy and of Catholic theology, whether of the time of St.
Augustine or of Rosmini, and reiterates it in almost unaltered
terminology. The moral law is absolute because it is an expres-

---

[19] "Justification of the devil."
[20] Natural theology.
[21] "Self law" into "no law."
[22] For example, the Professor of Pastoral Theology in the University
of Tübingen, later disavowed by his bishop. O.R., 17 May 1973.
[23] O.R., 31 August 1972.

sion of the eternal order of nature, fixed in the divine mind: *Lex naturalis est participatio legis aeternae et impressio divini luminis in creatura rationali qua inclinatur ad debitum actum et finem.*[24]

173. Catholic doctrine recalled.

The Catholic theory of the natural law is contained in three propositions. First: the natural law is an absolute order inherent in an ontological Absolute. Second: the natural law is immediately knowable in the structure of the rational creature. Third: the natural law contains the qualification of all possible human acts and that quality is recognized by a practical science. This practical science is followed by each agent in his own moral choices, but it also constitutes a systematic whole known as casuistry.

The natural law is thus a dictate of practical reason, that is, of reason judging the *should be* of human activity, and is parallel to speculative reason that judges the *being* of things.[25] Thus, just as all particular truths concerning non-practical matters are deduced from the principles of speculative reason, so all judgments on particular practical matters are deduced from the principles of practical reason; in both cases the possibility of error increases as the process of deduction moves further from principles and enters into the very complicated and variegated region of contingent events. Catholic theology has always distinguished between those deductions which are drawn immediately from principles and are certain, and remote deductions that decrease in certainty the further they are removed from first principles. This is what Paul VI is reiterating in the passage quoted. There is, on the one hand, something indefectible and unshakable about the moral imperative, and on the other something changeable about the world of the human actions that have to be modeled on that imperative. What this entails is often hard to know and always hard to desire. But the fact that something is difficult to know does not abolish the absoluteness or validity of the thing to be known.

---

[24] *Summa Theologica*, I,II,q.91,a.2. "The natural law is a participation in the eternal law and an impression of the divine light in the rational creature, by which it is inclined to its due action and end."

[25] *Summa Theologica*, I,II,q.94,a.2.

174. Grandeur of the natural law. The despising of it.

It has been the lot of our age to overthrow the absoluteness, the *tremendum* and the majesty of the natural law and to reduce it to the irrelevance of a mere opinion or an unreasoning mania for taboos. The Greek world lauded the law as something inviolable, immovable, unbegotten and indefectible. In the *Oedipus Rex* it "walks in the high places"[26] and forgetfulness does not put it to sleep.[27] In *Antigone* "it avails not today or yesterday but lives eternally."[28] Seneca is not less laudatory of the law of conscience when he says[29] "a right conscience and the spectacle of nature are the two most beautiful things under heaven." Then there is the famous remark at the end of Kant's *Critique of Pure Reason*: "Two things fill the spirit with an admiration and veneration that are ever new and increasing, the starry sky above me and the moral law within me."

The majesty of the moral law proceeds from its indefectible vigor, which is to be identified with the being of God himself. It shares in his timeless and absolute character and cannot be thought of as created. The natural law is in fact unbegotten in God and the Church's theological tradition has always rejected the idea that it is created: the world is created, but the moral law is not. The voluntarist school typified by William of Ockham maintained that the natural law was a contingent, created effect; but that view, with whatever attenuating interpretations, makes morality contingent and in effect abolishes it. Ockham in fact did say that one could without contradiction imagine another moral order freely willed by God like this present one, but in which good would be what is evil in the present system. The opposite view, namely that the law is absolute, means that evil acts are evil not only in this creation, but in every possible world. The natural law is thus impersonal, not in the sense that it does not affect persons: it does affect them at the highest level, but does not emanate from them; it affects them.

This ontological foundation of the moral law is attacked by the new theological currents of opinion, which try to deny the law is prior to human willing, and turn it into a subjective creation. The twelfth National Biblical Week held in Rome in 1972

---

[26] Lines 865-66.
[27] Line 870.
[28] Line 456.
[29] *Ad Helviam*, 8.

had as its professed aim to "renew moral theology not only in its method of exposition but also in its contents," saying it wanted "to give an authentic setting to morality." By replacing the Church's solid definitions with an enormous half philosophical and half poetical "circiterism," it said that "before being a teaching, the Christian religion is a presence of the day of the risen Lord, witnessed to ecclesially with authenticity."[30] This is a defective definition, because the root of religion lies in assent to objective doings and sayings, not in the subjective experience of a presence. Nor is it true that evil consists "in breaking the eschatological tension of the person in the history of salvation."[31] It does indeed break it, but the reason evil is evil, is not that it breaks a person's projection towards the future, but that it violates the relation between one nature and another, between the finite and the infinite; and that is quite independent of subsequent events. The Week meeting also cast doubt on the fixed character of the natural law because, using an unfamiliar and ambiguous terminology, it distinguishes between a transcendental and a categorical morality, alleges there are a variety of ethics in the New Testament, and says many New Testament precepts are mere products of their time. Finally it explicitly formulates its devaluation of commandments: "It is not primarily a case of observing a series of commands, but of submitting oneself to the truth of Christ, that is of living in profound faith."[32] It is not apparent that any good purpose is served by replacing precise words and ideas with "circiterising" ideas and ambiguous words as is being done here. The position expressed is compatible with Catholic theology if what is meant is that faith works through charity, and if there is no intention of refusing to recognize that Christ's commands express his spirit, and that Christ commands both the works and the spirit, that is, the intention of the works.

---

[30] O.R., 1 October 1972.
[31] O.R., 27 September 1972.
[32] O.R., 30 September and 1 October 1972.

CHAPTER XXI

THE NATURAL LAW

175. The natural law as taboo. Cardinal Suenens. Hume. Critique.

The allegedly changeable character of the natural law, which is a commonplace of the new theology,[1] cannot be separated from the attempt to deprive it of its absolute and timeless quality by reducing it to a mere irrational habit of thinking. The word *taboo*, which is borrowed from ethnology and signifies that ultimate degradation of the human spirit by which it takes an inanimate thing as being sacred and inviolable, has been taken up both by secular commentators and by bishops and theologians. For example, in his pastoral letter on sexuality, Cardinal Suenens says nothing about the procreative end of marriage, which is part of the natural law, and states that "a healthy evolution has removed *certain taboos* and has made relations between man and woman more natural and more genuine."[2] This is but one instance of the general demoting of moral virtues from the rank they possess in Christian ethics to the level of mistaken notions and superstitions.

Those who equate the natural law with taboos fail to realize that to deny the natural law is to deny the essence of a thing and to go against the principle of non-contradiction. Being has a make-up of its own, and resists the attempts of men to dislocate

---

[1] The case of Fr. Curran, one of the best known disciples of Fr. Häring and a leading spokesman on Catholic matters in the United States, is typical. He was removed from his position by the Archbishop of Washington after having taught that "the natural law and moral rules are in continuous evolution." But six thousand students and four hundred teachers protested on his behalf and the said archbishop restored him to his chair. I.C.I., No.288, 15 May 1968, p.7.

[2] O.R., 21 July 1976.

it, deform it or reduce it to non-being. The same thing applies to the natural law, which is *the order of being*. The modern father of this way of thinking is David Hume, in his "Essay" on justice, in which he states that: "The same species of reasoning, it may be thought, which so successfully exposes superstition, is also applicable to justice....But there is this material difference between superstition and justice, that the former is frivolous, useless, and burdensome; the latter is absolutely requisite to the well-being of mankind and existence of society."[3] However, in reality "it must be confessed, that all regards to right and propriety, seem entirely without foundation."[4] That adverb *absolutely* and the predicate *entirely without foundation* are too close together in Hume's text for forgetfulness to produce the obscurity in which contradictory assertions can coexist. Man's logical capacities cannot, in any case, be extinguished; man cannot be persuaded to accept the assertion that a thing is necessary (that is, that it cannot not be) and that it is devoid of any foundation in being. There can be no logical retreat; having once asserted that propriety, shame and obedience are taboos, one must also assert the same of paternal, filial and conjugal sentiments and of a repugnance to sodomy, cannibalism and necrophilia. This conclusion is now in fact being drawn, and accepted by society at large in its attitude to divorce, sodomy and abortion.

176. The law as a human creation. Duméry.

The attack on the natural law revolves around the attempt made by modern thought to cancel the difference between essences and abolish the dependence of the dependent. The individual's freedom to make and remake essences rises in revolt against the absolute character of the divine Legislator, of whom Victor Hugo said *il est, il est, il est éperdument.*[5] The attack is also based on the revolutionary philosophy which is a human revolt against any law deriving from an essence or nature. As Sartre would have it, there is no such thing as human nature, only a perpetual unmaking and remaking of man by man himself. The Catholic view denies that man can create, even as a

---

[3] David Hume, *Essays and Treatises on several subjects*, Vol. II, new edition, Dublin MDCCLXXIX, p.247.

[4] Ibid.

[5] "He exists, he exists, he astonishingly exists."

secondary cause, and instead holds that he draws out and actuates the potential of created realities. Man possesses, enjoys and elaborates upon his own nature and upon the things of this world, but he does not change the natures of those things: he is commanded to obey them. The revolutionary principle is, conversely, one of rejection and attempted destruction. *La nature des choses, voilà l'ennemi. L'homme qui fait son métier d'homme est celui qui refuse de s'y soumettre.*[6] This is an admirable formulation of the matter: it sees that fundamentally religion is a knowing and recognizing of the order in the natures of things, while irreligion is Beelzebub, that is, "the one without yoke." While the words quoted express the doctrine of a radical movement outside the Church, what St. Thomas used to call the *profundior intentio* of the same current of thought appears in the writings of Henri Duméry, who expressly maintains that human beings create values.[7] Values are the creation of the *cogito* which by its activity posits natures in an absolute sense. In the author's view, man possesses an axiological creativity, or a capacity to create values by living them. The author does not thereby mean the spirit's capacity to live out in experience moral values that are given in the intellect, and which the latter in some sense causes to be anew, by recognizing them. If that were what he meant, he would come within the ambit of the common teaching that allots the human person the role of making the values contained in the law appear in one's own free activity. In fact, however, the author is talking about a genuine creation of values. *La loi est celle du rapport de l'esprit à l'Absolu, de son retour à Dieu. Mais cette loi est posée par l'acte spirituel lui même qui tire de l'Absolu la force de se faire, de se donner un monde d'essences, un horizon des valeurs. Dès lors il est bien vrai que l'esprit dérive de l'Absolu et que les valeurs dérivent de la loi immanente à l'acte....Mais il n'est par vrai que les valeurs soient préformées dans l'Absolu, ce qui supprimerait tout pouvoir producteur de la liberté humaine.*[8]

---

6   "The nature of things, there is the enemy. The man who behaves as man should is someone who refuses to submit to it."

7   Principally in the book *La foi n'est pas un cri*, cited in the second edition, Paris 1957, and put on the Index in 1958. For the citation in the text, see p.210, note 20.

8   "The law is that of the relation of the spirit to the Absolute, of its return to God. But this law is posited by the spiritual act itself, which draws from the Absolute the power to make itself, to provide itself with a world of natures, a horizon of values. From then on it

This view implies the independence of the dependent,[9] that is, that the created spirit, thus created, has the power to create a world of values. That world is not secondary, a participation in the uncreated divine Idea: it is a truly primal, original world of values that are not preformed in God. It is the theory, so radically rejected by St. Thomas, that creatures are made with a capacity to create. Dependent being is seen as operating independently, without any efficient or exemplary cause.

I will not expand upon the similarities between this position and the Molinist position on the specific question of grace. In the final analysis it is always a matter of keeping at least some fraction of independence for nature: Molina makes the will's self-determination independent, but does not push it to the point of creating values, while the new theology assigns the human spirit not merely the positing of an act but the very creation of values. It could be said that as far as morals are concerned, man is his own God.

177. Rejection of the natural law by civil society.

The general breakdown of the Catholic system consists not only in the denial of the natural law by philosophical and theological thinkers, but in its ejection from the laws and customs of nations. Christian nations that, even under regimes hostile to the Church, used to regulate marriage and the family according to the maxims of natural justice are now separating individual, family and social legislation from the religious principles upon which those maxims rest and within which they are contained. Legal codes which, in these matters, were for centuries replicas of canon law, have broken free and are now shaping themselves by the principle of the independence of human life. This is apparent in the universal adoption of divorce, in the legality of abortion and its quasi-obligatory status (for obstetricians), and

---

is indeed true that the spirit derives from the Absolute and that values derive from the law immanent in the act....But it is not true that values are preformed in the Absolute, a state of affairs which would suppress any productive power in human freedom."

[9] This idea of an independent morality was upheld at the *Pax Romana* convention in Rome in September 1982. Its statement of position says that "ethical consciousness of itself gives force to its requirements, without resting on a religious or metaphysical foundation." O.R., 12 September 1982.

in the legalization of sodomy. It is worth undertaking a brief investigation of post-conciliar thought on each of these three points.

It should be remarked at the outset that there is an altogether new element in the change that has occurred. The many changes that history records regarding the political control of this or that country, or matters of internal political organization, or even the religion of whole nations, often depended in the past on the will of a monarch or the violent activity of minorities or tiny groups. It would be specious to see such changes as changes in the spirits or opinions of the mass of the people. The adoption of divorce and abortion by modern states does, by contrast, represent a general consensus. As a result of the general adoption of popular forms of government, laws, which were once the opinion of the few promulgated for the observance of the many, today represent the decision, the opinion, in short the philosophy of a whole nation. Thus, as Carlo Caffarra has accurately observed,[10] the legalization of abortion by nominally Christian peoples has supremely demonstrated the decay of our civilization, and its degradation (despite the remaining decency and sophistication of social life) to a level lower than that of the great non-Christian civilizations.[11]

[handwritten marginal notes:] Decent + sophisticated social life does not make a civilization, regardless of JPII's treatment. Christian should we treat it as such.

[10] O.R., 12 July 1978.
[11] In his speech at Santiago de Compostella on 9 November 1982, John Paul II nonetheless considered European unity as still existing, and as consisting of Christian values. O.R., 10 November 1982.

CHAPTER XXII

DIVORCE

178. Divorce. Mgr Zoghby.
Patriarch Maximos IV at the council.

The plebiscite of 1974, in which divorce was supported by the Italian people, obviously expressed the national will; and since it followed upon an extensive public debate, its anti-Catholic character could not be disguised.

The modern state's enmity to the Church had not previously been joined to an attack on the natural law, of which the Church is the chief guardian. In the post-conciliar period the defection of Italy in 1974 and Spain in 1981 completed the emancipation of European society from its religious base.

In paragraph 89 I mentioned the strenuous opposition the Church presented to the attacks that royal despots made upon the indissolubility of marriage, often assisted by the local ecclesiastical hierarchy. Last century, there were occasional instances of departure from the Church's perpetual teaching, even in the writings of churchmen, but they were always singled out for condemnation. The Church's weakness in this matter was obvious in Italy at the time of the referendum, when some priests campaigned in favor of the dissolubility of marriage and were permitted to do so by their superiors; some bishops even condemned priests' participation in the campaign for an anti-divorce referendum, and the Patriarch of Venice had to dismiss the priest responsible for Catholic universities when he had spoken out in favor of divorce. This abandonment of the struggle was also obvious in the protocol signed between the Holy See and Portugal in February 1975, amending the concordat of 1940. Where the latter, respecting the principle of indissolubility, had laid down that Catholic couples gave up their right to seek a divorce and that the Portuguese civil courts could not grant a divorce to canonically married people, the

1975 protocol went no further than reminding Catholic couples that marriage was indissoluble, and gave the civil courts the
right to dissolve marriages.[1]

These changes come as less of a surprise if one remembers
the statements that some council fathers made at Vatican II favoring divorce. They were eastern bishops who had been influenced by the matrimonial discipline of the Orthodox Church.
That Church allows divorce in various circumstances, including
the case of treason against the state on the part of one spouse.
During the CXXXIX session of the council, Charles Cardinal
Journet ably illustrated how this indulgent practice of the Orthodox Church is the historical result of its political dependence
on the Byzantine and Tzarist empires.[2] His speech was a reply to
the suggestion by Mgr Elias Zoghby, patriarchal-vicar of the
Melkites in Egypt, that the bond between an unjustly abandoned spouse and the guilty party be dissolved. When this suggestion stirred up an enormous row in the council and the
press, Mgr Zoghby felt bound to state in a further speech to the
council that in making his suggestion he in no way intended to
derogate from the principle of the indissolubility of marriage.[3]
The reply is obvious: it is not enough to maintain something
verbally while claiming that it can coexist intact with something
that destroys it.

The most developed attack on indissolubility was made by
the Patriarch of the Melkites, Maximos IV, who took up Mgr
Zoghby's proposals more forcefully and who collected his conciliar and extra-conciliar pronouncements in the form of a
book. Of course the abandonment of Catholic doctrine is not
admitted for what it is; it is advanced as a disciplinary rather
than a doctrinal change, in the form of a *pastoral solution*. At the
outset the book states the doctrine of indissolubility, solemnly
defined by the Council of Trent as an article of faith that shuts
the door on any discussion. Then, with the sophistical tactics
typical of the innovators,[4] it goes on to say: *Dans l'Eglise
catholique il se trouve des cas d'injustice vraiment révoltante, qui
condamnent des êtres humains, dont la vocation est de vivre dans
l'état commun de mariage...et qui en sont empêchés sans qu'il y ait*

---

[1]   O.R., 16 February 1975.
[2]   O.R., 1 October 1965.
[3]   O.R., 5-6 October 1965.
[4]   See paragraph 50.

de leur faute et sans qu'ils puissent humainement parlant supporter toute leur vie cet état anormal.[5]

The Church's constant tradition[6] and, at a theoretical level, the whole of Catholic dogma are opposed to the Patriarch's position. We will not elaborate upon the contradictory method that the innovators use when they proceed in one direction by verbally granting the principle of indissolubility, and then turn about and proceed to assert that marriages can be dissolved, as if contradictory assertions could coexist. The Patriarch's statements go beyond the boundary that divides free theological speculation from dogmas of the faith, and thus indirectly attack the principles that sustain religion. In effect he implicitly rejects the distinction between suffering and injustice when he asserts that the innocent spouse suffers unjustly at the hands of the Church. The whole operation of divine providence, and the Catholic doctrine of suffering, are involved here.

Injustice is evident on the part of the spouse who breaks communion, but the Patriarch asserts there is an injustice on the part of the Church, when in order to be faithful to the teaching of the Gospel as well as to the natural law, it declines to arrogate to itself the right to remove that suffering. The Church punishes the guilty party by depriving him or her of the Eucharist, for example, and by other withdrawal of rights, but it never grants a eudaemonological good precedence over moral good or over the law. The notion of the Just One suffering is at the heart of the Christian religion, a religion which does not promise freedom from suffering in this world, but in the life to come, and which regards suffering from an essentially supernatural point of view that integrates our present and future existence. The Patriarch's position is naturalistic. According to our faith, God does not arrange the course of events so that the just

---

[5] "There are in the Catholic Church cases of truly revolting injustice which condemn human beings whose vocation is to live in the common state of marriage...and who are prevented from doing so without any fault of their own and without being able, humanly speaking, to bear this abnormal condition all their lives." I.C.I., No.250, 1 April 1967, p.11.

[6] H. Rouzel's work *L'Eglise primitive face au divorce*, Paris 1971, is fundamental for this question. The only authorities against indissolubility are the anonymous writer known as Ambrosiaster, and an ambiguous and perhaps spurious passage in St. Epiphanius.

have good things in this world, but so that they may at the last
have every good from the One who is Himself All Good.

The removal of suffering is not the Church's particular concern. The Church does not accept the haughty words of the
ancient philosopher who said: *Nihil accidere bono viro mali potest*[7] or the opinion of the modern philosopher stating that:
"Talk of a good action accompanied by suffering is self-
contradictory."[8] Men should act to remove and punish injustice,
but everyone is exposed to it independent of his moral state.
Men suffer because they are men, not because they are personally bad. I will not here develop the line of theological reasoning
that shows all human evil originates in a fault. The sufferings of
the just are no stumbling block to the Christian religion and are
not seen by it as an injustice; it always views them as part of
man's overall destiny and in the context of a joy stemming from
the hope of a blessed immortality: *feliciter infelices*[9] in the
Augustinian phrase, deriving from St. Paul. The Patriarch, on
the other hand, sees suffering as an injustice rather than as an
experience in virtue, a participation in Christ, a purification
and expiation of one's own sins and those of others; and what is
more he shifts the blame for this injustice from the guilty party
to the guiltless Church.

179. Maximos IV, continued.
The formula "humanly speaking."

Maximos IV's theories on marriage thus call into question
the Catholic understanding of the workings of Providence, according to which neither the injustices of other men nor the
sufferings imposed by nature can ever prejudice one's eternal
salvation and the attainment of the goal for which one has been
created, irrespective of the situation in which the Christian may
find himself in this world. This difficult truth is directly
founded upon the transcendence of man's goal and on the in-
commensurable relationship between eudaemonological evil
(suffering) and moral good (virtue); between the sufferings of
this world and the rewards of the world to come. St. Paul's famous words come to mind: *Non sunt condignae passiones huius*

---

[7]   "No evil can befall the good man."
[8]   For the ancient Seneca, *De Providentia,* II,1, and for the modern
      B. Croce, *Filosofia della practica*, IV ed., Bari 1968, p.223.
[9]   "Happily unhappy." Enarr. in Psalm, 127, P.L., 37, 1632.

temporis ad futuram gloriam,[10] and *Quod in praesenti est momentaneum et leve tribulationis nostrae supra modum in sublimitate aeternum gloriae pondus operatur in nobis.*[11] We are in fact dealing with the counterweight of the infinite against every finite quantity. The fact is that the Patriarch is putting a purely human argument (*humainement parlant*) in a matter of faith and thus disregarding the doctrine of grace, which says things are possible with God that are impossible with men, as Christ teaches[12] on this very matter of marriage. The doctrine of grace teaches that man is never forced to sin: his insertion in the contingencies of history provides the concrete circumstances within which his will operates, but cannot determine its choices. When the Patriarch claims to *speak humanly* he is nullifying or weakening the doctrine reaffirmed by the Council of Trent, and denied by Luther.

The reserve expressed by the words *humanly speaking* is an invention of the thinkers of the Enlightenment, who pretended to correct their contradictions of Christianity by saying they were speaking from a merely human point of view. But the Patriarch's revival of this usage will not do. Anyone who believes in a supernatural religion can never speak merely humanly, or if you will, he can only hypothetically so speak, *ad personam* but not *ad rem.*[13] There are not three sorts of sentiment: just, unjust and human; nor are there three sorts of judgment: true, false and human. The third category figures largely in speech but does not subsist in itself. Any feeling is either appropriate or inappropriate and every judgment is either true or false. All human thinking or willing can be reduced to one or other of these categories. In short, Maximos IV's position proceeds from a humanism that is incompatible with Catholic doctrine. The Christian religion does not recognize a middle world between true and false, a kind of limbo that defeats Christ's redemptive

---

10 "The sufferings of this present life cannot be compared to the future glory." Romans, 8:18.

11 "This light and momentary affliction brings with it a reward multiplied every way, loading us with everlasting glory." II Corinthians, 4:17.

12 Matthew, 19:10 and 26.

13 To a particular person, not of the subject as such.

action by putting the human race back in a period before the Teacher had come.[14]

In 1967 the Canadian bishops issued a document supporting a law facilitating divorce. "The Church," they say, "when called upon to judge a civil law on divorce, must take account not only of its own legislation, but must also consider what better serves the common good of civil society."[15] The bishops consequently do not oppose a law that broadens and assists the legal right to dissolve marriages. The bishops do not elucidate the connection between the common good and an increase in divorce, but they do say that "divorce makes sense only in the context of an open and positive policy of strengthening family values." The bishops thus hold that divorce is a means of strengthening family values that contributes to the common good and makes sense to Christians. For all that, they can never obliterate the memory of their brothers in the episcopate who, during the last century, were prepared to go to prison for defending Christian marriage.

180. The value of indissolubility.

The rejection of indissolubility violates not only the supernatural law, as was asserted by some in the Italian divorce campaign, but the natural law as well. In proposition No.67 of the *Syllabus*, Pius IX condemned the doctrine that marriage was not indissoluble in virtue of the natural law. One cannot therefore accept the argument that since indissolubility derives simply from a religious obligation, the state must be allowed to dissolve the bond for those who do not consider themselves bound by an obligation of that sort.[16]

---

[14] This treatment of the subject is inspired by Manzoni in his *Morale cattolica*, Part One, Ch. III, ed. cit., Vol. II, pp.47ff.

[15] I.C.I., No.287, 1 May 1967, p.79.

[16] It is consequently also false to say that a Catholic citizen who requires that his marriage be indissoluble in civil law is violating the conscience of those who want it to be dissoluble. If the pro-divorcers have a right to a dissoluble civil marriage, the Catholic can claim an equal right to an indissoluble one. If the law does not provide him with that possibility, he is less favorably treated than those who support divorce. His civil marriage will not in fact be dissolved (because he wills it not to be), but in law it will not be

As a sacrament, matrimony is a figure and a realization of Christ's indissoluble union with His Church, and it is this mystical meaning that gives Christian marriage its unbreakable and enduring quality.[17] But even without its sacramental character, marriage as it exists *in puris naturalibus*[18] is still intrinsically indissoluble, and its reduction to a temporary union is a result of the modern mentality that puts the person above the law and makes him an independent self-legislator. Seen in that light, divorce might be redefined as *freedom of marriage*. Marriage ceases to be something endowed with its own proper structure that one decides to embrace, and becomes instead something that is entirely constructed by the subjective will; it thus falls into line with all the other freedoms that modern man demands. If the foundation of moral obligation is placed in the subject rather than the object, then there is no such thing as an obligation, but only a non-binding self-obligation.[19]

It is alleged that a contract that binds forever is impossible, as a man cannot know whether he will still believe and desire tomorrow what he does today, and because his present, real, will cannot be bound by a past will that is real no longer. This is Hume's sophism which, by denying any causal connection between successive states of consciousness, views man's volitional life as a series of independent and unconnected points. It also amounts to a denial of freedom. If liberty is the capacity to choose something, it is also the capacity to choose one of one's own free acts, and to fix oneself in it permanently.

According to St. Thomas, it is characteristic of the will to "fix" on one of a number of possible judgments. Why should the will not fix itself? To fix the will on one object and to achieve one's whole destiny in an instant is the characteristic perfection of the angelic nature according to Aquinas; for a human will to fix itself in a permanent and irrevocable pact can thus be viewed as an imitation of angelic stability on the part of a constantly changeable nature, and thus as a victory over mobility and time.

Be that as it may, the Catholic doctrine of the indissolubility of marriage is a great *celebration of the power of freedom*, and

---

indissoluble and thus there is no legal parity for the two schools of thought.

[17] Cf. Ephesians, 5:32.

[18] "In a pure state of nature."

[19] See paragraphs 172-5.

moreover of the *ordinary* power of freedom, as it involves every-body. It follows that every attempt to weaken that doctrine in order to "speak humanly," amounts to a lessening of human dignity. Through its intransigent permanence, the indissolubil-ity of marriage even rises above vows of religion. These latter are of the same nature; the will *vittima fassi...e fassi col suo atto,*[20] but are less excellent than the marriage vow, since the fact that they can be dispensed, and have in the post-conciliar Church be-come easily dispensable, lowers their standing to a level that is, in this regard, below that of a permanent communion of life in marriage.

The appropriateness of indissolubility, something closely connected with monogamy, can be demonstrated on social and psychological grounds and, in the final analysis justified eu-daemonologically as well as deontologically. These grounds range from the approximate equality in numbers of men and women, to society's need to produce a new generation, the need to control fluctuating human passions and the need to provide for the upbringing of children. Even setting aside the question of sacramentality and the divine law, the essential reason for indissolubility is profoundly spiritual. Marriage is the *full gift* of one person to another, by which two people of different sexes unite themselves as fully as is possible according to right reason. It is a union that presupposes the love all people owe to each other independently of sex, and to that it adds the natural sex-ual attraction between man and woman. I will say more about marriage and its procreative purpose later on.

Two concluding remarks are enough for the time being. First, indissolubility is a consequence of monogamy and mo-nogamy is the consequence of the totality of the mutual gift of the two persons, *solus ad solam.*[21] This totality is ultimately an expression of the fullness of God's own love. Second, since di-vorce is a giving in to the passions and, as we may add, to the promptings of fallen human nature, the Church's ban on it is an argument in favor of the Church's divine character and of its attachment to truth. The Church holds to a moral teaching that is higher and more perfect than that of other religions and phi-losophies, all of which regard the Church's high standard as im-practicable. The Church is able to set forth such standards be-

---

[20] *Paradiso*, V, 29-30. "Makes itself a victim...and does so by its own act."

[21] "A single man for a single woman."

cause it has a more noble and honorable idea of humanity, which it holds to be capable of the highest and most refined moral excellence.[22] Its idea is based on its consciousness of possessing a greater moral strength which both imposes high standards and gives the capacity and courage to adhere to them.

---

[22] This thought comes from Rosmini, *Filosofia del diritto*, No.1336 National Edition, Vol. XXXVIII, p.1107, note.

CHAPTER XXIII

SODOMY

181. Sodomy.

Some theological writers have supported the prevailing current of opinion that has led the whole of Europe to abandon its age-old faithfulness to the natural law and to legitimize homosexual relations, but we do not intend to enter into a discussion of the subject. It is sufficient to note that here as well there is a negation of natures, in particular of the natural and morally inviolable structure of the sexual act. It is alleged that heterophilia and homophilia are simply two modes of a single sexual dimension, and that the differentiation within that dimension is merely the result of social influences. Thus sodomy ceases to be a perversion severely condemned by philosophy, custom and the discipline of the Church, and becomes one expression of sexuality; it is also struck from the list of sins that cry out to heaven for vengeance, together with murder, the oppression of the poor and defrauding the workman of his wages. Natural differences are ignored in a sophistical idea of love as something that can establish a spiritual communion between persons beyond the limits laid in nature and in defiance of moral prohibitions. In the Dutch church the scandal passed from theological opinion into practice, and there were liturgical celebrations of homosexual unions and even a *Missa pro homophilis* that were deplored by *Notitiae*,[1] the official journal of the Commission for implementing liturgical reform.

---

[1] March 1970, p.102.

CHAPTER XXIV

ABORTION

182. Abortion. Historical development of doctrine. The formation of the foetus.

As defined both by medicine and by canon law, abortion is the expulsion of the immature foetus. It is thus formally distinct from craniotomy and embriotomy and other such obstetric operations that are also aimed at the deliberate killing of the foetus and which have been condemned by the Church in separate decrees.[1] Sixtus V launched an excommunication against anyone who procured or cooperated in an abortion *excepta matre*,[2] but the Code of Canon Law promulgated by Benedict XV removed the exception.[3]

Until after the Second World War, all European legal codes, including those promulgated by philosophically irreligious governments, punished a woman who had an abortion and all who cooperated in procuring one. There were no penalties for therapeutic abortions, which were termed interruptions of pregnancy, and were allowed at the discretion of informed medical opinion. Since the war, the law of almost all states has been amended to reject the natural law by legalizing abortion, making it a service provided free by the state, and has treated it, most improbably, as part of policy designed to safeguard the family.[4] The law now goes so far as to oblige a doctor to perform an abortion on a woman who requests it.

---

[1] Cf. Denzinger, 1889ff.
[2] "Except the mother."
[3] Cf. Canon 2350.
[4] The Holy See was obliged to condemn and secularize Sister Agnes Mansour, who had agreed to run an abortion center in Detroit. The sister replied to the notification from her bishop by saying that

It is important to note that there is an historically relative aspect to the question of abortion. A judgment about the licitness of an act is the conclusion of a syllogism in which the major premise is absolute and the minor contingent, and the conclusion is true because the contingent is seen to fall within the ambit of the absolute. In the matter of abortion the syllogism can be formulated as follows: The life of an innocent man is inviolable. The embryo is an innocent man. Therefore its life is inviolable. There is thus some latitude in weighing up the facts included in the minor premise. The universal law and the practical choice governing his behavior *hic et nunc* that a person must make, intersect at this point. It is also at this point that scientific knowledge necessarily enters into the empirical establishment of the facts presupposed in the minor premise. It is up to biology, not theology, to establish whether the embryo is a man at that stage or not. Like any other science, biology is subordinate to theology not in the sense that its theses are laid down for it by theology, but because the theses that it establishes by its own methods can be used by theology in another mode of enquiry.

Theories about abortion are, as it happens, a very good example of the historically conditioned character of moral judgments both among men in general and within the Church itself. Moral judgments concerning abortion have varied not because the principles involved have changed, but because knowledge of the facts governed by those principles has become more complete.

For some centuries Catholic theologians held that the expulsion of a foetus that had received a sensitive soul but had not yet received a rational soul was permissible and in some emergencies even a duty.[5] Opinions on the *status humanus* of the em-

---

since civil law had allowed abortion, he could not claim a right to defy the law. Cf. *L'actualité religieuse*, 15 June 1983, p.24.

[5]   This was the position held by Habert in his *Theologia dogmatica et moralis*, Venice 1770, Vol. VII, p.494: *Medicum non solum posse, sed etiam debere foetum eiicere, si saluti matris aliter consuli non possit.* (The doctor not only may, but even should expel the foetus, if the survival of the mother cannot be provided for in any other way). The theory of a late animation or hominization of the embryo was taken up anew by Mgr Lanza in 1939, arguing from the instance of monozygotic twins. L. Gedda rebuts the theory of late

byro were dominated by the Aristotelian theory of the three life principles: vegetative, sensitive and rational, that appeared successively in man, which meant that only the arrival of the last brought about the existence of a man.[6] In treating of homicide, St. Thomas makes no special mention of abortion[7] and Dante teaches that the rational soul that constitutes a man is added to the sensitive soul only at the moment when *l'articular del cerebro è perfetto.*[8]

The Church distanced itself from the natural philosophy of that period by teaching, in the dogma of the Immaculate Conception, that the Virgin was free from the infection of original sin from the first instant of her conception: she must therefore have been in that first instant a human person. Christ too had the *status hominis*[9] from the time of His conception; St. Thomas expressly notes that this means he was different from other men in whom *prius est vivum et postea animal et postea homo.*[10] Roman law, like dogmatic theology, also took a different position from Aristotelian philosophy inasmuch as it held the embryo was a person having rights, and assigned a *curator ventris*[11] with the task of representing it at law and safeguarding those rights.

The theory of the animation of the foetus by a rational soul on the ninetieth day after conception began to lose ground after the publication of Fienus's book *De animatione foetus* in 1620, and its teaching was defended and spread by Liguori.[12] Natural embriology thereafter accorded with supernatural as instanced

---

animation in his article *Quando incomincia la vita umana*, in O.R., 12 August 1983.

[6] It was only with the rediscovery of Aristotle's works in the 13th century that Catholic thinkers began to say abortion, though still wrong, was not homicide before the implantation of the rational soul a certain number of weeks after conception. The older view, like the modern one, was more severe. See also Denzinger-Schönmetzer 670. [Translator's note.]

[7] Cf. *Summa Theologica*, II,II,q.64.

[8] *Purgatorio*, XXV, 69. "The articulation of the brain is complete."

[9] "State of a human being."

[10] *Summa Theologica*, III,q.33,a.2, *ad tertium*. "First there is a living thing, then an animal and then man."

[11] "Guardian of the womb."

[12] St. Alphonsus Liguori (1696-1787), founder of the Redemptorist order and patron saint of moral theologians. [Translator's note.]

in Christ and the Virgin, and abortion at any stage of development was recognized as homicide.

A curious fact concerning the general drift of the new
thinking on this point is that where theology was once modeled
on the opinion of natural philosophers, and asserted the non-
homicidal character of abortion when it was performed prior to
the animation whereby *l'animal divenga fante*,[13] today's theological innovators stand in opposition to a consensus among ge-
neticists, who take the immediately and individually human
character of the embryo as an established fact.

183. The new theology of abortion. French Jesuits.

Some promoters of abortion openly attack the genetically
established truth that the zygote, that is, the entity produced by
the male and female gametes, is a human individual with its
own unrepeatable and unchangeable characteristics. The Meth-
odist church in the United States, for example, attacks it. It says
that the foetus prior to birth is a tissue not an individual and
that it can therefore be removed for therapeutic reasons as one
would remove a mass of cells. The notion is shared by the vulgar and irreligious wing of the feminist movement. By what
kind of leap a foetus that was previously a mere mass of cells
becomes a person at the moment of birth, is a question they do
not even address. The idea is mentioned by Tertullian[14] and
condemned by Blessed Innocent XI[15] and is thus not new. The
biological facts are definitely against it nonetheless. The embryo
is an individual *ab initio*.[16] If it seems undifferentiated and
lacking in individuality, it is simply because it is being looked at
from a macroscopic rather than a microscopic point of view.[17] It
is imprecise to say that a human being is always *generated* from a
fertilized human ovum: it is not generated, it *is* a human being,

---

[13] *Purgatorio*, XXV, 61. "The animal becomes a child."
[14] *De Anima*, 25.
[15] Denzinger, 1185.
[16] "From the beginning."
[17] Professor Blechschmidt of the University of Göttingen has produced decisive results on this question. He made seven hundred
cross sectional cuts in an embryo seven millimeters long while
taking two thousand photographs: the embryo is differentiated at
every level. See E. Blechschmidt, *Wie beginnt das menschliche
Leben*, Stein am Rhein 1976, p.11.

and its existence begins in the instant in which living parts detach themselves from two animals and unite to form an individual entity.

The real humanity of the zygote and the consequent illicitness of abortion is something the innovators try to escape by distinguishing between *human* life and *humanized* life. Human life is what the embryo has as a biological entity. The entity is called human and known to be human because it comes from two human gametes, not because it can be recognized as having the human *idiotropion,* or distinguishing characteristic. Humanized life, according to this theory, is what the embryo acquires inasmuch as it is accepted by human society, in particular by the parents that bring it to birth and love it. If the foetus is killed before it is accepted and loved, no crime is involved. This is the teaching of the Jesuits published in the French review *Les études*[18] and upheld in books by its editor Fr. Ribes.[19] The Italian politician Loris Fortuna cited these Jesuits and their opinion, as if they were spokesmen for the Church, when he put forward his proposal for the legalization and promotion of abortion in the Chamber of Deputies on 11 February 1969.

The theories of these French Jesuits are false, superficial and unprecedented in the Church, unless held to descend remotely from the casuists of the seventeenth century.[20] They contain a hidden denial of the essences of things, and also the vice of subjectivism. The infant is alleged to have no essential nature unless it is *accepted,* that is, given a nature by a subjective act of will on the part of its parents, when in fact the reverse is true; the fact of its acceptance is *called forth* by the ontological worth of the already existing infant. Since the baby exists, it has the right *to be wanted* as an existing thing, and its right to be wanted is rooted not in the fact of being wanted but in the fact

---

[18] January 1973.

[19] In a public discussion on abortion carried by *Le Monde* of 19 January 1973, Fr. Roqueplo states: "It is doubtful that the embryo's life is a human life." Fr. Ribes maintains that given that doubt, "there is not only no duty, but also no right, to insist on its being born."

[20] Seventeenth century casuists, as we have already noted, were able to hold that abortion could be legitimate, and in some cases even a duty, because the natural science of the time said that the foetus received the rational form, that made it human, only in its third month. Humanity's moral beliefs do in fact depend on the ideas men have about nature.

of simply being there.[21] This mistaken anthropology is derived from Marxism and, like it, makes the person a relation. The human person is certainly in relation with things and other persons, but it is not itself a relation: it is constituted as a being before entering into relations that conform with its nature.

184. The new theology of abortion, continued. The Beethoven argument. The Italian Constitutional Court.

Some theologians have argued in favor of abortion on the basis of a *weighing of values*[22] in which there is an unequal value between a mother and a baby, an adult and a child, a developed entity and one still to be developed, and in which the former is held to take precedence. Fr. Callahan, for instance, holds that Catholic moral theology has taken insufficient account of the value of a mother's life, and that when there is a clash between the child's right to life and that of the mother, or of the human species (allegedly threatened by an excess of population) a weighing up of all the elements can lead to an exception being made to the principle of the inviolability of innocent human life. The French Jesuits preferred to distinguish between one foetus and another on the basis of the parents' extrinsic desire to make it a human being or not. The American Father Callahan distinguishes between foetus and mother on the ground of the mother's prior existence and greater development. He assumes there is a difference in human value between foetus and mother and that therefore the former can be sacrificed to the latter.[23]

---

[21] In O.R., 28 August 1971, Ramsey notes that 40% of babies born are not wanted. But he makes a mistake in not distinguishing between wanting the baby to be conceived and wanting it to be born once it has been conceived. Here again St. Augustine is more profound than all the modern psychologies when, in the *Confessions*, he says of his bastard son Adeodatus that even children that are not wanted force us to love them once they have been born.

[22] Numerous Catholic associations, priests' assemblies and pastoral councils have expressed themselves in favor of abortion. See for example the resolution by the pastoral council of the city of Liège, that was immediately disclaimed by the local bishop, but not retracted by the council. Cf. *Itinéraires*, No.181, p.77.

[23] This comes from a metaphysical outlook that denies the existence of essences or natures. There is in fact an equality in essential worth between mother and child, since both have the same nature.

As in pagan times birth and survival depended on the *patria potestas*, the father's cruel right of life and death over the person of the newborn child, so today the alleged greater rights of the mother have conferred on her the power to make such decisions, subject only to feeble legal restraints, ignoring completely the husband's role in causing new life, and wiping out his responsibility for the future of the child. This destroys parity not only between the infant and the mother, but between the two spouses, as if the child were produced by parthenogenesis.

This widespread failure to recognize human equality is the result of a failure to recognize the existence of essences, that is, natures. If man is not a nature corresponding to a divine idea and dependent on the God who has made him as he is, it will no longer be true that *Ipse fecit nos et non ipsi nos.*[24] Human substance will be a form shapeable by the human substance itself. And what criterion will govern its shaping other than utility? And since technology is simply the organization of what is useful, it is hardly surprising that the great realities of human life are being removed from the religious sphere, and that birth, love, generation and death are gradually passing into the sphere of technology. Once the idea of the creature's absolute *dependence* on God is lost, an idea fundamental to philosophy even prior to its incorporation in religion, it is inevitable that the idea of one creature's *independence* of another will be lost as well. Only if I belong to God am I free from being enslaved by someone else; only if my axiological status rests on a divine idea am I free from being distorted and subjugated by another.

It can thus be seen that the *Beethoven argument* is uncatholic. This consists in forbidding abortion not on the grounds that mother and child have the same axiological status since both are human beings, but because one cannot tell whether the individual prevented from being born would not have turned out to be a great genius, or saint, or servant of the human race; one of Huxley's *alpha plusses*. This line of argument is uncatholic because it offends against three truths. First: all human individuals are axiologically equal, because their end or goal is God. Each one is of greater or lesser perfection by reason of natural gifts, moral merit or the gifts of grace (in which no two are equal), but this accidental gradation can never suppress the

Accidental quantity of being, which is greater in the mother, does not make a difference to the value of the persons concerned.

[24] Psalm 99:3. "It is He that has made us and not we ourselves."

equal worth of their natures. Second: no man should inflict any diminution in being upon another except by reason of a fault, and thus an innocent child is of itself immune to any penalty. Third: the value of one human being as such cannot be measured against another: one can be of greater or less virtue, more or less beauty, more or less learned, but none is thereby more or less of a man, despite the fact that it has become common to talk as if such were in fact the case.

Believing that men could be weighed up quantitatively was an error made by Nazi biologism. A court in Luneburg in Saxony made a famous ruling in 1937 that abortion should not be punished when the race of the foetus involved was Jewish, but that it was punishable in the case of an Aryan foetus. The SS *Einsatzgruppen* in Eastern Europe had the horrible practice, when taking reprisals, of shooting ten of the local people or, equivalently, fifty Jews.

In substance there is no difference between this and the philosophy of the Constitutional Court of the Italian Republic when it held article 546 of the penal code, which punished abortion, to be unconstitutional; it said someone who performed an abortion on a woman for whom giving birth would constitute a danger "to physical well-being and psychological equilibrium" should not be punished.

That judgment was more on a philosophical than a legal matter: that is, whether or not the embryo is a human person. The court's decision is in fact self-contradictory. It admits that the embryo is a subject possessing rights, as is apparent in the civil law that appoints a *curator ventris* for the child conceived and modifies testamentary bequests upon the arrival of new children; but it goes on to talk about a clash of rights between mother and child and concludes that those of the mother take precedence because she is a person while the child has still to become one, despite the fact that it has been recognized as a subject possessing rights. But what other than a person can constitute a subject possessing rights? And how and where does the transition to personhood take place? The court's decision is at odds with the certain findings of the science of biology; the Oracle is in this instance merely trying to reflect public opinion. The equal value of the foetus and the mother is an inviolable principle; it is even worse to give preference to the mother when it is not a matter of weighing one life against another, as was the case in the casuists' arguments about abortion, but simply a question of giving preference to her health or well being, or even to her arbitrary will. The right solution does not lie in suppressing one life in favor of another, but in accepting the ethical limits that govern obstetrics, and every other branch of technical expertise, while pressing ahead with improvements to those techniques themselves.[25]

185. Fundamental root of doctrine concerning abortion. Theory of potency and act.

One final observation is needed to uncover the underlying reason for the modern misunderstanding about abortion.

What we have said in these paragraphs is the same as we have said in many others, and constitutes the heart of this book, the primal truth that we are writing to assert. The crisis of the modern world consists in rejecting natures or essences, and in believing that man can give essences to things, as well as giving existence. To return to the question in hand, man is certainly the cause of the existence of the child conceived, but the latter is governed by the laws of its own nature, and its axiological status calls for recognition by every rational creature. As we have said, it is more a question of philosophy than of law. While recognizing the foetus as a subject having rights, the Constitutional Court holds that it is not a person because it is not at present conscious, or exercising a will, and the court thereby identifies the existence of a person with the present exercise of personal activities. This is a fallacy: at that rate comatose or sleeping people would not be persons, but they are universally recognized as such.

I believe this difficult point of doctrine can only be clarified by the theory of potency and act. Tertullian calls abortion *homicidii festinatio* since *non refert natam quis eripiat animam an nascentem disturbet: homo est et qui futurus est.*[26] This paradoxical

---

[25] Many advances in modern obstetrics are the result of the pressure exerted by the Church's moral teaching. The ideal would be the perfect matching up of methods assisting birth and the moral imperatives governing the matter.

[26] *Apologeticus*, Cap.9. "Anticipated murder" since "It makes no difference whether someone takes away a life already born, or undoes one that is in the process of being born: what will be a human being is one already."

formula is typical of Tertullian's style.[27] In fact, anybody who is already a human being cannot become one at some later stage; he is one already. This incompatibility between being and not being human disappears if one interprets it in the light of the Thomistic theory of act and potency, according to which the substance remains the same whatever stage it is in, whether its capacities are not yet realized or whether they are being put into act. A man remains a man even when he is not exercising certain human activities, just as a doctor remains a doctor when not acting as such, for example when he is asleep and somebody comes to wake him in order to exercise his skills. The solution to a moral problem can depend on what natural science has established on some point, but in the final analysis every possible solution conceals within it some presupposition containing a fundamental truth or error. In this case, the false presupposition ultimately makes the creature independent of itself. The true presupposition is that the creature depends on itself, that is, it is bound to its own essence that God alone has irrevocably given it within the realm of finite existence.

There is a supernatural corollary to the violation of the natural law through abortion. As well as ending his natural life, the act also cuts off man's access to the supernatural life to which he is called but from which he is excluded if, as usually happens, the aborted child is not baptized.[28] It should also be noted that all the errors spread within the Catholic world on this point were condemned in a document from the Sacred Congregation for the Doctrine of the Faith on 18 November 1974.

---

[27] Cf. De fuga,5.: si negaturus es, iam negasti; "If you are going to renege, you have reneged already." Taken literally, the formula does away with time.

[28] The opinion given by Fr. Gino Concetti, an editor of the Osservatore Romano, about the baptism of aborted foetuses is a good example of the decline in theological learning among the clergy. When asked about this question in the Giornale Nuovo of 5 June 1981, he recommended a completely invalid method of baptism. He was corrected in the same newspaper on 17 June by a layman who knew much more about the matter than he did.

CHAPTER XXV

SUICIDE

186. Suicide.

The change that has occurred regarding suicide appears more in practice than in theory. The principal fact involved is the abrogation by the new Code of Canon Law of the ban on giving ecclesiastical burial to those who have committed suicide.[1] The common teaching of the Church was that suicide involved a threefold evil: a lack of moral fortitude, inasmuch as the person gave in to misfortune; an injustice, inasmuch as he pronounced a death sentence against himself as if he were his own judge, when he had no right to do so; and an offense against God, inasmuch as life consists in the service of God, a service from which no one can spontaneously exempt himself, as Plato puts it in the *Phaedo*. This view has been replaced by another: namely that there are supreme earthly goods for which it is legitimate and noble to sacrifice one's life directly. So political suicides like those of Jan Palak, who burnt himself to death in a square in Prague, and Bobby Sands in Ireland, are no longer considered blameworthy and become instead an expression of the highest sort of spiritual freedom, and a sign of heroism. Following Palak's funeral, Cardinal Beran, the Archbishop of Prague said: "I admire these men's heroism, even if I cannot approve of their gesture." It seemed to escape the Cardinal's notice that heroism and despair, which is a lack of fortitude, cannot coexist.[2]

---

[1] Canon 1184.

[2] It has now become usual, in funeral addresses, to praise people who have committed suicide. In the address he gave at the funeral of one unfortunate twenty year old youth who was a student in an ecclesiastical house of studies, and who had committed suicide, the rector of the institution thanked the boy for the good he had done and asked his forgiveness for the guilt which the survivors had in-

Under the influence of psychology and psychiatry, it has become the received view that the mind of anyone committing suicide is convulsed by some irresistible disturbance and that his freedom is therefore seriously restricted or indeed totally annihilated. In the past the Church attributed broad bounds to a person's moral responsibility, but since the council it has increasingly accepted the idea that suicides are not responsible for their actions. As to the converse way of viewing it I mentioned above, the Church has always rejected the Stoic ethos that regarded suicide as a supreme expression of man's moral freedom, and the height of virtue.

---

curred through his death. (*Virtutis Palaestra*, Ascona 1983, p.121.) This is to dissolve personal responsibility into a sin committed by society, that is, by other people. When a sixteen year old boy and his girlfriend killed themselves in Rome in August 1983, they were given a full religious funeral and a panegyric. (O.R., 6 August 1983.) Giacomo Luvini-Perseghini, one of the leaders of the radical party in the Ticino, was much more accurate and frank in the words he said at the grave of Doctor Giuseppe Zola, buried as a suicide outside the cemetery at Lugano in 1834: "We hope that the God of our fathers, whose mercy is infinite, will deign to pardon the momentary mistake of one whose life was distinguished by many virtues."

CHAPTER XXVI

THE DEATH PENALTY

187. The death penalty.

Certain social institutions derive from the principles of the natural law and as such are perpetual in one form or another; for example the state, the family, a priesthood of some sort; and there are others that arise from a certain level of reflection on those principles and from historical circumstances, and which are abandoned when thought moves on to another level or when circumstances change; for example slavery. Until recently, the death penalty was philosophically defended, and used in practice by all countries as the ultimate penalty society imposes on evildoers, with the threefold aim of righting the balance of justice, defending society against attack, and dissuading others from wrongdoing.

The legitimacy of capital punishment is usually grounded on two propositions. First: society has a right to defend itself; second: this defense involves using all *necessary* means. Capital punishment is included in the second proposition on condition that taking the life of one member of the body of society is genuinely necessary for the wellbeing of the whole.

The growing tendency to mitigate punishments of all sorts is in part the product of the Gospel spirit of clemency and mercy, which has always been at odds down the centuries with savage judicial customs. With a certain degree of confusion that we need not go into here, the Church has always drawn back from blood. It should be remembered that canon law traditionally decreed the "irregularity," that is the banning from holy orders, not only of executioners, but of judges who condemned people to death in the ordinary course of law, and even of advocates and witnesses in trials that led to someone being put to death.

The controversy does not turn on society's right to defend itself; that is the undeniable premise of any penal code, but rather on the genuineness of the need to remove the offender altogether in order to effect that defense, which is the minor premise involved. From St. Augustine to St. Thomas Aquinas to Taparelli d'Azeglio,[1] the traditional teaching is that the decision as to the necessity and legitimacy of capital punishment depends on historical circumstances, that is, on the urgency of the need to hold society together in the face of the disruptive behavior of individuals who attack the common good. From Beccaria[2] onwards, proposals to abolish capital punishment have admitted the major premise, and allowed that the minor one depends on historical circumstances, since they allow the execution of offenders in some emergencies, such as war. During the last war, even Switzerland sentenced and shot seventeen people guilty of high treason.

188. Opposition to the death penalty.

Opposition to the death penalty[3] stems from two diverse and incompatible sets of reasons, and can only be evaluated in the light of the moral assumptions on which it is based. Horror at a crime can coexist with sympathy for human weakness, and with a sense of the human freedom that renders a man capable of rising from any fall as long as his life lasts; hence opposition to the death penalty. But opposition can also stem from the notion that every person is inviolable inasmuch as he is a self-conscious subject living out his life in the world; as if temporal life were an end in itself that could not be suppressed without frustrating the purpose of human existence. Although often thought of as religiously inspired, this second type of reason for

---

[1] Aloysius Taparelli d'Azeglio, S.J. (1793-1862), Rector of the Gregorian University in Rome, philosopher and sociologist. [Translator's note.]

[2] Cesare Beccaria (1735-1794), Italian economist and judicial theorist. [Translator's note.]

[3] Opposition to it has become almost universal, with the death penalty itself being regarded as an injustice. In 1983 several states belonging to the Council of Europe signed an additional protocol to the European Convention on Human Rights, obliging them to remove the death penalty from their legal systems. R.I., 1983, p.1077.

rejecting capital punishment is in fact irreligious. It overlooks the fact that from a Christian point of view earthly life is not an end in itself, but a means to life's moral goal, a goal that transcends the whole order of subordinate worldly goods. Therefore to take away a man's life is by no means to take away the transcendent end for which he was born and which guarantees his true dignity. A man can *propter vitam vivendi perdere causas*[4] that is, he can make himself unworthy of life by taking temporal life as being itself the supreme good instead of a means to that good. There is therefore a mistake implicit in the second sort of objection to capital punishment, inasmuch as it assumes that in putting someone to death, other men or the state are cutting a criminal off from his destined goal, or depriving him of his last end or taking away the possibility of his fulfilling his role as a human being. Just the opposite in fact. The condemned man is deprived of his earthly existence, but not of his goal. Naturally, a society that denies there is any future life and supposes there is a fundamental right to happiness in this world, must reject the death penalty as an injustice depriving man of his capacity to be happy. Paradoxically, those who oppose capital punishment on these grounds are assuming the state has a sort of totalitarian capacity which it does not in fact possess, a power to frustrate the whole of one's existence.[5] Since a death imposed by one man on another can remove neither the latter's moral goal nor his human worth, it is still more incapable of preventing the operations of God's justice, which sits in judgment on all our adjudications. The meaning of the motto engraved on the town executioner's sword in Fribourg in Switzerland: *Seigneur Dieu, tu es le juge*,[6] was not that human and divine justice were identical; it signified a recognition of that highest justice which sits in judgment on us all.

Another argument advanced is that capital punishment is useless as a deterrent; as witnessed by Caesar's famous remark during the trial of the Cataline conspirators, to the effect that a death which put an end to the shame and misery of the crimi-

---

[4] "For the sake of life, lose the causes of life."
[5] Sister Angela Corradi, a prison visitor, was therefore mistaken when she said at the *Comunione e Liberazione* Meeting in Rimini that prison could be an occasion for "finally crushing" someone. Our religion teaches that it is impossible for one man to crush another finally. O.R., 25 August 1983.
[6] "Lord God, Thou art the Judge."

nals would be a lesser punishment than their remaining alive to
bear them. This argument flies in the face of the juridical practice of pardoning people under sentence of death, as a favor,
and is also refuted by the fact that even infamous criminals
sometimes make pacts between themselves with death as the
penalty for breaking the agreement. They thereby give a very
apposite witness to the fact that capital punishment is an effective deterrent.

189. Doctrinal change in the Church.

An important change has occurred in the Church regarding
the theology of punishment. We could cite the French bishops'
documents that asserted in 1979 that the death penalty ought to
be abolished in France as it was *incompatible with the Gospel*, the
Canadian and American bishops' statements on the matter, and
the articles in the *Osservatore Romano*[7] calling for the abolition
of the death penalty, as injurious to human dignity and contrary
to the Gospel.

As to the biblical argument; even without accepting
Baudelaire's celebration of capital punishment as a supremely
sacred and religious proceeding, one cannot cancel out the Old
Testament's decrees regarding the death penalty, by a mere
stroke of the pen. Nor can canon law, still less the teaching of
the New Testament, be canceled out at a stroke. I am well aware
that the famous passage in Romans[8] giving princes the *ius
gladii*,[9] and calling them the ministers of God to punish the
wicked, has been emptied of meaning by the canons of the new
hermeneutic, on the grounds that it is the product of a past set
of historical circumstances. Pius XII however explicitly rejected
that view, in a speech to Catholic jurists on 5 February 1955,
and said the passage of St. Paul was of permanent and universal
value, because it refers to the essential foundation of penal
authority and to its inherent purpose. In the Gospel, Christ
indirectly sanctions capital punishment when he says it would
be better for a man to be condemned to death by drowning
than to commit the sin of scandal.[10] From the Book of Acts[11] it

---

[7] O.R., 22 January 1977 and 6 September 1978.
[8] Romans, 13:4.
[9] "The right to use the sword."
[10] Matthew, 18:6.
[11] Acts, 5:1-11.

seems the primitive Christian community had no objection to the death penalty, as Ananias and Sapphira are struck down when they appear before St. Peter guilty of fraud and lying at the expense of the brethren. Biblical commentaries tell us that the early Christians' enemies thought this sentence was harsh at the time.

The change in teaching is obvious on two points. In the new theology of punishment, *justice* is not considered, and the whole matter is made to turn on the usefulness of the penalty and its aptitude for bringing the guilty person back into society, as the saying goes. On this point, as on others, the new fangled view coincides with the utilitarianism preached by the Jacobins. The individual is held to be essentially independent; the state defends itself against a miscreant, but cannot punish him for breaking a moral law, that is, for being morally guilty. This guiltlessness of the guilty goes on to manifest itself in a reduced consideration for the victim, and even in giving preference to the guilty over the innocent. In Sweden people who have been imprisoned are given preferential treatment in examinations for public employment, as compared with other, unconvicted, members of the public. Consideration for the victim is eclipsed by mercy for the wrongdoer. Mounting the steps to the guillotine, the murderer Buffet shouted his hope that he would "be the last man guillotined in France." He should have shouted he hoped he would be the last murderer. The penalty for the offense seems more objectionable than the crime, and the victim is forgotten. The restoration of a moral order that has been violated by wrongdoing is rejected as if it were an act of vendetta. In fact it is something that justice demands and which must be pursued even if the harm done cannot be reversed and if the rehabilitation of the guilty party is impossible. The modern view also attacks even the validity of divine justice, which punishes the damned without there being any hope or possibility of amendment.[12] The very idea of the *redemption* of the guilty is reduced to a piece of social engineering. According to the *Osservatore Romano*,[13] redemption consists in "the awareness of a return to being useful to one's fellows" and not, as the Catholic system would have it, in the detestation of one's fault and a redi-

---

[12] See paragraph 316.
[13] O.R., 6 September 1978.

recting of the will back into conformity with the absolutes of the moral law.

To go on to assert that a life should not be ended because that would remove the possibility of making *expiation*, is to ignore the great truth that capital punishment is itself expiatory. In a humanistic religion expiation would of course be primarily the converting of a man to other men. On that view, time is needed to effect a reformation, and the time available should not be shortened. In God's religion, on the other hand, expiation is primarily a recognition of the divine majesty and lordship, which can be and should be recognized at every moment, in accordance with the principle of the concentration of one's moral life.[14]

Attacking capital punishment, the *Osservatore Romano*[15] asserts that where the wrongdoer is concerned "the community must allow him the possibility of purifying himself, of expiating his guilt, or freeing himself from evil; and capital punishment does not allow for this." In so saying, the paper denies the expiatory value of death; death which has the highest expiatory value possible among natural things, precisely because life is the highest good among the relative goods of this world; and it is by consenting to sacrifice that life, that the fullest expiation can be made. And again, the expiation that the innocent Christ made for the sins of mankind was itself effected through his being condemned to death. Remember too the conversions of condemned men at the hands of St. Joseph Cafasso; remember some of the letters of people condemned to death in the Resistance.[16] Thanks to the ministry of the priest, stepping in between the judge and the executioner, the death penalty has often brought about wonderful moral changes, such as those of Niccolo di Tuldo, comforted by St. Catherine of Siena who left an account of what happened in a famous letter of hers; or Felice Robol, assisted on the scaffold by Antonio Rosmini;[17] or Martin Merino who tried to kill the Queen of Spain in 1852; or Jacques Fesch guillotined in 1957, whose letters from prison are a

---

[14] See paragraph 202.

[15] O.R., 22 January 1977.

[16] See *Lettere di condannati a morte della Resistenza europea*, Turin 1975.

[17] The speech that Rosmini made on the stand in court at Rovereto in the Trentino can be found in his *Opere*, Milan 1846, Vol. XXVII, pp.132-184.

moving testimony to the spiritual perfection of one of God's elect.[18]

The most irreligious aspect of this argument against capital punishment is that it denies its expiatory value which, from a religious point of view, is of the highest importance because it can include a final consent to give up the greatest of all worldly goods. This fits exactly with St. Thomas's opinion that as well as canceling out any debt that the criminal owes to civil society, capital punishment can cancel all punishment due in the life to come. His thought is: *Mors illata etiam pro criminibus aufert totam poenam pro criminibus debitam in alia vita, vel partem poenae secundum quantitatem culpae, patientiae et contritionis, non autem mors naturalis.*[19] The moral importance of wanting to make expiation also explains the indefatigable efforts of the Confraternity of St. John the Baptist Beheaded, the members of which used to accompany men to their deaths, all the while suggesting, begging and providing help to get them to repent and accept their deaths, so ensuring that they would die in the grace of God, as the saying went.[20]

190. Inviolability of life. Essence of human dignity. Pius XII.

The leading argument in the new theology of punishment is however the one that asserts an inviolable and imprescriptible

---

[18] They were published by A.M. Lemonnier under the title *Lumière sur l'echafaud*, Paris 1971.

[19] *Summa Theologica*, Index, under the word *mors* (Turin 1926). "Even death inflicted as a punishment for crimes takes away the whole punishment due for those crimes in the next life, or at least part of that punishment, according to the quantities of guilt, resignation and contrition; but a natural death does not."

[20] It is extremely informative to read the records of the Roman Confraternity of St. John the Baptist Beheaded, for Thursday 16 February 1600, concerning the death of Giordano Bruno. Seven different confessors were provided for him, Dominicans, Jesuits, priests from the Oratory and Hieronymites, so that if one sort of spirituality could not convert him another perhaps might. See V. Spampanato, *Documenti della vita di Giordano Bruno*, Florence 1933, p.197. See also on this subject V. Paglia's book *La morte confortata*, Rome 1982, especially Chapter VII, *La morte del condannato esempio della morte cristiana.*

right to life, that is allegedly infringed when the state imposes
capital punishment. The article we have cited says: "To the
modern conscience, which is open, and aware of human values
and of man's centrality and primacy in the universe, and of his
dignity and his inalienable and inviolable rights, the death
penalty is repugnant as being an anti-human and barbarous
measure."

Some facts might be helpful in replying to this article,
which sums up in itself all the abolitionists' arguments. The
prominence the *Osservatore Romano* gives to the "modern conscience" is similar to the position accorded it by the French
bishops' document, which says *le refus de la peine de mort correspond chez nos contemporains à un progrès accompli dans le respect
de la vie humaine.*[21] A remark of that sort is born of the bad
mental habit of going along with fashionable ideas and of letting the wish become father to the thought; a crude rebuttal of
such unrealistic assertions is provided by the atrocious slaughter
of innocents perpetrated in Nazi Germany and Soviet Russia,
the widespread use of physical violence by despotic regimes as
an ordinary means of government, the legitimation and imposition of abortion by changes to the law, and by the increasing
cruelty of delinquents and terrorists, who are only feebly resisted by governments. The axiological centrality of man in the
universe will be discussed later.[22]

In discussions on the death penalty, the difference between
the rights of an innocent and a guilty man are generally ignored.
The right to life is considered as if it were inherent in man's
mere existence when, in fact, it derives from his moral goal.
Man's worth derives from his ordination to values that transcend temporal life, and this goal is built into his spirit inasmuch as it is an image of God. Although the goal is absolute
and the image indelible, man's freedom means that by a fault he
can descend from that dignity and turn aside from his goal. The
philosophical justification for penal law is precisely an axiological diminution, or shrinking in worth, on the part of a person
who violates the moral order and who, by his fault, arouses society to some coercive action designed to repair the disorder.
Those who base the imposition of penalties merely on the damage done to society, deprive penal law of any ethical character

---

[21] "The rejection of the death penalty is an indication that our contemporaries have an increased respect for human life."
[22] See paragraphs 205-10.

and turn it into a set of precautions against those who harm society, irrespective of whether they are acting freely or compulsively, rationally or irrationally. In the Catholic view, the penal system exists to ensure that the crime by which the delinquent has sought some satisfaction or other in defiance of the moral law, is punished by some corresponding diminution of well-being, enjoyment or satisfaction. Without this moral retaliation, a punishment is merely a utilitarian reaction which indeed neglects the dignity of man and reduces justice to a purely materialistic level; such was the case in Greece when recourse was had to the Prytaneum, or city council, to pass sentence against rocks, trees or animals that had caused some damage. Human dignity is something built into the natural structure of rational creatures but which is elicited and made conscious by the activity of a good or bad will, and which increases or decreases within that order of being. No right thinking person would want to equate the human worth of the Jew in Auschwitz with that of his killer Eichmann, or St. Catherine of Alexandria with Thais the Alexandrian courtesan. A person's worth can only be reduced by actions within the moral realm; and therefore, contrary to popular opinion, it cannot be measured by some level of participation in the benefits of technological progress: by a quota of economic welfare, by a level of literacy, by a better health service, by an abundance of the pleasures that life provides or by the stamping out of diseases. Let there be no confusion between an increase in a person's dignity or worth, which is a moral quality, and an increase in the possession of those utilitarian benefits which unworthy men also enjoy.[23]

The death penalty, and any other form of punishment, if they are not to descend to the level of pure defense and a sort of selective slaughter, always presuppose a moral diminution in the person punished: there is therefore no infringement of an inviolable or imprescriptible right involved. Society is not depriving the guilty person of his rights; rather, as Pius XII taught in his speech of 14 September 1952 *même quand il s'agit de l'exécution d'un condamné à mort, l'Etat ne dispose pas du droit de l'individu à la vie. Il est réservé alors au pouvoir public de priver le condamné du bien de la vie en expiation de sa faute après que par son crime il s'est déjà dépossédé de son droit à la vie.*[24]

---

[23] See paragraphs 210 and 218-9

[24] A.A.S., 1952, pp.779ff. "Even when it is a question of someone condemned to death, the state does not dispose of an individual's

If one considers the parallel with one's right to freedom, it becomes obvious that an innocent man's right to life is indeed inviolable, whereas a guilty person has diminished his rights by the actions of his depraved will: the right to freedom is innate, inviolable and imprescriptible, but penal codes nonetheless recognize the legitimacy of depriving people of their liberty, even for life, as a punishment for crime, and all nations in fact adopt this practice. There is in fact no unconditional right to any of the goods of earthly life; the only truly inviolable right is the right to seek one's ultimate goal, that is truth, virtue and eternal happiness, and the means necessary to acquire these. This right remains untouched even by the death penalty.

In conclusion, the death penalty, and indeed any kind of punishment, is illegitimate if one posits that the individual is independent of the moral law and ultimately of the civil law as well, thanks to the protection afforded by his own subjective moral code. Capital punishment comes to be regarded as barbarous in an irreligious society, that is shut within earthly horizons and which feels it has no right to deprive a man of the only good there is.

---

right to life. It is then the task of public authority to deprive the condemned man of the good of life, in expiation of his fault, after he has already deprived himself of the right to life by his crime."

CHAPTER XXVII

WAR

191. Christianity and war.

Even though it might appear from some episcopal pronouncements and from many of the views voiced among Catholics that there has been a *saltus in aliud*[1] in this area, the change that has occurred in the understanding of war is in fact a coherent development. The development in question shows the real meaning of the old adage: *what was not a sin can become one*, and vice versa. It can become one not because there is a change in the moral law, but in the circumstances that make an action more or less culpable, or altogether inculpable; and because further reflection can lead to a conscientious awareness of new duties. It is part of classical Catholic teaching that circumstances can change the quality of acts. The same act can be virtuous in marriage or culpable in fornication or still more culpable in adultery. To give a modern example, driving a car after having too much to drink used to be a venial sin in the days of empty roads, but it becomes a mortal sin in an age of crowded roads and dangerous traffic. Circumstances can change the moral evaluation that one must make of war, and can render illicit things which were licit and good in the different circumstances of times past.

The absolute condemnation of war is, however, alien to Catholic tradition; the profession of arms is not forbidden in the Gospel, is held to be an honest occupation by the Fathers, and has been followed by Christians, many of the martyr saints being soldiers. War was only regarded as illicit by movements of a Manichean or otherwise heretical stamp. Even the rule of the Franciscan tertiaries allows for carrying arms in defense of one's country. The same is true of the whole of Catholic theology

---

[1] "Leap into something different."

from Augustine to Thomas to Taparelli d'Azeglio. When discussing acts that disturb harmony among men, Aquinas describes war in a negative manner, by laying down that it is not always sinful. St. Augustine says[2] the evil of war lies in injustice, not in killing: *Quid enim culpatur in bello? An quia moriuntur quandoquidem morituri, ut domentur in pace victuri? Hoc reprehendere timidorum est, non religiosorum. Nocendi cupiditas, ulciscendi crudelitas, implacatus atque implacabilis animus, feritas rebellandi, libido dominandi et si qua similia, haec sunt quae in bello culpantur.*[3] After declaring that "everyone who violates the rights of others should be put into shaming isolation, under the ban of civilized society," Pius XII forcefully denounced pacifism in his Christmas message of 1949: "The attitude of those who abhor war because of its atrocities but not for its injustice as well, is preparing the way for the aggressor."

War can only be seen as the worst of evils by those who adopt an irreligious view of life, in which the supreme good is not a transcendent goal but rather life itself, and for whom pleasure is the reason for man's existence. War certainly is an evil; the Church lists it with hunger and disease among the scourges from which it wishes men spared. In his encyclical *Praeclara Congratulationis* of 1894, Leo XIII denounces the futility of war and looks forward to an international society of nations and a further development of international law. Benedict XV deplored the "horrendous butchery" and the "suicide of Europe" during the Great War, and denounced its "useless slaughter" in his Note of 1 August 1917.

192. Pacifism and peace. Cardinal Poma. Paul VI. John Paul II.

The kind of peace the Church supports is not the sort that absolutizes life, but the sort that subjects both peace and war to the demands of justice. By contrast Erasmus of Rotterdam, the

---

[2] *Contra Faustum*, ch.74.

[3] P.L., 42, 447. "What is wrong with war? Is it that some men, who are bound to die eventually, die now so that those who are defeated can be governed in peace? To object to that is a sign of men who are cowardly rather than religious. What is wrong in war is an eagerness to cause harm, a cruel vengeance, a remorseless and uncontrollable spirit, a rebellious wildness, a desire to dominate, and other things of that sort."

most forthright of pacifists, teaches in his *Querela pacis* and his paraphrase of the *Pater Noster*, that "there is no unjust peace that is not preferable to the most just of wars." Absolute pacifism has been widely taken up, and can appeal to some supporters in high places. The Archbishop of Milan, Cardinal Poma, says: "Nothing is so opposed to Christianity as war. It is *the synthesis of all sins*, since in it pride and the unleashing of the baser instincts are combined." An assertion so sweeping and so lacking in historical sense is at odds with centuries of Christian practice, at odds with the canonization of fighting saints such as Joan of Arc, and at odds with the praise of a just war that Paul VI made in a special document issued for the fifth centenary of the death of Scanderbeg.[4] When making a speech that recalled Pius XII's visit to the people of Rome after the bombing of the City in 1943, the same Paul VI described as "stupid" the cry of one young man who shouted: *Papa, papa, meglio la schiavitù che la guerra! Liberaci dalla guerra!*[5] Ghandi, great promoter of freedom and peace that he was, comes close to branding pacifism as cowardice: "It is a noble thing to defend one's welfare, one's honor and one's religion at the point of the sword. It is still nobler to defend them without attempting to harm the evildoers. But it is immoral and dishonorable to abandon one's partner in order to save one's skin by leaving his welfare, his honor and his religion at the mercy of evildoers."

There are indeed statements by Paul VI that assert "the absurdity of modern war" and "the supreme irrationality of war."[6] Then there is John Paul II's statement at Coventry in May 1982: "Today the scope and horror of modern war, whether nuclear or conventional, make war totally unacceptable for resolving disputes and disagreements between nations." Nevertheless, if one examines the terms of the two papal declarations, one sees that they do not depart from the traditional principles of the theology of war and that they constitute one of those developments in moral sensitivity that result from changed circumstances. The legitimacy of war depends on certain conditions: that it be declared by a competent authority; that it be aimed at righting a wrong; that there be a reasonable hope of

---

[4] Scanderbeg (1403-1467), leader of Albanian Christian resistance to the Turks. [Translator's note.]

[5] R.I., 1971, p.42. "Pope, Pope, better slavery than war! Free us from war!"

[6] O.R., 21 December 1977.

actually righting the wrong; that it be conducted with due moderation. These conditions reflect an uninterrupted tradition in Catholic scholastic theology, and are recognized, for example, in Article 137 of the "Social Code" drawn up by the International Union of Social Studies founded by Cardinal Mercier.

193. The teaching of Vatican II.

Vatican II reiterated the legitimacy of a defensive war, condemned offensive wars undertaken as a means of resolving disputes among nations, and absolutely condemned total war, especially of the atomic sort.[7] The council also allows military service by citizens, designed to ensure the safety and freedom of their country, and indeed says that "by fulfilling that duty they contribute effectively to the maintenance of the peace." The right to wage war had to be re-examined from a new point of view because one of the aforementioned conditions no longer applied, and thus the council decreed: "any act of war aimed at the indiscriminate destruction of whole cities or large areas together with their population is a crime against God and man which should be strongly and unhesitatingly condemned." Total war is forbidden even in cases of legitimate self-defense, since that too can become illegitimate through a lack of due moderation. While teaching that a defensive war against an aggressor is legitimate "until such time as an effective international authority equipped with adequate coercive force is constituted," the council teaches that such a war is wrong if it aims at the total destruction of the enemy. Thus, both wars begun offensively to resolve a dispute, and wars of any sort, offensive or defensive, that are fought without due moderation are condemned. But a

---

[7]   *Gaudium et Spes*, 79-80. This condemnation of unrestrained warfare is analogous to the decree against *artem illam mortiferam et Deo odibilem ballistariorum et sagittariorum* (the lethal art, hateful to God, of archers and those who operate mangonels) by the Second Council of Lyons under Innocent II in 1139. The condemnations result from the same moral objection to excessive destruction, manifesting itself differently amidst the relativities of history. Such condemnations also show the ineffectiveness of the Church's action in this field; an ineffectiveness also apparent in the banning of war by the Pact made in 1919, and again by the Kellog-Briand Pact of 1929 and yet again by the Charter of the United Nations in 1945.

defensive war conducted with the due restraint is not censured. As can happen with anything affected by circumstances, the moral judgment to be made about war has been changed by the new circumstance that total war has become a possibility.

A suggestion was made at the First Vatican Council to define that *Qui bellum incipiat, anathema sit*[8] but that proposition fails to address the moral aspect of the question since chronological priority in waging war does not determine the moral question involved.

The reason indiscriminate slaughter is condemned is that it alters the nature of war and changes it into something it cannot legitimately be. In the past, nations waged war through the specific actions of a specific organ, to wit, the army, while in recent times they have waged war with the whole body of society and everything is militarized; there is political war, commercial war, diplomatic war, propaganda war, chemical war, biological war and even meteorological war:[9] on the modern Olympus, Mars has been joined by Minerva, Mercury and a host of other gods.

Total war was begun in France in 1793 in the form of the *levée en masse*, involving the conscription of men, economic strength and even of minds, through the use of propaganda. The introduction of compulsory conscription, a kind of blood tax, by all modern states signifies the loss of freedom enjoyed by ancient societies, despite the fact that some people consider it a step forward in social equality.[10] It was the result of citizens being bound more closely together by the growing power of a state in the process of becoming a leviathan, in which the individual is merely a cell, and it led to war's losing its specific character. It should however be noted that military doctrine is now moving

---

8   "Let whoever begins a war be anathema."

9   In Geneva in 1977 the USA and the USSR signed a convention renouncing meteorological warfare. During the Vietnam war the United States rendered the Ho Chi Minh trail unusable by dropping fifty thousand containers of silver hydrate and carbon substances to make it rain.

10   Seneca praised the prince who assured such freedom, *Epist.*,LXXIII,9 and G. Ferrero also praises it in *Discorsi ai sordi*, Milan 1920. Rosmini, on the other hand, said that compulsory conscription was "the greatest benefit" left to Europe by the Napoleonic Empire, *Filosofia del diritto*, paragraph 2154, National Edition, Vol.XXXIX, p.1426.

away from the idea of war as something waged by the whole
people and the whole of a nation's resources, and is returning to
highly specialized professional armies. The idea of war as the
activity of a special group is thus being restored, and bloody
deeds are again Mars' peculiar concern. To fight with one arm
of the nation rather than with its whole body is more in accordance with the natural law, and brings us back to the situation
described by Frederick II of Prussia: "When I make war my
people don't realize the fact, because I do it with my soldiers."
Nonetheless, at the level of nuclear arms, the whole movement
of national life is still oriented towards total war and thus all the
organs of society become a single instrument aimed at the total
destruction of the enemy. Talleyrand's maxim to the effect that
states ought to do as much good as they can in peace and as
little evil as they can in war, is overturned by modern war,
which turns society into an engine of destruction.

194. War's unanswered questions.

War is moral subject to two conditions: that it be just, and
just use of force can only occur in the face of aggression; and
that it be moderate, and there can be no right to war that is not
bound to that moderation. We will not go into the theory propounded by Don Luigi Sturzo,[11] namely that wars are not produced by any intrinsic or necessary element in human nature,
and are merely a passing stage that can be overcome, like polygamy or slavery. We should note however that the use of force,
and therefore the principle of war, is essential to civilized society: namely a society that organizes the community towards
achieving the common good by means of law, but which also
restrains lawbreakers; and it is in its restraining functions that
its primary task admittedly lies, even if we do not agree completely with Hobbes on that point. Hence, if the races of the
earth are to climb down from their pretended absolute sover-
eignties, and realize the Catholic ideal of a community of nations by subjecting themselves to a supranational authority,[12]
that authority would have to have an effective power of repress-
ing lawbreakers, that is of making war on any rebel member. In
the present imperfectly organized condition of international life,
war is legitimate to defend the rights of individual states; in a

---

[11] In *La comunita internazionale e il diritto di guerra*, Paris 1932.

[12] See Vatican II, cited in the previous paragraph.

fully organized community of nations, war would be legitimate
to repress attacks on the community as such.

As to the justice of wars, some philosophers, including Cajetan, have held that a nation waging a war of legitimate defense
is performing an act of vindicatory justice, so that the just com-
batant *personam gerit iudicis criminaliter agentis*.[13] Others believe
such wars are acts of commutative justice, by which reparation
or restitution is sought for a good of which one has been unduly
deprived. The question does not have to be decided here. Cajetan's opinion nonetheless harmonizes with the Catholic principle, upheld in the *Syllabus of Errors*,[14] that one should defend
the rights of another innocent state under attack, rather than
adopt the notion of absolute non-intervention. Because a perfect international organization of society has not yet been established, with the three usual powers, legislative, governmental
and judicial, it remains difficult to show that a particular war is
just, and difficult to impose some sanction on an unjust war-
maker through the operations of a universal tribunal.

Even a just war is always a sad thing, for two reasons.
Firstly, because it is a form of fratricide and, if fought among
Christians, also a sort of sacrilege, given the sacred character of
a baptized man. Secondly, in war the actions of one side cannot
be good without those of the opposite side being bad.[15] The
defensive war of the side in the right is just, but can only be so
if the attacker is unjust. Thus it is that Kant, in his *Zum ewigen
Frieden*[16] says that on the day of victory both victors and van-
quished should wear mourning; and in Manzoni's *Carmagnola*
"homicidal choirs" raise "thanksgivings and hymns that Heaven
abhors."

Another unanswered question where wars are concerned is
the uncertainty of the outcome even for the party that is in the
right. Providence has decreed that earthly goods should *tend* to
accompany moral virtue, but this tendency is not enough in any
particular case to override the slings and arrows of outrageous
fortune. Anyone acquainted with history knows that it is full of

---

[13] "Plays the part of someone judging a criminal."

[14] Proposition No.62.

[15] Nonetheless, where the objective right and wrong in the quarrel are
unclear, as has often been the case, soldiers on both sides will be
subjectively acting in good faith by following their patriotic duty to
support their country. [Translator's note.]

[16] "Towards an eternal peace."

fortunate scoundrels and just men who suffer. The numerous instances in which nemesis overtakes the evildoer are not enough to turn the general tendency into a universal law. In the Catholic understanding of things, there are no inbuilt punishments, either individual or collective, that work infallibly; the just man can only look forward to security in the future. The uncertainties of war make the conflict two-edged right to the last, and Mars a faithless god. The outcome can depend on some minute accidental event, within which lurks the permanent power of a single moment.[17]

War is a kind of gambling, since chance plays a large part in it; indeed Manzoni said it should be regarded as gambling at the level of politics. Philologically, warfare and dueling are closely related, *bellum* = *duellum*. The good aimed at in fighting is itself something essentially obtainable without fighting. The same rational processes that tell us war is a bad thing in itself also tells us how we could obtain the desired good without war.

The chances of war tend to make the strength of the two sides irrelevant. Then again, as Jomini noted, the improvement in weapons that all states so assiduously pursue, only provides an advantage if the other side has not got the weapons in question, as in the case of firearms at Crecy in 1346 and the atomic bomb in Japan in 1945. The acquisition of the same weapons by both sides affords an advantage to neither. Weapons become more expensive and more lethal, but the outcome still depends on luck and bravery. In a combat of three against three, one side is no more likely to beat the other than in a fight between equal armies numbered by the million.

195. The question of moderation in war. Voltaire. Pius XII. Ultimate impossibility of modern war.

Moderation is essential to a just war. Even the party in the right is bound to exercise it. Defending oneself to the last by

---

[17] The fortuitous element in a general's fate was recognized by the ancients, who counted *felicitas*, or fortune, among the endowments of a successful leader, as well as leadership and expertise, and can be seen in the election of Pompey to lead the war against Mithradates (Cicero, *Pro Lege Manilia*). Bonaparte also set great store by fate; of General Mack whom he defeated at Ulm in 1805 he said: "He is incompetent: worse still he has a bad star."

useless sacrifices, when there is no hope of winning, is thus illegitimate.[18]

Whence derives this duty of moderation? Metaphysically, it comes from the principal of sufficient reason, which implies that it is irrational and therefore immoral to perform actions that are superfluous to the end in view. Actions should be directed towards an end, and those that are not are useless; war too must be conducted with a minimum of destruction since its aim is the universal restoration of justice and peace. The total destruction of the enemy is counterproductive of that end and thus illegitimate.

The moral reason for this restraint is even more important. One should never wish moral evil on one's neighbor. Nor should one ever will his physical evil *directly*, but merely as a means to some good, and to the minimum degree necessary. One does not desire war for its own sake, but as a means to a just peace.

Voltaire's opinion, given in his *Des droits de guerre*, to the effect that since war originates in a breakdown of law it cannot be expected to obey any rules, is a perfect justification of total war. It is incompatible with our religion. As G. Gonella argued,[19] a just war fought on moral grounds will naturally be governed by moral principles, including that of due restraint. This is where the difficulty arises. A state that wages war within due limits against an aggressor who observes no limits will often lose the battle and go down before an overpowering evil. A just war will thus be lost precisely because of its justice. A due restraint imposed on the slaughter will rule out the possibility of victory and make even a defensive war illegitimate. Justice in.cludes a due proportion between the damage entailed in upholding some good, and the importance of the good in question. When that proportion between means and end is lacking, it can become one's duty to tolerate a lesser injustice in order to avoid a greater. Pius XII teaches explicitly: *Il ne suffit pas d'avoir à se défendre contre n'importe quelle injustice pour utiliser la méthode violente de la guerre. Lorsque les dommages entraînés par*

---

[18] Examples of this are the defense of Stalingrad by General von Paulus during the last war, and the defense of Attu, where all two thousand Japanese holding the island were killed or committed suicide. The Hague Conventions of 1899 and 1907 forbid fighting without quarter and defending to the last man.

[19] In *Revue de droit internationale*, 1943, p.205.

celle-ci ne sont pas comparables à ceux de l'injustice on peut avoir l'obligation de subir l'injustice.[20]
The conundrum posed by modern war is clear. On the one hand it is legitimate to defend oneself by waging war; but then one is bound to exercise restraint in doing so, and may therefore be doomed to succumb before an unrestrained assailant. Circumstances can thus make even a defensive war immoral and create an obligation to submit to injustice. There are both ancient and modern examples of this. Pius IX's surrender on 20 September 1870 is a clearly justified instance of such submission;[21] the surrender by King Leopold of Belgium in June 1940 was also legitimate, although it was widely condemned. Should all wars be absolutely forbidden then, on the grounds that in modern circumstances they cannot but be unlimited; and should all defensive acts of war be forbidden, even in their initial stages?

196. Removal of the problem of war by an international confederation.

The Second Vatican Council teaches that: "Until a competent international authority equipped with forces adequate to restrain transgressors has been constituted, governments cannot be denied the right of legitimate defense."[22] In a future international society, consisting of a confederation of associated nations that are subject parts of one society rather than sovereign entities, the supreme authority would remove the right of individual nations to enforce justice for themselves, just as a single person's right to procure justice on his own initiative is removed at present by the authority of individual states. The human race

---

[20] Speech on 19 October 1953 to the XVI session of the International Office for the Documentation of Military Medicine, in *Discorsi ai medici*, IV, ed., Rome 1960, p.307. "The fact that one has to defend oneself against injustice of some sort is not enough to justify using the violent methods of war. When the harm caused by the latter are out of proportion to the harm caused by the injustice, one may have a duty to submit to that injustice."

[21] On that day the overwhelmingly powerful armies of the Italian state breached the walls of papal Rome, and to avoid useless bloodshed the Pope ordered his troops to surrender. [Translator's note.]

[22] *Gaudium et Spes*, 79.

should organize itself into a perfected *societas populorum*[23] of the sort that Leo XIII hoped for and that Benedict XV outlined in detail, leaving behind the wild state in which the community of nations still finds itself, and should thus conform to an ideal traditional in Catholic theology from the mediaeval thinkers to Suarez, Campanella and Taparelli d'Azeglio. War would of course not be eliminated, but it would be clear that persons who waged war to secure justice on their own account, as if they constituted a sovereign entity, would be acting unjustly and that a war conducted against such groups by the sole sovereign authority would be just. International order and peace can only rest upon the use of force by a supranational authority designed to put down those who act unjustly. Individual states dissolve into anarchy when the authorities have no force at their disposal: international society is no different.[24]

In a message for World Peace Day[25] John Paul II states that a solution to the problem of modern war is only possible through the recognition of a supranational authority, but the Pope envisages the community of nations as an institution for dialogue and negotiation, which it is already, while he says nothing about *force*, which is the backbone of authority. Nor does it seem that the Pope condemns the idea of a defensive war, for if he were to, there would be a *vacatio legis*[26] which would leave the world at the mercy of evildoers. The Pope's words at Coventry do not condemn the type of defensive war allowed by the council, but rather initiatives by those who resort to either nuclear or conventional weapons in order to resolve disagreements unilaterally. On the other hand, any party that is attacked and that defends itself, has a perfect right to use force. Nonetheless, the ambiguities remain because of the obligation to observe due restraint.

---

[23] "Society of peoples."

[24] In his *L'azione politica dell'ONU 1946-1974*, Padua 1983, M. Vismara shows with full documentation that the only clearly successful action by the U.N. was the solution of the Congo problem, and this was because it was obtained by the use of force; fifteen thousand men were deployed and soon put an end to the secession of Katanga under Tshombe and Kisai under Lumumba. The firm action taken by Hammarskjold, the Secretary General, was effective because of the use of an international military force.

[25] O.R., 21 December 1981.

[26] "A legal vacuum."

The duty to attempt to form the human race into a confederation of nations flows from the principle on which the whole of our argument is based, namely the idea of the dependency of dependent being; dependency on human law, on the moral law or on God. Parts must be considered precisely as parts, not as the whole. States must be reduced to their true status as relative rather than absolute wholes, subjects rather than sovereigns, creatures rather than mini-gods.

CHAPTER XXVIII

SITUATION ETHICS

197. Situation ethics. The practical and the praxiological. The law as a forecast.

If divorce, sodomy and abortion deny the natural law on specific points, situation ethics attacks its very principle and reduces morality to a purely subjective judgment that man makes about his own actions.

Situation ethics was condemned by Pius XII as a "radical revision of morality" in a speech he made to the World Federation of Catholic Young Women.[1] It is a moral philosophy that transfers the criteria determining the rightness or wrongness of an action from objective laws and essential structures to subjective intentions, that is "from the center to the periphery" as the Pope put it. An action is held to be right when there is a worthy intention and a sincere response to a situation. A knowledge of the situation is needed to decide the application of the law, but the law is held to be dictated by the conscience itself. The choice to be made is no longer determined by the nature of an action imposing itself on one's judgment; rather it is the judgment that creates the nature of the action and bestows legitimacy on it. The distinction between a subjective judgment that evaluates a particular action, and an objective judgment that evaluates the nature of the act by reference to universal standards is thus done away with.

It should be remembered that traditional ethics are also situation ethics. The knowledge of universal rules is only one half of morals. The other half, that goes to make up a complete moral judgment, consists in relating particular situations to the demands expressed in the law. This activity is what constitutes the genuine and permanent basis of casuistry. But situation

---

[1] O.R., 19 April 1952.

ethics eliminates universal laws and makes the conscience a rule unto itself, thus combining and compounding a praxiological judgment with a purely practical one.[2] The natural order, which is metaphysical and not simply biological, has vanished or at least become doubtful and unknowable. *Il y a des aspects de la vie où la complexité est telle qu'elle rend impossible ou inopportune une application littérale de la norme morale. Ici il faut faire confiance à la conscience personelle et au sens de responsabilité de la personne envers sa vie.*[3] If the intention here is to bring out the contingent difficulty people have in judging the rights and wrongs in particular situations, the point is obvious and gives rise to the science of casuistry as we have already noted. But it does not make sense to talk about a *literal* application of the law, precisely because the law is not something in writing, but a *sense* that must be transcribed or transliterated from the universal to the particular situation. Personal conscience, which is the same thing as a sense of personal responsibility, does indeed deal with actual life, but it deals with it as something that has to be judged, not as something that constitutes the criterion of judgment: and one's responsibility is not to one's own life, but to the demands of the law, through which God's will is made manifest.

It is also false to oppose general norms to particular cases, and to claim that the latter do not come under the former but are governed by some separate law of their own. Particular cases do come under general norms, and the reason is that the universal is nothing other than the individual case considered in its essence, as it exists when stripped of its individuating features.

Particular cases are also governed by general laws for metaphysical and theological reasons, not merely as a result of logical necessity. Moral laws include all possible cases. As a judgment of human reason, the law is a generalized abstraction to be applied to particular cases; but as an ideal order existing in the divine mind, it is a prevision of all historic cases occurring throughout the whole course of time: the God who gave the law "knows all the possible relations that feelings and actions can have with

---

[2]   The first deals with a universal subject, the second with a particular one. See Garrigou-Lagrange, *Dieu*, Paris 1933, pp.609ff.

[3]   Buelens-Gijsen, J. Grootaers, *Mariage catholique et contraception*, Paris 1968, p.88. "There are some aspects of life which are so complex as to make a literal application of a moral norm impossible or inopportune. In such cases one must rely on a person's conscience and on his sense of responsibility for his life."

eternal and unchanging justice."⁴ While claiming that particular cases do not come under general laws and that they can be interpreted by the subjective judgment of the person involved, situation ethics ignores the fact that the particular case is a case of something that occurs regularly and that, like the whole of the divine law, it is known to the divine lawgiver to whom all possible cases are present. Thus situations can seem extraordinary from man's point of view, because of the frequent gaps in his knowledge of the full realities of the case or because of his reluctance to accept the law, but remain nonetheless quite ordinary from the point of view of the law itself. Indeed, cases such as these manifest the law all the more clearly inasmuch as it appears in the guise of a naked command without anything else to recommend it.

Despite Pius XII's condemnation of situation ethics and the ambiguities by which the approach is beset, it has been taken up by some groups of bishops and put into practice by some Catholic movements. The bishops in question refuse to base themselves upon eternal principles and universal norms when dealing with particular situations, and set out instead from concrete situations which they analyze in order to arrive at the conclusions that humanity and the gospel require. It is a question of *une manière nouvelle de concevoir la conscience chrétienne, non plus comme une fonction appliquant par un syllogisme automatique un principe général à un cas particulier, mais plutôt comme une faculté qui, sous la conduite de l'Esprit de Dieu, est douée d'un certain pouvoir d'intuition et de création lui permettant de trouver pour chaque cas la solution originale qui convient.*⁵

---

⁴ Manzoni, *Morale cattolica*, First Part, ed. cit., Vol. I, p.35.
⁵ I.C.I., No. 581, 15 December 1982, p.51., discussing the Brazilian bishops' document on the methods of Catholic Action. "A new way of understanding the Christian conscience, so that it is no longer a function that applies a general principle to a particular case by an automatic syllogism, but becomes instead a faculty which, led by the Spirit of God, is endowed with a power of intuition and creation that enables it to find an original and suitable solution for each particular case."

198. Critique of creativity of the conscience.
Passivity of man's moral life. Rosmini.

By rejecting the law as an axiological order dependent on God rather than man, situation ethics is logically forced to adopt the principle of the creativity of the conscience. In commenting on the declaration *Personae humanae* published by the Congregation for the Doctrine of the Faith, the president of the French Episcopal Conference, Mgr Etchégaray, criticizes *la morale qui cherche à s'abriter seulement derrière les principes*;[6] he agrees with young people who *contestent l'anteriorité de la morale*;[7] he asserts that moral obligation *n'est pas semblable à la parole qui tombe de haut, mais plutôt à celle qui surgit de la relation avec l'homme et rend celui-ci coauteur de cette parole.*[8] Mgr Etchégaray thus condemns those who think the moral law exists before man comes to make a moral judgment; he insinuates that the moral law tries to take cover behind principles, when in fact it derives from principles and manifests them; and he pretends lastly that man is the coauthor of the law. Mgr Etchégaray's teaching is contrary to that of *Gaudium et Spes*[9] as recalled by John Paul II: *L'homme découvre au fond de sa conscience vraie et droite une loi qu'il ne s'est pas donnée lui-même et tend à se conformer aux normes objectives de la moralité.*[10] The Pope returned to the subject in a memorable speech he made on 18 August 1983 in which he reiterated the Church's teaching with wonderful clarity: "The individual conscience is not the ultimate criterion of morality; it must conform itself to the moral law. The moral law is present to man in his conscience. The conscience is the place where man reads, hears, sees the truth concerning

---

[6] "A moral philosophy that merely seeks to take cover behind principles."

[7] "Deny the *a priori* existence of the moral law."

[8] "Is not like a word that comes from on high, but rather like one that arises from relations with man, and which makes man a coauthor of that word."

[9] Paragraph 16.

[10] "Man discovers in the depth of a true and upright conscience a law that he has not made for himself and he tends to conform himself to the objective norms of the moral law." O.R., 2 April 1982.

good and evil. In his moral consciousness man is not alone with himself, but alone with God who speaks to him imperatively."[11]

Fr. Schillebeeckx, a spokesman for Dutch novelties, says of situation ethics: *Nous devons mettre l'accent aujourd'hui aussi bien sur l'importance des normes objectives que sur la nécessité de la créativité de la conscience et du sens des responsabilités personnelles.*[12] In reality of course, personal responsibility has always been at the center of moral theology. The more important point however is to pin down the error concealed in the idea that the conscience is creative, since in fact it is a contradiction in terms.[13] Conscience is the awareness of the otherness and absolute givenness of the law, to which man can add or subtract nothing except his free submission. If conscience were to create, it would be immoral in its very act of creating, because moral behavior is the harmony of the will with an ideal order, and the order is not created or creatable, even in God. Thus if conscience were creative rather than a faculty of recognition, there would be no order with which to harmonize, and conscience would be the canonization of an arbitrary will. Moral rules are a recognition of truth in practice, a kind of veracity whereby man presents truth to himself: presents it, not generates it.

It will be objected that moral life is an activity, indeed the supreme activity of the spirit. I would say as much myself. It is not however the creating of rules, but the actuation of a rule that is given and which man has only to receive. Rosmini is one of the Catholic thinkers who has most clearly recognized man's position before the law: "Duty affects and completely binds the man who is subject to it: if therefore the subject is wholly

---

[11] O.R., 18 August 1983. In its headline, the *Osservatore Romano* falsifies the content of the Pope's address, as it has done on other occasions: "The moral conscience is the place of God's dialogue with man." No, the word "dialogue" does not occur even once in the whole speech. On the contrary, the Pope teaches forcefully that the conscience is the place where man hears, accepts and obeys the voice of God: he does not dialogue, he has only to listen.

[12] "Today we ought to put the accent as much on the importance of objective norms as on the necessity of a creative conscience and of a sense of personal responsibility." In *Dieu et l'homme*, Brussels 1960, p.227.

[13] In his magazine *Filosofia*, 1983, pp.15-18, A. Guzzo has written some pages of rare clarity and depth on the *given* character of moral obligation and on consequent obedience in moral activity.

bound, everything about him is passive: no active principle remains in him that could have the effect of imposing an obligation....Man is merely passive with regard to the moral law: he
receives it within himself but does not form it: he is a subject
upon whom the law imposes itself, not a legislator who imposes
it."[14]

Situation ethics and Catholic ethics are therefore incompatible. The latter believes in an inviolable block or limitation
that confronts the conscience and before which the conscience
must halt. It is not right to talk about a dynamic as opposed to
a static morality either. From the point of view of the law, morals are static. From the point of view of the conscience, they are
indeed dynamic, but precisely because of the continuous effort
needed to conform and subject oneself to an unchanging law.

Man's passivity as a moral being is a consequence of his dependence on the Absolute as regards his essence, which is an
uncreated idea in the divine mind, and his existence, which is
something given to him; and his freedom, which, according to
St. Thomas, is a self-movement set in motion by God. In short,
the whole argument against situation ethics is summed up in
the Catholic affirmation of the dependence of the creature.

199. Situation ethics as an ethics of intention. Abelard.

By handing man the task of providing the criteria by which
moral judgments are to be made, and by claiming that judgments made about a situation are justified simply by reference
to the situation itself, situation ethics annihilates man by swallowing him up in the situation. It is alleged that decisions people make should not be judged abstractly, but historically, by
putting oneself in a particular person's position at the moment
he made his decision. But that is to compound the person in
the situation with the situation itself making them a single
whole, when in fact a person is confronted by a situation without being identical with it. So-called abstract judgments are
demanded by the nature of any law, since law is not something
that can be manipulated and picked apart at will: *fiat justitia,
pereat mundus: non enim perebit sed aedificabitur.*[15]

---

[14] *Principii della scienza morale*, Ch. V, Art. 2, National Edition,
Vol. XXI, p.170.
[15] "Let justice be done, and let the world perish: for it will not perish
but be built up."

To form a judgment about somebody's obligations, it is certainly necessary to be acquainted with the case in hand, that is, with the circumstances; nonetheless, as the word implies, the circumstances "stand around" the acting person and are not identical with him; when the circumstances change, he remains the same even though the judgments we may make about his obligations may change. If one were to pursue to its logical conclusion the idea that one should put oneself in the other man's position, one would inevitably end up sharing his opinions, because it would no longer be our judgment that would be brought to bear on the situation, but the other man's, produced by the circumstances of his own life.

Situation ethics resembles the ethics of intention of which Abelard is the most famous exponent, in his book called *Scito teipsum*.[16] He maintains that the moral state of an action depends on one's intention, that is, on the subjective judgment that the person performing the action makes on it. Thus one sins in performing a good act that one thinks to be bad, and one acquires merit in doing evil if one thinks it is good. He gives the example of those who crucified Christ, and says that since they thought they were doing the right thing, their actions were good; apart from one's good or evil intentions, there is only the material event of what is done, which is in itself morally indifferent. One should note nonetheless that Abelard could not consistently maintain his subjectivism since it so obviously exceeds the limits laid down by Christian theology. In fact, he formally contradicts himself in an important section of his twelfth chapter, and thus ruins his whole system: *Non est itaque bona intentio quia bona videtur, sed insuper quia talis est sicut existimatur, cum videlicet illud ad quod tendit si Deo placere credit, in hac insuper existimatione sua nequaquam fallitur.*[17] In any Christian ethic it is inevitable that there will be a reference to an objective law given to man, and passively received by him, since Christianity holds that the divine Idea, not man, is the measure of all things.

As can be seen in the passages quoted from Cardinal Etchégaray and Father Schillebeeckx, situation ethics silently and surreptitiously smuggles in the concept of a *right intention*. But

---

[16] "Know Thyself."

[17] "An intention is not good simply because it seems to be; it is good because it *is* what it seems to be, that is, if it is not mistaken in the object toward which it tends when it thinks it is pleasing God."

there can be no right or wrong intention if conscience is independent of law and stands in solitary detachment from any norm.

200. Whether Catholic morality removes the dynamic power of conscience.

The dynamism appropriate to one's moral life is not removed by the objectivity of the moral law. It remains true that *suae quisque fortunae faber*,[18] but in a legitimate sense of that expression. Man is the cause of his being good or evil, but not in the sense that he creates the framework of values by reference to which he is judged good or bad.

Is it correct to say "by freeing man from the law, the morality of the Gospel transfers the roots of moral law to a place within man himself"? One can put it that way, as Paul VI did,[19] but only if one rightly interprets words that can easily be ambiguous. It is not possible for the roots of the moral law to be within man, since man himself is not the root of being and cannot be the root of moral obligation either. The moral law is an absolute, whereas man is a contingent and relative being to whom the absolute is present and upon whom it imposes itself, but its origins do not lie in man himself.

Secondly, it is not possible for the moral law to spring up from one's own conscience, because the conscience is a *self* while the law is an *other*. The very word *conscience* proclaims indisputably that there cannot be a *con-scientia* without the self's feeling a duality, a presence with something else; and there cannot be a conscience unless man lives in connection with that law by which he is bound and to which he owes respect. One can talk, as Catholic theology always has, about the primary or remote source of moral law, namely God, and the secondary or proximate source, which is human reason inasmuch as it knows the absolute law. In the latter case however, one is talking about a root that is rooted in something else, which is in effect to admit that it is not really a root at all.

---

[18] "Each man is the maker of his own destiny."
[19] O.R., 17 June 1971.

CHAPTER XXIX

GLOBALITY AND GRADUALITY

201. Global morality.

The idea that one's moral life is a global entity, and the consequent undervaluing of individual actions is, I believe, without precedent in the history of moral philosophy and thus constitutes the most outstanding innovation that has occurred in this field. The idea developed during the years of grave uncertainty regarding the matter of contraceptives, after the council's decision to leave a pronouncement on the subject to the Pope, and before the promulgation of *Humanae Vitae*, which gave judgment in favor of the traditional teaching.

The new view is that the moral character of one's life and thus, theologically, one's eternal destiny, is determined by the whole, or the general color, or the globality of one's acts. This view does not, apparently, deny that individual actions affect the global result (if it did, what would one's moral activity consist of?) but it does maintain that a person's moral standing depends on general intentions, or what is called a "fundamental option" that one has made, orienting oneself towards God. During the course of the council itself, Patriarch Maximos IV and Cardinals Léger, Suenens and Alfrink spoke in favor of a global vision of the lives of married couples and said expressly that "one should pay less attention to the procreative goal of *each* conjugal act and more to that of conjugal life taken as a *whole*." The idea of globality became a major theme in the report of the commission that advised Paul VI to proclaim the legitimacy of contraception. The formula is: "Every act is naturally ordered towards procreation understood in a *global sense*."[1] The contradiction involved cannot be disguised: what is being said is that *every* act means *some* acts.

---

[1] This formula is quoted, and rejected, in *Humanae Vitae* itself.

The point is difficult to explain, but it is nonetheless true
that the idea of globality is a departure from the Church's
teaching. The Church has always asserted that one's moral life
exists at a certain point in time, and has always preached to the
Christian people accordingly. I have had occasion to study the
sermons given by parish priests in the Val di Blenio, in the
canton of the Ticino in Switzerland around the middle of the
nineteenth century, and I have found that insistently and without any exceptions, they maintain this idea of the importance of
a certain point in time: a Christian's eternal destiny depends on
the moment of death. The whole of Christian literature and
preaching contain no exceptions in this matter, which is dealt
with superbly by Bossuet, Bordaloue and Massillon in France,
and by Daniello Bartoli in Italy in his great work *L'uomo al
punto*. This universal consent is all the more striking for the fact
that the opposite point of view seems obvious and reasonable,
and is widely held: namely that the moral quality of someone's
life should be judged by the whole of his existence.

The global view of morality seems to be an offshoot of the
view that moral conduct should be judged by one's intentions,
given that the "fundamental option," or good intention that is
held to govern all particular acts and give them a collective orientation, is also held to make individual acts unimportant, because they are no longer to be measured singly by comparison
with a law, but are all deemed to be good by virtue of one's generally good intention. In this regard a global morality is the
same as Abelard's subjectivism.

202. Moral life as a point in time.

This is an important religious truth, but it is also difficult,
paradoxical and offensive to commonly held ideas. It seems
unjust and unreasonable that a man's moral worth should be
judged by reference to his state at the time he dies and not to an
overall balance of good and evil in his life.

Nonetheless, the Christian religion teaches that one's eternal
destiny depends on the moral state in which a man finds himself at the point of death: thus it does not depend on past historical states of affairs, but on the existing point that his moral
life has reached when death overtakes him. The other view, that
one's fate depends on a weighing up of good and bad deeds is

attributed by Segneri[2] to some of the rabbis, and is also held by the Muslims, who refer to a *mizan*, or balance of merits. But the teaching of the Catholic Church asserts the decisiveness of one's present moral state; and that teaching has been set forth in catechisms, preached in every pulpit and defined by a dogmatic decree of the second Council of Lyons.[3]

Rosmini explains this difficult truth very perceptively: "One should not consider a man's moral goodness like two qualities that exist contemporaneously, increasing and decreasing, canceling each other out; nor should one say that a man is damned when the quantity of evil accumulates and reaches a level established by God according to his free will and the laws of his justice. The whole man is good or bad, *quia nihil est damnationis in eis qui vere consepulti sunt cum Christo.*[4] Good cannot really exist in a bad man, because *quae societas Christi ad Belial?*[5] There are indeed venial sins in good men but these are not such as to make them cease being fundamentally good."[6] I know there are difficulties presented by common sense, and even by biblical texts, as well as by traditional depictions of divine judgment as a weighing up of souls. Nonetheless the importance of one's moral state at a particular point in time stems from a clear teaching of the Christian religion. Moral action is a relation of man to his last end, or to the law which mediates that end; it is not a relation with created things, or with worldly ends, or with the future of the human race. Now, the respect man owes to the law is owed and payable at every moment in time *independently of every other.* Past and future moments in life are absent here and now, but man's relation to his ultimate end, namely God, is always present, and it dominates what the whole of man is, and leaves no part of himself that he can give to finite things as subtracted from God. This is what gives moral life its seriousness. Not one instant of a man's life is free for him to devote to sin; this is a truth that has been preached in every age of Christian history. Every moment of wasted time

---

2   Paolo Segneri S.J.(1624-1694) the most famous preacher in seventeenth century Italy. [Translator's note.]

3   In 1274. See Denzinger, 464.

4   Cf. Romans 8:1. "For there is no damnation for those who are truly buried with Christ".

5   Cf. II Corinthians 6:15. "What company has Christ with the devil?"

6   Rosmini, *Epist.*, Vol. IV, p.214.

has to be *redeemed,*[7] that is, put into relation with the transcendent, apart from which there is nothing but non-being, whether metaphysical or moral.

203. Critique of globality.

In forming a judgment on the global view of morality, one should remember the principle mentioned in paragraph 153: when a truth is once firmly established, it stands fast in the face of all the objections that can be brought against it on particular points. In this instance, the absoluteness of moral obligation, which is binding at every moment of one's life, means that each and every moment in time should be devoted to honoring the Absolute, and that such honor cannot be withheld on account of a relation with other moments. But besides clashing with this firmly established truth, the global view of ethics collapses under the weight of the other difficulties by which it is confronted. It would seem that the global state of affairs is to be gathered from the sum total of good and bad acts. But how does one know if an act is good or bad if its value is derived from the global condition and the global condition is derived from the value of individual acts? Must not the individual act have a value of its own that it contributes to the sum total?

But the global system of morals labors under an even more grave and indeed invincible difficulty. It is alleged that a man's moral worth depends on the totality of his acts. But how can one know what this totality is, when it includes the future, which is unknowable? How can I depart here and now from the law, by my present actions, on the basis of an appeal to the globality of my acts, if I do not know how much of a future there is for me to integrate into the totality of my acts? I can judge the whole of a life when it is presented to me as a complete set of actions, but I can never regulate my own choices on the basis of the whole of my own life when that involves other uncertain and unknowable future acts. The truth of the matter is that a global whole can never provide a criterion by which to determine my present choices, because to make those choices would involve nothing less than my knowing my own future. Consider what would happen to conjugal fidelity if a moment of infidelity could be written off against a hypothetical moment of future fidelity; and consider what would happen to commer-

---

[7] Cf. Ephesians, 5:16.

cial honesty if today's fraud could be written off against tomorrow's hypothetical justice. Then again, a present intention to do evil is incompatible with an intention to repent and make reparation.

The global view destroys the moral order, which is a relation with the Absolute that must be maintained in each moment in time; but it destroys the order of time as well. It contradictorily presupposes that the global reality is, and is not, the sum total of moments in time. The global reality is alleged to be made up of moments and to be in fact the total of such moments. But it cannot be the sum total without including the final moments, which cannot be had because the future is unknowable. How can you establish a total without closing the account?[8]

204. The gradualist morality.

The moral philosophy of graduality is akin to situation ethics and globalist morality, being a synthesis of the errors of both systems. Situation ethics nullifies the demands of the law, and the globalist view nullifies the value of individual acts. The gradualist system, which cropped up at the Synod of Bishops in 1980, maintains that the demands of the moral law only impose themselves gradually, and thus the gradualness of a man's response to moral imperatives is transformed into an alleged gradualness on the part of the law itself. In fact, the moral law is an absolute that demands total obedience, even though the wills that have to conform to it may be weak and may often tend towards a conformity to the law without being strong enough to reach it. To assert a graduality in the moral imperative itself, would be to compromise the ideal and unchanging moral order of things; a graduality in one's responding to the law's requirements is, on the other hand, a simple psychological fact stemming from the changeableness of human wills. This gradual response to the law's demands has always been recognized in the Church's ethical and ascetical teaching. The fact that this doctrinal deviation has wormed its way into the hierarchy itself led John Paul II to issue a clear correction: graduality is a fact of human behavior, it is not a norm by which to guide con-

---

[8]   Yet again, if salvation depended on a global weighing up of one's moral activity, a repentance made late in a bad life would be incapable of rectifying the balance. [Translator's note.]

sciences: "A process of graduality can only be accepted on the part of someone who is trying sincerely to observe the divine law. Thus the so-called law of graduality cannot be identified with a graduality of the law, as if there were grades and different sorts of precepts in the divine law for men in different situations."[9] As the Pope's condemnation makes clear, the gradualist theory shifts the progressivity which exists in man's moral development, into the divine law itself.

---

[9] O.R., 27-28 October 1980.

CHAPTER XXX

THE AUTONOMY OF VALUES

205. The anthropocentric teleology of *Gaudium et Spes* 14 and 24.

All these deviations in moral philosophy are a response to the anthropocentric demands of the modern world, which is replacing the belief that the world is governed by the mind of God by the belief that man governs himself. This anthropocentric drive begets the technology that makes man believe he is the purpose for which the world exists, and that the exercise of control over the things of this world is the real task allotted to the human race.

This new teleology is echoed in some passages from the Second Vatican Council. The pastoral constitution *Gaudium et Spes* puts it thus: *Secundum credentium et non credentium fere concordem sententiam omnia quae in terra sunt ad hominem tamquam ad centrum suum et culmen ordinanda sunt.*[1] In more theological terms it says man *in terris sola creatura est quam Deus propter seipsam voluerit.*[2]

It is somewhat hasty to assert that believers and non-believers agree in recognizing that the world ought to be directed towards man, since all the pessimistic philosophies from Lucretius to Schopenhauer deny any anthropocentric goal to the world, and a very large part of modern science denies the

---

[1] *Gaudium et Spes* 14. "By the almost universal consent of believers and non-believers alike, all things on earth should be directed towards man as their center and culmination."

[2] *Gaudium et Spes* 24. Man "is the only creature on earth that God willed for *its* own sake." The generally used Italian translation mistakenly translates this as "for Himself," thus reversing the meaning and abolishing the change in teaching. John Paul II quoted the Latin text in a speech on conjugal love. O.R., 17 January 1980.

world has any goal at all. The mechanistic visions of these philosophies attack the anthropocentric idea, even when restricted to life on this planet alone. There is in Lucretius a memorable passage depicting man as an unhappy creature cast forth by his mother's spasms onto the shore of light, like a shipwrecked mariner *indigus omni vitali auxilio*[3] constrained to live between a zone of fire and a zone of ice, on the face of an earth that ignores him completely.

206. Critique of anthropocentric teleology. Proverbs 16:4.

If the anthropocentric concept of reality has a certain plausibility in a universe that is thought to be finite and enclosed within the planetary spheres, as the ancients thought it was, it is quite incredible in a universe that is infinite in every way and which infinitely surpasses Lucretius's *homullus*, now seen to be infinitesimal with respect to both space and time. By bursting the walls of Lucretius's world and driving the limits of creation into infinite retreat, modern science makes the anthropocentric view that the council adopted even more fragile. The universe cannot be made for man, because it infinitely surpasses him.

If one searches for God's reason for creating that infinite excess by which our world, and all the others, so greatly outstrip our tiny being, it is certainly legitimate to say that man has been placed in an infinite world so that he may recognize it for what it is, and thus recognize his own relative infinity as a spiritual being; this is Pascal's fantasy about the *roseau pensant*.[4] Be that as it may, when one considers how much there is that could be known about the universe, one is driven to admit that it surpasses man's limited being, both in regard to the infinitely large and the infinitely small. Hence the universe's infinite excess over man is really made to manifest God's infinity, not man's capacity to know the infinite.

The notion that man is the center of the universe is excluded by theology as well as by these cosmological considerations. The assertion that man is the only creature God has willed to exist *for itself* seems to deny the solemn affirmation of the Book of Proverbs that *Universa propter semetipsum operatus*

---

[3] Lucretius, *De Rerum Natura*, V, 195-234. "Bereft of life-sustaining help."
[4] "Thinking reed."

est Dominus.[5] In reality, it is impossible for the divine will to have anything other than its own goodness as its object; all finite goods only come to exist thanks to the Infinite Good, nor can the Infinite come forth from itself or become alien to itself by seeking something finite. As St. Thomas teaches, God wills the existence of finite things inasmuch as He wills Himself as creating finite beings: *Sic igitur Deus vult se et alia: sed se ut finem, alia ad finem.*[6] Thus He wills the finite things that He does will *for Himself*, not *for themselves*, because the finite cannot be the goal of the Infinite and the divine will cannot be attracted and passive before some finite entity. Finite things are not created by God because they are lovable; they are lovable because God wills them with their loveliness.[7] Just as God knows finite things by knowing Himself, so he wills them by willing Himself.

To allot man prime importance as the goal of existence is thus quite in harmony with contemporary trends, but it is quite unfounded from the point of view of the Christian religion, which orders everything towards God, not man. Man is not an end in himself; he is a subordinate end directed towards another higher end, and he is subject to the lordship of God who is the universal end or goal of the whole creation.

207. The autonomy of worldly values.

This setting aside of the theocentric goal of the whole of creation obscures the primordial sovereignty of God which, when recognized, prevents one seeing the things of this world as autonomous. It obscures one's view of Christ, the God-Man, as the supernatural goal of the world's existence; yet that is what our faith proclaims Him to be, irrespective of whether we see his incarnation as happening in consequence of man's sin, as Thomists do, or whether we see it as the primary goal for which the world was created, without reference to sin, as do the Scotists. Since only God exists by his own power, and since all finite things have the Infinite God as their goal, no creature can be said to exist by itself, either ontologically or teleologically. The council teaches that the things of this world *non solum sub-*

---

5   Proverbs, 16:4 "The Lord has made all things for Himself."
6   *Summa Theologica*, I,q.19,a.2 "So God wills Himself and other things: but Himself as the end, and other things for that end."
7   Op. cit., q.20,a.2.

*sidia sunt ad finem ultimum hominis, sed et proprium habent va-
lorem a Deo eis insitum sive in seipsis consideratae, sive ut partes
universi ordinis temporalis.*[8] But it also says they receive a particular worth *ex speciali relatione cum persona humana in cuius servi-
tium sunt creata.*[9] True, everything is summed up in Christ who
enjoys a primacy over all things,[10] but this, the council says, *non
privat ordinem temporalem sua autonomia...sed potius perficit.*[11]

But neither the world nor man himself can be man's goal,
since God did not have them as his goal in creating them. God
was his own goal in creating. Theology and religious feeling
have always regarded man's temporal goods as helps that serve
instrumentally in the exercise of the virtues.[12] On this matter–as
Paul VI put it–the council "has considerably modified attitudes
and judgments concerning the world."[13] In his speech to
UNESCO at Geneva in 1980, John Paul II declared: "Man
should be affirmed for his own sake and not for any other motive or reason: uniquely for his own sake. Still more, man
should be loved because he is man; love for man must be demanded because of the particular dignity which he possesses."[14]
The Pope's words are affected by the considerations he had to
bear in mind when addressing a gathering of a purely humanistic and non-religious sort, and perhaps too by St. Paul's desire to
be "all things to all men." They must be weighed up against his
explicit affirmation in the encyclical *Redemptor Hominis: Christus est centrum universi et historiae.*[15] This thorny question requires further development.

---

[8] *Apostolicam Actuositatem*, 7. "Are not only helps to man's ultimate
end but have their own worth that God has given them, whether
considered in themselves or as parts of the whole temporal order."

[9] Ibid. "From a special relation with the human person, for whose
service they have been created."

[10] Colossians, 1:18.

[11] *Apostolicam Actuositatem*, 7. "Does not deprive the temporal order
of its autonomy...but rather perfects it."

[12] The terms used by St. Thomas in his commentary on Aristotle's *Ni-
comachaen Ethics* are *co-operative* and *organice* Book I, lect. XV.

[13] O.R., 6 March, 1969.

[14] R.I., 1980, p.566.

[15] "Christ is the center of the universe and of history."

208. The true meaning of the autonomy of nature. Whether man should be loved or not.

The question of the autonomy of the created order is fundamentally metaphysical rather than religious. Every finite thing is essentially dependent, not autonomous or independent. Its existence is indeed its own and should not be confused with the existence of the Creator who causes it to be; the same is true of its activity. So the sun's action in heating things is genuinely an action of the sun and not an action of God in the sun, as some Arab philosophers held. The will's free activity is truly an act of free will, not an act of God. Every created thing genuinely has its own proper being and activity and laws: it is not a mere appearance of a single all embracing divine being or a single divine activity. Nonetheless, no existing thing is genuinely autonomous, since all things depend at every moment on divine influence; similarly no free act is autonomous because, as St. Thomas puts it, things are *moved by God to move themselves*. So the being and the activity of all creatures exist in an order that is radically dependent. St. Paul's famous words are not merely a theological truth: *non quod sufficientes simus cogitare aliquid a nobis, quasi ex nobis, sed sufficientia nostra ex Deo est.*[16] The autonomy of human goods is something internal to the created order, but the created order is itself dependent and excludes the possibility of any kind of primal, original or absolute independence on the part of those goods.

Believing in the autonomy of the created order leads directly to the idea that man is to be loved as an autonomous entity. This assertion fits ill with the Catholic doctrine which teaches that the motive for loving one's neighbor is the love of God. All the formulas of acts of charity, which were used so widely by Christians until Vatican II, maintain that God should be loved first and foremost and for his own sake, and that one's neighbor is to be loved for the love of God. The council says nothing about this.[17]

The command to love one's fellow men is connected in the Church's teaching with the command to love God, but it is put

---

[16] II Corinthians, 3:5. "Not as if we were sufficient to think something of ourselves, as if from ourselves, but our sufficiency is from God."

[17] Paul VI mentioned it in his speeches opening and closing the fourth period of the council in 1965. But he makes love of neighbor a precondition for loving God.

in second place and said to be *like* the former command.[18] The love of God remains primary and provides the form of the love that should be given to one's neighbor. It is therefore impossible to accept the notion of pure philanthropy, which is touted today as being superior to the love of God, since the latter is allegedly contaminated by a desire for a heavenly reward.

But how can the command to love one's neighbor be said to be *like* the command to love God? There are two reasons. First, because when one loves one's fellow man one is loving God in man, since man is made in the likeness of God. Second, when one loves one's fellow man one is acting in conformity with God's will, since God Himself loves man, and this too is a way of loving God.

In the Catholic understanding then, it is impossible to discover anything in man which is not derived from God's love for his creatures, and a reflection of it. Thus it is impossible to love man for his own sake, separately from the love of God. The particular qualities that a person has can be an important secondary influence on the love one has for him, and thus people love their mothers more than they do strangers, but these qualities cannot elicit the love due to that person in accordance with the new commandment to love, given in the Gospel. One man should love another because that other is loved by God: which means that it is God who makes him lovable. After all, how can one love some being for its own sake when it does not exist for its own sake?

The various grounds for the commands to love one's neighbor, which are elaborated by the Fathers in so many ways, can be reduced to a single absolute ground, which is the love of God. God hates nothing that He has made, and when one loves Him one necessarily loves all that He loves. Hence philanthropy is an extension of a theological love, and the two become one, not by a pantheistic confusion but because the love of man is contained within the love of God, since man belongs to God by both his creation and his redemption. St. Thomas explicitly teaches that we love both God and man with a single love: *Eadem caritas est qua diligimus Deum et proximos.*[19]

---

[18] Matthew, 22:39.
[19] *Summa Theologica*, II,II,q.103,a.3 *ad secundum*. This notion is common in Christian asceticism. For example Rosmini, *Epistolario ascetico*, Vol. III, p.178, Rome 1912: "In these exercises of charity

The stress that has been put in the post-conciliar period on human worth and on loving man for his own sake, clashes with the awareness men have of themselves as wounded and fallen creatures, and it also deprives love for one's fellow man of its true foundation, namely the fact that man is made for God, and the fact that the whole gamut of human goods has a divine origin. The detaching of human dignity from its religious base weakens the ground on which one can demand respect for that dignity, as can be seen from what has happened in the modern world, because to detach it thus is to leave it as an isolated and unsupported truth.

209. An objection solved.

The idea that man is the center of the universe and the goal of his own activity seems to derive support from the central idea of the Christian religion, which is that God *propter nos homines et propter nostram salutem descendit de caelis et incarnatus est.*[20] The whole divine nature is set in motion for man's sake. How then can man fail to act for the sake of man himself?

There are two opposing opinions about the reason for the incarnation. According to St. Thomas, the Word became incarnate to restore human nature after the fall; thus if Adam had not sinned the Word would not have been made man. For Scotus, on the other hand, the incarnation fulfills God's plan to communicate Himself in all his fullness, insofar as that can be communicated: thus even if Adam had not sinned, the Word would still have been made man with a fullness of self-communication such that a single person could be said to be both God and man. In St. Thomas's teaching at least, it would seem that man was taken as an end in himself, to which God freely subordinates Himself, making Himself a slave in order to achieve man's salvation. If God becomes man for man's sake, is it not right that men themselves should take man as the end in himself and love him for his own sake?

Anthropocentricity is nonetheless incompatible with the Catholic view of things: the whole of reality has only one center, and it is God viewed as transcendent. It is indeed true to say

---

towards one's neighbor one exercises and unfolds the love of God most effectively."

[20] "For us men and our salvation came down from heaven, and became incarnate." From the Nicene Creed.

that man is a synthesis or microcosm of the whole of creation, and as such has a primacy in the created order as, in a sense, its center. It is even more true to say that Christ is the synthesis of all creation.[21] But the chief truth that does away with any anthropocentric understanding of the incarnation is that the main goal of Christ's passion was to *satisfy the divine justice* for the offense committed against it by mankind, and to restore due honor to God; the saving of men was only the secondary goal. In all his incarnate activity, Christ's love was to do the will of the Father, even more than it was to love his brethren.[22] The whole of the Church's liturgy proclaims the subordinate importance of love for mankind in the process of the incarnation, inasmuch as the liturgy is neither anthropocentric nor Christocentric, but is addressed to the Father to whom sacrifice is offered.

In short, a purely human philanthropy is incompatible with the Christian religion. Man is not a creature that God wills *for itself,* He wills it *for Himself.*

---

[21] St. Bonaventure says: *Assumptio humanae naturae plus fecit ad perfectionem universi quam angelicae.* Commentary In *III Sentent.*, dist. II,a.I,q.2. "The assumption of human nature (by the Word) contributed more to the perfection of the universe than the assumption of an angelic nature (would have done)."

[22] Rosmini emphasizes this in his *Filosofia del diritto, Trattato della societa teocratica* Section 620ff., p.884 of Vol. XXXVIII of the National Edition. It is this truth that also does away with certain ambiguities connected with the question of the number of the elect, which was once the subject of lively debate: the purpose of the redemption is achieved whatever the number of those who are saved, because the offense done to God is repaired by Christ alone, even if the number saved is relatively small.

CHAPTER XXXI

WORK, TECHNOLOGY AND CONTEMPLATION

210. Anthropocentrism and technology. Work as dominion over the earth and as punishment.

Modern technology differs from that of the Greco-Roman world, and depends upon precise measurement and machines; although invented in principle by the Greeks of Alexandria, machines were never adapted by them for economic production, which was at that time entirely the task of servile labor.

For thousands of years, the idea of production was linked with that of effort, thus *ponos* can mean either effort or work; it was also linked with the idea of a penalty, the biblical "sweat of the brow." The separation of these two ideas and the trend towards the elimination of effort is the ideal pursued by the whole of modern society. Modern theology has considered the problem of work more than the theology of earlier times, thanks to the enormous development of machinery, which was more or less unknown in the ancient world.

Understood at first as a help to human activity, machines have slowly reduced the amount of human effort needed for production, and are tending to eliminate it completely. The assistance provided by machines is no longer a simple addition to human strength, but is now replacing the latter altogether.

Two ideas are contained in the Catholic concept of work, drawn from the Book of Genesis: the notion of mastery over the earth, and the notion of labor as a punishment and remedy for sin. In post-conciliar theology the first of these has been enormously developed, and the domination of the earth has been turned into a fundamental duty of the human race, as a kind of

religious obedience due to God: *replete terram et subiicite eam.*[1]
The religious character of this mastering of the earth is pushed
so much that it is even called a *cooperation* in God's creative
work, and a *fulfilling,* if not indeed a *correction* of it.[2] Dominion
over the earth is something man was called to before original
sin, and that calling is not abrogated by sin; it simply acquires a
penal aspect as a result of the fall. Thus man's task of operating
upon nature has remained as part of God's original design; what
is altogether novel is the *glorification of work* by modern society.
It is indeed a paradoxical glorification; on the one hand, new
constitutions assert that civil society is based upon work,[3] while
the whole drift of social organization is aimed at reducing
work,[4] thus undermining the alleged basis of society.

211. Modern technology. Genetic engineering.

It is generally recognized that the ruling principle of contemporary society is technology, seen as a means of controlling
and transforming nature. It is Bacon's principle of the
"terminorum humani imperii prolatio ad omne possibile."[5] When
technology first developed out of magic, leaving its chrysalis
behind, Bacon and Campanella set their sights on artificially
producing rain, flying machines, changes of sex, new species of
plants, and synthetic substances that would satisfy hunger and
thirst. The only thing that they did not propose to produce mechanically was man, since they had seen that even a machine
with the appearance of consciousness would still be only a machine.

As the council noted, modern technology has "changed the
face of the earth,"[6] and has realized these fantasies of the Renais-

---

[1]   Genesis, 1:28. "Fill the earth and subdue it."

[2]   This is a new idea, and is not found in, for instance, the "Social
      Code" drawn up by the International Union of Social Studies,
      Rovigo, 1927.

[3]   For example, Article 1 of the Constitution of the Italian Republic
      states: "Italy is a republic founded on work."

[4]   In an interview with Italian television in April 1981 Lech Walesa
      said: "As a worker I would like to work as little as possible."

[5]   In the "New Atlantis," in *Opera latine reddita,* London 1638 Vol.
      I, p.375. Sir Francis Bacon (1561-1626) "The extension of the
      limits of human control to the maximum possible."

[6]   *Gaudium et Spes* 5.

sance period. The fact that rain was artificially produced during the Vietnam war to block the Ho Chi Minh trail is recognized by the treaty of 18 May 1977 between the U.S.A. and the U.S.S.R. banning meteorological warfare.[7] Thanks to the limitless growth of atomic power, artificial earthquakes are now a possibility, as is the colonization of the moon contemplated by Kepler. It would only require a further change in degree, rather than in kind, to alter the axis of the earth and change climatic zones, thus realizing Dante's hypothesis:

E se dal dritto più o men lontano
Fosse il partire, assai sarebbe manco
E giù e su dell'ordine mondano.[8]

How far all this outstrips the amazement of the men of the Renaissance, recorded in their tracts *De dignitate et potentia hominis*[9] when they saw the blue flash at the muzzle of a gun as artificial lightning, and the miniature marvels of an infant technology as a proof of the majesty of man!

O leggi rotte! ch'un sol verme sia
Re, epilogo, armonia–fin d'ogni cosa.[10]

The importance of the glorification of technology becomes all the more apparent the higher the nature that that technology sets about to transform. We now have human genetic engineering, artificial insemination, *in vitro* conception, contraceptive technology and the possible production of particular sorts of human beings; Huxley's *alpha plusses*. The general idea is that technology will lead men to a perfectly rational view of reality and thereby make them happy; powerful movements of Marxist inspiration have set about realizing this goal of a perfect organization of the earth. Their conception of rationality is not theocentric or religious, but anthropocentric and scientistic and entirely shut within this world. This trend is apparent in the writings of Alexis Carrel, even though he was a Catholic convert; he envisages a scientific process whereby ordinary children

---

[7]   Article by O. Disch in *Science et Vie*, No. 719, August 1977.
[8]   *Paradiso*, X, 19-21. "The greater the departure from the vertical, the more the arrangement of the earth would move up or down."
[9]   "On the Nobility and Power of Man."
[10] Campanella *Poesie*, Bari 1915. *De la possanza de l'uomo*, p.172. "O broken laws! That a mere worm should be the king, the epilogue, the harmony–the end of all things."

would be transformed into supermen, just as bees make queens
out of workers by giving them special food. In this instance,
modern science fantasy falls far below the level of poetic inspiration of Campanella's *Cantica* on the potentialities of human-
kind.

212. The Moon landing. False religious interpretation.

The praise of technology reached its apogee with the landing on the moon by American astronauts on 20 July 1969. The
event was certainly memorable, but could not be described as
having any particular religious importance. A comparison with
another great discovery shows just how secular an event it was.
Columbus sailed to the New World in the ship *Saint Mary*, and
the cities founded there were called *Assumption, Holy Cross, St.
Paul, Holy Savior*: the whole enterprise was *christophoric*. In
1969 the ships and the rockets that soared through space were
named after pagan deities; Apollo, Venus, Saturn; they were
launched without being blessed; what they left on the moon was
an American flag and a plate with a secular inscription.[11]

Despite the secular character of the moon landing, Paul VI
quotes Psalm 18, *Caeli enarrant gloriam Dei* in a message honoring the astronauts, and attempts to give the event a religious
significance by saying it is God who has given such powers to
men. But what the psalm says is that nature sings the glory of
God quite independently of man; to have a religious character,
the exercise of the powers man has received from God must be
consciously recognized as something God has given, but in this
instance only man got a mention.

Again, despite the obviously secular character of the moon
landing, the deputy editor of the *Osservatore Romano* tried to
force some religious significance out of it[12] by asserting that "the
display of man's scientific and technical capacities has been a
major religious, not to say Christian event." Then, realizing that

---

[11]   "Here men from Earth set foot for the first time. July 1969 A.D. We
       came in peace, on behalf of all men." The only trace of religion is
       in the dating of the year.

[12]   A theologian at the Catholic University of Milan, Don Aceti, was
       interviewed in the *Europeo* on 27 July 1969 and replied to some-
       one who contrasted the religious character of Columbus's voyage
       with the lack of religion in the moon landing, by saying that "the
       presence of man in the universe is the presence of Christ."

he had gone beyond the bounds of plausibility, he concluded: "The first explorers of the moon did not materially plant the Cross in the soil of their new conquest, but they did so spiritually." This distinction will not hold water, because man's religious instinct is expressed in signs the senses can perceive, and the Cross is the most fundamental of all Christian signs; without some sensible expression, a spiritual presence by men can be taken as representing anything you like. The Muslims could just as well say that the presence of astronauts on the moon meant the planting there of the Crescent.

Father Gino Concetti was even more ecstatic in his piece in the *Osservatore*[13] in which we read that: "*Never before* has the divine image set by the Creator within human nature shone forth in all its grandeur as it has in this marvelous undertaking." Statements like that are either poetic approximations devoid of theological precision, or else a deviation from Catholic thought. In Christ's religion, the excellence of the divine image in man shines forth in a natural manner in moral goodness, and supernaturally in holiness of life. These alone represent an intrinsic good. The height of perfection lies not in the conquest of the universe, nor in Bacon's *prolatio ad omne possibile*, nor in anything which can be put to either good or evil use by technology, but in moral heroism and in that alone, because through it alone man conforms to the divine image in which he is created, and expresses the life of the Incarnation and of the Holy Trinity. The image of the divine that Father Concetti sees in technological sophistication is something that Catholic theology has only ever recognized in the heroic virtue of the saints and above all in the humanity of the Incarnate God, with which technology has nothing to do. It is not that technical achievements are worthless, or should be ignored; every rightly oriented human activity is good. It is simply that such goods should not be allotted an importance they do not deserve.

---

[13] O.R., 25 July 1969.

213. New concept of work.
The encyclical *Laborem Exercens*.

The doctrine of work has undergone important changes in post-conciliar thought.[14] These changes affect three points, and all display a certain anthropocentric and subjectivist tendency.

Firstly, work used to be treated as a special virtue called skill or exercise or industry, but is now treated as the universal category embracing all moral activity; man is alleged to fulfill his supposedly principal duty, of dominating the earth and perfecting creation, by working. The council says: *Labore suo homo...potest creationi divinae perficiendae sociam operam praebere. Immo per laborem Deo oblatum, tenemus hominem ipsi redemptionis operi Jesu Christi consociari,*[15] *qui praecellentem labori detulit dignitatem cum in Nazareth propriis manibus operaretur.*[16] Others go further in their bold theological speculations and even say that through the triumph of technology "man's likeness to God, which was lost at the fall, is beginning to be made manifest."[17]

---

[14] The encyclical *Laborem Exercens* of 14 September 1981 states in paragraph 2 that new meanings and purposes should be found for human work.

[15] In *Laborem Exercens* this assertion is softened by the addition of the words *quodam modo*, "in a certain way." See also the speech cited in O.R., 17 May 1981.

[16] *Gaudium et Spes* 67. "By his work man...can provide assistance in perfecting divine creation. Indeed, we hold that through work offered to God man is associated with the very work of redemption done by Jesus Christ, who bestowed a particular dignity upon work when he labored with his own hands in Nazareth."

[17] The Rector of the Lateran University in *Lavoro*, the journal of the Christian-Social unionists in the Ticino, 19 December 1969. The effects of grace are here attributed to technology. There is an excessively rhapsodic exegesis of *Laborem Exercens* in the O.R. of 28 October 1981, in an article by G. Ferraro which proclaims "the paschal character of work" by which a worker is alleged to participate in and renew the mystery of the death and resurrection of Christ. Participation in His death is supposed to come from the effort involved in work (though effort is not death) and participation in the resurrection is supposed to consist in "the new world that work helps to bring about." Clearly, when one detaches words from their normal meaning and ideas from a coherent pattern, one can assert anything about anything.

Thus the whole of moral activity comes to be included in the category of work in two novel ways: first, that work is man's primary duty in God's original design; second, that work is the all embracing means whereby man creatively realizes his personality.

As to the first point, one might say that it is characteristic of the Old Testament to see man as intended to dominate the earth by means of his labor because the Old Testament has a relatively earth-bound outlook on life, is little concerned with the life of the world to come, and envisages an earthly reward for virtue and for religious practice: "If you hearken to me, you will enjoy the goods of the earth."[18] This earthly conception of man's goal is left behind in the order of grace proclaimed in the New Testament, and in comparison with the New Testament message, the present lauding of work can be seen as a regressive tendency. There is not a trace of the glorification of work in Christ's preaching, which lifts the whole perspective towards the kingdom of heaven. It is true that God's kingdom begins to germinate here in this world by means of moral goodness, but it transcends all that mortal hearts can imagine: in comparison with that kingdom, the things of the world are so much refuse and dross.[19] The lauding of work as the universal category for all man's spiritual activity is a moving back towards a theology that the New Testament left behind, when it firmly subordinated the conquest of this earth to the quest for the kingdom of heaven.

214. Christ as a working man. Critique.

The depiction of Christ as a worker, *pertinens ad opificum ordinem* is also a novelty.[20] This presentation depends on Matthew 13:55 where He is called "the son of a carpenter" and Mark 6:3 where He is Himself called "a carpenter." But the scriptural foundations here are weak. The descriptions come from the mouths of the people of Nazareth, who had known Jesus as working with Joseph and who therefore continued to refer to Him as they had known Him, even though He was no

---

[18] Isaiah, 1:19.
[19] Cf. I Corinthians, 4:13.
[20] *Laborem Exercens*, 26 "Belonging to the working class." There was much amazement when Archbishop Montini met metal workers beneath a statue of Christ as a workman with a hammer and sickle.

longer doing that sort of work. In fact the Gospel contains no evidence that Christ was ever a workman. In the infancy narratives, which provide our information about his hidden life, no emphasis is put on any work Jesus may have done; on the contrary, even though He must have assisted Joseph as a boy, we can see from Luke 2:46 that his life was largely occupied by reading, reflection and intellectual activity. At twelve years of age He appeared in the Temple and sat "among the doctors listening to them and questioning them." Any work He did as a carpenter was done before beginning his messianic ministry; He stopped working as soon as He left Nazareth "to do and to teach." If Jesus can be put into any category, it is that of a mendicant or beggar who has given up all his goods.[21] He had nowhere to lay his head, and his disciples plucked heads of grain from other people's fields to feed themselves.[22] Jesus' state of life during his preaching of the Gospel is not that of a worker, but of someone who, like the apostles, has given up everything and taken on a complete poverty, which is a higher vocation than working.

The ideas of a "Gospel of Work" and of "Christ the Worker" are therefore unjustified. The incongruity of such titles was felt by Pius XII when, in order to emphasize the dignity of work, he instituted a feast of St. Joseph the Worker, not of Christ as worker. There can be no equality between a title drawn from a laborer's efforts and one drawn from a divine and human kingship, recognized by Pius XI in the feast of Christ the King.[23] Furthermore, as even *Laborem Exercens* recognizes, Christ utters not one word recommending work, but He does condemn that worrying about material well-being upon which so much work is based.[24]

---

[21] Cf. II Corinthians, 8:9. Lagrange says in his commentary on Luke 21:37 that the word used to describe Jesus' overnight stays "implies the condition of someone who is not at home."

[22] Matthew, 8:20 and 12:1.

[23] In 1960 in the suburbs of Rome a parish was dedicated to Christ the Divine Workman. But the Church has only ever celebrated saints under religious titles such as confessor, doctor, martyr etc. Pius XII's title for St. Joseph is a novelty.

[24] Cf. Matthew, 6:25-34.

215. Work as man's self-realization. Critique.

In the new view, work is presented as the very essence of all virtuous activity and is alleged to include intellectual pursuits and thus to embrace the whole of a person's existence. Every kind of virtue is attributed to work, but work loses its own character as a special virtue and becomes a fundamental structure of life. It is seen as both a transforming of the world and a self-realization by man, as well as an exercise of man's own creativity.[25] John Paul II has reiterated that all activity is work and that man discovers the meaning of life through it.[26]

The idea of creation, which has been examined in paragraph 198, cannot strictly speaking be applied to technological discoveries. As Dessauer showed in his *Philosophy of Technology* "the creation of technology actually consists in bringing down into the realm of sensible perception those forms that already exist in another 'kingdom.' The entirety of technical possibilities lies waiting to be found; the inventor does not produce them from within himself, nor does the human spirit generate them. This entirety can be described as a kingdom."[27]

The modern view holds that work is designed to achieve mastery over the earth and the perfecting of creation, but it also allots work a high moral character, asserting that through work

---

[25] This glorification of the creativity of work is rather peculiar in a system in which subjective participation by the worker in his own work is continually decreasing. There was a time when individual artisans produced all, or most, or a large part, of their own work. The contribution made by a factory worker today is over in half a minute and represents only a tiny fraction of the final product. To increase the personal meaning of work, a larger proportion of an individual product would have to be produced by an individual worker. Meaninglessness increases as the part played by machinery expands. In his speech to the International Labor Organization in Geneva on 16 June 1982, the Pope addressed the problem of the relationship between man and machine, but he referred the solution, somewhat surprisingly, to technology. For machines see paragraph 210.

[26] One suspects that the Marxist notion of "production" underlies this view. Marxists talk of "intellectual production" as well as the production of material objects, subsuming both sorts of activity in a single category. [Translator's note.]

[27] Friedrich Dessauer, *Philosophy of Technology*, Italian translation, Brescia 1933, pp.65 and 69.

man *seipsum ut hominem perfecit, immo quodam modo magis homo evadit;*[28] as the Pope says elsewhere, without work "man not only cannot feed himself, he cannot *realize himself* either, that is he cannot reach his true dimensions." Going on to state what these true dimensions are, the Pope says man "can reach his salvation by work."[29]

This morality of work is not a new teaching if it means that work has the limited value inherent in any virtuous activity; but it *is* new if it means that work is commensurate with the whole sphere of virtuous living, as if there were no particular virtues such as religion, justice, charity and so on. Inasmuch as each virtue implies an upright will, each one implies the presence of all the others, and thus perfects a man and brings about his salvation. This morality of work would be a novelty if it meant that work is the essence of moral virtue and that without work a man cannot attain his destiny as man. Pain and suffering, which are passive rather than active states, as well as the prayer and contemplation so highly valued in the Christian tradition, are part of truly human living, but they do not come under the heading of work. The Christian religion teaches that a man should deny himself, not realize himself.[30] This self-renunciation, be it noted, is brought about by conforming oneself to the law, that is, to the will of God, and is not a self-annihilation, but the cutting off of egoism and self-love. If one wanted to persist in the catachresis, or misuse of words, one could say that by this conforming, man fulfills his own nature and realizes himself, but he does not do so directly and intentionally (if he were to, the whole proceeding would be anthropocentric); he attains that end indirectly and secondarily. *Quaerite primum regnum Dei et iustitiam eius et haec omnia*

---

[28] *Laborem Exercens*, 9. Man "perfects himself as man, and indeed in a certain way becomes more of a man."

[29] O.R., 21-22 September 1982. Taken strictly, these remarks deny the legitimacy of a life of prayer and contemplation. Contemplatives, who certainly do not work, would be unable to reach their true human dimensions.

[30] Cf. Matthew, 16:24: *Abneget semetipsum.* "Let him renounce himself and take up his cross."

(including self-realization) *adicientur vobis,* and again: *Qui enim voluerit animam suam salvam facere, perdet eam.*[31]

216. The distinction between the speculative and the practical.

The undervaluing of purely speculative activity is a further consequence of the modern view.[32] The view held by the pagan philosophers has been stood on its head: they tended to despise manual labor, while we despise all speculation that does not have some utilitarian side effect. When he saw the mathematicians of Syracuse trying to invent machines, Plato accused them of trying to degrade their science by abandoning the contemplation of ideal reality. Aristotle justified slavery as necessary in one part of the human race, in order that another part could live a truly human, that is contemplative, life. The despising of work has been replaced in modern thought by the despising of purely theoretical activity, and people expect all scientific speculation to be directed towards our mastery over the external world, that is, towards technological improvements; even aes-

---

[31] Matthew, 6:33: "Seek ye first the Kingdom of God and his justice and all these things will be added unto you" and Luke, 9:24 "He who seeks to save his life will lose it."

[32] The equating of these two sorts of human activity is implied in paragraph 16 of *Laborem Exercens: Labor, multiplicem secundum huius vocis sensum, officium est sive obligatio.* "Work, in its many senses, is a duty or an obligation." Work and intellectual activity are put in the same category. One can indeed say that work is a duty for mankind; but not for individual men. Old people, children, the sick, the invalid, have no duty to work. The duty to work is incumbent on mankind as a species, as is the duty of procreation; it does not bind each individual. This idea underlies the foundation of the mendicant orders of friars and was defended by St. Thomas and St. Bonaventure and attacked by William of St. Amour, who held that the friars should perform manual work to support themselves, in virtue of their vow of poverty. In his *Quodlibet* VII, art. 17 and 18, Aquinas replies that the mendicant friars give themselves to intellectual activities and are therefore dispensed from the duty of manual work, provided they have someone who will give them sustenance. William of St. Amour's views would have meant the end of the mendicant orders, and were condemned by Pope Alexander IV.

thetic activities are affected by this utilitarian outlook.[33] Catholic philosophy has always divided life into two broad types: the contemplative life, in which internal activity predominates, and the active life, in which external activity is the main occupation. These two sorts of life are symbolized by Rachel and Liah in the Old Testament and Mary and Martha in the new.[34]

A form of life that is contemplative, or theoretic or intellectual, is made up of immanent activities, whether of the intellect or of the will, which spring from and are directed to the person involved, without producing anything in the exterior world. The active life is made up of *transitive* activities, which spring from the person but produce an exterior effect by modifying things around about. It is obvious that when one takes the transforming of this world as the goal of human existence, contemplative activity will lose its meaning. A contemplative life should not be confused with a life of academic study in the strict sense, because merely having the time to watch and be curious, and to cast one's eye upon the spectacle of nature, or upon some human event is also contemplation; in Pythagoras's image, it is behaving like the man who observes what is going on in the market place, without buying or selling. Another confusion to avoid is thinking that physical exertion and sweat is necessarily work; these occur in playing games, but games are not a form of work.

Work and contemplation are not merely distinct, they are actually incompatible. St. Thomas writes: *Manifestum est quod vita activa impedit contemplativam, inquantum impossibile est quod aliquid simul occupetur circa exteriores actiones et divinae contemplationi vacet.*[35] *Otium* or leisure, which is a state of being

---

[33] Mediaeval artists, who were often anonymous, would create beautiful objects not for the service of man, but so that they could proclaim the glory of God. Thus it was that they often placed their statues in the vaults of cathedrals, away from the light, though they were thus invisible to men, for whose benefit they had not been made.

[34] Be it noted that these two types of life are distinguished by being given predominantly, not exclusively, to one kind of activity or another. No contemplative life is devoid of some exercise of the active life and no active life is without some element of contemplation.

[35] *Summa Theologica*, II,II,q.182,a.3. "It is obvious that the active life impedes the contemplative, inasmuch as it is impossible for some-

free from bodily exertion and being given to the exercise of the intellect, is incompatible with work, which is occupation or business over external matters. This incompatibility is attested in ancient times by the distinction between freemen and slaves. It is also recognized by common consent and by language itself. When he reaches a certain age, a youth decides whether to go to work or to study, that is, whether his talents call him to the workplace or to a school, that is to "leisure," which is what the Greek word *schole* means. The distinctions in our society, and not in ours alone, turn on the difference between a contemplative life and a life tied to work.

217. Superiority of contemplation to work.

The superiority of the contemplative dimension over a working life is a commonplace of Christian philosophy and its greatest expression was the perfect poverty practiced by St. Francis of Assisi, which launched a great religious movement while also causing serious doctrinal controversies. The combination of the two lives, which St. Thomas taught was most suitable to our present mortal condition,[36] is fundamental to the Benedictine rule, which civilized Europe, but this does not alter the fact that the superior part in the mixture is the contemplative element; as Jesus said: *Maria optimam partem elegit.*[37]

St. Thomas gives many reasons for the excellence of contemplation[38] but the two principal ones are these. First: contemplation, that is intellectual activity, is fitting for man because of his own nature which is constituted by an incorporeal and immortal intellect which is intended to know the truth. Second: contemplation is an activity which continues in eternal life, whereas work is limited to a man's earthly sojourn. The excellence of contemplation corresponds with the repugnance[39] man feels for the exertion and pain which belong to work, inasmuch

---

one to be occupied with exterior activities and at the same time to give himself to divine contemplation."

[36] More precisely, St. Thomas said that contemplation and the passing on of its fruits through teaching, was superior to contemplation alone. [Translator's note.]

[37] Luke, 10:42 "Mary has chosen the better part."

[38] *Summa Theologica*, II,II,q.182,a.2.

[39] G. Rensi's pages on this matter in his *L'irrazionale, il lavoro, l'amore*, Milan 1923, pp.195ff. are worth noting.

as it has the character of a punishment. What man desires is contemplation, and it is given to him as a reward for his labor.[40]

The encyclical *Laborem Exercens* gives little attention to the contrast between intellectual and physical activities; indeed it groups the exertions of builders, metal workers and miners together with the intellectual work of scientific researchers and those who organize the life of a society.[41] The encyclical notes that the two forms of life have a common "tension of forces that is sometimes very heavy to bear," but it fails to distinguish between one sort of force and another, that is between predominantly intellectual and predominantly corporeal activities. This equating of work properly so called and work in the broad sense occurs more than once. After having presented Jesus as a workman, the encyclical goes on to list the various callings mentioned in Scripture and lumps manual workers with philosophers; and miners and barrow men with historians and those who interpret prophecies and fathom mysteries.[42]

---

[40] The praise of *otium*, or leisure, as the spirit's great goal is frequent in pagan authors, as for example Horace in Ode II, XVI. But Christian authors have been no less emphatic on the matter: Petrarch, *De otio religioso*.

[41] *Laborem Exercens*, 9.

[42] *Laborem Exercens*, 26. Cf. Ecclesiasticus, 39:1-5.

CHAPTER XXXII

CIVILIZATION AND SECONDARY CHRISTIANITY

218. The perfecting of nature and of persons.

The denial of the specific character and importance of the intellectual or contemplative life, and the accompanying glorification of work by which man changes the world, manipulates nature and directs everything towards his own control of reality, contains in principle a new civilization having man as its centre and goal. Modern theology cannot of course deny the transcendent goal of human existence, but it lets it fade away before the new found primacy of technological development, and the mastering of the here and now.

It is generally admitted that in modern culture there has been a disjunction between material and spiritual development, with the material outstripping the spiritual and leaving it behind. On the other hand, there is the commonly held but mistaken view that since technology is based upon an ever increasing knowledge of the material world, technological development represents an amazing development of man's intellect, that is, his spiritual side. It is this confusion in terms that led to the extravagant celebration of technology as a triumph of the spirit, that we have noted in connection with the moon landing.[1] The real distinction that needs to be drawn is not between matter and intellect, since, as we have said, even technical discoveries are the result of a highly developed intelligence. The crucial distinction is rather between a culture that aims at the perfecting of *nature*, including man's own nature, and a culture that

---

[1] See paragraph 212.

aims at the perfecting of the human *person*.[2] Human nature
consists of two .parts, the higher and dominant element being
the personal part, that is the spiritual soul in which man's intellect and will operate, and which is the seat of the virtues. Man
can perfect some part of his nature without perfecting his person. Thus he can improve his health, or physical dexterity, or
his knowledge of the world about, or his power to effect material changes in that world, without thereby perfecting his person, that is, without making any moral progress; as noted earlier, it is a sad but generally admitted fact that he can make great
strides in the material developments that are held today to
constitute *progress*, and be nonetheless slothful and corrupt
when it comes to his spiritual development, that is, his growth
as a person. The moral element is set aside, and the improvement of the material conditions of man's life on earth is pursued
eagerly by every available means. Modern culture is thus dominated by the perfecting of nature as it exists in and for man, but
leaves the personal element in him undeveloped.

It is difficult to establish the precise character of the relationship between progress with regard to nature, and the moral
progress of persons, but in any case it remains true that the personal principle is the ruling one in man and that everything else
must be governed by it, so that the progress of persons remains
unimpeded by developments with regard to nature. The con-
founding of a person with his nature is what gives rise to somatolatry, the glorification of sport, the abstract claiming of rights
without reference to moral duties, the worship of mechanical
inventions, the unfounded admiration of riches and power, in
short the pursuit of the Earthly City, devoted to unfolding the
full power of human nature in every field.

219. The City of the Devil, the City of Man, the City of God.

Two classes of men are portrayed in the book of Genesis.
One consists of the "famous men who are great in this world,"
the race of giants, the founders of cities, the bold, the conquerors: their goal is the development and expansion of human
things. The other class, the sons of God, aim at perfection as

---

[2]   I am here following Rosmini, in his *Antropologia sopranaturale*,
     Book II, Chapter 6, Article 10. National edition, Vol. XXVII,
     pp.308ff.

persons, that is, they will righteousness for men, and devotion to God absolutely and unconditionally and are concerned only incidentally and indirectly with the mastery of the earth. In the Gospel, these two classes are called the *children of this world* and *the children of light*, and the misdirection of energies which is so striking a fact of modern civilization is mysteriously portrayed in the saying that the children of darkness "are more prudent than the children of light, but *in their own kind*," that is, in the things of the world and in them alone.[3]

In his great work, the *City of God*, St. Augustine depicts the history of the human race as an intertwining of two cities, one theocentric even to the despising of this world, the other anthropocentric even to the despising of God. The former corresponds to the class of men who seek perfection as persons, the latter to those who seek the perfection of nature and of themselves as part of it. The latter are earthly through and through, the former earthly *in transitu* and heavenly *in termino*.[4] But the despising of God Augustine attributes to the earthly city is not always of the same kind. Some men positively exclude man's heavenly destiny from their view of life and attack the very idea of it as something inimical to the realization of mankind's true destiny here on earth. These are the men who are today attempting to establish an atheist civilization. Such is the true *civitas diaboli*[5] in an Augustinian sense, built on blood and lies and aiming at the extermination of Christianity. But there are other men, perhaps a larger group, who while not openly attacking the idea of a heavenly destiny for man, never strive to attain it themselves, and who push the whole of human society towards the ideal of a purely this-worldly perfection, or *Diesseitigkeit*. Such is the *civitas hominis*[6] that stands, as it were, between the other two. It detaches human good from moral good, that is, the well-being of humanity as part of nature from the well-being of the human person. It directs everything towards worldly progress, and takes mastery over this world as being the whole goal of human existence. But the Christian religion

---

3 Luke, 16:8.
4 "By the way" and "in aim."
5 "City of the Devil."
6 "City of Man."

teaches that man's whole goal is the service and enjoyment of
God: *hoc est enim omnis homo.*[7]

So there are three cities: the one directed towards a transcendent end, which it desires above all else; the one that attacks
that end and loves the world above all else; and lastly the one
that merely ignores the transcendent altogether. These three are
intertwined, and each runs its own, often indiscernible, course
through the world's history. Both the *civitas hominis,* towards
which the post-conciliar Church has turned in order to baptize
it and to be in turn unbaptized by it, and the *civitas diaboli* that
the post-conciliar Church attacks though in a feeble manner,
bring about a divorce between a man and his own soul by proclaiming the independence of what is in fact dependent.

220. Secondary Christianity.
Confusion between religion and civilization.

The *civitas diaboli* rejects Christianity; the *civitas hominis*
takes it as a fact of life, and assimilates it into itself, by treating
it as something that can be useful in achieving earthly purposes,
rather than something that orientates all earthly things towards
heaven in an absolute fashion. But given the fact that Christianity is either an absolute orientation of that sort, or else is
nothing at all, it follows that the merely partial acceptance of
Christian values by modern anthropocentric culture amounts to
a veiled rejection of Christianity. The post-conciliar Church has
a tendency to include all the values of the *civitas hominis* within
the ambit of the Christian religion. Frequent use is made of
such expressions as "human and Christian values" or "the
Church promotes human values" or "the Church has man as its
centre" or "religion makes man more truly man" and so forth.
Setting aside the solecism of qualifying a noun like "man," with
a comparative such as "more," this confusing way of speaking
blurs the distinction between religion and civilization; behind
this Giobertian philosophy[8] civilization is being regarded as the
primary effect of Catholicism. This is in substance the prevailing post-conciliar view, even though it is endlessly repeated that

---

[7]   Ecclesiasticus, 12:13. "This is the whole of man." [Cf. Cardinal
       Newman's lecture on "The Social State of Catholic Countries" in
       "Difficulties of Anglicans." Translator's note.]
[8]   Vincenzo Gioberti (1801-1852), Italian priest, political philosopher
       and nationalist. [Translator's note.]

Catholicism is not identified with any one culture, but acts as a leaven to them all. It is indeed true that religion has a civilizing effect, and the whole history of the Church bears witness to the fact; but Christianity does not primarily aim at advancing civilization, that is, at achieving an earthly kind of perfection. Modern society is pervaded by a spirit of independence and self-sufficiency: the world rejects dependence on anything other than itself. Faced with this fact, the Church seems to be afraid of being further rejected, as it already has been by a large part of the human race. Therefore it sets about watering down its own characteristic set of values and playing up the things it has in common with the world: all the world's causes are thus taken up by the Church. The Church offers its assistance to the world and is attempting to put itself at the head of human progress.

This is a tendency that arose in the nineteenth century and I have elsewhere given it the name of *secondary Christianity*. In the eighteenth century, unbelieving philosophers had denied the rationality or reasonableness of Catholicism and had hoped for its destruction, as something harmful to civilization and maintained only by *fabricateurs de divinités*,[9] but in the nineteenth century Christianity was seen as the supreme system of *human* values, as expressing the ideal of human perfection; but at the same time its transcendent and supernatural character was denied; the Word had become incarnate, but the Word in question was Hegelian Reason revealing itself in historical becoming. The reality is that anyone who denies the supernaturalness of Christianity, that is, who denies God's work in human souls by means of grace and denies the supernatural destiny of man, is abolishing real Christianity and reducing it to a means to an end in this world, even though he may still maintain that Christianity is an excellent thing. Secondary Christianity thinks it can maintain the ideal of Christianity while denying its status as a revealed and mysterious body of wisdom; it seeks to pluck its earthly fruits but will not accept the whole fruit that it produces. Secondary Christianity is what Benedetto Croce was talking about in his famous essay *Perché non possiamo non dirci cristiani*,[10] but real Christianity cannot but reject his view. That view grasps Christianity only under its earthly aspect, and reveres it, thus disfigured, as the foundation of human civiliza-

---

[9] "Manufacturers of gods."

[10] "Why we cannot but call ourselves Christians." [Benedetto Croce (1866-1952), Italian Hegelian philosopher. Translator's note.]

tion. Christianity is indeed a great tree, so fruitful that it eventually produces fruits that are, as it were, detached from the tree, but these have no value from the strictly religious point of view. In Manzoni's view, nothing could be falser than the idea of secondary Christianity, despite the fact that Carducci[11] in his speech at Lecco, and Italian Idealists in general, thought they could detect such a view underlying Manzoni's *Inni Sacri.*[12] Secondary Christianity, which some have also called *complementary* Christianity, inasmuch as Christianity is viewed as complementing this world's values, was described by Manzoni as reducing an end to a means, reducing what is *per se* to what is *per accidens.* "The Gospel as a means to an end," he exclaims, "the Gospel, which is unthinkable except as the sole end in itself!"[13] Manzoni lists the useful functions Christianity fulfills in this world: its commandments to be patient and charitable, its civilizing effect, the preservation of literature in the barbarian period, its inspiring beauties and its comforting hopes. Christianity, he says, is rightly praised for all these effects, which it truly has produced, since it is in its nature to foster order, culture and civilization; but, he says, it would be a grave mistake to identify Christianity with these effects, which are the least of its works, are merely worldly, and are producible by other causes, while simultaneously overlooking what is most important about Christianity, namely its essence, its inner workings and its supernatural end.[14]

---

[11] Giosue Carducci (1836-1907). Lapsed Jewish Italian poet of pagan and nationalist inspiration. [Translator's note.]

[12] "Sacred Hymns."

[13] For this line of thought, see *Morale Cattolica*, National Edition, Vol. III, pp.83ff. For the quotation, Vol. II, p.478.

[14] The 1974 conference on the Rome diocese's charitable and social work turned out to be a striking display of secondary Christianity; all sociology and politics, relief, housing, hospitals, schools, buildings. Not a jot of religion, but plenty of Marxist flavoring, and a condemnation of private business and professional activity, and a proposal that the Church should hand over all its goods to the state, in order to become more independent. O.R., 15 February 1974 and I.C.I., No. 451, 1 March 1974, p.24.

221. Critique of Secondary Christianity.
Theological error. Eudaemonological error.

The specific flaw in secondary Christianity which it shares in common with the *civitas hominis*, is its setting aside of the transcendent. This is the sin which St. Augustine calls *inadvertentia* and St. Thomas calls *inconsideratio*,[15] and which they both say was the sin of the angels who fell. This ignoring of our heavenly goal turns religion upside down by reversing its perspectives: *habemus hic manentem civitatem nec futuram inquirimus.*[16] Therefore: ultimate vision merely earthly, reduction of Christianity to a mere means to an end, apotheosis of civilization. This is to deny the "either or" the Gospel presents, and to replace it with a sort of "both and" that combines heaven and earth in a compound, in which the world is the predominant element that gives the character to the whole.

In a famous passage of his *Esprit de Lois*[17] Montesquieu points out the strange character of the Christian religion, which seems to have no other object apart from happiness in another life, but which makes us happy in this life nonetheless. But the contrast between the two lives does not go unnoticed, inasmuch as they imply two diverse conceptions of man's ultimate end. *Les deux mondes. Celui-ci gâte l'autre et l'autre gâte celui-ci. C'est trop de deux mondes. Il n'en fallait qu'un.*[18] Leopardi is just as pointed in his contrasting of the world and the Christian religion, when he brutally confronts the Christian ideal and the ideals of this world, alleging that the former constitutes a radical denial of the present life, the only life that actually exists.[19]

These antitheses presuppose that this earthly life is man's ultimate end, and they collapse if one presupposes instead that this life is simply a means to the ultimate end. Two ultimate ends are an impossibility.[20] When earthly life is reduced to a preparation and prelude to a life beyond this world, the sharp-

---

[15] "Inadvertence" and "inattention."

[16] The opposite of Hebrews 13:14, i.e., "Here we have an abiding city, nor do we look for any future one."

[17] Montesquieu, *Esprit des Lois*, Book XXIV, Ch. 3.

[18] "The two worlds. This one spoils the other and the other spoils this. Two worlds are too many. Only one was needed." Montesquieu, *Pensées*, Paris 1938, p. 77.

[19] Leopardi, *Zibaldone*, 2381.

[20] *Summa Theologica*, I,II,q.1,a.4 and 7.

ness of the contrast between the two worlds abates. Life in time can then be harmonized as an integral part of a larger whole and can be appreciated as a symbol, that is, as a fragment connected to that greater reality.

The eudaemonological error in secondary Christianity is no less significant than its error in theology. It asserts that the enjoyment of the worthy goods of this world is to be had more surely, genuinely and abundantly with the aid of Christianity than without it. But the idea of a Church that congratulates the human race on its temporal well-being is at odds with the Gospel, which contrasts heaven and earth or, more precisely, considers earth as relative to heaven, and heaven as absolute with regard to earth and relative with regard to God. The goal of this life is the life to come, and the goal of that life is God. Hence the excellence of the evangelical counsels,[21] which represent the sacrifice of earth to heaven, and are therefore incompatible with modern society, as eighteenth century rationalists and nineteenth century anti-religious governments so clearly saw. The true criterion by which the Christian religion should be judged is not its usefulness to society: Christianity is related in many significant ways to culture, but none of these relations is the essence of the Christian religion.

222. Church and society in the post-conciliar period.

The Church today finds itself in a cleft stick. On one hand it claims not to be identifiable with any particular society, and in doing so it is faithful to its own tradition; but on the other hand it wants to act as a ferment in all societies and push them towards a unified worldwide society which, allegedly, cannot exist without Christianity and which will give rise to a new world that is more just and more human. One could hardly say: more Christian.

The impossibility of simultaneously holding the anthropocentric and theocentric positions can only be disguised by forgetting the distinctive nature of distinct things, and by presenting some common basis upon which all things rest, so that Christianity and society can be subsumed into a single reality contained in that underlying element. It is the same metaphysical error that crops up in the much quoted formula Tertullian

---

[21] We have noted the decline in the following of them in paragraphs 140-45.

uses: *anima naturaliter christiana.*[22] As we have already said, there can be no such thing; people become Christians, they are never born such; the formula itself is contradictory since it means a *naturally supernatural* soul. This is the very same error that is now being made in equating the world and the Gospel; it is as if the Church were afraid of presenting the Gospel's divine values to the world unless they were somehow synonymous with the values of this world. There is endless talk about "Christian and human values," or worse still "human and Christian values"; there is a great desire to be faithful both to the world and to God. But that is not possible: *Nemo potest duobus dominis servire.*[23]

Let us say it again, the Church is of itself a *sanctifying* body not a *civilizing* body, and its activity is immediately directed to persons not to societies. But the post-conciliar Church, even its liturgy, talks about a new world, a free and just society, instead of just men renewed by the Holy Spirit. In this regard the Church is regressing. It is returning to the Old Testament, in which the people as a whole are saved or lost, women are saved through the circumcision of the other half of the human race, and the salvation looked for is quite earthly.

It is interesting to note that even in the Bible, civilization goes off on its own course: the first men named as founders of cities are Cain and the Cainites, while the inventor of metal working is Tubalcain, who came of the same fratricidal stock.

223. Catholicism and Jesuitism.

Until the present decline set in, the Society of Jesus was for centuries regarded by both Catholics and their enemies as one of the most authentic expressions of Catholicism and as the champion of the Roman Church. The great speculative theological school of Bellarmine and Suarez, the contributions made to positive theology by Petavius and the Bollandists, the missions in India, China and Japan, the extraordinary creation of the Reductions in Paraguay that lasted a century and a half, the leading role in education, the long struggle against royal absolutism and later against the liberal state, the splendor of holiness, of doctrine and of creativity, all render the famous Society one of the most imposing phenomena in religious history. The

---

[22] Tertullian, *Apologeticus*, 17. "A naturally Christian soul."
[23] Matthew, 6:24. "No man can serve two masters."

Jesuits infused a powerful new life into the Church and set about to organize the whole human race, and direct the whole earth towards heaven; indeed they aimed to subordinate all fields of learning and every branch of social life to that end. There was always a theocentric aim to their activity, but in the search for a dialectical harmony between the two worlds, which is always difficult to find, the Jesuits did from time to time tend to make Christianity a friend to human nature, inasmuch as it is good and from God, rather than to struggle against human nature, inasmuch as it is corrupted and recalcitrant.

In those circumstances, casuistry, which is a legitimate and necessary part of moral theology, sometimes slid into laxism. The latter is a tendency to remove the difference between vice and virtue, and to cover everything in a cloak of excuses, intended to make the way of salvation as easy as possible. I do not deny that the Jesuits' outlook was sometimes colored by this dangerous tendency, but it would be untrue to say that they ever adopted the ethos of secondary Christianity. The Jesuits' approach did indeed overestimate the part played by man's free will in the process of salvation, allow subjective opinion too large a say in making moral choices, lean in favor of human weakness, thus undermining the grace that comes to its aid, and did, lastly, ease the demands of Christian asceticism. Because they were so keenly aware of the antagonism between Christianity and the world, the Jesuits came to men's aid by trying to soften that antagonism and make life more easy and pleasant. Nonetheless, the Jesuits were never in any doubt about the absolutely transcendent nature of man's last end, and it was to facilitate the attainment of that end that they made such ambitious attempts to organize human life and society and so to assure the world's salvation. This outlook has something in common with the *utopia* of Plato's ideal societies and with what I have called the realistic *eutopia* conceived by Campanella. All three aim to subordinate earth to heaven.

224. The myth of the Grand Inquisitor.

Dostoyevski's tale of the Grand Inquisitor, in *The Brothers Karamazov*, is thus a caricature of the Jesuit ideal. The Inquisitor supports secondary Christianity in its most extreme form. In his view, the organization of the world and the direction of consciences have been rightly put in the hands of the few who have the biblical "knowledge of good and evil." They know that the idea of a life to come is a lie and a vain imagining, but they persuade men to believe in it in order to make them happy on this earth, by living and dying comfortably in a false hope that ends in an eternal void. The Grand Inquisitor upbraids Christ for having refused the kingdom of this world offered him by the devil, and for upsetting present attempts to perfect an earthly kingdom for mankind, by preaching his message of suffering and sacrifice.

The price the Grand Inquisitor demands is that men should hand over their souls and their freedom to their rulers, so as to be made happy by them; they receive in exchange, as Spitteler says in his *Prometheus and Epimetheus,* "*ein Gewissen, das wird dich lehren "Heit" und "Keit," und dich sicher leiten auf gerade Wegen.*"[24] In advancing the tale of the Grand Inquisitor, Dostoyevski was attempting an implicit caricature of the Jesuit ideal. The inspiration in this line of reasoning seems to have been the Jesuit Reductions, or colonies for the Indians, in Paraguay, which are the most perfect expression of a Jesuit inspired society, and in which social organization was directed towards our heavenly goal. As for their moral theories, the Jesuits want men to treat the transcendent God as a friend. And what is wrong with that: is He man's enemy?

---

[24] "A knowledge that will teach you "Hood" and "Ship" (e.g., brotherhood, friendship), i.e., abstract qualities, and lead you safely on the running path." The meaning is confusion of thought by application of abstract ideas. [Translator's note.]

CHAPTER XXXIII

DEMOCRACY IN THE CHURCH

225. The principles of 1789 and the Church.

Secondary Christianity, that is, Christianity regarded as something belonging to this world and useful for worldly purposes, began in the huge upheaval in France that engendered modern secular society. The antagonism between the revolution and the Christian religion was clearly recognized at first, but was later disguised by a benign interpretation of revolutionary principles and a weakening or adjusting of the true principles of Christianity. The revolution has provided a perfect example of words being detached from the principles they represent, and thereby acquiring a weak or equivocal meaning. The adoption of the rhetoric of secondary Christianity became a way of preserving Christianity, by securing recognition as part of the new system. The ideas of liberty, equality and fraternity are viewed by some people in the light of the ideology from which they sprang, while other people take them in isolation or even attach them to a different ideology altogether. Slogans detached from the principles they originally expressed, and reattached to another body of thought, are necessarily very ambiguous things. Liberty, equality and fraternity originally had a naturalistic, humanistic and immanentist meaning; a religiously acceptable interpretation has been foisted upon them since.

Apart from members of the French clergy who took the revolutionary oath to support the schismatic national Church, the first famous person to give a Christianizing interpretation to the revolution's ideals seems to have been Pius VII, while still bishop of Imola, and his remarks are often quoted.[1] Nonethe-

---

[1] Christmas sermon in 1798: "The democratic form of government adopted among us; no, it is not opposed to the maxims of the Gospel: it requires in fact all the sublime virtues which can only be learnt in the school of Jesus Christ."

less, each of the three revolutionary slogans is ambiguous.
Equality is a philosophical and theological truth, if it is held to
apply to human nature and its redemption. Liberty is not
merely a product of Christianity, but its very essence, if it is understood as the liberation of man from service to anyone other
than God. Fraternity is an outstanding feature of the Christian
ethos, if it is founded upon the Gospel commandment to love
God, and our neighbor for God's sake, and not upon the intrinsic excellence of man himself.[2] But it is quite obvious that in
the context of the ideology of 1789, the three principles constitute an autonomous and self-sufficient good, devoid of any axiological reference to God. This fundamental clash between
dependence on God and independence of Him is often ignored;
but worse still, the confusion often goes as far as believing that
the principles of 1789 are "the substance of Christianity" and
that "the Church was slow to take up their defense," slow, that
means, to recognize its own substance. Yet this is what the
French bishops have asserted.[3] All the Christian Democrat parties explicitly or implicitly adopt the declaration of the rights of
man, of 1789, and the United Nations' declaration on the same
subject.[4]

226. Change in doctrine concerning democracy. Passage from a species to a genus.

In his Christmas message for 1944, Pius XII drew a contrast between democracy and dictatorship: he recalled the sor-
rows and outrages that Europe was experiencing at that period,
and said that democracy was a necessary condition for peace
between peoples, for the restoration of authority and for the
respecting of the divine image in man. The Pope did not say
that popular representation is essential for every just political
order, but he did say it was essential for democracy. But then,
having touched lightly on the traditional doctrine that democracy is one species of political organization but not the very ge-

[2] See paragraph 169.
[3] Document of the French bishops, published in *La Croix*, 8 December 1981.
[4] See, for example, the French Christian Democrats, speaking
through their president when interviewed in *Itinéraires*, No.270,
p.71.

nus of all political life,[5] he launched that change that post-conciliar thought has turned into an accepted nostrum, namely that participation by all individuals in the government of the community is part of natural justice, and that in consequence monarchy, which is the exercise by one person of the right to govern society in accordance with the requirements of justice, ceases to be a legitimate species or form of government, and is to be regarded as illegitimate on the sole ground that it is at odds with an allegedly obligatory popular system.

It is worth noting in passing the enormous abuse of the word *democracy* that has now become common: every conceivable sort of existing government, *de jure* or *de facto*, legitimate or illegitimate, claims to be democratic. But the main point to be made here is that there has been a change in the Church's political philosophy whereby one species of government, namely democracy, has come to be treated as the sole legitimate form of civil organization.[6]

It is true that authority, which is a right to direct and to make rules, should be distributed among the different members of society, whether in families, or within a single society, or within the family of nations as a whole. Pius XII teaches that without this distribution of authority throughout society, the bulk of the population remains an unstructured mass, and that it can only be formed into a true people by some such organization. But modern democratic theory implies that *everyone* should form an opinion about the common good *as a whole*, and about the means that should be used to attain it. Consequently, given that it is impossible for everyone to govern society as a whole, democratic theory necessarily involves a representative system whereby one person's will is held to be represented by somebody else's.

In the traditional doctrine, a judgment about the merits of a democratic system depended upon the historical circumstances affecting a particular society; what used to be taught was

---

5   Pius XII returned to the theme of democracy in his message to the ACLI (Catholic Association of Italian Workers) on 1 May 1955, emphasizing the principle of the equal worth of all members of society, but pointing out that equality is useless if the organs of the state and public officials behave in an arbitrary way.

6   This false notion is corrected in the *Catéchisme de l'Eglise Catholique* of 1992, paragraphs 1901 and 1913-15. [Translator's note.]

that the three systems of government, namely monarchy, aristocracy and democracy, or government by the one, the few or the many, were not to be judged appropriate by reference to their own features, but by reference to circumstances, which might make one or other, or some combination of them, opportune, appropriate or useful in a given historical situation. It would therefore seem to be a major departure from tradition to teach now that wherever citizens are not held to share in the supreme governing authority, the system of government is illegitimate.

To realize the change in teaching, and indeed the crudeness of the change, it is useful to refer to the Catholic position as given in the collection of essays published by the Catholic University of Milan in 1940 entitled *Cento cinquant'anni dopo la Rivoluzione Francese.*[7] In it, the immortal principles of the revolution are declared "absurd," the revolution is presented as something that brought forth a host of evil consequences, and the fault of the *ancien régime* is said to have been not that it was too tough but that it was too feeble. As a matter of fact, the essays go to the opposite extreme and assert that a monarchical government is the only legitimate sort, and a clumsy assertion is made to the effect that "the people, the mob, needs a master and a ruler capable of restraining its passions."[8] The author also asserts that the aspirations of the revolution can be seen as legitimate if replanted in the Christian soil which is connatural to them, but even he fails to make the point that when uprooted from their native revolutionary soil they, like every other plant, are unlikely to flourish elsewhere: *com 'ogni altra semente, fuor di sua region fa mala prova.*[9]

227. Examination of the democratic system. Popular sovereignty. Competence.

The problems of democratic government have been debated from the beginning by the various currents of scholastic theology, including the school of Suarez, Bellarmine and Mariana, which elaborated the first philosophical statement of popular sovereignty; but it is not my intention to discuss the matter in

---

[7] "One hundred and fifty years after the French Revolution."
[8] Ibid., p.45.
[9] *Paradiso* VIII, 140-141. "As every other seed, outside its region, fares not well."

detail here. It should be noted, however, that the theory of the three writers mentioned differs profoundly from modern views of democracy. Their theory maintained that authority was lodged in the whole body of society, but derived from God and subject to divine law; they did not see authority as ultimately stemming from the will of the majority, as the moderns do.

The difficulties with democracy vary in kind and in importance, but they stem from a single root: the denial of the truth that all political action depends on a principle of justice more fundamental than public opinion and which should even prevail against public opinion. The doubtful premises of the modern democratic system are somewhat as follows.

Firstly: it is asserted that a greater wisdom is attained by getting everyone to *participate*, that is, by summoning a greater number of minds to deliberate on a matter. But politicians themselves know this is not necessarily the case. Guicciardini makes Antonio da Venafro say: "If you put six or eight wise men together they all go mad, because through their failure to agree they are more likely to launch a debate than find a solution."[10] The theories of Gustave Le Bon on crowd psychology also show that the average individual gets worse when acting as part of a mass.[11]

Secondly: it is assumed that deliberating on all matters concerning government is something that all people are capable of doing. That is, a right to a voice in policy making is alleged to stem from the fact that men are free spiritual beings, when in fact it stems from knowledge that particular men have acquired about the affairs in hand. It is a right derived from the historical development of some men, not from the nature common to all. It is a fault in logic to judge the validity of an opinion without reference to the knowledge and competence of the person advancing the opinion. This kind of logical error was condemned by Plato: he rightly says that when we want an opinion on things to do with horses, or gymnastics or medicine we do not consult indiscriminately; we ask an expert on the particular matter in hand.

This problem in the running of a democracy is aggravated by the complexity and the technical sophistication involved in state action in the modern world, which entail depending on

---

[10] Guicciardini, *Scritti politici e ricordi*, Bari 1933, p.309.
[11] G. Le Bon, *Psychologie des foules*, Paris 1917.

the advice of experts. If a course of action suggested by experts is referred for decision by the whole citizenry, as happens in direct democracies,[12] it is merely submitted to the judgment of a body unequipped with the knowledge needed to make a good decision, and which will either make an uninformed judgment or refer the matter once more to the experts for their opinion.

228. Examination of democracy.
The sophistry of taking a part for the whole.

Thirdly: as well as the assumption that the will of the majority is necessarily just and right, there is also a universal but equally false assumption that the will of the majority represents the will of the whole body politic. This is a sophistical synecdoche of the type that Manzoni identified in his *La Rivoluzione francese del 1789*, in which he criticizes the Abbé Sieyès'[13] view that because the deputies of the Third Estate represent the great majority of the nation, they had the right to regard themselves as actually *being* the nation as a whole. It is equivalent to saying that "some people" means "everybody." Thus it came about that the revolutionary acts of the National Assembly were said to be performed by "the people," and small and often unworthy cliques within that assembly were able to dignify their doings by cloaking them in the authority of "the people" as a whole.[14]

It is also obvious that majorities are not always right and that justice is not synonymous with the will of the people. In the Catholic view, civil laws are not themselves principles, but things that depend for their validity upon their own conformity with principles of justice. The laws of righteousness bind beyond the confines of civil law, and indeed against that law as well. As Cicero said: *Illud stultissimum, existimare omnia iusta*

---

[12] The author seems to have certain parts of the Swiss constitution in mind. [Translator's note.]

[13] Emmanuel Joseph Sieyès (1748-1836). Lapsed priest and revolutionary theorist. [Translator's note.]

[14] See *Opere*, National Edition, Vol.III, p.307. For this whole question see *Morale Cattolica*, ibid., pp.299 ff. This sophism, identified by Manzoni, reminds one of Condorcet's paradox asserting that the sum of rational choices made by individuals is inferior to a decision made collectively.

esse quae sita sint in populorum institutis aut legibus.[15] A majority is not the true source of law, because the moral authority of a law does not stem from the number of its human proponents, but from a higher source which Catholic doctrine, based upon revelation, has always expressed in the formula *omnis potestas a Deo.*[16]

It might be contended that a law that was unanimously supported by the whole of society would have a greater moral authority than one resting on a mere majority; the sophistry of taking a part as the whole would not arise in such a case, but God would still remain the source of all just and binding law.

229. Examination of democracy. "Dynamic majorities." Parties.

That moral authority does not really come from majorities is also proved by the fact that people sometimes appeal against a majority decision, by referring to a "dynamic majority," which is in fact a statistical minority. These minorities claim to be in tune with the movement of history, or the future, or the underlying will of the people, or the spirit of the age, or the signs of the times, or other slogans of the same kind. These are all pseudoconcepts and metaphors, called in to provide that ultimate source of moral authority which a numerical majority is deemed to provide in a pure democracy.

Opinion-forming minorities are woven into the fabric of representative systems; from the beginnings of the modern state, one school of thought has held that an elected representative should act to attain what he believes is the *good* of the people, irrespective of whether the people understand the good or not, while another school has held he should act in accordance with the people's *will*; to adopt the former view, while still adhering to the democratic ideology, produces the paradoxical result that the sovereign people are subject to a sovereign delegate, whom they have chosen, but who has the right to correct, direct and

---

[15] Cicero, *De Legibus*, I, XV, 42. "It is very stupid to think that everything contained in the customs and laws of the nations is just."

[16] Romans, 13:1. "All authority is from God."

contradict them. Long ago, Cicero had already said that: *magistratus populi utilitati magis quam voluntati consulat.*[17]

Since it is in fact impossible, amidst the current flux of contradictory opinions, to find any agreed philosophical basis for political authority, modern democracies are driven to base themselves on a pragmatism that opens the way to all kinds of cynical and machiavellian behavior. This is the origin of the deplorable sort of politics that "teaches men to violate justice at every turn in order to obtain some advantage or other, and when these repeated injustices have led society into dire straits, teaches that anything is legitimate to retrieve the whole desperate situation."[18]

Fourthly: there is Rosmini's objection to democracy inasmuch as democracy is to be identified with a party system. Since parties are expressions of disagreement in society, they cannot provide that integration which the body politic needs. They sometimes even represent different notions regarding the ends for which civil society exists, and the means to be employed in attaining them. In such cases, one party can only give in to another by admitting that it has had a less accurate vision of society than its rival, or by deciding that it has not the courage to continue its struggle. And in fact we know that in national emergencies, parties suspend hostilities for the good of the country.[19]

230. The Church and democracy.

It is a mistake to say that the political reforms in the papal states made by Pius IX from 1846 to 1848 constituted an

---

[17] Cicero, *De Republica*, Book V, fragments. ed. Castiglioni, Turin 1944, p.140. "A ruler of the people must think more about the good of the people than about what they want."

[18] Manzoni, *Morale Cattolica*, National Edition, Vol.II, First Part, Ch.VII, p.129.

[19] (In the Swiss context) the electoral system that produces the governing majority is open to criticism today, in a way it was not in the nineteenth century when there were only two parties. Although there are now several parties, the voter can still only cast his vote for one of them, and is denied the opportunity of expressing his view of all the parties, by voting preferentially. See my remarks in *L'anacronismo elettorale*, in *I giorni e le voci*, Locarno 1980 pp.33ff.

adoption by the Church of the principles of 1789. When Victor Hugo told the French House of Peers in 1848 that: "A pope who adopts the French Revolution and turns it into a Christian Revolution is not only a Man, but an Event," he was alleging an occurrence of something that is religiously, historically and philosophically impossible. The only revolution there can be in the Catholic Church is the continuing one, already complete yet ever new, which comes about through repentance in Christ.

It is true, however, that there has been a veering towards democracy since the Second Vatican Council, both because of the tendency we have already noted to regard democratic forms of government as the only legitimate kind, and because the Church's own institutions have taken on an egalitarian mentality, which has weakened the distinction between clergy and laity and led to the association of lay people with the government of the Church by means of representative bodies.

In 1963 in the encyclical *Pacem in Terris*, John XXIII approved the rights of man recognized in the charter of the United Nations Organization, but he based them directly on the dignity of man in an anthropocentric way, rather than pointing out that they stem from man's moral obligations, which derive from his link with the God who is the goal of his existence; this anthropocentric tendency was taken up by the council when it said that man is a creature that God wills for *its own sake*.[20] It is true that the Pope recalled the Catholic principle that all authority is from God, since human nature is the same in all men and provides no grounds for one to obey another; but he is silent about the fact that even when a majority may designate who is to hold authority, the authority still comes from God and not from the majority.

From the council onwards, there has been a movement towards the democratization of the Church by the creation of bodies which, although merely advisory, are designed to influence its government and to replace a single centre of authority with a decentralized form of control.[21]

---

[20] See paragraph 205.

[21] A document from the Pontifical Council for the Laity, published in the O.R. of 4 December 1981, makes the point that the Church is not founded on democratic principles: "The construction...of the Church is not brought about by the methods of a parliamentary system...even if the democratic model can teach us something for the internal life of the Church. Parliamentarianism in fact always

231. Influence of public opinion on the life of the Church.

Cardinal Suenens asserted in an interview that "most importantly, after the council there was a recognition of public opinion in the Church. This is something that is relatively new in the Church."[22]

This is hardly exact. What sort of recognition of public opinion is the Cardinal calling "new"? It is impossible to deny that the mass of the laity have had an important influence on the hierarchy. In early times, decisions were made in assemblies of the faithful that used the expression "It has pleased the Holy Spirit and us." And what were the swarms of heresies in the early centuries if not important expressions of public opinion? And when the mediaeval laity inaugurated movements like that of the Flagellants, or set off in search of martyrdom, or rose up against clergy who kept concubines or preached heresies; and when St. Thomas periodically attended gatherings at which he gave extempore answers to theological questions asked by the ordinary people of thirteenth century Paris; and when humble folk rioted in favor of the doctrine of the Immaculate Conception, and pulled those who preached against it from their pulpits in the seventeenth century; and when theological disputes on such matters as Jansen's teaching divided not only courts and intellectuals, but the unlettered multitude and overflowed into politics in the eighteenth century;[23] and when the doctrine of papal infallibility was debated in a thousand books, pamphlets and papers in the nineteenth;[24] was there then no public opinion in the Church? Again, to turn to perhaps the largest spiritual movement Christendom has ever seen, it is a notorious fact that Franciscanism was a popular lay movement which, like all the penitential movements of the thirteenth century, sprang to life before the clergy became involved in it; just as Boniface VIII decided to proclaim the first Holy Year of jubilee in 1300, be-

---

necessarily ends in conflict with the idea of unity in the Spirit - for which (the Church's) ministers are particularly responsible."
[22] C.I.D.S., 1969, No.13, pp.406ff.
[23] Of course, politics and theology were combined in these disputes, especially in France, but that only goes to show the importance of public opinion on religious questions.
[24] See the very full bibliography on the matter published during the period in question by the *Civiltà Cattolica*.

cause the people were demanding one on the grounds that a centenary jubilee was already customary, and indeed actually underway.

The customs which prevailed for centuries concerning the election of diocesan bishops are even clearer proof that the people did have a voice in ecclesiastical decision making. The bishop was not chosen by the people, but by the diocesan clergy with the participation of the people, who vouched for the worthiness of the candidates. Finally, one should not forget that in more recent centuries, especially after the Council of Trent, lay confraternities were incredibly flourishing; they devoted themselves partly to devotional activities and partly to charitable works, and governed themselves autonomously, so that the clergy were in fact involved in them only as servants of the confraternity.

In short it is historically inaccurate to talk about a "passive laity," as Pope Paul did in his speech of 22 March 1970. Even when all allowance is made for the abiding distinction between the hierarchy and the people, the latter have always been an integral part of the Church as a whole, imbued with the Holy Spirit, and have never been a merely passive or mechanical element moved by the clergy. What is today called public opinion has never ceased to drive the whole organism which is the Church, but to drive it in a way fitting for a subordinate part of the body.

232. The new role of public opinion in the Church.

What is new then, is not the existence of a public opinion in the Church, as Cardinal Suenens alleges, but the new strength that has been given to it by journalism and by other new and powerful means of spreading ideas. These not only express opinion, they reinforce it enormously, they change it and at times they even bring it into existence. Nourished by the underlying scepticism that pervades modern society, the modern communications media employ the old sophist tricks that were used to weaken the stronger argument and to color the implausible. Thanks to this new found and extraordinary psychological power, public opinion now rules the world more than it did in the past, when the great truths of natural reason and of revelation constituted, as it were, the solar system within which the epicycles of public opinion moved.

The greatest innovation in the post-conciliar Church in this matter is to have created juridically defined bodies whereby different groups are to express themselves: the standing synod of bishops, episcopal conferences, diocesan and national synods, pastoral and presbyteral councils and so on.[25]

But there is an internal contradiction in any purely consultative body, inasmuch as it is also a representation of public opinion. As a consultative body, it should be constituted on the basis of the competence of its members, but as a representative body it contains different experiences, as the saying goes, and different shades of opinion.

There is also a further contradiction. Even when such a body remains an expression of different points of view that the hierarchy can accept or reject, a synod of bishops or a pastoral council expresses opinions to which it can continue to adhere, even when the pope and bishops reject them. Thus it comes about that these participatory bodies within the Church turn, in fact, into means of expressing dissent, and independence of the bishops and the pope. This result was foreseen by some at the time these bodies were established, but has now been demonstrated *a posteriori* by the misguided proceedings of national synods, especially by the Dutch synod, which pushed the Church in Holland into a pre-schismatic state which has yet to be righted, despite the holding of a special synod of Dutch bishops in Rome under the eye of John Paul II. Almost all synods, diocesan or national, have tended to assert their independence and have taken up ideas and made proposals at odds with the stated policy of the Holy See, requesting such things as the ordination of married men, and of women, eucharistic communion with separated Christian brethren, and the admission of bigamous divorced people to the sacraments.[26]

We will not return to a discussion of the open manifestation of dissent by some bishops at the time *Humanae Vitae* appeared.[27] Let us note instead that there is a conflict between a process of democratization and the divinely constituted nature of the Church. There is a difference, indeed a contradiction, between the Church of Christ and a civil community: the latter exists prior to the form of its government, and hence societies

---

[25] See the decrees *Christus Dominus* (Vatican II, 1965) and *Ecclesiae sanctae* (Pope Paul VI, 1966) and the new Code of Canon Law.

[26] Cf. the German and Swiss national synods.

[27] See paragraphs 62 and 63.

are the source of every jurisdictional set of arrangements they may institute, and they retain the ultimate right to vary those arrangements as well. The Church, on the other hand, did not form itself, nor did it establish its own government; in its essentials it was established *in toto* by Christ, who established its laws and laid down its constitution before summoning mankind to join it: Christ's faithful are truly a new creation. The Church is therefore a unique kind of society, in which the head exists before the members and authority exists prior to the community.[28]

Any view that sees the Church as being based upon the people of God, conceived of in a democratic sense, or based upon public opinion among the laity, is at odds with the reality of the Church, in which authority is not something which is summoned forth from the body, but something which summons men to action, and in which all members are servants of Christ, bound by his commands. Any view that gives the laity a voice in decisions on the ground that the laity are "the sovereign people," is an inversion of the essential structure of the Church. The fact that this distinction between ecclesiastical and civil government is generally recognized, at least in words, is not enough to remove the *de facto* contradiction created by attempts to democratize the Church.

233. Episcopal conferences. Synods.

The setting up of episcopal conferences has had two effects: the distortion of the organic structure of the Church, and the enfeebling of individual bishops. According to pre-conciliar canon law, bishops, as the successors of the apostles, rule their own dioceses with ordinary jurisdiction in both spiritual and material questions, exercising legislative, judicial and coercive authority.[29] Their authority used to be clear, individual and indelegable, except for the case of vicars-general who are appointed and dismissed at a bishop's discretion.

It is true that in some countries, such as Switzerland, regular bishops' meetings used to be held, but these had no juridical structure and their purpose was to settle agreed pastoral policies to be pursued among people living under a single political regime; this was particularly appropriate in Switzerland where the

---

[28] This is a peculiar characteristic of the Church, as Laínez said at the Council of Trent. See Sarpi, *Istoria*, ed. cit., Vol. III, p.48.

[29] Cf. Canons 329 and 355.

people are of different languages, races and traditions and it was desirable to avoid striking diversities within a single sovereign state. These meetings were simple *de facto* gatherings, and each bishop remained throughout in full possession of his own authority and responsibility. The conciliar decree *Christus Dominus* talks about the collegiality of the whole body of Catholic bishops, saying that it has "full and supreme authority in the universal Church"; this would be equal with the authority of the pope but for the fact that it cannot be exercised without his consent. Such supreme authority has always been recognized as belonging to the bishops as a whole, when assembled with the pope in general council. It might be asked, however, whether an authority that can only be brought into operation at the instigation of an authority superior to itself, can properly be described as being "supreme"; the terminology seems somewhat otiose. The reality of the situation is that the conciliar decree has encouraged bishops to think that episcopal authority is exercised collegially within individual national episcopal conferences.

It is remarkable that the decree[30] bases its case for the new arrangements on the bishops' needs to work together within a single country, while failing to realize that a new juridical bond of this sort alters the Church's constitution, by replacing the authority of a bishop with a board of bishops, thus tending to replace a personal responsibility with a collective one, and leaving the individual bishop with a merely partial responsibility for his diocese.

As to the claim that bishops have authority directly as part of the apostolic body, Vatican I and Vatican II both taught[31] that the pope is the principle and foundation of the unity of the Church, and that it is through communion with him that the bishops have communion with each other. It is not possible to base episcopal authority on some common ground upon which the pope and bishops rest equally. But now, with the establishment of episcopal conferences, the Church has become a polycentric body, the centers being the national or regional episcopal conferences.

The first consequence of the new arrangements is a weakening of the bond of unity between each bishop and Rome, as can

---

[30] *Christus Dominus*, 37.
[31] The latter in its *Nota Praevia*. See paragraph 44.

be seen from the disagreements which have arisen on important points.[32]

The second consequence is the stripping of authority from individual bishops; they are no longer directly accountable to the Holy See or to their own people: individual responsibility is being replaced by a collegial responsibility which is dispersed throughout the whole body and cannot be located in any one member.[33]

In episcopal conferences, decisions are taken by two-thirds majorities, but although this may ensure unity of action, it still leaves the minority at the mercy of the majority.[34] Even though the decisions made by any of these new bodies may have been submitted to the Holy See for approval, their resolutions only have binding force if they are enacting what is already laid down in universal canon law, or if some special force is given to their resolutions by the Holy See when it approves them. It is hard to see how the episcopal conferences can be said to be imposing an obligation if the obligation already exists in canon law; but it is even harder to see how the individual bishop's responsibility can be recognized as long as it has to compete with the parallel authority of an episcopal conference. The incompatibility of these two lines of responsibility has led to deep divisions and, in places such as Holland, to a pre-schismatic state of affairs, in which bishops who think they have equal power with the pope have been allowed to go their own way by bishops loyal to Rome, who can, however, only accept union with their fellows on the basis of a common loyalty to the Roman Pontiff. There

---

[32] See paragraphs 61-65.

[33] It is worth noting that, in Europe at least, if the individual bishops are deprived of authority by their own episcopal conference, the national conferences themselves are losing authority to the confederation of European episcopal conferences.

[34] See paragraphs 227 and 228. It is thus no good saying that these ecclesiastical bodies are utterly different from the democratic assemblies of secular society. They have the same structures and modes of operation. By the force of their own internal logic, the episcopal conferences are becoming bodies representing the whole people of God, and are admitting the laity into their doings. In April 1983 the Italian Episcopal Conference admitted the active participation of priests and laity in its proceedings. On the third day of the meeting there were ten speeches by bishops, four by priests and six by laymen. O.R., 15 April 1983.

is also a general tendency for episcopal conferences to pro-
nounce their own judgments upon papal documents; instead of
giving obedience and consent as they did in the past, they now
often express a critical or dissenting opinion, as happened most
notoriously in the case of *Humanae Vitae.*

234. Synods and the Holy See.

Differences within the Church might be thought of as legitimate varieties of public opinion, were it not for the fact that
there is no room for differences of opinion once the Church's
teaching office has spoken; attempts are made to get round this
problem by distinguishing between the extraordinary and the
ordinary magisterium, with the latter being held never to be
infallible, and being in fact disputed by both clergy and laity.
Even if a minority does for a time embrace an unorthodox position, it ought to abandon it once an official pronouncement
has been made against the opinion in question, because it ceases
thenceforth to be a free opinion that anyone can hold. But in
fact, as we have noted, national synods have continued to treat
as open questions matters upon which decisions have already
been given, such as the abolition of celibacy, intercommunion
etc. At the Swiss Interdiocesan Forum held in 1981,[35] the whole
range of issues disputed throughout the entire post-conciliar
period, and upon which the Holy See had already given its decisions, were placed on the agenda yet again, with the approval
of the bishops. The fact that the papal nuncio to Switzerland
was allotted no part at all in proceedings was yet another sign of
the pre-schismatic independence asserted by the Church in
Switzerland.

The independence the bishops claim for themselves in relation to the Holy See is somewhat illusory, because the bishops
diminish and undermine their own authority by failing to weigh
and sift the unorthodox proposals that are foisted upon them by
others. Their authority as individual bishops is affected; I have
already mentioned the letter I received from a Swiss bishop who
had been asked to correct a particular doctrinal abuse and who
replied by saying: "As an individual bishop I am absolutely
powerless." He went on to say that "matters have been so arranged in the Church today, that an appeal by a bishop would

---

[35] The Forum was held as a substitute for the national synod the Swiss
bishops had proposed but which the Holy See had not allowed.

be ridiculed as well as going unheard."[36] Their authority as a bench of bishops is affected too, inasmuch as a group of men who individually feel they have no authority and responsibility will end up feeling they have no collective authority or responsibility either. This tendency is already manifest in the bishops' practice of referring matters to commissions of experts, who are often not experts at all, and then of allowing themselves to feel bound by whatever opinion the experts produce, as happened in the Charlot case.[37]

235. Spirit and style of synods.
The Swiss Forum of 1981.

Besides depriving bishops of their full authority, these synods also displayed much vagueness of thought and expression. The Swiss synod of 1981, which I have mentioned, met after some years of preparation to discuss the theme "For a living and missionary Church." In traditional theology, the idea of a living Church was acceptable inasmuch as it meant that there were spiritually living and dead members within the Church; not that the Church as such was living or dead. In the sense used here, however, it refers to the modern dynamist and vitalist view that change, rather than duration in one's proper state, is the true sign of life. The only precise and concrete proposals that the synod makes are ones that depart from tradition. The rest is abstractions, generalities and metaphors. There are such expressions as: "We must feel ourselves a community in which everyone accepts the experiences, the expectations, the ecclesial sensibilities of others in a climate of trust." It is obvious that a growing awareness of the needs of those in other parts of the world, and the development of connections between one continent and another, make new calls upon Christian charity, but the synod calls this "an opening to new relations of growth with other communities."

The modern Church is meant to be pursuing the goal of evangelization, but the Swiss assembly thinks that we must all become evangelizers, because Christians can only come to understand their own obligations through relations with their neighbors. Indulging in an even more superficial confusion of

---

[36] Bishops have been ignored and attacked in the past, but then it was by those outside the Church, not those within it.

[37] See paragraph 133.

ideas, devoid of any reference to the true operations of Providence, the assembly asserts, in the face of a world of travail, injustice and pain, that "we must communicate our joy to others, exchange hope in seeking out new forms of life for the Church." This substitution of joy for supernatural faith and hope, later led the Bishop of Lugano to jump in the pulpit, like the biblical goats, during his final sermon at the close of the gathering. But joy cannot be made the main theme of the Christian religion, since pain and evil are the greatest mystery in both life and religion, and anyone who shuts his eyes to them is rejecting religion itself.[38]

In conclusion, the Forum which claimed to represent the Church which is in Switzerland, consisted in reality of subdelegates appointed by delegates, who did not end up representing anything and who were for the most part people who knew little about Christian doctrine and who would not have survived the scrutinies as to suitability for office that were employed in ancient Greece.

The synod has two elements to it: one was based on confused and imprecise ideas such as "insertion into the world," "openness," "living community" and "becoming more human." There was a complete lack of reference to precise concepts like: divine commands, personal duties, a spirit of penance, supernatural faith and the exercise of the virtues. The other element was precise and unambiguous; the synod asserted that the demands that had already been advanced in the previous national synod, and rejected by the Holy See, were things that the Swiss church really wanted: the ordination of women, married priests, intercommunion, the admission of divorced and remarried people to the sacraments.

The underlying spirit at the synod was that subjectivism should carry the day in Church life, that the supremacy of public opinion should be canonized, and that in consequence, questions that the Church had declared closed should continue to be regarded as open. The dependence of the individual Christian on the Church is replaced by the dependence of the Church on the will of the crowd.

---

[38] For the quotations given here, see the account of the synod's activities in the *Giornale del Popolo*, 30 and 31 October 1981.

CHAPTER XXXIV

THEOLOGY AND PHILOSOPHY IN THE POST-CONCILIAR PERIOD

236. Philosophy and theology in Catholicism.

For the Catholic religion, as we have seen,[1] philosophy is a principle, not a corollary. The Christian religion is a revelation or unveiling of truths that are not naturally knowable, brought about by the Incarnation of the Word. The Word is the foundation of all; that is, the mind, rather than life or love: *In principio erat Verbum.*[2] When Doctor Faustus wished that action, *die Tat,* rather than mind were the primary principle in things, he was expressing man's rejection of religion. The theme pervading many of the pages of this book is the fundamental intellectuality of Catholicism, by which life proceeds from truth, just as the Holy Spirit proceeds from the Word within the Trinity, and does not come direct from the Father, as some of the Eastern Christians seem to think.

At no stage of its existence has the Church been able to avoid having some kind of philosophy, precisely because it has always needed to explain the natural truths upon which revelation rests, and has always needed to expound the supernatural truth itself, and to assist men to deepen their grasp of it, even though it can never be fully comprehended; these needs arise because man is an intellectual being, not a mere bundle of feelings. But while it is obvious that theology is intrinsically dependent on philosophy, it is much more difficult to grasp the relationship between Catholic doctrine and any one particular philosophical system as it exists in history. It is not possible to maintain that Catholic doctrine has an identical relationship

---

[1] See paragraph 147.
[2] John, 1:1.

with any and every philosophical system, because that would
mean that they are all equally compatible with Catholic teaching, or conversely, that where they disagreed among themselves,
pure scepticism should prevail and that all philosophy should
cease. Nor, lastly, will it do to assert the importance of philosophy for religion, if one is quite unable to say what particular
philosophy it is that can be of use to Christianity. This was the
problem besetting Cardinal Garrone when he made much of
the importance of philosophy, but could not tell us what philosophy was important.[3]

237. Misrepresentation of Thomism. Schillebeeckx.

It is indisputable that the Church has given a preference to
Thomistic philosophy, even when the cultural environment has
been decidedly un-Thomist; there is no good reason for regret-
ting that the *Summa Theologica* was, quite literally, enthroned
on the altar at the Council of Trent.[4] Later on, Leo XIII issued
the encyclical *Aeterni Patris* which, without denying the legitimacy of the other schools of Catholic thought, gave preference
to St. Thomas's doctrine and asserted that a restoration of
Thomism would lead to a cultural renewal in Catholicism, and
even to the curing of the ills of modern secular society.

Nonetheless, at Vatican II objections were made to the
privileged position accorded to Thomism. During session
CXXII, Cardinal Léger said that "Scholasticism is not suited to
non-western peoples" and that "the council should not express a
position on philosophical systems"; he further proposed to drop
the mention of St. Thomas in the text under discussion and said
that he could not be taken as a teacher who provided truths,
that is as the author of a system, but should be regarded only as
providing a method, that is as giving an example of the way in
which a Catholic thinker should keep in continual touch with
the cultural world of his own time.

The debasing of philosophy from a system of valid judgments to a mere method was also in evidence at the International Thomistic Conference of 1974, and was spread abroad in
popular Catholic publications too: what is relevant for today's
pluralist Catholicism is not what St. Thomas actually taught,
but St. Thomas's openness to and engagement with the general

---

[3] O.R., 23-24 October 1970.
[4] See Leo XIII's *Aeterni Patris* (§22). [Translator's note.]

culture of his period. Father Schillebeeckx O.P. maintains[5] two
theses which deprive Thomism of any real value. The first is
that, in opposition to the Augustinian school of thinking, St.
Thomas carried out "a kind of Christian secularization, which
accepts the value of things in themselves" and that "before talking about God, (St. Thomas) begins by analyzing created
causes." The second thesis is that "the content of what St.
Thomas says, even if it should not be ignored, is altogether secondary in comparison with the Thomistic method and approach." There follows a list of modernist ethical propositions,
which are attributed to St. Thomas.

Of these two theses, the first is pseudo-thomist rather than
Thomist, and savors of the new anthropocentrism. One can
only assert that St. Thomas treats secondary causes before talking about God if one ignores the very structure of the *Summa
Theologica* and forgets that in the introduction to that very work
Aquinas declares that he will treat first of God, then of the goal
of creation, and lastly of Christ[6] and that in theology all things
are discussed in relation to God.[7] How then can it be asserted
that St. Thomas first analyses secondary causes? He does indeed
discuss them; what philosophy could there be otherwise?; but
he does not deal with them first, and never deals with them in
themselves, but in their relation to God. The truth is that the
pseudothomistic theology of this Dutch Dominican views God
in relation to man, instead of viewing man in relation to God.

His second thesis entirely deprives specifically Thomistic
philosophy of any value at all. Where, in Schillebeeckx's view,
does the real importance of St. Thomas lie? Not in his content,
which is declared to be of secondary importance, but in his
method, by which is meant merely his external approach to a
problem. This approach is alleged to consist in a "horizontal"
openness, which Schillebeeckx contrasts with St. Bonaventure's
"verticalism," and which is said to have opened the way to the
"Christian secularization" which typifies the new post-conciliar
theology.

This attempted minimizing of the value of St. Thomas's
actual teachings is unsustainable. The importance of a system of
thought cannot be reduced to its method, which in fact is part
of logic; it must be sought in the actual propositions that a

---

5   In *Famiglia Cristiana*, 3 March 1974.
6   *Summa Theologica*, I,q.2 introduction.
7   Ibid., q.2,a.1.

theologian establishes by means of arguments appropriate to his
branch of knowledge. To say, as this Dutchman does, that what
is important about St. Thomas is not what he says, but merely
the position from which he says it, is equivalent to nullifying all
theology. Theology is a discussion centered on the reality of
God's being, not on the manner of conducting the discussion
itself.

238. Present and abiding importance of Thomism. Paul VI.

That the present relevance of Thomism lies in its example
in adapting Christianity to the prevailing culture is belied by the
fact that although it was indeed in contact with the culture of
its age, Thomism did not assimilate that culture, but rather
contradicted it vigorously on all those points on which it was at
odds with the teachings of the Christian religion.[8] Although it
was the dominant idea at the 1974 congress, and gave rise to the
founding of an international association for a syncretistic
Thomism, the idea that the value of Thomism lies in its method
rather than its content was not allowed to pass unchallenged by
Paul VI, who wrote a letter on the subject to the Master General
of the Friars Preacher on 14 November of that year. The Pope
restates the true grounds for the abiding importance of
Thomism. His letter concludes by saying that "to be a faithful
disciple of St. Thomas today, it is not enough to want to do in
our times, and with the methods available today, what he did in
his.[9] By merely proceeding upon a parallel path while not actually taking anything from him, one could scarcely arrive at a
very positive result, or at least scarcely offer the Church and the
world that endowment of wisdom of which they stand in need.
One cannot in fact speak of true and fruitful fidelity to St.
Thomas if one does not accept his principles, which are beacons
lighting up the most important problems in philosophy, or
without accepting too the fundamental notions in his system,
and his leading ideas. Only thus will the thought of the Angelic
Doctor undergo a rigorous development, by being brought into
contact with the ever increasing findings of secular disciplines."

---

[8]   See paragraph 5.
[9]   To do this would be merely to do what all the Fathers of the
      Church have done, from Tertullian in the third century, onwards.

239. Post-conciliar rejection of Thomism.

The all pervading characteristic of post-conciliar theology, when contrasted with the preceding period, is precisely this rejection of Thomism as a philosophy, that is as a system of theses, and its reduction to a mere methodological outlook, adjusted to the spirit of the age. The attacks upon Thomism in the council were not without their effect upon the drafting of the conciliar texts. The decree *Optatam Totius*, on the intellectual formation of the clergy says[10] that students should be led to acquire a solid and coherent conception of man, the world and God, *innixi patrimonio philosophico perenniter valido,*[11] but says nothing about Thomism, despite the fact that it is enjoined by Leo XIII's *Aeterni Patris* and by canon 1366, as well as by all the popes up to John XXIII.

The notion of a perennially valid philosophical tradition, which has replaced specific reference to Thomism, has no precise relevance to the question at issue. The truths that can be gleaned from the whole course of philosophy from Thales to Sartre do not constitute a philosophy, because a philosophy is a rational body of truths, setting forth a unified view of reality. Individual truths are simply *disiecta membra:*[12] they are the matter with which philosophy deals, but are not themselves an articulated philosophy. Then again, if the council is approving any and every philosophy, provided it can be harmonized with the truths of the Christian religion, there is no reason why the Church should not give equal approval to the Augustinian, Scotist, Suarezian and Rosminian philosophies, and the specific preference for Thomism would disappear entirely. As the Rosminian Hugh Honaan says,[13] in that case, within the meaning of official pronouncements, "Augustinians are Thomists, Scotists are Thomists, Suarezians are Thomists, Rosminians are Thomists, and so on." But to hold that position is obviously to nullify the specific characteristics of Thomism and of all the other philosophies mentioned, and to reduce them all to merely symbolic representations of the truth, all enjoying equal standing. The way is then open to say that heterodox philosophies are also symbolic representations of truth; and indeed the

---

[10] *Optatam Totius*, 15.
[11] "Based upon the perennially valid philosophical patrimony."
[12] Scattered limbs.
[13] In *Rivista Rosminiana*, 1949, p.287.

council decreed "that account should be taken of the philosophical enquiry made by contemporary thought," and this not
of course to refute modern errors, but "to derive support for the
truth from this contact."[14] It is impossible to disguise the eclectic streak in such an outlook, or to ignore the lessening of respect for Thomism, which is passed over in silence. In a view
such as this, philosophy has ceased to be a unified wisdom and
has become instead a variety of views.

240. Thomist theology in the post-conciliar Church. The setting aside of *Aeterni Patris*.

Although Thomism lost its privileged position at Vatican II
in the course of philosophical studies, it does rate a mention in
connection with theology; the mysteries of faith are to be expounded and integrated in theological speculation *Sancto
Thoma magistro.*[15] That the council was really non-Thomist in
outlook can be seen nonetheless in the fact that it never cites
Leo XIII's encyclical *Aeterni Patris* of 1879, which praised St.
Thomas's teaching, gave it a special standing, and commanded
that it be taught as the standard doctrine in Catholic teaching
institutions. This striking omission is repeated in John Paul II's
apostolic constitution *Sapientia Christiana*, which gives new
rules governing Catholic universities. It expatiates at length
upon freedom of theological research, but shows no concern for
unity of doctrine, while making great allowance for pluralism in
teaching. The mention of St. Thomas inserted in *Optatam
Totius* was ignored in the implementation of that decree, and
replaced by a so-called pluralism which has meant that ecclesiastical studies have lost their own specific flavor. As to the new
rules for universities, *Sapientia Christiana* lays down[16] that admission to a Catholic university involves having "those academic qualifications that are required for admission to secular
universities in the country in question." The effect of this
would be that to get into those Catholic universities in which
the clergy are often trained, one would need to be imbued with
Marxist or existentialist philosophy; it also means that the
originality and freedom of the Church in regard to the content
and methods of its own courses of study, which were so stoutly

---

[14] Paul VI, O.R., 15 September 1977.
[15] *Optatam Totius*, 16. "With St. Thomas as teacher."
[16] *Sapientia Christiana*, 32.

defended by the bishops of the nineteenth century against despotic state interference, are now to be abandoned in favor of those of a secular culture that either ignores or denies Catholic principles.

These changes the Church has made in its *ratio studiorum*,[17] abandoning both Thomism and the classics and adopting the spirit of syncretist pluralism, are yet another instance of the general loss of essences, and of the borders that mark off one kind of entity from another, thus enabling both to retain their specific characteristics. Everything typical of the post-conciliar Church is logically derived from this central problem of the loss of essences. Philosophy and theology are no longer seen as distinct fields of study, but are taught instead as a confused whole capable of being expressed in different ways, without worrying whether what is taught is coherent or incoherent, consistent or self-contradictory.

The reasons *Aeterni Patris* gives for according a privileged place to Thomism are as follows. First: Thomism is based upon a belief in the capacities of human reason, and rejects scepticism both partial and complete: the primary task of reason is to establish those naturally knowable truths which revealed truth presupposes. Second: on the basis of the spirit's capacity to grasp all truth, Thomism illuminates the truths of faith, inasmuch as they are capable of being understood by analogies with natural truths. Third: having thus demonstrated certain natural truths, and cast light upon the truth that has been revealed, Thomism goes on to defend the validity of these truths against objections. All three of these reasons can be summed up as constituting a recognition of the distinction between the natural and supernatural orders, that is between philosophy and theology, and it is upon this that all Catholic speculative thought turns.

As we have seen, Vatican II in effect abolished Thomism's privileged position by saying nothing about *Aeterni Patris*, by treating Thomism as a method rather than as a body of truth, and by encouraging contact with modern philosophies while failing to state what the purpose of such contact was meant to be. Since, as we noted earlier,[18] the modernizing school of thought often admits in words what it denies in practice; and

---

[17] "Program of studies."
[18] See paragraphs 49 and 50.

since it is an historical and psychological fact that the more
some good is undermined in practice the more lip service there
is paid to it, it is not surprising that the centenary of *Aeterni
Patris* in 1979 was marked by statements praising and honoring
the encyclical; empty praise indeed, for words cannot summon
to existence things that are not. The conference on St. Thomas
held in Rome in the centenary year of *Aeterni Patris* admitted
the change that had occurred: "With Vatican II, despite its reference to St. Thomas, the period of theological pluralism in
which we are now living opened."[19]

241. Theological pluralism in Catholic tradition.

Although the word *pluralism* is only used in the council's
documents to describe the differences and tensions within civil
society, and is never applied to the different theological schools
that have existed within Catholicism, it has become, with *dialogue*, the inspiring and directing idea in much post-conciliar
thought. While the notion of pluralism is appropriate within
the context of political communities, especially modern political
communities that are united by no principle other than the pursuit of liberty, it is by no means easy to reconcile it with dogmatic truth, or with Catholic theology. On the other hand, it is
certainly true that Christianity has from its beginnings contained a plurality of theological schools; if Johannine and Pauline thought do not constitute different theological schools, it is
nonetheless clear that the Alexandrian, Augustinian, Franciscan,
Thomist, Neo-thomist and Rosminian approaches do. Then
again, there have been the variety of answers to particular questions that have arisen within the ambit of orthodoxy on such
points as the purpose of the Incarnation, debated between
Thomists and Scotists; the Immaculate Conception, debated
between Dominicans and Franciscans: predestination and free
will, debated between Bannesians and Molinists; the various
answers given by moralists concerning the immediate rule conscience should follow, the role of contrition and attrition, and
many other points of moral theology.

Pluralism is thus clearly inherent in the very idea of theological research, and has always been a feature of Catholic

---

[19] *Atti* of the conference, Rome 1981, p.168.

thought.[20] The premises upon which theological pluralism rests have nonetheless changed in the post-conciliar period.

Pluralism has traditionally rested on two principles. The first is the inadequacy of the speculative human intellect, relative to the mystery of faith it is considering. The resources of any theologian's mind are limited, whether by the mind's essentially finite nature, or by the weaknesses of a particular individual. By faith, it can grasp the primary meaning of a doctrine with certainty, but the implications, consequences and why and wherefore surrounding the central doctrine may escape it. Thus one may grasp the central meaning of the eucharistic formula: *this is the body of Christ*, while still being uncertain about how this is so.[21] St. Thomas teaches that the body of Christ is in the sacrament by transubstantiation, and the remaining of the accidents of the previously existing substance; Giovanni Pico della Mirandola supports the idea of a kind of hypostatic union, Scotus proposes a multiplication of Christ's presence, Campanella hypothesizes the assumption of the bread into the quintessential sphere, Rosmini advances the idea of the transforming vivification of the substance of the bread by Christ. Error can creep into these rival theories if the forms of presence proposed do not preserve the primary meaning of the dogma, that is if they reduce the sacramental presence to an imagination rather than a reality, a mere representation or sign, rather than something affecting the real existence of the object. Once it goes beyond the doctrinal assertion: *this is the body of Christ*, theology runs into the doubt that stems from the limitations of our intellect with regard to both natural and supernatural truths.

The second principle upon which pluralism has traditionally rested is the intrinsic obscurity of the Infinite, that is the transcendent quality of the objects considered, which engenders a variety of lines of enquiry and of solutions proposed.

Both these traditional grounds for a plurality of theological opinion respect a fundamental principle of the Christian religion, namely that truth is convertible with being, and that man's

---

[20] There are even legal proofs that the Church has recognized the right to theological pluralism; in 1946 the Holy Roman Rota annulled two decrees by the Archbishop of Milan which had purported to suppress an ecclesiastical training college on the grounds, not of unorthodoxy, but of their theological tradition. See *Rivista Rosminiana*, 1951, p.158.

[21] See paragraph 266.

truth is a participation in the First Truth which is God, just as
finite being is a participation in God's primal existence.

242. The innovators' view of theological pluralism.

The reasons for post-conciliar pluralism are quite different,
and at odds with Catholic metaphysics. The 1979 Thomistic
congress, mentioned earlier, provided ample proof that it openly
accepted mobilism and the sceptical relativism upon which it
rests. It proclaims its belief that theology must update itself
from the classical mentality with which the Church identified
itself until Vatican II. The congress equates *aggiornamento* with
assimilation of the modern mentality, without first examining
whether such an assimilation is possible. It asserts that reality
should not be thought of as a system of natures which are finite
refractions of the divine idea, and which lead us towards the
truth by our knowing of them. It asserts instead that reality is
mere becoming or flux, and that human nature continually
changes, not in the sense that it comes into contact with
changing external realities while itself remaining the same, but
in the sense that change is the very essence of human nature.
The congress says that "the world which has been considered as
being almost wholly objective, is in fact a subjective construction, relative to social and historical points of view."[22]

If there are no fixed substances or truths to which the intellect can attain, then indeed the privileged position the Church
has accorded Thomism is unsustainable. Where nothing is stable and all is in motion, as Cardinal Alfrink puts it,[23] there can
indeed be no inviolate truth to which a privileged position
might be given. Where things are not fixed for eternity, but
merely fixed for the moment, philosophy can never be more
than a collection of shifting opinions, and nor can theology:
both simply dissolve.

A pseudo-thomism that makes all knowledge subjective is
equally incompatible with Catholic metaphysics. "In order to be
known, any reality must become part of our experience and
thus be invested with subjectivity in order to become an object
immanent within us and therefore relative to our knowledge."
To say that is to cast aside a fundamental feature of St. Thomas's

---

[22] *Atti*, cited above, p.169. We have already criticized Pyrrhonism in
paragraphs 148-9, and mobilism in 157-162.
[23] See paragraph 148.

philosophy. The object known must indeed be invested with a subjective form given by the intellect, but according to St. Thomas that form does not relativize or alter anything, because all the intellect does is to universalize the object known. That is, it leaves the intelligible content of the idea unchanged, while abstracting the idea from its material setting in the extra-mental world and considering it as a universalized concept.

In its relativist view of ethics too, the congress displays the consequences of scepticism and mobilism. Unchanging laws are rejected and individual consciences are declared to be creative, self-regulating and no longer subject to a rule before which they are merely passive.[24] If, as the congress asserts,[25] "not even human nature can be said to be the same everywhere," then there can be no common rule for consciences to follow and no way of even creating such a rule, because "meanings and values are products of the human mind."

In short, the centenary celebration of *Aeterni Patris* was little more than a ceremonial, or even theatrical, performance,[26] gone through partly for form's sake in order to demonstrate continuity, and partly the product of that dulling of logical thought, which stems from losing a sense of the difference between the natures of things, and which leads to a confusing of one thing with another.

At the supernatural level, mobilism and scepticism affect the idea of faith, and lead the congress to say faith is no longer understood as an act of assent to revealed truth, but as an existential commitment. The order of things is ignored, and the fact that faith is the cause of charity is taken as proving that the two virtues are in fact the same.[27]

What then is the value of the Thomism that the Church has so much praised? The congress cannot answer that question without contradicting itself. After having discovered that every philosophy is provisional, that all knowledge is relative and

---

[24] See paragraph 198.

[25] *Atti*, p.171.

[26] Reading the Acts of the congress reminds one of books published in times past, under religious or political censorship. A book with a titlepage bearing the words "Life of the Blessed Virgin" would contain a collection of anti-religious prints, and "Description of the Journey of Sir John Chasterly in China" would turn out to contain the ideas of the Young Italy movement.

[27] *Atti*, paragraph 169.

ephemeral, and that man himself has no permanent nature, the congress still goes on to assert that "in a notable manner," St. Thomas combined the static and dynamic mentalities, that is that he synthesized contradictory elements, broke free from the limits of his own time and "made, and gave expression to, fundamental insights about the basis of human thought and activity." But how can one say that without a firm foundation, provided by the recognition of an ideal human nature, and while asserting a simultaneous or successive multiplicity of first principles?

243. Dogma and its formulation.

As we have seen, the new theological pluralism is begotten of a sceptical relativism which maintains that it is impossible to think of anything at all without the thinker mixing himself up with the content of his thought; hence it follows that Catholic teachings are treated in this same way, with the result that they are held to represent an unknowable *quid*, a something or other that gives rise to a variety of mental experiences on the part of believers, who then formulate experience in a variety of ways, all equally valid from the subjective point of view. All theologies are nullified, because all are regarded as equivalent; the heart or kernel of religion is located in feelings or experiences, as the Modernists held at the beginning of this century.

This version of things inevitably raises questions about the formulas in which the Church has expressed her teachings, and makes them the product of historical and cultural circumstances; hence the formulas are no longer held to express the content of divinely revealed truth, and are seen as expressions of the subjective ways in which revelation is historically apprehended and lived out, in accordance with different cultures and schools of thought.

In *Mysterium Fidei* in 1965, Paul VI opposed this innovation by forcefully restating that the dogmatic formulations the Church uses represent actual realities that the human spirit really does attain to through its experience: thus experience is the means to understanding, not the content of what is understood. Hence these formulations of doctrine are in principle intelligible to all men at all times, and enjoy a supra-historical character as expressions of supra-historical realities. In the opening pages of *Humani Generis* in 1950, Pius XII had already taught that the mysteries of faith can be expressed in true and unchanging terms.

The new ideas in this field compromise the gnoseological foundations of Catholic doctrine and are a recrudescence of the Modernist errors of the early part of this century. These ideas imply that theology is not concerned with the grasping and expressing of unchanging truth; they lead instead to the now commonly held view[28] that it is the putting into words of believers' experiences, or, in the words of Zahrnt "a theological notion is merely an experience brought down to the level of reflective thought." Since experience is a subjective and changeable thing, it follows that theology must be so too; even when a theological view is widely held, it will be no more than the reflection of a large number of subjective experiences, and will still lack the fixed character of a truth that stands in its own right.

It is a fundamental proposition of Catholic philosophy that a mental concept is an expression of the reality of the object considered, and that linguistic constructions are an expression of the reality of the mental concepts.[29] There is thus a chain of certainty connecting being, thought and language. If, on the other hand, one accepts the new view that linguistic expressions have to do merely with subjective impressions rather than ontological realities, theology is reduced to psychology and dogmas of the Faith are reduced to a history of ideas.

It is admittedly difficult to give correct expression to the relationship between the truths of faith and doctrinal formulas. In his speech in Uganda, Paul VI said that the Church was "conservative of its own message" and emphasized that it conserves its message in formulas "that must be maintained to the letter."[30] He nonetheless left the matter unresolved by saying that the language of faith, that must be maintained, admits of a variety of expressions; how can this be when the formulas that must be literally maintained are themselves unique and definite linguistic expressions? This uncertainty had already occurred in the opening speech of the council, which distinguished between the deposit of faith and "the formulation of its clothing," or the

[28] See for example the very widely circulated *Nuovo Dizionario di Teologia, Edizioni Paoline,* Turin 1975.

[29] See my speech *Iam pridem nos vera vocabula rerum amisimus* in *Atti e memorie di Arcadia,* Third Series, Vol.III, Rome 1978.

[30] O.R., 2 August 1969.

ways of enunciating the faith *eodem tamen sensu eademque sententia.*[31]

The formulas in which the Church expresses its doctrines are not a clothing, that is an external covering; they are the expression of a naked truth. As the Latin text of the opening speech says, they are expressions of truth that have been received from God; it is impossible to maintain the sense of a proposition if one re-expresses it in terms that can be interpreted as having a different meaning. For example, if the formula expressing the Church's faith is: "the bread is transubstantiated into the Body of Christ," it is clear that the formula "the bread is transfinalized into the Body of Christ" does not maintain the truth in question, because changing the finality or goal or destiny of something is altogether different from changing its substantial being. It is alleged that a new interpretation of the same faith is all that is being attempted, a case of new words for old; but since words are not neutral in meaning, or a kind of hook on which any kind of idea can be hung, this process actually involves a movement from one meaning to another, a movement from truth to its denial.

244. Theology and Magisterium. Hans Küng.

Some post-conciliar theologians have attempted to change the substance of Catholic doctrine by advancing new *presentations* of the faith which in fact involve the introduction of new *meanings*. The proposition: "Jesus is Son of God" means that for some people Jesus is true God and true man subsisting in a single Person, while others take it as meaning that Jesus is a man who is perfectly conformed to the will of God, and morally united to Him. The new theology maintains that these two interpretations are not incompatible Christologies, but two modes of expressing the same faith. Cardinal Willebrands maintains that the doctrinal differences between Catholics and Eastern Orthodox are merely differences of language.[32]

During the 1967 synod of bishops, Cardinal Seper, the Prefect for the Congregation for the Doctrine of the Faith, denounced the heretical character of much post-conciliar theology in the following terms: "Things have got to the point where one cannot go on talking about healthy and fruitful research or le-

---

[31] See paragraphs 39 and 40.
[32] O.R., 16 July 1972.

gitimate adaptation; it has become a question of unwarranted novelties, false opinions and errors of faith."[33] This statement of the case is no different from Paul VI's, when he spoke of an internal dissolution of the Church.

The dissolution that theological pluralism has brought in its train stems at a deeper level from the freedom of opinion that the new school of thought has demanded with respect to the teaching authority of the Supreme Pontiff. I have already pointed out that the arm of this authority was foreshortened during Paul's pontificate.[34] It will suffice here to give a simple reminder of the Catholic position.

Freedom or space for theological enquiry has two defining criteria: Scripture and the Magisterium, or the Church's teaching authority. In the Catholic view, the theologian cannot be fully enlightened without the light that comes from both Scripture and the magisterium mutually enlightening each other; this reciprocal relationship was denied by the innovators of the sixteenth century, as it is by those of the present day.

Hans Küng's views have become notorious in this regard, divorced as they are from all Catholic doctrine on both philosophical questions, such as the existence of God, and questions of revealed truth, like the deity of Christ. These are but expressions of a radical denial of the Catholic principle of man's dependence on transcendent truth. Thought is dependent upon, and must conform to, the extra-mental objects it considers; faith is dependent upon and must adhere to the revealed Word; a theologian depends upon and must conform to a dogmatic truth deposited in the Church and set forth by her teachers. In Küng's view faith is a feeling of trust in the fundamental goodness of reality, a feeling expressible in any number of ways; so every religion is a way of salvation. The Church, he maintains, is not an organism centered on Christ, but a remembering of Christ by individuals, scattered throughout the human race.

It is obvious that theologians are no less qualified to exercise this kind of memory than are other Christians, and since the authority of the teaching office is no longer held to rest upon Christ's giving of teaching authority to Peter, but upon the knowledge of individuals, the duty of teaching will no longer belong specifically to the bishops together with Peter, but will

---

[33] O.R., 28 October 1967.
[34] See paragraphs 60-67.

instead be the function of theologians as a class. Hence the denial of the infallibility of the Church, which Küng holds to be *indefectible* but not *inerrant*, that is, there will always be a Church teaching truth but there will always be a certain amount of error mixed with the truth; the Church is thus a mixture of positive and negative elements like any human institution. In the final analysis, Küng's views are a compound of old errors propounded with a good deal of literary skill, amounting to a Lutheran belief in private judgment and faith as trust.

After the case had dragged on for some time, the Holy See brought the matter to a head by its decree of 15 December 1980 saying that Küng could no longer be regarded as a Catholic theologian; this, however, was a judgment about him personally and did not directly address his teaching;[35] it also gave yet further proof of divisions within the Church. The Roman decree was attacked in counterblasts from the staffs of some universities and some clergy. Küng continued to disseminate his views by word and in writing. St. Paul's command to Timothy not to teach strange doctrine[36] has been turned on its head: scepticism and mobilism lead people to look for strange doctrines as if they were a sign of a living faith. In commenting on St. Paul's text, St. Thomas Aquinas says superiors have a double responsibility: *primum cohibere falsa docentes, secundum prohibere ne populus falsa docentibus intendat.*[37] But today all such proposals are rejected in the name of freedom.

---

[35] Decrees of 1973 and 1975, the latter explicitly mentioning Küng and two of his books, had already been issued by the Congregation for the Doctrine of the Faith. [Translator's note.]

[36] Cf. I Timothy, 1:3.

[37] "First of all to restrain those who teach false doctrine, and secondly to prevent the people from listening to those teaching such doctrine."

CHAPTER XXXV

ECUMENISM

245. Change in the notion of Christian unity. The instruction of 1949.

The change in thinking about Christian unity is the most striking that has occurred in the Catholic system since Vatican II, uniting as it does all the elements of that attempted radical change that we have summed up in the phrase *loss of essences*.

Traditional teaching on Christian unity is set forth in the *Instructio de Motione Oecumenica*[1] published by the Holy Office on 20 December 1949, which takes up the teaching of Pius XI in his encyclical *Mortalium Animos* of 1928. The principles laid down are: First: "the Catholic Church possesses the fullness of Christ" that is, it does not need to acquire things that go to make up the fullness of Christianity from other denominations. Second: Christian unity must not be pursued by means of a process of assimilation between different confessions of faith, or by adjusting Catholic doctrine to the teachings of other de-nominations. Third: true union between the churches can come about only by the return, *per reditum*, of separated brethren to the true Church of God. Fourth: separated brethren who rejoin the Catholic Church lose nothing of the truth to be found in their own denominations, rather they retain it just as it was, but in its completed and perfected context, *complementum atque absolutum*.

The doctrine set forth in the *Instructio* therefore implies that the Church of Rome is the foundation and centre of Christian unity, that the Church's life in time does not revolve around a number of centers, namely the different Christian groupings, all of which have a single deeper center situated be-

---

[1] "Instruction on the Ecumenical Movement," A.A.S., 31 January 1950.

yond all of them, but rather that the Catholic Church is itself
the collective person or body of Christ; and lastly that the separated brethren must move towards the unmoving centre which
is the Church served by the successor of St. Peter. The rationale
or centre of Christian unity is therefore something that already
exists within human history and which the separated brethren
need to regain; it is not something to be constructed in the future. All the reserve that the Roman Church has exercised in
ecumenical matters, and particularly its continuing abstention
from the World Council of Churches, is motivated by this understanding of what Christian unity involves, and is designed to
exclude the idea that all denominations stand on an equal footing. This doctrinal position is merely the expression of the transcendent principle upon which Christianity rests, namely Christ
Himself, who is both God and man, and who is represented
within time by the Petrine office.

246. The conciliar change. Villain. Cardinal Bea.

The change introduced at the council is apparent in outward signs and in a shift in theory. In the conciliar decree *Unitatis Redintegratio*, the Instruction of 1949 is never mentioned,
and the word return, *reditus*, never occurs. It is replaced by the
idea of *convergence*. That is, the different Christian denominations, including Catholicism, should turn not to each other but
towards the total Christ who is outside all of them, and upon
whom they must converge.

It is true that in his speech opening the second period of
the council, in 1963, Paul VI reiterated the traditional teaching
that the separated brethren "lack that perfect unity that only the
Catholic Church can give them." He went on to say that the
threefold bond of this unity was constituted by a single belief, a
sharing in the same sacraments and "due adherence to a unified
ecclesiastical government," which latter included a great range
of languages, rites, historical traditions, local prerogatives and
currents of spirituality.

Despite this papal utterance, the council's eventual decree
on ecumenism, *Unitatis Redintegratio*, rejects the idea of a *return*
of separated brethren and adopts the idea of a simultaneous
conversion on the part of all Christians. Unity should be
brought about not by a return of the separated brethren to the
Catholic Church, but by a conversion of all the churches within
the total Christ, a Christ who is not identified with any of them

but who will be constructed by means of their coming together as one. The preparatory schemas drawn up before the council stated that the Church of Christ *is* the Catholic Church; but the council says only that the Church of Christ *subsists in* the Catholic Church, in effect adopting the idea that it also subsists in other Christian churches, and that all such churches ought to recognize their common subsistence in Christ. As a professor at the Gregorian University put it, the council recognizes that the separated churches are "instruments that the Holy Spirit uses to bring about the salvation of their members." On this egalitarian view of all Christian denominations, Catholicism is no longer seen as having any uniquely privileged position.

In his book *Introduction à l'oecuménisme*, published in Paris in 1959 during the period in which the council was being prepared, Father M. Villain had already attempted to do away with the contrast between the Catholic Church and Protestant denominations by distinguishing between central and marginal doctrines, and still more by distinguishing between the truths of the faith and the formulas by which they are expressed, which latter he said were not unchangeable. He maintained that doctrinal formulas do not *manifest* the truth, but rather *categorize* a datum that remains unknowable, and that Christian unity could be based on something more profound than truth, which he calls "the praying Christ." Prayer by all Christians is certainly needed to achieve unity,[2] but it is not itself unity; Pope Paul said unity in faith, sacraments and government is what is required.

Cardinal Bea put forward similar views on unity.[3] He said that ecumenism did not involve a movement of return to the Roman Church on the part of separated Christians; in accordance with established teaching, he pointed out that Protestants are not completely separate from the Church, because they are validly baptized. Having quoted Pius XII's encyclical *Mystici Corporis* of 1943 to the effect that Protestants "are directed towards the Mystical Body" by their baptism, he went further and said that they actually belonged to it and are therefore no worse off than Catholics when it comes to reaching God's salvation.[4] He views a reunion as a matter of making explicit a unity that is already there, and which has simply to be realized. He thinks

---

[2] See also what we have said in paragraph 243.
[3] See *Civiltà Cattolica*, January 1961 and the *Corriere del Ticino*, 10 March 1971.
[4] O.R., 27 April 1962.

the Catholic Church is in the same position, and that it too
needs to become aware of the deeper reality of the total Christ
which is a synthesis of all the scattered groups in Christendom.
No *reversion* of some groups towards another, but a *conversion* of
everyone to a new centre which is the hidden or deeper Christ.

247. Post-conciliar ecumenism. Paul VI.
The Secretariat for Christian Unity.

The replacement of the idea of a return to the Catholic
Church by that of a universal conversion to Christ figures
largely in the council's decree *Unitatis Redintegratio*,[5] which
teaches that the Church ought to be continually reformed. But
the meaning of conversion in this context is somewhat unclear.
Firstly, if one is to avoid mobilist errors, it must be emphasized
that there is a Christian condition or state of being within
which individual Christians work out their salvation and strive
for perfection, and that there is never any need to be converted
from that state to another. Secondly, this continual growth in
holiness, although needed as part of any growth towards overall
Christian unity, remains essentially a personal thing and can
never itself constitute Christian unity.

Although admitting there are differences between churches,
Cardinal Bea maintains that "the points that divide us do not
really concern doctrine, but rather the way doctrine is expressed,"[6] because all denominations are attached to a single
truth which underlies all other truths: as if the Church had been
mistaken for centuries, and all disagreements were merely a
matter of verbal misunderstandings. The task of the good shepherd in the Gospel parable is, on this view, no longer to lead
back those who have strayed, but just to leave the door of the
sheepfold open for any sheep who may choose to wander in.
This is hardly the sort of fold we expect from a good shepherd.

In a very convoluted sentence in a speech made on 23 January 1969, Paul VI seems close to adopting such views. *Dalla
discussione teologica può risultare quale sia l'essenziale patrimonio
dottrinale cristiano, quanto sia di esso communicabile autentica-
mente e insieme in termini differenti sostanzialmente uguali e
complementari, e come sia per tutti possibile e alla fine vittoriosa la*

---

[5]   *Unitatis Redintegratio*, 6.
[6]   O.R., 4 December 1963.

scoperta di quell'identità della fede nella libertà e nella varietà delle sue espressioni dalla quale l'unione possa felicemente essere celebrata.[7] It would seem, judging from this passage, that unity pre-exists everywhere, that there needs to be a universal recognition of the fact, and that truth is reached by deepening one's understanding of errors rather than by abandoning them. John Paul II takes up the same position in his speech to the Sacred College on 23 December 1982, which was later referred to at the time of the Sixth Assembly of the World Council of Churches in 1983: "In celebrating the redemption we go beyond misunderstandings and historical controversies in order to meet on the common foundation of our existence as Christians." The said assembly was composed of representatives of 304 Christian denominations who "expressed by song, dance and prayer the different ways there are of signifying an attitude of relationship with God."[8]

The document published, in French, by the Secretariat for Christian Unity in pursuance of the council's decree of Christian unity is very revealing.[9] It takes up the traditional formulation of the matter,[10] talking about: *"l'unité de l'Eglise une et unique, unité dont le Christ a doté son Eglise dès l'origine, et qui subsiste, nous le croyons, de façon inamissible dans l'Eglise catholique et qui, nous espérons, doit s' accroître sans cesse jusqu'à la consommation des siècles."*[11] Thus far the Catholic Church is presented as possessing unity and as making it increase, not in a formal sense, that is by itself becoming more unified, but rather in the material sense of adding hitherto separate denominations

---

[7] "From theological discussion it can emerge what the essential Christian doctrinal patrimony is, how much of it is communicable authentically and together in different terms that are substantially equal and complementary, and how it is possible for everyone to make the final victorious discovery of that identity of faith, in freedom, and in the variety of its expressions, from which union can be happily celebrated."

[8] O.R., 25-26 July 1983.

[9] O.R., 22-23 September 1970.

[10] Cf. *Lumen Gentium*, 8.

[11] "The unity of the one and only Church, a unity which Christ bestowed upon his Church from the beginning and which we believe continues to exist, in such a way as can never be lost, in the Catholic Church and which, we hope, is to grow unceasingly until the end of time."

to itself: this is an extending, rather than an intensifying, of unity. But thereafter the document talks exclusively about a unity to be *sought*, rather than *communicated*; it talks about a mutual recognition of each other's qualities, which will lead to *la resolution des divergences au delà des differences historiques actuelles.*[12] These historical differences could even be preserved as the doctrinal statements of particular denominations. Hence the proposal made by certain Reformed theologians to recognize the Petrine primacy as a doctrine of the Roman province of the universal church. A number of French parishes accept the idea of double membership, whereby the partners in a mixed marriage join equally in each other's worship.[13] Doctrinal differences are here regarded as merely contingent historical events; a return to the faith of the first seven general councils will make them irrelevant.[14] This view implicitly denies the homogeneous development of dogma since those seven councils; the development of doctrine is reversed, and an historical rather than a theological solution to the problem of Christian unity is proposed.

The assumption that Christian unity is to be sought through the reassembly of pieces, all of them of equal standing, has now completely supplanted the traditional view of the matter.[15] The appeal made during the LXXXIX session of the council by the Bishop of Strasbourg to the effect that "any expression alluding to a return by separated brethren should be avoided" has now become a doctrinal principle and a ruling norm for the ecumenical movement. Our critique of dialogue in general is particularly relevant when it comes to dialogue concerning Christian unity.[16]

---

[12] "The resolving of divisions beyond the level of differences currently existing."

[13] I.C.I., No.556, 15 November 1980.

[14] The first seven general councils were: Nicea in 325, Constantinople I in 381, Ephesus 431, Chalcedon 451, Constantinople II 555, Constantinople III 681 and Nicea II in 787. [Translator's note.].

[15] Even Paul VI spoke of the "recomposition of Christians who are divided among themselves, within the one Catholic Church, that is, the one universal and organic Church which is truly composite but united in a single, unequivocal faith." O.R., 27 January 1973.

[16] See paragraphs 151-6.

248. Consequences of post-conciliar ecumenism.
Drop in conversions.

This book cannot address all the points of faith and of theological discussion that have been affected by the doctrinal change which it sets out to examine. These points include the doctrine of salvation, the theory that distinguishes the Body of the Church from its Soul, the difference between faith and good faith, and the development of dogma. We cannot however ignore some of the obvious consequences of the present ecumenical policies, even though they are consequences that people prefer not to discuss. The principle that the separated brethren must *return* has been replaced by that of a conversion of everybody to a total Christ who is supposed to be immanent in all denominations.[17] As Athenagoras, the Patriarch of Constantinople, has openly declared *il n'est pas question dans ce mouvement d'union, de marche d'une Eglise vers l'autre, mais de marche de toutes les Eglises vers le Christ commun.*[18] If this is the essence of ecumenism, the Catholic Church can no longer seek to attract men to itself; it can only go along with other denominations in a movement towards a centre which is outside itself just as it is outside all other denominations. Mgr Le Bourgeois, the Bishop of Autun, states plainly: *Aucune Eglise ne peut prétendre être à elle seule l'authentique Eglise de Jésus-Christ tant que l'unité n'est pas réalisée.*[19]

In an article which was at odds with the *Osservatore Romano's* general policy, and which remained an isolated expression of opinion, Father Charles Boyer S.J.[20] said that the decline in conversions to Catholicism was due to society's abandonment

---

[17] The president of a Dutch ecumenical body has said: "The unity of the Church no longer means a return to the Catholic Church as it exists today, but a growth of all the churches towards the Church of Christ as it ought to be." I.C.I., No.281, 1 February 1967, p.15.

[18] "In this uniting movement there is no question of one church moving towards another; it is rather a matter of all churches moving towards the Christ they have in common." I.C.I., No.311, 1 May 1968, p.18.

[19] "By itself no Church can claim to be the authentic Church of Jesus Christ until unity has been achieved." I.C.I., No.585, 15 April 1983, p.20.

[20] Sometime Rector of the Pontifical Gregorian University in Rome. [Translator's note.]

of a theocentric outlook, and the attractions of the *civitas hominis* for the present generation; but he also blames ecumenism.[21] "It is alleged that all churches are more or less the same. Proselytism is condemned.[22] In order to avoid it, people avoid criticizing errors and giving clear expositions of true teaching.[23] Other denominations are advised to maintain their identity on the ground that there will eventually be a spontaneous convergence of churches." Although Father Boyer restricts the range of his argument by attributing these faults largely to the non-Catholic denominations, the truth is that what he says undercuts the essence of the new Catholic ecumenism too.

Conversions to Catholicism cannot but decline if conversion ceases to be regarded as a passage from one kind of thing to something very different, a matter of life and death for the individual concerned. If nothing essential changes on becoming Catholic, then conversion is an irrelevance and those that take that step may come to feel it was a waste of time doing so. Living in a country were religions are mixed, I have had occasion to discover that converts from Protestantism these days often come to regard the change they have made as being futile and mistaken. The great French writer Julien Green says frankly and bitterly that in today's circumstances he would not have become a Catholic: why leave one religion for another when there has ceased to be any difference between the two, barring their names?[24] I know of cases of Jews who had converted to Catholicism but who have returned to the synagogue in the wake of Vatican II's abdications and retractions. On the other hand, it is very difficult to un-convert today as well, because going back to Protestantism would often make no difference, just as it made no difference to move the other way.[25]

---

[21] O.R., 9 January 1975.

[22] This term is now used to describe calling people to join the Catholic Church, as missions have always done.

[23] This is in accordance with Pope John's policy announced at the opening of the council. See paragraph 40. [Translator's note.]

[24] Cited in *Itinéraires*, No.244, p.41.

[25] The Bishop of Chur told Dr. Melitta Brugger that in the ten years from 1954 to 1964 his diocese of 150,000 souls received 933 converts from Protestantism, but that in the following ten years it received only 318. The Bishop of Lugano said (17 January 1975) that he could not decide whether the decline in conversions was a good or a bad thing. In the United States before the council there

249. Political character of ecumenism.

Formerly, personal conversion was seen as the important thing; the idea of a spiritual *metanoia* occurring on mass as the result of negotiations by hierarchies was seen to be incongruous. Mass conversions occurred in times when rulers decided the whole course of a society's action and could thus also lay down what religion it should follow. Much of the Christianization of the barbarian peoples came as a result of the conversion of chiefs who then proceeded to assist in the evangelization of their peoples. As late as the eighteenth century, missionary activity often took the form of influencing rulers and ruling classes rather than preaching directly to the ordinary people. The fact that whole nations defected from the Church at the time of the Reformation was often due to a single ruler abandoning the faith. Frederick of Saxony and Henry VIII of England are instances of the importance of rulers in bringing about religious change, because in their cases a whole country broke with Rome at the instigation of its prince.

Despite the continual talk today about religious liberty, ecumenical reunions seem to be envisaged on lines not very different from those that prevailed in the age of *cuius regio, eius religio*.[26] Such methods are at odds with the intrinsic nature of an assent of faith; I see no difference between rulers negotiating their people's religion with the assistance of theologians and the heads of different denominations doing the same. I do not, on the other hand, deny that the Catholic Church has negotiated on matters of Christian unity whether at Lyons in 1274, or Florence in 1439, or Poissy in 1561 or Malines in the 1920's, and that these negotiations were carried on by small groups of men. However, it must be admitted that while authoritative decisions on such matters are possible in the Catholic system, which rests upon the authority of the Church, such decisions are impossible for denominations based on the principle of private judgment, and which repudiate the idea of a hierarchy: in such denominations as these, agreement is impossible without a prior consultation of the community as a whole.

---

were about 170,000 conversions each year: now the figure is vastly less.

[26] "Whosoever the region, his the religion" i.e., subjects must adopt the religion of their rulers. This was the principle adopted at the Peace of Augsburg in 1555. [Translator's note.]

To think that a reconciliation of opposing doctrines can be brought about by pragmatic negotiation is characteristic of worldly minds; it ill becomes philosophers and men of faith.

The efforts of Aulus Gellius while Roman pro-consul in Greece provide an amusing and appropriate parallel to what is happening today; Gellius was an energetic, or what would today be called a dynamic character, who thought it ought to be possible to put an end to the controversies between the Greek philosophers once and for all, so he called them all together for a meeting that was to produce agreement: he imagined he could establish order in ideas just as he was attempting to restore order in public affairs. Cicero gently mocks his efforts.[27] Gellius's assembly is something of a joke; but there have been serious meetings of that sort, that produced real results in the course of the centuries, and which involved Catholics and Greeks, Catholics and Protestants, or Protestants of one sort or another. One of the more memorable of such unions was the one effected in the Duchy of Nassau in 1817 at the instigation of the ruler. This was a somewhat peculiar union in which each denomination kept its own beliefs, but all were nevertheless organized into a single church system.

It is undeniable that religious changes affecting whole populations have been brought about by political means, or negotiated, or even commanded by autocratic decree; the people involved went along with the measures either willingly, or because they had been forced to conform. A recent example of this proceeding is what happened to the Eastern Catholics in the Ukraine after the Second World War; they were isolated from Rome and forcibly subordinated to the Moscow patriarchate by the Soviet government.

While admitting that Christian unity is often promoted for partly political reasons, we must not forget that there are two sorts of human beings; those who manage affairs and those who manage ideas, and the two matters are not to be managed in the same way; to treat ideas other than in accordance with their own inner logic can only lead to merely verbal agreements devoid of substance.

---

[27] Cicero, *De Legibus*, I, XX, 53.

250. Unsuitability of current ecumenical methods.

The methods adopted by the present ecumenical movement are at odds with the ends it is ostensibly aiming at. Firstly, it tends to obscure the fact that Protestantism cannot be negotiated with as an entity, because it is in fact an amorphous mass of beliefs. Secondly, there is an internal contradiction within ecumenism itself, in that it says that union will come from believers deepening their own personal faith and conversion of life, while it also proceeds to seek union through negotiations carried on by small groups acting without the authorization of their own denominations, which latter is essential in bodies based on the principle of private judgment. Whence do these small groups of theologians derive their authority as representatives when they negotiate about reunion? The Catholic Church alone can avoid this problem, inasmuch as it is based on the idea of authority, and its members would accept union were the hierarchy to tell them to do so. But the hundreds of separate Protestant denominations have no principle of authority; they are in essence civil corporations and lack the means whereby a decision to unite could be translated into a united act of the whole community. Catholic ecumenism proceeds on an hierarchical basis; the other denominations have no real right to represent the amorphous mass on behalf of which they claim to be negotiating. That is why Pius IX addressed an appeal *ad omnes protestantes*[28] when convoking the First Vatican Council, and did not treat them as communities. However they are looked at, the present proceedings ignore the much celebrated principle of private judgment; matters of intimate religious conviction are handed over to be dealt with politically by small groups of negotiators, and it is openly admitted that union is to result not from individual conviction and conversion, but from agreements between collective entities, namely the denominations in question.

251. Movement towards non-Christian ecumenism.

The change in teaching we have been considering hitherto is that all churches should unite not in the Catholic Church but in a Church of Christ, through their all moving towards a centre which is outside all of them.

---

[28] "To all Protestants."

The proposed alteration of the foundation of unity between differing Christians inevitably flows on to non-Christian religions as well, and alters the conception of missionary activity. Non-Christians are also to form part of a religiously unified humanity, but in their case as in that of non-Catholic Christians, unity is to result not from their conversion to Christianity, but from a deepened understanding of the intrinsic merits of non-Christian religions, so that all men will eventually be united on the basis of a deeper truth that underlies all religious belief.

Jean Guitton develops this idea.[29] He maintains that diversity is good, and that nobody need abandon anything. It is, however, obvious that some diversities stem from the contradiction between true and false, and that there are certain errors in non-Christian religions that ought to be abandoned. But Guitton seems to say Catholicism has no specific doctrine to advance, and that it should merely assist in deepening the understanding of values that are implicit in all religious experience. Thus for a Mohammedan, conversion would mean becoming a deeper sort of Muslim, and the same for a Jew or a Buddhist as well, and so on. Efforts to convert people have now been widely abandoned, that is, specifically religious activity has been given up, and summoning men to join the Catholic Church is regarded as deplorable proselytism.

While not abandoning the traditional formulas that define missionary activity as "leading men to Christ," the conciliar decree on missions accepts the novel outlook, and justifies it on the basis of the present state of the world *ex quo nova exsurgit humanitatis conditio*.[30] This change deprives missions of their theoretical justification. It is yet another example of the tendency to set aside the uniquely divine status of the Catholic religion. Unity between separated Christians is supposed to be achieved by a movement towards a Christ who dwells in the souls of all believers in virtue of their baptism. Thus a supernatural character still attaches in some way or other to the movement toward unity. But if non-Christians are not to join with Christians on the basis of a movement beyond themselves and towards Christ, but by a deepening of their own beliefs instead, then it would seem that Christ, as the principle of unity,

---

[29] O.R., 19 November 1979.

[30] *Ad Gentes*, 1. "From which a new condition of humanity is arising."

must somehow exist in the depths of the human soul as such; to
say that, however, is to deny the supernatural or to equate nature with supernatural grace. The saving principle then comes
from *below* not from *above*: it is immanent in human nature
and can be manifested in all men as such.[31]

Paul VI was not altogether clear on the matter. In his *Conversations* with Jean Guitton we mentioned earlier, he says: *Il n'y
a qu'une seule Eglise axe de convergence, une seule Eglise en qui
toutes les Eglises doivent se réunir.*[32] But to unite *in* the Church is
not quite the same as to *join* the Church as something already
existing which itself brings about the unification in question.
When he goes on from faith to charity and says: *Mais la charité
nous pousse à respecter toutes les libertés,*[33] he fails to make the
point that neither conscience nor liberty are self-sustaining, and
that Catholicism is based upon truth rather than liberty.

252. Naturalist character of non-Christian ecumenism. Teaching of the Secretariat for Non-Christians.

From the writing of the prologue of the Gospel of St. John
right up to the time of Rosmini and beyond, Catholic theology
has devoted a great deal of attention to the idea that religious
truth is given by a light that enlightens every man from within
his own conscience. The Word, as the light of nature, enables us
to recognize the good qualities to be found in non-Christian
cultures, but the same Word prevents us from regarding those
cultures as self-sufficient when it comes to attaining salvation.

Despite that, the head of the Secretariat for Non-Christians
reduces Christian missionary activity to a dialogue "not designed to convert, but to deepen the truth." We read that "in
order to grow in accordance with God's designs, the Church
needs to acquire the values contained in non-Christian religions."[34] This line of thought is not new; it confuses culture with
religion, when what is needed is a careful distinction between

---

[31] In accordance with such thinking, the 1983 *Missel des Dimanches*,
(Sunday Mass booklet) published by the French bishops, prays on
All Saints Day *avec les Saints de toutes croyance et incroyance*s,
"with saints of every kind of belief and unbelief."
[32] "Only one Church is the axis of convergence, one Church in which
all churches should unite."
[33] "But charity drives us to respect all due freedom."
[34] O.R., 15 January 1971.

them. The idea is that Christianity lies hidden in the breast of non-Christian religions, so that a deeper understanding of the *Logos* of nature will reveal the supernatural realities of the Incarnation and grace. Islam, for example, is treated as containing the seed of Christianity which has simply to germinate and grow.[35] As in the case of separated Christians, so here the path suggested is not conversion to Christian truth, but the making explicit, or maturing, of a truth immanent within all religions. This approach goes beyond the conciliar decree *Ad Gentes* which says that "all the elements of truth and grace that are to be found among unbelievers thanks to this secret presence of God, are to be purged of the dross of error and restored to Christ their author...Thus all the good that is to be found sown in the minds and hearts of men, or in their culture and religions, does not perish but is purified, elevated and brought to completion."[36]

The opinions of Mgr Rossano, the head of the Secretariat for Non-Christians, given above, raise a question about *ecclesiology* and another about *theology*. To say, as he does, that the Church is lacking in some way and needs to be complemented by non-Christian religions, seems to deny that the Church is the fully adequate means established to procure men's salvation. Religion and culture are here being confused. Cultures are human constructs, they are always partial or one-sided, they are mutually connected and influence each other, they all stand on the same foundation, namely human nature; but this is not so with religions, inasmuch as the Catholic religion is not the product of human thinking but a supernatural creation which would never have sprung forth from human nature no matter how much the latter was *deepened*. There is a sophistical confusion of religion and culture at work here, which disguises the transcendent origins of Christianity. In Mgr Rossano's view, the Church is no longer seen as a perfect society, that is, as a body possessing all the means necessary to achieve its ends; it is seen instead as an imperfect society that stands in need of the lights

---

[35] Mgr Capucci, the vicar of the Latin Patriarch of Jerusalem, said in an interview on Italian Swiss Television on 11 September 1982 that all men are sons of the Church and that the Pope draws *no distinction* between Mohammedans and Christians.

[36] The very same text is also found in *Lumen Gentium*, 17. "Religions" is the correct translation of *ritibus*, which the editions of conciliar documents often translate as "customs."

and values of other religions. Culture is not religion; thus the universal religion, namely Catholicism, is not to be conceived of as something constructed out of all the cultures of the world.

Theologically, Mgr Rossano's view undermines the catholicity of the Church, inasmuch as a Church that needs to be combined with something else, as opposed to being preached to other men, can hardly claim to be universal in its range.[37] In a course devoted to *aggiornamento* at the Catholic University of Milan, Mgr Sartori, who is a lecturer in dogmatic theology in the Northern Italian Theological Faculty, also asserted this defective or partial character of Catholicism: "Catholicism," he says, "has discovered its partiality, that it is a contraction within universality, and it has rediscovered the All within which its own Christian partiality is situated."[38] Christianity is here presented as merely one of an infinity of possible historical forms in which the universal natural religion is expressed, and its supernatural claims are absorbed and naturalized.

253. Theory of anonymous Christians in the new ecumenism.

The conciliar declaration *Nostra Aetate* quotes the famous Johannine text about the "light that enlightens every man" that gives what genuine basis there is in every religion. But the council says nothing about what John Paul II has described as a mystery parallel to that of the Incarnation, namely that the light was rejected by men. It is thus impossible for the light to be truly the foundation of all religions.[39] The Pope says that Christmas contains the double mystery of belief in the birth of the Incarnate God and of His non-reception by the world and by His own people.

The council refrains from speaking about a supernatural light coming from the Word and talks instead about a "fullness of light." That the two documents, *Ad Gentes*, and *Nostra Aetate*, are stamped with a certain naturalism can be seen even

---

[37] In an interview with the *Civiltà Cattolica*, Father Spiazzi says that "no church is perfectly identical with Christ. Hence the need for every church to accept this centripetal movement towards the Redeemer." O.R., 27 January 1982.

[38] See *Vita e Pensiero*, September-December 1977, pp.74-77.

[39] O.R., 26-27 December 1981.

from their terminology; the word "supernatural" does not occur in either of them.[40]

This optimistic view of non-Christian religions inevitably led to an emphasizing of those elements of natural religion that Islam and Christianity have in common. The council mentioned the Islamic belief in a provident and omnipotent God and in a last judgment, but it ignored the denial of the Trinity and the divinity of Christ, that is, the denial of the two most important truths of Christianity which some have held to be necessary for salvation.

Within the new ecumenism lurks the old problem of the salvation of unbelievers, which has beset Christian theology from it beginnings, and has been compounded with the question of the number of the elect, the presumption being that a relatively small number of persons attaining salvation would somehow reduce the credibility of Christianity. The divine Word, who is incarnate as Christ, is the origin of all created good; thus to follow the Word at the supernatural or the natural level is in fact to follow the same principle. Campanella took Christ, the universal source of rationality, as the foundation of his whole philosophy and made this insight the explanation of Christian missionary activity. "Christ is not the leader of a sect, as are the heads of other peoples; he is the wisdom, the word, the reason of God, and thus himself God, who assumed humanity as the instrument of our renewal and redemption; since all men are rational in virtue of their sharing in Christ as primal Reason, all men are implicitly Christians; they need to recognize this fact explicitly within the Christian religion, in which alone man returns to God."[41]

While knowing nothing of Campanella, the new theology has taken up his idea of *implicit* Christians and turned it into that of *anonymous* Christians. These persons are alleged to adhere to Christ by an unconscious desire and to attain eternal life by so doing.[42]

---

[40] See the cited *Concordantiae* under this word.

[41] R. Amerio, *Il problema esegetico fondamentale del pensiero campanelliano*, in *Rivista di filosofia neoscolastica*, 1939, pp.378ff.

[42] The view of K. Rahner's school, *in Das Christentum und die nichtchristlichen Religionen*, in *Schriften zur Theologie*, Cologne 1972.

254. Critique of the new ecumenism.
Pelagian coloring. Unimportance of missions.

The principal characteristic of the new system is its Pelagian flavor. The new view does not in fact maintain the unique divine status of Christianity because what brings salvation in the new view is not grace, that is, God's special communication of his own being through *historical events*, but rather God's universal self-communication to men's minds through the *natural* light of reason. Historical reality is abandoned for a timeless ideal; a real presence is replaced by the intuition of an idea. Man's ordering towards natural goods, which is the foundation of human culture, is distinct from an ordering towards supernatural goods, which is the foundation of Christianity; it is illegitimate to disguise the leap from one to the other by teaching Christianity as if it were immanent within the religious sense of the human race. It is impossible to discover the supernatural by the light of nature. The supernatural is implanted in the depths of man's heart by a special historical action; it does not spring up from within those depths themselves.[43]

The new ecumenism also does away with *missions*. If the nations already have saving truth buried in the breast of their own religious sense, the proclaiming of such truth by Christianity becomes unnecessary and futile. The spreading of Christianity will end up seeming like nothing more than an attempt to subject souls to the missionaries, rather than to the truth, if in fact the souls in question are held to possess the truth already. The truth however is, that in preaching the Gospel the Church is not preaching its own doctrine, and that not even Christ himself preached his own message.[44] Instead of integrating other religious truth into itself, as Gioberti rightly saw that Christianity did, the new ecumenism integrates Christianity into other religions. Mgr Rossano expressly talks about the "perpetual

---

[43] Thus, to say, as the *Osservatore Romano* does on 11 January 1972, that "the council has ruled out once and for all the assumption that only Catholics possess the truth" is rash and erroneous, because it fails to draw the crucial distinction between the specific truth coming from Christ and the universal truths coming from human nature. Again, to say the Church is not monolithic is to deny that it has a single foundation stone that stretches beneath both the visible and invisible worlds.

[44] Cf. John, 7:16.

problematicity of the Christian subject"; a formula that does away with the certainty of faith, and plants scepticism in the very heart of all religion.[45]

In the Catholic view, the preaching of the Gospel must take precedence over the advancement of technology, which is in fact what culture has come to be in modern society; Paul VI said it was wrong to reverse this order by giving precedence to "human promotion" and liberation.[46] Nonetheless, the reversal has occurred in much post-conciliar activity. Father Basetti Sani[47] says that the Koran is a divinely inspired book; Mgr Yves Plumey states that "beyond differences in dogma and morals, Christianity and Islam teach the same truths and aim at the same end";[48] the *Osservatore Romano* says[49] "Hinduism is already oriented towards Christ and already in fact contains the symbol of Christian reality"; therefore the Church's missionary activity can be nothing more than literacy programs, irrigation schemes, agricultural improvements and health services, that is, the advancement of civilization rather than religion. The notion of non-missionary missions has become the essential idea in the annual World Missions Day; in 1974 the latter was the occasion for disseminating hundreds of thousands of leaflets saying: "What does it (the Missions Day) mean? It means working to-

---

[45] Syncretist ideas have spread widely among ordinary people; the Rimini Meeting for Friendship between Peoples, organized by the great Catholic movement, *Comunione e Liberazione*, in August 1982 turned into "a colloquium in several voices, (Protestants, Buddhists, Jews, etc. took part in it) on the subject of the religious experiences of people of different faiths, but having the common denominator of communion for man, and for his reserve of the sacred." O.R., 30-31 August 1982. This commonality was at odds with the teaching that John Paul II was giving during the same few days, in his sermon in San Marino in which he developed the idea that "in this world good is separated from evil, and is set against it by the very will of God" and that this opposition manifests itself in man's conscience; the same human consciousness which the Rimini Meeting made the ground of man's unity.

[46] O.R., 25 October 1971.

[47] In *Renovatio*, 1971, p.229. This statement was widely objected to, but defended by the editor Don G. Baget Bozzo, who rejects the criticism in a letter he sent me on 9 September 1971.

[48] Cited in *Ami du Clergé*, 1964, p.414.

[49] In a review of a work by R. Panikkar. O.R., 28 July 1977.

gether to eliminate hatreds, wars, famine and misery. It means
cooperating in the spiritual, human and social redemption of
peoples in the light of the Christian message. What does it ask
of us? Maternity homes, sheltered accommodation, schools,
hospitals, dispensaries, orphanages, old people's homes, lepro-
sariums, hospitals for tuberculosis. The missionaries are waiting
for a generous act of solidarity." The whole appeal is devoid of
any trace of the Catholic religion as such; it is entirely devoted
to philanthropic undertakings. The common basis of all mankind's religions, to which the new ecumenism appeals, is not
Christ, the Incarnate God known by revelation, but Christ conceived of as representing an ideal humanity, the perfect man
desired by naturalist humanitarianism. It is hardly surprising
then if missionaries become disenchanted with missions that are
primarily directed at a merely earthly renewal of humanity; nor
is it surprising that an ecumenism of a merely natural sort
should have found its pantheon at Marseilles, thanks to Mgr
Etchégaray.[50] It is, lastly, no surprise that at an Islamic-Christian
seminar in Tripoli in 1976, Cardinal Pignedoli agreed, as point
17 of a document, to accept the condemnation of all missions
aimed at conversion, on the basis that the founders of both religions were "messengers of God."[51] It has now become commonplace among Catholics to regard as proselytism what used
to be called missionary activity; Catholics have completely accepted the World Council of Churches' view on this matter.
Pastor Potter, the secretary of the council, said in his speech to
the world ecumenical conference in Vancouver in July 1983
that the mature fruit of the ecumenical movement in the Christian world at large was that: "From mistrust, from refusal to
recognize each other as churches, from *proselytism*, from apologetics in favor of one's own particular faith, we have moved on
to discourage proselytism so as to make our common witness to
Christ more faithful and more convincing." The *Osservatore
Romano* reports all this without any reservations, and seems to
accept that this is the Catholic Church's position too.[52] It is

---

[50] The attempt to transform a chapel in Notre-Dame de la Garde into a
merely monotheist centre, with the statues of saints being replaced
by texts from the Koran and the Torah, aroused strong popular objections, which led to its being in part frustrated. *Itinéraires*,
No.205, pp.113 and 167.
[51] O.R., 13 February 1976.
[52] O.R., 28 July 1983.

hardly surprising, in the midst of this doctrinal confusion, that an enormous Red Indian totem pole was erected as a symbol at the site of the meetings. The *Osservatore Romano* reports the fact under the headline "Diverse cultures converging in a single faith."[53]

255. Changing religion into culture. Campanella's ecumenism.

The new ecumenism thus tends to move out of the properly religious sphere, based on supernatural premises, and to move into the secular sphere, thus modeling religious unity more and more on the humanitarian internationalism supported by the United Nations Organization. The World Council of Churches admits as much, and commits itself "to the triumph of the rights of man, rather than to mutual disagreements on *questions of truth.*"[54] At the Fourth Italian National Missionary Congress, Cardinal Ballestrero took up the notion of development as the goal of missionary activity. He said that the idea of missions "has become fuller, because missions are understood today as human promotion: it is by passing down the road of human progress that the missionary *also* comes to proclaim the faith."[55] The fulfillment of human destiny in this world is no longer seen as a leading of the whole of humanity back to the God-Man, who grants it experience of divine things; it is rather the complete unfolding of the full power of human reason, which is still a shaft of light from the divine Word, but is only acknowledged as operating *in puris naturalibus.*[56] This tendency can be seen in every step that modern civilization takes, imbued as it is with a technological spirit and a desire to dominate the earth.

In the seventeenth century, Campanella's theology had already given powerful expression to the ideal of earthly perfection, but his was a theology based on the presupposition that Christianity had the capacity to restore man as a whole, and to inaugurate an earthly perfection of which mere nature was incapable. Campanella was concerned to refute the charge, made by Machiavellian politicians, that the earthly well-being of nations was incompatible with Christian law. He was attempting to

---

[53] O.R., 31 July 1983.
[54] R.I., 1972, p.887.
[55] O.R., 23 September 1982.
[56] "In merely natural things."

prove earthly perfection came to the human race as a fruit of Christianity. Nonetheless, his *theocosmopolis* preserved the theocentric outlook that is essential to Christianity; all temporal authority was to be subject to religious authority, indeed to the papacy, so that it could be led towards a supernatural end. Campanella's vision adumbrates the reduction of the human race to unity by means of its being led to Christ, who is both the natural and the supernatural light of the world. This unity was to be achieved by a break involving conversion to the Catholic Church, not by the perfecting of natural good. Thus his great treatise on the theology of missions, the *Quod Reminiscentur*, proposes the drawing of all earth's religions towards what he calls a "superadded" religion, that is, one revealed and implanted in men's minds from on high.

256. Influence of modern psychology on the new ecumenism.

The Bishop of Castellammare di Stabia writes that "in the missionary context, the position of the ecumenical movement is not the one traditionally assigned to it."[57] Ecumenism has no real relation to missionary activity, because it leads to the conclusion that there is no need to *send* anyone to the unbelievers; each religion has simply to manifest the Christ latent within it. An *unconscious desire* for Christ is said to drive non-Christian religions towards manifesting their Christian content, and by following this desire everyone can attain salvation.

The problem of the salvation of unbelievers was addressed in various ways by classical theology; by the theory of special supernatural help being given to them, or by the idea of a state of natural happiness, similar to that of unbaptized infants dying before the age of reason, to which those who have lived generally in accordance with natural virtue attain. But no Catholic theologian has ever taught that eternal salvation, that is, a supernatural reward, could ever be attained without the grace of God that lifts the soul above itself, and which is absolutely discontinuous with respect to man's natural state. So firmly was it maintained that it is impossible for nature to produce an act transcending its own goals, that theologians inevitably reached the conclusion that there are two kinds of last end for human nature, one state that it can naturally attain, and another that it

---

[57] O.R., 22 May 1981.

can attain only with supernatural help. But whatever the theory adopted, it was always held that salvation involved an enlightening of the mind; the unconscious mind was never given any determining role in achieving man's salvation.

The modern theories about unconscious desires deny that religious acts occur at the level of intellect and will, and place them instead in the mind's obscure depths. Thus the question of salvation is removed from the ambit of a man's moral choices, involving knowledge, deliberation and freedom.

But it is unsatisfactory to maintain that man's eternal destiny is decided by involuntary acts produced by obscure instincts. Man cannot be saved without exercising his freedom. It is all the more peculiar and paradoxical that the new theologians should adopt these theories about unconscious desires, since their general emphasis is on the importance of self-realization or self-determination. Or are we to say that self-determination is, in the final analysis, an act of man's unconscious mind? The influence of certain schools of psychology has seriously affected the Catholic doctrine of salvation, and has produced the pseudo-concept of an unconscious desire, that is, of a willing without an act of will; a kind of act which can have neither merit nor reward.

257. A "Summa" of the new ecumenism in two articles in the *Osservatore Romano*.

In two articles, the importance of which is shown by their being in large part identical *ad litteram*, Mgr Piero Rossano presents a *summa* of the new ecumenism.[58] We will give attention to the points that most clearly illustrate the fundamental change that has occurred.

The first point to notice is that the author completely changes the theory of the origins of the religious division of the human race. This division has always been held to stem from mankind's abandonment of a divine unifying principle. By breaking man's link with God, original sin also broke the har-

---

[58] O.R., 17 November 1979 and 11 October 1980. The thinking contained in these two articles is repeated by the author in Bulletin No.48 of the Secretariat for Non-Christians, issued in April 1982. He there asserts that the Church's function is to safeguard the religious sense and the worship of God wherever they occur; but this is a naturalist and syncretist aim. See also O.R., 18 April 1982.

mony there would have been among the sons of Adam. Campanella[59] has provided the most impressive systematic statement of the idea of the religious unification of the human race; he teaches that *metaphysically* the origin of the different religions lies in the nothingness that is part of all finite being; *historically* it lies in the sin of Adam, which has wounded man's spirit with weakness, ignorance and malice and has led to religious divisions by leading man away from the unity of view with which he was originally endowed by the divine Reason that enlightens every man who comes into the world. That men can believe that they are performing a sacred act by worshipping scarab beetles or dung, or by sacrificing a parent on the altar of their gods, or by prostituting their daughters in temples, or by enslaving women in polygamy, has always been seen as an effect of original sin.[60] Giambattista Vico[61] believed that the purpose of human culture is to reconstruct the unity of humanity damaged by Adam's sin.[62] Variety is indeed part of God's original providential design, and would have existed even if the state of innocence had lasted, but it would not have involved hostile divisions, conflicts or mutual attack. There would have been a single religion containing variations that did not affect its essence. These differences would have been something like those between rites within the unity of the Catholic Church; they would not have been like the difference between Buddhist pantheism and nihilism and the Catholic belief in a transcendent God, or the difference between polytheism and monotheism, or that between Islamic monotheism and the Christian Trinity.

---

[59] Campanella is totally ignored by the new theology.

[60] Mgr Rossano ignores Vatican II's explicit statement in *Apostolicam Actuositatem*, 7 that: *homines originali labe affecti in perplures saepe lapsi sunt errores circa verum Deum, naturam hominis et principia legis moralis: unde mores et institutiones humanae corruptae et ipsa persona humana non raro conculcata.* "Men, being affected by the stain of original sin, have often fallen into numerous errors about the true God, the nature of man and the principles of the moral law: thus human behavior and institutions have been corrupted, and the human person itself often attacked."

[61] Giambattista Vico (1668-1744). A Neapolitan lawyer and philosopher, was one of the first antiquaries to develop a comparative sociology and philosophy of history. [Translator's note.]

[62] See VI Inaugural Oration.

Mgr Rossano, however, maintains that Adam's sin is not the cause of religious division; he says it is part of the original design of creation. "What is the historical origin of the different religions? Apart from the complexity of the whole question of religion, involving as it does a host of particular and detailed questions, we must undoubtedly look to ethnic characteristics, differing ecological, historical and cultural experiences, the incomprehensibility of the object of man's quest and the limits of human nature. On the other hand, the determining importance of religious founders and leaders should not be undervalued."

There is a certain peculiarity about all this: when dealing with Christian denominations, a variety of religious bodies is always said to be a *scandal* and an injury to Christ, but here, in the case of non-Christians, division is seen as a thoroughly good thing, as a "fruit of the inexhaustible richness of the human family that the creative Wisdom of God has divided among individuals, families, nations" and, as he does not say, but ought to, religions. Mgr Rossano's conclusions are very frank: "Every religion represents one people's traditional way of replying to God's gift and God's enlightenment." It would seem that the Secretariat for Christian Unity also now officially maintains, in contrast to what was said immediately after the council, that a variety of Christian denominations is not a scandal but a sign of communion, and an enrichment. Cardinal Willebrands, the head of the secretariat, says in his letter to the World Council of Churches Assembly at Vancouver in August 1983 that: "Today the different ways of bearing witness are no longer considered as a sign of division in faith, but rather as an element that assists in enriching our comprehension of that faith." He is here adopting the new ploy of presenting different things as if they were merely varying manifestations of the same entity.

258. Critique of the new ecumenism.
The unimportance of missions, continued.

In this whole presentation of the matter there is no reference at all to original sin as the beginning of disorderly divisions within the human race.

It is true that the Fathers of the early centuries, such as Justin Martyr and the Alexandrian writers, taught that the seed of the Word had been scattered abroad among the human race; but they also taught that man's religious insights had been darkened by the effects of original sin, and even by evil spirits who, as St. Augustine says, tempted man to adore them or to adore other mere mortals.[63]

The truth is that the wisdom discernible in the pagan world is a remnant of what man enjoyed in his unfallen state. But Mgr Rossano entirely abandons the idea that man's state has been changed by an original fault. The notion plays no part in his interpretation. But Vatican II teaches[64] that in the course of history the human race has been stained by serious vices *quia homines originali labe affecti, in perplures saepe lapsi sunt errores circa verum Deum.* Mgr Rossano takes what is derivative as being original, and what is pathological and irrational as being right and proper.

One irrefutable consequence of Mgr Rossano's system is the unimportance, indeed the impossibility, of missions. If religions are by God's design many and varied, and if all of them express the same innate impulse, and in so doing constitute an enriching variety, then the whole idea of missions collapses. On this view, all religious experiences are positive because they express a common reality to which they all have access. Furthermore, if variety is richness it follows that we should not impoverish the human race by bringing it all to the same form of religion.

The classic treatises "On the true religion" collapse. The specific problem posed by a variety of religions no longer exists, because there is no one true religion to be found among the many now existing; the true religion is the one and only religion that lives in all the cults that are its diverse legitimate forms of expression.

What I might call the orthodox naturalism to be found in Campanella's writings can serve here to illustrate where the bounds of orthodoxy are crossed by today's innovations. Campanella recognized that there is a natural religion implanted in the souls of all men by God as Prime Reason, and that this religion is the same in all men. This he calls *religio indita.* He posits that this universal and innate impulse is translated into voluntary acts and thus moves into the realm of conscious knowledge. This he calls *religio addita.* But he denies that these varied expressions of religion are all equally good, since they all in fact contain varying amounts of error, and it is precisely because of this that a divinely revealed religion is necessary. *Religio posita a*

---

[63] For all this see the classic work of Pinard de la Boullaye, *L'étude comparée des religions*, Paris 1922, Vol.I, p.54.

[64] See note 59 above.

nobis est imperfecta et falsa interdum, indita vero perfecta et vera:
et quia contingit homines errare ob additas, idcirco ad Deum spec-
tat religionem et iter ad se propalare.[65]

In Mgr Rossano's system however, Christianity, Islam, Bud-
dhism and Hinduism all *correctly* express man's religious instinct, all of them are means of salvation which, he says, "they
reach or can reach,"[66] all of them come immediately from God
"who gave them birth"; there is no trace of original sin. Admittedly, Mgr Rossano protests that he does not intend to confuse
the historical revelation made in the Incarnate Word with the
natural revelation of the Word in creation, as if God had revealed himself contradictorily and differently in all the differing
religions. But, firstly, he has already explicitly stated that a variety of religions is positively willed by God and that it is an expression of the riches of the human spirit. And, secondly, this
rider of his does not remove the confusion between the natural
and supernatural in his thinking, because he insists[67] on using
the terms *Word* and *Holy Spirit* interchangeably, which amounts
to abolishing the distinction between natural religion, which
depends on the former, and the supernatural Christian religion,
which depends on the latter. The admission that there are differing degrees of excellence between one religion and another is
not enough to establish a difference in kind between Christianity and the rest.

The difficulty of creating anything other than a kind of
syncretist amalgam of religions on the basis of Mgr Rossano's
opinions is so great, that at the end of his article the author is
reduced to saying it is an open question "how one can con-
cretely reconcile the universality of the Christian message with
respect for the spiritual identity and traditions of others; how,
and whether, one can reconcile faithfulness to Christ with

---

[65] Campanella, *Metaphysicorum Libri*, Paris 1638, p. III, cap. 3, art.
1, p.204. "The religion posited by us is imperfect and sometimes
false, while the originally innate religion is perfect and true and because it happens that men err in the religions they posit, God has to
reveal a religion and a way to himself."

[66] Note the equivalence: reach or can reach. Here reality and possibility are the same.

[67] In O.R., 10 October 1975, Karl Rahner is even less able to disguise
this confusion: "Notwithstanding its supernatural character and its
not being due, grace can be considered as something belonging to
man's existence."

faithfulness to one's own non-Christian religious tradition; what
the relationship is between universal enlightenment by the
Word and the historic revelation in the Gospel; how a religious
tradition which is foreign to Christ, and apparently opposed to
him, can be called a vehicle of Christ's grace." Mgr Rossano fails
to see that these problems, which he calls *residual*, are in fact the
main issue that he was trying to resolve and that in fact a resolution of the sort he desires is impossible on the basis of orthodox teaching. The fundamental issue in Catholic apologetics is
precisely this question of the relationship between the *Logos* in
nature and the *Logos* Incarnate, that is, between the natural and
supernatural dispensations, between Christianity and non-
Christian religions; it is the old debate *de vera religione*.[68] It is
the main issue. It is not some residual problem left over when
the main issue has been decided. It is the crucial religious issue,
in all its inescapable urgency.

259. Theological weakness of the new ecumenism.

I have already drawn attention elsewhere to the fact that the
doctrine of predestination has suffered a total eclipse in the
conciliar sky. The new ecumenism suffers from this weakness as
well, inasmuch as the debate about the true religion is part of
natural theology, or theodicy, that is, the explanation of God's
operations in this world. In Catholic thinking, the predestination of the elect is the summit or crowning effect of all God's
providential workings in creation. It is not the business of a
book of this sort to go into a subject like predestination, but we
must at least draw attention to the fact that it is impossible to
address the subject of the salvation of those who belong to non-
Christian religions without addressing the theological issues
which underlie it. If we were to go into the matter, it would
become apparent just how much the change that has occurred
in the Church has cut the roots of Catholic thought.

260. Real state of ecumenism. The movement from a religious to a humanitarian ecumenism.

Ambiguity, propaganda and the *loquimini nobis placentia*[69]
have been more obvious in ecumenical matters than in any

---

[68] "On the true religion."
[69] "Tell us what we want to hear."

other area of post-conciliar activity. Around 1970, posters depicting the meeting between Paul VI and the Patriarch Athenagoras of Constantinople were put in church porches in Italy and
Italian Switzerland, bearing a text announcing the reunion of
600 million Catholics and 250 million Eastern Orthodox. Setting aside the inaccuracy of the statistics, and the almost total
lack of jurisdiction enjoyed by the patriarch, one should not
forget the solemn declaration that the same patriarch made
shortly after his meeting with the Pope: *Il n'est pas question en ce
mouvement d'union de marche d'une Eglise vers l'autre, mais de
marche de toutes les Eglises vers le Christ commun, de reconstruction de l'Eglise une, saint, catholique et apostolique.*[70]

For the Catholic Church, the biggest obstacle to ecumenical
endeavors is the residual core of its traditional teaching. It is this
core that has stopped the Church joining the World Council of
Churches, which is based on the equality of all denominations.
This core of teaching is at odds with the conciliar spirit, which
regards religious unity as its chief priority. It is as if the demand
for unity had itself become a kind of doctrine and, as Cardinal
Siri said,[71] as if the truth had to be changed to suit the requirements of non-Catholics. To avoid facing unpleasant truths the
heart of the matter is rarely addressed, despite the fact that there
are plenty of optimistic and triumphalist expressions of opinion
after every meeting of the ecumenical theological committees.[72]

In a very important and dramatic speech in January 1978,[73]
Paul VI dissipated some illusions, moved by a realism that must
have gone against his utopian tendencies: "The difficulties in
establishing a genuine union between the different Christian
denominations are so great as to paralyze any human hope that
it can be historically achieved. The breaks that have occurred

---

[70] "In this uniting movement there is no question of one church
moving towards another; it is rather a matter of all churches moving towards the Christ they have in common, a question of the reconstruction of the one, holy, catholic and apostolic Church." See
footnote 18 above.

[71] In *Renovatio*, 1970, p.489.

[72] The auxiliary bishop of Paris, Mgr Gouet, the Grand Mufti of
France, and a Calvinist minister jointly distributed pendants to the
students of the college at Montgeron, bearing the united signs of
the Torah, the Cross and the Half Moon. Reported in *L'Aurore*, 15
March 1971.

[73] O.R., 19 January 1978.

have ossified, solidified and become institutionalized to such an extent as to make it utopian to attempt to reconstruct a body dependent on Christ as head, and which is, in St. Paul's words, well structured... The problem of Christian unity seems insoluble, especially because it is a real unity that is sought. One cannot accept any and every illegitimate pluralistic interpretation of the sacred word "unity." This need for a genuine unity, when faced with the concrete historical conditions of the various Christian denominations, seems to disappoint any ecumenical hopes: history never goes backwards." The Pope ends his anguished speech by abandoning himself to prayer, and by appealing against his historical despair on the basis of a theological hope.[74]

Paul VI had already said [75] that it is easy to be an optimist if one knows nothing about the question, but for anyone who knows the doctrinal, historical and psychological problems involved, it is clear that "much time will be needed, and a special *almost miraculous* intervention of the grace of God." As on other occasions, the Pope's forecasts move from historical argument to the idea of a miracle.

A similar realistic view of the matter was put by John Paul II in a speech of 21 January 1982 reaffirming the genuine core of differences that exist among Christians. "It is not merely a question of prejudices inherited from the past; it is often a matter of differing judgments rooted in deep convictions that touch the conscience. Then again, *new difficulties* are unfortunately arising." As had been explained by the Archbishop of Poznan in an important speech during the LXXVI sitting of the council, the core of differences consists of the primacy of the

---

[74] In 1975 the Greek Catholic synod went against Pope Paul's thinking when it accepted a proposal by Mgr Zoghby, the Archbishop of Baalbek, that deplored the creation of the Eastern Catholic Churches in union with Rome, and suggested a double communion in which the Greek Catholics would join the Eastern Orthodox Church (from which it is alleged they were separated "without sufficient grounds") without breaking communion with the Bishop of Rome. The synod wanted the teaching of the First Vatican Council on papal primacy reviewed and reformed. The proposal was rejected by the Holy See. See E. Zoghby, *Tous schismatiques?* Beirut, 1981.

[75] On 20 January 1965, in a speech important enough to be reported in R.I. 1965, p.125.

Roman Pontiff, ecclesiastical celibacy and the eucharist:[76] the archbishop made the point that it is untrue to say that Protestants do not know the Catholic Church; they do know it, and they consider it the principal obstacle to union.[77]

The present temper of ecumenism, involving an effective renunciation of an expansion of the Catholic faith, is clearly evident in John Paul II's speeches in Nigeria in 1982: there is no mention of conversion to Christ, but in a special message to Muslims, which was not actually received by any Muslims or in any way replied to, the Pope hoped for cooperation between the two religions "in the interests of Nigerian unity" and "to make a contribution to the good order of the world as a new civilization of love."[78] As we have noted, harmony in the world is no longer presented in terms of a single religion, but of a single civilization, or, if you will, of a single natural religion of worldliness and immanence. Religious ecumenism is dissolving more and more into a humanitarian ecumenism, of which the different religions are said to be equally valid, but changeable, historical expressions. The religious organization of mankind is to be modeled on its secular condition; the order of the day is taken from the prophet Micah, and was used by Shazar, the Israeli president, in January 1964 in his speech to Paul VI when the Pope was leaving the Holy Land: "Let every nation work in the name of its own God, and we in the name of the Lord our God."[79]

---

[76] The infallibility of the universal ordinary magisterium is surely the heart of the matter? [Translator's note.]

[77] K. Rahner was thus proceeding realistically when he said in an address given in the Protestant church of St. Peter in Basle on 20 January 1982: "Either recognize the irreconcilability of the different denominations, or be content with a merely verbal unity, or admit that the different denominations constitute a single faith."

[78] O.R., 14 February 1982.

[79] Micah 4:5. See R.I., 1964, p.50. There was an even stronger note of syncretism in the statement by Cardinal Lustiger, the Archbishop of Paris, in an interview on 3 February 1981 in *France-Soir*: "I am a Jew. For me the two religions are one." He was immediately contradicted by Kaplan, the Chief Rabbi of France: "For us, it is impossible to be a Jew and a Christian at the same time," and his successor, Chief Rabbi Sirat, said the same: "One cannot, without abusing language, talk about a Judeo-Christian religion. You are either a Jew or a Christian." There is an obvious contrast between

people who have lost their grip on the essences of things, and those
who have retained it.

CHAPTER XXXVI

THE SACRAMENTS. BAPTISM

261. Change in the theology of the sacraments.

Change in this matter was put into effect by the alteration of the liturgy, all the sacramental rites being in some way affected, but here we wish to discuss the actual or proposed changes in the meaning of the sacraments themselves. There is a consistent bent to these changes; the subjective elements are played up and there is a corresponding reduction in the ontological importance of the sacraments. Without actually abandoning the classical definition of a sacrament as a sign that produces a supernatural effect, the sign value is emphasized and the ontological content is devalued thus making a sacrament a symbol of subjective events in the life of the person receiving it.

One could say that the whole world is a sacrament, inasmuch as every created thing is a reflection of the Word, and inasmuch as the word *sacrament* can be taken broadly as a sign of the sacred. But above and beyond that kind of sacramentality, the Christian religion recognizes sacraments in the strict sense, that is, certain things, actions or words that God uses as signs that produce and represent supernatural realities.

There are thus two elements that make a sacrament: the *supernatural reality* that is communicated to man and the *signifying* of that reality in some rite. It is obvious if one does away with the ontological reality of the supernatural realm, what is left to be signified will be merely what a human person experiences in receiving the sacrament, that is, a subjective change in the recipient. Symbols remain, the ontological realities depart. In that case, sacraments slip into the realm of mere psychology and become symbols like those used in the old covenant, or simply occasions for arousing and expressing faith.

This reduction of the supernatural and ontological element is apparent in the new rites for all the sacraments, but we will confine ourselves to baptism, the eucharist and marriage.

262. The practice of baptism down the centuries.

The new theology of baptism shows its subjectivist leanings in its rejection of infant baptism, based on the naturalist principle that the receiving of a sacrament ought to follow upon a free choice by the person receiving it, and that the act of receiving it should itself form part of the conscious psychological and moral experience of the person concerned.

It is an historical fact that infant baptism was always practiced by the Church, even in the earliest centuries before the pagans had been converted in any numbers. When large numbers of adults came to be converted, adult baptism became more common than the baptism of new-born children, with the result that an elaborate system of instruction developed with a catechumenate, scrutinies, exorcisms and all sorts of examinations, which were preserved in the baptismal ceremonies right up until the recent changes. Obviously, the requirement that adults approaching baptism should have freely chosen to do so on the basis of a knowledge of the faith and right moral dispositions, cannot be extended to infants who are unable to meet such requirements, nor can their inability be allowed to prevent their reception of the sacrament. In St. Augustine's time[1] the children of Catholics were often not baptized until later life, St. Ambrose and St. Augustine being among their number. But this practice was an abuse occasioned by the desire to escape the strict moral requirements of Catholicism and the rigors of its penitential discipline, which imposed prolonged or life-long penances on its baptized members, if they fell into serious sin after baptism.[2] St. Augustine tells us that the delaying of baptism was an excuse for moral laxity, and led by logical extension to the practice of delaying baptism until one was on one's deathbed, as did the so-called *clinici*. Infant baptism became virtually universal when

---

[1]   The fourth century, when adult pagans were being converted in the largest numbers but with sometimes limited initial knowledge of Christianity. [Translator's note.]

[2]   St. Augustine, *Confessions*, I, XI: *Sine illum, faciat quod vult, nondum enim baptizatus est.* "Leave him alone, let him do what he likes, because he has not been baptized yet."

the whole of society was Christian from the fifth century onwards. Decrees both civil and ecclesiastical uphold and approve the practice and lay down penalties for those who are slow to have their children baptized. To let a child die without baptism in a Christian society is a grave fault, as baptism is the means to eternal life.

The subject of the *limbus puerorum*, or state of natural happiness, for the souls of unbaptized infants, has been much discussed in theology ever since the Pelagian controversy of the fifth century, but lies outside the scope of this book. The urgency of the need to baptize newborn infants sometimes led people to divide the baptismal ceremony, with the actual baptism being performed by anyone to hand, giving rise to the expressions *dare l'acqua* in the Lombard dialects, and *ondoyer* in French, and the rest of the liturgical ceremonies being performed later in Church by a priest. For the same reasons, the ancient times for the conferring of baptism, namely Easter and Pentecost in the period when most candidates were adults, were subsequently not observed when infant baptism had become the universal practice.

263. New tendency to subjectivize baptism.

The modern theology of baptism is tending to shift the emphasis of the sacrament from the objective gift of grace to the subjective exercise of freedom, by saying that the saving power of the sacrament lies primarily in the consciousness of the gift of faith on the part of the one baptized. Hence the revival of the controversy about infant baptism, which some people maintain lacks an essential element of the sacrament inasmuch as it does not involve conscious participation by the infant.

It should not be forgotten that there has always been an element of subjective assent that the Church requires for children to be baptized; this is represented by the faith and desire of those adults who present a child for baptism. The faith involved is the faith of the Church and it is held by others, not by the child, who is unconscious of it; it is nonetheless the child's own faith inasmuch as the child is not an isolated unit but a member of its family, which is in turn a part of the Church,[3] in which all members are enlivened and united by the Holy Spirit.[4]

In baptism, as in every other sacrament, there is also an objective element that goes beyond the current moral condition of the recipient and has an effect independent of his subjective dispositions, and leads him towards holiness.[5] The main effect of baptism is the fulfilling of the famous prophecy of Jeremiah[6] which proclaims a difference between the sacraments of the old and new Israels, the former being material and unfruitful, the latter spiritual and productive because they write the law on men's hearts. This implanting of what St. Paul calls a *character* is brought about within the nature and operations of the soul, though it is explained differently by different schools of thought; its essential feature is that it is supernatural and that it marks out those who receive it by bestowing on them a new birth in Christ. This regeneration takes place in an infant without any awareness, or will, or act on its part, and it remains quite unconscious of what it has received, even though the gift is designed to effect great changes and instill new inclinations into the one who is thus reborn. Clearly, this Catholic vision of baptism is the absolute opposite of a subjectivism that would place all the emphasis on self-consciousness and self-fulfillment, and despises anything that is not produced by the personal activities of the individual in question.[7] In the Catholic view, the supernatural virtues are bestowed upon the soul through baptism, obviously not *in act*, but as a *habit*, so that in the course of

---

[3] There is a parallel with the admission of infants to the People of God by circumcision under the old covenant. [Translator's note.]

[4] This subjective element was so strongly felt in Carolingian times (i.e., the ninth century) that the unconscious infants were present with their parents at the instructions before baptism, the scrutinies and throughout the whole preparatory series of ceremonies.

[5] This effect is there even if an adult to be baptized is in a state of serious sin. See Gasparri, *Catechismus*, p.197.

[6] Jeremiah, 31:33.

[7] The *Déclaration des évêques de France sur le baptême des enfants* is full of this subjectivist spirit: infant baptism is treated as something that might be abandoned; the document proposes a gradual initiation into the mystery of the risen Christ involving a delaying of baptism. The Cathars in the Middle Ages also objected to infant baptism and said conscious acts were what were needed for salvation. See *Esprit et Vie*, 1966, p.503.

a Christian's spiritual growth he will become capable of performing free and conscious acts of supernatural virtue. Obviously, what is today called *conscientization*, that is the reduction of man to self-awareness and sensory experience, is radically incompatible with Catholic theology; because they are not psychological experiences, and because they involve none of those personal acts in which post-conciliar anthropology locates the whole of a person's worth, the new theology cannot accept the reality of the changes wrought in the soul by the grace of baptism, which lifts a soul above its natural level and directs it towards a life composed of supernatural activity.

It is the rejecting of the primordial idea of man's dependence on God that leads, by necessary consequence, to this tendency to remove infant baptism from the Church's practice, on the grounds that it takes place without conscious action by man, and to replace it with an adult baptism immune to such objections. Because baptismal grace is independent of the individual person who receives it, there is no room for it in a system in which everything turns on the primacy of subjective experience.

I will not go into the matter further, but I cannot end this treatment of baptism without remarking that here too, theological opinions are the offspring of philosophical ones: the denial of the theory of potency and act necessarily leads to denying that a baptized infant has *in potentia* a virtue which will in due course be produced *in actu* as it grows up. In the new view, an infused and invisible faith cannot exist. This is a corollary of the rejection of the fact that God creates invisible things as well as visible ones; *Creatorem...visibilium omnium et invisibilium.*[8]

264. Baptism on the strength of the parents' faith.

The view that infants who die without being able to be baptized are saved on the faith of the parents, who commended them to God, is another expression of subjectivism. It is not a new theory, as its most famous historical proponent was Cardinal Cajetan.[9] As advanced by the new theology however, it does

---

[8]   Cf. The Nicene Creed. "Creator of all things...visible and invisible."

[9]   Tommaso de Vio, Cardinal Cajetan (1469-1534) Master General of the Dominicans 1508-1518 and Bishop of Gaeta, his birthplace; whence his name. [Translator's note.]

away with the specific purpose of the sacrament, because it
equates desiring something with necessarily obtaining what is
desired, thus making everything turn on subjective wishes; it is
also a misrepresentation of the Catholic doctrine of *baptism of
desire*. This latter involves a desire for baptism on the part of the
one who needs baptism, not a vicarious desire on the part of
someone else. Nonetheless the new liturgy presupposes that unbaptized infants *are* part of the Church; besides a rite for the
funeral of baptized infants, there is now one for infants who die
unbaptized.[10]

---

[10]   It should be noted, however, that this Mass "At the Funeral of an
       Unbaptized Child" does *not* pray for the soul of the child, but only
       for its parents and others who mourn. See Mass *In Exsequiis par-
       vuli nondum baptizati* in the typical edition of the Roman Missal.
       Libreria Editrice Vaticana MCMLXXVII Vol. I p.1878, Vol.II
       p.1818, Vol.III p.1930, Vol. IV p.1734. [Translator's note.]

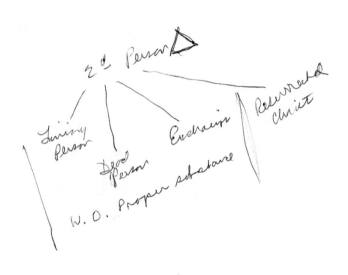

CHAPTER XXXVII

THE EUCHARIST

265. The Catholic doctrine of the Eucharist.

The eucharist is the summit of the Catholic religion and the consummate expression of the sacred. All the other sacraments are, as it were, mere sacramentals that lead towards it as preparatory ceremonies. The mystery of the real presence of the historical individual who is Jesus Christ, in the midst of his Church, does not take away from the structure of created or uncreated Being, but rather adds something to both. That presence is in fact the highest expression of the attributes of the Holy Trinity: its power, wisdom and love reflected in the structure of creation.

It is the highest expression of the divine *power* because it contains the great miracle of Transubstantiation, that is, of the persistence of the accidents of bread and wine without their metaphysical substance, and contains too the mystery of the simultaneous presence of the same body in many places. It is also the highest expression of God's power in human creatures, who are enabled to perform the miracle of transubstantiation, who receive a pledge of their eschatological glorification, and who are strengthened in all their own moral energies.

The eucharist is the highest expression of the divine *wisdom* because here God has established a marvelous way of communicating himself sacramentally in the form of food, over and above his self-communication in creation, in the Incarnation, and through grace. Just as human nature exists without a human person in the Incarnation, because that nature has been taken up into a divine person, so in the eucharist the accidents continue to exist without their proper substance, because they are sustained miraculously by the substance of Christ's body. The eucharist adds too to man's wisdom, because by reflecting

Jesus was not a human being: He was always a divine being.

on its mystery, our minds are raised above the clash of material
reality and attain to purely spiritual concepts.

Lastly the eucharist is the highest expression of divine *love*
because, desiring to communicate himself to his creature in
every possible way, the Infinite Love that had already communicated itself in creation, in the Incarnation and through grace,
now communicates itself in a new way, as man feeds on the
body of Christ and in a mysterious manner takes on divinity.
The eucharist adds too to man's love, because man is enabled to
respond to God's infinite love with a love that runs through an
infinity of space, to pour itself out and be dissolved in the Be-
loved.[1]

266. Theology of the Eucharist.

Any interpretation of the eucharist must respect the real
presence of the body of Christ in the sacrament, and stands or
falls according to whether or not it does so. It is, however, not
the business of this book to go into the different, daring and
difficult theologies that have been advanced on the matter.

The heart of the mystery is that the body of Christ, or better the whole of Christ, God and man, is *really* present after the
consecration, with the whole substance of the bread having been
changed into that body. The deception of our senses, which
perceive the properties of bread when the body of Christ is
really present, is not really a deception, because the senses continue to focus on their own proper object, namely the qualities,
accidents or appearances of things, and not on the metaphysical
substance of bread, which is no longer what sustains the sensory
object before us, but has been replaced by the substance of
Christ's body. The body is not present in its own properties, but
in those the substance of bread possessed before the consecration.[2] This is the doctrine of the encyclical *Mysterium Fidei* of
1965, in which Paul VI sets forth anew the teaching of the
Council of Trent, down to the letter.

---

[1]   This line of thought is inspired by Campanella's *Theologia*, Book
      XXIV, Ch.12, aut. 7, pp.46ff. Rome 1966.

[2]   Be it noted that since extension in space is not held to belong to the
      substance of a body in this metaphysical system, but is simply one
      of the qualities of the substance, a change in substance does not
      entail any change in extension in space, as it would in the Cartesian
      metaphysics in which extension is the essence of any body.

It is worth noting Rosmini's attempt in modern times to understand transubstantiation as the replacement of the body of the bread by the body of Christ, as a result of the words of consecration. The substantial principle of the individual God-Man who is in heaven, is held by Rosmini to vivify the substance of the bread and make it become his own substance, in a manner analogous to that in which our bodies take sustenance and turn bread into man.[3] Rosmini, at any rate, upholds the dogmatic truth that the substance of bread is intrinsically changed into the substance of the body of Christ.

267. The new theology of the Eucharist.

The heart of traditional doctrine on this matter lies in the obvious sense of the word *estin* in the Synoptic Gospels and in I Corinthians 11:24, which Luther admitted could not be got round, saying: "The text is too strong."[4] There are obviously passages in the Bible in which the predicate *to be* has a manifestly metaphorical meaning, not an ontological one. For example, in the explanation of Pharaoh's dream where *septem spicae...septem anni sunt*[5] the seven ears of corn are clearly not substantially a period of time. In other places likewise, the word *to be* means *to symbolize*, as is clear from the context. In this case, however, Christ really does intend the word in its ontological sense, which clashes with the impression derived from the senses, and which alienated a good many of Christ's disciples.[6] It is in this ontological sense that the primitive Christian community understood these words,[7] and in this sense that the faith of the Church has held them down the centuries.[8]

---

3   See the large treatise on the eucharist in *Antropologia sopranaturale*, National edition, Vol. XXVIII, p.275. Rosmini's theories were, however, censured by a decree of the Holy Office in 1888 embracing 40 propositions.

4   In the formula *Hoc est enim corpus meum* the particle *enim* means *really*, not *in fact*, as is shown even by its position in the sentence. This, at least, was the opinion of a commission of Latinists in the University of Bologna, presided over by G.B. Pighi.

5   Cf. Genesis, 41:27. "The seven ears of corn...are seven years."

6   Cf. John, 6.

7   Cf. Ignatius of Antioch, Epistle to the Smyrneans, 6. [Translator's note.]

8   Ambiguities on eucharistic matters are very common in writings having an official character. In No.2 of the working documents

The new theology, as expressed in the Dutch Catechism which became a textbook in Catholic schools, has shifted its explanation of the eucharist from the level of being to that of ideas, and teaches that the change brought about by the words of consecration has to do with purposes and meaning: bread which naturally signifies the food that sustains our bodily life and is produced in order to do so, is said to change its meaning so as to signify the body of Christ, and to acquire a new purpose as the nourishment of Christian spiritual life. It is wrong, however, to claim that the words *transignification* and *transfinalization* more clearly express the personal nature of religious activity, as these writers pretend: the theory of transubstantiation also maintains that it is Christ, as a divine and human individual, who offers himself up in love as both victim and food. It is even more sublime, and an even greater offering, to give one's own substance than to offer something else which merely signifies one's substance.

A non-substantial theory of the eucharistic change is at odds with both Sacred Scripture and the Council of Trent. The new theories do away with the depth of the mystery. The innovators try to emphasize that the purpose of any artifact is inherent in its existence, but they cannot avoid the fact that meanings and purposes exist over and above the very being of the bread in question. It is indeed true that bread is naturally nourishing, but nourishment does not sustain the actual existence of the bread; an idea, including an idea about a thing's purpose, is not

---

published by the organizing centre for the XX Eucharistic Congress held at Milan in 1983, it is asserted that "the bread and wine in themselves, neither as realities nor as signs, even after the consecration, have any title to support and reveal the equation established by Christ (this is my body)." Here the efficacy of the words of consecration is denied, and the truth of the Real Presence is at least obscured. The ambiguity of doctrine in this document, which is inspired by Rahner and Schillebeeckx, was pointed out in *Renovatio* 1982 pp.198ff., and its authors made a feeble defense of it in *Renovatio* 1983 pp.255ff. They maintain, among other things, that only the magisterium of the Church can judge the orthodoxy of a doctrinal position. In fact, it is certain that every member of the faithful has the right to compare the teaching of individual theologians with that of the universal Church, and by so doing to recognize whether an author is expressing the truth of the Faith or a private surmise of his own, contrary to the Faith.

identical with the existence of that thing. A bread that was not designed to be eaten would not be bread, but bread is able to be eaten because of its own internal constitution that makes it nourishing for man. Any mere transfinalization, as a change in the relation of one thing to others, presupposes the prior existence of some thing in itself.

268. Decline in adoration.

The chief and inevitable consequence of reducing the eucharistic mystery to a mere change in the meaning of the bread and wine, which leaves them substantially unchanged, is to abolish them as objects of worship, and thus to put an end to the worship of God present in the sacramental signs. It is impossible to adore the eucharistic bread in any sense if it has a purely metaphorical significance, and if its purpose is considered to be derived entirely from the human mind without any special relation to God as the efficient cause of its being: on such a view, the bread really remains exactly what it was before the consecration. When transubstantiation is admitted, however, the bread is accepted as having become the true body of Christ, and there is an object to which adoration can truly be given; we adore beings, not relations; or more precisely, we adore persons. Thus if the eucharist is thought of as a new kind of relationship, rather than a new real object, adoration will lose its object. We do not adore metaphors; we adore beings. Even in pagan polytheism, when ideals or abstract entities like goodness, beauty and justice became objects of worship, they were turned into symbolic persons; worship was paid to those persons, not to the abstractions as such. The Graces, the Furies, Memory, are all hypostatizations.

When substances go, duration goes too, because duration is the remaining in being of a substance, and without a substance there can be no duration. A purely symbolic body, given as a symbolic food, has meaning only with regard to eating. If the bread of the eucharist is reduced to a symbol of nourishment, no importance attaches to it except when it is being eaten. This is the origin of the view, now widely held among Christians, that what is placed in the tabernacle after Mass is over is in no sense divine. But if, on the other hand, the bread is not merely a symbol, but a real substance, the sacrament remains after the conclusion of the ceremony which gives it a new purpose, and after the act of eating.

269. Worship of the Eucharist outside Mass.

This decline in worship of the eucharist has manifested it-self both at Mass and outside Mass; at Mass the sacrament is now consumed without any signs of adoration, and outside Mass, the cult of the Blessed Sacrament, visits, solemn exposi-tions, the Forty Hours and acts of reparation have fallen out of use and are now often avoided as deviant forms of piety. Dis-taste for these devotions has spread rapidly and has been en-couraged by bad theology, and tolerated by the bishops in their usual accommodating way, despite the publication of *Mysterium Fidei* in 1965 and the instruction *Eucharisticum Mysterium* in 1967, both of which strongly recommended devotion to the Blessed Sacrament, whether public or private, as an extension of a Christian piety that is centered on the Mass. In his letter enti-tled *Dominicae Cenae* addressed to all the bishops in 1980, John Paul II thought it appropriate to ask forgiveness "for everything that may have caused scandal or anxiety concerning the inter-pretation of the doctrine of this great sacrament, and the ven-eration due to it, as a result of a sometimes partial, one-sided, or mistaken application of the provisions of Vatican II." In 1981 the Pope presented the International Eucharistic Congress at Lourdes with a monstrance, rather than a chalice and paten; that is, he gave something that is exclusively used in the worship of the Blessed Sacrament outside Mass, in order to correct the deviant teachings that the congress's preparatory meeting in Toulouse had already noted and deplored.[9]

The abandonment of adoration, both within the Mass and outside it, is undoubtedly the result of desubstantializing theo-ries about the eucharist, which reduce it from a sacrificial act directly recalling the action of the Divine Redeemer, to a con-vivial gathering celebrating the fraternal fellowship of those pre-sent. This decline in adoration is also a retrograde step; it is pre-sented as being a return to a more ancient tradition. It is now emphasized that until the eleventh century the eucharistic spe-cies were reserved primarily for giving Holy Communion to the sick and dying, as indeed is still the case today; that fact, how-ever, cannot alter the nature of the mystery, which is essentially concerned with the Adorable God Himself. It is not possible to

---

[9]   See *Congrès eucharistique Lourdes 1981*, Paris 1981, p.100. See
      also Cardinal Siri's deploring of the "notable decay in the cult of
      the eucharist" in his magazine *Renovatio*, 1982, p.5, n.1.

force the Church backward[10] towards a less explicit formulation
of the faith and a correspondingly less developed practice of
eucharistic piety on the part of the People of God. As we have
already said, the historical development of doctrine and piety is
the product of a deeper appreciation of the content of divine
revelation; therefore if one repudiates the principle of development and canonizes instead some particular past stage of development, and attempts to force the Church's movement to return
to that stage and remain there, one implicitly annihilates a great
part of Christian doctrine regarding both faith and morals,
since the body of doctrine is now much more developed than it
was at the beginning, or during the Middle Ages.

270. The degradation of the sacred.

If the bread of the eucharist is merely ordinary bread used
for a special purpose, the Blessed Sacrament, that is, the presence of the Sacred One Himself, is abolished altogether.

The traditional attitude that the Christian people have
maintained towards the Blessed Sacrament down the centuries
has varied somewhat, but it has always remained an attitude of
reverence, awe and profound religious tenderness that is altogether different from the new tendency to see the eucharist as a
fellowship meal that expresses the loving union of the community celebrating.[11] Some people go so far as to assert that
Christ's presence in the eucharist is no more than his spiritual
presence in the community gathered in fraternal charity.[12]

---

[10] From the thirteenth century onwards, eucharistic adoration outside
Mass has been desired by Christians at large, practiced and spread
by saints from Francis of Assisi to Charles de Foucauld, taken as
the object of some religious orders, propagated by Guilds of the
Blessed Sacrament, depicted in art and has penetrated deeply into
popular thinking. In the eighteenth century St. Alphonsus Liguori's
little book *Visits to the Blessed Sacrament* went through 24 editions during the author's life time and had a further 95 during the
nineteenth century after his death. See *Esprit et Vie*, 1982, p.273ff,
in an article by J. Roche, *Le culte du Saint Sacrement hors messe*.

[11] F. Biffi, the Rector of the Lateran University, says in the *Giornale
del Popolo* of 27 March 1980 that "the Mass is a breaking of bread,
that is, a sharing of friendship, affection and help." Nothing about
transubstantiation or sacrifice here.

[12] The anti-latreic attitude is obvious in the full scale inquiry into the
subject published in I.C.I. No.564, 15 July 1981, p.26, where "the

The attempt to portray the Lord's Supper as a friendly and *cheerful* gathering has given rise to sacrilegious convivial meetings that are a scandal and a sorrow to the Church, involving as they do improper matter for consecration, arbitrary ritual, illegitimate consecrators, non-religious places of worship and irreligious ways of behaving. The Last Supper was indeed an act of divine love, but it had a *tragic* character to it. It took place with a premonition that the Son of God was about to be killed, under the shadow of a betrayal, with the disciples afraid and uncertain about their own loyalty to their own Master,[13] and amidst the tension that led up to the bloody sweat of Gethsemane. Christian art has always depicted the Last Supper as a tragic event rather than as a cheerful meal.[14]

The desubstantialization of eucharistic theology has inevitably reduced reverence towards the sacrament, and the recent liturgical reform has been influenced by this tendency and has in turn reinforced it, perhaps because of ecumenical considerations.[15] The eucharistic fast prior to receiving Holy Communion has been almost entirely abolished; the use of the candles has tended to disappear; bows, kisses and genuflections have become rarer;[16] the Blessed Sacrament has been removed from the most honorable place in the churches, that is, at the altar;

---

excesses of the Counter-Reformation" are deplored, and in which a non-realist interpretation of the sacrament is dominant.

[13] None of the disciples was certain that he was not to be the traitor, and they all asked the Master; "Is it I?" This tragic uncertainty about one's own moral standing is marvelously portrayed in Leonardo da Vinci's *Last Supper* at Santa Maria delle Grazie at Milan.

[14] In a speech on 9 June 1983, John Paul II said that since the eucharist is a memorial not only of the death of Christ, but also of his resurrection, it makes us sharers in his triumphant risen life, and thus has about it a joyful atmosphere. It is however obvious that the memorial turns primarily and immediately on the Supper and the Passion that the eucharist portrays.

[15] Irreverence has reached such proportions that the Austrian bishops decided to publish a document specifically addressing the question. See Mgr Graber, the Bishop of Regensburg, in *Die fünf Wunden der heutigen Kirche*, Regensburg 1977, p.10.

[16] Nowadays reverence is not only not required, it is even forbidden. The Bishop of Antigonish in Canada formally banned kneeling to receive Holy Communion. See *The Globe and Mail*, New Glasgow, 19 August 1982.

tabernacles have been taken down from high positions and put
in low ones, or have been removed from the centre and put at
the side; public and private paraliturgical devotions worshipping the Blessed Sacrament have been abandoned; Corpus
Christi has been abolished in many places as a public holiday,
and the processions that formerly took place during that day
have been moved to the evening, as rites of a *lucifuga natio*;[17] the
eucharist has been invalidly celebrated with any substance,
even sweet pudding;[18] sacred words, of which the initial letters
were traditionally printed with some elaboration, are now
printed in ordinary type; formulas used in preparation and
thanksgiving for Holy Communion have been discarded;[19] the
duty of making a confession in preparation for Holy Communion at Easter is widely ignored; pews with kneelers have been
replaced by chairs that make no provision for kneeling; the duty
of confessing serious sins prior to receiving the Body of Christ
is regarded as out of date; the sacred species are handled by all
and sundry and Holy Communion is distributed by non-
consecrated persons; there are unheard of familiarities with consecrated hosts, with priests even sending them in envelopes
through the post to people wanting to make a communion;[20]
the instruction *de defectibus in celebratione missarum occurrenti-
bus* printed in the Missal has been dropped.[21] In short, there are

---

[17] "A people that flies from the light."
[18] The archdiocesan newspaper in Seattle, in the United States, the *North-West Catholic Progress*, printed a recipe in March 1971 for confecting a substance with which to celebrate Mass: "Milk, Crisco (a sort of margarine), eggs, baking powder and honey."
[19] Whenever the young St. John Bosco was going to go to Holy Communion, his mother used to put away his toys and games for three days; and so distinguished a character as Antonio Fogazzaro (1842-1911; writer, poet and philosopher) used to begin preparing in early November for Holy Communion on the feast of the Immaculate Conception on 8 December; he maintained that Holy Communion produced little fruit without a long period of preparation. (See his *Epistolario*, p.328).
[20] See the newspaper *L'Est républicain*, 8 February 1977, for a statement by the Bishop of Verdun, who finds nothing reprehensible in the practice.
[21] "Concerning defects occurring in the celebration of Mass." These possible mishaps and irregularities were very carefully considered in the old Missal. But obviously, when the sacrament ceases to be

thousands of indications of this degradation of the eucharist on every hand.[22]

Since the eucharist is the supreme expression of the sacred, and the means by which all souls are led back to the One God who is their origin, we could conclude that the current crisis in the Church is a crisis of the eucharist, a crisis of faith in the eucharist, and that this crisis includes all the secularization and desacralization that is visibly expressed in the particular changes that are occurring.

271. The Eucharist as *venerandum* and *tremendum*.

Setting aside the sometimes improper use that was made of the eucharistic species in judicial proceedings and as a means of working miracles,[23] it is an undeniable fact that the sacrament, considered more as something to be adored rather than as food, aroused profound feelings of awe, faith and love in the hearts of the faithful. The deacon used to sing the warning to the people at Mass as they were about to approach to receive Holy Communion: *Accedite cum fide, tremore et dilectione.*[24] This attitude lasted until Vatican II in the popular practice of reciting acts of faith, adoration, humility, contrition, thanksgiving, hope and charity in connection with receiving Holy Communion, as can be seen in a host of devotional booklets that were widely used.

The *tremendum*, the awe connected with the Blessed Sacrament, is apparent in the upset aroused in ordinary Christians by the spread of the Berengarian heresy in the eleventh century; but today there is little of it left, when people go to communion

---

sacred in its very essence, defects in its celebration become matters of no importance.

[22] See also *Esprit et Vie*, 1971, p.11, a list of improprieties that commonly occur in the celebration of Mass; see also the list of often sacrilegious abuses given by Cardinal Renard in *Documentation Catholique*, 1992, col.933. Then there is the unspeakable and incredible fact we recently noted in a house of male religious, namely that the Blessed Sacrament chapel was placed right beside the latrines.

[23] There is the famous instance of the oath sworn by Pope St. Gregory VII at Canossa in the presence of the Blessed Sacrament and of the Emperor Henry IV. At the abbey of Münster in the Grisons, Carolingian paintings show St. Peter throwing the sacrament at dogs to quieten them(!)

[24] "Approach with faith, fear and love."

as absent-mindedly as they take holy water at the stoups in church porches. In those days the power of faith in the real presence could really be seen, and a shaking of that faith upset the morals of the masses. When Berengarius[25] denied transubstantiation and took away the *tremendum* from the sacrament, there was a reaction on the part of the ordinary people. Guitmund of Aversa, a contemporary of Berengarius, records what happened: *Homines scelestos ad Berengarium concurrere solitos fuisse, qui laetabantur se magno metu liberatos, cum intelligerent eucharistiam non esse rem tam divinam, ut propter eius perceptionem a sceleribus et flagitiis se continere deberent.*[26] For these men the eucharist, when regarded as the true body of Christ, was an impediment to sin, or at least their sin was an impediment to receiving the sacrament. This aspect of awe in respect of the sacrament, connected with transubstantiation, did not exclude loving adoration, but it took precedence over it in their minds.

At other times and places, love of the sacrament was the prevailing note; orthodox piety contains the whole range of feeling, and it was love of this sort that led to the foundation of religious houses, especially women's ones, which had perpetual adoration of the eucharist as their primary purpose. Popular devotion among the laity sounded this same note of tenderness. It can be seen, for example, in a little fourteenth century book of pious practices.[27] At the elevation of the host the faithful and fervent soul of the believer sees the very body of Christ, rather than the consecrated host: words fail with which to recognize adequately the unspeakable privilege that "the Lord has allowed himself to be seen by thee." The soul then pours out its overflowing sense of veneration in a moving expression of humble adoration.

The decline in eucharistic piety was mentioned by Paul VI in his encyclical *Mysterium Fidei* and in the instruction *Memo-*

---

[25] Berengarius of Tours (c.1010-1088) a theologian who upheld a symbolical theory of the real presence in the eucharist. [Translator's note.]

[26] P.L., 149, 1447. "Berengarius used to be approached by wicked men who rejoiced at having been liberated from a great fear when they learned that the eucharist was not such a divine thing as to oblige them to abstain from their wickedness and their crimes in order to receive it."

[27] Published by Mgr Carlo Marcona in *Memorie storiche della diocesi di Milano*, 1960, pp.185 ff.

riale Domini of 20 May 1969. The Pope connects this with a
decline in faith, because "wherever the truth and efficacy of the
eucharistic miracle, and of Christ's presence in it, have been
most profoundly understood, respect for the sacrament has been
more deeply felt."

272. Priesthood and eucharistic *synaxis*.

The centrality of the eucharist in the mystery of the Catholic religion means that its degrading leads to the degrading of all
the other sacraments that lead up to it. This lowering is particularly obvious when it comes to the sacrament of Holy Orders,
which gives a man the ontological capacity to perform the act of
transubstantiation. On this point of religion, as indeed on all
points, realities and their manifestation are bound together by
bonds which cannot be broken; to try to break them is *nelle fata
dar di cozzo.*[28]

We have already drawn attention[29] to the attempts the new
theologians make to equate the priesthood common to all the
faithful, who are set apart for the worship of God by their baptism, with the sacramental priesthood, by which certain individuals are marked out by an added character which gives them
a new level of being and enables them to effect the transubstantiation of bread and wine in the eucharist.

This ontological element in the priesthood exactly corresponds to the ontological element in the eucharist, and it obviously follows that if the sacrament does not involve an ontological transmutation of substance, but merely a transposition in
meaning that does not go beyond the order of human mental
processes, then there is no need for the priest to have any special
level of being, any ontological peculiarity, to enable him to effect a change which is itself not ontological. If what is present in
the eucharist is Christ, as He is present spiritually in the community gathered together to remember the Last Supper, all
specifically priestly activity is superfluous because it is the *synaxis*, or meeting, of faithful people that constitutes the eucharistic presence of Christ. In that view of things, the priest does
not give effect to any substantial change in the elements of
bread and wine. Rather, on the basis of an equality shared by all
members of the Church in their exercise of their common

---

[28] *Inferno* IX, 97. "To clash with the fates."
[29] See paragraphs 80-82.

priesthood, the priest simply presides at the symbolic change performed by the community.

The reduction of the eucharist to a memorial *synaxis* or meeting was officially approved by article 7 of the *Institutio Generalis Missalis Romani*[30] promulgated by Paul VI on 3 April 1969. It defines the Mass in these terms: "The Lord's Supper or Mass is the *holy assembly (synaxis)* or meeting of the people of God, gathered together under the presidency of a priest to *celebrate the memorial* of the Lord." This definition is based upon Matthew 18:20: "Wherever two or three are gathered together in my name, I am there in their midst." According to Charles Cardinal Journet, Paul VI admitted that he had signed the *Institutio* without reading it, even though it was an important doctrinal pronouncement.[31] It is an accepted and inevitable fact that most papal documents are drawn up by the Roman Curia and are merely reviewed by the pope, or even signed by him on trust. It is therefore possible that that is what happened in this instance, even though the nature and circumstances of the document make it quite unique in the history of the Church. The obligation to acquire a personal knowledge of a document that one is signing, varies in accordance with the nature of the document; in this case, it was an annex to an apostolic constitution.

The fact that the definition of the Mass advanced is objectionable on various grounds, and dubiously orthodox[32] becomes obvious upon inspection, and was also confirmed *a posteriori* by its retraction some months after it was promulgated, and its replacement by a doctrinally correct formula. This almost immediate retraction is unprecedented in the history of the

---

[30] *General Instruction of the Roman Missal.*

[31] See Fr. Joseph Boxler in *Mysterium Fidei*, February 1982, p.3.

[32] The dubious orthodoxy of the original version of article 7 is the result of a compromise between the requirements of traditional doctrine and the influence of non-Catholics, who attended the labors of the post-conciliar committee on the liturgy not merely as observers (as their title suggested) but as consultants and participants in the drafting of the texts. Mgr Baum, then president of the American Bishops' Committee for ecumenical matters said in the *Detroit News* of 27 June 1967: "They are not there simply as observers, but also as expert advisers and they *participate fully* in discussions on the Catholic liturgical renewal. If they had only listened there wouldn't have been much sense in it, but they contributed."

Church's dogmatic pronouncements; there are indeed examples
of retractions and abjurations of errors in practical and political
matters, like those of Paschal II and Pius VII, but there is no
example of so sudden or swift a retraction of a previous statement on a doctrinal question.[33]

273. Analysis of Article 7.

An analysis of the definition given soon reveals the doctrinal change. Up until Vatican II, all schools of theology and all
catechisms defined the Mass as a true and proper sacrifice, in

---

[33] The correction of article 7 was carried in the May issue of *Notitiae*,
the official publication of the Sacred Congregation of Divine Worship. It is preceded by a preface from which we learn that "the
members and the experts of the Consilium, having examined article
7 both before and after its promulgation, found no doctrinal error
in it, *nor any reason to change it*. However, in order to avoid difficulties and to render certain expressions more clear, it was decided
that the document would be touched up here and there." Article 7
was not "touched up," it was entirely recast to bring out the essential elements of the Church's doctrine, though it still made no
mention of transubstantiation, even though Paul VI had already
seen the need to reiterate that doctrine in the encyclical *Mysterium
Fidei* in 1965. Here is the recast text: *In Missa seu Cena Dominica
populus Dei in unum convocatur sacerdote praeside personamque
Christi gerente, ad memoriale Domini seu sacrificium eucharisticum celebrandum. Quare de huiusmodi sanctae Ecclesiae coadu-
natione locali eminenter valet promissio Christi: "Ubi sunt duo vel
tres congregati in nomine meo, ibi sum in medio eorum." In Mis-
sae enim celebratione, in qua sacrificium Crucis perpetuatur,
Christus realiter praesens adest in ipso coetu suo nomine congre-
gato, in persona ministri, in verbo suo et quidem substantialiter et
continenter sub speciebus eucharisticis.* "In the Mass or Lord's
Supper, the people of God is called together under the presidency
of a priest acting in the person of Christ, to celebrate the memorial
of the Lord or the eucharistic sacrifice. Wherefore, Christ's promise is especially true of this local meeting of Holy Church: "Where
two or three are gathered together in my name, I am there in the
midst of them." For in the celebration of Mass, in which the sacrifice of the Cross is perpetuated, Christ is really present, in the
gathering itself met together in his name, in the person of the minister, in his word and substantially and continually under the
eucharistic species." Anyone can judge whether these changes are
only "touchings up."

which through the ministry of the priest, Christ offers his body and blood to the Father for the remission of our sins.[34] But according to the *Institutio*, the Mass is not a sacrificial act performed by the priest *in persona Christi*, but is identified with a meeting: *Cena Domini vel Missa est synaxis.*[35] *Synaxis* is a novel term, used by Protestants, but unknown to Catholics at large. There is, moreover, a logical fallacy contained in the predicate. The Mass, which is a series of sacred actions, cannot be identified with a meeting, which is a moral entity. Nor can it be reduced to a remembering of the Lord, since memory is a matter of merely mental attention. It is true that Christ said: *hoc facite in meam commemorationem,*[36] but the remembering is consequent upon the doing. We are not commanded to remember what Christ has done, but rather to do the same thing that Christ did (*hoc facite*) and to do it to remember. It is significant that in the Missal all the commemorative and operative words in the Roman Canon occur under the heading *infra actionem.*[37] The Mass is a real action directed towards a remembering at the mental level. Nonetheless, whole episcopal conferences have adopted the idea that the Mass is merely a memorial; the French bishops' *Missel des dimanches* of 1969, republished in 1973, expressly says that in the Mass *il n'est question que de faire mémoire de l'unique sacrifice déjà accompli.*[38] This is grammatically the same formula as the *nudam commemorationem* condemned by the Council of Trent.[39]

The new fangled conception of which article 7 of the *Institutio* is redolent, basically implies a subjectivization of the sacrament, because by saying nothing about transubstantiation, the objective side of the matter is ignored. Everything is reducible to the congregation's experience of its own faith. The renewal of the sacrifice, which is actually effected in very truth according to traditional teaching, is here reduced to its metaphorical and purely mental renewal. This kind of eucharistic subjectivism is collective however: it is the community as a body, not the individual, that makes the presence of Christ real. Then again, the

---

[34] Cf. Gasparri's *Catechismus* cit., p.205.
[35] "The Lord's supper or Mass is a meeting."
[36] Luke, 22:19 and I Corinthians, 11:24. "Do this in memory of Me."
[37] "Within the action."
[38] "It is simply a matter of making an act of remembering the one sacrifice already accomplished."
[39] Session XXII, Canon 3. "Mere commemoration."

reference article 7 makes to Matthew 18:20 is obviously inappropriate because it refers to Christ's moral presence in the Church, not to his real presence in the sacrament.

274. The degrading of the priesthood in the Eucharist. Cardinal Poletti.

Emptying the sacrament of its real content has two main results. First: if there is no supernatural ontological change in the eucharist, there will be no need for a supernatural ontological power to bring about Christ's presence in the eucharist: this causes the priestly office to be lowered from the level of a *sacerdos*, that is, a *dator sacri*, a giver of the sacred, to that of a first among equals at the assembly's celebration. Second: since Christ's presence is conceived of as a presence in the community, brought about by the communal remembrance of him, the fact of the consecration of the elements by the priest at a given point will wane in importance, compared with the fact of the *synaxis* and the coming together in unity of the congregation, with or without any idea of an ontological basis for such unity dependent on the sacrament.

We will not attempt to give examples of all the aberrant, arbitrary and sacrilegious celebrations in which lay people purport to consecrate the eucharistic elements: they are, however, very common, especially in Holland, and photographs exist to substantiate their occurrence. We will not give examples because it would appear that no bishop has ever approved of such practices, even though bishops have failed to condemn them authoritatively; it is obvious too, that the enormity of such things, in the strict sense of the word, cannot be denied. It should nonetheless be said that in many German speaking dioceses, the lay people join in the priest's act of consecrating the bread and wine, saying the words along with him, thereby equating the priesthood of all believers with that of a ministerial priest. What really proves that errors have crept into the Church regarding the doctrine of the eucharist, is not so much the fact that these things happen, as that the bishops connive at them or at least say nothing about them. But here is one example.

On Tuesday 24 April 1980, in Rome, in the church of the Gesù, which is one of the busiest churches in the centre of the city, I was present at a Mass during which the whole congregation said the words of consecration together with the priest. Having mentioned the incident to Cardinal Seper, the Prefect for the Congregation of the Doctrine of the Faith, I wrote at his suggestion soon afterwards to Cardinal Poletti, the papal Vicar for the diocese of Rome denouncing the happening as *abolitio sacerdotii, deiectio sacramenti, irrisio rubricarum, humanarum divinarumque rerum confusio ac permixtio* and all the more amazing *quia in urbe Roma, quod fuit orbis catholici caput, sacrorumque exemplum et speculum orthodoxiae et orthopraxeos, tam monstrosa denormatio apparuit.*[40] I received no reply to my complaint until July, after I had written another letter requesting one; I did not intend to allow the ignoring of my rights, as a member of the Church, to have the Church's service conducted in accordance with the Church's own regulations, nor did I intend to forgo my right to obtain satisfaction after a legitimate complaint. Cardinal Poletti then informed me that he had not replied to my letter because he had considered it as "a simple report of a passing episode, rather than an official complaint about an occurrence regarding which he ought to give an explanation." He did nonetheless acknowledge that the "absurd abuse" had actually occurred; he assured me it was an exceptional event; and he defended the propriety of the way the liturgy was usually celebrated in Rome "which is perhaps better than elsewhere."

The obvious reply is that a bishop is responsible for the due conduct of the liturgy in his diocese, and that he is accountable to those who demand it of him; the fact that the abuse was exceptional in Rome did not alter the fact that it was frequent in the Catholic world at large, and the seriousness of the misbehavior should have aroused pastoral concern, a careful reply to the complaint, and prompt action to remedy the problem.[41]

275. Dominance of *synaxis* over sacrament.

We have seen how article 7 appealed to Matthew 18 to emphasize the spiritual presence of Christ in the assembled people, and how it failed to draw a clear distinction between that pres-

---

[40] "The abolition of the priesthood, the overthrowing of the sacrament, the mocking of the rubrics and the confusing and compounding of human and divine things" and "that so monstrous an aberration should manifest itself in the city of Rome, which has always been the capital of the Catholic world, a model in religious matters and the mirror of orthodoxy and right behavior."
[41] The correspondence is preserved among my papers.

ence and the real presence in the sacrament. The classical term *transubstantiation* is also missing. The first consequence flowing from the new importance given to the *synaxis* as opposed to transubstantiation is that the people should share in the consecration, as is also insinuated by the ambiguous language in one of the new eucharistic prayers to the effect that the whole congregation is admitted "to priestly service."[42] But if Christ is present in the assembly gathered around the Lord's table, and if an *agape* is the principal element in the celebration, the *synaxis* will be more important than any act performed individually by the consecrating priest: from this it follows that if a priest is not available to say Mass where the community is, then there is no need to go looking for a priest elsewhere at the cost of an inconvenient journey, as was done in times past by more devout and thoughtful generations; Sunday worship should instead take the form of a simple meeting of God's people.

This is what the French bishops have in fact taught in official documents that approve and encourage the practice that has recently sprung up of getting people to attend Sunday meetings without a priest. The bishops encourage the faithful not to leave parishes that do not have a priest to celebrate Mass, and go to other parishes that do; they exhort them instead to stay with their local communities for two reasons: first, because they assert that the most important thing is the ecclesial community, that is, the social unit, as they allege the Council teaches.[43] Secondly, *on ne se met pas en règle avec Dieu en se soumettant à une obligation.*[44] In so saying, the Bishop of Evreux seems to be unaware of the fact that religious practice is nothing other than an obligation on man's part towards God, and that the whole of

---

[42] Mgr Riobé, the Bishop of Orléans, thinks the community should choose itself a consecrating minister simply by nominating someone. I.C.I. No.451, 1 March 1974, p.21.

[43] In the 1983 *Missel des dimanches* the French bishops say: *L'eucharistie est sans doute la meilleure manière d'animer un ressemblement de chrétiens, mais elle n'est pas la seule.* "The eucharist is doubtless the best way of animating a group of Christians, but it is not the only one." Here the difference in kind between the Mass and a meeting is reduced to a difference in degree.

[44] Thus the Bishop of Evreux in *Documentation Catholique*, 6 April 1975, col.348. "One does not put oneself right with God by submitting to an obligation." This is repeated in hundreds of parish bulletins and in official and semi-official publications.

the Christian religion is expressed in the fulfilling of such obligations; this is so even under the Gospel dispensation, which is a new law, but a law still. In the view of some bishops, it is not merely a matter of bending to hard necessity, in instances where a parish has no priest. They believe instead that a meeting is actually better than a Mass; that having a community of believers is better than having a consecrating priesthood, and that the common priesthood of all believers is superior to that of the ministerial priesthood. They hold that all this is a rediscovery of the true nature of the Church, for which we are allegedly indebted to Vatican II. The Vicar-General of the diocese of Belley says that such priestless Sunday gatherings are recommended *par l'ensemble des évêques de France*, and as a doctrinal basis for the practice he says *le Concile nous a aidés a redécouvrir ce qui est premier, c'est le peuple des baptisés....Dans cette nouvelle perspective l'important c'est que le peuple de Dieu se rassemble.*[45] To regard this sort of Sunday meeting as positively desirable in itself, is to allow a *synaxis* to have a greater importance than the eucharist: *La prise en charge par les chrétiens de leurs assemblées mène à aller plus loin que la Messe du dimanche.*[46] The Mass is thus relativized and abandoned, despite the fact that it is the most sacred of all things, the mystery around which the Church revolves, and the sacred act that priests are specifically ordained to perform. This is an example of the drastic kind of change we have mentioned;[47] a devaluing of the Mass and the consequent abolition of the duty of attending the eucharist on Sundays and holy days of obligation.[48]

---

[45] See the periodical *Contact*, No.42, April 1976. Recommended "by the French bishops as a whole" and "the council has helped us to rediscover what is of first importance, namely the baptized people...In this new perspective, the important thing is that the people of God should gather."

[46] "Christians taking responsibility for their own Sunday assemblies leads to more than does a Sunday Mass."

[47] See paragraph 37.

[48] This line of thought had already been heard at the CIX and CX congregations of the council, coming from Mgr La Ravoire, an Indian bishop, and from the Patriarch Maximos IV, who said that "it is difficult to justify the precept to attend Mass under pain of sin; nobody believes in it and unbelievers make fun of it." O.R., 26-27 October 1964; *Le Monde*, 20 October 1964. See, on the other hand, the marvelous defense of the reasonableness, the devotional impor-

This degrading of the eucharist, which is the most striking feature of the contemporary Church, is in the final analysis a result of the desubstantialization and consequent subjectivization of the mystery. If the eucharist is nothing more than an act of remembering, an expression of love between believers, an expression of hope for a better world, then it must descend from its uniquely exalted position and be considered as belonging to the same class of rites as the sacred meals catalogued in religious ethnography, in which devotees seek identification with their god. In the Dionysian mysteries, the participants became goats, only mentally of course, and by way of notional assimilation. But in all of this there is nothing of the uniqueness of the Christian mystery, in which God is actually present and actually received.[49]

---

tance, and the legitimacy of this precept, given by Manzoni in his *Morale Cattolica*, First Part, Ch. VI, in Vol. II, p.111, ed. cit.

[49] Paul VI attacked this aberration in a speech to the bishops of south-western France, in which he said *la célébration de l'Eucharistie se situe bien au-delà d'une rencontre fraternelle et d'un partage de vie.* O.R., 18-19 April 1977. "The celebration of the eucharist is far beyond the level of a fraternal meeting and a sharing of life's experiences."

CHAPTER XXXVIII

LITURGICAL REFORM

276. Liturgical Reform.

The reform of the Catholic liturgy is the most obvious, visible, universal and practical effect of the Second Vatican Council. It is a reform that has contradicted what the council actually laid down in its decrees, and which has been deeply affected by the ambiguous character carefully instilled into those decrees by the men who drafted them, and exploited by those who implemented them appealing all the while to "the spirit of the council."[1] The forest of material is almost limitless, but we will attempt to deal with the main principles, both explicit and implicit, that have governed the reform, and thus to show its fundamental meaning; here too there is a prevailing tendency towards independence and subjectivism, both historically, through a breaking with tradition,[2] and dogmatically, not indeed by the rejection of any article of faith, but by a setting aside and a watering down of doctrine, of the sort we have seen in connection with the eucharist.

Since objective reality is one, and subjective apprehension is multiple, the first manifestation of the subjectivist mentality that dominated the council took the form of an abandonment of unity in favor of pluralism; since the western church almost from the beginning had been one in speech by its use of Latin,

---

[1] See paragraphs 48-50.

[2] Reading the ancient liturgies, as given for example in the Sacramentary of Biasca, [a tenth century manuscript of the Ambrosian Rite. Translator's note.] and coming across the same formulas with which the Church has prayed for more than the last thousand years, one feels very acutely the calamity that has overtaken the Church, inasmuch as it has stripped itself of *antiquitas*, which even the pagans knew *proxime accedit ad deos* ("nearly approaches the gods"), and of a sense of the divine changelessness amidst the flux of time.

the obvious move in a pluralist direction was to destroy that oneness by abandoning Latin as the language of the Church.

The extermination of Latin in the liturgy nonetheless contradicts article 36 of the council's constitution on the matter, which decreed: *Linguae Latinae usus in ritibus Latinis servetur.*[3] Its use was in fact restricted first of all to the canon, and then dropped altogether in favor of an integral vernacularization of the Mass.[4] It also contradicts Pius XII's encyclical of 1947, *Mediator Dei* which reiterated "the serious reasons the Church has for firmly maintaining the unconditional obligation the celebrant has to use the Latin tongue." It also contradicts John XXIII's *Veterum Sapientia* of 1962: "Let no innovator dare to write against the use of Latin in the sacred rites... nor let them in their folly attempt to minimize the will of the Apostolic See in this matter."[5] Lastly, it contradicts Paul VI's own apostolic letter *Sacrificium Laudis*, which speaks against a delatinization that "attacks not only this bountiful spring of civilization, this rich treasure of piety, but attacks too the decorum, the beauty and the original vigor of the prayer and song of the liturgy."[6]

The stamping out of Latin is, furthermore, at odds with the egalitarian spirit which pervades the modern world, and the modern Church. Egalitarians want to raise the cultural level of the masses, but the abandonment of Latin displays a kind of despising of the people of God, as if they were unworthy in their coarseness to be elevated to a level at which they could appreciate the sublime and poetical, and it damns them instead to drag everything down to the lowest common denominator.

---

[3]   "The use of Latin is to be retained in the Latin rites."

[4]   This despite the fact that in a pastoral letter Cardinal Lercaro [a leading figure in the reform. Translator's note.] had given assurances that the canon would stay in Latin, since it was, as he said, a priestly prayer rather than one designed to be said by the congregation. The rapidity of change shows the weakness of the initial scheme and the inconstancy of the human spirit.

[5]   See paragraph 32.

[6]   It is a mystery how Paul VI could reproach the Italian state for abolishing Latin in middle schools, when receiving the Mayor of Rome in January 1970; he called that step "an offense to Rome, and a self- inflicted mutilation of Roman culture."

277. Popular involvement in the Latin liturgy.

The Council of Trent ordered[7] that the priest should explain to the people the texts that were read at Mass. This was done not only during the sermon, but in a wealth of devotional books in general use up until Vatican II, which enabled people to follow the various parts of the Mass with ease. These books contained suitable prayers, often adapted from the liturgical texts, and even had little drawings showing the arrangement of the altar, the movements of the celebrant, the position of the sacred vessels and furnishings, all set out as clearly as could be. Obviously, when the people were illiterate, there could not be a perfect correspondence between the successive texts of the sacred ceremonies and the private devout thoughts of the unlettered crowd. Nonetheless, the whole congregation, literate or illiterate, could understand the structure of the ceremony and recognize its important moments, especially when the latter were pointed out by the ringing of a bell. There was thus no lack of spiritual participation in the liturgy on the part of the people. This was especially true after the Second World War when, in all European countries, in Italy especially thanks to the *Opera della Regalità di Cristo*, leaflets carrying the parallel Latin and vernacular texts of the Masses of Sundays and greater feasts were made available. It is important to remember that from the eighteenth century, if not earlier,[8] people's missals carrying the Latin text, with a vernacular translation printed in parallel, were already in use. In Manzoni's library at Brusuglio there is a Latin-French missal printed in Paris in 1778 that Julia Manzoni used to use.

It is customary to object that in the Latin liturgy the people are detached from the act of worship and that there is none of that personal and vital participation which the reforms are aimed to produce. But as against that, there is the fact that for centuries the popular mind was full of the liturgy, with the

---

[7] Session XXII. Ch.8

[8] There was progress on the question of translating and publishing liturgical texts in the vernacular languages. Alexander VII's decree of 12 January 1661, condemning a French translation of the Roman Missal, was inspired by an unduly metaphysical and insufficiently historical understanding of that genuine connaturality between sacred matters and the use of Latin, which we will discuss a little further on.

speech of ordinary people being full of words, metaphors and solecisms drawn from Latin. Anyone who reads Giordano Bruno's *Candelaio*, with its vivid portrayal of the life of the masses, will be amazed at the knowledge people of the lowest classes had of the formulas and ceremonies of the liturgy, not always of course properly used, and often bearing a twisted meaning, but attesting nonetheless the influence the Church's rites had on the popular mind. Today such influence has entirely vanished, and popular speech takes its style from anything rather than the liturgy, especially from sport. The reform is an important linguistic phenomenon that has changed the ritual language of half a billion people, and has removed the last traces of liturgical influence upon ordinary speech.

278. The value of Latin in the Church. Universality.

Pius VI's bull *Auctorem Fidei* of 1794 rejected the Synod of Pistoia's proposal to put the liturgy into the vernacular.[9] Rosmini's *Five Wounds of Holy Church* argued that the right remedy for lack of participation in worship lay not (as it is sometimes incorrectly alleged) in abolishing Latin but in giving the people a better and more vital instruction in the faith.[10]

If we say that Latin is *connatural* with the Catholic religion, we do not mean to assert a metaphysical connaturality involving the essence of the thing itself, but rather an historical connatu-

---

[9]   Cf. Denzinger 1566.

[10]   *Delle Cinque Piaghe della Santa Chiesa*, "On the Five Wounds of Holy Church," reprinted at Brescia 1966, p.74: "By wanting to put the sacred rites into the vernacular languages, one would run into greater difficulties and advance a cure worse than the ill. The advantages in maintaining the ancient languages are chiefly: the expression that the ancient liturgies give to the fact of the unchangeability of the faith; the uniting of many Christian nations in a single rite, using the same sacred language, that makes them feel the unity and grandeur of the Church, and their common brotherhood all the more strongly; the fact that an ancient, sacred language has something venerable and mysterious about it, as if it were a superhuman and celestial tongue ...; the instilling of a feeling of trust in those who are able to pray to God with the same words with which numberless holy people, who are our fathers in Christ, prayed to Him for so many centuries." The vernacularization of the rites "would introduce a serious division among the people" and "an endless changing of sacred things."

rality, that is, something acquired in the course of events that has bestowed a unique association and a unique suitability on Latin as the idiom of Catholicism. Catholicism was, as it were, born Aramaic, rapidly became Greek, and was then Latin for so many centuries that Latin has become connatural to it. To say that a language has become historically connatural to Christianity, is to say that it has adapted itself in many ways to the requirements of the Christian religion, and has been perfectly molded along the Church's lines.

So then, first of all the Church is a universal thing; not merely in the geographical sense of being, as one of the new eucharist prayers puts it, "diffused" throughout the earth.[11] Its universality comes from the fact that all men are called to join it, and from its connection with Christ who is the head and the source of unity for the whole human race. The Church educated the peoples of Europe and created their alphabets in some cases, as with the Slavic languages and Armenian, and gave the people their first written documents. In conjunction with the civilizing activities of European states, the Church has also educated many nations in Africa. It is therefore impossible for it to take as its own the language of any one particular people, thus discriminating against the rest. Despite the centrifugal tendencies apparent in the post-conciliar period, the modern Catholic Church still seems to fail to understand how important linguistic unity is in building up the unity of a vast assemblage of men. But Islam has understood it very well, and continues to use ancient Arabic in its worship, even in non-Arabic countries; nor have the Jews failed to grasp this point, and thus they continue to use ancient Hebrew for religious purposes. The newly independent states that have only just achieved national unity since the Second World War have understood the point as well: they have not adopted a local dialect as their official language, but have instead all taken on the English or French that were the languages of those who colonized and civilized them.[12]

---

[11] In fact it is *dispersed* in separate places throughout the earth, not *diffused*: the latter word is a metaphor drawn from liquids that spread uniformly, giving a continuous cover over some surface.

[12] That the use of a supranational language is a factor making for unity and harmony in civil life as well, is proved by the fact that when certain multi-lingual Asian and African states have attempted to install a single local tongue as the official language of the coun-

Secondly, the Church is in its substance unchangeable, and
it therefore naturally expresses itself in a language which is in a
certain sense unchangeable and exempt, relatively speaking but
in a unique degree, from the alterations that affect languages in
common use, and which occur so steadily as to have made the
first written works in all of today's European languages unintel-
ligible without the aid of dictionaries. The Church needs a language that reflects its timeless truth and is immune from historical change. Given the fact that no human language can escape change altogether, the Church has attached itself to one
which does so as far as possible. I am choosing my words carefully, because I know that some degree of change is inseparable
from any living language, and that even Church Latin has
changed in the course of time. Setting aside the current decay in
the knowledge of Latin, whether in secular or ecclesiastical circles, one can realize the fact of change by comparing the papal
encyclicals of the last century with those of recent pontificates.

279. Relative changelessness. Distinguished character
of the Latin language.

Thirdly, the Church's language should have a certain nobility or character of distinction about it, because the things it is
trying to express are the flower of the human spirit, or better, a
foretaste of superhuman realities. This is not to say that the
Church despises the *profanum vulgus*:[13] the Church sanctifies
whatever it touches, and the uneducated, the poor and the
simple are the object of its special care. It treats prince and pau-
per alike in its sacraments, it instructed people in their own language so that, for example, St. Thomas preached at Naples in
the Neapolitan dialect, Gerson[14] preached in the dialect of the
Auvergne, and parish priests in Lombardy preached in the village patois until the late nineteenth century. The Church
founded religious orders for instructing the masses, even identifying with them by taking humble names, such as that of the
Ignorantelli. The fact that Latin is the Church's special language
is not therefore a sign of any haughty disdain for the unedu-

---

try, they have provoked civil disturbances and have had to abandon
their plans.
13 "The vulgar crowd."
14 Jean Gerson, 1363-1429, French theologian and spiritual writer.
[Translator's note.]

cated. The real reason the Church acquired its Latin culture is that it stands in historical continuity with the culture of the ancient world, as we have already pointed out.[15] But the single most important reason for maintaining that culture is the need to guard dogma in a language that is immune to changes caused by human temperament. The appetites or passions, from pride down to hasty judgment, are an element of instability in human minds, that cause distortions of the truth and division among men. To guard against their influence, clear thought and precise expression are needed. It is therefore unreasonable to complain about arguments over subtle differences between one definition and another, as if all such discussions were the ridiculous trifling of wordspinners. A word is the very expression of an idea itself, and so to change a word is to change an idea or a doctrine, as can be seen in the consistent development of dogma along orthodox or unorthodox lines, depending on the words used. We have seen this process at work in the case of transubstantiation.[16]

Just as the supernatural life establishes a new kind of communion between those who share a common human nature, but without taking away any of the things they already had in common, so Church Latin has a *suprahistorical* character that establishes a new communion among men, without removing any of the connections that they already share. When discussing the excellences of different languages, Lorenzo the Magnificent attributes Latin's universal status to the *prosperità della fortuna.*[17] One does not necessarily have to believe with the medievals that both the Roman Empire and the Roman language were established by Providence *per lo loco santo u'siede il successor del maggior Piero.*[18] Even without accepting that opinion, one can still recognize the importance and appropriateness of the Church's use of Latin.

We cannot end this discussion without recalling the fact that until a short while ago, Latin was the most widely spread common language of the cultural world. This common tongue could have been preserved within the Catholic Church for purposes of teaching, worship and administration, if a pusillanimous and feeble spirit had not frustrated the reinvigoration of

---

[15] See paragraph 32.
[16] See paragraph 275.
[17] *Scritti scelti*, Turin 1930, p.46 "The favor of fortune."
[18] *Inferno*, II, 23-24. "For the holy place, where sits the successor of great Peter."

Latin ordered by John XXIII.[19] Contemporary governments
have displayed a tougher spirit than the Church in imposing or
encouraging entire peoples to speak unknown and foreign languages, as has happened in Israel, which has revived Hebrew, in
China, and in many African states.

280. The new version of the liturgy.

The adoption of vernacular languages has certainly split up
Catholic worship, and put an end to the harmonious chorus of
praise that used to rise to blend with that of the angels. But the
official Latin text of the Mass, promulgated on 3 April 1969,
should have at least imposed a limit on the disintegration. The
different vernacular translations, all of which had to be approved by Rome, should have adhered to the new Latin texts.
They should have adhered to them closely, because an exact
conformity is required in any translation, since as the word
implies, a *translation* is a *carrying over* of the same idea from one
idiom into another. But in fact, a spirit of novelty and change,
typical of the post-conciliar period, has had a powerful influence on the new Latin biblical and liturgical texts, a spirit expressing the general drift towards subjectivization and detachment from any fixed point of reference, whether in the Church's
tradition or in the apostolic deposit of faith.

So far as the Italian translation is concerned, this independent spirit is strikingly obvious at those many points at which the
translation diverges from the original Latin. What is meant to
be an Italian version is in many respects a new text embodying a
wholesale reform within the original reform. We will give some
examples drawn from the rite of Mass published by the Italian
Episcopal Conference in 1969.

The changes cover the whole field, from vocabulary to syntax, but they all display the same profound change in mentality.
Sometimes they seem to be the expression of a set policy.
Propositions expressing an intent, for example, are generally
eliminated and replaced by propositions of fact. There is certainly a tendency in modern languages to avoid organizing one's
thought in a strongly synthetic structure, and to break up
thoughts into a string of short statements instead. But this
mode of expression also reflects a distaste for ontological or
metaphysical theories of causation: a real connection between

---

[19] See paragraph 32.

one thing and another is replaced by a mere succession of one thing after another.

In the prayer said immediately after the *Pater Noster* we read: *Da propitius pacem...ut a peccato simus semper liberi* etc. These words mean "Grant peace so that we may be always free from sin." But the Italian version says: *Concedi la pace...e saremo sempre liberi.*[20] Similarly, in the first Advent preface the Latin says: *Nobis salutis perpetuae tramitem reservavit, ut capiamus quod nunc audemus exspectare promissum,* that is: "He opened the way of eternal salvation to us so that we should obtain what we now dare to hope for as promised." But the Italian says: *Egli ci aprì la via...e potremo ottenere.*[21] The events of being granted peace, and of being free from sin as a result; and the events of opening a way, and of obtaining what we now hope for as a result, lose all causal connection and become a mere sequence of events. One thing happens after the other, but the whole event is no longer portrayed as the achievement of a goal willed by God but requiring our cooperation for its achievement. It is like saying that the two propositions: "Titus drinks the medicine in order to get better" and "Titus drinks the medicine and he gets better" are identical. There are no effects any more, just happenings; no goals or responsibilities, just facts. Anyone who pauses to reflect on the implications of this abolition of goals, will recognize a profound connection with the desubstantializing and anti-metaphysical mentality of modern philosophy.[22]

281. The new version of the liturgy.
Change in vocabulary. Pelagian tendencies.

As to vocabulary, the changes are no less significant, and suggest a tendency towards innovation and a bending of doctrine.

---

[20] "Grant peace...*and we will* be always free from sin."

[21] "He opened for us the way...*and we will* be able to obtain."

[22] Because the whole translation has a varied and uneven character, it sometimes happens that statements of fact are turned into statements of intent. In the offertory the words *ex quo nobis fiet panis vitae* are rendered as *perché diventi per noi cibo di vita,* i.e., "Which will become for us the bread of life" becomes "In order that it may become for us the bread of life."

Deus Sabaoth has been translated as *Dio dell'universo*,[23] but
this is to change the meaning of the Hebrew *Sabaoth* and the
Latin *exercituum*, which both refer to the strength, warlike and
other, of a God whose power is revealed. However, the translators have resolved to avoid any hint of militaristic language,
despite the fact that the Old Testament is a history of wars, and
that Job and St. Paul both call human life itself a struggle or a
warfare. Again deferring to the anti-militarist spirit of contemporary western society, the words *militia coelestis exercitus* become *moltitudine dei cori celesti*.[24] A musical image replaces a
military one.

In a place where the Latin was not changed, the Italian
translation has changed even the words of consecration, departing not only from a formula that had been preserved intact for
centuries, but from the implications of Sacred Scripture, and
abandoning too that delicate reverence which once led theologians to debate the legitimacy of changing even the slightest word.
Thus, where the Latin says *qui pro vobis et pro multis effundetur*
the translation changes it to *versato per voi e per tutti*.[25] The difference is obvious. The change is not theologically wrong, since
Christ's redemptive sacrifice does indeed merit eternal salvation
for all men, even though salvation is only in fact attained by
those who respond to that sacrifice through a voluntary acceptance of the grace it brings. Since, however, the two versions are
meant to be saying the same thing, it is obvious that there
would have been no reason for introducing this unwonted and
unhelpful change, if the translators had not been intending to
get rid of even the slightest hint of the Catholic doctrine of predestination, and to insinuate the idea of universal salvation instead.[26] There is thus a Pelagian tinge to this flight from an idea
of a distinction between some men and others.

---

[23] "God of all."

[24] "Militia of the heavenly army" becomes "Multitude of the heavenly
choirs."

[25] "Which will be poured out for you and for many" becomes "poured
out for you and for all."

[26] It is useless to try and justify the change philologically by saying
that "many" is a Semitic turn of phrase meaning "all." Such is not
the case: *the* many does indeed mean the mass of men, but *many*
simply means many. To assert that ancient peoples did not draw a
distinction between the idea of all and the idea of many, is to accuse them of lacking a grip on the fundamental elements of reason.

The same Pelagian tone may be detected in the translation of the ferial Lenten preface; where the Latin says *virtutem largiris et praemia*, "You give virtue and its rewards," the Italian says *infondi la forza e doni il premio*.[27] Setting aside grammatical objections that might be made over the doubling of *largiris* in two verbs, *infondi* and *doni*, the main point is that the translation weakens an important principle of Christian ethics, namely that virtue, like every other good, is a gift from Heaven. This is Pelagian in the sense that Pelagius could not imagine virtue except as something exclusively produced by the autonomous human will; he thought of God as simply setting moral standards, and that any further action by God was incompatible with man's moral choices; he strongly rejected the idea that merit proceeded from grace rather than from the inner resources of human freedom. In accordance with such thinking, the new Missal has omitted all references in the collects, and similar prayers, to asking God for virtue, and has failed to express the fact that when the liturgy says *grant*, it is implying that both virtue and the reward that crowns it are gifts of God. Infusing strength is not the same as granting virtue. To get that rendering, the translator has had to take the word *virtus* in its classical sense, rather than in its obvious Christian one.[28]

Pagan ethics, especially in its two last and greatest forms, Epicureanism and Stoicism, held that earthly goods should be sought from God, but that moral virtue was something that man had to attain entirely of his own resources. Cicero says in a well known passage: *omnes mortales sic habent, externas commoditates, vineta, segetes, oliveta...a diis se habere, virtutem autem nemo umquam a deo acceptam deo rettulit*.[29] Sartre echoes the same sentiments for modern man in Orestes' defiance of Jupiter: *Tu es le roi des pierres et des étoiles mais tu n'est pas le roi des hommes*.[30] If one is not firm in upholding God's dominion over the human will, then one restricts the operations of Providence,

---

[27] "You provide strength and give the reward."

[28] In so saying, I do not deny that *virtus* sometimes does mean *strength*, or that *virtutes* in the Bible are sometimes "miracles."

[29] *De Natura Deorum*, III, XXXVI, 86-87. "All men agree that they receive external blessings as vineyards, fields and olive groves...from the gods, but nobody has ever received virtue from a god, or traced its origin thither."

[30] *Les mouches*, Act III, Scene II. "You are the god of stones and stars, but you are not the god of men."

compromises God's infinite power, and changes the nature of Christian teaching.[31]

282. The new version of the liturgy. Dogmatic ambiguities.

Many passages in the new Missal reflect the egalitarian spirit we have mentioned,[32] and tend to deny the ontological differences between the ministerial priesthood and the priesthood of the laity. There is an undeniable ambiguity on this point when the Italian version of the Roman Canon translates *nos servi tui* and *famuli tui* equally as *noi tuoi ministri.*[33] Then again, *Ci hai chiamati a prestare il servizio sacerdotale* are words which should in their context apply to the ordained priest, but which are used for the people of God as a whole.[34]

On another subject altogether, there is an equally important variation introduced when *Domine non sum dignus ut intres sub tectum meum* becomes *non sono degno di partecipare alla tua mensa.*[35] That Christ should enter my dwelling, that is my inmost self, is quite different from eating at table with him; there is here an implicit denial of the fact that in the eucharist God really does enter man; that idea is converted into a mere sharing at the same table, a simple friendship.

Since we are limiting our discussion to the Italian Missal, we cannot treat of all the others, and the changes they make; in the case of African languages, there are hundreds of versions and it is hard to see how they can have been reviewed and approved in the Roman curia, in which nobody knows the many languages in question; the translators themselves must have been treated by the curia as the reviewers of their own productions.[36]

---

[31] On this point see paragraphs 207-209 on the autonomy of natural values.

[32] See paragraphs 80-82.

[33] "We your servants" and "your familiars," i.e., we of your household, as "we your ministers."

[34] Cf. Second eucharistic prayer. "You have called us to offer priestly service."

[35] "Lord I am not worthy that you should enter under my roof" becomes "I am not worthy to share at your table."

[36] In the Upper Volta, or Burkina Faso, a country of some five million people, in which sixty languages are spoken, the bishops have chosen seventeen of them as liturgical languages.

The *Missel Romain* published by the French bishops[37] translated the word *consubstantialem* in the Creed, as "of the same nature." This is obviously inadequate theologically: the Father and the Son are of one and the same being, they are not two beings that happen to have the same nature. Martin and Titus have the same human nature, but they are not one in being, that is, of one substance. The same *Missel* is also at odds with Catholic doctrine in its translation of Philippians 2:6 : *qui cum in forma Dei esset, non rapinam arbitratus est esse se aequalem Deo.* In the 1970 lectionary this was correctly translated, in accordance with the Jerusalem Bible version: *Etant de condition divine il ne retint pas jalousement le rang qui l'égalait à Dieu.*[38] But subsequent editions had: *Le Christ Jésus est l'image de Dieu, mais il n'a pas voulu conquérir de force l'égalité avec Dieu.*[39] The error is obvious. Christ is God, and he cannot therefore *conquer* equality with God. There is an Arianizing tendency here.[40]

283. General collapse of Latin.

The collapse of Latin is the most obvious and undeniable fact about the post-conciliar Church, and a sign that the Church has abandoned itself unreservedly to the drift of current events.[41] The machinery of Church government is now polyglot;

---

[37] A detailed analysis of it has been published by J. Renié, *Missale Romanum et Missel Romain*, Paris 1975. This shows how the heterodox nuances of the French version reflect the heterodox beliefs of the French bishops, 20% of whom do not accept the divinity of Christ. See pp.33-34.

[38] "Being of divine status, he did not cling jealously to the rank by which he was equal to God."

[39] "Christ Jesus is the image of God, but he did not want to seize equality with God by force."

[40] It should be noted that in still later editions, the *Missel* returned to the correct translation, as a result of strong protests.

[41] The collapse of Latin is obvious in the results of an enquiry carried out by the Congregation for the Sacraments and Divine Worship, and published in *Notitiae*, December 1981, pp.589-611: "As far as Latin is concerned, it is clear from the enquiry that its use is tending to disappear." The liturgical reform "has produced, and continues to produce *abundant fruit.*" This report does not view the disappearance of Latin as a bad thing; it views it positively, while completely ignoring the fact that the most striking and obvious ef-

theological teaching is given in the vernacular; in giving his
Christmas and Easter greetings, the Pope now goes on at length
using dozens of foreign phrases. Even in consistories, the cardinal who speaks on behalf of all the newly nominated cardinals
uses French, while John Paul II replies in seven languages.[42]
When opening the General Congregation of the Jesuits in September 1983, the Pope spoke in five modern languages, while
Paul VI at an earlier gathering of the same body had spoken to
the assembled Jesuits in Latin. Not the least significant fact
about John Paul II's speech on that occasion was the order in
which he used the different languages, first place being given to
Italian, which was the least widely spoken of the five languages
involved. When attending Mass in some tourist centre in Italy
today, one is more likely to come across German or English
than Latin. When the Pope visited Great Britain for six days in
May 1982, all his Masses were celebrated in the language of the
country.[43] At the triennial world synod of bishops held in Rome,
the participating bishops do their work in *circuli minores*,[44] that
speak French, German, English, Spanish etc., one of which is a
Latin speaking group. Thus the synod is divided by language,
when once its labors would have been conducted in a Latin that
unified all the participants. Latin, and its related Gregorian
chant, have not only been abandoned, despite contradictory and
feeble appeals by Paul VI; they are now actually despised and
mocked by most clergy as things fit only for a society of dead

---

fect of the reform was that people stopped going to Mass. In 1975,
Cardinal Marty, the Archbishop of Paris, revealed that in his diocese the number of Mass-goers has dropped by 47%
(*Documentation Catholique*, 19 October 1975) and the percentage
has increased further since then. The enquiry carried out by the
Congregation was directed at the bishops of the world, and made
reference to the *spirit* of the council, but did not refer to the actual
text of the conciliar document decreeing that the use of Latin
should be retained. To top it all, there is the fact that Roman congregations now publish certain documents addressed to the universal Church in English. (O.R., 25 June 1983.)

[42] O.R., 3 February 1983.

[43] This is generally the case in all the Pope's foreign visits. He now
often uses Italian in Rome and in the Vatican. [Translator's note.]

[44] "Small circles."

souls.[45] Paul VI's self-contradictory proceedings are manifest yet
again in his establishment of the *Latinitas* office, with its head-
quarters in the Palace of the Cancelleria in Rome, with the purpose of promoting the restoration of Latin as a language of
scholarly interchange and general communication. It is to be
hoped the foundation does not have the same fate as the Institute for Higher Latin Studies, established by John XXIII in pursuance of *Veterum Sapientia.*

The descent to this nadir in the use of Latin in worship,
and for religious purposes in general, was begun by the *Consilium* or committee, set up to implement liturgical changes in
the wake of the Second Vatican Council's decree on the liturgy;
and in particular by its "Instruction" of September 1964. In the
usual self-contradictory way, the Instruction states that the
recitation of the Divine Office in choir should always be in
Latin, but then it at once proceeds to open the way for dispensations from this rule on the grounds that "the use of Latin
constitutes for some a *grave impediment* to the recitation of the
Divine Office." So the document actually ends up asserting that
Latin is not only unnecessary and antiquated, but a positive
obstacle to prayer. But the council had decreed, when dealing
with ecclesiastical studies, that the learning of Latin is necessary
for the understanding of the Church's documents.[46]

In one memorable speech, Paul VI recognized and sorrow-
fully regretted the enormous loss to the Church represented by
the casting aside of Latin and Gregorian chant.[47] Nonetheless, so
far as the Pope was concerned, the seriousness of this loss was
not to be allowed to stand in the way of the advantages that it
was hoped would flow from delatinization, nor was it to dis-
suade him from proceeding with his reform, nor could it restrain its hasty implementation, nor would the Pope even moderate the baneful and unhappy effects of that reform through
the exercise of the wisdom that once characterized the Roman

---

[45] See P. Buscaroli's article in the *Giornale Nuovo*, 13 April 1982.
When he was in Venice looking for a Holy Week celebration in
Latin, using Gregorian chant, Buscaroli was insulted by the priests
he approached: "Latin? Gregorian chant? That is stuff for bigots,
aesthetes and pietists." What used to be typical of the more rabid
anti-clericalism of the nineteenth century has become a permanent
state of mind among today's Catholic clergy.

[46] Cf. Optatam Totius, 13.

[47] Cf. O.R., 27 November 1969.

See. Thus when addressing the transition to what he improperly
calls the "spoken language," because Latin too was a spoken
language for liturgical purposes, Pope Paul recognizes that the
abandonment of Latin is "a great sacrifice," and he feels the
rupturing of tradition acutely. He effectively admits that the
new rite breaks with the ancient one that has been handed
down the centuries, and that it is content with an eclectic rifling
of some ancient sources,[48] thus cutting off the present Christian
generation from the ones that have gone before. Nor does the
Pope fail to appreciate the inestimable riches of liturgical Latin.
"We are losing the language of the Christian centuries, we are in
the process of becoming, as it were, profane intruders within the
sanctuary of sacred letters, and we thereby lose a great part of
that stupendous and incomparable artistic and spiritual reality
which is Gregorian chant. We do indeed have reason for regret,
and to feel as it were, that we have lost our way. What will be
put in the place of this angelic language? It is a sacrifice of *inestimable value*." The Pope says that Latin "brought to our lips
the prayers of our ancestors and gave us the comfort of a fidelity
to our spiritual past, which *we made present* in order to transmit
to coming generations." But if we made it present, then it seems
obvious to remark that there was no need for a reform allegedly
introduced in order to make the liturgy relevant to the present.
"In these circumstances, we understand better the value of tradition": these words of the Pope can only mean that in the act
of abandoning tradition, we understand better that the value of
tradition is less than we thought it was.[49]

In the end the Pope attempts to justify the abandonment of
all these riches. Even so high a price is worth paying, he says,
"because the understanding of prayer is worth more than the
ancient silken vestments in which it is royally arrayed. There is a
greater value in *participation by the people*, this modern people,
hungry for clear, intelligible words that can be translated into its
everyday conversation." He then cites I Corinthians 14:19: "In
the church I would rather speak five words which my mind ut-

---

[48] And with an even larger amount of new compositions and new
      structures. [Translator's note.]

[49] Much of the loss Pope Paul deplored would have been avoided if
      he had promulgated vernacular versions of the traditional Missal in
      each of the major modern languages, and if any new additions to
      the liturgy had been introduced merely as options. [Translator's
      note.].

ters for your instruction, than ten thousand in a strange tongue."[50]

284. Critique of the principles of the liturgical reform. Human expressiveness.

Before examining the principles of the reform, it is worth dealing with the sophism to the effect that a multiplicity of languages is no detriment to liturgical unity. This unity is alleged to be secured, as long as the different translations all have the same meaning. That is true up to a point, provided the translations really are accurate; and we have seen that they often are not. But even when the translations are good, they differ in vocabulary, construction and syntax, and thus a variety of languages is inevitably a less satisfactory expression of liturgical unity than that provided by the use of Latin.

Liturgical prayer is distinguished from *mental prayer* precisely by the fact that it is exterior, sensible and communitarian. To say that a variety of languages expresses unity is a contradiction in terms, because the unity that is allegedly expressed is neither visible nor audible and is therefore a unity that exists at a non-liturgical level. If a diversity of languages will do as an expression of unity, then why should one stop there; why not go on to a diversity of ritual gesture?[51] But to do that is to destroy the liturgy, precisely because the liturgy goes beyond internal acts, and comes forth into the external world; and the more

---

[50] This citation is not relevant to the use of the vernacular in the liturgy, for it is the passage in which St. Paul checks the abuse of excessive speaking in foreign tongues. [Translator's note.]

[51] This has in fact already happened. African dances have been used liturgically at papal Masses. At one bishop's funeral, the coffin was danced through a whole village. In the experimental period prior to 1969, Masses of every kind were celebrated: at Turin, Cardinal Pellegrino experimented with a new rite for Holy Week in his cathedral and in five of his parishes; at Milan, Cardinal Colombo used a new rite for funerals. In Africa, liturgical innovations have been based upon tribal rites in order to *faire comprendre qu'il y a continuité entre le projet ancestral et le christianisme.* I.C.I., No.577, 15 August 1982, p.38 and No.279, 1 January 1967, p.7. "To make the Africans understand that there is a continuity between their ancestral customs and Christianity."

perfectly an internal unity is given a unified external expression, the more perfect is the liturgical form involved.

As Paul VI said in his speech mentioned above, the principal and decisive reason for the reform is that the understanding of prayer is more important than the ancient regal vesture in which it is clothed. But to say that the understanding of a liturgical formula is more important than the formula itself, is like saying that the understanding of an idea is more important than the idea, when in fact the importance of understanding depends upon the importance of the content of the idea in question.[52]

Furthermore, the text cited from St. Paul does not actually support the idea that understanding is the supreme value in the liturgy. The Apostle is in fact referring to teaching, *ut et alios instruam*,[53] which must necessarily be intelligible to the hearer. Now the Church has always given instruction during Mass in the different vernacular languages, either by re-reading the Gospel or other material in the vulgar tongue, or by propounding and explaining the meaning of the liturgical texts during the sermon. If we remember the distinction between the liturgy of the word, that is, the first half of the Mass, and the liturgy of sacrifice, or the eucharist proper, which is the second half, then we realize that the intellectual comprehension of the forms of prayer, of which even an unbeliever is capable, can never be more important that the lifting up of the mind and heart to God, which is the essence of prayer. The council did indeed allot a fundamental importance to "conscious, active and fruitful"[54] participation of the faithful at Mass, but by participation it means that "the faithful should be present at the mystery of faith not as strangers or silent[55] spectators, but really understanding it by means of the rites and prayers."[56]

---

[52] This line of reasoning is especially relevant in the light of the fact that most of the new liturgy is not a translation of the old, but an assemblage of new material. It is not therefore a question of understanding the traditional liturgy, but of replacing it with another. *Four-fifths* of the collects, secrets and postcommunion prayers of the traditional Missal are dropped or altered in the new rite. [Translator's note.]

[53] I Corinthians, 14:19. "In order that I instruct others also."

[54] *Sacrosanctum Concilium*, 11.

[55] The obvious answer is that a man can be full of thoughts and full of love while saying nothing with his lips, and that conversely, some-

The motivation underlying the reform combines various significant departures from traditional thinking, all of them connected with an incipient change in doctrine.

The first change comes from supposing that the liturgy should give expression to the *feelings of modern men*,[57] when in fact it is designed to express the timeless vision of the Church. Precisely because it is timeless, the Church's vision does include the mentality of contemporary men, but it is not restricted to it; the Church's mentality is not historical, but suprahistorical, and embraces the whole compass of every generation of Christians. According to the classic definition, repeated by the council,[58] the liturgy is the priestly action of Christ and of his mystical body which is the Church: this gives rise to the public worship of God the Father. The priestly action of Christ at Mass cannot happen without the action of an ordained priest; the priesthood given by baptism is utterly incapable of consecrating the Lord's Body which is the centre of the liturgy. This point of faith was clearly reiterated in a document entitled *Sacerdotium Ministeriale*, put out by the Congregation for the Doctrine of the Faith in September 1983. Without a priest there can be no eucharist and, in that sense, no public prayer of the Church, but conversely, a priest who celebrates Mass without a congregation is nonetheless fulfilling a "public and social" act.[59] Mass is now coming to be thought of by some people not as an action essentially of the priest acting *in persona Christi*,[60] but as an action of the community, in the sense that the community not only offers the sacrifice together with the priest who effects it, but that the community co-offers and con-celebrates on an equal footing with the celebrant himself.[61]

one can pay God a merely verbal honor. The fact is that before the reform the congregation often used to pray and sing with one voice at the various liturgical functions.

[56] *Sacrosanctum Concilium*, 48.

[57] Ibid., 37 and 38. The *Osservatore Romano* of 15 March 1974 proclaims this idea in the headline of a special article: *Celebriamo ciò che viviamo* "We celebrate what we live." No, what we celebrate in the liturgy is not our own life, but the mystery, the life, the glory of the Lord.

[58] Ibid., 7.

[59] Ibid., 27.

[60] "In the person of Christ."

[61] Cf. Ibid., 48.

All of this demonstrates that the new rite, as actually celebrated, has been influenced by theological schools of thought
that weaken the special ontological status of the ordained priest,
that attempt to enlarge the role of the people of God in worship
at the expense of the sacred functions of the priest, that make
the meeting of the people more important than the act of consecration, and that promote the subjectivization and thus the
instability of the whole of Christian worship. In this view, the
essence of divine worship is no longer the unchanging sacrament, and a consequently unchanging worship, but rather a
changing set of human feelings that demand expression, and
that stamp upon the liturgy the mentality and customs of different peoples. Thus the Church no longer aspires to a strict
uniformity in rites but instead "looks favorably upon whatever
is not strictly connected with superstition, and preserves it intact, if possible, and sometimes even introduces it into the liturgy itself."[62]

285. The principle of creativity.

The new liturgy is thus psychological rather than ontological, subjective rather than objective, anthropological rather than
theological, and expresses not so much a transcendent mystery
as the feelings with which the people react to that mystery.[63]

---

[62] Ibid., 37.

[63] *La Croix*, the daily newspaper of French Catholics, openly expressed the principle of the new liturgy on 11 and 12 April 1982:
different generations, different social groups, different age groups
should tell the Church what they want, and the Church should respond to these aspirations in the liturgy. A plurification of liturgy is
thus required, and the Children's Masses that aroused so much opposition are a first step in this direction. The hierarchy too has
made it plain that the new liturgy is driven by a movement for continual change. *Présence et Dialogue*, the official bulletin of the
archbishopric of Paris said in September 1969: *Il n'est plus possible, à un moment où l'évolution du monde est rapide, de considé-
rer les rites comme définitivement fixés. Ils sont appelés à être
révisés régulièrement sous l'autorité du Pape et des évêques et
avec le concours du peuple chrétien, pour mieux signifier en un
temps la réalité immuable du don divin.* "It is no longer possible, at
a time when the world is rapidly evolving, to consider the rites as
definitively fixed. There is a need for them to be regularly revised
under the authority of the pope and the bishops and with the help

The specific function of worship is to stimulate man's sense of the divine rather than to convey the reality of a divine gift; hence the congregation is more important than the eucharistic rite, and the laity more important than the priest.

This change in turn produces another, which might be described as the principle of liturgical creativity. According to this view, the people of God pour their own culture and their own spirit into the Church's rites, and the priest acts as the means of expressing all this in the celebration.[64] The objectivity of the liturgy, which is a reflection of the absolute Object, must retreat before the importance of a human subject seeking self-expression. *Sacrosanctum Concilium*[65] distinguishes between a changeable and an unchangeable part of the liturgy, but without saying what the latter actually includes. If even the words of consecration are changed, it is hard to see just where the immutability of the liturgy lies. Of course, there has been change down the centuries in the changeable elements of the liturgy, but it has occurred cautiously, modestly, and prudently. The recent reform could certainly find antiquated elements in the liturgy, which were in need of change. One example would be the Ember Days or Quarter Tense, now out of place in a Church that has spread to countries that have only two seasons,[66] or again the prayer *pro Christianissimo Imperatore*[67] in the liturgy of Good Friday. It was also certainly time to abolish the oath taken by a bishop at his consecration not to murder, or conspire to murder, the pope; and this has been duly abolished. But it is one thing to change rites like this in order to accommodate them to conditions which have obviously changed, and quite another to lay down a general principle that the Church's

---

of the Christian laity, so as to better express, at a given moment, the unchangeable reality of the divine gift."

[64] In an important article in *Esprit et Vie*, 1977, p.248, the Benedictine G.M. Oury states that many liturgical reviews consider the prayers of the new missal to be out of date, and that they therefore have no hesitation in proposing new "more appropriate" formulas for the various feasts through the year, and that individual priests should arrogate to themselves the right to express their own creativity likewise.

[65] *Sacrosanctum Concilium*, 21.

[66] The Ember Days were originally connected with prayers for good weather and an abundant harvest. [Translator's note.]

[67] A prayer for the Holy Roman Emperor. [Translator's note.]

rites ought to be dependent on the psychology, customs, or spirit of particular peoples, or even of private individuals.

The principle of creativity stems from the false presupposition that the liturgy ought to express the feelings of the faithful, and that it is something that they themselves produce; what it really expresses is the mystery of Christ, Christ being the true source of the liturgy. The new view implicitly reduces the liturgy to the level of poetry.

The new liturgy legitimates and encourages the idea of creativity, even though creativity is not a legitimate concept even in artistic matters, because underlying all artistic invention there is something uncreated, indeed uncreatable. Firstly, there are hardly any binding rules in the new liturgy; at many points the celebrant is presented with a range of options as to what he should say or do, from which he can choose freely. The idea of creativity does away with conditions and limits, and thus tends to remove the very idea of breaking the rules. This optional spirit means that every celebrant can adjust, add or omit, and thus create whatever form he finds most congenial; as if it were a case of expressing himself instead of adoring God, as if he had to give a form to the mystery, rather than conform himself to it. Hence the enormous variety in the celebration of Mass, which ought to be the same throughout the Catholic world. When the reform was introduced in 1969, a typical edition of the *Missale Romanum* was published, from which all vernacular Missals were to be translated, and the translations were to be approved by the Holy See. But in fact, the idea of creativity has deprived the typical edition of its binding force. In an article in the *Osservatore Romano*[68] commemorating the twentieth anniversary of the opening of the council, a Benedictine liturgist deplores the fact that "we have often been content with a mere translation of the Roman texts" when in fact "what is needed is the progressive elaboration of a liturgical language and a euchology composed directly in the national language." This diversity will be a reflection of the different national spirits and cultures one is trying to express, but it is also encouraged by the many options included in the rubrics themselves,[69] by the personal in-

---

[68] O.R., 20 October 1982.

[69] In the *Rite of Mass* published by the Italian Episcopal Conference, which contains only the Common of the Mass, three options are provided at six points, and two options at a further nine points. A

ventions of individual celebrants, and by the transference of liturgical authority from the Apostolic See to episcopal conferences or individual bishops.

This transformation of the liturgy, from a stable form of sacred drama into a poetic drama begotten of the inventive capacities of particular individuals, is one of the most visible and most widely lamented effects of the reform. It has been fostered by the paralysis of authority we have already discussed.[70] The idea of creativity thus completely abolishes the binding force of the rubrics; by rejecting the idea of a fixed essence or nature in things, and by asserting independence from the mystery as it stands fast in eternity, this creativity transforms a transcendent sacred reality into an expression of mankind's own poetic capacities.

The policy of creativity, which is intended to make the liturgy "more lively and participatory," produces two effects. Firstly, it changes a sacred action into a theatrical display. Secondly, it changes the celebrant's activity into something private, or idiosyncratic, when in fact it always has a public and social character, even when it takes place in private; creativity thus obstructs that common sharing in public worship expressed by "a common mind and a common voice."

286. Movement from the sacred to the theatrical.

It has been asserted by way of attack upon the traditional Mass, that it was a spectacle staged by priests under the gaze of a mute and passive congregation. The accusation is extravagant and baseless. It is the new liturgy that has really become a theatrical performance, not only in practice but in theory.

In a special article headed "For a new style of celebration," the *Osservatore Romano*[71] asserts that the liturgy should be turned into a kind of theater. It says "The celebration of Mass has now become an art involving different degrees of emphasis and tone, highlights, pauses, rests and recommencements, crescendoes and diminuendoes, as in a symphony." But all of this already existed in the traditional rite, which has parts to be sung, or spoken, or said aloud, or in a low voice, or said secretly,

---

mathematical calculation shows that an endless variety of Masses can thus be generated.

[70] See paragraphs 65 and 71.

[71] O.R., 15 March 1974.

as well as having musical tones that are ordinary, or solemn or particularly solemn. The difference between the old liturgy and the new lies not in the fact that the old lacked such "differing degrees," but in the fact that they were fixed, prescribed and regulated in accordance with the sacred and objective character of the rite, while in the new they are left to what might be described as the Dionysian invention of the celebrant and the concelebrating assembly. "From the do-all celebrant of the former Missal, we must move to the figure of a "director"-celebrant who knows how to bring the liturgical action to life."[72] To talk like that is both unfair and illogical. The celebrant does not do everything in the old rite, as the article claims; first of all, he is assisted by a server, and more importantly, he cannot say or do anything other than what is clearly laid down in the rubrics; yet in the face of all this he is still called a "do-all celebrant." It is really in the new rite that the celebrant can do whatever his powers of invention can devise, without rules, without limits, using every means available, with the congregation falling in at random with whatever his imagination may suggest; and this is held up as the ideal new liturgical style. This *ad hoc* invention of liturgy means that it is difficult to find any two celebrations that are alike, especially on solemn occasions, when the liturgy is specially arranged, with its own actions, music and readings being chosen by the congregation rather than being what is laid down by the official liturgical books. Priests are encouraged (by the *Osservatore Romano*) to "make use of all available resources to get themselves accepted as 'leaders'[73] able to create contacts." The objective character of the mystery and the power inherent in it are completely overlooked, and the liturgy is thus reduced to a psychological, indeed a mechanically psychological, impression of the sort produced by a mime or the *commedia dell'arte*.

The *Osservatore Romano*[74] says "the attempts at reform are still in their initial stages. A single contact with certain lively liturgies celebrated in some African or Latin-American Church could knock us out of our senile torpor." The president of the

---

[72] So anyone who is not a good film or theater director will be a bad celebrant, and the rite will no longer depend on the objective sacrality of what is being done, but on the efficiency of the subjective performance that is produced.

[73] The English word is used in the Italian text. [Translator's note.]

[74] O.R., 7 October 1978.

committee of the Italian Episcopal Conference preparing a revision of the Missal, Archbishop Magrassi, gave an interview to
the magazine *Il Regno*[75] in which he deplored stagnation in the
liturgy due to a reluctance to accept the principle of creativity;
he says that "if the thing in the liturgy is the expression of a
people manifesting its religious feelings, then the way is open to
a liturgy that has enormous space for creativity."

Thus the Mass becomes a spectacle *pris en charge*,[76] as the
French bishops put it, by the whole people of God. The Mass
adjusts itself to times and people, expresses human emotions,
incorporates readings from newspapers and novels, draws all
worldly activities into worship, life's experiences, the daily
round; and all under the direction of someone analogous to a
stage or film director. To concoct a new rite for particular people is a form of flattery; an example of it occurred at the Mass
celebrated at Poigny-Forêts for Giscard d'Estaing and Aldo
Moro during the Rambouillet summit in April 1971. The parish priest decided that the epistle and gospel of the Sunday in
question were unsuitable for such high personages and might
have irritated them, so he chose others instead. This was a form
of deference to the powers of this world.

The Mass celebrated on French television on 20 February
1972 was an even clearer indication of the novelties being introduced, both because it was celebrated with the authority of
the episcopal conference and because it was seen by millions of
the faithful. There was no altar, but five tables instead; the celebrants wore none of the vestments prescribed in the *General
Instruction to the Roman Missal* in paragraphs 297 and following; the opening prayers were specially composed and differed
from the official forms; prior to the *Kyrie* various participants
made little speeches telling the gathering about their personal
thoughts; the *Creed* was not said; the words of the *offertory* were
made up; the canon (which was the second eucharistic prayer)
was interlarded with songs and newly composed texts; before
the *Lord's Prayer* a statement was made by one of the partici-

---

[75] *Il Regno*, 15 September 1981.

[76] "Taken in hand." Continual change in the liturgy is approved by
the French bishops in the 1983 *Missel des Dimanches* (Sunday
Mass booklet) *car chaque année, et c'est la joyeuse liberté des
chrétiens, tout est toujours nouveau.* "Because each year everything is always new; and that is part of the joyful liberty Christians
have."

pants concerning the situation in Ireland; at communion, a man and woman went to the priest's table, picked up a plate with hosts on it and took communion themselves; they then passed the plate to the other lay people who likewise gave themselves communion; then they made communion under the species of wine and passed the cup on to the others similarly.

These creative Masses are now common in different parts of the Catholic world, and mean that the liturgy is different in different countries, dioceses, parishes and even in different churches within the one parish.[77] Sometimes the elevation is done with the paten, thus avoiding showing the host to the people; sometimes host and paten are offered simultaneously; sometimes they are elevated with open arms; sometimes the host is broken at the consecration and elevated in two pieces; texts are interpolated at will; new eucharistic prayers are invented;[78] readings from newspapers and secular writers are introduced in place of Scripture, as was proposed by the Swiss Synod of 1972; whole parts of the rite are left out, especially the Creed; any and every kind of dress is adopted; sometimes no candles are lit; sometimes leavened bread is used (which is illicit in the Latin rites) and a variety of wines or liquors of every type; ordinary plates and wine glasses are used instead of the chalice and paten; sometimes the priest standing at the altar consecrates altar breads that the participants are holding in their hands. Then there are the dances, the mimes, the percussion instruments and all the other violations of liturgical norms, that are rarely criticized or stopped by bishops.[79] We have already dealt with irreverence to the Blessed Sacrament in paragraph 270.

---

[77] I have some hundreds of examples among my papers, bearing witness to these practices in Italy and Switzerland. It is obvious how little notice is taken of *Sacrosanctum Concilium*, 23, which lays down that there should not be great differences in the liturgy between one region and another.

[78] In France, books containing new eucharistic prayers have been published. See for example *A la recherche de prières eucharistiques pour notre temps*, Various authors, Paris 1976. As appears from the title, what the Church has theoretically found and established has not been found or established, and has still to be searched for.

[79] A dossier of abuses arising from this creativity was published in *Esprit et Vie*, 1975, pp. 11 ff., by J.C. Didier; it is all the more

287. Transition from public to private.

In degenerating from the sacred to the merely poetic, the liturgy also moves from the communal to the private realm, and it is ironical that a reform launched to emphasize the communal aspects of the Church's rites should in the event grant such leeway to an imaginative individualism which is the very antithesis of anything genuinely communitarian. The sacred of its nature leads to what is universal, it leads to the subordination of the individual to God and to the community that is the means of union with God; creativity, on the other hand, leads to a heightening of individualism and gives a private character to liturgical action. Whenever the celebrant creates a new word or a gesture that is not in the liturgical books, he is separating himself from the Church, if not indeed opposing it, and if he is still praying nonetheless, his prayer has a private character and a private worth. It can no longer be said that he is acting *in persona Christi*[80] in the strict liturgical sense, but only in the broad sense in which, assuming he is in a state of grace, it can be said that his prayer has a supernatural Christian value. Conversely, insofar as the liturgy degenerates into something private, a true liturgical coming together of the Church is prevented, since a consensus of that sort is possible only if the celebration in question is a true celebration of Christ and of his Church, rather than an event staged by some private person.

In a conversation that occurred in 1942, Max Picard, the writer who made so much of objectivity and of things appreciated in themselves, propounded to me the absolute objectivity of the sacred; he rightly pointed out that when celebrating, a priest has to lose himself in the objective reality of the rite and thus efface his own personality. He added picturesquely that the Mass could almost celebrate itself, the bells could ring themselves and the host could elevate itself of its own accord. The objective character of the sacred is diametrically opposed to the "living" liturgy aimed at by the reform, which confuses life with liveliness, movement and change. To live is in fact to perdure with the same identity, it is a succeeding, that is, a self-

---

noteworthy for the fact that the journal in question is generally in favor of the reform.

[80] "In the person of Christ."

preservation amidst a series of changes, as we said when dealing
with mobilism.[81]

288. Bible and liturgy.

The change in the relationship between the Bible and the
liturgy, in pursuance of the conciliar decrees[82] is also of some
significance: *In celebrationibus sacris abundantior, varior et aptior
lectio Sacrae Scripturae instauretur*, that is, "In sacred celebrations let there be a wider, more varied and more appropriate
reading of Sacred Scripture."[83] At the theoretical level, there has
been a change in emphasis, reversing the cautious line followed
hitherto, and supported by Pius VI against the Pistoians;[84] at the
practical and liturgical level, the usage of centuries has been
abandoned.

It should, however, be remembered that the Church's
preaching to the ordinary people has always been based upon
the explaining of the Scriptures, as had been laid down at the
Council of Trent.[85] St. Augustine explained all 150 psalms in

---

[81] See paragraphs 157-62. The reform was lauded in extravagant
terms by Father Bugnini, its principal author, in many of his writings, especially in the statement reported in *Carrefour* of 22 October 1969 to the effect that the new Missal "has a richness greater
than anything that has been seen in twenty centuries." In the same
year, he says in *Notitiae*, the official publication of the council for
the reform of the liturgy, p.295 "There is no shadow then (in the
reform), only a sea of light." Such expressions hardly signify a
sound state of mind, whether judged by liturgical or diplomatic
standards.

[82] Cf. *Sacrosanctum Concilium*, 35 and 51.

[83] Note the insinuation that the Church's traditional use of Scripture
has been inappropriate. [Translator's note.]

[84] In the Bull *Auctorem Fidei* of 28 August 1794, Pope Pius VI censured a list of propositions drawn from the acts of the synod of the
diocese of Pistoia, in Tuscany, held in 1786 under the presidency
of the Jansenist bishop of Pistoia and Prato, Scipio de Ricci. The
synod had taught that everyone capable of reading the Bible was
morally obliged to do so.[Translator's note.]

[85] In this regard one might note a fact that bears witness to a general
decline in the intellectual level of the clergy; I mean the abandonment of the custom of delivering a sermon already committed to
memory, and its replacement by a reading of a text already written
out. Thus in modern Masses the readings are not followed by a

sermons preached to his North African congregation, but it is not only the ancient Fathers whose sermons are based on some biblical text; the same is true of more recent preachers such as Segneri, Bartoli, Bossuet, Massillon and the great preachers at Notre Dame in Paris; even if the sermon was not based on some precise section of a Gospel, it was always accompanied by scriptural quotations that the preachers would make in the Vulgate Latin, and then translate, even though they were preaching in the vernacular.

The Church's traditional reserve in the matter of indiscriminate Bible reading is based upon one undeniable fact about the Bible. It is a *difficult* book, that records and approves doings whose meaning can only be rightly grasped by those who have a good deal of knowledge; doings that appear scandalous, and present difficulties to the general run of men. These include such things as the harlot in the Book of Hosea, Oolla and Ooliba in the Book of Ezechiel, Judith's ensnarement of Holofernes, Tamar's incest, David's adultery, the extermination of the Jews' enemies, the *herem*. Voltaire's satirical genius reached its peak in his *Instruction du gardien des capucins de Raguse à frère Pediculosus partant pour la Terre Sainte.*[86] His mockery is atrocious, his irony bubbling and superb; the attack is not so much upon the Scriptures as upon the imprudent, crass and supposedly educational use of them that is being suggested, but which the Church had traditionally declined to adopt. By his blasphemous miniature masterpiece, Voltaire, a non-Christian, implicitly provides strong support for the Church's belief that Bible reading is not necessarily a good thing in all cases.

That there are linguistic, historical and moral difficulties with the Bible is obvious from a mere glance at it; indeed the Bible says as much about itself. As to language, *Cunctae res difficiles; non potest eas homo explicare sermone.*[87] And as to the Bible as a whole, and some passages in St. Paul in particular, II Peter

---

homily, but by another reading. See *Piccola apologia della memoria*, in R. Amerio, *I giorni e le voci*, Locarno 1980, p.60. [On the other hand, men of outstanding intellect have often insisted on reading their sermons. Translator's note.]

[86] "Instruction of the Custodian of the Capuchins at Ragusa to Brother Pediculosus leaving for the Holy Land."

[87] Ecclesiastes 1:8. "All things are complex, the word of man shall not unravel them."

says: *in quibus sunt quaedam difficilia intellectu, quae indocti et instabiles depravant sicut et caeteras Scripturas.*[88]

Nonetheless, the most striking proof that there are difficult passages in Scripture, likely to cause problems if they are set before all and sundry, is provided, ironically, by the present reform itself. It has done to the Bible what was done to the Latin classics in the expurgated editions prepared for students, but which nobody had ever dared to do to the Scriptures until now. The reform has actually torn out of the psalms the so-called "imprecatory" or cursing verses that were deemed to be at odds with the Second Vatican Council's irenical views, thus mutilating the sacred text and, as it were, surreptitiously removing knowledge of it from the minds of both clergy and laity alike.[89] The reform has also, in twenty-two places, expunged whole verses from the text of the Gospels used at Mass in order to remove references to the Last Judgment, the condemnation of the world, and sin.[90]

Because of these linguistic and historical difficulties, because of the various levels of meaning at which theologians hold that the Scriptures can be read, and because of the Catholic principle that the Church, as opposed to the Synagogue, possesses not only the Scriptures but the true meaning of the Scriptures, the discipline of the Church used to prescribe that the Bible should be mediated to the people of God as a whole by the clergy;[91] that a prudent judgment ought to be made as to what should be emphasized and what passed over; that in general a knowledge of the sacred text should be set in the context of the liturgy, catechesis or sermons; that the Vulgate Latin

---

[88] II Peter, 3:16. "In which there are some things difficult to understand, that uninstructed and unreliable people distort, as they do the other Scriptures."

[89] Archbishop Bugnini, the principal overseer, if not architect, of the changes tells us that the censoring of the psalms was done at the personal insistence of Pope Paul. See A. Bugnini, *The Reform of the Liturgy: 1948-1975*, Italian edition 1982, trans. Matthew J. O'Connell, Collegeville, Minnesota, 1990. [Translator's note.]

[90] See the study by R. Kaschewsky in *Una Voce Korrespondenz*, 1982, No. 2/3.

[91] It should be remembered that at most times, and in most places, most of the laity have been at best semi-literate and half-educated; a state of affairs that is perhaps returning even in the western world. [Translator's note.]

should be taken as an official and dependable text and that translations should be made from it; and lastly that vernacular versions should be approved by ecclesiastical authority and should contain explanatory notes in accordance with the Church's understanding of the text.

All of these rules have been done away with, either by the new shape imposed on the liturgy after the council, or by a progressive violation of what norms the council retained. In the face of the Protestant and Jansenist popularization of the Scriptures, Pius VI laid down in 1794 that the reading of the Bible was not obligatory or expedient for everyone who could read.[92] The Second Vatican Council on the other hand warmly recommends frequent reading of the Bible to all the faithful.[93] The Church's reason for insisting that vernacular versions be authorized by ecclesiastical authority and accompanied by explanatory notes was that the unchanging truths of faith should stand fast amidst changing fashions of thought and aberrant private interpretations.[94] The council retained the requirement that notes should be provided, but left it up to the bishops to exercise supervision over the versions produced. There have in fact been a great number of new translations, some of which have retained the genuine meaning of the texts and have been sound from a linguistic point of view, while others have often suffered from ambiguity, heterodox tendencies and linguistic imprecision. The resultant state of affairs is rather like that which prevailed in early Christian times when, as St. Augustine records, there was a host of translations in circulation, because every Christian who thought he knew a little Greek and Latin attempted to produce his own version.[95] But in those days it was a matter of limited parts of the Bible being translated out of personal devotion, for personal devotional purposes. Today, it is a matter of whole Bibles being published, sometimes by mixed

---

[92] Cf. Denzinger 1507 and 1429.

[93] *Dei Verbum* 25. It should however be remembered that in 1898 an indulgence was attached to the practice of reading the Bible for a quarter of an hour a day, thus encouraging all to read the Bible during the 64 years prior to Vatican II. See *Enchiridion Indulgentiarum. S.C. Indulgentiarum* 13 December 1898. [Translator's note.]

[94] Cf. Denzinger 1603.

[95] Cf. *De Doctrina Christiana*, II, 6, 8.

committees of Catholics and others, often without notes and not always with ecclesiastical approval.

289. Variety and imprecision of the new version.

The council's requirements gave rise to a useful general revision of St. Jerome's Vulgate, of which a critical edition was already being produced, Pope Pius XI having founded the monastery of St. Jerome at Rome to further the undertaking in 1932. Nonetheless, the host of different versions appearing one after another, with or without official approval, produced a confusion and bewilderment unknown previously.

The traditional names of some books were changed, *Qoheleth* instead of *Ecclesiastes*, *Sirach* instead of *Ecclesiasticus* and so on; the biblical readings at Sunday Mass were increased so as to require three annual cycles to get through all of them; in some vernacular Missals, injunctions and instructions and prefaces and commentaries have been interspersed freely among the liturgical texts, against the council's express provisions,[96] with the names of their authors printed above them, also in violation of the norms; thus the official texts giving the Church's prayer are often found mixed in among private reflections, fly-by-night opinions, quotations from non-Christian authors both ancient and modern, and effusions of the sociological opinions of the compilers. The traditional Missals were beautiful and sober productions, containing everything in one manageable volume; there were also pocket editions that were very easy to handle. Some modern Missals, vastly enlarged by additions both sacred and profane, as heterogeneous as a Latin *satura* or miscellany, now have the character of semi-ecclesiastical collective productions, divided into three volumes which, with all their festive and ferial parts, form a total whole of about 4,000 pages.

The policy of putting as much as possible of the treasures of the Bible before the people of God during worship runs into a serious difficulty, inasmuch as its frustrates the use of the memory as an educational principle. In the traditional rite, in the course of the liturgical year the people would hear on Sundays a single annual cycle of Gospel passages (some of which admittedly presented difficulties, like the parable of the Unjust Steward). The annual recurrence of these readings, with an accompanying sermon, eventually had the effect of stamping no small

---

[96] Cf. *Sacrosanctum Concilium*, 34.

part of the Master's teaching upon the minds of the faithful. The principal element in remembering something is the repetition of a single impression. Because man's knowledge comes to very little without memory, the knowledge of the Bible produced by the new lectionary is very slight, inasmuch as the same thing only recurs every third year, and thus cannot become clearly stamped in one's memory. There was a time when the people of God knew some psalms and hymns and sequences and other liturgical prayers by heart, and would use them, sometimes in a distorted form, in their own popular speech; but now the people hardly know anything more than those few fixed texts that constitute the common of every Mass. This violation of the principle of memory and of the rules of psychology means that the general knowledge of the Bible and of liturgical texts, that the reform was meant to increase, has in practice been greatly reduced.

Apart from an excess of material, the new liturgical books also contain errors of interpretation. I will give just one example.

The second reading of the Easter Mass contains a passage from I Corinthians 5:7; *kai gar to pascha hemon etuthe Christos*, which means "Christ was in fact sacrificed for us as our Passover." But the new Missals put it: "Our Passover is Christ sacrificed," or "Christ, our Passover, has been sacrificed"; and the communion antiphon of the same Mass says: "Christ, our Passover, is sacrificed." All of these translations miss the predicative force of the expression *to pascha* in the original setting. However, in a book of this sort it is not possible to track down all the unjustifiable renderings; as the poet puts it, they are innumerable as the sands of the shore, and the waves of the sea.

290. Altar and table in the liturgical reform.

The changes that have been made to the structure and position of the altar as part of the liturgical reform are evidence of changes, whether conscious or unconscious, in the mentality prevailing in the Church at large. As we have often said before, ideas develop in accordance with an inexorable internal logic of their own.

The primary idea that was lost was that of the altar as a massive base, immovable and exalted, upon which to offer sacrifice. The altar symbolized the "mount of vision" upon which Abraham prepared to sacrifice his son in obedience to the Lord, and represented too Mount Calvary upon which the God-Man offered his sacrifice. The notion of God as stable, eternal and exalted was also connected with the form of the altar. With an analogous kind of symbolism, Homer sets Ulysses' nuptial couch within the living form of an olive tree to express the nature of marriage. The altar thus stood *in excelsis*; it was the place of sacrifice, it signified the unchangeability of God. From a specifically Christian point of view, it is the place where the eucharistic sacrifice is offered, and thus deserves the most worthy, prominent and visible place in the church.

I am well aware that the structure and position of altars has varied somewhat with the centuries and that the arrangement generally seen prior to the reform does not date much further back than the Council of Trent; but, on the other hand, I do not believe that the mere fact of proving that some now vanished opinion or custom once existed in the Church is any reason at all for returning to a previous state of affairs. To justify the resuscitation of an earlier form, it would be necessary to show that, were it to be revived, it would effect a fuller realization of the Church's faith and teachings than do the forms now in use. The fact is that many of the customs that used to exist at previous periods in the Church's history represent a less developed level in the understanding of faith, and of the *sensus Christi*[97] that unfolds progressively within the Church. To return to them would imply a backward step. This can be seen in connection with doctrine and devotions connected with Our Lady, but also in regard to the doctrine of the Incarnation itself, and is true in general of the greater explicit knowledge of revealed truths as it now exists in the Church, as compared to earlier periods.[98] As a matter of fact, the more perfect awareness of eucharistic doctrine which is the foundation of venerating and adoring the Sacrament, and of guarding it with the greatest care, is certainly given less adequate expression by the forms adopted in the wake of the council.

As I have said, the fixed and immovable character of the altar was the first idea that was lost; the notion of the Mass as a meal came to prevail over the understanding of it as a sacrifice, and that led to plain, light, movable tables replacing massive, monumental and immovable altars. The old altars were demol-

---

[97] "Sense of Christ."
[98] See paragraph 269.

ished, unless the civil authorities protected them for artistic reasons; or else the altar table was detached, leaving the rest of the construction as a kind of reredos; or else they were left as they stood, with another altar placed in front, thus rendering them useless.

Secondly, instead of occupying an elevated and dominant position, the altar is often now placed at the lowest point, with rows of seats for the people rising above it, as in an ancient theater.

Thirdly, instead of being reserved in a tabernacle contiguous with the back of the altar, the Blessed Sacrament has often lost its central and most noble position, and has been placed to one side; or else put in a separate chapel where it is not immediately visible; or, lastly, it has been left in its old central tabernacle but with the result that the celebrant stands with his back to it when he is at the new altar.

291. The altar facing the people.

The introduction of altars facing the people is the most important ceremonial change to have occurred since the council. Post-conciliar liturgical decrees stated that such an arrangement was "not essential," and ordered that existing altars should be kept whenever historical, artistic or religious considerations suggested it; it was also forbidden to set up two altars in the same sanctuary, with one standing in front of the other.[99]

Nonetheless, whenever the civil authorities have not prevented it, the altars have generally been demolished, or at least duplicated by the introduction of a free standing altar so the priest can celebrate facing the congregation.

Altars facing the people were allowed in the liturgy even before the reform, but apparently this depended on the orienta-

---

[99] See the letter of 30 June 1965 from Cardinal Lercaro, the president of the *Consilium* to implement liturgical change, in *Orientamenti dell'arte sacra dopo il Vaticano II*, published by the Central Commission for Sacred Art in Italy, Minerva Italica, 1969. For the ban on having two altars in one sanctuary, see the reply of 19 February 1972 by the Congregation for Divine Worship, published in the *Rivista* of the archdiocese of Genoa, and by me in *Colloqui di S. Silvestro*, Lugano 1974, p.258. It is there laid down that the added altars should be removed. But in fact new altars go on being put in everywhere.

tion of the building, because the rubrics say: *Si altare sit ad ori-entem versus populum.*[100] But the celebrant's position must in any case respect the absolute pre-eminence of the Blessed Sacrament, whether the congregation gathers on all sides of the altar as it did in antiquity, as is still apparent from the words *omnium circumstantium*[101] in the canon, or whether the people gather in the nave only.

An altar facing the congregation presents serious difficulties. If, as often happens, it stands in front of the tabernacle, then the celebrant most unbecomingly turns his back on the Blessed Sacrament in order to face the people. This arrangement recalls the "abomination" deplored in Ezechiel 8:16, where the priests sacrifice with their backs turned to the *Sancta Sanctorum*, the Holy of Holies. The unsuitability of this arrangement is all the more obvious when one considers that under the Old Law the *Sancta Sanctorum* was merely a prefiguration of what was to come, whereas in a Catholic church we are dealing with the *Sanctissimum*; the Holy One Himself. Again, it should be remembered that pulpits were built at the side of the nave so the preacher would not have to turn his back on the host,[102] and during the exposition of the Blessed Sacrament, if there was to be a sermon, the host and monstrance were veiled, as it was held to be irreverent even to be in sight of the Sacrament without directing one's attention to it.

But apart from questions of reverence to the Blessed Sacrament, the celebration of Mass facing the congregation has specific difficulties of its own. The spaces in which we move have an emotional and symbolic significance; common space, within which all material bodies exist, is divided not only by physical objects but by non-physical meanings that are the basis of symbolism, which in its turn provides the intelligible face of the sacred. For example, forwards means hope and backwards means something suspect; the right is favorable, the left unfortunate; high signifies divine, low signifies evil; straight is truth, oblique is uncertainty, etc. Thus in the liturgy too, the placing and arrangement of persons and things has an underlying

---

[100] "If the altar is towards the east facing the people."
[101] "Of all those standing around." In the Roman basilicas, the people have always stood to right and left of the main altar, as well as in the nave. [Translator's note.]
[102] This was also the best place, acoustically, to put the preacher in the days before the electronic liturgy. [Translator's note.]

meaning that either does or does not conform to the sacred realities involved. For the priest to turn his face to the people and the people to face the priest during the most sacred parts of the ceremony expresses a completely different ethos from that which prevailed when they both faced the same way. This face to face celebration breaks the symbolic unanimity of the whole assembly. As Mass was usually celebrated in the pre-conciliar period, priest and people were all of them turned towards a God who is symbolically before and above them all. These positions reflect a hierarchical arrangement and a theocentric orientation; they look God-ward. In the new "back to front" Mass, *à l'envers* as Paul Claudel put it,[103] both people and priest are turned towards man, in an anthropocentric arrangement. The united sense of the Church is spoiled, because the God towards whom the people are turned stands, as it were, in the opposite place to the God whom the priest is facing. The priest's right also becomes the people's left. The celebrant stands before a God on whom the people turn their back, and vice versa. Of course one can ignore this arrangement of persons and concentrate instead on the host upon the altar, but it is nonetheless natural for human piety to proceed figuratively and to think of people in symbolic places. As I have said then, the united sense of the Church is spoiled by face to face celebration, because the Church's sense of worship depends on a united looking towards God, and not upon its members contemplating one another. The Church is reduced to a closed community of human beings, when by nature it is really a community directed outwards beyond itself, towards a single transcendent point.

292. The new church architecture.

The new style of church architecture, which is hardly new in fact, has also been influenced by the idea that what is sacred is produced by man and for man, and has lost all feeling for the sacred as such. The functionalism that is so characteristic of modern architecture, and that has become the first principle of all building, governs the design of churches as well; they are now conceived in a utilitarian spirit which, while keeping their religious use in view, does not exclude other uses either; hence the so-called multi-purpose churches that are used as places for

---

[103] In an article published in 1955 not long before his death.
[Translator's note.]

non-religious meetings, as concert halls, as shelters for those on strike, etc.

The ideas of adoration, and of the sacred as something essentially separated or set apart, are lost in all this. The new church architecture treats the sacred as something diffused throughout the whole of reality, and hence any attempt to localize it in church buildings must be abandoned.

The new cathedral in Taranto designed by Luigi Nervi, which is considered to be a masterpiece of church architecture, is in fact entirely at odds with Catholic doctrine. In the traditional understanding the altar should be on high, as should the church if possible inasmuch as it symbolizes the mount of meeting with God; thus the people should lift their eyes to the altar. At Taranto the altar is in the lowest place rather than the highest, as if God were below and man were above Him. As opposed to the idea of the sacred as something marked off or set apart, the vault is thrown open to the sky in order to signify, as Nervi himself asserts, that the space outside is sacred as well.[104] This is to destroy the idea of the sacred in general, and the specific Catholic localization of the sacred in the eucharist as well. At Taranto too, the Blessed Sacrament altar is set to one side, and is no more significant than any of the other side altars dedicated in honor of various saints, and no more significant than the altar that is a memorial to those who died during the war.[105]

Paul VI was once presented with a model of the new church at Tagba, which has no walls so as to be completely open to sacred nature breaking in with its beauty on every hand.[106]

San Carlino ai Morti was the church of the Milan hospital for the incurable and was open at the sides in order to allow the sick to follow the Mass from their bedrooms; the idea there

---

[104] Expanding the sacred is the same as abolishing it, just as pantheism is a kind of atheism. When Giacomo Manzu, the famous modern artist, was asked what the sacred was, he replied: "Everything is sacred." O.R., 23 November 1978.

[105] Despite the general abasement of altars, and their replacement by tables, the usual euphemistic style of writing leads people to assert that one of the merits of the liturgical reform has been *la remise en valeur de l'autel, de son symbolisme et même de son mystère*. In *Esprit et Vie*, 1983, p.457. "The restoration of the importance of the altar, with its symbolism and even its mystery."

[106] O.R., 10 June 1968.

however, was not to do away with the sacred by rejecting a *templum*, a *temenos*, a hearth, a *limen*, strengthened by the presence of the eucharist.

Whenever this expansion of the sacred beyond the sacred is attempted, the nature of things is violated, yet again, in a relativistic attempt to detect everything in every other thing, and to equate everything with everything else.[107]

The desire to extend the sacred unlimitedly, as if there were no inherent contradiction in talking about something as sacred yet in no sense set apart from anything else, runs into particular difficulties in a Catholic context because of the Catholic doctrine of the eucharist. This states that there can be a uniquely special presence of God, over and above his universal presence throughout his creation. This is the sacramental presence of the God-Man, body and blood, soul and divinity, who enters the space and time of transient creatures only by means of his body, whether in its earthly or glorified state. True, he does not enter it in a three-dimensional way, or as the theologians put it, circumscriptively;[108] but he does nonetheless really enter it in such a way that the Being of the Holy One is present in this particular place but not in that.[109] The eucharist is the thing that is sacred in its very being; from it, all sacred places, times, persons and actions flow, and to it they all refer. It is only through the eucharist that the divine can be localized. Without belief in the eucharist, then of course the divine presence can in no sense be contained within four walls, and any attempt to localize it verges on being superstitious. Without belief in the eucharist, a church must logically be regarded as nothing more than a place where people meet for worship and other ritual activities; it can

---

[107] It is appropriate here to note the changes made to the Way of the Cross. In their eagerness to assert their independence of tradition, modern architects put all the Stations in a line two or three metres long, so that they are right next to each other; thus the person doing the Stations can see them all at once, and is also denied the opportunity of moving from one to another. The *Via Crucis* has become a *Statio Crucis*. Walking has been turned into staying put. This too is an instance of the violation of the essence or nature of something.

[108] Cf. *Summa Theologica*, III,q.76,a.5.

[109] Theresa of Konnersreuth could distinguish the presence of the Blessed Sacrament in Catholic churches, as distinct from Protestant ones, even when passing by in the street.

no longer be regarded as the tabernacle of the Holy One whence all sanctification is derived.

An over-emphasis on the merely functional aspects of a church building diminishes one's sense of the sacred. A church is indeed a place where the faithful meet to pray and to take part in the liturgy, but it has a sacred character even when such functions are not being exercised within it; a sacred building, like every other artistic creation of a religious sort, exists in itself as distinct from the use which may subsequently be made of it. *Si hi tacuerint, lapides clamabunt*[110] is a saying applicable to sacred architecture; or as Rouault said, churches ought to be *maisons priantes*,[111] not merely places that people use for prayer, but places which themselves pray. This is true of those mediaeval churches in which an artist has hidden some beautiful carving or painting high up in a remote corner, away from the light, where nobody sees it, but where all by itself it still sings the glory of the God for whom it was made; made by an artist content that his own name too should be similarly forgotten, that the name of God alone might be glorified.

293. Summary of the liturgical reform.

The practical results of the reform have been to nullify what the council itself laid down concerning the maintenance of Latin and Gregorian chant.[112] This is an instance of the alleged

---

[110] Luke, 19:40 "If these (people) kept silent, the stones would cry out."

[111] "Houses that pray."

[112] Cf. *Sacrosanctum Concilium* 36 and 116. The destruction of Gregorian chant is attested by Father R.M. Baratta, O.S.B., director of the Roman Gregorian Choir, in O.R., 15 April 1983: "In seminaries and religious institutes the chant has generally been lost. Even the printer's photographic plates of the *Liber Usualis* have been destroyed, and it was the book that was most widely used; anybody wanting to learn about Gregorian chant today will find it impossible to buy a single copy of the Ferretti or Sunol editions. The last copies of the *Liber* were sold off as waste paper, along with Missals, and were salvaged here in Rome, though only to a very limited extent, and almost entirely by lay people who bought them at the Porta Portese." [The Roman flea market. Translator's note.] A *Graduale Romanum* appeared in 1974 "but it left out the introductory part, which at least used to explain some basic concepts, and it has no psalm tones, no antiphons, no hymns, nothing. These are

spirit of the council preventing a legitimate implementation of
the council's own decrees. The chief result of the reform was a
drop in Mass attendance, which, taking an average of national
averages, now amounts to about 40% of what it was. It is true
of course that this desertion cannot be wholly attributed to the
adoption of a new liturgy, as it was also provoked by the clergy's
distaste for their own priestly office, an overvaluation of the
ecclesiastical functions of the laity, the degradation of the
eucharist, a decline of supernatural vision in religion as a whole,
and a conforming of the Church to the secularist opinions of
the world. Nonetheless, in this concatenation of causes, the de-
formation of the Church's rites and wholesale innovation in the
life of the Church in general have played a conspicuous part.
Those who sponsored the reforms have usually denied that they
amount to something approaching a fundamental change, but
there is decisive evidence that that is precisely what has occurred. There are numerous statements by Protestants to the
effect that the new Mass can be celebrated in conformity with
their beliefs, and is thus acceptable for use at eucharistic celebrations in their own communities. Max Thurian of the Protestant Taizé community has stated that one of the fruits of the
new Mass will probably be *que des communités non catholiques
pourront célébrer la Sainte Cène avec les mêmes prières que l'Eglise
catholique: théologiquement c'est possible.*[113] It must therefore be
recognized that the reform has changed a Catholic Mass that
was *unacceptable* to Protestants into a Catholic Mass that *is* ac-

---

things one cannot do without when teaching." Gregorian chant is
still sought after by music lovers, quite apart from its liturgical setting of which the Church has now robbed it; concert halls are
crowded for performances of Gregorian chant and records and
disks of it sell very well.

[113] *La Croix*, 30 May 1969. "That non-Catholic communities will be
able to celebrate the Lord's Supper with the same prayers as the
Catholic Church: theologically it is possible." The prior of Taizé,
Brother Roger Schutz has said: "*Les nouvelles prières eucharistiques présentent une structure qui correspond à la Messe luthéri-
enne.*" *Itinéraires*, No.218 December 1977, p.116. "The new
eucharistic prayers have a structure corresponding to that of the
Lutheran Mass." In *Pope Paul's New Mass*, Dickinson 1980, M.
Davies has shown that the new Roman rite is similar to, and sometimes identical with, Cranmer's Anglican Mass produced in the
sixteenth century.

ceptable to Protestants. This judgment implies that there has
been a profound change: Protestants are, after all, the best
judges of what is acceptable to Protestants. Max Thurian's declaration is merely one among many of a similar kind; and the
joint celebration of the eucharist by Catholic priests and Protestant ministers, with only feeble opposition from the bishops,
confirms the fact that there has been a change in teaching.[114]

---

[114] The omissions, ambiguities and options embodied in the 1969 Missal mean that it can be made acceptable or unacceptable to some
Protestants depending on what choice of ritual, texts and ceremonial actions the celebrant makes. [Translator's note.]

CHAPTER XXXIX

THE SACRAMENT OF MATRIMONY

294. New concept of conjugal love and marriage.

Although the changed thinking on this matter is not set down in black and white anywhere in the council's texts, and although it has been attacked by the more active supporters of tradition, Cardinal Felici being the chief among them, it has nonetheless now been widely accepted and has become a common opinion in the Church. The council itself does state that among the new developments in the Church, the "spirituality of matrimony"[1] is undergoing continual reformulation, and that changes in modern society "are manifesting ever more clearly[2] in various ways the true character of marriage." Obviously the council was not intending to deny that matrimony had always had a spirituality of its own in the Catholic system. What it is talking about then is a *new* spirituality. The change is accompanied by the usual euphemisms[3] praising the various kinds of help that modern society is supposedly providing for marriage and the family. Nothing, it would seem, could make the scales fall from the council fathers' eyes: neither the adoption of divorce by all formerly Christian states, nor the fact that trial marriages have now become common, nor the fact that contraception has been made legal or even compulsory, not even the widespread legalization of abortion, though all of these phenomena were known to the council and deplored by it.

The departure from traditional teaching does not affect the *supernatural* side of Christian marriage, by which it embodies and expresses the union between Christ and his Church. What

---

[1] *Unitatis Redintegratio*, 6.

[2] The expression *saepe saepius* means *more and more*, not *very often*, as many of the translations put it.

[3] *Gaudium et Spes*, 47.

IOTA UNUM

it affects is the unitive and procreative aspects of marriage as a *natural* institution.

The anatomical and physiological differentiation of the sexes shows that, from a natural point of view, their exact organic complementarity is ordered towards the union of two biological entities so that they become in the Biblical phrase "one flesh"; in Campanella's picturesque image the organic complementarity is like that of one glove with another glove turned inside out. This union is in turn ordered towards the moral union of the two persons who, without actually becoming one, enter into as full a communion as possible by means of that physical union. Conjugal union is in fact the fullest possible union into which two rational creatures of different sex can enter.

However, it is not through physical union that perfect personal union is actually achieved. Paradoxically, considered in itself and at its most intense, physical union is a moment when the two persons are separate, inasmuch as conscious awareness both of oneself and of the other is lost at that point. Perfect personal union is of a moral rather than a physical order, and exists in the realm of love between friends, a love by which neither of the parties desires the other, but, at a higher level, desires perfect good *for* the other and *with* that other.[4]

The natural effect of physical union is procreation, and procreation is without doubt the intrinsic purpose of a conjugal relationship; two persons love, and their natures generate a third. From the point of view of Catholic metaphysics, these natures are, as it were, ideas uttered by the divine Word and thrown into real existence. As such, natures become criteria of ethical behavior, inasmuch as man's moral function is realized in taking on his own nature, following the laws immanent within it, and fulfilling its purpose.

There are thus two drives that urge human beings towards marriage. The first is the natural instinct by which people seek to reproduce themselves in another human being, in whom they feel they in some sense re-exist, and thanks to whom they seem to escape the full power of death. The second is the desire to fulfill themselves by giving themselves in person as a gift of love

---

[4] This, it would seem, is what John Paul II was teaching when he said, during his catechesis on the first chapters of Genesis given at Wednesday general audiences in the winter of 1980, that it was a disorder to desire one's spouse.

to some other person. The first might be called the natural good of marriage and the second its moral good, always remembering that the natural good becomes itself morally good if it is taken on in the right spirit.

295. The primary and secondary goods of marriage.

The procreative goal of marriage was called its primary end, and the mutual perfecting or fulfilling of the spouses was called its secondary end. The latter expression can be taken in various senses, but what it meant in substance was "an end consequent upon the primary end"; it did not mean "an end of lesser or secondary importance." The real meaning is that it is in the goal of generating offspring that the spouses find their personal fulfillment, and if that full physical union and its possible consequences were not there, then there could indeed be a moral union of another kind, but it would not be a conjugal relationship.

Procreation and union are thus equally true goals in marriage, but tradition has tended to emphasize the former. In this view, the spouses pursue the goal of generating offspring and of educating that offspring, and it is in so doing that they exercise their mutual love and find fulfillment as spouses; or could one put it the other way and say that they aim at exercising their mutual love which fulfills them spiritually, and that the generation of offspring is the result of that? The opinion that seems generally to have been held is that parents exist for the benefit of children, not vice versa; that marriage is for procreation, not the other way round. But it is difficult to define the relation between the natural end of marriage, namely procreation, and the personal end, namely fulfillment as a person. The Book of Genesis bears witness to the fact that the propagation of the human race is one of the purposes of marriage: *Crescite et multiplicamini*,[5] but it bears similar witness to the fact that the mutual perfection or fulfillment of the spouses is likewise one of its purposes inasmuch as Eve is created as an *adiutorium simile*[6] through whom Adam is brought out of his solitude and drawn into a reciprocal love. At the supernatural level, the propagation of the human race is the more important of these two ends, because the multiplication of human individuals is ultimately designed to fill up the predestined number of the elect.

---

[5] Genesis 1, 22. "Increase and multiply."
[6] Genesis 2, 18. "Help of like kind."

The question must be looked at more closely. Does the goal of procreation have to be consciously adverted to and intended by the spouses in each specific act of union? Or can they not advert to it, and concentrate instead on the unitive goal, that is, on the reciprocal gift of themselves to each other, with its attendant positive qualities, provided always that they do not positively exclude the natural goal of the act by any deliberate deed on their part?

Antonio Fogazzaro disagreed with the views of Alessandro Manzoni on this same question, presented in another guise. In *Fermo e Lucia,* Vol. II, Ch. I, Manzoni portrays human love as stemming from the natural impulse towards procreation: its depths relate to a goal greater than any individual, and its dangers come from the power of a strong instinct to stifle reason. Fogazzaro disagrees in his *Sopra un'opinione di Alessandro Manzoni,*[7] and says that love is not merely an overpowering vital drive or an instinct of the species: the chief of its many ends is *unum fieri cum eo quod amas*[8] as Augustine and Thomas say. Even when the propagation of the species is not involved, love is concerned with an irrepressible desire for unity which relates directly to religion and the quest for immortality.[9]

---

[7]   Published in Milan in 1912.

[8]   "To become one with that which you love."

[9]   Fr. E. Gentili's theory set forth in *L'amour dans le célibat*, Paris 1968, is related to Fogazzaro's view and is echoed by Louise Rinser in *Une femme d'aujourd'hui et l'Eglise*, Paris 1970. Gentili maintains that there can be a chaste and spiritual, but nonetheless loving, relationship between persons vowed to celibacy. He gives as examples St. Francis of Assisi and St. Clare, St. Teresa of Avila and Father Gratian, St. Francis de Sales and St. Jane Frances de Chantal. One could add Frederick Borromeo and the Dominican sister Catharine Vannini (see the letters published by Mgr C. Marcora in *Memorie storiche della Diocesi di Milano*, Vol. XI, pp.177ff.). But on the other hand there is the dilemma of "either fleeing or marrying" that has been held by the generality of Catholic moral theologians. Then there is "the spiritual use of the flesh" referred to by Teilhard de Chardin in the sad pages published posthumously by his friend Jeanne Mortier. That sort of "ascending as a pair towards the divine centre" is an error psychologically, morally and theologically.

296. Predominance of the procreative end of marriage in traditional teaching. Luke, 20:35-36.

The traditional doctrine on marriage as a union directed essentially towards procreation is given a new twist by the council when it describes it as a "communion of life and love," with procreation following upon that.[10] Thus in the council's teaching, the essential equality of the two ends is maintained,[11] but the procreative end can be seen as "secondary" to the personalist end, if "secondary" is taken in its true sense, explained above, of following upon something else: *secundum est quod sequitur*.[12] The council's treatment of the matter has nothing in common with the notion that human love is a blind force that makes use of individuals as instruments for the expansion of life within the universe. Such was Schopenhauer's view, and it also inspired the Platonic myths of Eros with his net and Venus as a huntress, who ensnare us by pleasure and make us serve the end of procreating the species so that *ci mugne Dio amore a far un cacio di nuovo uomo*.[13]

The reason the council's teaching is so distinct from such an outlook is that it proclaims marriage to be based upon friendship rather than desire, and teaches that conjugal affection is directed from one person to another[14] as an act of will; thus the marriage bond itself is brought into being by a consent of wills. The tendency of American ecclesiastical tribunals to define marriage by reference to its persistence as a communion of life and love, rather than by reference to a specific and irrevocable

---

[10] *Gaudium et Spes*, 48.

[11] It was not maintained by Doms in his book *Sinn und Zweck der Ehe*, which holds that the goal of mutual fulfillment is primary. The proposition was censured by a decree of the Holy Office on 1 April 1944.

[12] "The secondary is what follows." Pius XI, quoting the catechism of the Council of Trent, teaches that the mutual fellowship and perfecting or fulfillment of the spouses is the primary end of marriage in the broad sense, but not in the narrow sense. In the latter sense he teaches that its primary end is the procreation and education of offspring. See Denzinger 2232 (or 3707). [Translator's note.]

[13] Campanella, *Poesie*, Bari 1915, p.22 "The God of Love drives us to make a clot of new humanity."

[14] *Gaudium et Spes*, 49.

act of consent, has been condemned by Paul VI and John Paul II.

The tendency after the council to give equal emphasis to procreation and love, even in the specifically sexual sphere as distinct from marriage as a whole, leads on to a separation of these two ends, and then further to placing the expression of love above procreation, and then ultimately to the legitimacy of contraception; this tendency is obviously out of harmony with the teaching the Church has hitherto maintained. As Cardinal Felici showed,[15] the council itself maintained in the drafting of *Gaudium et Spes* that *bonum prolis primum locum tenet.*[16]

This *objective* priority of the procreative end of marriage seems to require a corresponding *subjective* priority in the intention of the spouses during sexual relations. Innocent XI[17] censured the opinion that the conjugal act is free from fault when performed without any procreative intention, motivated simply by pleasure.[18] If the goodness of conjugal union is compromised by the lack of a positive intention regarding its procreative effect, it seems marital relations must necessarily include a procreative intention. It amounts therefore to a change in doctrine to allege that the perfecting and reciprocal gift of the spouses is a sufficient intention to make conjugal relations morally good.[19]

[15] O.R., 11 October 1972, note 3; in a lengthy article.
[16] "The good of offspring takes first place."
[17] Blessed Innocent XI, Odescalchi (1676-1689); beatified by Pius XII in 1956. [Translator's note.]
[18] Denzinger, 1159.
[19] The full text of Denzinger 1159 runs as follows: *Opus coniugii ob solam voluptatem exercitum omni penitus caret culpa ac defectu veniali.* "The conjugal act performed solely for pleasure is altogether free of any fault or venial defect." Together with 64 other propositions, this one is condemned as being "at least a cause of scandal and pernicious in practice." It will be seen that the proposition makes no mention of the duty of a procreative intention. [Translator's note.]

In dealing with the Sadducees' captious question about the woman who had been married seven times,[20] Jesus gives the desire to generate offspring as the reason for the existence of marriage. He says that in heaven "they will not take wives or husbands, because they will no longer die." Here marriage is identified with the work of procreation; there is no hint of a communion of life and a reciprocal gift of personal love, which would necessarily last as long as the persons in question. In this gospel passage both procreation and life together are relegated to the passing world of earthly reality. In his long catechesis on the meaning of marriage, John Paul II never referred to this passage in Luke, which certainly gives priority to procreation as the *raison d'être* of marriage; when mortal life ceases, procreation ceases, and when procreation ceases so does marriage. Of course, there is no objection to the idea that conjugal, filial and parental affection still exist in our heavenly life; Dante describes this beautifully in the fourteenth canto of the *Paradiso*; but these affections will exist in persons whose bodies have been resurrected and glorified, and they will be, so to speak, memories of the affections felt in this life, an instance, as Dante says elsewhere, or how *al mondo di sù quel di giù torna.*[21]

Pius XI teaches[22] that the mutual perfecting of the spouses "can be called the primary reason and motive for marriage," but it must be remembered that in his teaching, the mutual integration of lives that perfects the spouses includes the mutual gift of their bodies, which in the natural course of things is the source of offspring; and he regards offspring as the highest good marriage can produce. Without believing in the myths of the ancient world, we can still say that in their act of love, the spouses *are their offspring*: "the marriage bed upon which" as Penelope says to Odysseus "we were together our son Telemachus."

The question we set out to answer in the previous paragraph, namely whether the procreative end of marriage must be subjectively intended by the spouse, or whether it is legitimate merely to intend the expressing of conjugal love, is something it is not particularly important to settle here.

---

[20] Luke, 20:35-36.

[21] *Paradiso*, IX, 108. "This world below is ordered towards the one above."

[22] *Casti connubii*, 24 and 25.

297. Marriage and contraception.

It becomes possible to separate conjugal relations from procreation, if one loses sight of the fact that the essential coexistence of the two ends of marriage means that in order to express
a perfect union, conjugal relations must remain open to their
natural procreative effect. But people now imagine that the full
union in which marriage consists can in fact be separated from
its natural effect, which is the generation of new life. This view
was supported strongly by the majority of the advisory committee which Paul VI set up to examine the question, but the traditional doctrine was maintained despite its opinion. *Humanae
Vitae* and *Mysterium Fidei* are the outstanding documents of
Paul VI's pontificate, because in the latter the Pope upheld the
core of supernatural dogma, and in the former he upheld the
core of the natural law, that is, by the two combined, he upheld
the two levels of truth that the Church must maintain.

Humanae Vitae is the document that most bitterly manifested the divisions in the Church, and was thus the most
painful and, for the Pope personally, the most glorious act of his
pontificate.[23] As long as the unitive end of conjugal relations
was held to be subordinate to the procreative, contraception
could not be held to be legitimate. As we have seen in the
teaching of Pius XI, one can say that spiritual communion is the
primary end of marriage, but it remains indissolubly linked to
the procreative end. It would perhaps be more verbally precise
to say that the communion of the spouses is *co-primary*, that is,
of the first order but always in conjunction with the other end,
so that without the latter the former could not attain the status
either of an end or of a primary end.

This duality of purpose is a difficult matter. It is difficult to
maintain that the two ends are equal, because a single action, in
this case conjugal relations, cannot have two ends without one
being inferior to, and a means towards, the other. Now, in traditional teaching every act of conjugal union must implicitly
include the procreative end, since conjugal love is of its nature

---

[23] Cf. paragraphs 61-63. *Humanae Vitae* was also the most ill-timed
of utterances. Had it been issued three years earlier, without the
uncertainty created by delay and a hostile committee report, there
would have been no occasion for a crisis. [Translator's note.]

fertile.[24] It is in the process of loving that procreation occurs, and in the process of procreating that love is expressed.

This structure of the conjugal act is distorted by contraception. The assumption is made that love and procreation can conflict with each other, and the conclusion is drawn that the conflict can be overcome by downplaying and excluding the procreative end, to give free reign to the expression of love. There is an alleged clash of duties which the spouses resolve in their concrete circumstances, adopting contraception so as to give preference to love, in order to maintain their unity, their faithfulness and the good of the family itself. That is, for example, what the French bishops and many others teach, as we have seen in certain paragraphs above.

In the address that he delivered to a group of priests attending a convention on the pastoral care of families, John Paul II outlined another profound philosophical reason for the illicitness of contraception.[25] He pointed out that contraception not only violates the natural association of the unitive and procreative ends of marriage, but that it also mars the very act of reciprocal self-giving in personal union. "The contraceptive act," the Pope says, "introduces a substantial diminution into this reciprocal giving, and expresses an objective refusal to give to the other *the whole good* of femininity and masculinity." In short, as well as offending against the procreative end of marriage, contraception also offends against the total reciprocal giving of the two persons, by subtracting something, namely the procreative part, of the human nature in which those persons subsist.

298. Critique of the theory of contraception.

Various themes in the new theology which we have already examined come together in defense of contraception, and we may now point them out.

Views on this matter are often infected with a subjectivism stemming from *situation ethics,* and presuppose that it is impossible to make any objective and universally binding judg-

---

[24] Canon 1013, §1 (1917 Code of Canon Law). [Translator's note.]
[25] O.R., 18 September 1983.

merit on a practical matter; it is thus left up to the conscience of the human agent to establish both the nature of the situation to be judged, and the criteria wherewith to judge it.

Views on this matter are also infected with the false concept of *globality*. The fertility of conjugal acts is seen as a characteristic of conjugal acts in general, rather than as being the fertility of this or that act in particular; it relates to the sum total of such actions and is not connected intrinsically to any of them. I have already pointed out that this notion involves an impossible nullification of time and the abolition of any binding moral rules.[26]

Contraception effects a dissociation between what nature intends and what the human will intends, or to put it in terms of an old but precise distinction, between the *finis operis* and the *finis operantis*.[27] What is at issue here is the whole Catholic philosophy that maintains that essences or natures, including the nature of the human body, are forms or fundamental principles of reality, deriving from archetypes in the divine intellect; in his terminology Goethe called such forms "mothers." In the Catholic view, essences are internal principles governing the development of a thing, and they participate in the divine immutability. They are also subsistent forms: both understanding and willing are parts of man's essence; though the latter is independent of such activities. Man's liberty is confronted by these natures, not so that he may deform or remodel them to his own liking, but that he may conform *himself* to them, because it is precisely insofar as these natures *confront* man's liberty that they acquire the character of a law imposing itself upon that liberty. When confronted with a law, liberty can harmonize itself with it and become one with the law, which is what constitutes the moral goodness of an act; or else it can defy the law, fail to harmonize with it, and set out on its own, which is what constitutes moral evil.

As we have said elsewhere, in order to be morally good, human activity must recognize essences and the order of things, and must conform to being in its own structured axiological reality. Now the sexual act is of its nature directed towards procreation: the anatomy, physiology and psychology of human beings as sexual creatures bear witness to the fact, and the

---

[26] See paragraph 201-3.
[27] "The goal of the work" and "the goal of the worker."

common convictions of different peoples confirm the conclusion in language and customs. There is a biological connection between the act and its end, that cannot be broken so as to reject the end and seize the eudaemonological content of the act, frustrating the end aimed at by nature.

The physiological, or what used to be called the vegetative, part of man is not capable of moral virtue, which is why the latter does not exist in animals and plants; but it can be taken up into morally virtuous activity when the physiological system is part of a higher whole, as it is in man. In such cases the higher ruling element in the whole unites itself to physiological activity and regulates it by restraining or encouraging it as the case may be. This is the origin of the virtues of temperance, regulating the appetite for food, and chastity, regulating the appetite for sexual pleasure. If however the will intervenes in order to detach a physiological function from its end, so as to pursue pleasure while rejecting the natural effect of the function, a vice exists in the man in question, which will be more or less grave depending on whether the detachment is more or less deliberate. If one seeks a parallel to contraception, one can be found in the ancient practice of taking emetics to provoke vomiting to empty one's stomach, in order to be able to renew the pleasures of tasting food, even though this frustrated the natural end of eating, which is nutrition. In conjugal acts, man should not split up the natural purposes which are connected with such acts, but must instead "respect the unbreakable connection that God has willed to exist between the two meanings of the conjugal act, namely the unitive and the procreative."[28]

---

[28] *Humanae Vitae*, 12.

CHAPTER XL

THEODICY

299. The new theodicy.[1]

When discussing commonly held opinions about the present crisis in the Church,[2] the autonomy of earthly goods,[3] anthropocentrism and technology,[4] and secondary Christianity,[5] we have necessarily touched on new currents of thought in philosophical theology or theodicy. The overall conclusion emerging from those opinions was that the modern mind thinks man's purpose in the world is realized within the world itself; that any further transcendent goal is only a means to realizing some set of values immanent within man himself; and that in a world adjusted and developed by human energies, God has no place, or else has, as it were, a relative and auxiliary role in partnership with man. In accordance with this trend, the Church is setting aside its specifically supernatural nature, and blending its mission with the task of advancing civilization, fitting itself in as a help towards a more just and brotherly world. The aim is to create a *civitas hominica*[6] without denying a higher *civitas dominica*,[7] but the links between the two are deliberately loosened with the aim of establishing a purely humanitarian world order. The position Christianity will occupy in this new world will not

---

[1] The continental word "theodicy" is not commonly used in English, but no single word will do as an equivalent, so it is here retained. It means the consideration of the divine government of the world, the operations of Providence, and the rational justification of belief; a mixture of natural theology and apologetics. [Translator's note.]
[2] See paragraphs 10-11.
[3] See paragraphs 207-8.
[4] See paragraph 210.
[5] See paragraphs 220-1.
[6] "City of Man."
[7] "City of the Lord."

rest upon its possession of natural and supernatural truth, but upon a liberty common to all men.

In treating the new ecumenism,[8] we saw that the ideal of the Catholic unity of the human race, of which we presented Campanella's vision as an example, has been replaced by a purely rational and natural ecumenism which all religions can promote when dissolved into a purely humanitarian system of values. At present then, the Church is drawn paradoxically towards an *incarnation* of one sort, whereby it would attempt to leaven the world as part of a humanitarian world order, and a *disincarnation* of another sort, whereby it would abandon involvement with worldly things in the name of an alleged greater purity, ignoring the fact that its real task is to invest worldly realities with a religious significance. It should not be forgotten that at the Roman diocesan conference on "The requirements of charity and justice" in 1974, it was proposed that the Church should give all its property to the state, so as to be independent, and that no more church buildings should be constructed.[9]

The question of the relationship between this world, and a Church which is at heart other-worldly, is misrepresented by this false understanding of religion, and leads us to re-examine the doctrine of divine causality.

300. New conception of divine causality. The French bishops.

The change on this point was manifested by the French bishops in the published proceedings of their plenary meeting in 1968, and contradicts the Church's teaching, practice and traditional liturgy. The Church teaches that any creature's action is caused, in a metaphysical sense, by God's universal causality, with the result that all its activity is simultaneously the product of a created cause and the Uncreated Cause. The French bishops, however, teach that because certain entities have a natural capacity to produce certain effects, there is no need to refer further back to a divine transcendent cause of creaturely causality, underlying all changing being.

In the Church's view, prayer of petition is justified both by metaphysics and by divine revelation, inasmuch as *a Deo omnia*; that is to say, as we read upon the portals of some medieval

---

[8] See paragraphs 247-9.
[9] O.R., 15 February 1974.

churches, "all things come from God." But according to the French bishops this is a false, pagan idea. *Sans doute un héritage païen venant du fond des âges a-t-il sédimenté l'âme chrétienne, et les sequelles de cet héritage sont loin d'être totalement disparues, même de notre rituel. Au scandal ou à la risée de l'homme moderne, une partie de notre liturgie continue a demander à Dieu ce que le paysan demande à l'engrais, un salut cosmique que fait de Dieu le suppléant de nos insuffisances.*[10] Launching into the usual denigration of the Church as it has actually existed in history, they continue by saying: *Saint Paul n'a pas transigé avec les usages païens. L'Eglise a tenté de le faire, mais avait l'excuse de ne pouvoir faire autrement. Aujourd'hui l'avènement de la civilisation scientifico-technique lui donne une chance appréciable parce qu'elle travaille dans le même sens et le cultivateur compte plus sur les engrais que sur les rogations pour faire lever sa moisson.*[11]

To say that Christian civilization was in fact pagan and that it has been redeemed by the present technological culture is to question the fundamental truth of the Catholic faith. It is also manifestly false; or are we to pretend that peasants of a pre-technological type did not know about manure, or that they scattered it around indiscriminately as if they had no idea what made for flourishing fields?

The French bishops' thesis contains both a religious and a philosophical error. It compromises the universality of Providence, which extends in fact to individual things and to the hairs on one's head.[12] By compromising the universality of Providence it also compromises the principle of creation, the prime principle upon which Christianity rests; it is precisely

---

[10] "Undoubtedly, a pagan heritage dating from the beginning of time has left traces in the Christian soul, and the consequences of this heritage have far from totally disappeared, even in our ritual. To the scandal or scorn of modern man, part of our liturgy continues to ask of God what the farmer asks of his fertilizer, a cosmic well-being that makes God an agent who makes good our deficiencies."

[11] "St. Paul did not compromise with pagan customs. The Church attempted to do so, but had the excuse that it could not do otherwise. Today the arrival of scientifico-technological civilization is a piece of good fortune for the Church, because technology works towards the end that has always been aimed at, and the farmer now relies more on fertilizers than he does on the rogational prayers to make his crops grow."

[12] Matthew, 10:30.

because the whole of the world is caused by God, that each and every created thing falls under the control of Divine Providence, a truth which is also taught by the First Vatican Council.[13] Philosophically, the French bishops' position is not a new development, but a return to the Aristotelian view that since God was simply a self-contemplating intellect, the things of this world were not the object of the divine attention, but were left to chance or fate instead. In the final analysis, their position denies the infinity of the divine wisdom and power upon which the idea of Providence depends, and implies that there must be finite beings that do not derive from the Prime Being, and a causality that does not come from the Primal Cause.

301. Change in the doctrine of prayer.

Nor is it true that the Church's teaching removes the operation of secondary causes, and of human activity in particular; these operate under the influence of the First Cause which makes them exist and exist as causes. To say that human acts are really the causes of their effects, while nevertheless performed under the influence of a universally operating Cause, is not to remove the operation of secondary causes but simply to set things in their right order. Human acts do not change the dispositions of Divine Providence but fulfill them, because that particular human activity or prayer is included in the divine design.[14] Of course the farmer sows his seed and applies his manure, but the fruit is the result of a thousand concomitant causes over which neither he nor technology have any control; and all of this depends on God.

This is not the sort of book that can enter into dispute about the relation between primary and secondary causality. It is sufficient to keep in mind the distinction between the transcendent Cause and a cause operating within the natural order, and to avoid the mistake of thinking of them as equal and concurrent when they in fact operate in different orders; the farmer, the sun and the rain produce the effect of fertile soil, but that effect is produced by agents that are themselves conditioned by the transcendent Cause. There is no difficulty in attributing a single effect simultaneously to a primal and a secondary cause, but at different levels.

---

[13] Constitution *Dei Filius*, Cap. I.
[14] *Summa Theologica*, I,q.22,a.3, *ad secundum* and II,II,q.83,a.2.

The reasonableness of petitionary prayer depends on the doctrine of Providence. Man can ask God for temporal and spiritual blessings without denying a genuine causality on the part of creatures, because their causality is itself produced by that divine power that bestows existence and operation upon all created things.[15] Does the healing of a sick man not proceed from God because it comes via a doctor? Is the doctor an independent cause, separate from the Prime Cause? The answer is not an "either or" but a "both and."

We have seen[16] that while paganism thought it absurd to ask God for virtue and a rightly ordered will, Christianity prays for these things above all else: *Adesto, quaesumus Domine, supplicationibus nostris, ut esse, te largiente, mereamur et inter prospera humiles et inter adversa securi.*[17] Clearly, if it makes sense to ask God for a rightly directed will, which one already has by the fact of desiring it, then *a fortiori* it makes sense to ask for temporal blessings, which we do *not* possess by desiring virtue; this remains true even though temporal blessings are a less important thing to have than virtue itself.[18]

The French bishops' teaching is contradicted even by the Lord's Prayer, in which we ask for our daily bread, although it is the "fruit of the earth and the work of human hands" as the offertory of the new Mass puts it; it is indeed the product of human labor, but Christ nonetheless commands us to ask it of the

---

[15] The Church recognizes, approves and orders prayers of petition: all goods are sought from God, but moral good, that is to say virtue, is sought absolutely, and the rest relatively, and as a means towards moral good. This is a difficult doctrine. In sanctuary churches, for every thousand *ex voto* memorials put up in thanksgiving for the restoration of health, or for having been preserved in danger or having come unharmed through some peril, you will hardly find one giving thanks for conversion of life, or for having been able to put aside an undue hatred or for having persevered in some good intention.

[16] See paragraph 281.

[17] "Be present at our praying we beseech thee O Lord, that by thy gift we may be worthy to be humble amidst good fortune and undisturbed in adversity."

[18] Perhaps the rejection by the French bishops of the Rogation prayers is also a result of their aversion for the cult of the saints, since the litany of the saints is sung during Rogation processions.

Father; the bread is *ours* but we are nonetheless commanded to ask for it.

The pre-conciliar liturgy made frequent use of prayers for temporal blessings, with votive Masses *pro vitanda mortalitate, pro infirmis, tempore belli,* and with special prayers *tempore famis, tempore terraemotus, ad petendam pluviam, ad postulandam serenitatem*[19] and so on. But obviously, in the context of a civilization that puts all its hopes in technology, and which claims it is removing the supposed remnants of ancient polytheism from Christianity, the Rogation prayers that were so devout, expressive and sound in their inspiration had to cede place to the enlightened use of chemical fertilizers.[20] Nonetheless, the first transcendent Cause remains active in secondary causes and we can go on praying to that Cause even if the invocation *ut fructus terrae dare et conservare digneris*[21] has been expunged from the litany.

302. Providence and misfortune.

The *Osservatore Romano*[22] suggests a change in doctrine concerning the meaning of evil in the world, similar to the French bishops' ideas on petitionary prayer; a change principally concerned with explaining the great disasters that strike whole countries, involving good and bad alike in a common distress.

---

[19] "For preventing epidemics," "for the sick," "in time of war" and "in time of famine," "in time of earthquakes," "for asking for rain," "for asking for good weather."

[20] When much of Italy and large parts of the United States were parched by a serious drought that burnt up the fields and threatened to produce a famine in the summer of 1976, Paul VI exhorted his hearers in an Angelus address "to have recourse to that God, our heavenly Father, who controls even the inexorable laws of nature and who is perhaps waiting for the humility and the faith of our filial prayers in order to restore equilibrium to the seasons, fruitfulness to the soil, water to the rivers and refreshment for the thirst of all living things." O.R. 5-6 July 1976, which then prints a prayer for rain.

[21] "That thou wouldst deign to give and protect the fruits of the earth."

[22] O.R., 17 January 1971.

The problem of evil is the fundamental one in theodicy,[23] and indeed the chief spur to man's reflection upon his own destiny. Though it admits of partial solutions at the purely theoretical level, its full explanation–and much more–can only be found in Christian revelation. This problem constitutes the greatest temptation against faith, inasmuch as an evil that afflicts the innocent seems to be a kind of injustice on God's part; it can even be a temptation against faith when such evils befall the guilty. Philosophy attempts to satisfy the mind by logical considerations, such as the disproportion between the human and divine intellect, and the need to know the whole of reality before judging whether some part of it is disordered; and by metaphysical considerations, such as the idea that finitude may always imply imperfection, that is, evil. Only theology can surmount the difficulty, by combining the mystery of human suffering with that of a Christ who suffered even though he was innocent.

J. Galot attempts to show that human suffering is not a form of punishment.[24] But he then goes on to say that "Christ took upon himself the weight of suffering that man's sins *are deemed*[25] to have deserved." He ought to have said "that man's sins *had* deserved"; he fails to realize that what he is talking about is precisely a *punishment* that Christ underwent on behalf of the human race. Even in Christ's case, suffering is a penalty for sin; its meaning does not change even in that unique instance.

The fundamental Catholic idea is that all natural evils among men, such as death, disease and pain, are the consequence of some moral evil. It is not true that all misfortunes that befall some particular person are the result of a personal

---

[23] English readers should note again how the notion of "theodicy" is charged with an apologetical intent, absent from straightforward natural theology. [Translator's note.]

[24] O.R., 17 April 1981.

[25] In Italian, *avrebbero meritate*; literally "would have merited." This use of the conditional in Italian is a way of distancing the speaker from the content of what is being said. Like the use of inverted commas in English, it leaves it somewhat unclear as to whether the speaker does or does not accept the truth of the sentiments in question. [Translator's note.]

fault of his own;[26] that view reflects the sort of servile and materialistic pragmatism upheld by Eliphaz in the Book of Job:[27] you are afflicted therefore you have sinned. Nonetheless a Christian may reasonably take misfortune and treat it as an expiation, penalty or correction for his own sins or those of others, given the fact that he is in some sense a sinner, and that the attainment of true virtue is incomparably more important than any suffering.

Suffering on the part of children evokes "a bitter protest," as John Paul II said when visiting the children's hospital of the Bambino Gesù in Rome.[28] But that difficulty is removed from the point of view of a believer by the fact that Christians suffer in conjunction with the sufferings of the Incarnate God;[29] theologically, all human suffering is a consequence of the sin of Adam *in quo omnes peccaverunt;*[30] and from the natural point of view man is subject to suffering because of his nature, prescinding from questions of guilt and innocence.

It is not so much individual injustice of the sort that led Odoacer to exclaim "Where is God?" when he was put to death by Theodoric, but rather, great collective disasters such as earthquakes, floods, famines and plagues, that arouse our bitterest complaints, inasmuch as they affect guilty and guiltless alike and thus apparently give the lie to the idea of cosmic justice.

303. Moral origin of human suffering.

Whatever be the meaning of God's vengeance mentioned in the Old Testament, the punishments inflicted by God under the Christian dispensation are part of his justice and mercy, and have a moral purpose; they lead us to realize more vividly that life is an undeserved gift from God; they lead us to employ our lives in those activities by which the moral purpose of our existence is fulfilled;[31] they lead us to become more helpful and

---

[26] A proposition insinuating this idea was condemned by Clement XI (Denzinger 1420.)
[27] Job, 4 and 5.
[28] O.R., 10 June 1982.
[29] Cf. Romans, 8:17.
[30] Romans, 5:12. "In whom all have sinned."
[31] In an address to the people of Rome, after the bombing raid in which people were killed on 19 July 1943, Pius XII prayed that that misfortune should be transformed into a strengthened faith, so

compassionate to our neighbors; they allow us to expiate our sins and those of others. The following prayer from the traditional liturgy sets God's scourges correctly in the light of his justice and mercy: *Parce Domine, parce populo tuo, ut dignis flagellationibus castigatus in tua misericordia respiret.* [32]

The error in the *Osservatore Romano* article of 1971 mentioned above, and entitled *La Parte dell'Uomo*, is twofold. Firstly, there is no metaphysical notion of causality, because the author fails to see that creature and Creator are not two causes of the same sort that work together on the same level, and that a created cause operates in virtue of the uncreated Cause. Secondly, the author believes that Providence should guide men to happiness in this world and that if the latter is not achieved, Providence is defective and unjust. In fact, Providence is a universal order, embracing the whole of time and eternity, which achieves a just uniting of moral virtue and happiness only eschatologically, in the life to come. Thus Providence would only be defective if the just man were left suffering eternally. The happiness of the just man in the present life is only a hoped-for happiness which is directed not towards finite goods but towards the infinite and ultimate Good.

Because of its ignoring of transcendent causality, the *Osservatore Romano* proposes to detach Providence in part from God and to hand it over to man, thus introducing a sort of dualism. "What we must learn," it says, "is a truth that has been obscured by a very aberrant line of argument concerning what is called Divine Providence. It is man, not God, who has responsibility for a world that God indeed has created, but has consigned to man's care. What we call Providence is exercised by means of man's decisions." If asserted in the sense that the Prime Cause rules the world by means of the secondary causes inferior to it, the last statement can bear a true sense; but it bears a false sense in this case, because the author thinks secondary causes are equal with the First Cause, that is, that they are themselves prime causes. When discussing the problem of great natural catastrophes, the author attributes them all to human causality and thinks that earthquakes, floods and lightning can one day be entirely eliminated. It is true that he immediately

that "each person may fulfill his own Christian duties by conforming fully to the will of God." O.R., 21 July 1943.

[32] "Spare O Lord, spare thy people; that chastened by the scourgings they deserve, they may take rest in thy mercy."

proceeds to moderate his anthropocentric providentialism by
talking about the elimination of the consequences of catastrophes rather than of the catastrophes themselves. It is nonetheless
obvious that the Catholic concept of Providence is here being
mutilated and that there is an implicit adoption of a technological *regnum hominis*.[33]

Because he fails to understand such scourges as "providential misfortunes" that exist to further the moral purposes of
creation, the author brashly asserts: "The statement that human
suffering is a punishment for man's sin will hardly convince us
when we think of the terrible maladies that afflict infants...
Whatever our doctrine of original sin may involve, it does not
allow us to maintain that children have deserved sufferings of
that sort." Without realizing it, the author is doing away with
part of the doctrine of original sin because, as St. Thomas
teaches, *mors et omnes defectus corporales consequentes sunt
quaedam poenae originalis peccati*.[34] Nor is this merely the thesis
of a particular theological school; it is part of revealed truth:
Stipendia peccati mors and *Corpus...mortuum est propter pecca-
tum*.[35]

The theory concerning these evils that emerges from the
Osservatore Romano article is faulty because of its naturalism, in
that it attributes to nature things that are the consequence of a
moral decision, and it fails to recognize that there is a sin of
nature, to wit original sin, which is distinct from any personal
sin, and lastly, it fails to recognize that it is the existence of
original sin that explains the evils in the world and that justifies
divine Providence.[36]

---

[33] "Kingdom of Man." See paragraphs 210 and 218.
[34] *Summa Theologica*, I,II,q.85,a.5. "Death and all bodily defects
following (upon the loss of original justice) are kinds of penalties
for original sin."
[35] Romans, 6:23 and 8:10. "The wages of sin is death" and "the body
is a dead thing because of sin." John Paul II has reaffirmed this
truth: "Suffering has its theological root in the mystery of sin."
O.R., 24 December 1982.
[36] See nonetheless the footnote to paragraph 97. If, as some Doctors
of the Church explicitly teach, human nature survived the fall of
man intact *in puris naturalibus,* then *a fortiori,* so did the rest of
nature. The loss of man's preternatural dominion over nature alters
his relation to nature without altering nature itself, whether animal,
vegetable or inanimate. [Translator's note.]

304. Death as an evil.

According to the Catholic Faith, death, like the universe in general, has a moral cause, meaning and purpose that Providence will fulfill, even by turning evil itself to that end. But the outstanding feature of the modern attitude to death is the denial of its moral importance, and its removal from the religious context which it has enjoyed in all previous civilizations.

Epicureanism took death as the fundamental problem facing man and the supposed mortality of the soul as the key to happiness. It took the form of a perpetual struggle against the fear of death, a search for serenity that would overcome that terror which pervades the whole of life in overt or hidden ways and disturbs it at its most profound level. This struggle had a moral purpose for Epicurus, inasmuch as the fear of death as he understood it was fear of an immortality devoid of any sort of moral fulfillment or reward or punishment; an abyss of netherlife inhabited by shades. It was thus the opposite of the Christian vision of the life to come, in which man's moral life, and indeed the whole universe, attains its fulfillment through the realization of justice. The Epicurean celebration of mortality, inasmuch as it was a denial of a meaningless eternity, can therefore be regarded as a preparation for Christian faith and hope.

The Christian conception of death is characterized by two ideas: that death is an act that a man performs; and that death is a moment that decides the whole of a man's destiny. Both these ideas are set aside and downplayed by contemporary thinking.

As we have seen,[37] the Christian religion teaches that the death of human beings is a penalty for sin; it does not therefore deny the sadness that stems from it; even the Incarnate God felt it.[38] But death is also a point at which this life of trial ends, and at which the mixture of goods and evils therefore ceases, and justice is done; that is, there is a definitive conjunction of virtue and happiness, in which the latter is achieved through the perfection of the former.

---

[37] See paragraph 303.
[38] Cf. Matthew, 26:38 and Luke, 22:44.

305. Preparation for death and forgetfulness of death.

Since death is the decisive point in the whole of a man's existence, it is a definite act, indeed the supreme act, that a man performs; it is not a mere breaking off, a falling away from individual existence into an undifferentiated non-existence, as happens as a beast falls to earth in a slaughterhouse beneath the butcher's blow. We have already discussed the moral life as something existing at a particular point in time.[39] What is important here is to emphasize the sovereign importance that Christianity assigns to the act of dying: like all moral acts, it ought to be considered and meditated upon.

This preparation for death is not something that only Christianity teaches; the Platonists used to say *meditatio mortis, id est meditatio vitae*,[40] and Stoics and Epicureans looked upon philosophy as an exercise that strips man of his last garment, the most difficult of all to remove, namely the fear of death. So then, it is not true that the ancient philosophical schools taught men to abandon the consideration of death by losing themselves in pleasure; it is, in fact, the pragmatic approach to life that leads in that direction.

For many centuries, an important part of ascetical teaching was that one should prepare for death, in order to acquire the moral dispositions one needed in order to die well; the *ars bene moriendi*[41] gave rise to a myriad of books great and small used by ordinary people, it was a common theme for sermons and it reached its heights in masterpieces like *L'uomo al punto* by Daniello Bartoli, and Pascal's letter to Madame Périer. Until Vatican II, preparation for a good death was a subject treated in manuals of piety and a practice followed by the devout. A "Mass for imploring the grace of dying well" figured among the votive Masses of the old Missal. To keep one's attention fixed on the idea of death is a difficult exercise that requires a precise technique, since death conflicts with our natural energies and the mind recoils from it, and from the inert and motionless quality that is its principal accompaniment. Nonetheless, Christianity requires us to make this effort to prepare for death, inasmuch as a Christian's death is an action, not simply a ceasing of action. The Epicureans tried to deny that death had any contact with

---

[39] See paragraph 202.
[40] "To meditate upon death is to meditate on life."
[41] "The Art of Dying Well."

man. The Jacobins put the same idea in the famous couplet: *Pourquoi pour la mort tant de cris superflus? Tu es, elle n'est pas; elle est, tu n'es plus.*[42] But in fact the idea of death is part of the idea of man's total destiny; the old saying chiseled the idea into men's minds: *memorare novissima tua et in aeternum non peccabis.*[43] This right disposition towards death is difficult to acquire inasmuch as we have not experienced death yet, only thought about it; thus, as the Stoics said, we can never know whether we are really prepared for it or not. Spiritual writers insist on the difficulty of dying well and on the need to prepare to do it. The clouding of the mind that often precedes a man's passing, illusions arising from within or suggested from without and temptations to despair coming from the Evil One all make it difficult to confront death in the right frame of mind.[44]

306. An unprepared death. Pius XI.

Sentiat se mori[45] was a form of studied cruelty, as intended by the Roman Emperor Caligula in instructions to executioners, but becomes in the Christian sense a grace and a moral duty. Death is the supreme evil for animals, for in them the sensitive principle is not joined to an immaterial, immortal intellectual principle. But it is not the supreme evil for the Christian, since for him both the greatest good and the greatest evil lie beyond the destruction wrought by death.

The outlook of the men of our age has undergone a marked change in this matter; they fly from the consideration of death and remove anything that might remind them of it, because death is for them merely anti-life, a cutting off, a non-being. Every word, idea, gesture or symbol, including even the Cross inasmuch as it signifies suffering; anything that pertains to our ending is removed from social relations with a diligent care fed by a hidden fear. A desire to prepare for death, in order to make sure that one's last act was consciously and deliberately performed, has now been replaced by a desire for a death of which

---

[42] "Why so many unnecessary cries because of death? Where you are, it is not; where it is, you are no more."

[43] Ecclesiasticus, 7:40. "Remember your last end, and you will not sin forever."

[44] Cf. The first section of the third part of Segneri's, *Il Cristiano Istruito, The Christian Instructed.*

[45] "Let him feel that he is dying."

one is unconscious. That sudden, unprepared death people once abhorred, or even regarded as a punishment, and from which they prayed to be spared in the marvelous litany of the saints,[46] has become what people hope for, and procure, so far as they can, by anesthetics.[47] Once upon a time people used to ask: "Did he receive the sacraments? Did he make his confession? Did he forgive his enemies?" but now it is: "Did he know he was dying? Did he suffer?"

This change in outlook involves two convictions: that this life is the whole of life and that what gives value to life is the enjoyment of pleasures; and the consequent conviction that this life is not a preparation or a ripening for a life to come. The two together amount to a belief in *Diesseitigkeit*, or this-worldliness.

Pius XI told his *Maestro di Camera*, Mgr Arborio Mella di Sant' Elia, that he hoped for a sudden death. He used to pray to St. Andrew of Avellino for the grace of dying thus, which is curious because that saint is usually invoked *against* sudden seizures. The way the Pope defended his devotion in the face of lively objections from Mgr Arborio is also odd. He said a Christian should always be prepared for death and should not need to get ready for it. It is odd because dying is still an action, and so we need to prepare ourselves for doing it, not for not doing it; we prepare to die, not to be dead.

307. Death and judgment.

There are many considerations that make death less terrible to the eyes of a believer. Beyond those provided by pagan philosophy, there are others peculiar to the Christian faith: the death of the Incarnate God, the example of the saints, the merit stemming from consenting to die which is what makes a good death, hope for the Kingdom; for these reasons St. Jerome applied to death the words of the Song of Songs: *Nigra sum, sed formosa*.[48] There is something terrible, or at least fearful about death nonetheless, essentially because it leads to an absolute and

---

[46] One of the invocations of the litany is: *A subitanea et improvisa morte, libera nos Domine*, "From a sudden and unprepared death, deliver us O Lord." [Translator's note.]

[47] An unforeseen death seemed the *summa vitae felicitas*, "the crowning happiness of life, to the pagans." See Pliny, *Nat. Hist.* VII, 180.

[48] Song of Songs, 1:4. "I am black but beautiful."

inevitable judgment upon a man's works and his faithfulness to the law, whether he has conceived the latter as being merely an absolute, impersonal idea in an abstract system of values, or whether he has seen it as a command coming from a divine Person.[49]

The Christian's attitude while awaiting God's judgment is primarily one of hope which, in Catholic teaching, is a looking forward to the final triumph of perfect justice. This brings with it the happiness of heaven. But this hope, this lively hope, does not remove all uncertainty on man's part. Though justice and mercy co-exist in God, the point at which they meet escapes man's understanding. But we do know that virtue must finally be rewarded by happiness; Kant posited the necessity of the immortality of the soul on this ground; and we do know that punishment is just and right, inasmuch as the God who established the moral order cannot be indifferent to its observance. He cannot therefore ordain that obedience and disobedience to it should ultimately come to the same thing.

So a Christian has a lively hope, but it does not exclude uncertainty as to his own eternal salvation. Calvin thought that there was a contradiction in this view, and taught that every Christian must be certain that he is going to arrive at eternal life through the mercy of Christ.[50] He says "only he is truly faithful who, trusting in the promises of the divine favor towards him, awaits in advance his eternal salvation, with full certainty."[51] But a solution like this, that attempts to remove all uncertainty from Christian hope, is a mixing up of two elements: faith, which is certain, and hope, which is an anticipation. The two are in-

---

[49] Mgr Favreau, coadjutor bishop of La Rochelle, and later Bishop of Nanterre, denies that judgment is a future event, in the book *Des évêques disent la foi de l'Eglise*, Paris 1978, in which the French bishops set forth Catholic teaching: *Le jugement c'est maintenant. Aussi avons-nous à comprendre et à faire comprendre: c'est notre vie d'aujourd'hui qui nous juge,* p.275. "The judgment is now. That is what we must understand, and get others to understand: it is our life today that judges us." The obvious reply is that judgment and the act it is judging cannot exist at the same time.

[50] This was also Luther's view, and is still held by traditional Protestants. [Translator's note.]

[51] Cited by Manzoni in chapter VIII of *Morale Cattolica*, ed. cit., Vol II, p.160. The whole treatment given here is inspired by Manzoni's teaching.

compatible, since one cannot hope for something which is certain, and one cannot believe that one will inevitably receive something that is merely hoped for. That God rewards the just with eternal life is a certainty of faith, not an object of hope; the object of hope is that God will reward me specifically. This hope is very real and lively considering the faithfulness and power of the one who promises me eternal life; but it remains a pure hope, that is a waiting in suspense, considering that the promise is conditional upon my behavior.

The element of uncertainty in our hope for salvation is a truth of faith defined by the Council of Trent,[52] which taught that man's will is always changeable during this life and that therefore one is not normally certain of one's own salvation.

We might allege in support of this doctrine the statement in "Ecclesiastes,"[53] "Nor can any tell whether they have earned his love or his displeasure." Certainly, by consulting his conscience a man can grasp his own moral condition, but an uncertainty is thrown upon his own conclusions by the profundity of the soul which, as the Fathers say, *scatet mysteriis*;[54] it produces apparently humble sentiments that are rooted in pride, loving thoughts that are a disguised hatred, good thoughts that are demons transfigured into angels of light. Well before Freud, these depths of the soul that make true self-knowledge so difficult were known to spiritual writers, who were well aware that unrecognized thoughts and desires can stain and deflect our good intentions. Hence the exercise of purifying one's motives, that has become common in Catholic ascetical practice. Thus preparation for death includes both hope, and fear at the prospect of meeting God's judgment; our preparation is hopeful and awesome at once inasmuch as an eternity of bliss or woe depends upon the outcome.

308. Justice and mercy in Christian death.

Modern theology tends to amalgamate the point of death and the meeting with Christ the Savior, while saying nothing about Christ as judge. Of the two things that make death awesome theologically, namely that it is a consequence of sin, and

---

[52] Session VI. Chapters 12 and 13. Canons 15 and 16.
[53] Ecclesiastes, 9:1-2.
[54] "It spouts mysteries."

the fact that it is the moment of judgment, the latter is only lightly touched upon.

But revelation itself leaves no room for doubt. There is no need to cite the Old Testament, which is full of the terribleness of God's judgments, whether in this life or in the next. It is enough to recall Christ's depiction of the last judgment bringing reward or condemnation, or his parables of the foolish virgins or the unprofitable servant, all of which teach a divine rejection of some men.[55] The idea of the separation of the reprobate and the elect is very clearly articulated; sheep and goats, the merciful and the cruel, *venite benedicti* and *discedite maledicti*.[56] In Hebrews the idea of judgment is no less clearly put; *mihi vindicta et ego retribuam* and *horrendum est incidere in manus Dei viventis*.[57] It has admittedly always been difficult to keep the balance between hope and fear; generations of men, either beaten down by misfortune or flattered by prosperity, have oscillated between a carefree hope seasoned with awe, and a waking terror shot through with hope. The two ends of the chain ought to be joined in a unified circle.

Fear of judgment is essential to the Christian religion; it has always moved Christian peoples from their innermost depths, and inspired great artistic works; Michelangelo's Sistine Chapel, the anonymous *Dies Irae*, or the baroque ossuaries. Prior to the liturgical changes, the liturgy of the dead was shaped by the notion of judgment, which is the primary reality death brings; the judgment in itself implies neither a favorable nor an unfavorable outcome, it is judgment simply as such that is so awesome. But within that preoccupation the joyful notion of hope had free reign; in Masses for the dead God was asked to give the dead eternal light and over and over again came the phrase *quia pius es*, "for Thou art faithful"; the Lord was addressed as *veniae largitor et humanae salutis amator, indulgentiarum Dominus*, as one *cui proprium est misereri semper et parcere* and *cuius misericordiae non est numerus*.[58] All of this was united however to the idea of judgment, and in the first of the three Masses for the dead the

---

[55] Cf. Matthew, 25.

[56] "Come you blessed" and "Depart you cursed."

[57] Hebrews, 10:30-31. "Vengeance is mine and I will repay" and "It is a fearful thing to fall into the hands of the living God."

[58] "Bestower of forgiveness and lover of human salvation," "Lord of forgiveness," one "whose nature it is always to be merciful and to relent" and "whose mercy is beyond measuring."

Gospel is taken from John, chapter five, and announces the judgment at the end of time: *Et procedent qui bona fecerunt in resurrectionem vitae, qui vero mala egerunt in resurrectionem iudicii.*[59]

St. Francis of Assisi's *Canticle* also shows that the idea of a Christian death contains both hope and fear in that it praises the Lord for "our sister death," but immediately adds: "woe to those who die in mortal sin" and conversely "blessed are those whom it finds in his holy will." The prospect of judgment was mentioned in the rite for funerals, but no more than the divine mercy; in the opening prayer of the absolutions following immediately after the Mass it is nobly proclaimed that nobody is justified except by the pardoning grace of Christ, and the prayer says: *non ergo eum tua iudicialis sententia premat, sed gratia tua illi succurrente mereatur evadere iudicium ultionis.*[60] In the responsory *Libera me Domine* that follows, the grandiose scene of the last judgment, with its passing away of heaven and earth, is certainly fit to astound human hearts and the whole of nature itself, but even in this *dies magna et amara valde*[61] there comes at last the consolation of eternal light, *lux perpetua luceat eis*, even though it be on a day of wrath, a *dies irae*.

Hope often led to a sort of joy in death. In the famous *Triumph of Death* at Clusone in the Val Seriana, which is one of the most striking displays of the idea of death entertained in the past, in this case the fifteenth century, one of the captions explaining the scene carries the words: *O tu che servi Dio di buon cuore; non aver paura a questo ballo venire; ma allegramente vieni e non temire; poiché chi nasce gli convien morire.*[62]

---

[59] "And those who have done good will go into the resurrection of life, but those who have done evil, into the resurrection of judgment."

[60] "Let not the sentence of thy judgment oppress him, but, thy grace coming to his aid, may he be worthy to escape the judgment of condemnation."

[61] "Great and very bitter day."

[62] "O thou that servest God with a good heart,
Be not afraid to come into this dance,
But come thou joyfully and do not fear;
Who'er is born, befits it him to die."

309. Marginalization of the fear of judgment.

In the post-conciliar mentality, and in the liturgical reform, the idea of death as a judgment or final *discrimen* is downplayed and is obscured by the idea of eternal salvation; no more appearing for trial, as it were, but an immediate continuity between earthly life and eternal salvation.[63] Death is stripped of its two-edged character and presented as an event which brings one immediately into the glory of Christ. Words that allude to judgment, hell or purgatory, which prayers for the dead used to mention without embarrassment, are generally expunged from the new rite. The invocation: *In die judicii, libera nos Domine*[64] was cut out of the litany of the saints. Death is presented as having only one univocal aspect; it is not seen as a meeting with Christ our judge but as being exclusively a meeting with Christ as savior, despite the fact that the Apostles' Creed says *venturus est judicare vivos et mortuos*.[65] Hence the so-called paschal character of the new liturgy for the dead, the introduction of the

---

[63] Connected with this is the new fangled theory that the soul takes on an incorruptible body at the death of each individual, and thus enters into glory no different from that of the Virgin whose earthly body was assumed into heaven. It is just as if everyone had been assumed likewise. It would be a waste of words to spend time going into the absurdity and superficiality of this opinion. It constitutes a denial of the general resurrection of the bodies of the dead that is asserted in the Creed to be an event that will happen in the future at the end of time; it means we are not the same in our risen identity materially (as Christ was); and it abolishes the special privileges of the Blessed Virgin, despite the fact that her special status is expressly referred to in Pius XII's solemn definition of the Assumption, a reference which the innovators think was out of place or unwarranted. These heretical views are popularized in Catholic papers. See for example S. Vitalini in *Giornale del Popolo*, 14 August 1982.

[64] "In the day of judgment, deliver us O Lord."

[65] "He will come to judge the living and the dead."

Alleluia,[66] the expulsion of the *Dies irae*,[67] and the changing of
the color of the vestments from black to violet or rose.[68]

These changes have not been introduced through a concern
to give greater emphasis to a particular aspect of a complex reality, but are presented rather as the one true understanding of
Christian death which, allegedly, has been rediscovered at last.
And of course there is the usual denigration of the historic
Church; not content merely with emphasizing hope more than
was usual when the idea of judgment was dominant, the innovators go on to assert that to think of judgment at all in connection with Christian death, and thus to regard it with a feeling of awe "is a very feeble sort of Christianity."[69] It is true that
the second formulary of Mass for the dead in the new rite uses
the eschatological Gospel from Matthew, chapter 25, but the
preceding acclamation only mentions the blessed who are called
to heaven; in the interpretation of this gospel text given in the
people's *Messale dell'assemblea cristiana*[70] published by the Italian
Episcopal Conference, the meaning is reduced to the "coming
of Jesus the Messiah-King who transfers his elect from his kingdom to that of the Father." But the real meaning of the word
"elect" is in fact rejected by the new theology of death, because
it involves the ideas of distinguishing, passing over, and drawing
out of a mass, and so refers to the idea of predestination. The
instruction prefixed to the liturgy of the dead in this people's

---

[66] This *Alleluia* is an archaizing restoration. St. Ambrose mentions it.

[67] Still occasionally used; as at the solemn requiem for Pope John
Paul I in the Church of the Holy Sepulchre at Jerusalem in 1978.
[Translator's note.]

[68] The new Missal introduces violet merely as an alternative to black,
but in fact the latter is hardly ever seen. Many bishops and priests
now use white, even in countries where black is the traditional
color. This is a direct violation of the new Missal's provisions.
[Translator's note.]

[69] S. Vitalini, *Preghiamo Insieme*, "Let us pray together," Lugano
1975, p.19. The Fribourg professor has forgotten about the Last
Judgment in the Sistine Chapel, and how Savonarola used to stir
Guicciardini (F. Guicciardini, *Estratti Savonaroliani*, in *Scritti*,
Bari 1936, pp.285 ff.) and how Don Bosco used to move his hear-
ers to groans and cries when preaching about judgment (*Memorie
Biografiche*, Vol. IV, p.421).

[70] *Missal of the Christian Assembly.*

Missal states that "death is essentially not death, but life, glory, resurrection."[71]

This is an illegitimate assertion of identity between two distinct ideas; that of the general resurrection whereby the bodies of all the dead are raised to life, which happens universally without respect to anyone's moral standing; and that other kind of resurrection whereby faithful souls receive glorified bodies that will live in heaven forever. The resurrection in the general sense is not the result of a judgment about an individual's merits, but in the limited sense it is; and the alternative to a glorious resurrection, that is, a resurrection of the former sort, is referred to as a second death; but this is not mentioned at all in the Missal in question. The Missal does make a fleeting reference to the need for purification on the part of souls that have been saved, and it gives an inchoate statement of the doctrine of purgatory, without ever using that term although it is the one adopted by the Church; but it makes no mention at all of the possibility of eternal loss. In short, the Four Last Things, death, judgment, heaven and hell, seem to be reduced to two; death and heaven. The history of the Christian religion nonetheless contains thousands of examples of a lucid death, without any exultant expression of hope, but free too of any display of an undue lack of trust in God that would have upset or disturbed life's end. Rosmini and Enrichetta Manzoni gave examples at their deaths of a Catholic faith of this sort.[72]

310. Dignity of burial in Catholic ritual.

If death ceases to be an action by which one consents to die and offers oneself to God, and thus loses the character of a crisis or separating out, that is, of a discrimination of a sort which gave rise to the depiction of a sieve in mortuary painting,[73] then burial too loses its solemn quality. When belief in eternal life weakens, the gravity and solemnity of death declines as well,

---

[71] *Messale dell'assemblea Cristiana*, p.1300.

[72] For Rosmini see the bulletin *Charitas*, July 1971, p.15 and for Manzoni, *Epistolario*, ed. cit. Vol. II, p.26.

[73] The profound quality of this kind of art is developed in my article in the *Introduzione alla Valsolda*, referred to earlier, describing the paintings in the ossuary at Loggio. It is also obvious in those at Clusone in the Val Seriana in the province of Bergamo, and at Pinzolo in the Val Rendena in the province of Trent.

because it comes to be seen as a mere accident within the world's history; and by the same token funeral rites and customs must also decay and give place to a mere removing of the corpse. The Italian expression *mettere via un morto*[74] then displays all its tragic cruelty; burying someone is the same as getting rid of him, separating him from all human fellowship. Having identified life with pleasurable sensations, the *civitas hominis* abhors any concern with death. But to "put someone away" is quite alien to the Christian religion, which believes not only in another life, but in the continuity of life, with one sort being the preliminary to the other. There is not in fact that strong opposition between this life and the life to come that modern thinkers imagine, and which they assume leads to each life spoiling the other. Inasmuch as it was related to an eternal destiny, the act of dying acquired a grandeur and a dignity through this sense of continuity, and was also an object of attention for the community and for the Church.

It did not happen everywhere, but in some French dioceses the whole community would gather round the person dying and continue over several days with psalms, prayers, and other acts of piety and devotion. A man was not abandoned to himself to perform what was regarded as the decisive and difficult act of dying. The wonderful *Ordo Commendationis Animae*,[75] which combines tenderness and compunction with the most daring of hopes, used to accompany the dying person moment by moment with supplication addressed to God, the invocation of the angels and the saints, and reprimands warning off the Evil One. The rite was very communitarian, associating as it did the Church of the angels, the Church of souls triumphant in heaven and the Church on its way here on earth; it was based on the ideas of judgment and mercy, it surrounded the dying person with all the power and beauty of the Christian religion, it provided for the whole of the Passion to be read through, it recalled and proclaimed all the acts of deliverance the Lord has worked, all during the last moments of a dying brother. When the moment of death was drawing near, it became more urgent and pressing: *Cum vero*, the rubric says, *tempus expirationis institerit, tum maxime ab omnibus circumstantibus flexis genibus*

---

[74] "Putting away a dead one."
[75] The prayers for commending the soul of one dying.

vehementer orationi instandum est.[76] Thus it was, after the praying of the *Proficiscere anima christiana*, and of the *Libera Domine*, and of the *Agnosce, Domine, creaturam tuam*, that the act of death took place in the midst of a community truly united *ad convivendum et commoriendum.*[77] The rite was an action of the whole Church, in heaven and on earth, that supported the dying person, who himself took part in so much of it as he could, and whose place was supplied by others in what was beyond him.

The funeral service, next, was an expression of piety and an occasion of intercession, and the body was honored with candles, incensation and aspersion with holy water. The officiating priest pronounced no panegyric, and was even forbidden to stay and listen to a funeral oration delivered by someone else.[78] Remembrance and prayers for the deceased were repeated on the seventh and thirtieth days after his death, and on the anniver-

---

[76] "When the time of expiring has drawn near, then especially should all those present give themselves fervently to prayer on bended knee."

[77] The opening words of various prayers in the ritual for the dying: "Set forth O Christian soul," the litany with the invocation "Deliver O Lord the soul of thy servant," and the prayer containing the words "Acknowledge O Lord, thy creature." Thus there was a community "for living together and dying together."

[78] The norm of the Church's liturgy was *fiat aequalitas*, let equality rule. The rite itself was the same for everyone, and was not altered by the fact of accidental additions of pomp and ceremony for some people. Praise was not to be given to anyone, but prayers were offered for all. The importation of the Protestant custom of laudatory speech about the dead person is wholly undesirable. Often the priest has not known the person in question and then, invidiously, says nothing, or says something inappropriate about him. The humbler sort of people often have nothing said about them at all, while at the funerals of those who have held some prominent position in the world, the priest goes on at length, irrespective of whether the man was religious or not, as if the Church were keen to annex him to itself in posthumous triumph. The words spoken by the Archbishop of Florence when attending the funeral of Eugenio Montale were just such an attempt, as was the proposal by Cardinal Colombo to transfer Manzoni's remains to Milan Cathedral. On this last matter, see *Il Giornale*, 23 and 29 September 1983, where I showed that the arguments in favor of such a transfer were not well grounded.

sary, when the Office of the Dead was often sung. Detailed provisions were made regarding these matters in wills, including the endowment of Masses, bequests for pious works, indulgences to be offered up, and specifications regarding the tomb.

311. Indignity of burial today.

Care for the dead is bound up with belief in another life, with belief that a man is eternally saved or damned at the moment of death, and with the consequent belief that everything connected with death has a genuine importance for human beings. These convictions give value to the whole of life and to each of its parts, as is suggested by the fact that tombstones used to state the orbit of a man's life in years, months and days. The marginalization of belief in another world has occasioned a change in behavior that many writers have studied.[79] Technological civilization, obscurely conscious that it will never be able to *frangere anche alla morte il telo*,[80] has nonetheless sought to dispel the awesomeness of death from human affairs, by annihilating its moral value and pushing it out of the field of moral calculation as being the only event that has no consequences and no meaning. Thus where once everything was done to ensure that death was prepared for and consciously confronted,[81] today's medicine multiplies the means of saving life but sees its ultimate perfection in providing a comfortable death; thus whenever it cannot actually defeat death, it makes it unconscious.

Sickness and death happened at home during the centuries in which medical knowledge was in its infancy and lacked sophisticated accoutrements, and when doctors called on patients rather than vice versa; and so a sick or dying man was assisted by his own circle of family and friends. Because of the amazing

---

[79] See for example P. Aries, *Essais sur l'histoire de la mort en Occident*, Paris 1975.

[80] "To snap even Death's dart in twain." (V. Monti)

[81] When Louis XIII was on his death bed, sleeping, and the doctors decided that his end was nigh, his confessor was called to wake the king and tell him that the moment had come. The fact is recorded by St. Vincent de Paul, whom the king had called to be with him as he died. Pascal had himself carried to the Hospice for Incurables so that he could die among Christ's poor.

growth in medical techniques, sickness and death occur today in hospitals, which were originally only hostels for the helpless.

Care for the bodies of the dead, which naturally was of prime importance when it was an expression of familial devotion, is now entrusted to funeral businesses. In consequence, the rites by which the Church showed what importance it placed upon one's eternal destiny, the immortality of the soul and resurrection of the body, have largely fallen out of use. No care for the dead can now be exercised in the family setting, despite the fact that the new theology makes much of the idea of the family as a domestic church. Once a man used to live through his sickness in the midst of his family, go through his last moments at home and die at home. His relatives would dutifully hasten from distant parts to be present at his last breath. The body was laid out near the domestic hearth, honored with flowers and candles, watched over uninterruptedly through the night; within sight of it people talked in hushed voices,[82] and the curtains were drawn in the windows of the house in mourning. Today, bodies are taken from the hospital ward to the hospital's mortuary, and thence to a public mortuary where they lie side by side distinguished only by a label. The escorting of the body from the house, to the church, to the graveyard, has largely vanished. In many large cities, the bodies are collected in the public mortuary and, without any family or friends present, they are all hastily blessed by a priest who calls three or four times a month, and then taken off to be buried or cremated.[83]

312. Cremation

A Christian funeral is not always a sign of Christian faith on the part of the deceased, as the clergy sometimes perform a funeral for decency's sake, or for human or social reasons; but this is at odds with Christian law, by which a Christian funeral should only be given to Christians who have died with the right dispositions, such as faith, contrition and that acceptance of God's will that makes a good death. In his short work *De Cura pro Defunctis Gerenda*,[84] St. Augustine says that although the

---

[82] A sacred silence is not now observed even at funerals; at Paul VI's funeral the crowd clapped and cheered as the coffin passed.

[83] Even two centuries ago, Mozart's burial was somewhat similar. [Translator's note.]

[84] "On the care to be had of the Dead."

dead do not know about happenings now occurring on earth, funeral observances do indirectly benefit them inasmuch as the living visit their tombs and are thus brought to remember them and to pray for them.

Care should be taken of the bodies of the dead, because they have been companions of the soul in life's activities, and still more because having been part of a human person during his earthly course, they will be part of that person once more in the final resurrection of which Christ's resurrection is the cause. While most religions believe in the immortality of the soul, the resurrection of the body is an exclusively Christian doctrine,[85] and it is of all beliefs the one that reason finds hardest to accept; it is an object of faith pure and simple, and the greatest of paradoxes. When St. Paul came to Athens in A.D.51, where every shade of Gentile thought existed, Epicurean and Stoic philosophers took him from the market place to the Areopagus so that they could hear the extraordinary man; but when the Apostle started talking about the resurrection of the dead, they left him to himself saying: "On this point, some other time."[86]

In paganism the immortality of souls is sometimes accepted, but the idea of a distinction in the rewards that they receive is not: they all fall into the same darkness amounting to a life without life.[87] The ancient mystery religions had an inkling of the idea of a reward for virtue, and a blessed perfection in a future life. But no religion at all, apart from Christianity, holds clearly that our bodies will rise again one day and continue the course of our life, our personal identity having been restored in full, *tutta quanta* as Dante puts it.[88]

It was to nourish faith in this doctrine, that reason finds so difficult but which is so characteristic of Catholicism, that the Church has always been opposed to burning the bodies of Christians, while at the same time allowing a great variety of forms of burial, whether in churches, first allowed in the case of martyrs, or in churchyards or in consecrated ground outside the town, or in secular cemeteries. Man is no more when death has struck, but the body *was* that of a human being and will be again in the final resurrection, and so it deserves respect and care.

---

[85] The Pharisees, at the time of Our Lord, believed in it. [Translator's note.]

[86] Cf. Acts, 17:16-34.

[87] See however paragraph 162. [Translator's note.]

[88] *Paradiso*, XIV, 45.

The ancient and continuous Christian practice of burying the dead stems from what the Gospels and St. Paul say about the body's being like buried seed, and being sown corruptible and raised incorruptible.[89] Christian burial is first and foremost an imitation of what happened to the body of Christ. The Church has never said that the reduction of a body to ashes by incineration is an obstacle to its resurrection, but in a religion that accepts the validity of symbolism, the Church could hardly fail to regard cremation as a counter-sign of the resurrection of the body. That is, cremation does not directly contradict the idea of resurrection, but it does do away with all the symbolism connected with burial, and also deprives of meaning a vocabulary dating from early Christian times; a cemetery means by origin a "sleeping place"; the Italian *camposanto*, for a burial ground, means a "holy field" dedicated to God; the word *depositio*, used in Latin for Christian burial, is derived not so much from the physical act of putting down into the earth, as from the legal act of depositing something, so that a Christian's body is seen as being put down on deposit to be restored at the day of resurrection. This symbolism is so powerful that it led the Church to make a principle of the matter; to have one's body burnt was, in the nineteenth and twentieth centuries, a commonly accepted sign that one was not a believer. Sometimes people wanted to be cremated through an irrational fear of being buried alive, rather than as a sign of unbelief, but in any case Canon 1203 of the Code of Canon Law of 1917 refused to allow or recognize requests for cremation on the part of Catholics. Canon 1176 of the new Code of 1983 allows cremation, thus reinforcing the great change on the matter made by Paul VI. In cities where a crematorium exists, the number of cremations has rapidly outstripped the number of burials.

This loss of a distinctively Christian practice, even in matters that have come down in immemorial tradition and which have a genuine religious significance, is part of a general accommodation of Catholicism to the world, a watering down of the sacred, a pervading utilitarianism and an eclipsing of man's fundamental call to something beyond this world.

---

[89] Cf. I Corinthians, 15:42.

CHAPTER XLI

ESCHATOLOGY

313. The triumph of justice. Hell.

Catholic Christianity sees eternal life or reprobation as the highest expression of absolute justice; these things are difficult for the mind to accept, as we have said when explaining how our moral status can vary from moment to moment; and people who don't believe in a future life obviously don't believe in salvation or damnation at all. They object to the idea that this life needs any fulfillment in another world.

The idea of hell was almost completely neglected by Vatican II; some council fathers complained of the fact during the LXXX congregation, when the eschatological character of the Christian vocation was being discussed. Hell is never mentioned by name in the council's texts, but is referred to once indirectly as "eternal fire."[1] Nothing was said about the actual doctrine of hell.

Paul VI complained that "the subject of hell is not heard about any more."[2] His complaint should have been about the priests who fail to mention it; how can the faithful hear about it if the clergy say nothing? Having vanished from teaching, hell has vanished from the belief of most people,[3] its eternity is denied by some theologians and it is reduced by others, as it was by Epicurean philosophers, to the status of a myth expressing the suffering caused by a bad conscience.

The French bishops as a body have pronounced against the doctrine of hell, thus reinforcing what is taught by many of

---

[1] Cf. the cited *Concordantiae*. [See *Lumen Gentium*, 48. Translator's note.]

[2] O.R., 29 April 1971.

[3] From statistics published in the *Osservatore Romano* of 19 November 1970, it appears that 50% of the people of Rome calling themselves Catholics believe neither in heaven nor hell.

their parish priests: *L'enfer c'est simplement une manière de parler du Christ à des hommes peu évolués religieusement: nous avons évolué depuis.*[4] Hell is here clearly referred to as an idea believed in by crude or childlike peoples, and which today's Catholicism rejects. There is of course no objection, in our opinion at least, to theologians distinguishing between the doctrine of hell and the poetic and fantastic imaginings with which it has been overlaid in literature and art, sometimes of the highest quality. Nor is there perhaps anything wrong with saying that hell is not a place but a moral state.[5] But Catholic theology condemns the reduction of dogmas to myths. The French bishops however do not hesitate to reject the doctrine head on. Hell remains, for all that, the final assertion of justice, rising eternal above the ashes of man's justice; an eternal sanction maintaining the difference between right and wrong.

Voir dans l'enfer, the bishops' spokesman says, *un châtiment que Dieu enfligerait à quelqu'un qui, conscient de ses fautes, ne s'en repentirait pas, est inacceptable. Inacceptable aussi la peur engendrée par l'enseignement selon lequel si la mort nous surprend en état de péché mortel, c'est la damnation.*[6] But this is precisely what is taught by the Councils,[7] and thus the attack the bishops make

---

4   In *Des évêques disent la foi de l'Eglise*, Paris 1978. The chapter on hell is by Mgr Favreau, the auxiliary bishop of La Rochelle. "Hell is simply a manner of speaking that Christ used when addressing people whose religious outlook was somewhat primitive; we have developed further since."

5   Ibid., p.296.

6   Ibid. "To see in hell a punishment that God imposes on someone who is aware of his faults but refuses to repent of them, is unacceptable. Also unacceptable is the fear engendered by the view that if death should overtake us in the state of mortal sin, then we are damned."

7   The principal statement touching on hell approved expressly by a general council seems to be that contained in the Byzantine Emperor's profession of faith, read out at and approved by the Second Council of Lyons in 1274: *Illorum autem animas qui in mortali peccato vel cum solo originali decedunt, mox in infernum descendere, poenis tamen disparibus puniendas.* "The souls of those who die in mortal sin, or merely in original sin, descend at once into hell, but (the two categories) to be punished by different kinds of punishment." Denzinger 464 or 858. This doctrine was solemnly reaffirmed in identical terms by the general council of Florence in 1439. Denzinger 693 or 1306. [Translator's note.].

on it involves the whole question of the infallibility of the Church. It is part of divine and Catholic faith, that is, truth divinely revealed and formally defined by the Church, that hell exists; and it is part of divine faith merely, that is, divinely revealed but not formally defined by the Church, that some people go there. The latter proposition is supported by Christ's words about Judas, "the son of perdition who had to perish,"[8] about the last judgment,[9] and about the wheat and the tares in the parable.

Authors counted as Catholics have rejected hell as repugnant to reason. Giovanni Papini would have to be numbered among them, were it not for the fact that the doctrinal substance contained in his book *Il Diavolo* is, as the *Osservatore Romano* noted in an article entitled "An unnecessary condemnation," so slight as to be non-existent, and were it not for the fact that he quotes the Gospel while thinking he is merely quoting St. Augustine; did he not need, in a word, to go back to his catechism.

Jacques Maritain's denial of hell in his posthumous work *Approches sans entraves*[10] is more worthy of consideration; he maintains that Satan will finally be pardoned and consigned, by the prayer of Christ, to the natural happiness of Limbo, together with infants who died without baptism.[11]

Karl Rahner maintains that the denial of the eternity of punishment and the assertion of universal salvation are a new development due to Vatican II, and constitute a milestone for the faith of the Church.

---

[8] Cf. John, 17:12.

[9] Matthew, 25.

[10] J. Maritain, *Approches sans entraves*, "Unshackled Approaches," Paris 1974.

[11] Whatever degree of happiness unbaptized infants who die in original sin enjoy, they are still subject to the penalty attaching to original sin, namely absence of the Beatific Vision, and they are thus in hell, but with a merely *negative* penalty. See footnote 7 above, and also the teaching of Innocent III in 1201 and Pius VI in 1794. Denzinger 410 or 780, and 1526 or 2626. Limbo is a part of hell. Hence although Maritain does not, strictly speaking, deny the existance of hell by assigning Satan and the damned to Limbo, he does, however, deny the reality of hell. For he denies the *positive* punishment, the fire of hell and the eternity of the sufferings of the damned, which are defined dogmas of Faith. [Translator's note.]

These are the fantasies entertained by Victor Hugo in his *La Fin de Satan*. Following in his footsteps Maritain says: *un jour tous les habitants des Enfers...tous les réprouvés seront des pardonnés.*[12] This hosanna that goes up to God from hell has precedents, all of them heretical, including Origen's famous theory of *apocatastasis,* if that is what it does in fact involve. Many theologians have devoted themselves to deepening the philosophical and theological meaning of hell, and many others to emptying it of meaning. In his principal work, Campanella upholds the orthodox position and refutes the arguments against it that had seemed convincing to him in his youth. Theological literature even contains defenses of the devil; the many modern ones have a precedent in the curious work of Bartolo of Sassoferrato in the fourteenth century called *Tractatus Procuratorius.*[13]

314. Defense of Hell.

The errors worming their way through eschatological teaching prompted the Congregation for the Doctrine of the Faith to send out a corrective document to episcopal conferences.[14] It draws attention to a "slow corrupting and progressive dissolving of some articles of the Creed" in opinions common among the faithful. It says the cause of the problem lies in an excessive liberty of speculation, and an undue publicity given to disputes among theologians, but in the usual euphemistic way, it says nothing about the fact that many bishops connive at this false doctrine. The document reaffirms the very important doctrine of the resurrection of the bodies of the dead at the end of time; it reasserts the traditional belief in the survival of a conscious and willing element in man after death; it defends the

---

[12] "One day all the inhabitants of Hell...all the reprobate will be pardoned." Maritain, op. cit., p.30.

[13] The denial of the existence of hell is paralleled by the denial of the existence of the devil. Cardinal Suenens delivers a remarkable palinode on this subject in the *Osservatore Romano* of 20 November 1982; after having said nothing for a long time about the existence of the devil, he now presents the warfare waged upon the human race by evil spirits as one of the principal truths of Christianity. "I do not hesitate to admit to not having given enough emphasis, during my pastoral ministry, to this role of the Spirit of Darkness. I feel it my duty today to draw attention to it."

[14] O.R., 16-17 June 1979.

word "soul," by which the Church has always referred to that element, and it denies there is any need to change this terminology; it reiterates the doctrine of a life beyond this world, in which the just enjoy eternal life in paradise, and the reprobate inherit an eternal absence of such life, which is referred to as a second death.

The eternity of happiness seems reasonable and proper to the human mind. Reasonable, because the intuition of infinite truth and the possession of infinite good exclude the possibility of falling into error or wanting any good independently of the Good that includes all others. Our objections arise when it comes to an eternity of punishment. Abbadie's acute observation is relevant here.[15] Self-love finds nothing disproportionate about eternal happiness, but eternal punishment disgusts it. Why so, he asks, if not because self-love likes to deceive itself?

Nonetheless, difficulties in coming to terms with hell are not simply the expression of superficial feelings; there are deep problems to which the solution has to be sought at a deep level; here supremely Democritus's adage rings true, namely that truth lies in the depths.

The French bishops say that hell *est un scandale pour Dieu lui-même, une souffrance pour lui, l'échec de son amour sauveur.*[16] This sort of objection to hell flows from certain metaphysical assumptions. People conclude that because the providential plan for the universe includes certain evils, the system itself is bad and thus incompatible with a divine love that is free to will into being whatever it wants, and which is good in all its works. But hell is nevertheless the product of love; Dante does not hesitate to join "eternal suffering" with "the primal Love":

> *Giustizia mosse il mio alto Fattore;*
> *Fecemi la divina Potestate,*
> *E la somma Sapienza e il primo Amore.*[17]

All existing things are good in themselves, but the finite and interlocking nature of things means that something can be good or bad in relation to other things. The act of adultery is a good inasmuch as it is an exercise of one's living power, and is itself

---

[15] *Traité de la vérité de la religion chrétienne*, Vol. II, p.402.

[16] French bishops, op. cit., p.292. "Is a scandal for God himself, a source of suffering for him, a block to his saving love."

[17] *Inferno*, III, 4-6. "Justice moved my high Maker; the divine Power made me, and the supreme Wisdom and the primal Love."

productive of life; but it is an evil if considered in relation to the
moral law and to the damage it inflicts on one's neighbor's
rights. There can be no evil in God, because evil exists in relation to some set of finite things, and God is infinite and unrelated to anything else in that sense; He is good in Himself and
in relation to all creatures. These latter are existent and intelligible and good by participation in his Existence, Truth and
Goodness. From God's point of view death and hell are not
evils; the latter is good for punishing evil and vindicating justice, and the former is good for allowing one thing to be made
out of another, for sustaining the cycle of life within nature, and
for displaying God's immanent infinity in a quasi-infinite series
of limited existences in the material world. There would only be
a flaw in the system, that is an absurdity spoiling the rationality
of the whole, if hell were an accident spoiling the divine plan.
But in fact it is an integral part of the whole of reality, and that
whole is good; its goodness is made up of parts that, taken individually, are either congenial or antipathetic to each other but
which, taken together, form a composite whole that is excellent
and which God wills to exist by the power of his perfect will.

To conclude this brief apology for hell, I might say something to remove, as far as is possible, the general difficulty attaching to the notion. The Catholic conception of hell ought to
be presented in its theological essentials; fantasizing about it
ought to be left to the free play of private imagination. Man's
imagination can attain to great heights in the matter, as Dante
and Michelangelo are enough to demonstrate. But Catholic
teaching on hell does not present it as a sort of perpetual parox-
ysm "in which one suffers every evil without any good" as some
catechisms have put it, though not the well-known one written
by Cardinal Gasparri. Such a state of existence is metaphysically
absurd because it excludes the divine mercy, which operates
even in hell, and it leaves out the sense of order born of the fact
that the lost soul is in its appropriate place within the moral
scheme of the universe. If one may risk a metaphor, the condition of the lost should be thought of as being not so much an
agony, as an infinitely long day of dimness and somber boredom.[18]

---

[18] St. Thomas Aquinas teaches that hell is compatible with varying
       degrees of real though imperfect natural happiness: Cf. *De malo*, 5,
       3 and the commentary on the *Sentences*, II,d.33,q.2,a.2.
       [Translator's note.]

315. The eternity of punishment

One only thinks of hell as a flaw or an irregularity if one has fallen into the error of anthropocentrism. If human beings were the centre of the world, creation would itself fail to attain its own end if certain human beings did not attain heaven; and this would be a flaw.[19] But in reality the goal of God's action in producing creatures is no different from the "goal" of his own existence, namely Himself; all creation exists for the glory of God, not for the glory of man. One could say that the goal of God's creation is man, but only in the sense of being Christ, the God-Man who recapitulates within Himself the whole of creation.[20]

The denial of hell springs from anthropocentrism, and as Abbadie says, its root is human self-love, which forgets that God does not perish because some men do. But mankind itself does not perish anyway, inasmuch as it is saved in Christ. The fundamental point of Catholic theodicy is that one must have an overall view of reality before one can make judgments about a particular creature and its purposes. Death is a negative thing, but it fits into the order of the world nonetheless, because all things are meant to have only as much life and goodness as God gives them; even hell itself is good, because it is given existence by God.

The liturgy gives clear expression to this truth in the invitatory verse of the Office of the Dead: *Regem cui omnia vivunt, venite adoremus*, which echoes Luke: *omnes enim vivunt ei.*[21] That individuals do not exist for themselves, but are directed out of themselves towards God is taught even more clearly in Romans: *Nemo nostrum sibi vivit et nemo sibi moritur. Sive ergo vivimus, Domino vivimus, sive morimur, Domino morimur. Sive ergo vivimus, sive morimur, Domini sumus.*[22] This complete and

---

[19] The encyclical *Humani Generis* of 1950 emphasizes the fact that no created spirit, whether angel or man, is called by nature to the Beatific Vision. Thus for a human being not to attain heaven is not a frustration of his nature at all, but of his supernatural vocation in Adam. [Translator's note.]

[20] See paragraphs 205-9.

[21] "Come let us adore the King for whom all things are alive." Echoing Luke, 20:38, "For Him all men are alive."

[22] Romans 14:7-8. "None of us lives as his own master, and none of us dies as his own master. While we live, we live as the Lord's ser-

permanent subordination of man to God means that even if an individual does not attain the heavenly happiness God has offered, the goal of his existence is still not frustrated, because he exists for God's purposes and not for the realization of his own maximal perfection. To recur to an Augustinian analogy, contrarieties within the universe, including evils and hell itself, are like semitones in music and shadows in pictures; that is, they are beautiful as part of a harmony and as an overall picture, even though in themselves they are absences of a tone or of light.

There remains the objection to the eternity of hell. It would seem at first sight that an eternal penalty and an unchanging unhappiness for any soul are at odds with the purpose of punishment.[23] In this view, a punishment only works insofar as it re-establishes the moral order of things by correcting a moral fault. Admittedly it is not just that evil men should be happy; the universal voice of conscience continuously asserts that fact loud and clear. But, on the other hand, if the same punishment is inflicted permanently, it must mean that it is failing to effect a moral reformation in the man being punished and is therefore failing to work as a punishment should. It may in fact continue as a form of suffering, but degraded to that level it becomes irrational and unworthy of a perfect God.

The reply to this objection is that even though the damned are not reformed by their punishment, the order of justice is re-established nonetheless. It is helpful here to remember the hard truth that one's moral state exists at a point in time, that is, it exists in the present.[24] Man owes obedience to God all the time. Now, in that special kind of duration in which souls exist in

---

vants, when we die, we die as the Lord's servants; in life and in death we belong to the Lord."

[23] The idea that any punishment is legitimate only if it is directed towards the improvement of the guilty party is becoming common in contemporary penal law. If it is accepted, the only alternatives are to believe in an end to the punishments of hell at the point at which the offense has been purged, or else in a progressive diminution *in infinitum* of those punishments, and thus in a hell which is eternal but forever getting less bad, as Gioberti maintains in his *Filosofia della Rivelazione*, Turin 1856. In that case, just as heaven is an unending and never exhausted growth, so hell would be an unending reduction both of guilt and of its punishment. Gioberti, p.351.

[24] See paragraph 202.

hell, which is a kind of participated eternity, man's guilty will permanently refuses the obedience that God demands of it, and a corresponding punishment is thus inflicted on it continually. It is not true therefore that the punishment continually fails to work; on the contrary it works all the time, achieving what it is meant to achieve, and the reason it continues is because the act of defiance continues. A lost soul continuously makes due satisfaction to divine justice, and is not exempted from doing so in the future by the fact that it does so at present, any more than we in this life are freed of our obligation to obey God tomorrow by the fact that we are obeying him today. Eternal loss rests on the same grounds as eternal beatitude; one way or another, homage is paid ceaselessly to God's infinite excellence; not intermittently by oscillating human souls, but continually by souls that have no desire to sin or no desire to repent.

316. Hell as pure justice.

In hell there is consequently no secondary function attached to punishment, such as the reformation of the guilty or the defense of society; what remains is the essential reason for punishment, namely the vindication of justice. The damned do not repent, nor does heaven need to be defended from them; they have found their place in the final order of the world, not exactly by their free choice, but again, not as the result of coercion either. The last judgment merely manifests the moral state of the world, and opens up men's consciences to a self-knowledge that was previously hidden from them by their own evil. The Bible refers to this process under the image of the opening of the books. This is in reality an intellectual operation that occurs within the minds of those who are judged, and involves the remembering of their own actions and the revealing of those of others; the last judgment is also a spontaneous thing, because the wicked are accused not by some external agent but by the interior action of their own consciences, conflicting among themselves as Romans profoundly expresses it: *testimonium reddente illis conscientia ipsorum, et inter se invicem cogitationibus accusantibus aut etiam defendentibus.*[25] The immanent hell experienced by a bad conscience and described by Epicurus and Bos-

---

[25] Romans 2:15: "Their conscience utters its own testimony, and when they dispute with one another they find themselves condemning this, approving that."

suet is very real, but it is only an anticipation and foretaste of
the hell to come.

Mystics, theologians and poets have emphasized the spontaneous element in damnation. In Dante's hell, souls are impa-
tient to throw themselves into their punishment:

e pronti sono a trapassar lo rio
ché la divina giustizia li sprona
sì che la tema si volve in disio.[26]

The reason is this. The lost souls dislike being lost because
it is a radical disorder in their being, which latter has missed out
on the prize it was offered. But they desire their punishment
because, at least extrinsically, it brings some order to their radical disorderliness. St. Catherine of Genoa says that "if the soul
did not find at that point an order proceeding from the justice
of God, it would be in a greater hell than it is, due to the fact of
finding itself outside that order." In this sense even hell itself is a
work of mercy. This idea of an impatience to undergo punishment being greater than the fear of punishment, shows yet again
that man's purpose lies outside himself; he is part of the order of
the world.

So if punishment does not reform the lost, does it therefore
fail in any way to improve the state of things? Not at all. God's
operations not only conserve things in being, but also perfect
them; this necessity applies to the lost as well, so that some
good is brought out of their evil. This does not happen because
each being is perfected but because, through all the good and ill
involved, being as a whole is perfected. In regard to the lost, this
means that the universe receives an added perfection because
their eternal punishment is, as we have seen, an eternal assertion
of justice. Even the damned give an added meaning to the
world, because though they are never themselves reformed, they
serve a purpose with respect to the whole in that the blessed see,
and rejoice over, the divine justice as it is displayed in them:
*Laetabitur justus cum viderit vindicta*m;[27] and also in that they
see the evils from which the divine mercy has preserved them.

There remains the obvious objection that there is a disproportion between a sin of limited duration and a sanction for it

---

[26] *Inferno*, III, 124-126. "And they are ready to cross the river, the
divine justice urging them on, so that their fear turns into desire."

[27] Psalm 57:11. "The just man will rejoice when he sees the punishment."

that lasts forever. The answer is that the proportion does not have to do with the time it took to commit the sin, but with the moral condition created by that sin. Even in matters of earthly justice, penalties are imposed not in proportion to the time involved in the committing of crime, but to its seriousness. This is the classical answer to this difficulty; it has been given before but is none the worse for that. When viewed existentially as an action occurring within the context of someone's life, a sin is an event that takes place within a finite period, but it is not finite when viewed as an event by which a creature actuates or negates its own relation to the infinite principle of value, namely God. In this sense even the most fleeting act of will, if it really is an act of will, is imbued not only with the moral importance proper to its transient character, but with a kind of surcharge by which it gives expression to higher realities that put it in touch with the archetypal and eternal world. In the Christian view it is this relationship that is the basis of man's moral dignity and of the seriousness of his moral life. This gives a timeless quality to morality that was appreciated by Stoics and Epicureans. The latter thought, wrongly, that happiness could be real without being lasting. But in fact to be real, happiness must last. Kant thought a lasting happiness could not be proved by reason but had to be deduced from feelings instead, but in the Catholic view the happiness of heaven is part of the law by which rational creatures are related to their Creator; the law by which finite goods are related to God, the source of goodness. The bestowal of eternal happiness is thus the point at which the transcendent world of the archetypes intersects with the finite creation.

The limitless quality of the life to come whether for good or ill, is in the last analysis a trans-temporal expression of the absolute importance of the soul and its life. It is connected too with the difference between the nature of things, that is, the different essences of different things, that have been referred to so often in this book. These different qualities in things would go on existing only within the mind of God if they could not survive the end of the world; and that they can only do if heaven and hell do not end up being the same thing. The argument is obvious but of irresistible force. It is not a question of punishing an offense to an infinite God by a punishment that lasts an infinite time. It is, rather, a matter of maintaining the difference between one kind of moral behavior and another and of proclaiming that no amount of time can abolish it. If all things will return happily to God, by an *apocatastasis* of an Origenist sort, then after the passage of a sufficiently long time, virginity and prostitution will come to the same thing and the past action of all human beings will be of absolutely no importance, given that what we care about is not what we were, but what we ultimately will be for the rest of eternity. The permanent reality of heaven and hell means that even though the whole temporal order, and the sequence of events that occurs within it, will be gone at the end of the world, the values of right and wrong cannot be done away with. True, the good exists unchangeably in God; but if moral goodness were not also woven into or stamped upon the order of the world as well, then the whole content of time would not alter the final state of things, and might therefore just as well not have existed. Justice, no less than mercy, is a good that must be conserved forever. The Jew from Auschwitz remains in eternity the Jew who was in Auschwitz, and the executioner Eichmann remains in eternity the executioner Eichmann. Hell is the difference between the one and the other; it is the preservation of the moral distinction between them, and thus of their moral natures. The only thing that can be destroyed is guilt, which is wiped out by forgiveness and which comes about through God's mercy and man's repentance, but not without that repentance.

EPILOGUE

317. The change in the Church as *Hairesis*.
Notional and real assent.

Our book closes by returning to its beginning and taking up the theme of its opening paragraphs: namely, is the change that we have examined fundamental, or is it only on the surface of things; is it development or corruption; an unfolding of what was already there or a drastic transmutation? In his famous *Histoire des Variations des Eglises Protestantes*, Bossuet took change and novelty in doctrine as a symptom of error, and traced heresy to an act of *hairesis*, that is, a subjective act of choosing what doctrines one would accept or reject, that is, to the erection of private judgment upon tradition into a dogmatic principle.[1] On the other hand, a subjective choice of a kind that does not distort the truth, but appropriates it all the more deeply, can very properly be exercised in religious matters. What is it that causes the endless flowering of new ideas in asceticism, mysticism and religious aesthetics if not this heightened subjective awareness of one aspect of the truth rather than another? Thus subjective choice, or *hairesis*, is only un-Catholic when it goes so far as to lose the right understanding of the essence of some doctrine and, in so doing, distorts the correct overall meaning of Christianity.

When discussing secondary Christianity,[2] we based our argument on the distinction between essences, which is reducible to the principle of contradiction; that is that something cannot both be and not be in the same respect at the same time; and we

---

[1] See paragraphs 14-18. The very word heresy implies the infallibility of the Church, since choice can only be synonymous with error if the Church's teachings, from which the choice is made, are inevitably correct. [Translator's note.]

[2] See paragraphs 220-1.

showed that Christianity has an absolute or ultimate character
to it, which human society in this world does not. From this it
follows that the present decline of Catholicism towards a purely
earthly system of values constitutes a substantial mutation in the
nature of the religion. Nonetheless, to justify the theory that a
fundamental change of this sort is occurring, one must show
that the goods of this earthly life have acquired such independent status with respect to the goods of the life to come that the
former are now being accorded equal importance with the latter.

But even here one needs to draw a distinction. Although
one grasps a truth and assents to it theoretically, this assent can
be accompanied by a greater or lesser degree of enthusiasm or
feeling; it is one thing to understand and accept a truth and
another to have strong feelings about it, and one would not be
justified in saying that someone did not understand and accept
a truth just because he did not feel it very strongly. The whole
cycle of thoughts that can be entertained about an intelligible
object is too vast for all the parts of a system to be equally
strongly felt, even though they are all equally assented to at the
notional or theoretical level. Thus the Christian belief about the
dependence of this world on a higher one can legitimately be
imbued with a more lively appreciation of the goods of this
world than was common in the past, but it cannot be reconciled
with the assertion that this world's goods are an end in themselves. Christianity is incompatible with the reduction of heaven
to earth, and a complete *Diesseitigkeit.*

318. The unchanging character of Catholic doctrine. St. Vincent of Lerins and Cardinal Newman.

The impossibility of changing the essence of Catholicism
coexists with a need for it to change in its accidental properties
as history takes its course. But the passage of time, through
which Catholicism lives, cannot change the essence of religion.
This is true not only because the distinct natures of things, even
from a philosophical point of view, are uncreated ideas that exist
changelessly in the mind of God, but still more because the
foundation of Christianity as a revealed religion is the divine
Word entering history, clothed in our humanity, but without
change to his changeless Godhead. This distinction between the
changing and the unchangeable elements in Christianity was
upheld, even as regards essential dogmatic questions, by St.

Vincent of Lerins in the fifth century and, with the increased development of an historical sense, was taken up in the nineteenth by Cardinal Newman as a means of understanding the development of Christian doctrine. It was also laid down at the outset of the council by John XXIII, but was not taken up by the council itself.[3] The council failed to emphasize the changeless foundations underlying the development of religious truth because it was preoccupied with the changeable and dynamic aspects of the Church.

In his *Commonitorium*, St. Vincent first of all sets forth an external test for discerning what constitutes part of the Catholic faith, and for distinguishing it from extraneous additions that it may have acquired in the course of time. These extraneous elements do not share in the suprahistorical character of revealed truths of faith; they are essentially part of history and not part of Christian doctrine. St. Vincent says that the Catholic faith is *quod ubique, quod semper, quod ab omnibus creditum est.*[4] But Cardinal Newman pointed out how difficult it is to show that this *ubique* and *semper* and *ab omnibus* is true in respect of each article of faith.[5] It is only a rough rule of thumb. Does "everywhere" mean everywhere in the Church or in the world? Does "always" mean all the time in every place or continually only in some places? And "by everyone" must surely mean by almost everyone, or by a majority; and is the majority a majority of the people or of the wise, or of those in authority? The phrase is obviously based upon a limited view of the dimensions of the Church, human society, and history.

St. Vincent's real criterion is the second one he expounds in his *Commonitorium*, namely that a doctrine is Catholic if it represents a genuine development of revealed principles laid down at the historical origins of the Church and preserved as part of the apostolic deposit of faith. Of course in the Catholic system the guarantee that a development is genuine is provided by the supreme teaching authority of the Church, but the legitimacy of a development can also be seen from an examination of the

---

[3] See paragraphs 38-40.
[4] "What has been believed everywhere, always, and by all."
[5] This is precisely what Newman had to establish to embrace the Catholic Faith. [Translator's note.]

matter in the light of our own logical thinking and historical knowledge.[6]

It is really a matter of the essential nature of the Christian religion, which does not change endlessly as do its external historical accompaniments. The preservation of type is an even more fundamental concept in thought than it is in biology. The whole question of the present condition of the Church can be summed up as follows: is the essence of Catholicism preserved? Do the changes that have occurred allow the same essence to continue in existence amidst changing circumstances, or do they turn it into something else? The mere clarification of an idea is not a shift to another idea: as St. Vincent says *intelligitur illustrius quod ante obscurius credebatur. Eadem tamen quae didicisti, doce, et cum dicas nove, ne dicas nova.*[7] A legitimate development of an idea occurs when it expands within itself; a mutation happens when it goes beyond its own limits and moves towards something else. It is right therefore, says St. Vincent, that there should be an increased awareness of the full content of the faith both on the part of individuals and on the part of the Church as a whole at successive historical periods *sed in suo dumtaxat genere, in eodem scilicet dogmate eodem sensu eademque sententia.*[8]

319. Substance interpreted as mode by the innovators.

Development in understanding of the truths of the faith implies that the elements that are brought to light in the developed form of the dogma really were contained in its initial form. There is thus no development without conservation of what was there before; development necessarily means that what was already there comes to be more clearly identified within the mind of the Church, that is, that it is set in new relations and seen to produce new consequences that were not realized previously: so the Immaculate Conception was contained within the divine motherhood, and the Assumption within the Immaculate

---

[6] Cardinal Newman's *Essay on the Development of Christian Doctrine*, 1845, sets forth several criteria for discerning a true development. [Translator's note.]

[7] "There is a clearer understanding of what was more obscurely believed before. Teach those same things that you have learned, and when you put them in a new way, do not say new things."

[8] "But provided it be in its own type, that is, within the same dogma, and with the same meaning and the same content of belief."

Conception. It is thus true, as we have said before, that there is a successively more perfect understanding of the faith, and the Christian of the twentieth century has a greater explicit knowledge of the truth than did the primitive Church and the Apostles themselves.

From this it also follows that we should reject the view that we need to go back to the sources and carry out what the French call a *ressourcement* of the Church. As Cardinal Newman remarked, the full nature of a river is known by examining the whole course of the river, not simply by looking at its source. It is by reaching its mouth that a river fulfills its destiny as a river, that it expresses its potential and reveals its character. The parts of the river beside which people build cities tend to be not at the source but at the estuary. In other words, in attempting to return to the sources of Christianity by jumping backwards over the Church's historical developments, or as Father Congar puts it, by leaping back across fifteen centuries, the innovators, though they do not realize it, are proposing in the interests of purity to set aside all the *ressourcements* that the living Church has carried out as the centuries have flowed along. It is the substance of these developments that must always be conserved, not the historical accompaniments that went with the developments. The truth is relevant to every age.

It might be objected that the historical character of doctrinal development lowers Christian doctrine to the level of any other set of ideas. The objection does not hold. The fundamental idea of Christianity is the lowering, or condescending or humiliation of the Word within time, a lowering which does not compromise the divine, but brings it down to the level of an historical manifestation. It is only the preservation of type that assures the historical identity of Catholicism.

If the present crisis is tending to overthrow the nature of the Church, and if this tendency is internal to the Church rather than the result of an external assault as it has been on other occasions, then we are headed for a formless darkness that will make analysis and forecast impossible, and in the face of which there will be no alternative but to keep silence.

To prevent this breakdown in continuity and intelligibility, even the innovators who are promoting the cause of a fundamental mutation within Christianity are obliged to uphold the historical continuity of the Church in some way or other; to admit they support a transformation of substance would be equivalent to apostatizing openly, and would confound all their arguments, because their new predicates would have no continuing subject to which they could be attached. They therefore attempt to disguise the leap to a different kind of reality by describing it in other terms, namely in terms of another mode of being. They put forward the view that the new idea of Christianity is only a new mode of existence for the same religion, rather than a transition to a different entity, which would imply the disruption and destruction of what previously existed. The whole of our book is, however, a collection of evidence showing that just such a transition has occurred. The idea of a purely symbolic presence of Christ in the Eucharist is presented as a new mode of understanding his Real Presence. The idea that the life of the Risen Christ exists in the faith of his disciples is put forward as a new mode of saying Christ really rose from the dead at a given moment in time, and this notion is alleged to be faithful to Catholic doctrine. The idea of the Ascension of the Lord as a symbolic and spiritual ascending of Christians by means of their faith is substituted as an equivalent to believing in his bodily ascension. The idea that original sin is simply an expression of the solidarity of the human race, which leaves each individual perfectly innocent, is put forward as being in unbroken continuity with the Catholic doctrine of the corruption of man's original condition, passed on by propagation to every human being. The idea of the taking on of a glorified body the instant after death, the material body being permanently abandoned thereafter, is advanced as a new presentation of the doctrine of the resurrection of the flesh.

Besides being unsupported by the magisterium of the Church, all these ideas are riddled with logical flaws and assume, for example, that saying "Christ did not ascend bodily" is the same as saying "Christ ascended bodily." The one is no *mode* of the other; the two are contradictory. Equivalences of this sort can be sustained only by supposing that the human intellect can make contradictories identical, that is, that it can tell itself that being coincides with non-being. This is the Pyrrhonism we examined earlier.[9] This pseudo-rationalism has triumphantly installed itself in post-conciliar theological schools and is tending, by a fatal lack of logical force, to extinguish and annihilate the specifically supernatural character of Christian-

---

[9] See paragraphs 147-50.

ity.[10] We have drawn particular attention to this denial of the supernatural in the change that has come over the notion of ecumenism, as set forth in documents from the Secretariat for Non-Christians;[11] but as a general tendency it can be seen in the whole of our analysis. Nor should it be forgotten that this corruption of Catholic dogma is being spread among the people by the clergy and the Catholic press. When the Vicar-General of the diocese of Lugano preached against the Ascension and was publicly criticized by a layman, who reminded him of Catholic teaching on the matter, the Vicar-General was supported by the bishop, Mgr Ernesto Togni, who made a public declaration of his solidarity and trust.[12]

320. Loss of unity of doctrine in the Church.

Since a thing's *unity* is a sign of its *being*, the condition of its being can be judged from the degree of its unity, inasmuch as it falls to pieces as its unifying principle weakens. *Ens et unum convertuntur*[13] is true of moral entities no less than physical ones. A molecule ceases to be with the breakup of the atoms of which it consisted. An animal ceases to be the moment its mass of cells loses the vital link that made it one organism. By the same token a moral entity loses its being when it loses its own unity. The Church consists of numbers of people undivided among themselves and divided from all other groups, and insofar as it is a community, that is a Church, it is one. This one Church is kept in being by a unifying principle through which individuals become members of a society, that is, parts of a whole in which individuals exist as one. The level of being of that community which is the Church can be determined from the level of its unity.

Now, in the present circumstances, its unity is fractured in three respects: doctrine, worship and government.

---

[10] Lest the reader assume the author is overstating the logical fatuity current in post-conciliar theological schools, the translator can state that he was taught by a Jesuit at the Pontifical Gregorian University in Rome, that the assertion in the Nicene Creed that Christ "rose again on the third day" did not exclude the assertion that his material body never rose, any more than anybody else's.

[11] See paragraphs 245-54.

[12] Cf. *Giornale del Popolo*, 23 December 1982.

[13] "Unity is convertible with being."

The doctrine taught and preached by the Church's ministers used once to be uttered with united voice. Now, however, it varies within the same country from diocese to diocese, within the same diocese from parish to parish, and within the same parish from preacher to preacher. Instead of being merely that difference in color, presentation or feeling regarding a single body of truth which is right and inevitable when speaking on any subject, these differences represent an alteration of dogma, cloaked in a policy of adapting the presentation of the faith to the character and expectations of contemporary men. Private theorizings grow ever bolder. The doctrinal corruption of priests either precedes or follows that of the bishops. The latter, in turn, issue individual pronouncements that differ among themselves, and by generally tolerating or sanctioning the deviations of their priests, the bishops have allowed a general confusion to reign in the Church on matters of faith, and have thus caused a deplorable weakening of unity among the faithful. Doctrinal unity used to be a peculiar characteristic of the Roman Church and was recognized and admired by those outside; it was also a reflection of the internal processions within the Holy Trinity, since *in principio erat Verbum*[14] and nothing can be achieved in the Church without the Word.

The lack of doctrinal unity that had already begun to emerge at the council, but which was there treated as a symptom of freedom and vitality, was manifested very openly by the appearance of *Humanae Vitae*,[15] and thereafter in a host of publications that bishops consented to by their silence, that is, when they did not actually intervene publicly to defend the errors of their priests against complaints by the laity. The faithful have a right to compare the teaching of an individual minister with that of other ministers and ultimately with that of the supreme teaching office. This right comes from their sharing in the teaching office of Christ conferred by baptism, and carries with it an obligation to reject false teaching in the internal forum, that is, in their own minds, and, if circumstances require, to attack it publicly as well.

As we have seen[16] this doctrinal corruption has ceased to be restricted to small esoteric circles and to be governed by a kind

---

[14] "In the beginning was the Word."
[15] See paragraphs 62-63.
[16] See paragraphs 131-41.

of *disciplina arcani*:[17] it has now become public in the body of the Church through sermons, books, schoolteaching and catechesis, which latter has often fallen into the hands of lay people with insufficient knowledge and a thirst for novelty. This obscuring of Catholic doctrine is not altogether unconnected with the procedures of the Congregation for the Doctrine of the Faith, which have replaced those of its predecessor the Holy Office, and which have delegated the watch over orthodoxy that used to be exercised by the Holy See to the care of bishops, who are less doctrinally instructed and less firm; nor is it unconnected with the lack of attention given to the cultural level of candidates when appointing new bishops to dioceses.

321. Undermining of dogma and doctrinal indifferentism. *Etudes.* Mgr Le Bourgeois.

There is at present a general tendency in the Church to shift the goal of Christian life from heaven to earth and to twist the Gospel law that proclaims the primacy of God into a primacy of man. The truths of faith are thus tamed and stripped of whatever in them is of a supernatural nature to which secularized man objects; the salt of the earth thus loses its savor. The depth of the error that now dominates general thinking among the people of God can be gauged by the lack of objections and the feebleness of the complaints that the faithful now offer in the face of these doctrinal perversions.[18] This indifferentism is hardly surprising in the circumstances. Whole peoples in the past have defected from the Church when led to do so by their clergy, whether in England and Germany in the sixteenth century, or in the recent instances of the Rumanian Catholic Church in 1945, the Ukranian Catholics in 1947 or the Chinese Catholics in 1957.[19] It cannot be denied that this dying down of resentment of false teaching among the people in general is a sign of the gravity of the crisis.

This loss of the very idea of dogmatic truth is not just a popular state of mind; it is now theoretically defended in intel-

---

[17] "Guarding of the secret."

[18] An extraordinary number of Catholics pay so little intellectual attention to doctrinal matters, that they are still unaware anything much is happening. [Translator's note].

[19] In the last three instances there was no noticeable unorthodoxy among the clergy. [Translator's note.]

lectual circles within the Church. To give just one authoritative
example, Mgr Le Bourgeois, the Bishop of Autun writes that:
*Aujourd'hui je dis haut ma joie de voir mon Eglise, trop souvent
perçue comme toujours sûre d'elle-même, propriétaire et juge de la
vérité totale, briser cette image pour s'ouvrir, comprendre, accueillir
la pensée des autres, reconnaître ses propres limites, accomplir fi-
nalement une "opération vérité," ce qui est tout autre chose
qu'exposer et défendre des "vérités."*[20] The French Jesuit review
Etudes puts the new principle bluntly: *La foi d'aujourd'hui à
l'état adulte peut se passer des dogmes: elle est assez grande pour
pouvoir découvrir Dieu par contact personnel. La foi ne doit pas se
fonder sur les vérités révélées, mais à travers les événements de
l'histoire.*[21] The modernist origin, indeed the modernist content
of this doctrine, is obvious. Faith is said to have grown up,
when faith properly so called has shrunken and vanished; everything is based on feelings which are regarded as an experience of
God; Christianity is alleged to rest not upon truths revealed by
an historical act of revelation, but upon human experiences
transcribed into shifting intellectual categories; the mediation of
the Church gives place to private judgment, that is, to the principle upon which the Lutheran movement and most modern
philosophy is based.

The spirit of modern philosophy, which had already been
accepted by the modernist heresy, has also led to the great
changes that have taken place within Catholic biblical exegesis,
even within its official institutional expression, namely the
Pontifical Biblical Institute. It is this change that has caused the
lapse into insignificance of the Pontifical Biblical Commission
as well. This change in thinking, sometimes covert and sometimes open, can be summed up under three heads.

---

[20] I.C.I, No.586, 1983, p.19: "Today I state clearly how glad I am to
see my Church, which has too often been seen as always sure of itself, the master and judge of all truth, breaking that image in order
to open itself up, to understand, to welcome other people's thinking, to recognize its own limitations, and to carry out at last a 'truth
finding operation'; which is quite a different thing from explaining
and defending 'truths.'"

[21] Father Varillon, *Abrégé de la foi catholique*, in *Etudes*, October
1977: "Today's faith in its adult state can do without dogmas: it is
big enough to be able to discover God by personal contact. Faith
should not be founded on revealed truths, but on events unfolding
in history."

The first point is the overthrow of the relationship between the Old and New Testaments: the doings and sayings of the Old Testament are no longer taken as prefigurations of those in the New, that is they no longer have a prophetic sense; quite the reverse in fact, since the New is said to be merely a construct modeled on the contents of the Old. Thus, for example, the special conceptions and angelic messages involving mothers of Old Testament figures that are recorded in the history of the chosen people are no longer seen as anticipatory signs of analogous events in the Gospel; it is the Gospel events that are regarded as figments elaborated by believers using models drawn from the earlier writings. The essentially forward looking march of events in the Bible is reversed into a mentality that looks backward instead. On this basis the Gospel accounts of Christ's infancy are regarded as a compilation of Old Testament *motifs* that do not refer to actual events, but display instead different stages of religious experience.

The second point is the shift from history to poetry. It is now commonly taught that the New Testament is merely the expression of the faith of the primitive Christian community. This is a new teaching, and is at odds with the whole doctrine of the Church from its very beginning, which maintains that the Gospels do not proclaim faith, but facts upon which people based their faith. Before being objects of faith, Christ's words and deeds existed in the real, historical world and it was from there that they passed into the content of belief; they could be believed in only because they had already happened. This new fangled exegesis is bluntly contradicted by what the evangelists say; they never purport to be preaching what they believe, but rather reporting what they have heard and seen so that we may believe. Let St. John speak for them all: "Our message concerns that Word who is life; what He was from the first, what we have heard about Him, what our own eyes have seen of Him; what it was that met our gaze, and the touch of our hands (*epselaphesan*)."[22] The modernist substance of the new exegesis can be easily recognized: Christianity is not based on what is *true*, but on what is *experienced*; not on *knowledge* but on *feeling*.

The third point is the placing of Sacred Scripture on the same level as any other piece of writing; what we should seek to gather from it is not a series of events that really happened in

---

[22] I John, 1:1.

So much of the confusion seems a result of comparative religion studies. G.K.C. once said, "He who studies comparative religions will become comparatively religious."

720   IOTA UNUM

the past, but an understanding of the cultural state of a particular people and the nature of their mythology. The whole Mosaic history is sometimes dismissed on this basis as being a myth; the inspiration of Scripture itself is interpreted as nothing more than an intense popular credence in a set of baseless beliefs. The accounts of miracles in sacred history are likewise denied, particularly the value of Christ's miracles as proof of his divine mission, despite the fact that their nature in that regard has been dogmatically defined by various councils.[23] This, for example, is what Cardinal Gantin says: "We are not called to believe on the strength of Christ's power to work miracles; rather it is faith in Him as Son of God that makes us able to believe in his miracles."[24] One might be amazed at the Cardinal's bland contradiction of a defined dogma of the Church, were it not for the fact that causes for amazement of a similar nature are now so common that their very frequency has deprived them of their capacity to amaze.

While considering this loss of unity in doctrine we might remind ourselves of its depth and, above all, of its swiftness by referring to the false analyses and forecasts made about the Church's doctrinal unity around the time of the council. In his pastoral letter for Lent 1962, Cardinal Montini, the Archbishop of Milan said that "today there are no errors in the Church, or scandals or deviations or abuses to correct" and when he had become Pope he said in his first encyclical *Ecclesiam Suam* in 1964 that: "At the present time it is no longer a matter of ridding the Church of this or that particular heresy or of certain specific disorders. Thanks be to God there are none in the Church." The precisely opposite kind of statements the same Pope Paul VI was making towards the end of his reign, proclaiming that there was a grave crisis in the Church,[25] arouse questions concerning not only psychology, but also principles of interpretation and the nature of God's dealings with the world. But we are here concerned with emphasizing the loss of unity in doctrine. If it is not entirely true to say, as Cardinal Suenens has, that there are a goodly number of propositions that used to be taught in Rome before the council as definite truths, that the council itself proceeded to discard, it is nonetheless true to say that what used to be a single voice in matters of doctrine is now

---

[23] Denzinger, 1790 and 1813.

[24] O.R., 7 December 1984.

[25] See especially paragraphs 7-9, 77 and 78.

a host of discordant voices instead. This is the effect of a loss of the virtue of faith itself, rather than the result of a series of disagreements in detail. In that sense, what Paul VI said is true; there are no particular errors to condemn; what needs to be condemned is an error of principle, because the host of particular errors in question do not relate to some subordinate aspect of Christianity but flow from a distinct anti-principle which was identified and condemned by St. Pius X under the name of Modernism.

322. Loss of unity of worship.

We have discussed this matter in detail already.[26] There has been a universal fragmentation, nationalization and individualization of the liturgy. From diocese to diocese the rites of the Church differ not only in language, in pursuance of the principle of vernacularization, but in ceremony, in pursuance of the principle of expressing national characteristics. This variety is due to the fact that priests and laity have acquired a kind of creative sharing in the Church's power to fix its liturgy, which results in worship being shaped and reshaped from one occasion to the next to match the taste and preferences of the celebrant or congregation. These distortions are particularly common at funerals and weddings, the mourners or the spouses being allowed to turn the rite into an expression of their own personal religiosity. Funerals sometimes now include an address in praise of the deceased, sometimes not; sometimes there is a sprinkling and incensation of the coffin, sometimes not; sometimes the celebrant accompanies the body to the cemetery or crematorium, sometimes not; sometimes the coffin is escorted in the first place from the home of the deceased, sometimes not. This ritual variety means that it is hard to detect much uniformity about funerals. St. Paul's pronouncement *fiat aequalitas*[27] is more or less overlooked, at least in death.

We will not repeat all we have said about the abolition of Latin as the language of the Church.[28] It has had the paradoxical result that at a time when different governments are laboriously working to unite their peoples across national boundaries, the

---

[26] See paragraphs 276-93.
[27] II Corinthians, 8:14 "Let there be equality."
[28] See paragraphs 277-83.

Catholic liturgy is erecting barriers[29] that were not there before, and is thus at odds with the universalist spirit of the age.[30]

John Paul II protests against the distortion of the liturgy, that has sprung from this idea of creativity, in all his addresses to bishops coming to Rome for their *ad limina* visits. He continually renews his admonitions to the effect that the liturgy should be celebrated in strict conformity with the Roman rules; but the persistence of his appeals simply shows their lack of effect, while very effectively demonstrating the breadth of the problem.

Nor does the Pope believe in combating disobedience by issuing commands that would be universally binding, because that would clash with the post-conciliar practice of merely urging people to do the right thing and it would also be at odds with the ideal of flexibility enshrined in the new liturgy itself. Speaking to the Swiss bishops, the Pope deplored "the arbitrary liturgical experiments which the faithful are sometimes forced to attend, and the one-sided manner in which subjects are treated in parish sermons." He asked for faithfulness to the liturgical rules promulgated by the Holy See, saying it was a sign of the reverence due to the Blessed Sacrament itself "which is measured in no small way by the fidelity and obedience shown to the Church, and above all by the conscientious observance of the norms promulgated by the Holy See regarding the liturgy."[31]

---

[29] When the Catholic Scouts from Lugano went to visit Canada, they did not go to Mass, even on Sundays, because in that country Mass was in English, which they did not know.

[30] The loss of unity in worship is defended and indeed commended in the *Osservatore Romano* of 20 October 1982, which applauds the "progressive elaboration of a liturgical language and a euchology composed directly in the local languages. This gradual transition is necessary in every country." The article laments the fact that "this adaptation of the liturgy to the national spirit has not been pushed too far and we have often been content with a mere translation of the Roman books." It would seem the author wants the process to be pushed "too far."

[31] O.R., 9 July 1982. The Pope's speech on the state of the Church in Switzerland was concealed from Catholics by the Catholic press. Only after the *Gazetta Ticinese* of 4 August 1982 had published its translation of it, did the Catholic daily papers in Lugano feel obliged to let Catholics know about a papal speech concerning their own Church.

An unexpected confirmation of this break up of unity in worship was provided by the indult of 3 October 1984 by which the Pope once more allowed the celebration of Mass according to the traditional rite in use before the council, which had been eliminated by Paul VI in 1969 when he made the new Missal obligatory.[32] The indult aroused the ire of those who saw it as a retrograde step and a retraction of the reform, and the enthusiasm of those who saw it as the granting of a not unreasonable request. What is surprising is the contradiction between the indult and the enquiry carried out in 1981 regarding the reception given by the people to the new rites, and the abandonment of Latin. The conclusion had been that Latin and the old rite of Mass had gone out of use everywhere without causing any regrets except among a few small groups doomed to rapid extinction.[33] The conclusion was accompanied by a prediction: the Latin liturgy, and indeed any desire for it, would disappear within a relatively short time. The indult for its part declares expressly that after the 1981 enquiry it was clear there was no longer any problem regarding Latin and the old Mass: *Attentis eorum responsionibus fere in totum solutum visum est problema eorum sacerdotum et christifidelium qui ritui Tridentino nuncupato inhaerentes manserant.*[34] But after having said this, the indult continues: *Cum autem problema idem perduret.*[35] How can a problem be said to persist if it has been almost totally resolved? One might be justified in conjecturing that this change in policy was due to the fact that the 1981 enquiry was badly conducted, or badly interpreted or not carried through in good faith; but in any case, however one explains the turnabout, the Holy See has reversed its policy on a matter upon which Paul VI had been very firm.

---

[32] It is now widely recognized that it is impossible to point to any document signed by Pope Paul that ever made the use of the new Missal obligatory. It is also certain that Pope Paul said late in his reign that its use *was* obligatory, but he at no time indicated what decree was alleged to have made it so. [Translator's note.]

[33] See paragraph 283.

[34] "Having considered their answers (the bishops' that is) the problem of those priests and faithful who remained attached to what is called the Tridentine rite seems to have been almost totally resolved."

[35] "However, since the same problem persists."

It must, however, be recognized that with a new liturgy that varies so much according to national tastes as to make the way it is celebrated in one country unrecognizable to Catholics from another, and when a rite in one language, of one heart and mind, has been replaced by a rite lacking all these qualities, it was an affront to the much vaunted principle of liturgical pluralism that the traditional rite of Mass should be the one thing that was *not* allowed, because to ban it was to deny one of the best options that a pluralist spectrum should include.

The indult came out at the very time at which a convention of the heads of the liturgical commissions in various countries was meeting in Rome, at the invitation of the Congregation for Divine Worship, to mark the twentieth anniversary of the appearance of *Sacrosanctum Concilium*, the council's decree on the liturgy. In the usual euphemistic way, it praised the fruits of the reform. There was talk of a "new Pentecost, a springtime, a new Epiphany": it was asserted that the reform "has offered the possibility of maturing a personal and communitarian relationship with God," that was not offered before the council. Just when the Catholic liturgy is becoming a motley aggregation of rites and a discordant chorus of voices, the convention announced: "No longer two voices (priest and people) but a single chorus."[36]

This lauding of the new regime did not completely succeed in hiding the real state of affairs. The pro-Prefect of the Congregation for Divine Worship, the Benedictine Mayer, tended to doubt that interior participation by the people had actually been increased by the reforms; he pointed to a declining sense of the sacred and a declining reverence for the liturgy; he drew attention to the incongruity of frequent communion among people who have ceased using the sacrament of penance. In fact, the reports made by the different national liturgical officials showed that in every corner of the Church a rapid differentiation of rites is underway, governed by the two principles we have mentioned, a self-expression that leads to a modeling of the rite in accordance with national characteristics, and a creativity that looks for the authentic sources of liturgy within human beings themselves and which rejects the notion of an objective sacrality. These two principles are to be put into effect by the national episcopal conferences. These are the bodies whose task it is to develop and fix their own ways of worship, and the

---

[36] O.R., 24 October 1984.

role of the Holy See in the matter is to confirm what they have done. The pre-conciliar norm, which was that the Holy See was the appropriate legislating authority in liturgical affairs, is thus reversed.[37]

From a liturgical unity that was guaranteed by unity of language, ceremony and material objects, there has been a transition to a syncretism in which very varied elements coexist, in language, in ceremonies, in vestments and in singing. Assertions are still made to the effect that there is a single Roman rite, but such unity is not actually expressed in deeds, and is therefore nullified. The Roman authority, which used to guarantee unity, is bending and weakening before the centrifugal forces of the new democratizing ecclesiology.

323. Loss of unity of government.
Deromanization of the Sacred College.

A society, of whatever sort, is usually not created by authority, but an authority is nonetheless needed in society to unite a mass of individuals by directing their energies towards a common end. But in the Church, authority is of a special kind because it exists prior to the society it governs. While other societies first exist and then articulate themselves through their governing institutions, the Church owes neither its existence nor its governing authority to its members, but receives both from Christ: the Head exists before the Church, which is an effect or an expansion of the Head. Of course authority is only one part of the organism of the Church, and should not be identified with the Church as such; it is a service within the Church, as they say these days. But Catholicism necessarily involves a reference to authority for the reason we have just mentioned and which Christ formulated clearly when he said: "He who hears you hears Me."[38] Authority is essential to the unity of the Church. The pre-eminent authority of Peter and the Petrine ministry has always been held to be the foundation and centre of the unity of the Church on earth; any decrease in loyalty to Rome is necessarily accompanied by a cracking in the unity of the Church as a society.

The problem of lack of unity among bishops that Rosmini lamented in his famous work "The Five Wounds of Holy

---

[37] For all this, O.R. special edition, 1 November 1984.
[38] Luke, 10:16.

Church" has become strikingly apparent in the contemporary
Church. Indeed it has worsened considerably. In Rosmini's day
it was merely a negative thing, due to a lack of any frequent
communication or correspondence among the bishops; they
were united nevertheless by their common connection with the
Roman Pontiff. Today their lack of unity has turned into positive disagreement and dissent among themselves. While there
has been a vast increase in meetings, committees, symposia, and
assemblings of episcopal conferences, the bishops in individual
countries are internally divided, as can be seen in Holland, the
United States and Brazil; episcopal documents are at odds with
other episcopal documents, as if to demonstrate that there is
now no *sensus communis* in the Church. This intestine disagreement is a necessary result of disagreement with the Roman
Pontiff to whom verbal allegiance is still given, but whose
teaching is subjected to review and judgment by the bishops, as
was glaringly obvious in the case of *Humanae Vitae*[39] and as can
be seen from the continual examination by local synods of
points on which the Holy See has already delivered a solemn
decision.

Using official sources,[40] we have already described the weakening of ecclesiastical authority, whether from a failure to exercise such authority, or because of resistance to it, due to an independent spirit that has been stirred up among the people of
God. We have mentioned the recent secessions of the Rumanian
and Ukranian Catholic Churches and of the Church in China,
all motivated by a rejection of Roman authority and a mistaken
belief that one could maintain Catholic doctrine and ethics
while detaching oneself from papal authority, and that one
could maintain unity while rejecting the principle sustaining it,
namely Rome.[41] We have also mentioned the serious signs of
independence shown by various bishops at the time of *Humanae Vitae*, and by the pre-schismatic crisis in Holland which
the holding of an extraordinary synod of the bishops of that
country in Rome, attended by the Pope in January 1980, failed
to resolve. Then again there is the lack of unity shown by theological deviations on the part of individuals and whole faculties,
the dissolution of catechesis, and disciplinary variations from

---

[39] See paragraphs 62 and 63.
[40] See paragraphs 60-64.
[41] Communist persecution was the real reason for these secessions.
[Translator's note.]

one diocese to another. We have also drawn attention to a paralysis of authority and a *breviatio manus* on the part of the papacy.[42]

Given that, in the Catholic Church, a decline in authority always manifests itself in a decline in Roman authority, I will mention a significant change showing how this has happened in regard to the College of Cardinals. The change compromises the principle upon which papal authority rests, and alters the character of the Sacred College. As John Paul II said when creating eighteen cardinals in the consistory of 2 February 1983, the College of Cardinals was in origin a group of priests of the diocese of Rome gathered round their bishop, and that is what it continues to be, because each cardinal is the titular holder of a church in Rome and "by being assigned his own titular church, he becomes in a certain way part of the clergy of the diocese of Rome."[43] After there had been sharp disputes about precedence between Oriental Catholic Patriarchs, who had traditionally never been cardinals, and some of the members of the Sacred College, Paul VI decided in 1965 to make the patriarchs cardinals, but without assigning them any Roman titular church, since they belonged to oriental rites and did not form part of the Latin Roman clergy.[44] This change, which was little noticed,

---

[42] See paragraphs 65, 66 and 71.

[43] O.R., 3 February 1983.

[44] Thus when Antoine Pierre Khoraiche, the Maronite Patriarch of Antioch, was made a cardinal in the consistory of 2 February 1983, he was not assigned any titular church in Rome. A further oddity regarding the Sacred College was that when Henri de Lubac was made a cardinal deacon in the same consistory, he was allowed to remain merely a priest, against the rule made by John XXIII that cardinals of all three orders should be consecrated as bishops. [As the author points out, a cardinal is a cardinal because he belongs to the clergy of the church at Rome. He is assigned a church in Rome that he holds as its titular priest, or in a much smaller number of cases, as its titular deacon. There are also seven small episcopal sees in the neighborhood of Rome of which the titular bishop is a cardinal; these men are "cardinal bishops" as distinct from the "cardinal priests" and "cardinal deacons." These are the "three orders" the author is referring to, which constitute the College of Cardinals or Sacred College. Originally, and logically, only the seven cardinal bishops needed to be bishops; cardinal priests only needed to be priests and cardinal deacons, deacons. The last cardi-

is of great theoretical importance because it ignores the historical basis of the institution, alters its structure, and takes away a
sign of the primacy of the church which is at Rome. The Sacred
College is no longer theoretically a body bound to the Roman
See and forming part of the Roman clergy; it is instead a
council of bishops who are part of the college in virtue of the
episcopal or patriarchal sees that they hold in other parts of the
world. We may also note here the incongruous character of the
Pope's speech, which spoke about the holding of Roman titular
churches as the basis of membership of the Sacred College,
when at least one of those created cardinal that day was made
cardinal in virtue of holding a patriarchal see in the East. This is
a clear proof of the weakening of the primatial authority of the
church at Rome, and thus of the papal primacy that holds local
churches together in a single Catholic Church.

The weakening of a unifying papal authority began institu-
tionally with the transfer in 1966 to local bishops of certain
faculties previously reserved to the Holy See, effected by the
decree *De episcoporum muneribus*. The bishops' law-making
power was subsequently further enlarged, with a corresponding
contraction of Roman jurisdiction, and received a definitive
status in the new Code of Canon Law.[45]

324. Condition of the Church today. Cardinal Siri. Cardinal Wyszynski. The French bishops.

The twentieth anniversary of the opening of Vatican II led
various people to attempt to summarize the condition of the
Church today. As usual, the whole range of opinion was

---

nal deacon to be merely a deacon died in 1876, but it was only
Pope Benedict XV (1914-1922) who decreed that a mere deacon
should not in future be a cardinal deacon, but had to take priest's
orders. It was only Pope John XXIII (1958-1963) who decreed that
cardinal priests and deacons had to be ordained bishop. Cardinal de
Lubac's remaining a priest when made a cardinal is thus perfectly
traditional. Pope Paul decreed in 1965 that the Eastern Catholic
patriarchs should be made cardinals and given rank after the cardinal bishops, but before the cardinal priests and cardinal deacons.
Eastern Catholic patriarchs have never been assigned Roman titular
churches. Translator's note.]

[45] See paragraph 61 for the limited effective authority of individual
bishops. [Translator's note.]

sounded, reflecting the opposing opinions and directions of thought in the post-conciliar Church. We may set aside the *Osservatore Romano's* paeans of praise, including the headline: "We are the most gospel-minded century in history,"[46] a refrain taken up by Father Congar: "Our age is one of the most gospel-minded in history."[47] We can also set aside the denigratory statements to the effect that "to renew itself, the Church must rediscover the Gospel, that is, be more gospel-minded. In the past it has indulged in politics and war." Nor do we need to answer those who admit the facts of decline in religious practice, but who claim that this desertion has been accompanied by a growth in the gospel spirit. We must consider, however, the opinion delivered by Cardinal Siri after a calm observation of the facts.[48] He recognizes that some people at the council had "the intention of getting the Church to live protestantly, without tradition and without the papal primacy: to achieve the first end they created a lot of confusion, and to achieve the second, they tried to use arguments in favor of collegiality." Siri distinguishes between the council, which was "a great barrier against the principle of disintegration" and "the prevailing tendency of the post-conciliar period during which the sad habit grew up of swallowing private individuals' ideas along with the decrees of the council."

This distinction is often used in papal speeches, and analyses of the situation made by those who seek to maintain the Church's continuity through history, and its internal unity. How far this interpretation holds and how far it does not, can be judged from the whole of our book. A distinction of this sort is rejected by people who are often accused of a one-sided pessimism, but who in fact are guilty of no such thing, because they are the only ones who are really coming to grips with the profound significance of the evolution occurring in the Church at present. They are the ones who have got through to the essence of the matter, and who understand that the spirit of the present age, as we have said,[49] is not something composite, made up of parts that can be separated and judged one by one, but is instead the ruling principle that gives the age its consistency and its spiritual unity.

---

[46] O.R., 20 October 1982.
[47] O.R., 21 August 1983.
[48] In *Renovatio*, 1982, p.325.
[49] See paragraph 25.

In a homily in Warsaw Cathedral on 9 April 1974, Cardinal
Wyszynski, the Primate of Poland, gave his diagnosis of the state
of the Catholic Church in a synthetic rather than an analytical
fashion. He described a post-conciliar church "whose life is distancing itself appreciably from the event of Calvary; a Church
that is reducing its demands and no longer resolving problems
in accordance with the will of God, but in accordance with
man's natural capacities; a Church in which the Creed has become elastic and morality relativistic; a Church wrapped in
clouds and lacking the Tables of the Law; a Church that shuts
its eyes to sin, and is afraid of being reproached for not being
modern."

Although he was one who assisted and praised the conciliar
reforms, even Ugo Cardinal Poletti, the Vicar of His Holiness
for the City of Rome, was recently forced to give in to facts, and
wrote in the *Osservatore Romano* that: "In the years after the
council (perhaps it is inevitable after every important council) a
great deal of doctrinal and pastoral confusion arose in the
Catholic Church, which has moved a scholar above all suspicion, such as Rahner, to speak of a crypto-heresy. Unfortunately
this atmosphere generates a deep disorientation among the
faithful themselves. We must put an end to this situation by
following St. Paul's invitation to speak the truth in charity."[50]
Going on to analyze the details of the doctrinal decay, Poletti
traces its origin to a change in ecclesiology: the idea that the
Church is an aggregation of local churches, which idea, we
might add, was greatly advanced by the imprudent increasing of
the power of episcopal conferences and the consequent weakening of the Petrine authority. It should also be noted that what
the Cardinal says in parentheses, about the inevitability of doctrinal confusion, will not hold. Doctrinal confusion traditionally preceded councils, because the councils were called precisely
to resolve the confusion, even if they did not always succeed in
doing so immediately as can be seen in the case of Nicea. The
Council of Trent was followed by a period of great doctrinal
clarity and a firm condemnation of errors. There can be no reform of the Church when doctrinal pronouncements are vague.
It is a peculiarity of Vatican II that it generated confusion rather
than cleared it up and *the reason the council had this unprece-*

---

[50] O.R., 7 October 1984.

dented effect lies back in Pope John's opening speech,[51] *in which the traditional principle that errors should be refuted was replaced by the novel principle of entering into a trusting dialogue with everything non-Catholic.*

The turning of the tide of praise that marked the twentieth anniversary of the council's opening, definitely arrived with the declarations made by Cardinal Ratzinger, Prefect of the Congregation for the Doctrine of the Faith, in an interview in the summer of 1984, reproduced in the *Osservatore Romano* on 9 November of that year. It is true that there had already been many signs that the scales were beginning to fall from the eyes of the better informed, but Ratzinger's pronouncements definitely tore away the veils that had been hiding the truth, despite the fact that the Cardinal's personal opinions are not endowed with the authority they would have had had he been speaking in an official capacity. "The results of the council," he said, "seem cruelly to contradict the expectations everybody had, beginning with John XXIII and Paul VI: it was expected to produce a new unity among Catholics, but instead dissension has increased to a point where it has moved from self-criticism to self-destruction... it was expected to produce a leap forward, but we have been confronted instead with a continuing process of decay that has gone on largely on the basis of appeals to the council, and has thus helped to discredit the council in the eyes of many people. The result would therefore seem negative... It is undeniable that this period has been decidedly unfavorable for the Catholic Church. I believe that the council cannot really be held responsible for developments and turns of events that contradict both the spirit and letter of its documents. It is my impression that the misfortunes the Church has met with in the last twenty years are not due to the true council itself, but to an unleashing within the council of latent aggressive, polemical and centrifugal forces." The Cardinal links the crisis to four causes: a loss of faith in God, in the Church, in dogma and in Scripture as the Church reads it. Ratzinger's remarks on the shift in ecclesiology are very striking; the authority of Peter has been weakened by an undue strengthening of episcopal conferences, which has also destroyed the individual authority of bishops. "The bishops must be given back full personal responsibility."

[51] See paragraph 40.

It is paradoxical that this loss of authority by individual bishops has taken place at the very time that the importance of local churches has been so emphasized, and when the local bishop is given precedence over the papal nuncio at ceremonies, reversing what used to be the case. Cardinal Ratzinger's views on the matter of local churches are, at any rate, in agreement with those of Cardinal Poletti we mentioned earlier.

As a final demonstration of the variety there is in assessments of the present condition of the Church, we will mention a work on the state of the Church in France, edited by the secretary of the French Episcopal Conference.[52] It is in large part written by cardinals and bishops. In its first section, the post-conciliar Church is regarded as a *return to the sources*, a refoundation of the Church on its original and authentic base. Father Congar's idea that we need to *enjamber*, that is to leap over, fifteen centuries, crops up again combined with a desire for the kind of fundamental shift we have mentioned,[53] and some more denigration of the historic Church.[54] This attempt to set aside history is based on an imperfect understanding of the development of ideas. An idea itself is regarded as identical with one of its historical expressions; there is an attempt to latch on to, and recreate, a particular past historical period, namely the state of the Church as it existed in the pagan Roman Empire; the so-called pre-constantinian Christianity. But as we have already said more than once, the historical development of a principle is distinct from the principle itself; the principle is expressed historically in a series of states, but never exhaustively, and it transcends any one particular historical moment. In order to prove that Catholicism as it existed during the centuries one wants to *enjamber* was a mistaken development of Christianity, one would have to show that those stages of its history are a contradiction of the very nature of the Christian religion, rather than states of affairs that actuated and suitably expressed that nature; that is, one would need to assert that there was a vacuum of Christianity at the time: the historical continuity of those ages with what precedes and follows them would become theoretically inexplicable. Since it cannot support its favorable judgment on the post-conciliar period by reference to the statistical

---

[52] G. Defois (ed.), *Le Concile: vingt ans de notre histoire*, Desclée, 1982.

[53] See paragraphs 53 and 54.

[54] See paragraph 55.

evidence available, the book says nothing about it,[55] and attempts instead to give a positive air to things by listing all the initiatives that have been launched, even the ones that failed, as they are all seen as signs of life. This method of interpretation stems from the mobilism characteristic of the modern world,[56] which holds that moving is more important than arriving anywhere, seeking more important than finding anything, and that value is bestowed on human living by the act of living itself. The arbitrary assumption that the post-conciliar tendencies are in harmony with the *movement of history*, allows the authors of the book to envelop the unpleasant realities of a Christianity that has lost its salt, and an internal disintegration of the Church, within a gush of unrealistic optimism.[57] So instead of conclusions drawn from historical facts, we are left with a projection of human hopes that are regarded as inspired by the Holy Spirit, seen no longer as the soul of the Church, but of the world at large.

325. Crises in the Church and the modern world. Parallel between the decline of paganism and the present decline of the Church.

The crisis in the modern Church is obvious from the fact that the latter has not succeeded in making the increased impact on the world that its own renewal was allegedly designed to produce. The contradiction between the council's intentions and what has actually happened can be seen in three ways.

The condition of the world at the moment is rather like that of the decaying Roman civilization of the fourth century.

---

[55] According to the 1980 census, the population of France had grown by three million in ten years, but according to Vatican statistics, which count all baptized Catholics as Catholics, there had been no increase in the Catholic population, which thus shrank proportionally. But according to Barret, writing in the *World Encyclopedia of Statistics* (*Enciclopedia statistica mondiale*), who only counts those who call themselves Catholics, there were three million professing atheists in France in 1980 where there had been only two and a half million in 1970, and 130,000 in 1925. There had, however, been a large increase in Mohammedanism, with some Catholics even converting to Islam.

[56] See paragraphs 157-62.

[57] See paragraph 228.

There are many parallels and similarities: the breakup of society,
the increased eroticism, the passion for the circus or sporting
arena and other spectacles, divorce, abortion, a bloated public
administration, the declining value of the currency, sodomy, the
abandonment of agricultural work, the drift of the masses to the
cities, an increase in robbery and similar crimes. The only
things lacking in the fourth century were the elements deriving
from technology, which was of little consequence then, but
which has now brought human existence to a level of artificial-
ity which involves the gradual replacing of all natural processes,
whether of love or birth or death.

But what is more important than this series of similarities
in detail, is the similarity in the shift in thinking that is common to both eras. At the very time when a dying paganism was
defending the presence of the statue and altar of the goddess of
Victory in the Roman Senate,[58] that very paganism was undergoing the same change that has now begun in the Catholic
Church. The specific character of Christianity is being lost, and
Catholicism is being dissolved into a combined universal religion, of which all particular religions are regarded as valid expressions, because religions are, on this view, simply the expressions of the different cultures in which they exist. The seed
from which this view has sprung is clearly detectable in a speech
by Paul VI that we have already discussed.[59] Pope Paul maintained in that speech that the Catholic religion is not a cause for
division among men, because it draws distinctions between
things without opposing one to another, just as languages, customs and races constitute distinctions, but not necessarily oppositions, within a single humanity. In the post-conciliar period, the ecumenical movement has moved more and more towards viewing all religions as an expression of a set of natural
values that are more or less present in all cultures, in a manner
that varies according to historical circumstance.[60] No unique
virtue can be assigned to Catholic Christianity: all religions are
held to participate in humanity's religious quest, and all of them

---

[58] The presence or absence of this statue in the Senate house was a
continuing bone of contention between the Christian and pagan
parties in Rome in the last quarter of the fourth century. It was removed for the last time by the Emperor Theodosius in the early
390s. [Translator's note.]
[59] See paragraph 59.
[60] See paragraphs 252-60.

do so as well as they can in their particular historical circumstances, but all are inadequate in comparison with the mystery that they seek to express. Catholicism has no transcendent superiority to other religions but is seen as belonging to the same category as all the rest, it is, as Pope Paul says in his speech "a value that distinguishes itself from all other values" and the difference between it and all other religions is like the difference among men that "is brought by language, culture, art or a profession."

Now this is just the line taken in the famous *Relatio Symmachi*,[61] and rebutted by St. Ambrose. *Aequum est quidquid omnes colunt, unum putari. Eadem scrutamur astra, idem nos mundus involvit. Quid interest qua quisque prudentia verum inquirat? Uno itinere non potest perveniri ad tam grande secretum.*[62] This allows us to see the similarity between the crisis of paganism and that of contemporary Christianity. Both stem from a scepticism that flies from any kind of certainty about truth; or from a religious pluralism, based on scepticism, which regards all religions as equally inadequate to the immense mystery of the universe.

If this is the theoretical side of the crisis, its practical manifestation is the universal breakdown in morals that we have described; it is very diverse in its effects but they all originate from the same belief that human actions are to be measured not by any natural or divine law, but by what is useful in this life, and ultimately by what is pleasurable. John Paul II has defined both the present situation and its cause exactly. "The situation," he says, "can be reduced to two basic tendencies; on one hand a continual and systematic attack on the principles of morality, and on the other, the tactic of multiplying types of corruption and models for it to imitate." The reasons for this development are metaphysical, because once the idea of God has been rejected or obscured, all true systems of value crumble. "We must recognize that there is in man a being that demands an 'ought to be,' and that this is due to an overarching law: namely the natu-

---

[61] "Symmachus's Statement." Symmachus was a rich pagan aristocrat, the leader of the party referred to in the first footnote to this paragraph. [Translator's note.]

[62] "It is reasonable to regard what people worship as being one and the same. We all study the same stars, the same world contains us all. What does it matter what scheme each man adopts to seek out truth? No one way can bring us to grasp so great a mystery."

ral law that is witnessed to by the inner workings of conscience."[63]

As we have shown,[64] the moderns think the natural law is an
incoherent and superstitious taboo that should be done away
with, indeed, has already been done away with. We have seen
how the origins of all the particular corruptions of contemporary culture can be traced to that primal denial.

In his speech, the Pope sets forth anew the abiding doctrine
of the Church and insists upon the fact that the natural law, far
from being arbitrary, is innate within human beings as God's
creatures. Then, going beyond the limits of our natural wisdom,
he shows that it is not enough to base the moral law simply on
the existence of God; "that is still not enough to determine the
content of morality in an absolute way." Philosophical morality
is in fact fulfilled and perfected by a theological morality: "we
must say that only Jesus Christ, the Revealer of the Father, is the
safe paradigm for morality, since He alone is its divine paradigm."[65]

Human dignity and the rights of man are one of the subjects most frequently dealt with in papal preaching, but it is
impossible to assert such rights with any conviction if one does
not first establish that they are derived from the absolute and
inviolable character of man's relation to God. Rights are correlative to, and dependent upon, duties. Thus even Mazzini[66]
wrote about *I doveri dell'uomo*, the Duties of Man, rather than
about rights. But the modern world has inverted this relationship, making rights the chief good and claiming that duties exist
only to secure rights. In any case it is a bad thing for isolated
truths to be asserted independently of religious truth, because
they then lack any internal regulating principle of their own
when thus detached from their foundation, and also because in
such circumstances the Church is deprived of its primary task of
teaching the whole moral truth.[67]

---

[63] O.R., 29-30 November 1982.

[64] See paragraphs 172-77.

[65] O.R., 29-30 November 1982.

[66] A deistic, republican revolutionary in 19th century Italy.
[Translator's note.]

[67] See what Manzoni says on this subject in his *Morale Cattolica*, ed.
cit., Vol.II, pp.577-78.

326. Decline of the Church's social influence in the world.

Catholicism's loss of its specific character weakens the Church's social influence, which is unifying, and exercises a healthy moral effect. This unifying power is compromised by the schisms we have noted in Russia, the Ukraine and China and by the incipient schisms of the type seen in Holland. These include the schism in Nicaragua, where a so-called Popular Church, inspired by "liberation theology," has openly repudiated papal authority.[68]

Deluded by the glamour of an unprecedented expansion of papal diplomatic representation, some people imagine that the pope's religious authority in the modern world has increased; but it is in fact diminishing continually, not only because of the spread of a worldly and secular spirit among ordinary people, but also because of the inoperativeness of that same authority, which is no longer merely a prudent and circumstantial restraint, as it was in the past, but has become instead a systematic and deliberate default. As we have seen,[69] this is apparent within the Church, where the Holy See's orders are ignored or disobeyed by the masses, and are either unrecognized or neglected by the bishops.[70]

Civil society, which once bore a Christian stamp in its laws and customs, has now almost everywhere removed it by adopting divorce and abortion (except in Portugal and Ireland), by legalizing sodomy and incest, by the official introduction of contraceptive instruction in schools,[71] by the increasing refusal

how even there! 2007

---

[68] Priests who are committed to revolutionary struggle and are ministers in the Nicaraguan Marxist government rejected Pope John Paul II's appeal to them to abandon their political offices and return to their pastoral duties. The statement made by Father D'Escoto, the Minister for Foreign Affairs, is revealing: "I will not be in Managua on 5 March for the Pope's visit, but in New Delhi for the non-aligned summit which is *infinitely more important* than the visit of a Pope." R.I., 1983, p.126.

[69] See paragraphs 65, 66 and 71.

[70] See paragraphs 61-64.

[71] In O.R., 17 February 1983, Cardinal Suenens noted the scandal caused by the introduction into French high schools of a booklet on sexual matters, by authority of the Ministry of Youth and Sport. It illustrates different contraceptive techniques and amounts to an of-

to acknowledge diversity in human rights stemming from the diversity among human beings, by the total secularization of schools, education, the press, the calendar[72] and what were once called charitable institutions, by the statutory enshrinement of religious indifferentism and atheism as the basis of civil society and by the reduction of public religious ceremonies to purely civic rituals attended by believers and unbelievers alike.[73]

It is not possible to attribute this desacralization of life to the personal tastes of Paul VI, who despite the fact that he "had a mentality of a lay sort"[74] according to Jean Guitton, the layman who had the deepest discussions with him and who perhaps best understood his mind. In a Catholic theodicy one cannot attribute such a fundamental shift to the effect of a single person. Nonetheless, for anyone who manages to avoid the natural tendency to believe what it would be nice to believe, and to divert one's mental gaze from whatever is displeasing, it is impossible to deny that the shift from a still largely Christian culture to an entirely anthropocentric one happened during Pope Paul's reign and immediately thereafter.[75] Paul VI himself recognized the crisis both in public speeches[76] and in his private talks with Guitton. He spoke to Guitton, a member of the French Academy, *avec effroi*[77] about what was happening, and said that *à l'intérieur du catholicisme une pensée de type non catholique semble parfois avoir le dessus et il se peut que cette pensée*

---

ficial encouragement of sexual indulgence and the abolition of all moral restraints. The Cardinal deplores the absence of any strong protests against the process of corruption, but its causes are manifold, and the Church itself must carry a good part of the blame.

[72] One should not overlook the progressive replacement of liturgical festivities by purely secular ones: Mothers' Day, Sick People's Day, Social Communications Sunday, World Peace Day, etc,. etc.

[73] This even happens at papal Masses now that non-Catholics and non-Christians have begun to be appointed as ambassadors to the Holy See.

[74] J. Guitton, *Paul VI secret*, Paris 1979, p.17: "*Avec lui on n'était pas en présence d'un clerc, mais d'un laic qui aurait été soudain promu à la Papauté.*" "With him one was not in the presence of a cleric, but of a layman who seemed to have been suddenly elevated to the papacy."

[75] This is most strikingly true of Italy. [Translator's note.]

[76] See paragraph 7.

[77] Guitton, op. cit. p.149 "with dismay."

non catholique à l'intérieur du catholicisme devienne demain la plus forte.[78] Even if that were to happen, heterodoxy would still never amount to the same thing as genuinely Catholic thought.

327. Decline of the Church's vital influence in international affairs.

By *vital influence* we mean an action that produces visible effects in the international field. In the past these effects were quite significant, despite the fact that the Church's influence was opposed, combatted and frustrated where possible, both theoretically and politically, by the philosophies of different states. We do not deny, indeed we emphatically assert, the importance of the teaching role that the Church continues to fulfill and we do not underestimate its effects; but truths in the abstract are not necessarily connected with any acceptance of them by particular people and societies. One should continue to respect a true moral system even if other people call it out of date or dead. But we must recognize the ineffectiveness of papal teaching in contemporary life. We will not repeat what we have said about the growing detachment of ordinary people from Christian ethics: but it was very apparent in the Italian referendum of 1981 to reverse the recent legalization of abortion; in Rome, the See of Peter and the centre of Christendom, only 22% of those voting, voted against abortion. In some countries, secularist groups are urging young people to go to their parish priests and formally demand to be crossed out of the baptismal register as a way of abolishing their own status as Christians.[79] As for non-Christian states, there have been terrible violations of human rights in China and India, where attempts are made by the state to control human reproduction by despotic methods. These methods are presented as being democratic, and concerned to promote national welfare. The ruling dogma of modern political philosophy is the absolute sovereignty of the state, condemned in proposition 39 of the *Syllabus of Errors*: *Reipublicae status, utpote omnium iurium origo et fons, iure quo-*

---

[78]   Ibid., p.168. "Within Catholicism, a kind of non-Catholic thinking sometimes seems to have the upper hand; and it could be that tomorrow this non-Catholic thought within Catholicism might be the stronger."

[79]   Cf. *Esprit et vie*, 1982, p.615.

dam pollet nullis circumscripto limitibus.[80] Nonetheless, absolute sovereignty is still the ruling principle today, and is recognized even in the Charter of the United Nations. This means that the General Assembly of that body, which is the highest expression of today's humanistic ideology, is in fact ineffective, because relations between member states are determined by the balance of power, and censures passed by the Assembly are disregarded; the Security Council, which is meant to be an instrument for practical decision making, is itself run on opportunistic Machiavellian lines and bows before a *fait accompli.*

The lack of authority on the part of the papacy has been obvious during John Paul II's reign. His teaching on human dignity, peace, and human rights is untiring but ineffective. He did not succeed in interposing himself between the belligerents and effecting a cease fire, before or during his visits to Argentina and Great Britain, when they were fighting each other in 1982; that is, he failed to insist successfully on the incompatibility between his visit as a messenger of the Gospel of peace, and the existence of a state of war between the countries he was visiting; as if the difference between peace and war were of no importance in the conscience of Christian peoples.

The Pope's visit to Central America at the beginning of March 1983 occasioned the biggest humiliation inflicted on a pope this century. On the very day he landed as a bringer of peace and mercy, the Guatemalan government shot five members of opposition groups, ignoring his repeated requests for clemency. The Guatemalan president, General Rios Montt, who received him as Head of the Church, is a renegade Catholic who belongs to a Protestant sect. In Belize, where the majority of the population is black and Protestant, the Pope came face to face with the new phenomenon of the formal abandonment of the Catholic religion due to proselytism by sects, which he described as "improper and unworthy."[81] The greatest affront was delivered in Nicaragua. There the Pope was opposed by priests and laity of the "Popular Church." These Catholics who defied Roman condemnations were benignly described by the *Osservatore Romano* as Christians "who opt for revolution, taken as a concrete way of putting the ethical values of the gospel message

---

[80] "Since it is the source and origin of all rights, the state is endowed with a jurisdiction confined by no limits."

[81] R.I., 1983, p.354.

into effect."[82] The celebration of Mass in the main square of the capital developed into a mass defiance of the Pope, who was prevented from speaking, and drowned out by irreverent revolutionary cries. The *Osservatore* spoke of a "profanation of the Mass"[83] and the episcopal secretariat for Central America published a statement "condemning strongly the unprecedented mistreatment and outright affront to the person of the Holy Father."[84] It is also worth noting that San Salvador's request that the Pope should intervene to bring an end to the guerrilla war in that country, and Nicaragua's that he should urge the United States to begin a dialogue, could neither of them be accepted because, according to the papal spokesman, "the Pope's journey was primarily religious." In short, Papa Wojtyla's apostolic journey occasioned a sorry display of the internal divisions in the Church, Catholicism's retreat in the face of Protestant proselytism, and its political and moral ineffectiveness despite the long Catholic traditions of the countries in question.

On the other hand, people point to the enormous crowds that gathered for the occasion; but everyone knows what superficial, fickle and deceptive things crowds are, how their moods change from moment to moment, and how little can be deduced from their existence regarding the real mentality of a people.

328. The Church thrown off course by secondary Christianity. The encyclical *Populorum Progressio*.

We have already traced the present decline of Catholicism to its desertion of its own primary purpose, in order to direct its attentions to the perfecting of man in this world.[85] It is true that Christianity tends to produce an improving effect; Campanella and Gioberti made the fact the central point in their philosophies; but Christianity can never take man's temporal perfection as its primary or even co-primary end without negating its own nature. This change involves the whole theory of natural goods which we have treated earlier and here presuppose.[86] The Church aided the development of European civilization, as a

---

[82] O.R., 2 March 1982.
[83] O.R., 6 March 1983.
[84] O.R., 7-8 March 1983.
[85] See paragraphs 220 and 221.
[86] See paragraphs 205-10.

real but secondary effect of the practice of Christianity; it has also assisted in civilizing much of the rest of the world as well; but at Vatican II it took on the role of directly advancing man's temporal welfare and has thus attempted to make secular progress part of the purpose of the Gospel. *Populorum Progressio* develops this line of thought. It claims to be a development of *Rerum Novarum*, which aimed to reconcile the richer and poorer classes within the ambit of individual nations; Pope Paul's encyclical aims to reconcile rich and poor nations with each other, now that increasing international awareness has led to a stronger and closer sense of fellow feeling and it is hungry races, not hungry individuals, who make demands upon the rich. In a speech to the International Labor Organization, John Paul II has also said that the chief social task of our day is the promoting of a *world-wide common good.*[87]

In *Populorum Progressio* there is a widened conception of the requirements of justice, with its correlative rights, as distinct from the spirit of benevolence, which is a non-legally enforceable moral obligation. This widened conception is justified from a Catholic point of view because, as I have said, a change in historical circumstances can change not only the degree but the kind of moral obligation one has, thus turning a minor fault into a major one, and an act of kindness into a legally binding obligation. I will not enter into the encyclical's detailed proposals, such as the establishment of a world fund to help poorer countries; these proposals have been criticized by sociologists and economists, but they have perhaps evaluated them from a rather one-sided point of view.

What is more relevant to our purposes is the change in perspective that tends to undermine Catholic doctrine by making technological progress and an increase in wealth a necessary precondition for man's spiritual perfection, and for any activity by the Church, in accordance with the views of Father Montuclard.[88] It is true that the encyclical presents the goal of development as being "an integral growth," a humanism destined to be integrated into Christ, thus becoming a transcendent hu-

---

[87] O.R., 16 June 1982.

[88] See paragraph 117. This idea of a necessary precondition was explicitly adopted in the new constitutions of the Dominican Order, promulgated in 1968, but it has been struck out by decrees of General Chapters meeting in later years. It is perhaps not merely a coincidence that Montuclard was a Dominican. [Translator's note.]

manism. But all this leaves the connection between man in his humanly developed state and man in his supernaturalized state quite undetermined.

Paul VI expresses his hope for a world in which the parable of Dives and Lazarus is corrected "so that liberty is not an empty word, and Lazarus, the poor man, may sit at the same table as the rich."[89] But this is to reverse the meaning of the parable. In the Gospel the rich man *accepit bona in vita sua*[90] and for that reason he ends up being punished; Lazarus, on the other hand, *recepit mala et nunc consolatur*.[91] To want Lazarus to enjoy life in the same way as the rich man would mean saying he is better off with worldly goods than with heavenly consolation; or else would imply that the enjoyment of earthly goods is tied to the enjoyment of God, and necessarily brings a man to Him.

As the Sermon on the Mount solemnly teaches, weeping and being consoled, thirsting for justice and receiving it, are mutually exclusive.[92] And in fact it is impossible to argue that weeping is consolation or that thirsting leads to having one's thirst quenched. What precedes a thing is not the thing itself. Christianity sees an "either or" that governs heavenly and earthly loves, not a "both and." It is perhaps possible to talk about loving both heavenly and earthly goods, but not by putting them on an equal footing, because this world's goods should only be desired conditionally, as a means to an end, while the goods of the life to come are desired absolutely since God is the ultimate goal of all things.

The thought underlying Pope Paul's encyclical is really that of Father Lebret, who drafted it:[93] the Church's action in improving the state of this world is not incidental or a side effect, rather, it is essential to the preaching of the Gospel; what the 1971 Synod of Bishops in Rome called "the Church's mission for the redemption of humanity and for liberation from every oppressive situation." This duality of redemption and liberation is another version of the sophistical "both and": redemption and liberation are not two things, but they are one and the same

---

[89] *Populorum Progressio*, 47.
[90] "Received good things in this life."
[91] Luke, 16:25. "Received evil and is now consoled."
[92] This fact is often smoothed over these days.
[93] See V. Cosmao, *Changer le monde*, Paris 1981. The author is the director of the *Centre Lebret*.

because redemption means liberation, but a liberation that is eschatological and spiritual, and which happens through Christ.

329. Obscuring of Catholic doctrine regarding the last things. Humanistic ecumenism.

To integrate earthly well-being into the Gospel message is to obscure Christianity's ultraterrestrial goal. It means that justice is no longer seen as a turning of men towards God,[94] and becomes instead a turning of man to man; the religious outlook merges with the humanistic one, the Kingdom of God turns into a Kingdom of Man. Hence the ever greater resemblance between the doings of a culture that organizes life without any reference to the things of God, and the activities of a Church that is no longer concerned with things Christian merely, but which, to use the current jargon, "promotes human and Christian values."

The religious syncretism that we noted earlier is but one expression of a human syncretism that is the very soul of the modern world. It is this spirit that has led to the setting aside of specifically Catholic rules, principles or fundamental convictions, and to putting the emphasis exclusively on things Catholics hold in common with others; this constitutes an attempt to equate all shades of opinion with each other and to base the opinions one really cares about on human nature alone, that is on a merely human set of values.[95] Not one state in the world today has a constitution based explicitly on the Christian religion.[96] Catholic doctrine about the end of the world is never mentioned, and the idea of predestination has disappeared from teaching. Instead, the ends or interests or subjects that are discussed are those that are accepted as valid by everyone in general, that is, subjects connected with this world only; the Church is now attempting to put itself at the service of man-

---

[94] Ecclesiastes, 12:13. "Fear God and keep his commandments; this is the whole meaning of man."

[95] The author was writing shortly before the pan-religious proceedings presided over by the Pope at Assisi in October 1986. They are a good example of what he is talking about at this point. They were planned, it seems, by Cardinal Etchégaray, which is hardly surprising in the light of paragraphs 135 and 254. [Translator's note.]

[96] Liechtenstein does, but here indeed, *exceptio probat regulam*, "the exception proves the rule." [Translator's note.]

kind in matters of worldly concern, and it is on that basis that its activity is accepted or even positively encouraged.[97] The tension between heavenly and earthly aspirations still sets a great part of the human race against the Church, insofar as men are inspired and guided by communism;[98] it is strange to record the fact that this tension is more acutely felt by the communists than by the Church, which is setting about to weaken and water down the contrast between the two states of mind. So-called "lay," that is non-Christian, humanism is beginning to make common cause with the new ideal advanced by the Church, because that ideal has so much in common with the secularist outlook; it is as if heaven and earth were supposed to be the same thing, and as if Christianity had altered its nature, even though in fact it cannot.[99]

In pursuance of our aim of using official documents to illustrate what is happening, we can see this process of levelling down between the world and the Church in a speech made by Sandro Pertini, the President of the Italian Republic, in 1983: "I am firmly convinced that true progress for our country will not come from an opposition between different beliefs, but from their capacity for mutual understanding and esteem. Europe and Italy are born of the joint efforts of Catholics and non-Christians, from the whole contribution made by the Christian cultural tradition and also from secular values such as an appreciation of diversity, mutual respect, tolerance; all of which are also part of Christianity itself. It is no longer the time for opposition, but for mutual integration for the good of man. In this field, believers and unbelievers can go a long way together."[100] We may note the weakness of the historical analysis in these remarks, in that they assume that secular values were at work in Europe when as yet they did not exist, being as they are the offspring of the modern age. The main point, however, is

---

[97] In his speech to the fishermen of Flutrock the Pope said: "Men and women are born to contribute by their work to the building up of the human community, and thereby to realize their full human stature as co-creators with God and builders with Him of his Kingdom."

[98] A decidedly smaller part of the human race is covered by these remarks in the 1990s than was the case at the time of writing. [Translator's note.]

[99] See paragraph 53.

[100] O.R., 27 January 1983.

that the President clearly has a syncretist humanitarian outlook. This matches nicely with the aspirations expressed by *Comunione e Liberazione* in its annual meeting at Rimini in 1983; in its message to Pertini it said it was "committing itself to the building of a society that puts man at the centre, to dialogue between different cultures and identities, to the rights of every man, and to peace."[101] But comprehension and integration presuppose some more fundamental common good that underlies the various lesser values that are to be comprehended, that is, taken together and integrated; in the humanist scheme of things, this good is man in himself, seen as the crown of the world's existence; the ultimate good is no longer transcendent as it is in the Christian view. This humanist ideal pushes Christianity aside and aims at building a kingdom of man which, according to Auguste Comte, is the final stage in human development, and which amounts to a new version of the "Age of the Holy Spirit," realized within this world's history.

President Pertini went even further in his speech on the occasion of the Pope's visit to the Quirinale on 2 June 1984. What he said amounted in fact to an assertion that all religions were irrelevant to the progress of the human race. For him, they are nothing more than possible expressions of the human spirit, which develops independent of all of them. He believes that they *cannot impede* the growth of a common identity among men, but he does not see them as necessary to the creation of a united humanity: "Neither religious denomination, nor philosophical belief, nor political allegiance can constitute an obstacle on the road to understanding."[102] For his part, the Pope framed his reply in terms of a humanist world order, and when talking about the Italian people, said that their distinguishing national characteristic was their humanitarian spirit and he attributed the achievements of St. Camillus of Lellis and St. Joseph Cottolengo to that, rather than to their Christian faith. But in fact, the similarities that exist between actions motivated by Christian faith and those inspired by some secular set of values are, as the scholastics put it, merely material rather than formal similarities: they do not constitute, in essence, the same activity, because of the radically different reasons for which they are performed. In the Catholic vision of things, the human race

---

[101] O.R., 31 August 1983.
[102] O.R., 4 June 1984.

can be united while still retaining its diversity, provided that the diversity does not interfere with recognizing a common transcendent goal which is the genuine principle of unity, and which exists over and above all differences. In the humanist view, this transcendent ground of unity is done away with, and man is put in its place as the centre and crown of reality. This humanism can make room for Christianity, but only as one expression among many of what it is to be human.

In his sermon at Pentecost 1983, John Paul II emphasized the unifying effect the Church has in the world, and tried to depict the Church as playing an important role in forming the humanist and secularist world order towards which the nations are moving. "From Pentecost on, reconciliation is no longer a dream for a distant future. It has become a reality that is destined to grow continually through the universal expansion of the Church."[103] The Pope mentioned two ways in which the Church exercises its unifying effect. First, "by making men adhere to Christ, the Holy Spirit binds them in unity in a single body, the Church, and thus reconciles in one friendship people who are far removed from each other by geography and culture." Furthermore, "the Holy Spirit exercises his activity outside the Church, inspiring men with a desire for a greater unity between all nations." The utopian inspiration of such talk is obvious. The universal expansion of the Church is today at a full stop, because of the internal decomposition deplored by Paul VI and the new sort of ecumenism that has sterilized missionary activity. The Holy Spirit's activity outside the Church is a doctrine of the faith, but it cannot be seen or made the basis of historical predictions except insofar as it brings each individual into the Church.[104]

The Church's ineffectiveness in producing worldly improvements is the expression of a law: *suum quisque officium agat*.[105] The physical or moral nature of a thing is the cause of its activity, and thus the Church's supernatural nature is primarily expressed in a supernatural activity. Any other activity, such as the effecting of secular improvements, is something that, as the history of civilization demonstrates, the Church does perform, but only in a consequential and dependent way. Thus the

---

[103] O.R., 26 May 1983.

[104] Cf. Council of Trent. Canon 3 on Justification, Denzinger 813 or 1553. [Translator's note.]

[105] "Let each man perform his own function."

Church does indeed have a contribution to make to the current
development of society, but not by reinforcing current trends;
its task is to redress and oppose the imbalance of much of what
is now taking place. The Church cannot put itself in the van of
a kind of progress that is really produced by other agents of a
non-ecclesiastical sort; yet this is what it now seems keen to do.
The ambiguous, uncertain and ineffective character of Christian
socialism is an illustration of this principle. In putting forth its
supernatural strength, the Church does actually defend the
natural foundations of human society, but it does so precisely by
deploying that supernatural strength of its own. As a matter of
fact the Catholic Church is at present the only major body that
does uphold the objective duties and obligations of the natural
law, but its defense of that law is conducted in the face of a host
of violations of it, of every possible kind.[106] The moral order is,
moreover, connected with the Church's eschatological teaching,
because the moral law provides the true order in human living,
of a kind that finds its fulfillment and goal in the realities of the
world to come: *non contemplantibus nobis quae videntur, sed
quae non videntur. Quae enim videntur temporalia sunt, quae
autem non videntur aeterna sunt.*[107]

330. Laws of the Spirit of the Age.
Pleasure. Forgetfulness.

One of the most striking aspects of the modern world is its
perpetual agitation of mind, the endless shifting of opinion, the
swiftly changing character of society, the uninterrupted discussing and hypothesizing on all subjects and by all parties, the incessant pullulation of congresses, learned conventions and study
groups. This is the outward sign of the scepticism and mobilism
that have so profoundly corrupted the modern state of mind.
But all this activity is a phenomenon without a noumenon, and
stems from a law we mentioned earlier: the more things pass out
of real existence in the external world, the more they are likely
to be talked about; so that words cease to be the sign of things
and become instead things in their own right that replace real
existence. Thus, for example, when the monastic life is languish-

---

[106] See paragraphs 172-77, and the following chapters in detail.

[107] II Corinthians, 4:18. "We fix our eyes on what is unseen, not on
what we can see. What we can see, lasts but for a moment; what is
unseen is eternal."

ing, there is an outburst of writings about its renewal, and about the discovery or rediscovery of monastic values, so that the whole subject becomes a problem to be discussed, an occasion for wordspinning. Or again, when adoration of the Blessed Sacrament has fallen to its lowest ebb, the Sacrament becomes a subject for discussions, study meetings and the publication of books on a scale that was never seen in periods of deep eucharistic piety. The Eucharist is discussed in relation to everything else; tourism, sport, the theater or what have you. Far from being a sign of life, this excess is a sign of an emptiness: when a thing really exists, it does not need to be made a problem for discussion, or to invade the world of mere chatter.

This turning of reality into words cannot be adequately explained unless one remembers the mind's arcane power of acknowledging or ignoring what is present to it, that is, of setting something before itself and giving it attention, or of removing it and not noticing it, just as if it did not exist. This is a mystery touched on several times in the Bible, especially in the words: *ut videntes non videant et audientes non intelligant.*[108]

This forgetfulness, whether individual or social, that is such an important factor in life, is begotten of the mind's capacity to illumine or obscure this or that aspect of a known reality. Forgetfulness is the grand driving force of history, and shapes the spirit of an age. The kind of forgetfulness I mean is the sort that does not remove our knowing a fact, but that makes us pay no attention to it, so that, as Leibniz says, we perceive something, but do not apperceive it.

This is the kind of forgetfulness that sets the spirit of a particular period. Together with passion and the will, this kind of forgetfulness is, as I have just said, the grand driving force of history. The human spirit cannot contain several different values at the same time,[109] and it is thanks to forgetfulness that the old world endlessly renews itself. History, which itself consists of memory, like Danae, pours one event on top of another endlessly into the vessel, but the vessel is never filled, and events escape and are lost outside the inadequate and leaky jar of

---

[108] Luke, 8:10. "So that they can watch without seeing, and listen without understanding."

[109] This remark, and the general treatment of this matter, is heavily indebted to a continental idealism deriving from Hegel via Croce and Gentile, which Anglo-Saxon minds may find unfamiliar. [Translator's note.]

memory. From stage to stage, the state of the world is compounded of memory and oblivion. "The span of one hundred
years at most" writes Virgilio Malvezzi "is the width of the bed
of the river of forgetfulness. The men who knew that rebellions
were useless, not without danger, and extremely damaging, are
long dead. No one thinks any more about the burnt towns, the
scorched trees, the sterile fields, the cities deserted, destroyed or
damaged. No one believes the damage occurred, or if they do,
they do not attribute much importance to it, because they know
it was reparable, because they see it has been repaired."[110] History, I have said, is Danae. By remembering, each generation
would recapitulate the history of the world; by forgetting, each
one begins it anew. Thus the centuries go through the same cycle of misfortune, palliated only, as Francesco Chiesa says in his
Martire, by the "gentle forgetfulness of children." One particular generation's efforts will not do to fix a memory and abolish
oblivion. After the Persian Wars, the Greeks left the burnt temples standing, to perpetuate the memory of the cruel impiety of
the barbarians. In 1945 the Americans contemplated not re-
building the German cities, so that the German people would
not forget their guilt and the misfortune that had followed from
it. But to contend against oblivion is to kick against fate, because forgetfulness is the law of history, indeed it is the constitutive element of history, which is a struggle of living and dying,
that is, of things appearing and disappearing to the spirit. In
temporal life, forgetfulness has such a beneficial effect that it is
even institutionalized in law in the various devices governing
the extinction of obligations, rights and liabilities contained in
all legal systems. Then again, there is the act of pardon, which is
a kind of voluntary forgetfulness, which does not undo past
events, but wipes them out of the memory of the one granting
the pardon.[111]

Oblivion plays a large part in the history of nations and of
the Church. A *damnatio memoriae*[112] is usual with all regimes
that rise upon the ruins of their predecessors. But here we are
concerned with forgetfulness as a phenomenon in the modern

---

[110] In *Policiti e moralisti del Seicento*, Bari 1930, p.233.

[111] When Pope Pius IX granted a general "amnesty" at the beginning
of his reign, Metternich objected to the concept on the grounds that
God Himself never forgets anything, but does grant pardons.
[Translator's note.]

[112] "Damnation of the memory."

Church. All the changes, and their consequences, considered throughout this book investigating what has occurred in Catholicism in the twentieth century, are a kind of forgetfulness, a sort of Augustinian *inadvertentia*.[113] The new emphases at Vatican II are a highlighting of parts of Catholic doctrine, with a corresponding obscuring of other complementary parts. This forgetfulness veils the doctrine of predestination with the truth of a universal offer of grace; it veils hell with the truth of divine mercy; the Real Presence with the truth of Christ's spiritual presence in the congregation; absolute obedience to the divine law with the truth that personal perfection is its result; it veils man's eschatological destiny with the truth of his duties in this life; the infallibility of Peter with the truth of the collegial teaching authority of the bishops; the unchanging character of the moral law with the truth of the historical changes in its application; the ministerial priesthood with the truth of the priesthood of all the baptized; the dogmatic character of the Church's teaching with the truth that there is a value in investigative discussion.

Vatican II represents a massive series of innovations that have marked every aspect of ecclesial life, whether theoretical or practical, but the fact of these innovations is less revealing than the phenomenon of forgetfulness which underlies them. Any genuine renewal of the contemporary Church must consist of a restoration of memory, always of course retaining the distinction between that essential remembering which is identical with the very being of the Church, and the remembering of its changing historical expressions that is necessary only to the well-being of that same Church.

331. Instances of forgetfulness in the modern Church.

If we turn to look for instances of forgetfulness in the contemporary Church, many of which are commonly regarded as long overdue adjustments of opinions that needed refining or moderating, we do not have far to go. First of all there is the forgetfulness of the sufferings of the Church in the nineteenth century at the hands of liberal regimes, and during the present century at the hands of dictatorships. This particular forgetting of the past is begotten of weakness and an abhorrence of any kind of conflict, even with unjust aggressors. John XXIII pro-

---

[113] "Lack of attention."

vided an example of it in his message to President Fanfani at the time of the centenary of the unification of Italy. The Pope denies that there was a conflict between the Italian nation and the papacy during the struggles of the Risorgimento, and says the idea that there was is the fruit "of certain disreputable writings." He tries to show "that the beneficent star and luminous sign inviting the triumph of the magnificent ideal (of national unity) was Pope Pius IX, who understood it in its most noble sense." In his benign and eirenical enthusiasm, John XXIII was deliberately forgetting the confutations, condemnations and anathemas that Pius IX pronounced in the face of liberal risorgimentist ideas; he was also attempting to remove from historical memory the anti-Catholic hostility of much of the national movement, and to suppress the dramatic conflict that beset some Italian Catholics at the time.

In this and other historical matters, Paul VI was more moderate, and stuck to the limits imposed by both truth and the dignity of the papacy, since he was not possessed of the same optimistic outlook as his predecessor.

John Paul II, however, has often indulged in this deliberate forgetting of things; but it is hard to know to what precise psychological trait, or doctrinal view or political policy the phenomenon should be ascribed. We will give just two examples of his condemning to Lethe of important events in European history during the last half century. During his visit to Poland in 1979, the Pope went to the site of the torments of Auschwitz and solemnly recalled the death of millions of innocent people under the rod of a godless tyranny, and called the place a "sanctuary of human suffering," a "Golgotha of the modern world." But then, in a spontaneous outburst, he broke forth unexpectedly into an ardent tribute "to the enormous contribution of blood paid by Russia in the struggle for the liberty of nations in the last great war."[114] The enslavement of Latvia, Estonia, Lithuania, Czechoslovakia, Hungary, Rumania and Poland by soviet despotism, which changed the fate of half of

---

[114] This section of the Pope's speech is missing in the Polish text, and was delivered spontaneously. It does appear in the Italian translation of the speech. Correspondents from the Swiss ATS and the Italian ANSA, who heard the speech in the flesh, reported the remarks in their news services. See for example the *Giornale del Popolo*, 8 June 1979.

Europe and did grave harm to Christianity is here condemned to oblivion.

The forgetting of the sufferings of the Church in Spain, during the civil war there from 1936 to 1939, was no less extraordinary in the speeches John Paul II made during his visit in November 1982. I would be among the first to admit that in that bloody national upheaval there were a great many diverse and ill-assorted elements at work: rival political outlooks, indeed fundamentally different views of life, both religious and secular; and I am also aware how difficult it is to distinguish one element from another among all the forces embroiled in the conflict. Amidst this compound of mixed motives, instances of martyrdom strictly so called must have been less common than they appeared to be. It is nonetheless impossible to overlook the fact that twelve bishops, four thousand priests and religious and more than a thousand nuns[115] were massacred during the bloody conflict, and that some of them at least must have been killed *in odium fidei*,[116] as indeed people on the other side openly admitted, and that they were true martyrs in the sense in which the Church uses that term. At the time, the war was regarded as a religious struggle first and foremost, for example by Pius XI in a solemn allocution on the matter, and as being only secondarily a merely political event. Despite all this, none of the many speeches made by the Pope during his visit to Spain contain the slightest reference to the sufferings the Church there underwent. Yet only a few weeks before the visit, the *Osservatore Romano* carried a major article by Father Isidoro da Villapadierna on "94 Capuchins, victims of the Revolution in Spain," whose cause for recognition as martyrs has been launched in the Roman Congregation for the Causes of Saints.

The capacity to forget has another name: opportunism, and yet another: the effect of time. In this epilogue to the whole of our discussion we must make an attempt to trace its origin and its meaning.

---

[115] Hugh Thomas, in his major history of the Spanish Civil War, broadly favorable to the anti-Catholic Republic, says that 6,000 priests but only 300 nuns were slaughtered. [Translator's note.]

[116] "Out of hatred of the faith."

332. Metaphysical analysis of the crisis.

That there is a crisis in the Church and that it is connected with the crisis in the world at large, is universally admitted except by a few odd voices that insist on saying only what people would like to hear, and that prevent themselves from being taken seriously by the very absurdity of their assertions. It is also universally admitted that the crisis takes the form of an imbalance between what may be briefly described as the material development of the human race on one hand, and its spiritual development on the other. The truth is that this imbalance is the result of an inability to keep technical developments within the ambit of moral developments, and thus to put things in any coherent order. The root cause of the confusion that has characterized the centuries of the modern era is a lack of unity, that is, the absence of a principle to coordinate and unify the various goods with which man is confronted. Unity is the essential condition for the existence of any being, and also for its perfection. The Good, which is in itself supremely One, is reflected in creatures in a multiplicity of ways, but that multiplicity is itself contained within an order, that is, in another unity since order is the coming together of many into one; it is the existence of that unity which makes the multiplicity of lesser goods a true image of the single, primordial, eternal Good.

What then is the reason the modern world has lost this unity? I ought here to point out that the unifying principle can never be one of the elements that has to be unified, but must instead be something external and superior to them all; thus mankind's problems cannot be resolved from a standpoint within man himself. The modern world, by contrast, attempts to unify its goods on the basis of one of the goods internal to it. But none of them in fact has this unifying capacity, because all of them are partial and they are often at odds with each other: economics, pleasure, personal development, freedom. The good that can unify these multiple goods is that ultimate Good by which all things are made and towards which they all converge. This ultimate Good is external to the order of goods it unifies. It is the thing that makes an ordered series of connected things out of the disordered series of unconnected things of which life apparently consists, in such a way that one answers to another and the whole interlocks in a graded series of goods mounting towards an end.

But to return to the question: why is it that the modern world cannot make these connections, and set things in a definite order? Obviously as has been often, perhaps too often, said in this book, because it has lost the concept of an ultimate goal by shutting itself within an absolute *Diesseitigkeit*. Something that disposes men to set aside any last end, but does not force them to do so, is the limitation of the human spirit itself. It is this limitation that tends to make men incapable of doing what needs to be done to grasp the order in the world, and of establishing a scale of values. The task is threefold. First, to appreciate individual goods for what they are; second, to grasp the relation that each good has with the primal Good which is both the world's first cause and its last end. Third, in the light of that relation, to understand the synthetic connection of each good with every other, and set them all in a unified vision of the good as a whole.

When knowledge of the world was limited and not very detailed, the various goods in life that man was aware of were perceived indistinctly in a unitary whole, informed by a single set of values, which was in fact religious in character. An awareness of the relation of things to ultimate reality dominated the human mind and constituted an all embracing form that unified experience. But although the mind of man can contain the whole range of goods in this way, it cannot do so when they become clearly distinguished and fully developed, each within its own sphere. In such circumstances, the mind can no longer envisage different kinds of goods in a single view, as it could when they were less clearly distinguished, but instead considers them one after another, individually. Thus in the modern world we frequently come across the phenomenon of people who base their existence on some particular kind of good and who live it out as if it were autonomous and could subordinate all other goods to itself: this particular good arrogates to itself the role which properly belongs to the prime transcendent good alone. This is in effect to bestow on one kind of worldly good a sort of religious significance amounting to idolatry. Different kinds of good are artificially separated from each other, torn out of their true setting, and cut off from the primal good that sustains them: *la forma universal di questo nodo*[117] is thus lost. Individual goods thus tend to take an unlimited hold upon men, and since

---

[117] *Paradiso*, XXXIII, 91. "The universal form of this knot."

their relation to the supreme good is not grasped, their autonomous existence, and the muddying of vision that they cause when not harmonized in a religious view of life, tend to produce an anti-religious or at best a non-religious attitude in men. Religion then becomes an element in this world; which is what produces secondary Christianity.[118] A transcendent goal beyond this world is first of all restricted within the bounds of changeable individual minds, under the protection of liberal principles, and then is watered down into a complete this-worldliness, since the force of logic ends up dissolving it into an absolute *Diesseitigkeit*. The Archbishop of Avignon regards the dissolving of Christianity into this world as the distinctive achievement of Vatican II: "The Church," he says, "has sought a new definition of itself and has begun to love the world, to open itself to it, to turn itself into a dialogue."[119] This constitutes an attempt to get away from a plurality of goods, too diverse for the mind to contain, and to return to a unified view of the good. But the return is not to be effected, as it should be, by a restoration of the supremacy of a unifying, transcendent good lying beyond the world, but by setting up a pseudo-principle immanent within the world, that refuses to look yonder for an ultimate explanation or to seek an end for man beyond his life in time. The reef upon which this attempt founders is the impossibility of an independent dependency, which is the key idea in the whole of our analysis.

An unconnected range of goods amounts to a sort of polytheism. Simone Weil describes very clearly the flaw in a pluralist set of values: "To believe there is a variety of goods, each independent of the other, such as truth, beauty, or virtue, is the sin of polytheism; the imagination should not be allowed to play with Apollo and Diana."[120] That this was in fact the case, had already been recognized by Nicholas Malebranche. He denies any causality on the part of created things, because he says that if they did have any true, that is independent, causality, they would become prime causes themselves and thus be worshipped in themselves.[121] It is a very easy move from metaphysics to ethics: if there were in fact a plurality of goods that were unconnected, independent and not derived from a primal good, each

---

[118] See paragraphs 220-1.

[119] O.R., 3 September 1976.

[120] Simone Weil, *La prima radice*, Milan 1954, p.268.

[121] Nicholas Malebranche, *De la recherche de la vérité*, Lib. VI, cap.3.

one of them would indeed be a primal good and could become the principle of a religious cult.[122] To regard individual goods as autonomous is thus to do away with all true religious faith.

333. Diagnosis and prognosis. Two final conjectures.

It is difficult, indeed impossible, to conclude the analyses that extend throughout this book by making a guess or forecast about what is to come. The raising of guesswork to the level of a science by giving it the ill begotten name of futurology, is an incoherent, vulgar, theatrical and vain proceeding. It is true that in general like causes produce like effects, but this is only a general rule that does not permit of syllogistic application in individual cases; probabilities, not certainties, are all we can arrive at. We cannot account for the operations of free will, for contingent failures in finite natures, or for extraordinary divine intervention, whether in the order of nature or of grace. There is thus no getting away from the old adage: *de futuris contingentibus non est determinata veritas.*[123] The Catholic faith provides only one certainty about future events: creation and the whole course of the world are under the control of divine Providence and their purpose is to glorify God. Nonetheless, the meaning of the world's changes is not apparent in each and every moment of history. That meaning can only be gathered from the whole of those changes, and can only be guessed at so long as change is still happening and has not reached its eschatological conclusion. But let us risk a few guesses.

The first conjecture would be that the process of the dissolving of the Catholic religion into the substance of this world will continue, and that the human race will move towards a complete levelling down of all political structures, religious beliefs, economic systems, juridical institutions and types of culture. This would happen under the sway of a technology directed towards the advancement of mankind as an end in itself,

[122] In his works on the history of philosophy, Mgr F. Olgiati says the characteristic of the modern age is concreteness, that is, a perception of reality, and that the Middle Ages were characteristically abstract. It seems to us that the word 'concreteness' would be better used to mean a grasping of all the real relations of things, and that without an awareness of a relation to a transcendent reality, thought wanders about in sophistical abstractions.
[123] "We can know no certain truth about contingent future events."

and with reference to this world alone. The establishment of a kingdom of man, by Bacon's *prolatio terminorum humani imperii ad omne possibile*[124] would thus lead to a radically new kind of existence, prophesied by the new theology no less than by marxist philosophy. The religious hue still attaching to liberation theology would, in this view, vanish away and leave the humanistic essence of such theories nakedly exposed.[125]

This first conjecture implies the absolute historicity of Christianity, the abandonment of belief in divine revelation in the face of the development of the human spirit, and the elimination of any idea of an absolute, whether in reason or in religion. The active principle of this destruction of religion might be considered to be atheistic communism, but all the other philosophies that were historically connected with its appearance also have a role in producing the end result.

Some eighteenth and nineteenth century thinkers, possessed either of a certain cleverness or else of a noble and penetrating vision, had premonitions of a vague and confused kind as to the crisis of the modern world. Jean-Jacques Rousseau says: "*L'empire de Russie voudra subjuguer l'Europe et sera subjugué lui-même. Les Tartares ses sujets deviendront ses maîtres et les nôtres.*"[126] Giacomo Leopardi says: "I do not hesitate to predict it. Europe, civilized as it is, will be the prey of the semi-barbarians who threaten it from the far North; and when the conquerors have become civilized, the world will return to normal."[127] Balmes is even more precise: "Some people believe that Europe can never again know conflict like that of the barbarian and Arab invasions. They have not considered what an Asia governed by Russia might produce in the way of revolutions."[128] This kind of change in civilization, involving a change in religion, or the annihilation of all religion, is also hinted at in the majestic pages at the end of Vico's *Scienza Nuova*: "But, if the nations are caught in that greatest of civil evils, such that they can neither

---

[124] "The extension of the boundaries of human control to their greatest possible extent."

[125] See paragraphs 218 and 255.

[126] Jean-Jacques Rousseau, *Contrat Social*, Lib. II, cap.8. "The empire of Russia will decide to subjugate Europe and will be subjugated itself. Its Tartar subjects will become its masters and ours."

[127] Giacomo Leopardi, *Zibaldone*, 867.

[128] Balmes, *Il Protestantesimo comparato col Cattolicismo*, Florence 1882, p.187.

consent among themselves to be ruled by one monarch nation, and yet no better nations come from outside to conquer and conserve them, then to this their extreme misfortune Providence shall apply this last remedy: that...they go and make wastes of their cities, and human habitations of their wastes; and in such manner, in the course of long ages of barbarism they may wear away the ill-begotten subtleties of malicious minds, that had made them more fearsome savages through the barbarism of thought[129] than they had first been through the barbarism of the senses."

This first conjecture is incompatible with the Catholic faith. As we have said,[130] man has no other root than that with which he was created and upon which the supernatural rests: there can thus never be any change affecting the root. There can, moreover, never be any renewal of man other than that affected by grace, and this renewal is of a kind that continues in his life beyond the end of the world, without creating any new age within the world's history. A state of grace is man's first and last condition, and there are no new heavens or new earths to be had under our present skies or on our present earth.

The second conjecture about the future of the Church is the one Montini began as a bishop and completed as pope.[131] The Church will continue to open itself to the world and to conform itself to that world, that is, it will continue to undo its own nature; but its supernatural life will survive, restricted to a faithful remnant, and its supernatural end will continue to be pursued faithfully by that part of it which is left in the world. The misleading well-being of a Church that is dissolving itself into the world will be matched by the progressive contraction and wretchedness of a small number of people, a tiny minority that seems insignificant and doomed to die, but which in fact contains the concentration of God's elect, an indefectible witness to the true faith. The Church will be a handful of defeated men, as Paul VI foresaw in his speech of 18 February 1976.

This emptying and abasement of the Church fulfills rather than invalidates the words of St. John: *haec est victoria quae*

---

[129] The barbarism of thought is what befalls reason when it is detached from its transcendent principle and its moral goal, as happens in a technological world.

[130] See paragraphs 53-54.

[131] See paragraph 36.

vincit mundum, fides nostra.[132] This process cannot be understood merely historically, since it is closely connected with the
mystery of predestination. The faith is not "greedy for tri-
umphs"; the story of the Church is not one of completed victories, but of battles being won, that is, of an endless struggling in
which the Church never definitively loses, but in which it can
never cease from struggling. This darkening of faith, foretold in
Luke 18:8, may be accompanied by drastic changes in society,
but they will not destroy the reality of that remnant of the
Church, even if they include the ruin of Rome, so often referred
to in extracanonical prophecy, the migration of the Church
from east to west (perhaps to the Americas, perhaps to Africa),
the change from one world order to another in accordance with
the biblical scheme, and the destruction and reconstruction of
nations.[133]

Half dying of poverty and persecution, and despised by the
world, the Church will share the fate of Thomas Mann's *Elect*:
while the world goes down in barbarism, he takes refuge in penance and devotion in the inhuman solitude of an inaccessible
retreat; there he lives in the wild, he is reduced to eating grass
and earth, he becomes a living creature that is human but can
hardly be recognized as such. Then, in a decisive moment for
Christendom, Providence seeks out the semihuman creature,
Roman legates carry him off to the City, raise him to the pontifical throne, and consecrate him to the renewal of the Church
and the salvation of the human race.

From abasement to exaltation; this is the old road familiar
to faith. It is from Isaiah's wall,[134] broken into minute fragments
so small that not even a scrap can be found big enough to carry
a lighted coal, that the building of the heavenly or earthly Jerusalem is achieved, in the hope coming from God's promise. A
movement of this sort goes against the laws of human history,
but has precedents in the unexpected resurrection of the Church
after the Arian and Lutheran crises, in which its transcendent
truths seemed to be in danger of destruction. This rising again

---

[132] I John, 5:4. "Our faith, that is the triumphant principle which tri-
umphs over the world."

[133] I am thinking chiefly of the "Revelations" of St. Bridget of Sweden, and of the synthesis of mediaeval prophecy that Campanella
gives in his *Articuli Prophetales*, edited by G. Ernst, Florence
1976.

[134] Isaiah, 30:14.

from disaster *oltre la difension di senni umani*[135] is in accordance with the laws by which Providence operates in governing the world.[136] The divine action runs from one extreme to the other, so that creation touches the lowest point of evil and then rises to the height of all good. Moral struggle drives the universe to its end, which is the realization of its predestined quantity of moral good or, theologically speaking, the filling up of the number of the elect. It is this struggle alone that provides occasion for the internal development of rational creatures and the expression of all the possible degrees of goodness. It is not that evil is needed for this development to occur; but a victory over evil is a good included in the design, and one of which intellectual beings are capable.

Faith in Providence thus proclaims the possibility that the world might rise and be healed by a metanoia which it cannot initiate but which it is capable of accepting once it is offered. The Church's task in this critical moment is not to attempt to "read the signs of the times," because *non est vestrum nosse tempora vel momenta;*[137] it is rather to read the signs of the eternal will, that are there to be read in every age, and stand steadfast before the face of every generation that passes with the centuries.

The last certitude is that the very warp and weave of history is constituted by the mystery of predestination, and that here, as Manzoni sublimely wrote, human thought must fold its wings and come to earth.

334. The burden against Duma.

It must seem that our considerations have come to a conclusion that amounts to a negative, hypothetical, shadowy and twilight understanding, if not indeed to a knowledge that is

---

[135] *Inferno*, VII, 81. "Beyond the limits of human understanding."

[136] Expounded by Rosmini in the third book of his *Teodicea.*

[137] Acts, 1:7. "It is not for you to know the times and seasons."

night. And so it is. The veil cannot be pierced; we feel our way
beneath a darkling light. "*Custos quid de nocte? Custos quid de
nocte? Dixit custos: Venit mane et nox. Si quaeritis, quaerite, con-
vertimini, venite.*"[138]

---

[138] Isaiah, 21:11-12. "Watchman, what of the night? Watchman, what
of the night? The watchman says: Morning comes, and with it the
night. If you seek, seek on; come back and ask again."

SUBJECT INDEX

INDEX OF PERSONS